TWELFTH EDITION

TOURISM

Principles, Practices, Philosophies

Charles R. Goeldner

J. R. Brent Ritchie

WILEY

JOHN WILEY & SONS, INC.

Library of Congress Cataloging-in-Publication Data

Goeldner, Charles R.
    Tourism : principles, practices, philosophies / Charles R. Goeldner, J.R. Brent Ritchie.—12th ed.
      p. cm.
      Includes bibliographical references and index.
      ISBN 978-1-118-07177-9 (hardback)
  1.   Tourism. I. Ritchie, J. R. Brent.   II. Title.
      G155.A1M386 2011
      338.4'791—dc22
                                                                              2011016026

Printed in the United States of America
10 9 8 7 6

Contents ✢

Space travel, only a few years ago the dream of a few space pioneers, is now a featured story in the travel sections of leading newspapers. Billionaires write checks for a place in line to go into space while ordinary travelers note the emergence of the megaplane, the Airbus A380, with potential capacity of over 800. Meanwhile Boeing has responded with the smaller, lighter Boeing 787 Dreamliner about to enter commercial service. Most important, tourism planners recognize that technological change, peak oil prices, climate change, and other environmental issues necessitate adaptation if tourism is to thrive. And while tourism planners remain human, just over the horizon they foresee the imminent arrival of nonhuman robots who are about to change the future face of tourism—particularly as it pertains to the provision of routine services and the fulfillment of repetitive tasks required to keep the tourism product functional.

The industry must respond to these challenges and opportunities plus deal with options generated by the proliferation of travel blogs and social networking sites such as Facebook, Linkedin, YouTube, Twitter, and MySpace, which change the stream of communication about travel and tourism. Furthermore, security continues to present challenges and added cost. These factors underscore why the globe's most dynamic industry demands constant reassessment.

Although basic tourism principles remain, applications must constantly be reevaluated in light of new developments and more challenging economic times. Nevertheless, the world's largest industry, tourism, continues to grow even more as millions of travelers from such booming economies as China, India, Brazil, and Russia seek culture, comfortable climates, and recreation in offshore destinations. At the same time, additional millions of retiring baby boomers from industrialized nations will take advantage of leisure time to enjoy increased travel. All are lured to pack their bags as increasing access to the Internet and television whet appetites to see the modern wonders of the world. The travel industry must respond. Accordingly, *Tourism, Twelfth Edition* is designed to examine changes and relate them to the basic concepts of tourism.

This book is intended to be used primarily as a textbook for college and university courses in tourism. However, the book also provides valuable information and guidance for national/state/provincial/local tourism offices, convention and visitors bureaus, chambers of commerce, tourism planning and development organizations, tourism promoters, tourist accommodations, attractions and other businesses, transportation carriers, oil and automotive companies, and any other organization that is interested or involved in the movement of people from their homes or businesses to destinations.

NEW TO THIS EDITION

The *Twelfth Edition* updates the Eleventh Edition of this leading comprehensive tourism text. Because the tourism industry changes so rapidly, the revision involves adding new developments, updating data, updating profiles, expanding some sectors, adding new Web sites, adding selected references, and expanding the glossary. B&Bs, timeshares, meetings and conventions, sustainable tourism, climate change, social media, and mobile marketing are some topics given expanded coverage.

The *Twelfth Edition* has been revised and updated to explore new trends in travel and tourism and discusses changes to the industry since the publication of the previous edition. New elements in the *Twelfth Edition* include:

■ *Profiles of travel industry leaders* such as J. R. Marriott Jr. of Marriott International and Roger Dow of the U.S. Travel Association. Their comments about the future are included. These industry leaders have introduced practices that have transformed the nature and quality of the vacation experience. We are also proud to acknowledge the outstanding ethical and moral leadership that Taleb Rifai, the secretary-general of the United Nations World Tourism Organization (UNWTO), has brought to tourism.

■ *Global Insights* are short features that cover timely, interesting, and even whimsical topics that are intended to serve as a stimulus for discussion. Examples are Dark Tourism, Tourism Forecasts, Travel Advisories, The Power of Travel, Emerging Markets, and Travel Experiences. These *Global Insights* facilitate and strengthen the ability of the instructor to identify selected areas of emerging importance in tourism. In addition, they assist the instructor in exploring the significance of these areas, without requiring extensive background reading.

■ Chapter 3 has new information on technology, convention centers, arenas, stadium and public facilities management jobs, and an updated internship section.

■ Chapter 5 has new information on the airline industry, updated cruise industry information, and added train travel as a tourist attraction.

■ Chapter 6 has a new section on culinary tourism.

■ Chapter 7 has extensive treatment of the changing world of travel distribution, with new information about the future and mobile marketing.

■ Chapter 11 has added information on seniors, as well as a new section on gay and lesbian tourism.

■ Chapter 15 has information on passports, visas, ethics, and government policy impacts, with clarified differences between destination vision and mission statement.

■ Chapter 17 has been substantially revised to update information on sustainable development and climate change.

■ Chapters 18 and 19 discuss the use of the Internet in tourism research, marketing, and promotion.

■ Chapter 19 also has new material on social media, blogs, and podcasting.

■ Chapter 20 takes a new look at the future of travel by identifying new trends such as space tourism.

■ There is additional coverage of crisis management in Chapter 15 and Chapter 20.

■ Updated and additional Internet Exercises are included at the end of each chapter to keep information current.

■ Selected references for each chapter have been gathered in an appendix.

■ Updated Internet sites for each chapter can be found on the companion Web site for the book at www.wiley.com/college/goeldner.

ORGANIZATION AND CONTENT

This book explores major concepts in tourism, what makes tourism possible, and how tourism can become an important factor in the wealth of any nation. It is written in broad, global terms, discussing the principles, practices, and philosophies of tourism that have been found to bring about success. In this *Twelfth Edition* of *Tourism,* even greater attention has been paid to the global impact of tourism, both economically and socially.

For tourism to be successful, a great variety of components must work together seamlessly to create a positive travel experience. This book is divided into six parts, which examine the various components of tourism, their function, and their significance.

Part 1 provides a broad overview of tourism, with chapters devoted specifically to the global impact of tourism, a history of travel, and career opportunities.

Part 2 looks at the governmental and private-sector organizations that provide services, products, and destinations for travelers. Individual chapters discuss tourist organizations, passenger transportation, lodging and food service providers, travel agents and wholesalers, and tourism attractions.

Part 3 examines travel motivation, travel behavior, and the sociology of tourism.

Part 4 is devoted to tourism planning and a further examination of the components of tourism. A chapter on formulating tourism policy is included in this part. Other chapters cover topics such as tourism supply, forecasting demand, the economic impact of tourism, tourism planning, and environmental issues. In light of the growing importance of the environment, a particular effort has been made to explore fully the managerial issues at the tourism/environment interface—a point at which there is much potential for conflict.

Part 5 examines the important fields of tourism research and tourism marketing.

Part 6 looks at projections for tourism in 2020 and 2030, and suggests how today's industry can prepare itself to accommodate future growth and meet tomorrow's challenges.

FEATURES

To help students better understand and process the information presented, a number of pedagogical features have been integrated into this textbook.

The Learning Objectives at the beginning of each chapter alert students to the important concepts that will be covered.

LEARNING OBJECTIVES

- Understand what tourism is and its many definitions.
- Learn the components of tourism and tourism management.
- Examine the various approaches to studying tourism and determine which is of greatest interest to you.

- Appreciate how important this industry is to the economy of the world and of many countries.
- Know the benefits and costs of tourism.

The chapter Introduction sets the scene and provides some context for what students are about to read. When appropriate, boxes, tables, illustrations, photos, and Internet sites have been included to help illustrate important topics and ideas. The chapter discussion concludes with a written Summary to help students reinforce what they have read.

SUMMARY

Transportation services and facilities are an integral component of tourism. In fact, the success of practically all forms of travel depends on adequate transportation. Transportation services and facilities are the arteries through which the lifeblood of the travel industry flows. Travel by air dominates long- and middle-distance travel in the United States. But private automobiles carry the bulk (about 80 percent) of all travelers on short trips. Automobiles are also very important on long and international trips. Rental cars are popular, because they supplement air travel. Rail travel in the United States has declined substantially since the 1950s but is still important in commuting and longer-haul traffic. Motorcoach transportation is available in far more places than either air or rail, but it constitutes a rather small percentage of total vehicle miles. Vacationing on cruise ships has become the fastest-growing segment of the U.S. travel industry. New and refurbished cruise ships are appearing regularly.

The list of Key Concepts serves as a valuable checkpoint for understanding the chapter topics. These terms are boldfaced and green within the chapter to call them to the reader's attention.

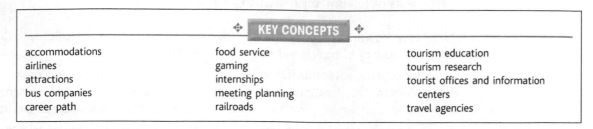

⬧ KEY CONCEPTS ⬧		
accommodations	food service	tourism education
airlines	gaming	tourism research
attractions	internships	tourist offices and information
bus companies	meeting planning	centers
career path	railroads	travel agencies

An updated directory of Internet Sites lists Web sites referred to in the chapter as well as additional sites students can turn to for more information. This directory can be found on the companion Web site for the book at www.wiley.com/college/goeldner.

Three types of exercises have been provided to gauge student understanding of the subject matter. The Questions for Review and Discussion test student recall of important chapter concepts and include some critical thinking questions.

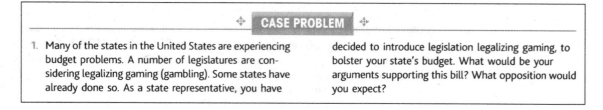

⬧ QUESTIONS FOR REVIEW AND DISCUSSION ⬧

1. The United Nations World Tourism Organization (UNWTO) has made poverty alleviation through tourism one of its leading priorities. Do you believe this is feasible? What are the major problems you anticipate UNWTO will encounter in its efforts to develop and implement this priority?

2. If you were minister of tourism for Thailand, what types of assistance might you request from UNWTO? from PATA?

The Case Problems present hypothetical situations that require students to apply what they have learned. They can be used for written assignments or as the catalyst for class discussions.

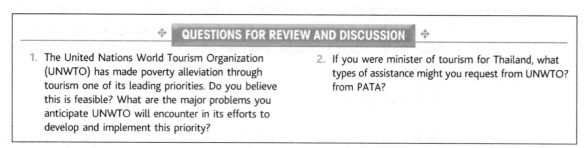

⬧ CASE PROBLEM ⬧

1. Many of the states in the United States are experiencing budget problems. A number of legislatures are considering legalizing gaming (gambling). Some states have already done so. As a state representative, you have decided to introduce legislation legalizing gaming, to bolster your state's budget. What would be your arguments supporting this bill? What opposition would you expect?

Also included is a series of Internet Exercises, designed to increase students' familiarity with technology by having them visit important travel industry Web sites and answer questions based on their investigation. This section has been expanded in this edition.

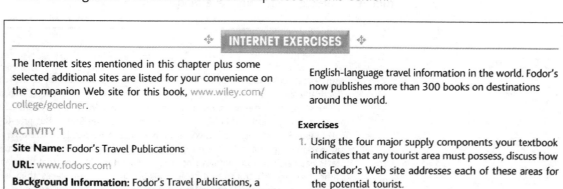

⬧ INTERNET EXERCISES ⬧

The Internet sites mentioned in this chapter plus some selected additional sites are listed for your convenience on the companion Web site for this book, www.wiley.com/college/goeldner.

ACTIVITY 1

Site Name: Fodor's Travel Publications

URL: www.fodors.com

Background Information: Fodor's Travel Publications, a subsidiary of Random House, is the largest publisher of English-language travel information in the world. Fodor's now publishes more than 300 books on destinations around the world.

Exercises

1. Using the four major supply components your textbook indicates that any tourist area must possess, discuss how the Fodor's Web site addresses each of these areas for the potential tourist.

Features updated to this edition are Global Insights on timely subjects that can serve as a springboard for lively discussion and as the basis for encouraging deeper study into key issues of the day.

❖ GLOBAL INSIGHT ❖

New Wonders

Bernard Weber, a Swiss filmmaker, created a popularity contest to choose seven new world wonders since the Great Pyramids of Egypt are the sole remaining wonder of the Seven Wonders of the Ancient World. Nearly 200 early candidates chosen by Internet ballot were reduced down by a panel of experts to 21 finalists. Online and telephone call-in voting on finalists began in 2005. Nothing prevented multiple voting by travelers, fans, citizens, governments, tourism organizations, and so on. The poll was decidedly unscientific.

Even so, millions of people from around the world voted via the Internet to choose a new list of the Seven Wonders of the World. The winners were announced on the seventh day of the seventh month in the year '07 (07/07/07). Winners were: the Great Wall of China; the ancient city of Petra in Jordan; the statue of Christ the Redeemer in Rio de Janeiro; Machu Picchu in Peru; the Maya ruins of Chichen Itza in Mexico; the Colosseum in Rome; and India's Taj Mahal.

All are sites well worth visiting, but it will be interesting to see if Weber's "New Seven Wonders" become an accepted list because his campaign did not receive the backing of major mainstream monument designation organizations or at UNESCO's World Heritage agency.

DISCUSSION QUESTIONS

1. What marketing opportunities are present from being named a new "wonder of the world"?

2. What do you think of Weber's methodology to choose the new seven wonders?

Also featured are Profiles of eight travel and tourism leaders and WATG, one of the top destination design firms in the world. Our goal in including these profiles is to acknowledge the very special contributions that these industry leaders have made to tourism.

PROFILE

DAWN DREW,
Founder and CEO The M.O.S.T.E., Inc.,
International Marketing and
Entertainment

Dawn Drew joined the National Geographic Society as advertising director of *National Geographic Traveler* magazine in December 1994. During her nine years with the Society, she has been promoted twice, first to publisher of *Traveler* in 1998 and two years later to vice president.

- Publication of *National Geographic Traveler On Campus*, an edition sent to nearly 1 million college students interested or involved in study abroad programs and education travel

- Publication of *National Geographic Traveler* Special Supplements, in-book editorial supplements that focus on a single destination from a cultural perspective

- Creation of National Geographic Traveler Destination Immersion Programs, local market events that allow the general public consumers and readers of *Traveler* magazine to "sample" a destination via seminal experiences with food and wine tastings, photo gallery exhibitions, live photography presentations, and live music concerts featuring artists from around the globe

In addition to her publishing responsibilities for the magazine, Dawn has remained active in the travel industry. Since 1996, she has served as a member of the Travel Industry Association (TIA) board of directors, has been chair of the research committee for three consecutive years, is currently chair of the marketing committee, has held officers' positions for five years, and is currently the second vice chair of the organization. In 2009, Dawn became national chair of the TIA, the first magazine publisher ever to hold that post.

During her tenure as chair of the research committee, National Geographic Traveler successfully collaborated with the TIA research division to produce a landmark study, "Geo-Tourism," the first major piece of research to examine the awareness and travel habits of Americans with regard to sustainable tourism. An updated version of this study was introduced in October 2007 at the TIA Marketing Outlook Forum.

ADDITIONAL RESOURCES

An *Instructor's Manual* (ISBN 978-1-118-15224-9) is available to professors who have adopted this textbook. The *Instructor's Manual* contains teaching suggestions, sample syllabi, and test questions and answers. An electronic version of the *Instructor's Manual* is available to qualified instructors on the companion Web site at www.wiley.com/college/goeldner. The Web site also includes PowerPoint slides and Internet resources.

The *Test Bank* for this text has been specifically formatted for Respondus, an easy-to-use software for creating and managing exams that can be printed to paper or published directly to Blackboard, WebCT, Desire2Learn, eCollege, ANGEL, and other eLearning systems. Instructors who adopt *Tourism: Principles, Practices, Philosophies* can download the *Test Bank* for free. Additional Wiley resources also can be uploaded into your LMS course at no charge. To view and access these resources and the *Test Bank*, visit www.wiley.com/college/goeldner, click on the "Visit the Companion Sites" link, then click on "Instructor Companion Site."

ACKNOWLEDGMENTS

As *Tourism, Twelfth Edition* goes to press, we celebrate the thousands of students who have already begun their education in travel and tourism with previous editions of this book. We acknowledge their participation through their letters to us and to our publisher.

We are grateful for the help of all of the educators who have contributed to this and previous editions through their constructive comments and feedback at conferences, via telephone, and written correspondence.

Many thanks go to the current and past reviewers of the manuscript for their helpful comments. They include:

Jim Clark, president and CEO, Fort Collins Convention & Visitors Bureau

Dogon Gursoy, Washington State University

Tammie J. Kaufman, University of Central Florida

Richard F. Patterson, Western Kentucky University

Wayne W. Smith, College of Charleston

Daniel M. Spencer, Black Hills State University

Victor Teye, Arizona State University

Dallen J. Timothy, Arizona State University

We cannot emphasize too much the extent to which their comments have provided guidance to us in our revision efforts and as we constantly seek to maintain the pioneering standard for quality set for us by the founder of this textbook, Dr. Robert W. McIntosh. We once again salute him.

We especially wish to thank Philip L. Pearce, Department of Tourism, James Cook University, Townsville, Queensland, Australia, for his contribution of Chapter 9, "Motivation for Pleasure Travel." A special word of thanks must also go to Dr. Richard F. Patterson, Western Kentucky University, who developed a number of the Internet exercises for this textbook, and Cindy DiPersio, University of Colorado, who proofread the manuscript.

We also acknowledge the support of the staff at John Wiley & Sons, especially JoAnna Turtletaub, Mary Cassells, Julie Kerr, Jenni Lee, and Amy Weintraub. Special recognition must go to Deb Angus at the University of Calgary, who tirelessly prepared the manuscript, artwork, index, and *Instructor's Manual*.

Charles R. Goeldner
University of Colorado

J. R. Brent Ritchie
University of Calgary

PART 1

Tourism Overview

Florence, Italy, is a favorite destination in Europe for travelers around the world. *Photo courtesy of Corbis Digital Stock.*

CHAPTER 1

Tourism in Perspective

LEARNING OBJECTIVES

- Understand what tourism is and its many definitions.
- Learn the components of tourism and tourism management.
- Examine the various approaches to studying tourism and determine which is of greatest interest to you.
- Appreciate how important this industry is to the economy of the world and of many countries.
- Know the benefits and costs of tourism.

Tourism is visiting the exquisite canaled city of Venice, Italy; exploring the waterways and walkways; riding in a gondola; taking the vaporetti (public "bus" ferries); admiring the bridges, museums, palaces, and churches. This magical city with its unique beauty provides tourists from all over the world enjoyment. *Photo courtesy of PhotoDisc, Inc./Getty Images.*

INTRODUCTION

Bon Voyage!

You are setting off on a voyage to learn about the subject of **tourism**. Assuming that the forecasters and futurists are correct, you are studying the world's largest industry. Tourism is alive with dynamic growth, new activities, new destinations, new technology, new markets, and rapid changes. Record numbers of tourists are traveling the globe, attracted by an increased variety of tour packages, cruises, adventure experiences, and independent itineraries. All of these visitors and the activities they generate change local communities. They have an economic and social impact that cannot be ignored. In today's society, attention must be paid to environmental issues, cultural issues, economic issues, the way landscapes are created to appeal to tourists, and how tourists behave.

The **tourism industry** is global. It is big business and will continue to grow. Meeting this growth with well-planned, environmentally sound development is a challenge for planning all over the world, whether it is Indonesia, Nepal, the United States, Australia, Thailand, or France. The goal of this chapter and the book is to raise issues, provide frameworks, and generate your thoughtful consideration of the issues and changes facing this complex field as it operates in an increasingly technological and global age.

WHAT IS TOURISM?

When we think of tourism, we think primarily of people who are visiting a particular place for sightseeing, visiting friends and relatives, taking a vacation, and having a good time. They might spend their leisure time engaging in various sports, sunbathing, talking, singing, taking rides, touring, reading, or simply enjoying the environment. If we consider the subject further, we may include in our definition of tourism people who are participating in a convention, a business conference, or some other kind of business or professional activity, as well as those who are taking a study tour under an expert guide or doing some kind of scientific research or study.

These visitors use all forms of transportation, from hiking in a wilderness park to flying in a jet to an exciting city. Transportation can include taking a chairlift up a Colorado mountainside or standing at the rail of a cruise ship looking across the blue Caribbean. Whether people travel by one of these means or by car, motorcoach, camper, train, taxi, motorbike, or bicycle, they are taking a trip and thus are engaging in tourism. That is what this book is all about—why people travel (and why some don't) and the socioeconomic effects that their presence and **expenditures** have on a society.

Any attempt to define tourism and to describe its scope fully must consider the various groups that participate in and are affected by this industry. Their perspectives are vital to the development of a comprehensive definition. Four different perspectives of tourism can be identified:

1. *The tourist.* The tourist seeks various psychic and physical experiences and satisfactions. The nature of these will largely determine the destinations chosen and the activities enjoyed.
2. *The businesses providing tourist goods and services.* Businesspeople see tourism as an opportunity to make a profit by supplying the goods and services that the tourist market demands.
3. *The government of the host community or area.* Politicians view tourism as a wealth factor in the economy of their jurisdictions. Their perspective is related to the incomes their citizens can earn from this business. Politicians also consider the foreign exchange receipts from international tourism, as well as the tax receipts collected from tourist expenditures, either directly or indirectly. The **host government** can play an important role in tourism policy, development, promotion, and implementation (see Chapter 15).

In the United States, the definition of a person-trip is one person traveling 50 miles (one way) or more away from home, or staying overnight regardless of distance. U.S. residents take over two billion person-trips a year—mostly by motor vehicle on the nation's highways. *Photo courtesy of The Adirondack Regional Tourism Council.*

4. *The host community.* Local people usually see tourism as a cultural and employment factor. Of importance to the **host community**, for example, is the effect of the interaction between large numbers of international visitors and residents. This effect may be beneficial or harmful, or both.

Thus, tourism can be defined as the processes, activities, and outcomes arising from the relationships and the interactions among tourists, tourism suppliers, host governments, host communities, and surrounding environments that are involved in the attracting and hosting of visitors. (See the Glossary for definitions of tourist and excursionist.)

Tourism is a composite of activities, services, and industries that deliver a travel experience: transportation, accommodations, eating and drinking establishments, shops, entertainment, activity facilities, and other hospitality services available for individuals or groups that are traveling away from home. It encompasses all providers of visitor and visitor-related services. Tourism is the entire world industry of travel, hotels, transportation, and all other components, including promotion, that serve the needs and wants of travelers. Finally, tourism is the sum total of tourist expenditures within the borders of a nation or a political subdivision or a transportation-centered economic area of contiguous states or nations. This economic concept also considers the income multiplier of these tourist expenditures (discussed in Chapter 14).

One has only to consider the multidimensional aspects of tourism and its interactions with other activities to understand why it is difficult to come up with a meaningful definition that will be universally accepted. Each of the many definitions that have arisen is aimed at fitting a special situation and solving an immediate problem, and the lack of uniform definitions has hampered the study of tourism as a discipline. Development of a field depends on: (1) uniform definitions, (2) description, (3) analysis, (4) prediction, and (5) control.

Modern tourism is a discipline that has only recently attracted the attention of scholars from many fields. The majority of studies have been conducted for special purposes and have used narrow

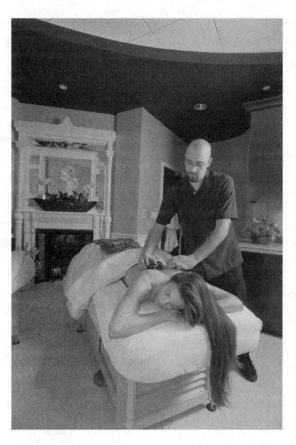

Tourism is relaxing and enjoying a vacation with a stone massage at the Spa of the Rockies. A massage allows a comfortable escape from the complexities of the modern world and encourages a stress-free vacation. *Photo courtesy of the Spa of the Rockies at Glenwood Hot Springs in Glenwood Springs, Colorado.*

operational definitions to suit particular needs of researchers or government officials; these studies have not encompassed a systems approach. Consequently, many definitions of tourism and the tourist are based on distance traveled, the length of time spent, and the purpose of the trip. This makes it difficult to gather statistical information that scholars can use to develop a database, describe the tourism phenomenon, and do analyses.

The problem is not trivial. It has been tackled by a number of august bodies over the years, including the League of Nations, the United Nations, the United Nations World Tourism Organization (UNWTO), the Organization for Economic Cooperation and Development (OECD), the National Tourism Resources Review Commission, and the U.S. Senate's National Tourism Policy Study.

The following review of various definitions illustrates the problems of arriving at a consensus. We examine the concept of the movement of people and the terminology and definitions applied by the United Nations World Tourism Organization and those of the United States, Canada, the United Kingdom, and Australia. Later, a comprehensive classification of travelers is provided that endeavors to reflect a consensus of current thought and practice.

United Nations World Tourism Organization Definitions

The International Conference on Travel and Tourism Statistics convened by the United Nations World Tourism Organization (UNWTO) in Ottawa, Canada, in 1991 reviewed, updated, and expanded on the work of earlier international groups. The Ottawa Conference made some fundamental recommendations on definitions of tourism, travelers, and tourists. The United Nations Statistical Commission adopted the UNWTO's recommendations on tourism statistics on March 4, 1993.

Tourism

The UNWTO has taken the concept of tourism beyond a stereotypical image of "holiday making." The officially accepted definition is: "Tourism comprises the activities of persons traveling to and staying in places outside their usual environment for not more than one consecutive year for leisure, business, and other purposes." The term *usual environment* is intended to exclude trips within the area of usual residence, frequent and regular trips between the domicile and the workplace, and other community trips of a routine character.

1. International tourism
   a. Inbound tourism: Visits to a country by nonresidents
   b. Outbound tourism: Visits by residents of a country to another country
2. Internal tourism: Visits by residents and nonresidents of the country of reference

3. **Domestic tourism:** Visits by residents of a country to their own country
4. **National tourism:** Internal tourism plus outbound tourism (the resident tourism market for travel agents, airlines, and other suppliers)

Traveler Terminology for International Tourism

Underlying the foregoing conceptualization of tourism is the overall concept of **traveler**, defined as "any person on a trip between two or more countries or between two or more localities within his/her country of usual residence." All types of travelers engaged in tourism are described as **visitors**, a term that constitutes the basic concept of the entire system of tourism statistics. International visitors are persons who travel for a period not exceeding 12 months to a country other than the one in which they generally reside and whose main purpose is other than the exercise of an activity remunerated from within the place visited. Internal visitors are persons who travel to a destination within their own country, which is outside their usual environment, for a period not exceeding 12 months.

All visitors are subdivided into two further categories:

1. **Same-day visitors:** Visitors who do not spend the night in a collective or private accommodation in the country visited—for example, a cruise ship passenger spending four hours in a port or day-trippers visiting an attraction
2. **Tourists:** Visitors who stay in the country visited for at least one night—for example, a visitor on a two-week vacation

There are many purposes for a visit—notably pleasure, business, and other purposes, such as family reasons, health, and transit.

United States

The Western Council for Travel Research in 1963 employed the term *visitor* and defined a **visit** as occurring every time a visitor entered an area under study. The definition of *tourist* used by the National Tourism Resources Review Commission in 1973 was: "A tourist is one who travels away from home for a distance of at least 50 miles (one way) for business, pleasure, personal affairs, or any other purpose except to commute to work, whether he stays overnight or returns the same day."

The United States Travel Association (USTA) research department defines a **person-trip** as one person traveling 50 miles (one way) or more away from home or staying overnight, regardless of distance. Trips are included regardless of purpose, excluding only crews, students, military personnel on active duty, and commuters.

Canada

In a series of quarterly household sample surveys known as the Canadian Travel Survey that began in 1978, trips qualifying for inclusion are similar to those in the United States. The 50-mile figure was a compromise to satisfy concerns regarding the accuracy of recall for shorter trips and the possibility of the inclusion of trips completed entirely within the boundaries of a large metropolitan area such as Toronto.

The determination of which length of trip to include in surveys of domestic travel has varied according to the purpose of the survey methodology employed. Whereas there is general agreement that commuting journeys and one-way trips should be excluded, qualifying distances vary. The province of Ontario favors 25 miles.

In Canada's international travel surveys, the primary groups of travelers identified are nonresident travelers, resident travelers, and other travelers. Both nonresident and resident travelers include both same-day and business travelers. Other travelers consist of immigrants, former residents, military personnel, and crews.

United Kingdom

Visit Britain, Visit Scotland, Visit Wales, and the Northern Ireland Tourist Board jointly sponsor a continuous survey of internal tourism, the United Kingdom Tourism Survey (UKTS). It measures all trips away from home lasting one night or more. These include: (1) trips taken by residents for holidays, (2) visits to friends and relatives (nonholiday), or (3) trips taken for business, conferences, or any other purposes. Tourism is measured in terms of volume (trips taken, nights away) and value (expenditure on trips).

The International Passenger Survey collects information on both overseas visitors to the United Kingdom and travel abroad by U.K. residents. It distinguishes five different types of visits: holiday independent, holiday inclusive, business, visits to friends and relatives, and miscellaneous.

Australia

The Australian Bureau of Industry Economics in 1979 placed length of stay and distance traveled constraints in its definition of *tourist* as follows: "A person visiting a location at least 40 kilometers from his usual place of residence, for a period of at least 24 hours and not exceeding 12 months."

In supporting the use of the UNWTO definitions, the Australian Bureau of Statistics notes that the term "*usual environment* is somewhat vague." It states that "visits to tourist attractions by local residents should not be included" and that visits to second homes should be included only "where they are clearly for temporary recreational purposes."

Comprehensive Classification of Travelers

The main types of travelers are indicated in Figure 1.1. Shown is the fundamental distinction between residents and visitors and the interest of travel and tourism practitioners in the characteristics of nontravelers as well as travelers. The figure also reflects the apparent consensus that business and same-day travel both fall within the scope of travel and tourism.

Placed to one side are some other types of travelers generally regarded as being outside the area of interest, although included in some travel surveys. Foremost among these exclusions are commuters, who seem to fall outside the area of interest to all in the travel and tourism community. Other travelers generally excluded from studies on travel and tourism are those who undertake trips within the community, which for convenience are described arbitrarily as trips involving less than a specific one-way distance, such as 50 miles. These "other travelers" have been focused on in the Nationwide Personal Transportation Surveys conducted by the U.S. Department of Transportation. The broad class of travelers categorized as migrants, both international and domestic, is also commonly excluded from tourism or travel research, on the grounds that their movement is not temporary, although they use the same facilities as other travelers, albeit in one direction, and frequently require temporary accommodation on reaching their destination. The real significance of migration to travel and tourism, however, is not in the one-way trip in itself, but in the long-term implications of a transplanted demand for travel and the creation of a new travel destination for separated friends and relatives.

Other groups of travelers are commonly excluded from travel and tourism studies because their travel is not affected by travel promotion, although they tend to compete for the same types of facilities and services. Students and temporary workers traveling purely for reasons of education or temporary employment are two leading examples. Another frequently excluded group consists of crews, although they can be regarded as special subsets of tourists.

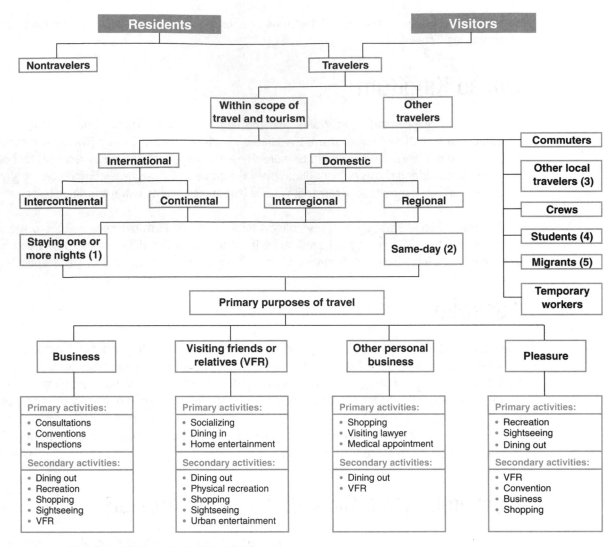

Figure 1.1 Classification of travelers.

(1) *Tourists* in international technical definitions.
(2) *Excursionists* in international technical definitions.
(3) Travelers whose trips are shorter than those that qualify for travel and tourism: e.g., under 50 miles (80 km) from home.
(4) Students traveling between home and school only—other travel of students is within scope of travel and tourism.
(5) All persons moving to a new place of residence, including all one-way travelers, such as emigrants, immigrants, refugees, domestic migrants, and nomads.

Of those travelers directly within the scope of travel and tourism, basic distinctions are made among those whose trips are completed within one day. The same-day visitors are also called day-trippers and **excursionists** because they stay less than 24 hours. Although they are important travelers, their economic significance pales in comparison to travelers who stay one or more nights. An additional meaningful division can also be made between those international travelers whose travel is between continents and those whose international travel is confined to countries within the same continent. In the case of the United States, the distinction is between (1) trips to or from the neighboring countries of Canada and Mexico or elsewhere in the Americas and (2) trips made to or from countries in Europe or on other continents.

The purposes of travel identified in Figure 1.1 go beyond those traditionally accepted because of the growing evidence that "visits to friends and relatives" (VFR) is a basic travel motivation and a distinctive factor in **marketing**, accounting for a major proportion of travel. In any event, "primary

Tourism is engaging in wonderful, fun, family experiences while on vacation. Visiting an interactive zoological park such as Jungle Island and enjoying an encounter with lorikeets is a memorable experience. *Photo courtesy of Jungle Island.*

purpose" is an arbitrary concept because many journeys are undertaken for a combination of reasons, such as "business and vacation."

COMPONENTS OF TOURISM AND TOURISM MANAGEMENT

Tourism is a complex phenomenon, one that is extremely difficult to describe succinctly. Any model of tourism must "capture" the composition—or components—of the tourism system, as well as the key processes and outcomes that occur within tourism. These processes and outcomes include the very essence of tourism, the travel experience, and the supporting means by which tourism is made possible. Figure 1.2 attempts to describe the complexity of the relationships among the many components of the tourism phenomenon.

The Tourist

The very heart of the tourism phenomenon model is unequivocally the *tourists* and the travel experiences that they seek when visiting a tourism destination. In order for a destination to provide stimulating, high-quality experiences, it is critical that both policy makers and managers be able to understand tourists' motivation for pleasure travel, as well as the multiple factors that influence their selection of a destination, their mode of travel, and their ultimate choice among the myriad activities that may fulfill their travel needs. It is only when we understand the tourist as fully as possible that we can proceed to develop the facilities, events, activities, and programs that will distinguish a given destination, thus making it uniquely attractive to the tourist.

Natural Resources and Environment

A fundamental dimension of the model—indeed, the very basis of much tourism—is the natural resources and environment component. Any given destination is primarily and unchangeably characterized by its **physiography** (the nature and appearance of its landscape) and its **climate** (the kind of weather it has over a period of years; i.e., the conditions of heat and cold, moisture and

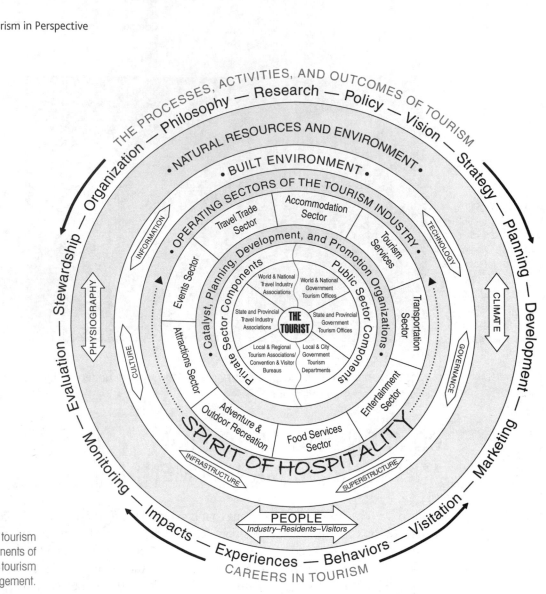

Figure 1.2 The tourism phenomenon: components of tourism and tourism management.

dryness, and wind). Finally, the third component of the natural environment is people. In the case of people, we must distinguish between two very important categories of individuals: (1) those who "belong" to the destination (its residents), and (2) those who are current or potential visitors to the destination (the tourism market).

The Built Environment

Another dimension of the tourism phenomenon is the **built environment** that has been created by humans. This built environment first includes the culture of the residents of the host region. As discussed in Chapter 10, the culture of a people reflects many dimensions of its past development and its current way of life. *Culture* is a very permanent characteristic of a destination, and one that cannot (and should not) be changed simply to enhance tourism development.

The *infrastructure* of a tourism destination is yet another dimension that has not been put in place mainly to serve tourism. Such basic things as roads, sewage systems, communication networks, and many commercial facilities (supermarkets and retail stores) have been put in place to meet the needs of local residents. Although these components of the infrastructure can also be important to visitors, their primary functions are related to the ongoing daily needs of residents. In contrast, a destination's *tourism superstructure* includes those facilities that have been developed especially to respond to the

Tourism is visiting the Indian Peaks Wilderness Area near Denver, Colorado, and marveling at all that nature has to offer. Outdoor recreationists recognize their responsibility to maintain the environmental integrity of the areas they explore. *Photo by Richard Grant, courtesy of Denver Metro Convention and Visitors Bureau.*

demands of visitors. The most obvious examples include hotels, restaurants, conference centers, car rental locations, and major attractions. Because of their special tourism orientation, the characteristics of components of the superstructure are essentially determined by visitors' wishes rather than residents' desires, even though residents often desire many benefits from certain elements of the tourism superstructure.

Technology is one of the most recent, and still increasingly influential, dimensions of the built environment that is shaping the nature of both tourism products/services and travel experiences. In many ways, technology can be viewed as one of the most distinctive and most powerful characteristics of the built environment since the dawn of modern tourism following World War II. The advent of jet aircraft and the massive invasion of telecommunications technology, linked closely with computer technology, have had a dramatic impact on the very essence of the tourism phenomenon. Indeed, these aspects of technology have become so pervasive and so important that they, in fact, represent very specialized elements of both the tourism infrastructure and superstructure. However, because of their unique identification with the modern era of the built environment, each aspect—transportation, telecommunications, and computer technology—merits specific identification. See Chapters 5, 7, 18, and 19.

A recent addition to the built environment of a destination is *information*. Increasingly, the success of a destination is determined by its ability to assemble, interpret, and utilize information in an effective manner. Information is of several types: information concerning the potential tourism market, which is essential for destination design and development; information on the level of satisfaction of current visitors regarding the quality, or enjoyment, of their visitation experience; information regarding competitors and their activities; information concerning the functioning or performance of the destination in its efforts to profitably provide attractive experiences to visitors; and information concerning the extent to which residents of the host region understand and support tourism as a long-term component of the socioeconomic system.

Finally, a dimension of tourism that often receives inadequate attention is the overall system of *governance* within which the tourism system functions. This topic is discussed in greater detail in Chapter 15. For present purposes, it should be noted that the system of governance surrounding tourism (the legal, political, and fiscal systems regulating its functioning) has a profound impact on the ability of a destination to compete in the international marketplace and subsequently plays a major role in determining the profitability of individual firms. Although the system of governance of a country or region may be viewed as an evolutionary dimension of overall culture, it is subject to influence and change within an observable time frame. Sometimes these changes can be quite dramatic and can occur in a relatively short period of time in cultural terms. Recent high-profile examples include the worldwide phenomenon of deregulation and privatization and the more focused process of economic (and eventually social) integration brought about by the formation of regional trade blocs such as the European Union (EU) and the countries of North American Free Trade Agreement (NAFTA). Parallel initiatives in Asia are Asia Pacific Economic Cooperation (APEC) and the Association of Southeast Asia Nations (ASEAN). Even more recently, the events of September 11, 2001, have incited many governments to introduce new regulations concerning airline travel and entry to countries that impact both domestic and international travel.

Operating Sectors of the Tourism Industry

The **operating sectors** of the tourism industry represent what many of the general public perceive as "tourism." First and foremost, the **transportation** sector (see Figure 1.2), comprising airlines, bus companies, and so on, tends to typify the movement of people and travel (see Chapter 5). The **accommodation** sector, which includes many well-known brands such as Hilton, Marriott, Howard Johnson, Best Western, and so on, is highly visible to the public. Similarly, the **food services** sector also contains a broad spectrum of brands and logos that have become part of everyday life in many communities. Examples include world-famous fast-food chains (McDonald's, Pizza Hut, Burger King, KFC) and internationally known gourmet restaurants such as Maxim's in Paris and Alfredo's in Rome. The accommodations and food service sectors are covered in Chapter 6.

The **attractions** sector also contains many well-known icons in the tourism industry. The undisputed leader of the attraction world is Disneyland/Walt Disney World. Other world-famous attractions include the upscale Louvre museum in Paris, France; the Hermitage in St. Petersburg, Russia; Marineland and Knott's Berry Farm in the United States; the pyramids in Egypt; Stonehenge in the United Kingdom; the Acropolis in Athens, Greece; and Niagara Falls, Canada. Attractions are the primary focus of Chapter 8.

Closely related to attractions is the **events** sector. Its icons include the Oktoberfest in Munich, Germany; the Calgary Stampede in Canada; the Mardi Gras of New Orleans and Rio de Janeiro, Brazil; the Boston Marathon; and the Super Bowl in the United States, as well as such transient events as World Cup Soccer and the International Summer and Winter Olympic Games.

The **adventure and outdoor recreation** sector is one of the most rapidly growing components of modern tourism. Changes in demographics, values, and lifestyles are creating increasing demand for activities such as golfing, skiing, snowboarding, whitewater rafting, parasailing, hang gliding, mountain biking, and mountaineering. Most of these activities are characterized by both an element of thrill seeking and an element of being outdoors. An allied, related desire for closeness to nature has given rise to the phenomenon of **ecotourism**, an ill-defined and often abused term for any type of travel activity in a natural setting (see Chapters 8 and 17).

At the other end of the "natural-manufactured" spectrum is the equally fast-growing component of **entertainment**. Certain destinations, most notably Las Vegas, Nashville, and Branson, Missouri, have grown up on a heavy diet of world-famous entertainers. More traditionally, New York/Broadway and Los Angeles/Hollywood have used various aspects of the entertainment industry to consolidate their worldwide reputations as "must see" destinations.

Less glamorous, but still essential to the success and well-being of the tourism industry, are the travel **trade sector** and **tourism services** (see Chapter 7). **Travel trade** is composed of the retail travel agent and the wholesale tour operator. Both of these entities are critical to linking "experience suppliers" and the tourist. The multifaceted travel industry services sector provides yet another type of critical support for successful tourism. Computer support services, retail services, financial services, specialized consulting services, and tourism educators all make an important and usually unique contribution to the effective and efficient functioning of the complex tourism system. While the public (and even many firms themselves) do not identify themselves as part of the tourism juggernaut, the fact remains that, as soon as any one of these services becomes deficient, tourism suffers.

Spirit of Hospitality

As already discussed, the operating sectors of tourism are responsible for delivering high-quality memorable experiences. Care must be taken, however, to wrap these experiences in a warm spirit of hospitality. Quite simply, it is not enough to deliver all the attributes of an experience in a cold or detached manner. Each individual visitor must feel that he or she is more than a source of cold cash revenue for the business or destination. Rather, visitors have a natural human desire for warm acceptance as they seek to enjoy the range of experiences the destination has to offer. Thus, the challenge facing destinations is to deliver their experiences in a way that enables the visitors to believe they are welcome, that they truly are guests.

While tourists naturally recognize that they are transient visitors, destinations must first train industry personnel to treat the tourist with fairness, respect, and a level of politeness. Second, the destination must encourage its permanent residents to behave as friendly hosts to visitors who are in unfamiliar surroundings. They should convey a friendly attitude and, when required, offer basic information and a helpful hand. These small but important gestures will do much to foster a destination spirit of hospitality that will, in turn, greatly enhance the perceived value of all the other aspects of the visitation experience.

Planning, Development, Promotion, and Catalyst Organizations

It is widely acknowledged that the success of tourism ultimately depends on the competence and ability of all of the operating sectors discussed above (i.e., the front line of tourism) to deliver a high-quality experience to each tourist—one person at a time. There is another hidden component of tourism that is equally important in determining the success of a tourism destination. It is known by the unwieldy name of planning, development, promotion, and catalyst organizations (PDPCO). It is the visionaries, policy makers, strategic planners, and individuals and groups who "make the right things happen" that are increasingly a determinant of successful tourism. In effect, in tourism it is as critical that we "do the right things" as that we "do things right." This means simply that policy makers need to ensure that their destination offers the kinds of travel experiences that are most appropriate to the visitor, always keeping in mind any limitations imposed by the resources of the destination.

Once the appropriate experiences have been identified through effective planning, it is essential to ensure that plans are translated into the facilities, events, and programs that are necessary to provide the visitor with the given experience "on the ground."

The organization responsible for providing the insight and leadership necessary to envisage and bring policies and plans into reality is increasingly referred to as the destination management organization (DMO). The specific identity of this organization depends on the "level" of the destination. In most countries, policy and planning involve two very important categories of stakeholders, namely, the public sector (governments) and the private sector (see Figure 1.2). At the *national* level, governments are usually represented by a national tourism office (such as a department of tourism or a national tourism corporation). A national travel/tourism industry association typically represents the private sector.

At the *state/provincial* level, the public/private sector organizations are usually known respectively as the state/provincial government tourism office and the state/provincial travel industry association. The parallel equivalent at the *city/municipal* or *regional* level are local and city government tourism departments and local and city tourism associations or, more commonly, a convention and visitor bureau (CVB) (see Chapter 4).

The Importance of Integrated/Collaborative Planning and Development

One dimension of Figure 1.2 that is essential to note is the "wavy line" that forms the interface between the public and private sectors at all levels. This line is intended to convey the importance of integrated or collaborative planning and development efforts. Because both the public and private sectors each control (and often operate) an important percentage of tourism facilities, events, and programs, it is critical that policy, planning, and development efforts be continuously carried out within a joint, cooperative, collaborative organizational framework. Failure to acknowledge the importance of this reality leads only to antagonism, strife, and disjointed strategic planning and development. Therefore, each destination must strive to create DMOs where collaboration is built into the design. The actual name of the organization (be it a tourism authority, a tourism council, or a tourism partnership) matters little. What is important is the quality of the collaboration that occurs.

The Processes, Activities, and Outcomes of Tourism

Another dimension of Figure 1.2 that needs to be understood is the nature of the processes and activities that both surround and occur within the tourism system and that in the end create the outcomes that are the essence of the phenomenon we call tourism.

We have previously addressed the issue of organizing the components of tourism so that they work together effectively. As indicated, a common result of these organizational efforts is the creation of a DMO. For successful tourism, the DMO, in collaboration with all stakeholders, must define the **tourism philosophy** of the destination and formulate a supportive *policy, vision,* and *strategy* (see Chapter 15). These, in turn, provide direction and guidance for the detailed *planning* and *development* initiatives that will ultimately determine the nature and quality of the *experiences* the destination is capable of offering (see Chapter 16).

The availability of these "experience offerings" must be made known to potential visitors through effective *marketing,* defined in the broadest sense (see Chapter 19). Such marketing includes highly visible promotional efforts as well as the less glamorous dimensions of pricing and distribution of the travel products/experiences.

Successful marketing will attract a broad range of visitors whose behaviors provide them with enjoyment and the memorable experiences associated with these behaviors. These behaviors can give rise to both positive and negative impacts. The positive impacts pertain largely to the economic benefits (income and employment) that tourism provides. The negative impacts largely concern the ecological, social, cultural, and commemorative integrity of the destination.

The success of the policy, development, and marketing programs is measured by the levels of visitation achieved, the type of visitors attracted, the appropriateness of their behavior—and especially by the quality of visitor experiences. Each of these impacts must be rigorously **monitored** in order that a systematic **evaluation** of the strengths and weaknesses of the above programs can be made. Finally, a comprehensive program of **stewardship** is required to ensure that the success of tourism does not destroy the natural resources on which tourism depends so heavily (see Chapter 17).

The final activity that is essential to long-term success of tourism is an ongoing process of **evaluation**. Evaluation is simply an attempt to carefully assess the appropriateness, effectiveness, efficiency, and overall performance of all components and processes in the tourism system. The results of the evaluation provide a critical source of information for the next ongoing stages of policy formulation, visioning, and strategic planning and development.

Careers in Tourism

All of the foregoing segments, sectors, and organizations require people to make the various processes work and to make the broad range of activities and experiences available to travelers. It is these "experiences" that are the tourism product, the intended outcome of the tourism phenomenon. The people in the tourism industry who provide these experiences, as in any industry, must perform a vast number of organizational functions. These functions range from relatively simple jobs to highly sophisticated and demanding tasks (see Chapter 3). All are important in providing a truly memorable vacation experience or efficient business travel.

The tourism industry is often characterized by the large number of front-line service jobs that must be performed for tourism to function effectively. For example, the accommodation sector requires bell staff, front desk staff, and room maintenance staff. The food services sector requires cooks, waitstaff, bartenders, and kitchen maintenance staff. The attractions sector requires facilitation and equipment operators, as do the entertainment, event, and transportation sectors. The adventure and outdoor recreation sector needs guides and group leaders. The travel trade and tourism services sectors must have the personnel to assist travelers as they plan their trips and then to meet their many needs for information and assistance throughout their travel experiences. As can be surmised, the performance of the many tasks identified requires many thousands of individuals who are trained to perform each specialized task in an effective and friendly manner.

But this is only the "face of tourism" that encompasses the many service jobs for which tourism is sometimes criticized, and even ridiculed. Behind this face (which, incidentally, provides many essential part-time and first-time jobs for students and less-skilled members of our society) are an extremely large number of highly attractive career positions that require sophisticated technical skills and/or managerial training. These career positions are attractive in two very different ways. First, they provide challenges equal to those in virtually any other industry. Second, the nature of tourism means that many of these careers are pursued in very attractive physical settings and among people who generally like to see others enjoy life. The career path of the manager of a large vacation resort, while just as challenging as the path of those in many other sectors, offers both an attractive income and a lifestyle that is simply not available in many other sectors or professions.

BASIC APPROACHES TO THE STUDY OF TOURISM

The study of tourism is commonly approached through a variety of methods. However, there is little or no agreement on how it should be undertaken. The following are several methods that have been used.

Institutional Approach

The institutional approach to the study of tourism considers the various intermediaries and institutions that perform tourism activities. It emphasizes institutions such as the travel agency. This approach requires an investigation of the organization, operating methods, problems, costs, and economic place of travel agents who act on behalf of the customer, purchasing services from airlines, rental car companies, hotels, and so on. An advantage of this approach is that the U.S. Census Bureau conducts a survey every five years on selected services that includes travel agents and lodging places, thus providing a database for further study.

Product Approach

The product approach involves the study of various tourism products and how they are produced, marketed, and consumed. For example, one might study an airline seat—how it is created, the people who are engaged in buying and selling it, how it is financed, how it is advertised, and so on. Repeating this procedure for rental cars, hotel rooms, meals, and other tourist services gives a full picture of the field. Unfortunately, the product approach tends to be too time-consuming; it does not allow the student to grasp the fundamentals of tourism quickly. However, it is an excellent source of examples.

Historical Approach

The historical approach is not widely used. It involves an analysis of tourism activities and institutions from an evolutionary angle. It searches for the cause of innovations, their growth or decline, and shifts in interest. Even though tourism has been practiced for centuries, real growth did not start until after World War II. In the 1960s and 1970s, places such as Mallorca and Southern Spain were destinations that realized a massive influx of tourists arriving on package tours. Thus, mass tourism was born, creating the need to study the effects that large numbers of people have on a destination. Because mass tourism is a fairly recent phenomenon, this approach has limited usefulness.

Managerial Approach

The managerial approach is firm-oriented (microeconomic), focusing on the management activities necessary to operate a tourist enterprise, such as planning, research, pricing, marketing, control, and the like. It is a popular approach, using insights gleaned from other approaches and disciplines. Although a major focus of this book is managerial, readers will recognize that other perspectives are also being used. Regardless of which approach is used to study tourism, it is important to know the managerial approach. Products change, institutions change, and society changes; this means that managerial objectives and procedures must be geared to change to meet shifts in the tourism environment. The *Journal of Travel Research* and *Tourism Management,* leading journals in the field, both feature this approach.

Economic Approach

Because of its importance to both domestic and world economies, tourism has been examined closely by economists, who focus on supply, demand, balance of payments, foreign exchange, employment, expenditures, development, multipliers, and other economic factors. This approach is useful in providing a framework for analyzing tourism and its contributions to a country's economy. The disadvantage of the economic approach is that, whereas tourism is an important economic phenomenon, it has noneconomic impacts as well. The economic approach does not usually pay adequate attention to the environmental, cultural, psychological, sociological, and anthropological approaches. *Tourism Economics* is a journal utilizing the economic approach.

Sociological Approach

Tourism tends to be a social activity. Consequently, it has attracted the attention of sociologists, who have studied the tourism behavior of individuals and groups of people and the impact of tourism on society. This approach examines social classes, habits, and customs of both hosts and guests. The sociology of leisure is a relatively undeveloped field, but it shows promise of progressing rapidly and becoming more widely used. As tourism continues to make a massive impact on society, it will be studied more and more from a sociological perspective.

Geographical Approach

Geography is a wide-ranging discipline, so it is natural that geographers should be interested in tourism and the spatial aspects of travel. The geographer specializes in the study of location, environment, climate, landscape, and their economic aspects. The geographer's approach to tourism sheds light on the location of tourist areas, the movements of people created by tourism locales, the changes that tourism brings to the landscape in the form of tourism facilities, dispersion of tourism development, physical planning, and economic, social, and cultural problems. Because tourism touches geography at so many points, geographers have investigated the area more thoroughly than have scholars in many other disciplines. Because the geographers' approach is so encompassing—dealing with land use, economic aspects, demographic impacts, and cultural problems—a study of their contributions is highly recommended. Recreational geography is a common course title used by geographers studying this specialty. Because tourism, leisure, and recreation are so closely related, it is necessary to search for literature under all these titles to discover the contributions of various fields. Geographers were instrumental in starting both the *Journal of Leisure Research* and *Leisure Sciences*. Another journal, *Tourism Geographies,* was launched in February 1999 with the aim of providing a forum for the presentation and discussion of geographic perspectives on tourism and tourism-related areas of recreation and leisure studies.

Interdisciplinary Approaches

Tourism embraces virtually all aspects of our society. We have cultural and heritage tourism, which calls for an anthropological approach. Because people behave in different ways and travel for different reasons, it is necessary to use a psychological approach to determine the best way to promote and market tourism products. Because tourists cross borders and require passports and visas from government offices, and because most countries have government-operated tourism development departments, we find that political institutions are involved, thus calling for a political science approach. Any industry that becomes an economic giant affecting the lives of many people attracts the attention of legislative bodies (along with that of the sociologists, geographers, economists, and anthropologists), which create the laws, regulations, and legal environment in which the tourist industry must operate; so we also have a legal approach. The great importance of transportation suggests passenger transportation as another approach. The fact simply is that tourism is so vast, so complex, and so multifaceted that it is necessary to take a number of approaches to studying the field, each geared to a somewhat different task or objective. Figure 1.3 illustrates the interdisciplinary nature of tourism studies and their reciprocity and mutuality. The *Annals of Tourism Research,* an interdisciplinary social sciences journal, is another publication that should be on the serious tourism student's reading list.

The Systems Approach

What is really needed to study tourism is a systems approach. A system is a set of interrelated components coordinated to form a unified whole and organized to accomplish a set of goals. It integrates all approaches into a comprehensive method dealing with both micro and macro-issues. It examines the tourist firm's competitive environment, its market, its results, its linkages with other institutions, the consumer, and the interaction of the firm with the consumer. In addition, a systems approach takes a macro-viewpoint and examines the entire tourism system of a country, state, or area and how it operates within and relates to other systems, such as legal, political, economic, and social systems.

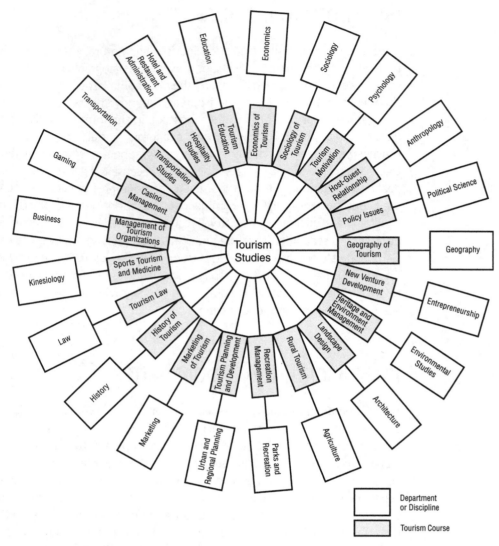

Figure 1.3 Disciplinary inputs to the tourism field. Adapted from Jafar Jafari, University of Wisconsin-Stout, *Study of Tourism: Choices of Discipline and Approach.*

ECONOMIC IMPORTANCE

The World Travel and Tourism Council (WTTC) has been measuring the economic impact of travel and tourism for the world, regions, and Organization for Economic Cooperation and Development (OECD) countries since 1991. In 1992, the WTTC released its first estimates indicating that travel and tourism (T&T) is one of the world's largest industries and a generator of quality jobs. The WTTC continues its measurement efforts; Table 1.1 shows its most recent world estimates for 2010 and forecasts for 2020. In 2010, the global travel and tourism industry was expected to generate $5.75 trillion of economic activity and more than 235.8 million jobs (direct and indirect). Travel and tourism is projected to grow to $11.15 trillion of economic activity and over 303.0 million jobs by 2020.

Globally in 2010, the travel and tourism economy (direct and indirect) employment is estimated at 235,758,000 jobs, 8.1 percent of total employment, or 1 in every 12.3 jobs. By 2020, this should total 303,019,000 jobs, 9.2 percent of total employment, or 1 in every 10.9 jobs. The world travel and tourism economy's contribution to gross domestic product is expected to total 9.2 percent ($5.75 trillion) in 2010 and rise to 9.6 percent ($11.2 trillion) in 2020.

The economic figures cited show that tourism has grown to be an activity of worldwide importance and significance. For a number of countries, tourism is the largest commodity in international trade. In

TABLE 1.1 World Economic Impact: Estimates and Forecasts

World	2010			2020		
	US$ Billion	% of Total	Growth	US$ Billion	% of Total	Growth
Personal T&T*	3,111	8.4	1.6	5,793	8.8	4.1
Business Travel	819	1.3	−1.8	1,589	1.4	4.3
Government Expenditures	436	3.8	2.6	744	4.0	3.1
Capital Investment	1,241	9.2	−1.7	2,757	9.4	5.3
Visitor Exports	1,086	6.1	0.9	2,160	5.2	5.2
Other Exports	850	4.8	5.9	1,908	4.5	6.5
T&T Demand	7,543	9.4	1.1	14,950	9.5	4.7
T&T Industry GDP	1,986	3.2	0.7	3,650	3.2	4.0
T&T Economy GDP	5,751	9.2	0.5	11,151	9.6	4.4
T&T Industry Employment (000)	81,913	2.8	−0.1	104,740	3.2	2.5
T&T Economy Employment (000)	235,758	8.1	−0.3	303,019	9.2	2.5

*Travel and tourism

Source: World Travel and Tourism Council.

many others, it ranks among the top three industries. Tourism has grown rapidly to become a major social and economic force in the world.

The 2010 WTTC estimates for the world is the tenth set of Tourism Satellite Accounting (TSA) that Oxford Economics has prepared for WTTC. The first, commissioned in 2001, reengineered the models previously developed during the 1990s. The second, prepared in 2002, served an important role in helping to quantify the effects of the tragic events of September 11, 2001, on tourism. The third, in 2003, significantly upgraded and enhanced the quality, sophistication, and precision of the TSA research and presented a second (worst-case) scenario for the Iraq war. The 2004 research increased the world coverage by adding 13 countries not previously included in the TSA research, bringing the total number of countries included to 174. The 2007 research is now firmly anchored in the international standard for tourism satellite accounting that was developed by UNWTO, OECD, and Eurostat, and approved by the United Nations Statistical Commission in 2000 (see Chapter 14 for further discussion of tourism satellite accounting). Visit the WTTC Web site (www.wttc.org) for the latest estimates and forecasts for 181 countries.

As tourism has grown, it has moved from being the province of the rich to being accessible to the masses, involving millions of people. The UNWTO attempts to document tourism's growth in its annual publications titled *Tourism Highlights* and *Compendium of Tourism Statistics.* Table 1.2 shows UNWTO international tourist arrival data up to 2010 and the strong rates of growth for the last several decades, marred only by no growth in 2001, a downturn in 2003, and a decline in 2009, when

STATISTICAL DATA AVAILABILITY

One of the problems in collecting and reporting statistical data for a book is the data lag. As this book was being revised, 2009 data were just becoming available. Unfortunately, data lags are increasing rather than decreasing. This disturbing reality is especially upsetting when one considers that travel is a dynamic and changing industry. The data in this book provide a perspective on the size and importance of the industry and its sectors. Users are encouraged to access the sources provided to update the information and determine if trends are continuing or changing. One of the best ways to do that is to get on the Internet. Web site addresses are provided in many cases to enable you to locate the latest information available.

TABLE 1.2 International Tourist Arrivals: 1950, 1960, 1970, and 1980, 1990, 1995–2010

Year	Arrivals (millions)	Percent of Growth
1950	25	—
1960	69	176
1970	166	141
1980	288	73
1990	456	58
1995	528	16
1996	561	6
1997	586	4
1998	602	3
1999	626	4
2000	675	8
2001	675	0
2002	695	3
2003	684	−1
2004	755	10
2005	795	5
2006	839	6
2007	894	6
2008	913	2
2009	877	−4
2010	935[a]	7

[a] Estimated

Source: United Nations World Tourism Organization (UNWTO).

tourism (and other sectors) were hit hard by the credit and housing market collapses experienced in many countries, as households cut back on leisure travel and corporations cut travel expenditures. However, UNWTO states that tourism is the world's largest growth industry with long-term signs being very positive. Their study, *Tourism 2020 Vision,* forecasts that international arrivals will exceed 1 billion by 2010 and 1.6 billion by 2020. Whether the projections are made by UNWTO or WTTC, growth appears to be in the future forecasts.

UNWTO's 2003 estimate of 684 million tourist arrivals was a result of an exceptionally difficult year in which negative factors came together (the Iraq war, terrorism fears, the severe acute respiratory syndrome [SARS], and a persistently weak world economy), causing a 1.3 percent decline in arrivals compared to 2002.

Thus, this growth of tourism has been irregular this past decade. Rapid growth, medium growth, and even declines have marked tourism's performance the last decade. Long term, it is believed that underlying factors will keep travel on a growth pattern. Travel is resilient and history has shown us that travel bounces back from problems and crises. However, travel will always be vulnerable to economic downturns, terrorism, earthquakes, tsunamis, volcanic ash, and oil concerns.

Preliminary arrival data from UNWTO for 2010 shows international tourism arrivals recovered strongly in 2010. Worldwide, the number of international tourist arrivals reached 935 million, up 58 million, almost 7 percent from 2009. Following the year of global recovery in 2010, tourism is expected to grow in 2011 at a 4 to 5 percent rate, slightly above the long-term average.

TABLE 1.3 World's Top Ten Tourism Destinations by Arrivals, 2009

| Rank | Country | INTERNATIONAL TOURIST ARRIVALS (MILLION) | | % Change |
		2009	2008[a]	09/08
1	France	74.2	79.2	−6.3
2	United States	54.9	57.9	−5.3
3	Spain	52.2	57.2	−8.7
4	China	50.9	53.0	−4.1
5	Italy	43.2	42.7	1.2
6	United Kingdom	28.0	30.1	−7.0
7	Turkey	25.5	25.0	2.0
8	Germany	24.2	24.9	−2.7
9	Malaysia	23.6	22.1	7.2
10	Mexico	21.5	22.6	−5.2

[a] Data as collected in UNWTO database April 2010.

Source: United Nations World Tourism Organization (UNWTO).

Top Ten

The world's top ten tourism destinations are shown in Table 1.3. France ranks number one in tourism arrivals, with 74.2 million, followed by the United States, Spain, China, and Italy. These five leading destinations account for 31.3 percent of the world volume of tourism flows. The top ten countries account for about 45.3 percent of the flows. Although this represents a heavy geographical concentration, the trend is toward a gradual diversification with the emergence of new destinations in the Asia–Pacific regions. China has moved to fourth place and Malaysia to ninth. Turkey has moved to seventh place.

A similar concentration pattern emerges if countries are classified according to their tourism receipts. Table 1.4 shows the rank of countries by international tourism receipts, with the United States leading, followed by Spain, France, Italy, China, Germany, United Kingdom, Australia, Turkey, and Austria. In terms of receipts, the United States benefits from attracting a greater share of higher-spending, longer-staying, long-haul tourists than its European competitors, which rely more on short-haul tourism. For world tourism statistics, a visit to the United Nations World Tourism Organization's Web site is a must: unwto.org/en.

Be alert to the fact that most tourism data go through a series of changes; first, preliminary data are released allowing an early look at trends, then additional data become available improving the database, and revisions are made. Revision is a typical process for improving and reporting data. Make it a rule to always go to the source to get the latest data for tourism planning purposes.

Canada

Canada was the world's fifteenth most popular tourism destination in 2009, with 15.8 million international visitors according to the UNWTO. In receipts, Canada ranked sixteenth with $13.6 billion.

Results from Canada National Tourism Indicators (NTI) show that tourism spending in Canada decreased 2.0 percent in real terms in 2009, as spending by international visitors fell to its lowest level in 15 years. As a result, the domestic share of tourism spending increased for a fifth consecutive year to 80 percent from 70 percent in 2004.

TABLE 1.4 World's Top Ten Tourism Earners, 2009

Rank	Country	International Tourist Receipts (US$ billion)		% Change
		2009	2008[a]	09/08
1	United States	93.9	110.0	−14.4
2	Spain	53.2	61.6	−9.0
3	France	49.4	56.6	−7.6
4	Italy	40.2	45.7	−7.2
5	China	39.7	40.8	−2.9
6	Germany	34.7	40.0	−8.5
7	United Kingdom	30.1	36.0	−1.6
8	Australia	25.6	24.8	11.2
9	Turkey	21.3	22.0	−3.2
10	Austria	19.4	21.6	−5.2

[a] Data as collected in UNWTO database June 2010.

Source: United Nations World Tourism Organization (UNWTO).

The decline in international tourism spending in Canada mirrored a worldwide trend that saw a decrease in international tourism receipts (constant prices) in the first three quarters of 2009. According to UNWTO, international tourism has shown some resiliency toward the global economic crisis, falling at about half the pace of estimated exports worldwide.

In Canada, spending by international visitors decreased 8.7 percent in real terms to its lowest level since 1994. In comparison, Canada's exports of goods and services declined 14.0 percent. Overnight travel from the United States and overseas fell 6.4 percent and 12.3 percent, respectively. This was the first decline in travel from overseas since 2003, when the severe acute respiratory syndrome (SARS) outbreak occurred.

Canadians love to travel; consequently, Canada's international travel account deficit was at $12.6 billion in 2008, the highest level ever. Over the past 20 years, Canadian spending overseas has decreased only twice, in 1994 and 2002.

United States

In the United States, tourism is ranked as the third largest retail industry behind automobile and food sales. In employment, it is second to health services. Although tourism is often thought of as leisure travel, it also encompasses business and convention travel, meetings, seminars, recreation, student travel (if less than a year), transportation services, and accommodations. According to the United States Travel Association (USTA) research department, travel and tourism generated $731.3 billion in spending in 2009. This total includes expenditures by foreign travelers, domestic travelers, and international passenger fares.

These travel expenditures, in turn, generated 7.4 million jobs for Americans, with $186.3 billion in payroll income as well as $113.0 billion tax revenue for federal, state, and local governments. International visitors spent $121.1 billion traveling in the United States in 2009, including international passenger fares, while U.S. resident travelers spent $99.1 billion traveling in foreign countries. As a result, a travel trade surplus of $22.0 billion was generated.

Traveler spending in the United States is projected to total $738.5 billion in 2010, $805.7 billion in 2011, $858.70 billion in 2012, and $895.5 in 2013 according to USTA's forecasts. Readers are

Tourism is a family taking a vacation and enjoying a beautiful beach. The sea offers a fun place to enjoy the sun, sand, water, and other resort amenities. *Photo courtesy of Amelia Island Convention & Visitors Bureau.*

encouraged to examine the USTA Travel Forecast, which is based on USTA's Travel Forecast Model. It also includes inbound travel data from the U.S. Commerce Department's International Trade Administration. It is the opinion of the authors that USTA is the most authoritative source of information on the U.S. travel industry, and you should visit its extensive Web site (www.ustravel.org).

Directly or indirectly, tourism is part of the fabric of most of the world's industries, including transportation, retailing, advertising, sports, sporting goods and equipment, clothing, the food industry, and health care. Tourism also plays a part in most communication media, particularly in the travel sections of newspapers and on the Web. There are many print and visual media of direct interest to tourism. Media are also important to those engaged in marketing tourism, such as airlines, cruise lines, motorcoach and rail lines, tour companies, travel agencies, auto rental companies, accommodations, attractions, and tourism educational organizations.

Politicians at all levels are typically very concerned with tourism. They look increasingly at tourism as a tool for economic development. In development, they have enacted laws requiring land-use plans with subsequent zoning and building codes to control location, number, and manner of construction of tourist facilities. Parks and recreation programs are enjoyed by tourists as well as local residents. Many governments impose taxes, all or part of which are paid directly or indirectly by tourists and their suppliers. The power of tourism politically is sometimes manifested in unusual ways. An example was the threat of a travel boycott of Alaska by environmental groups protesting the state's planned aerial shooting of 300 wolves. The plan was canceled.

Many industry analysts project a doubling of tourism by the year 2020, with constructive government policies. We believe that such policies will indeed be forthcoming if tourism leaders convey their message effectively. It is in all our interests to achieve this growth, provided that it is accomplished in an intelligent, planned, and thoughtful manner by developers and the public alike. There is an unequivocal responsibility to review the social and environmental factors vigilantly in order to preserve and enhance those qualities that give any destination its special appeal and character. These include its culture, natural resources, host population, and the spirit of the place. We hope that you will strive to assist in the achievement of these ultimate worthy goals.

BENEFITS AND COSTS OF TOURISM

Tourism brings both economic and noneconomic benefits and costs to host communities. Some of the considerable economic impacts and benefits were described in the preceding section. There are additional areas of benefit that have not received much research attention. These relate to the benefits of tourism to the traveler, such as the contribution of pleasure travel to rest and relaxation, the educational benefit, the understanding of other people and cultures, and the physical and mental well being of the traveler.

There is no question that tourism delivers benefits, but tourism is not perfect. Even advocates for tourism such as your authors (we have been accused of being cheerleaders for tourism) acknowledge that tourism is not an unqualified blessing. There are also costs of tourism, and they do not accrue equally. Many of the social costs incurred are difficult or impossible to measure. Books such as *The Golden Hordes, Tourism: Blessing or Blight,* and *The Holiday Makers* (see the Selected References) point out some of the unpleasant aspects of tourism. Improperly planned and developed tourism can create problems. The demands of tourism may come into conflict with the needs and wishes of local residents. Thoughtless development, inappropriate development, overdevelopment, or unfinished development can easily damage the environment.

Tourism has been blamed for polluting beaches; raising the price of labor, land, goods, and so on; spoiling the countryside; contaminating the values of native people; crowding; congestion; noise; litter; crime; loss of privacy; creating social tensions; environmental deterioration; lack of control over a destination's future; and low-paid seasonal employment. These problems are common to many forms of development and in many cases represent dissatisfaction with the status quo or overdevelopment. They emphasize the need for a coordinated overall economic development plan, of which tourism will be one part.

We must accept that tourism is neither a blessing nor a blight, neither poison nor panacea. Tourism can bring great benefits, but it can also bring social problems. The world has experience in how to increase the benefits of tourism and at least some experience in how to lessen social problems. What has to be done is to balance the benefits and costs to come up with the best cost/benefit result.

Tourism students and executives must have a clear understanding of both the positive and the negative impacts of tourism on the quality of life of a nation, a province or state, or a community. What are the positive aspects? The negative aspects? We need a balance sheet. First, we look at the plus side of the ledger. Tourism:

- Provides employment opportunities, both skilled and unskilled, because it is a labor-intensive industry
- Generates a supply of needed foreign exchange
- Increases incomes
- Creates increased gross domestic product
- Can be built on existing infrastructure
- Develops an infrastructure that will also help stimulate local commerce and industry
- Can be developed with local products and resources
- Helps to diversify the economy
- Tends to be one of the most compatible economic development activities available to an area, complementing other economic activities
- Spreads development
- Has a high multiplier impact
- Increases governmental revenues
- Broadens educational and cultural horizons and improves feelings of self-worth
- Improves the quality of life related to a higher level of income and improved standards of living

- Reinforces preservation of heritage and tradition
- Justifies environmental protection and improvement
- Provides employment for artists, musicians, and other performing artists because of visitor interest in local culture, thereby enhancing cultural heritage
- Provides tourist and recreational facilities that may be used by a local population
- Breaks down language barriers, sociocultural barriers, class barriers, racial barriers, political barriers, and religious barriers
- Creates a favorable worldwide image for a destination
- Promotes a global community
- Promotes international understanding and peace

On the minus side of the ledger, we find a number of problems that can be created by tourism, especially by its overdevelopment:

- Develops excess demand for resources
- Creates the difficulties of seasonality
- Causes inflation
- Can result in unbalanced economic development
- Creates social problems
- Degrades the natural physical environment, creates pollution, and contributes to global warming
- Degrades the cultural environment
- Increases the incidence of crime, prostitution, and gambling
- Increases vulnerability to economic and political changes
- Threatens family structure
- Commercializes culture, religion, and the arts
- Creates misunderstanding
- Creates conflicts in the host society
- Contributes to disease, economic fluctuation, and transportation problems

Like all change, tourism exacts a price. However, it is here, it is huge, and it needs to be planned and managed. The challenge is to get the right balance, which is to have the benefits outweigh the costs and take steps to lessen the unfavorable impacts that are a part of change. Tourism development must be a part of overall economic development and must be done in a manner that is sustainable.

SUMMARY

In this chapter, we have examined the subject of tourism. The rapid growth in the movement of people, both domestically and internationally, has brought about an industry of vast proportions and diversity. Also, the industry is universal—found in all countries of the world, but in greatly varied qualities and proportions.

The economic importance and future prospects are also worthy of careful study. These considerations lead to the ways in which the study of tourism can be undertaken. There are a number of basic approaches to the study of tourism, and in this book we include all of them in the various chapters. By the time you complete the book, you will know a great deal about the social and economic implications of tourism, and you will have developed a keen interest in our world and the fascinating panorama of places, peoples, cultures, beauty, and learning that travel provides in such abundance.

KEY CONCEPTS

accommodation	excursionist	same-day visitors
adventure and outdoor recreation	expenditures	stewardship
attractions	food services	tourism
benefits of tourism	host community	tourism services
built environment	host government	tourism philosophy
climate physiography	inbound tourism	tourist
costs of tourism	internal tourism	trade
destination management organization (DMO)	international tourism	tourist industry
	marketing	transportation
domestic tourism	monitoring	travel trade
economic impact	national tourism	traveler
ecotourism	operating sectors	usual environment
entertainment	outbound tourism	visit
evaluation	PDPCO	visitor
events	person-trip	

 INTERNET EXERCISES

The Internet sites mentioned in this chapter plus some selected additional sites are listed for your convenience on the companion Web site for this book, www.wiley.com/college/goeldner.

ACTIVITY 1

Site Name: World Travel and Tourism Council

URL: www.wttc.org

Background Information: The World Travel and Tourism Council (WTTC) is the global business leaders' forum for travel and tourism. Its members are chief executives from all sectors of the travel and tourism industry, including accommodations, catering, cruises, entertainment, recreation, transportation, and travel-related services. Its central goal is to work with governments to realize the full economic impact of the world's largest generator of wealth and jobs, namely, travel and tourism.

Exercise

1. Visit the WTTC site and identify the organization's strategic priorities.

ACTIVITY 2

Site Name: United States Travel Association

URL: www.ustravel.org

Background Information: USTA, the U.S. Travel Association, is a nonprofit trade organization based in Washington, D.C., that represents and speaks for the common interests of the U.S. travel industry.

Exercises

1. Visit the USTA site and find its mission and objectives.

2. Explore its economic research section and determine the economic impact of travel and tourism in the United States.

 QUESTIONS FOR REVIEW AND DISCUSSION

1. Identify and describe the four perspectives contained in the definition of tourism, in terms of your home community.

2. Why do bodies such as the U.S. Travel Association need specific tourism definitions? Why does a state or country need them? A county? A city?

3. What approach to tourism study does this course take? Which approach interests you most?

4. What are the components of tourism?

5. How important are tourist attractions?

6. Why are geographers, sociologists, anthropologists, and economists interested in tourism?

7. What will the tourism industry be like in the year 2020? 2030?

8. How can an industry that contributes 9.2 percent of global gross domestic product and creates over 235 million jobs still be in search of recognition?

9. What are the benefits of tourism?

10. What are some negative aspects of tourism?

11. Why is tourism so popular?

 CASE PROBLEMS

1. Suppose that you are a high school economics teacher. You plan to visit your principal's office and convince her that tourism should be included as part of one of your courses. What arguments would you use?

2. You are the minister of tourism of Jamaica, an island country. Identify the instructions you would issue to your statistics department concerning collecting data on tourist arrivals and expenditures.

CHAPTER 2 ✤

Tourism through the Ages

LEARNING OBJECTIVES

- Recognize the antiquity of human travel over vast distances on both sea and land.

- Understand how these journeys have evolved from trips that were difficult and often dangerous, to mass travel for millions today.

- Learn about some of the great travelers in history who wrote astonishing accounts of exotic places they had visited.

- Discover the many similarities in travel motivations, economic conditions, political situations, attractions, and tourist facilities during the period of the Roman Empire and today.

For generations, travelers have flocked to the Great Wall of China. At least 2,600 years old and some 3,946 miles long, it is the only manmade structure on earth visible to the naked eye from the moon. *Photo courtesy of the China National Tourist Office.*

INTRODUCTION

We travel long roads and cross the water to see what we disregard when it is under our eyes. This is either because nature has so arranged things that we go after what is far off and remain indifferent to what is nearby, or because any desire loses its intensity by being easily satisfied, or because we postpone whatever we can see whenever we want, feeling sure we will often get around to it. Whatever the reason, there are numbers of things in this city of ours and its environs which we have not even heard of, much less seen; yet, if they were in Greece or Egypt or Asia . . . we would have heard all about them, read all about them, looked over all there was to see.

The Younger Pliny, second century C.E.[1]

Twenty-first-century travelers, tiredly pulling their carry-on bags from the overhead bin and waiting to walk down the jetway to a foreign destination, might think their experience is uniquely modern. But they are the latest in a long line of travelers reaching back to antiquity. From earliest times, "all modes of carriage (from animal to the sonic jet) and accommodations (from the meanest hovel to the five-star luxury hotel) have given a livelihood to countless legions."[2] Like today's travelers, these travelers did not do it alone. "Guiding, counseling, and harboring the traveler is among the world's earliest vocations."[3]

Today, modern travelers can book online making their own travel arrangements or enlist a travel agent to make plane reservations, book hotels, and make recommendations for special tours upon arrival at the destination. Even with the specialized help of a travel agent, travelers frequently arrive feeling dirty and tired, complain about the crowded flight, and hope to clear customs without waiting in a long line. A middle-aged couple ruefully recalls that the travel agent was not able to book a hotel that she could recommend. (An automobile festival or a visit by the pope had filled major hotels, and there was little choice.) Also, the local bank was out of euros or zlotys or won, or whatever the name of the destination country's currency. So the couple has to exchange money before getting a cab to that unpromising hotel and are sure that the driver won't speak English, will spot them as greenhorns, and will drive them all over—with the meter running on and on. Even with these possible problems and irritations, they are excited and join multitudes that have gone before them to enjoy the rewards of travel.

EARLY BEGINNINGS

The invention of money by the Sumerians (Babylonians) and the development of trade beginning about 4000 B.C.E. mark the beginning of the modern era of travel. Not only were the Sumerians the first to grasp the idea of money and use it in business transactions, but they were also the first to invent cuneiform writing and the wheel, so they should be credited as the founders of the travel business. People could now pay for transportation and accommodations with money or by barter.

Five thousand years ago, cruises were organized and conducted from Egypt. Probably the first journey ever made for purposes of peace and tourism was made by Queen Hatshepsut to the land of Punt (believed to be on the east coast of Africa) in 1480 B.C.E. Descriptions of this tour have been recorded on the walls of the temple of Deir el-Bahri at Luxor. These texts and bas-reliefs are among the world's rarest artworks and are universally admired for their wondrous beauty and artistic qualities. The Colossi of Memnon at Thebes have on their pedestals the names of Greek tourists of the fifth century B.C.E.

Beginning in 2700 B.C.E., the pharaohs began to take advantage of the abundance of good building stone in the Nile valley to build their elaborate burial tombs. They included the Step Pyramid of Djoser, the Sphinx, the three great pyramids at Giza, and the pyramid complex at Abusir. These great outdoor wonders began attracting large numbers as early as the New Kingdom from 1600 to 1200 B.C.E. "Each monument was a hallowed spot, so the visitors always spent some moments in prayer, yet their prime motivation was curiosity or disinterested enjoyment, not religion."[4]

They left evidence of their visits in inscriptions such as the following: "Hadnakhte, scribe of the treasury, came to make an excursion and amuse himself on the west of Memphis together with his brother, Panakhti, scribe of the Vizier."[5] Like tourists through the ages, they felt the need to leave evidence of their visits. Some hastily painted their names; others scratched their names in the soft stone with a sharp point. The latter method was so common that the technical term we give to such scribblings is graffiti, Italian for "scratching."

A second recognizable tourist trait was the urge to acquire souvenirs. Harkhuf, an envoy of the pharaoh to the Sudan, brought home a Pygmy trained in native dances to present to his ruler! Early **Egyptians** also purchased bargains or specialties abroad for their friends and relatives. In 1800 B.C.E., young Uzalum received this request: "I have never before written to you for something precious I wanted. But if you want to be like a father to me, get me a fine string full of beads, to be worn around the head."[6]

Herodotus reported:

The Egyptians meet to celebrate festivals not once a year but a number of times. The biggest and most popular is at Bubastis . . . the next at Busiris . . . the third at Saïs . . . the fourth at Heliopolis . . . the fifth at Buto . . . the sixth at Papremis. . . . They go there on the river, men and women together, a big crowd of each in each boat. As they sail, some of the women keep clicking castanets and some of the men playing on the pipes, and the rest, both men and women, sing and beat time with their hands. . . . And when they arrive at Bubastis, they celebrate the occasion with great sacrifices, and more wine is consumed at this one festival than during the whole rest of the year.[7]

When this holiday throng arrived at its sites, there were no commercial facilities offering food and lodging. Like modern attendees at a Grateful Dead concert, they had to sleep in the open and feed themselves as best they could.[8] In contrast, government officials such as Harkhuf, the provider of the dancing pygmy, enjoyed the comforts of temples and government depots in their travels.

Early Roads

The wheel led to the development of a heavy wagon that could be drawn by teams of oxen or onagers, a type of wild ass. "A walker or animal needs only a track,"[9] but a vehicle needs a road.

Ancient Egyptian pyramids and the Sphinx were some of the world's first tourist attractions.
Photo courtesy of PhotoDisc, Inc./Getty Images.

There were not many **early roads** that could take wheeled traffic. A king of Ur bragged that he went from Nippur to Ur, a distance of some 100 miles, and back in a day. This boast, sometime around 2050 B.C.E., implies the existence of a carriage road.[10] Even the best of the highways, however, were minimal. Paving was almost nonexistent until the time of the Hittites, who paved a mile and a third of road between their capital and a nearby sanctuary to carry heavily loaded wagons on festal days. Even then their war chariots, light horse-drawn carts invented for war, rolled over the countryside on dirt roads. Also, bridges were rare in a land that experienced frequent flooding. A hymn tells of King Shulgi exulting "'I enlarged the footpaths, straightened the highways of the land' . . . but not every Mesopotamian monarch was a Shulgi, and there must have been long periods with nobody to 'straighten' the roads."[11]

Roads were better on the island of Crete, where the Minoans flourished from 2000 to 1500 B.C.E., and on the Greek peninsula of the Mycenaeans, who flourished from 1600 to 1200 B.C.E.[12] A two-lane road, 13½ feet wide, ran from the coast of Crete to the capital at Knossos. In Greece, roads were usually one lane, although some were as much as 11½ feet wide, making two-way traffic possible. Bridges and culverts kept them passable.

Who traveled? Mainly three groups: the military, government officials, and caravans. The warlike Assyrians, like the Romans after them, realized that roads were basic to moving their war chariots efficiently. As their empire expanded from the Mediterranean in the west to the Persian Gulf in the east, the Assyrians improved roads, largely for military use.

The Epic of Gilgamesh (c. 2000 B.C.E.) recounts the travels of a Sumerian king who is given directions by a deity. By only a slight stretch of the imagination, Gilgamesh's deity might be regarded as the first travel guide! This adds a fourth reason—in addition to money, writing, and the wheel—to credit the Sumerians with the beginnings of the travel industry.

The history of roads is thus related to the centralizing of populations in powerful cities. Alexander the Great found well-developed roads in India in 326 B.C.E. In Persia (now Iran), all the cities and provinces were connected to the capital, Susa, by roads built between 500 and 400 B.C.E. One of these roads was 1,500 miles long.

The **Romans** started building roads in about 150 B.C.E. These were quite elaborate in construction. The roadway was surveyed using a cross staff hung with plumb bobs. Soldiers and laborers dug the roadbed, and then stones and concrete were evenly placed. Paving stones were then laid on top, and the highway was edged with curbstones and contoured to a sloping crown to shed the rain. Some of these roads are still in use.

By the time of Emperor Trajan (ruled from 98 to 117 C.E.), the Roman roads comprised a network of some 50,000 miles. They girdled the Roman Empire, extending from near Scotland and Germany in the north to well within Egypt in the south and along the southern shores of the Mediterranean Sea. To the east, roads extended to the Persian Gulf in what is now Iraq and Kuwait.

The Romans could travel as much as 100 miles a day using relays of horses furnished from rest posts five to six miles apart. Romans also journeyed to see famous temples in the Mediterranean area, particularly the pyramids and monuments of Egypt. Greece and Asia Minor were popular destinations, offering the Olympic Games, medicinal baths and seaside resorts, theatrical productions, festivals, athletic competitions, and other forms of amusement and entertainment. The Roman combination of empire, roads, the need for overseeing the empire, wealth, leisure, tourist attractions, and the desire for travel created a demand for accommodations and other tourist services that came into being as an early form of tourism.

Roman tourists went about sightseeing much as we do today. They used guidebooks, employed guides, left graffiti everywhere, and bought souvenirs. The examples are diverse and often amusing. The only guidebook to survive from ancient times is a guidebook of Greece, written by a Greek named Pausanias between 160 and 180 C.E. (during the reigns of emperors Hadrian, Antoninus Pius, and Marcus Aurelius). This guide "marks a milestone in the history of tourism. He [Pausanias] is the direct ancestor of the equally sober and unimaginative, painstakingly comprehensive and scrupulously accurate Karl Baedeker."[13]

The Silk Road

In 1889, Rudyard Kipling penned the oft-quoted line "East is East and West is West and never the twain shall meet." Actually, East and West had already met more than 2,000 years earlier on the now-fabled **Silk Road**.

Indeed, it is a misnomer even to call it a road. From the beginning, some *Silk Route* sections were mere directions across trackless steppe or desert rather than visible paths: "the majority of states on the Silk Routes traded with their nearer neighbors, and travelers were like participants in a relay race stretching a third of the way around the world."[14]

Marco Polo, who traveled to China from Italy in the thirteenth century, became the first Western explorer to compose a popular and lasting account. Though his chronicle is probably more fiction than history, since it draws from the tales of many traders, his observations often ring true. In spite of omissions and exaggerations, his book has remained an international bestseller.[15]

Just as the Silk Road was not a road, so silk was but a part of the trade. Westbound caravans carried furs, ceramics, spices, the day lily for its medicinal uses, peaches, apricots, and even rhubarb.[16] Eastbound ones carried precious metals and gems, ivory, glass, perfumes, dyes, textiles, as well as the grapevine, alfalfa, chives, coriander, sesame, cucumbers, figs, and safflower.[17]

For protection against marauders, merchants formed caravans of up to 1,000 camels, protected by armed escorts. Each two-humped Bactrian camel could carry 400 to 500 pounds of merchandise. The long route was divided into areas of political and economic influence. "The Chinese traders escorted their merchandise as far as Dunhuang or beyond the Great Wall to Loulan where it was sold or bartered to Central Asian middlemen—Parthians, Sogdians, Indians, and Kushans—who carried the trade on to the cities of the Persian, Syrian, and Greek merchants. Each transaction increased the cost of the end product, which reached the Roman Empire in the hands of Greek and Jewish entrepreneurs."[18]

The Classical World

The lands of the Mediterranean Sea (2000 B.C.E. to 500 C.E.) produced a remarkable evolution in travel. In the cradle of Western civilization, travel for trade, commerce, religious purposes, festivals, medical treatment, or education developed at an early date. There are numerous references to caravans and traders in the Old Testament.

Beginning in 776 B.C.E., **Greeks** from the city-states came together every four years to honor Zeus through athletic competition. Eventually, four of these national festivals emerged: **Olympic Games**, Pythian Games, Isthmian Games, and Nemean Games. Each festival included sacrifice and prayer to a single god. The games honored the deity by offering up a superlative athletic or artistic performance:

> [T]hese festivals furnished in one unique package the spectrum of attractions that have drawn tourists from all times and places: the feeling of being part of a great event and of enjoying a special experience; a gay festive mood punctuated by exalted religious moments; elaborate pageantry; the excitement of contests between performers of the highest calibre—and, on top of all this, a chance to wander among famous buildings and works of art. Imagine the modern Olympics taking place at Easter in Rome, with the religious services held at St. Peter's.[19]

Greek inns provided little more than a night's shelter. A guest who wanted to wash had to carry his own towel down the street to the nearest public bath. Once there, he took off his clothes in a dressing room and put them in someone's care, lest they be stolen while he bathed. "The bath itself was a big basin over which he leaned while an attendant sloshed water over him."[20]

Everyday folk could also be found wending their way to the sanctuaries of the healing gods, especially Aesculapius. Such places were usually located in a beautiful setting that included pure air and water (often with mineral springs). The sanctuary at Epidaurus also included facilities for rest and diversion, including the temple with admired sculptures, colonnades for shaded walks, a stadium for

The Acropolis of Athens, the site of four of the greatest masterpieces of classical Greek art—the Parthenon, the Propylaca, the Erechteum, and the Temple of Athena Nike—illustrates the civilizations, myths, and religions that flourished in Greece over a period of more than 1,000 years. The Acropolis is a UNESCO World Heritage Site and was proclaimed as the preeminent monument of the European Cultural Heritage list of monuments in 2007. *Photo courtesy of Corbis Digital Stock.*

athletic events, and the second-largest theater in Greece. The Greeks recognized rest and diversion as important elements in treatment of the sick. People also traveled to seek advice of the oracles, especially those at Dodona and Delphi. Statesmen, generals, and other powerful figures sought advice before taking an important action. Socrates' disciple inquired about his master's wisdom at the temple of Delphi.[21]

Although festival visitors, businessmen, the sick, and advice seekers comprised the bulk of travelers in the fifth and fourth centuries B.C.E., there was also another small category, the tourist. Greece's "Father of History," Herodotus, would undoubtedly have qualified for the top category of frequent-traveler miles if such awards had been given.

In addition to traveling all over Greece and the Aegean Islands, he sailed to Cyrene in North Africa, explored southern Italy and Sicily, and sailed from Ephesus on the west coast of Asia Minor to Sardis. He got as far east as Babylon by sailing to Syria, then striking east to the Euphrates and following a caravan track for weeks. There he looked upon the ancient city of Babylon:

square in shape, with each side 14 miles long, a total of 56 miles. Babylon is not only of enormous size; it has a splendor such as no other city of all we have seen. The city wall is $85^1/_2$ feet wide and 342 high. Its circuit is pierced by one hundred entrances, with gates, jambs, and lintels of bronze. The town is full of three- and four-storey houses and is cut through with streets that are absolutely straight, not only the main ones but also the side streets going down to the river.[22]

His figures are inflated, probably because he got them from his guides. He loved doing the sights and, like most modern tourists, was dependent on guides for information. A Greek entering Asia Minor would encounter strange tongues and Oriental ways.

Not until Alexander conquered the Persian Empire would the Greek ways spread into the ancient East.

Possibly, Herodotus's travel combined business and pleasure, as did that of Solon, who led Athens through a crisis, then took a trip abroad. Athens developed into a tourist attraction from the second half of the fifth century on, as people went to see the Parthenon and other new buildings atop the Acropolis.

Today's traveler who gets into trouble in a foreign city usually turns to his country's consulate. The ancient Greek turned to his *proxenos* (from the Greek *pro*, meaning "before" or "for," and *xenos*, foreigner). The primary duty of the proxenos was to aid and assist in all ways possible any of his compatriots who turned up in the place of his residence, particularly those who had come in some official capacity.[23] His more mundane duties might include extending hospitality, obtaining theater tickets, or extending a loan for someone who had run short of funds while visiting. More complex duties included negotiating ransom for relatives of someone taken as a prisoner of war. The heirs of someone who died in the city might ask the proxenos to wind up essential financial matters there.[24]

As the fourth century B.C.E. came to a close in Greece, people traveled despite the discomfort and dangers. Traveling by sea, they worried about storms and pirates; by land, about bad roads, dismal inns, and highwaymen. Only the wealthy described by Homer could escape the worst pitfalls.

Those who traveled for business, healing, or entertainment at festivals represented the majority. A small minority traveled for the sheer love of it—like Herodotus, the world's first great travel writer.

The museum, born in the ancient Near East, came of age with the Greeks. Sanctuaries such as Apollo's at Delphi and that of Zeus at Olympia gradually accumulated valuable objects donated either as thank-you offerings for services rendered or as bribes for acts the supplicant hoped would be rendered. Herodotus describes six gold mixing bowls dedicated by Gyges of Lydia and weighing some 1,730 pounds and a gold lion from Croesus weighing 375 pounds. While Herodotus singled these out because of their cost, others were notable for their aesthetic qualities. The Greeks had few precious metals but hewed the plentiful marble with consummate skill. The temple of Hera exemplifies the scope and quality of sculpture acquired from the seventh through the third centuries B.C.E.:

All over the Greek world through generous gifts of statues and paintings from the hopeful or the satisfied, temples became art galleries as well as houses of worship—exactly as Europe's cathedrals and churches were destined to become. . . . And they drew visitors the same way that art laden churches do today to see the treasures and only incidentally, to say a prayer.[25]

In Asia Minor, beginning with the installation of a democratic government in Ephesus by Alexander the Great in 334 B.C.E., some 700,000 tourists would crowd the city (in what is now Turkey) in a single season to be entertained by the acrobats, animal acts, jugglers, magicians, and prostitutes who filled the streets. Ephesus also became an important trading center and, under Alexander, was one of the most important cities in the ancient world.

Early Ships

The Phoenicians were master shipwrights, building tubby wooden craft with a single square sail. By 800 B.C.E., they had built a network of trading posts around the Mediterranean emanating from their own thriving cities along the coast in what is now Lebanon. Acting as middlemen for their neighbors, they purveyed raw materials and also finished goods, such as linen and papyrus from Egypt, ivory and gold from Nubia, grain and copper from Sardinia, olive oil and wine from Sicily, cedar timbers from their homeland, and perfume and spices from the East. Presumably, these early ships also occasionally carried a few passengers. They were the first creators of a maritime empire.

The Greeks followed the **Phoenicians** in becoming great sea traders. Improved ships accelerated a flourishing Mediterranean trade. Merchant ships also carried paying passengers (although Noah with his ark probably deserves credit for being the first cruise operator, even though his passengers were primarily animals). Unlike Noah's passengers, those sailing on Greek ships had to bring their own servants, food, and wine. Widely varying accommodations aboard, stormy seas, and pirate attacks were worrisome realities.

Chinese

Several tourism history scholars decry the eurocentricity of writings about the history of tourism. Most notable of these is Trevor Sofield, of the University of Tasmania, who states:

> *The emperors of China had ministers for travel 4,000 years ago—well before imperial Rome and Herodotus. So, this is a plea to move beyond Chaucer's pilgrimage to Canterbury and Marco Polo's ventures from Venice, and go further back in time to explore other civilizations and their histories of travel besides (mainly western) Europe and North America. The history of pilgrimage travel in countries such as India, China, Nepal, Thailand, Iran, Vietnam, Sri Lanka, Myanmar and others pre-dates much European travel history. Inns and hospitality industries in these countries pre-date European examples.*[26]

Sofield and Li in their article "Tourism Development and Cultural Policies in China" report that one of the main features of China's domestic tourism lies in the traditions about travel and heritage sites established over a 4,000-year period when ancestral gods and animistic spirits resided in mountains, rivers, lakes, and other natural features:

> *Stretching in an unbroken chain from the beginnings of the Shang dynasty (CA 1350–1050 BC) to the final demise of the emperors in the fall of the Quing dynasty and the declaration of a Republic in 1912, each successive emperor and his court paid homage to a wide range of gods and goddesses. The sites multiplied over the centuries and as Buddhism became established, even more sacred sites were added. Much ancient travel was thus for pilgrimage, embedded in the beliefs of the godkings.*[27]

Polynesians

Among early voyages, those in Oceania were amazing. Small dugout canoes not over 40 feet in length were used for voyages from Southeast Asia southward and eastward through what is now called Micronesia across the Pacific to the Marquesas Islands, the Tuamotu Archipelago, and the Society Islands. About 500 C.E., **Polynesians** from the Society Islands traveled to Hawaii, a distance of over 2,000 miles. Navigation was accomplished by observing the position of the sun and stars, ocean swells, clouds, and bird flights. Considering the problems of fresh water and food supplies, such sea travel was astonishing. Later, navigation by the early explorers was facilitated by using a sandglass to measure time, a "log" line trailed behind the ship to measure distance, and a compass to gauge direction.

Europeans

The collapse of the Roman Empire in the fourth and fifth centuries spelled disaster for pleasure travel and tourism in Europe. During the Dark Ages (from the fall of the Western Roman Empire, 476 C.E., to the beginning of the modern era, 1450 C.E.), only the most adventurous Europeans would travel. A trip during this period in history was dangerous; no one associated travel with pleasure. The most notable exception to this in Europe during the period was the Crusades.

By the end of the Dark Ages, large numbers of pilgrims were traveling to such popular shrines as Canterbury in England (immortalized in Chaucer's *Canterbury Tales*) and St. James of Compostela, the pilgrimage to the Cathedral of Santiago de Compostela in Galicia in northwestern Spain. Fewer made the long, expensive, and often dangerous journey to the Holy Land. Beginning in 1388, England's King Richard II required pilgrims to carry permits, the forerunner of the modern passport. Despite hardship and dangers, they went by the thousands to pay reverence to hallowed sites, to atone for sins, or to fulfill promises they had made while ill.

A fourteenth-century travelers' guide gave pilgrims detailed directions about the regions through which they would pass and the types of inns they would encounter along the often-inhospitable routes. Innkeeping had nearly disappeared except for local taverns, and a few inns were scattered throughout Europe. They typically were filthy, vermin-infested warrens. Inns in Spain and Italy provided a bed for each guest, but in Germany and other areas, guests commonly had to share beds. At the other end of the spectrum lay an inn of quality, such as the one described in Mandeville's guide. He quotes the mistress of the inn: "Jenette lyghte the candell, and lede them ther above in the solere [upper room], and bere them hoot watre for to wasshe their feet, and covere them with uysshons."

Travelers of any social distinction, however, were generally entertained in castles or private houses. Church monasteries or hospices offered accommodations for the majority. They offered services well beyond bed and board. They could provide a doctor and furnish medicines, replace worn garments, provide guides to show a visitor around the sights, or even grant a loan of money. They also offered opportunities for meditation and prayer.

The most famous stopover was the French Alpine hospice of Grand-Saint-Bernard, established in 962. (The Saint Bernard dogs that were sent to find and rescue travelers have been made famous by ads showing a little flask of wine appended to the dogs' collars.) St. Catherine's monastery at the foot of Mount Sinai still flourishes. Those who could afford to pay were expected to leave a generous donation.

Eventually, providing hospitality services for increasing numbers became burdensome to the religious houses. They could not turn the poor away, because Christian charity was an important element in the church's mission; nor could they turn away the nobles, who made generous financial contributions. But they could, and increasingly did, refer the middle classes to taverns, inns, and wine shops. Thus, the church played an important role in the development of the hospitality industry during this period.

The Grand Tour

The **Grand Tour** of the seventeenth and eighteenth centuries was made by diplomats, business-people, and scholars who traveled to Europe, mainly to the cities of France and Italy. It became fashionable for scholars to study in Paris, Rome, Florence, and other cultural centers. Although making the Grand Tour began as an educational experience, it has been criticized as eventually degenerating into the simple pursuit of pleasure. The following description from *A Geography of Tourism* describes the Grand Tour:

> *One of the interesting aspects of the Grand Tour was its conventional and regular form. As early as 1678, Jean Gailhard, in his* Compleat Gentleman, *had prescribed a three-year tour as customary. A generally accepted itinerary was also laid down, which involved a long stay in France, especially in Paris, almost a year in Italy visiting Genoa, Milan, Florence, Rome, and Venice, and then a return by way of Germany and the Low Countries via Switzerland. Of course, there were variations to this itinerary, but this was the most popular route. It was generally believed that ``there was little more to be seen in the rest of the civil world after Italy, France, and the Low Countries, but plain and prodigious barbarism."*[28]

The term *Grand Tour* persists today, and the trip to Europe—the Continent—can be traced back to the early Grand Tour. Today's concept is far different, however: the tour is more likely to be three weeks, not three years.

Americans

The vast continent of North America, principally in what is now Florida and in the Southwest, was originally explored by the Spanish in the sixteenth century. Remarkably long journeys were made, often under severe conditions. The Spanish used horses, which were unknown to the American Indians until that time. In the East, Cape Cod was discovered by Bartholomew Gosnold in 1602, and the Plymouth Colony was established in 1620.

Early travel was on foot or on horseback, but travel by small boat or canoe provided access to the interior of the country. Generally, travel was from east to west. As roads were built, stagecoach travel became widespread, and "ordinaries" (small hotels) came into common use. Among the most remarkable journeys were those by covered wagon to the West across the Great Plains. This movement followed the Civil War (1861–1865). Construction of railroads across the country (the first transcontinental link was at Promontory, Utah, in 1869) popularized rail travel. The Wells Fargo Company organized the American Express Company in 1850. This pioneer company issued the first traveler's checks in 1891 and began other travel services, later becoming travel agents and arranging tours. Today, American Express is known throughout the world for its traveler's checks, credit cards, and various travel and financial services.

One of the most significant phenomenons in America's travel history is the amount of travel done by servicemen and -women during World War II. Over 12 million Americans served in the armed forces from 1941 to 1945. Most were assigned to duty in places far removed from their homes, such as the European and Pacific theaters of war.

Extensive domestic travel also became commonplace, introducing the military traveler to different and often exotic places and bringing a broader perspective of what the North American continent and foreign countries had to offer visitors. Travel thus became a part of their experience. Following the war, a large increase in travel occurred when gasoline rationing was removed and automobiles were again being manufactured. Air, rail, and bus travel also expanded.

Nowhere in the United States can visitors experience so extensively life in the eighteenth century as in Colonial Williamsburg, with its mile-long Duke of Gloucester Street, horse-drawn carriages, and hundreds of restored colonial homes and gardens. *Photo courtesy of Virginia Tourism Corporation.*

EARLY (AND LATER) TOURIST ATTRACTIONS

Sightseeing has always been a major activity of tourists; this has been true since ancient times. Most of us have heard of the Seven Wonders of the Ancient World, but few could win a trivia contest by naming them:

1. The Great Pyramids of Egypt, including the Sphinx
2. The Hanging Gardens of Babylon, sometimes including the Walls of Babylon and the Palace, in what is now Iraq
3. The Tomb of Mausolus at Halicarnassus, in what is now Turkey
4. The Statue of Zeus at Olympia in Greece
5. The Colossus of Rhodes in the Harbor at Rhodes, an island belonging to Greece
6. The Great Lighthouse (Pharos) in Alexandria, Egypt
7. The Temple of Artemis (also called the Temple of Diana) at Ephesus, at the time part of Greece, now in Turkey

The Great Pyramids of Egypt are the sole remaining wonder.

Just as tourists in ancient times traveled to see these wonders, modern tourists travel to see such natural wonders as the Grand Canyon, Yosemite National Park, Yellowstone, Niagara Falls, the oceans, the Great Lakes, and human-built wonders such as great cities, museums, dams, and monuments.

Spas, Baths, Seaside Resorts

Another interesting aspect in the history of tourism was the development of spas, after their original use by the Romans, which took place in Britain and on the Continent. In the eighteenth century, spas

The Great Pyramids of Egypt are the sole remaining wonder of the Seven Wonders of the Ancient World.
Photo courtesy of United Nations.

New Wonders

Bernard Weber, a Swiss filmmaker, created a popularity contest to choose seven new world wonders since the Great Pyramids of Egypt are the sole remaining wonder of the Seven Wonders of the Ancient World. Nearly 200 early candidates chosen by Internet ballot were reduced down by a panel of experts to 21 finalists. Online and telephone call-in voting on finalists began in 2005. Nothing prevented multiple voting by travelers, fans, citizens, governments, tourism organizations, and so on. The poll was decidedly unscientific.

Even so, millions of people from around the world voted via the Internet to choose a new list of the Seven Wonders of the World. The winners were announced on the seventh day of the seventh month in the year '07 (07/07/07). Winners were: the Great Wall of China; the ancient city of Petra in Jordan; the statue of Christ the Redeemer in Rio de Janeiro; Machu Picchu in Peru; the Maya ruins of Chichen Itza in Mexico; the Colosseum in Rome; and India's Taj Mahal.

All are sites well worth visiting, but it will be interesting to see if Weber's "New Seven Wonders" become an accepted list because his campaign did not receive the backing of major mainstream monument designation organizations or at UNESCO's World Heritage agency.

DISCUSSION QUESTIONS

1. What marketing opportunities are present from being named a new "wonder of the world"?

2. What do you think of Weber's methodology to choose the new seven wonders?

---

became very fashionable among members of high society, not only for their curative aspects but also for the social events, games, dancing, and gambling that they offered. The spa at Bath, England, was one such successful health and social resort.

Sea bathing also became popular, and some believed that saltwater treatment was more beneficial than that at the inland spas. Well known in Britain were Brighton, Margate, Ramsgate, Worthing, Hastings, Weymouth, Blackpool, and Scarborough. By 1861, the success of these seaside resorts indicated that there was a pent-up demand for vacation travel. Most visitors did not stay overnight but made one-day excursions to the seaside. Patronage of the hotels at these resorts was still limited to those with considerable means.

Thus, tourism owes a debt to medical practitioners who advocated the medicinal value of mineral waters and sent their patients to places where mineral springs were known to exist. Later, physicians also recommended sea bathing for its therapeutic value. While spas and seaside resorts were first visited for reasons of health, they soon became centers of entertainment, recreation, and gambling, attracting the rich and fashionable with or without ailments. This era of tourism illustrates that usually a combination of factors rather than one element spells the success or failure of an enterprise. Today, hot springs, although they are not high on travelers' priority lists, are still tourist attractions. Examples in the United States are Hot Springs, Arkansas; French Lick, Indiana; and Glenwood Springs, Colorado. The sea, particularly in the Sun Belt, continues to have a powerful attraction and is one of the leading forces in tourism development, which is evident from the number of travelers to Hawaii, Florida, the Caribbean, and Mexico.

EARLY ECONOMIC REFERENCES

As tourists traveled to see pyramids, visit seaside resorts, and attend festivals and athletic events, they needed food and lodging, and they spent money for these services. Traders did the same. Then, as now, the economic impact of these expenditures was difficult to measure, as evidenced by the following quotation from Thomas Mun, who in 1620 wrote in England's *Treasure by Foreign Trade*: "There are yet some other petty things which seem to have a reference to this balance of which the said officers of

His Majesty's Customs can take no notice to bring them into the account; as mainly, the expenses of the travelers."[29]

THE FIRST TRAVEL AGENTS

In 1822, Robert Smart of Bristol, England, announced himself as the first steamship agent. He began booking passengers on steamers to various Bristol Channel ports and to Dublin, Ireland.

In 1841, Thomas Cook began running a special excursion train from Leicester to Loughborough (in England), a trip of 12 miles. On July 5 of that year, Cook's train carried 570 passengers at a round-trip price of 1 shilling per passenger. This is believed to be the first publicly advertised excursion train. Thus, Cook can rightfully be recognized as the first rail excursion agent; his pioneering efforts were eventually copied widely in all parts of the world. Cook's company grew rapidly, providing escorted tours to the Continent and later to the United States and around the world. The company continues to be one of the world's largest travel organizations.

The first specialist in individual inclusive travel (the basic function of travel agents) was probably Thomas Bennett (1814–1898), an Englishman who served as secretary to the British consul general in Oslo, Norway. In this position, Bennett frequently arranged individual scenic tours in Norway for visiting British notables. Finally, in 1850, he set up a business as a "trip organizer" and provided individual tourists with itineraries, carriages, provisions, and a "traveling kit." He routinely made advance arrangements for horses and hotel rooms for his clients.

HISTORIC TRANSPORTATION

Another element in the tourism equation is transportation. The early tourists traveled on foot, on beasts of burden, by boat, and on wheeled vehicles.

Stagecoach Travel

Stagecoaches were invented in Hungary in the fifteenth century and provided regular service there on prescribed routes. By the nineteenth century, stagecoach travel had become quite popular, especially in Great Britain. The development of the famous English tavern was brought about by the need for overnight lodging by stagecoach passengers.

Water Travel

Market boats picked up passengers as well as goods on ship canals in England as early as 1772. The Duke of Bridgewater began such water travel service between Manchester and London Bridge (near Warrington). Each boat had a coffee room from which refreshments were sold by the captain's wife. By 1815, steamboats were plying the Clyde, the Avon, and the Thames. A poster in 1833 announced steamboat excursion trips from London. By 1841, steamship excursions on the Thames were so well established that a publisher was bringing out a weekly *Steamboat Excursion Guide*.

Rail Travel

Railways were first built in England in 1825 and carried passengers beginning in 1830. The newly completed railway between Liverpool and Manchester featured special provisions for passengers. The

Older-style rail travel is still available in many places across the United States so that tourists can experience this memorable mode of transportation. The steam train shown here carries visitors in, "gold, country" California. Docents provide history and make the ride more enjoyable. *Photo courtesy of Tuolumne County Visitors Bureau.*

railroad's directors did not expect much passenger business, but time proved them wrong. The typical charge of only 1 penny per mile created a sizable demand for rail travel—much to the delight of the rail companies. Because these fares were much lower than stagecoach fares, rail travel became widely accepted even for those with low incomes.

Early rail travel in Britain was not without its detractors, however. Writers in the most powerful organs of public opinion of that day seemed to consider the new form of rail locomotion a device of Satan. When a rail line was proposed from London to Woolrich to carry passengers at a speed of 18 miles per hour, one aghast contributor to the *Quarterly Review* wrote, "We should as soon expect the people of Woolrich to be fired off upon one of Congreve's ricochet rockets as trust themselves to the mercy of such a machine going at such a rate." Another writer deemed the railroads for passenger transportation "visionary schemes unworthy of notice." Between 1826 and 1840, the first railroads were built in the United States.

Automobile and Motorcoach Travel

Automobiles entered the travel scene in the United States when Henry Ford introduced his famous Model T in 1908. The relatively cheap "tin lizzie" revolutionized travel in the country, creating a demand for better roads. By 1920, a road network became available, leading to the automobile's current dominance of the travel industry. Today, the automobile accounts for about 84 percent of intercity miles traveled and is the mode of travel for approximately 80 percent of all trips. **Automobile travel** brought about the early tourist courts in the 1920s and 1930s, which have evolved into the motels and motor hotels of today. Motorcoaches also came into use soon after the popularization of the automobile and remain a major mode of transportation.

Automobiles dominate travel today, but visiting the National Automobile Museum (Harrah Collection) in Reno, Nevada, provides an appreciation of the old days, when cars were not quite so comfortable. *Photo courtesy of Reno News Bureau.*

Air Travel

Nearly 16 years after the airplane's first flight at Kitty Hawk, North Carolina, in 1903, regularly scheduled air service began in Germany. This was a Berlin–Leipzig–Weimar route, and the carrier later became known as Deutsche Lufthansa. Today, Lufthansa is a major international airline. The first transatlantic passenger was Charles A. Levine, who flew with Clarence Chamberlin nonstop from New York to Germany. The plane made a forced landing 118 miles from Berlin, their destination, which they reached on June 7, 1927. This was shortly after Charles Lindbergh's historic solo flight from New York to Paris.

The first U.S. airline, Varney Airlines, was launched in 1926 and provided scheduled airmail service. However, this airline was formed only 11 days before Western Airlines, which began service on April 17, 1926. Varney Airlines later merged with three other lines to form United Air Lines. On April 1, 1987, Western merged with Delta Air Lines. At first, only one passenger was carried in addition to the mail, if the weight limitations permitted. The first international mail route was flown by **Pan American Airways** from Key West, Florida, to Havana, Cuba, on October 28, 1927. Pan Am flew the first passengers on the same route on January 16, 1928. The trip took 1 hour 10 minutes, and the fare was $50 each way.

The various U.S. airlines gradually expanded their services to more cities and international destinations. During World War II, their equipment and most staff were devoted to war service. Development of the DC-3 and the Boeing 314A transoceanic Clipper in the early 1940s established paying passenger traffic and brought about much wider acceptance of **air travel**. The jet engine, invented in England by Frank Whittle, was used on such military planes as the B-52. The first American commercial jet was the Boeing 707. The first U.S. transcontinental jet flight was operated by American Airlines on January 25, 1959, from Los Angeles to New York City, and the jumbo jet era began in January 1970, when Pan American World Airways flew 352 passengers from New York to London using the new Boeing 747 equipment.

The Concorde ushered in the era of supersonic flight. The Concorde was a product of a joint British–French venture. A prototype was unveiled in 1967, and the jet made its first test flight in

Flight museums such as the Virginia Aviation Museum remind us what a short history the airplane has.
Photo by Cyane Lowdon, courtesy of the Science Museum of Virginia.

1969. The Concorde was a marvel of engineering and design. The white bird with its distinctive tilted needle nose and broad wingspan was an icon of the modern world. The Concorde traveled at 1,350 miles per hour, twice the speed of sound. It flew at 60,000 feet, almost twice as high as other commercial jets. Probably no other civilian aircraft has captured the imagination of the traveling public as the Concorde.

The Concorde carried passengers for the last time on Friday, October 24, 2003, when British Airways retired its fleet. Air France retired its fleet of Concordes on May 31, 2003. Thus, after 34 years, a chapter in supersonic aviation ended. This marked the first time in aviation history that a major innovation was retired without a more advanced technological product replacing it.

British Airways has its fleet of Concordes on display. They are to be found in the United States at the Museum of Flight in Seattle and the Intrepid Sea, Air and Space Museum in New York; in Britain at Airbus UK in Filton, near Bristol, at Manchester Airport, at Heathrow Airport, and at the Museum of Flight near Edinburgh; and in Barbados, at Grantely Adams Airport in Bridgetown.

Because of its speed, comfort, and safety, air travel is the leading mode of public transportation today, as measured in revenue passenger miles (one fare-paying passenger transported one mile).

ACCOMMODATIONS

The earliest guest rooms were parts of private dwellings, and travelers were hosted almost like members of the family. In the Middle East and in the Orient, caravansaries and inns date back to antiquity. In more modern times, first the stagecoach and then railroads, steamships, the automobile, motorcoach, and airplane expanded the need for adequate **accommodations**. The railroad brought the downtown city hotel, the automobile and motorcoach brought the motel, and the airplane led to the boom in accommodations within or near airports. Accommodating—housing, feeding, and entertaining—travelers is one of the world's most important industries.

CHRONOLOGIES OF TRAVEL

Herein are two chronologies of travel: (1) a chronology of ancient migrations, early explorers, and great travelers, and (2) a chronology of travel arrangers of their business and their suppliers. The selected travelers and explorers not only made remarkably long and arduous journeys to little-known (and often mistaken) places, but also wrote vivid descriptions or had scribes write for them. They faced sometimes unbelievably difficult, often dangerous, and occasionally fatal hardships.

The comfortable and pleasant (even sometimes inspiring) traveling facilities of today are truly a tribute to the development of modern technology, design, and engineering.

Chronology of Ancient Migrations, Early Explorers, and Great Travelers

1 million years ago	*Homo erectus* originates in eastern and southern Africa; makes extensive migrations north to the Middle East and to Asia.
350,000 years ago	Early *Homo sapiens* evolves from *H. erectus*; dwells in Africa, Europe, and Asia.
50,000–30,000 years ago	Anatomically modern man, *H. sapiens*, evolves and expands into Australia from southeastern Asia and into northeastern Asia.
15,000 years ago	Upper Paleolithic people cross into northern latitudes of the New World from northeast Asia on a land bridge.

B.C.E.

4000	Sumerians (Mesopotamia, Babylonia) invent money, cuneiform writing, and the wheel; also, the concept of a tour guide.
2000–332	Phoenicians begin maritime trading and navigating over the entire Mediterranean Sea area. They may possibly have sailed as far as the British Isles and probably along the coast of western Africa and to the Azores.
1501–1481	Queen Hatshepsut makes the journey from Egypt to the land of Punt, believed to be an area along the eastern coast of Africa.
336–323	Alexander the Great leads his army from Greece into Asia, crossing the Hindu Kush mountains (Afghanistan–Kashmir area), and to the Indus River.

C.E.

500	Polynesians from the Society Islands sail to Hawaii, a distance of over 2,000 miles.
800–1100	Vikings establish trade and explore Iceland, Greenland, and the coast of North America.
1271–1295	Marco Polo, a Venetian merchant, travels to Persia, Tibet, the Gobi Desert, Burma, Siam, Java, Sumatra, India, Ceylon, the Siberian Arctic, and other places.
1325–1354	Ibn Battuwtah, the "Marco Polo of Islam," a Moroccan, makes six pilgrimages to Mecca; also visits India, China, Spain, and Timbuktu in Africa.
1492–1502	Christopher Columbus explores the New World, including the Bahamas, Cuba, Jamaica, Central America, and the northern coast of South America.
1497	John Cabot, an Italian navigator, sailing from Bristol, England, discovers North America at a point now known as Nova Scotia.
1513	Vasco Núñez de Balboa, a Spanish explorer, discovers the Pacific Ocean.
1519	Ferdinand Magellan sails west from Spain to circumnavigate the globe. He is killed in the Philippines, but some of his crew complete the circumnavigation.
1540–1541	Francisco Vásquez de Coronado, a Spanish explorer, seeks gold, silver, and precious jewels (without success) in what is now Arizona, New Mexico, Texas, Oklahoma, and other areas of the American Southwest.
1602	Bartholomew Gosnold, English explorer and colonizer, navigates the eastern coast of the (now) United States from Maine to Narragansett Bay; discovers and names Cape Cod. In 1606, his ship carries some of the first settlers to Virginia.

Prague, in the Czech Republic, has become one of the most popular destinations in Eastern Europe since the fall of the Iron Curtain in the early 1990s. *Photo courtesy of Corbis Digital Stock.*

1768–1780	James Cook, an English naval officer, explores the northeastern coast of North America, and in the Pacific discovers New Caledonia, New Zealand, Australia, and Hawaii. He is killed in Hawaii.
1784–1808	Alexander Mackenzie, a Scot, makes the first overland exploration across North America north of Mexico; discovers the river now named for him, which flows into the Arctic Ocean, and the Fraser River, which discharges into the Pacific.
1804–1806	Meriwether Lewis and William Clark, Americans, lead an expedition that opens the American West, discovering the Columbia River and traveling to the Pacific coast.
1860–1863	John H. Speke, an Englishman, discovers the source of the Nile River to be the Victoria Nile flowing out of Ripon Falls, issuing from the north shore of Lake Victoria.
1925–1934	William Beebe, American underwater explorer and inventor, develops the bathysphere and dives to 3,034 feet offshore Bermuda.
1951–1955	Elizabeth Marshall Thomas, an American, explores the Kalahari Desert in central Africa.
1969	Neil Armstrong, Edwin (Buzz) Aldrin Jr., and Michael Collins, American astronauts, make their pioneering journey to the moon in the Saturn V space vehicle. First Armstrong and then Aldrin step out of the lunar module onto the moon's surface. Collins continues to pilot the command and service module, which later joins with the lunar module for their return to Earth.

Chronology of Travel Arrangers, Their Businesses, Facilities, Equipment, and Suppliers

B.C.E.

2000	Caravansaries (inns) are established in the Near East and the Orient in ancient times. Located on caravan routes, they provide overnight rest needs for travelers and traders and

for their donkeys and camels. These people travel in groups for mutual assistance and defense.

776   Greeks begin travels to the Olympic Games. Subsequently, the games are held every four years.

C.E.

500–1450   During Europe's Middle Ages, a royal party in unfamiliar territory sends out a harbinger to scout the best route, find accommodations and food, then return to the group as a guide.

1605   The hackney coach is introduced in London.

1801   Richard Trevithick, in England, perfects a steam locomotive capable of pulling heavy railcars.

1815   John L. McAdam and Thomas Telford, Britishers, invent all-weather roads, subsequently with a bituminous top.

1822   Robert Smart of Bristol, England, starts booking passengers on steamships sailing to Ireland.

1826–1840   Railroads begin service in the United States, first hauling minerals such as coal and, later, passengers.

1829   The Tremont House opens in Boston, the first "modern" hotel.

1830   The first passengers are carried by rail in England.

1838   Stendhal, the pseudonym of Marie-Henri Beyle of France, writes *Mémoires d'un touriste*, believed to be the first disseminated printed use of the French word *tourist*.

1841   Thomas Cook organizes a special excursion train carrying 570 passengers from Leicester to Loughborough, England, a trip of 12 miles.

1850   Thomas Bennett, secretary to the British consul general in Oslo, Norway, sets up a "trip organizer" business as a sideline. He provides individual pleasure travel itineraries and other services.

1873   The American Express Company is created by joining the original American Express Company formed in 1850 with the Wells Fargo Company, founded in 1852.

1902   The American Automobile Association (AAA) is founded in Chicago.

1903   Wilbur and Orville Wright make the first successful gasoline-powered airplane flight at Kitty Hawk, North Carolina.

1908   Henry Ford introduces the famous Model T automobile.

1918   Deutsche Lufthansa provides the first scheduled air passenger service from Berlin to Leipzig and Weimar.

1920   The U.S. road system begins great improvement.

1926   Varney Airlines and Western Airlines become the first airlines in the United States.

1927   Charles A. Lindbergh flies solo from New York to Paris nonstop.

1927   Charles A. Levine becomes the first transatlantic passenger, flying from New York to within 118 miles of Berlin, his destination, because of a forced landing.

1927   Pan American Airways flies first international commercial mail flight from Key West, Florida, to Havana, Cuba.

1928   Pan Am flies first passenger flight on the same route.

1931   The American Society of Steamship Agents is founded in New York.

1936   The Air Transport Association (ATA) is formed in Chicago.

1939   Frank Whittle, an Englishman, develops the first jet engine capable of powering a full-size airplane.

1944   The American Society of Travel Agents (ASTA) is founded from the American Society of Steamship Agents.

1945   End of World War II and the beginning of the era of mass tourism.

1951   Founding of Pacific Asia Travel Association (PATA) in Honolulu, Hawaii.

1952   The U.S. Congress creates the National System of Interstate Highways.

1954   Great Britain produces the Comet, the first passenger jet plane.

1958   The Boeing Commercial Airplane Company produces the B-707, the first commercial jet plane built in the United States.

1959	American Airlines flies the first transcontinental B-707 flight from Los Angeles to New York.
1961	The U.S. Congress creates the U.S. Travel Service.
1964	American Airlines inaugurates the SABRE computerized reservation system (CRS).
1970	Pan American World Airways flies the first Boeing 747 "jumbo jet" plane with 352 passengers from New York to London.
1978	British Airways and Air France begin passenger service on the supersonic Concorde airplane. The U.S. Airline Deregulation Act is passed.
1990	The Berlin Wall falls.
1994	The "age of travel," wherein the most complex trip can be planned and arranged by a single phone call from the traveler; might involve numerous airlines, a cruise ship, sightseeing tours, a local rental car, other ground services, and entertainment—all reserved by amazing computerized reservation systems worldwide, the entire trip, except for incidentals, paid for by a single credit card.
1994	The "Chunnel" undersea railway opens, providing rail travel under the English Channel between England and France.
1995	Delta Air Lines introduces commission caps, putting a ceiling on payments to travel agents for domestic tickets. Denver International Airport (DIA) opens as the first new U.S. airport in 20 years. The first White House Conference on Travel and Tourism is held.
1996	Alaska Airlines becomes the first carrier to accept online bookings and take payment through a Web site on the Internet.
1998	Hong Kong opens new $20 billion airport.
2001	Dennis Tito takes the world's first paid space vacation. September 11 attacks on the United States.
2003	The Concorde is retired.
2006	Anousheh Ansari is the first woman to take a paid space trip.
2007	Singapore Airlines launched the Airbus A380 in commercial service.
2009	The travel industry took a tremendous hit in 2008 and 2009 as the Great Recession took hold in the United States, Europe, and elsewhere and kept travelers at home.
2011	ANA launched the Boeing 787 in commercial service.

SUMMARY

Early explorers, traders, and shippers laid the groundwork upon which our modern age of travel is based. Human needs to arrange trips and facilitate movements have not changed over the ages: building roads, vehicles, and ships and providing overnight rest accommodations go back into antiquity. The brave explorers who went into the unknown made available to their contemporaries knowledge of what the world was really like.

Over the centuries, inventions such as the sandglass to measure time, the "log" line to measure distance, and the compass to gauge direction made possible successful sea exploration. The roads of early Persia and those of the Roman Empire were used for exploration, for military purposes, for transporting tribute, and for pleasure trips and recreation.

Subsequent inventions of better roads, stagecoaches, passenger railroads, passenger ships, automobiles, motorcoaches, and airplanes created an ever speedier and more pleasant means of travel. Hotels and inns became more commodious and comfortable, with the added convenience of location, services, and appointments.

However, the conditions for an ever-expanding tourism market are little different now than from Roman times. Tourism will flourish if prospective travelers are convinced that they will be safe and comfortable and well rewarded by their trip. When the Roman Empire declined, tourism declined. The wealthy class was reduced, roads deteriorated, and the countryside was plagued by bandits and scoundrels. Today, wars, unrest, and terrorism are similarly detrimental to tourism. Peace, prosperity, effective marketing, and reasonable travel costs remain the essential ingredients needed for the universal growth of travel.

❖ KEY CONCEPTS ❖

accommodations	Grand Tour	Romans
air travel	Greeks	Silk Road
American Express	Olympic Games	stagecoaches
attractions	Pan American Airways	Sumerians
automotive travel	Phoenicians	Thomas Bennett
early beginnings	Polynesians	Thomas Cook
early roads	rail travel	travel agents
Egyptians	Robert Smart	water travel

❖ INTERNET EXERCISES ❖

The Internet sites mentioned in this chapter, plus some selected additional sites, are listed for your convenience on the companion Web site for this book, www.wiley.com/college/goeldner.

ACTIVITY 1

Site Name: The National Amusement Park Historical Association

URL: www.napha.org

Background Information: The National Amusement Park Historical Association (NAPHA) is an international organization dedicated to the preservation and enjoyment of the amusement and theme park industry—past, present, and future.

Exercises

1. Trace the evolution of the amusement park from medieval Europe to the present day.

2. What is the prognosis for the amusement park industry in the United States today?

ACTIVITY 2

Site Name: National Trust for Historic Preservation

URL: www.preservationnation.org

Background Information: The National Trust for Historic Preservation is a privately funded nonprofit organization that provides leadership, education, and advocacy to save America's diverse historic places and revitalize our communities.

Exercises

1. What are National Trust historic sites?

2. Where does the National Trust get its operating funds?

3. Does the National Trust decide which buildings are historic?

❖ QUESTIONS FOR REVIEW AND DISCUSSION ❖

1. Of what value is learning the fundamentals of tourism's long history?

2. Do today's travelers have motivations and concerns similar to those of travelers who lived during the classical era?

3. What were the principal travel impulses of such early sea explorers as Columbus, Cabot, Balboa, Magellan, and Gosnold?

4. Give some examples of how guides operated in early tourism. Why were they so important? Are their functions the same today? Their ethics? (When discussing, include tour escorts.)

5. Describe the parallels that exist between tourism in Roman times and that of today.

6. Why have the Olympic Games survived since 776 B.C.E.?

7. In the twenty-first century, how consequential for the international traveler is an ability to converse in foreign languages?

8. Can one's money be converted to that of any other country?

9. What countries use the euro for currency?

10. Are museums, cathedrals, and art galleries really important to most visitors? Provide some outstanding examples.

11. How significant were religious motivations in early travel? Do these still exist? If so, list examples.

12. Early religious houses such as churches and monasteries often accommodated travelers. Give reasons for this.

13. What, if any, were the impacts of Marco Polo's writings on the growth of travel by Europeans during the Renaissance (fourteenth through sixteenth centuries)?

14. Specifically, why did travel by rail supersede that by stagecoach?

15. Are medical and health travel motivations still important?

16. Describe ancient tourist attractions. How significant are they now?

17. Why has air travel become the primary mode for middle- and long-distance trips?

18. Who was the first travel agent, and what services did he provide? The first rail passenger agent? Tour operator? Steamship agent?

19. How have computerized reservations systems (CRSs) aided travel agencies and the traveler?

20. What do you think travel will be like 20 years from now?

❖ **CASE PROBLEM** ❖

1. Mrs. Harris is a successful museum curator. She is approached by the Museum Director to develop a special nine month exhibit on "the history of travel" that would occupy an entire floor of the museum. She is very excited about the project, and has hired you as a travel consultant to help with the exhibit. What advice would you give her on what to include in the exhibit?

   What time periods would be best to focus on? What advice do you have on modes of transportation, people, and technological innovations? What features would ensure a large audience?

ENDNOTES

1. Lionel Casson, *Travel in the Ancient World* (London: Allen and Unwin, 1974), p. 253. A note on style: B.C.E. (Before the Common Era) and C.E. (Common Era), used by some authors and often used in scholarly literature, are the alternative designations corresponding to B.C. and A.D.

2. Eric Friedheim, *Travel Agents: From Caravans and Clippers to the Concorde* (New York: Travel Agent Magazine Books, 1992), pp. 27–28.

3. Ibid., p. 5.

4. Casson, *Travel in the Ancient World*, p. 32.

5. Ibid., p. 32.

6. Ibid., p. 34.

7. Ibid., p. 31.

8. Ibid., p. 35.

9. Ibid., p. 25.

10. Ibid.

11. Ibid., p. 27.

12. Ibid.

13. Ibid., p. 299.

14. Peter Neville-Hadley, *China: The Silk Routes* (Old Saybrook, CT: Globe Pequot Press, 1997).

15. J. D. Brown, *Frommer's China: The 50 Most Memorable Trips* (New York: Simon & Schuster, 1998), p. 371.

16. Neville-Hadley, *China*, p. 61.

17. Stephen G. Haw, *A Traveller's History of China*, 2d ed. (New York: N.W. Publishing Group, 1998), pp. 84–85.

18. Judy Bonavia, *The Silk Road from Xi'an to Kashgar*, revised by William Lindesay and Wa Qi, 2d ed. (New York: W.W. Norton & Co., 1999).

19. Casson, *Travel in the Ancient World*, pp. 76–77.

20. Ibid., p. 89.

21. Ibid., pp. 84–85.

22. Ibid., p. 99.

23. Ibid., p. 93.

24. Ibid., pp. 240–241.

25. Ibid., pp. 240–241.

26. Internet correspondence.

27. Trevor Sofield and Sarah Li, "Tourism Development and Cultural Policies in China," *Annals of Tourism Research*, vol. 25, no. 2 (1998), pp. 362–392.

28. H. Robinson, *A Geography of Tourism* (London: Macdonald and Evans, 1976), p. 13.

29. Quoted in George Young, *Tourism: Blessing or Blight?* (Middlesex, UK: Pelican Books, 1973), p. 1.

CHAPTER 3

Career Opportunities

LEARNING OBJECTIVES

- Evaluate future job opportunities in the tourism field.

- Learn about the careers available.

- Discover which careers might match your interests and abilities.

- Know additional sources of information on careers.

An airline employee checking in air travelers. *Photo courtesy of Corbis Digital Stock.*

INTRODUCTION

Every student eventually must leave the college or university campus and seek a career-oriented job. This is a difficult decision-making time, often filled with doubt as to what goals or ambitions should be pursued. Coming face to face with the problem of getting a first major career-oriented job is a challenging task. You are marketing a product—yourself—and you will have to do a good job of communicating to convince a prospective employer that you have the abilities needed and that you will be an asset to the organization.

JOB FORECASTS

The World Travel and Tourism Council (WTTC) estimates that in 2010, there were more than 235.8 million people worldwide, some 8.1 percent of the total workforce, employed in jobs that exist because of the demand generated by tourism. Although tourism contributes to gross domestic product (GDP), capital investment, employment, foreign exchange, and export earnings, it is the job-creation capacity of tourism that is its most significant feature. According to the WTTC, by 2020, **employment forecasts** are that 303.0 million people around the globe will have jobs created by tourism, accounting for 9.2 percent of total employment, or 1 in every 10.9 jobs.

In brief, tourism is one of the world's fastest-growing industries, and some employers are worried that they will not be able to find enough employees to fill open positions. Tourism is a growth field that will continue to offer great opportunities.

JOB REQUIREMENTS

Are you suited to work in the tourism field? Do you like working with people? Can you provide leadership? Would you be genuinely concerned for a traveler's comfort, needs, and well-being even if the customer might be rude and obnoxious? If you can answer in the affirmative,

One of the best jobs in tourism is to serve as the head of a city convention and visitors bureau. Shown here is Richard W. Scharf, president and CEO of Visit Denver, The Convention & Visitors Bureau. *Photo courtesy of Visit Denver, The Convention & Visitors Bureau.*

you can find a place in this industry. You have to like to do things for other people and work helpfully with them. If not, this is not the industry for you. Courtesy comes easily when customers are pleasant and gracious. But a great deal of self-discipline is required to serve every type of person, especially demanding or indecisive ones. In tourism settings, the customer might often change his or her mind. This requires patience and an unfailingly cheerful personality.

You must also ask if you have the physical stamina required to carry out many of the jobs available. It is difficult to work long hours on your feet or to work in a hot, humid, or cold environment. You might be involved in the pressure of a crush of people, such as at an airline ticket counter. A travel agency counselor must have keen vision, excellent hearing, and strong nerves. A large-resort manager is constantly required to deal with sophisticated budgeting and investment decisions. The chief executive officer (CEO) of a major convention and visitors bureau must provide leadership to and coordinate the efforts of a very diverse membership. Try to evaluate your physical and mental attributes and skills to determine if you can perform.

To enhance your chances of getting a job and deciding if you would like it, visit several types of tourist-related organizations. Watch the activities being performed. Talk to managers, supervisors, and employees. Try to obtain an internship. Work experience means a great deal. Once you have had work experience, you can utilize those skills in a wide variety of tourism enterprises in any number of locations around the world.

CAREER POSSIBILITIES

Tourism today is one of the world's largest industries. It is made up of many segments, the principal ones being transportation, accommodations, food service, shopping, travel arrangements, and activities for tourists, such as history, culture, adventure, sports, recreation, entertainment, and other similar activities. The businesses that provide these services require knowledgeable and imaginative business managers.

Familiarity with tourism, recreation, business, and leisure equips one to pursue a career in a number of tourism-related fields. Tourism skills are critically needed, and there are many opportunities available in a multitude of fields.

Because tourism is diverse and complex and each sector has many job opportunities and career paths, it is virtually impossible to list and describe all the jobs one might consider in this large field. However, as a student interested in tourism, you could examine the following areas, many of which are discussed in more detail in Chapters 5 to 8.

An effort has been made in the industry segments to provide a fairly comprehensive list of jobs, including entry-level jobs requiring few skills. Entry jobs are listed because they are part of the tourism industry and provide examples of the kinds of jobs managers will have the task of recruiting and supervising.

Tourism Technology

Opportunities for technology jobs permeate the tourism industry at virtually every level. Although information technology has always been important in the field, its importance increases as the variety of new devices and improvements on existing ones appear. For instance, application of advanced information technology to provide tourist information via navigation systems, PDAs (personal digital assistants), or mobile phones is growing.

Consequently, additional technical manpower will continue to be needed for tourism managers to achieve the best results. People skilled in Web technologies, user interface, modules, database management, programming, business intelligence, business analysis, market research, and computer graphics are among those who can look forward to opportunities in the industry.

In addition to information technology, a number of new tourism products have emerged as tourism technology has been combined with other industries. These include medical tourism, educational tourism, agricultural tourism, marine tourism, and space tourism.

Another technology creating tourism jobs is the Global Positioning System (GPS). GPS has become a widely used aid to navigation worldwide, and is also a useful tool for mapmaking, land surveying, and commerce. Indeed, there is hardly a field that is not employing GPS; its many capabilities are applied by scientists, pilots, military troops, hikers, bikers, business travelers, vacationers, off-road adventurers, mariners, fishermen, hunters, and balloonists, to cite a few. Visit www.garmin.com and www.tomtom.jobs for more information.

Airlines

The airlines are a major travel industry employer, offering a host of jobs at many levels, ranging from entry level to top management, including reservation agents, flight attendants, pilots, flight engineers, aircraft mechanics, maintenance staff, baggage handlers, airline food service jobs, sales representatives, sales jobs, computer specialists, training staff, office jobs, clerical positions, ticket agents, and research jobs. Because airlines have to meet safety and other requirements, opportunities also exist with the Federal Aviation Administration (FAA). The FAA hires air traffic controllers and various other specialists. Airports also use a wide range of personnel, from parking attendants to airport managers. Other policy and air safety–related jobs are available with associations such as the Air Transport Association.

People in tourism tend to enjoy their work. The opportunity to service visitors on vacation or on family outings is more satisfying than many other forms of employment.
Photo courtesy of The Broadmoor.

Bus Companies

Bus companies require management personnel, ticket agents, sales representatives, tour representatives, hostesses, information clerks, clerical positions, bus drivers, personnel people, and training employees.

Cruise Companies

The cruise industry is the fastest-growing segment of the tourism industry today. Job opportunities include those for sales representatives, clerical workers, market researchers, recreation directors, and CEOs. Because of their similarity in operations, cruise lines have many of the same jobs as the lodging industry.

Railroads

Passenger rail service in the United States is dominated by Amtrak and in Canada by Via Rail. In Europe, Japan, and elsewhere, rail passenger transportation is much more developed and widespread, offering greater opportunities than in North America. Railroads hire managers, passenger service representatives, traffic analysts, marketing managers, sales representatives, reservations clerks, information specialists, conductors, engineers, coach and lounge car attendants, and station agents.

Rental Car Companies

With increased pleasure, air travel, and the growth of fly/drive programs, rental car companies are becoming an ever-more-important segment of the travel industry. This sector of tourism employs reservation agents, rental sales agents, clerks of various kinds, service agents, mechanics, and district and regional managers.

Hotels, Motels, and Resorts

The range of jobs in accommodations is extremely broad. The following list is representative: regional manager, general manager, resident manager, comptroller, accountants, management trainees, director of sales, director of convention sales, director of personnel, director of research, mail clerks, room clerks, reservation clerks, front-office manager, housekeepers, superintendent of service, bellhops, lobby porters, doormen, maids, chefs, cooks, kitchen helpers, storeroom employees, dishwashers, waiters, bartenders, apprentice waiters, heating and air-conditioning personnel, maintenance workers, engineers, electricians, plumbers, carpenters, painters, and laundry workers.

Resorts tend to have the same jobs as those mentioned for hotels and motels; however, larger resorts will have greater job opportunities and require more assistants in all areas. Resorts also have a number of additional job opportunities in the areas of social events, entertainment, and recreation, such as for tennis and golf pros. At ski resorts there will be ski instructors, members of a safety patrol, and so on. The American Hotel and Lodging Association has launched the AH&LA Online Career Center, which lists open positions in the lodging industry. Visit its Web site at www.ahla.com and click on *career center*.

Global Distributions Systems and Online Companies

There are currently three large global distributions systems (GDS) companies and a number of smaller ones. GDSs are computer reservation systems that sell tickets for multiple airlines, book hotels, reserve rental cars, and conduct other transactions related to travel.

A five-star resort such as The Broadmoor in Colorado Springs provides a wide range of managerial job opportunities in attractive surroundings. *Photo courtesy of The Broadmoor.*

The big three companies are Amadeus, Sabre, and Travelport GDS, which includes the Galileo and Worldspan systems. They own some of the largest online travel companies, providing thousands of jobs. For example, Sabre has over 6,800 employees and also owns Travelocity. Other large online agencies are Expedia, Orbitz, Priceline, CheapTickets, and Hotwire. In addition, many smaller companies provide services ranging from search to purchase. Some representative job titles are principal IT strategist, senior software design engineer, network engineer, IT voice network engineer, director of software development, senior software design engineer, database developer, senior manager of strategy and marketing, marketing manager, sales manager, director of customer care, customer service quality director, customer service representative, marketing analyst, account manager, global recruiter, art director, fraud analyst, financial analyst, customer analyst, merchandising analyst, lodging operations manager, product manager, corporate counsel, and call center representative.

Travel Agencies

Travel agencies range from very small to very large businesses. There exist both online travel agencies and the traditional bricks-and-mortar agencies. The smaller businesses are very much like any other small business. Very few people carry out all the business operations, and jobs include secretarial, travel counseling, and managerial positions. In large offices, job opportunities are more varied and include branch manager, commercial account specialists, domestic travel counselors, international travel counselors, research directors, and advertising managers. Trainee group sales consultants, accountants, file clerks, sales personnel, tour planners, tour guides, reservationists, group coordinators, trainees, operations employees, administrative assistants, advertising specialists, and computer specialists are other possibilities.

❖ GLOBAL INSIGHT ❖

Top 10 Things Tourism Employees Like about Their Jobs

1. **Variety.** Person after person said how much they enjoyed the variety in their jobs. Every day is different. "I rarely have a boring day," a lot of them said. "There is never a dull moment," others agreed. Tourism offers many different challenges. Most employees were grateful not to be stuck in a routine, predictable job.

2. **Dealing with people.** Tourism employees enjoyed the opportunity to meet and deal with people from all over the world. Many felt good when they knew they had helped or entertained this diverse group of customers.

3. **Working with other tourism employees.** Employees praised their fellow employees. People in tourism, they said, tend to be dynamic, interesting, and upbeat. Many people liked the fact that tourism had a lot of younger employees. Some 50 percent of the employees in the tourism industry fall within the 15- to 24-year-old age group.

4. **Opportunities.** Because the industry is growing, employees said, there are so many different types of jobs and opportunities in the tourism industry. It is possible, they said, to get experience in many different kinds of tourism. There are lots of career paths available. There are so many opportunities to learn new skills.

5. **Advancement potential.** Employees were also enthusiastic about the opportunities for relatively quick advancement in tourism. If you work hard, they said, you can move up to the next level faster than you could in many other industries.

6. **Developing global skills.** Another positive was the fact that your tourism skills are transferable all around the world. Once you have experience, employees said, you can work in many different parts of the world.

7. **Easy to get started.** Many tourism employees were grateful at the ease of getting an entry-level job in tourism. "You don't need postsecondary school education. It is desirable, however, to get tourism training and education if you want to build a career in tourism."

8. **Training opportunities.** At the same time, employees were pleased that there were many tourism training and educational programs available to expand their knowledge about the industry. Many of these can be pursued part time while you are working.

9. **Tips!** Many tourism employees were happy to supplement their income with tips. They enjoyed being able to influence their tip amount by providing good service.

10. **Creativity.** A great variety of tourism jobs, they said, allow you to think on your feet and be creative.

Source: Canadian Tourism Human Resource Council.

DISCUSSION QUESTIONS

1. Which one of these things is the most appealing to you when considering job opportunities?

2. How important is the factor "enjoy working with people" in tourism?

Tour Companies

Tour companies offer employment opportunities in such positions as tour manager or escort, tour coordinator, tour planner, publicist, reservations specialist, accountant, sales representative, group tour specialist, incentive tour coordinator, costing specialist, hotel coordinator, office supervisor, and managerial positions. Often a graduate will begin employment as a management trainee, working in all the departments of the company before a permanent assignment is made.

Food Service

Many job opportunities are available in the rapidly growing food service industry, such as headwaiters, captains, waiters and waitresses, buspersons, chefs, cooks, bartenders, restaurant managers, assistant managers, personnel directors, dieticians, menu planners, cashiers, food service supervisors, purchasing agents, butchers, beverage workers, hostesses, kitchen helpers, and dishwashers. In addition, highly trained managers having a strong background in this sector are required to oversee the development and performance of large restaurant chains.

Professional chefs find great satisfaction in creating tasty, nutritious, and virtually irresistible food items. Photo courtesy of Doral Golf Resort and Spa.

Tourism Education

As global tourism continues to grow, the need for tourism education grows. In recent years, many colleges and universities have added travel and tourism programs, existing programs have been expanded, vocational schools have launched programs, trade associations have introduced education and certification programs, and private firms have opened travel schools. There are job opportunities for administrators, teachers, professors, researchers, and support staff.

Tourism Research

Tourism research consists of the collection and analysis of data from both primary and secondary sources. The tourism researcher plans market studies, consumer surveys, and the implementation of research projects. Research jobs are available in national tourism offices, state/provincial travel offices, and private firms.

Travel Communications

A number of opportunities are available in the field of travel communications—editors, staff writers, and freelance writers. Most major travel firms need public relations people who write and edit, disseminate information, develop communication vehicles, obtain publicity, arrange special events, do public speaking, plan public relations campaigns, and so on. A travel photographer could find employment in either public relations or travel writing. Television is a medium with increasing opportunities. The Internet has become a major communication medium for the travel industry and provides a range of job opportunities.

Recreation and Leisure

Jobs in recreation and leisure are numerous. Some examples are activity director, aquatics specialist, ski instructor, park ranger, naturalist, museum guide, handicapped-program planner, forester, camping director, concert promoter, lifeguards, tennis and golf instructors, coaches for various athletic teams, and drama directors. Many recreation workers teach handicrafts. Resorts, parks, and recreation departments often employ recreation directors who hire specialists to work with senior citizens or

Club Med (Mediterranée) is a vacation concept that has flourished over many years. Started in 1950, the first village opened on the Spanish island of Mallorca. "The Club Med Experience," unique when it began, saw each resort (or village) provide an extensive list of services and activities in a single package. Thus, all lodging, food, and facilities were included in the price charged. The sailboat shown is but one example of the high-class facilities available to all "Gentils Membres" (guests). While Club Med originally focused on the "young singles" market, it later changed its emphasis to families as the composition and lifestyles of the "boomer" market evolved. *Photo courtesy of Club Med.*

youth groups, to serve as camp counselors, or to teach such skills as boating and sailing. Management, supervisory, and administrative positions are also available.

Attractions

Attractions such as amusement parks and theme parks are a major source of tourism employment. Large organizations such as Disney World, Disneyland, Six Flags, Europa-Park, Tivoli Gardens, and Sea World provide job opportunities ranging from top management jobs to clerical and maintenance jobs.

PROFILE

DAWN DREW
Founder and CEO The M.O.S.T.E., Inc.,
International Marketing and
Entertainment

Dawn Drew joined the National Geographic Society as advertising director of *National Geographic Traveler* magazine in December 1994. During her nine years with the Society, she has been promoted twice, first to publisher of *Traveler* in 1998 and two years later to vice president.

During her tenure at the Society, Dawn has led the magazine to multiple years of advertising page and revenue growth. She has also overseen the development of a national sales staff and the successful transition from *Traveler*'s bimonthly status to publication eight times a year with several brand extensions. Examples of some of the magazine's achievements include:

■ Publication of its largest issues in both ad pages and revenue

■ Publication of its first newsstand edition, "Discover Europe"

■ Selected as one of *AdWeek*'s "Hot List" publications two years in a row

■ Publication of *National Geographic Traveler On Campus*, an edition sent to nearly 1 million college students interested or involved in study abroad programs and education travel

■ Publication of *National Geographic Traveler* Special Supplements, in-book editorial supplements that focus on a single destination from a cultural perspective

■ Creation of National Geographic Traveler Destination Immersion Programs, local market events that allow the general public consumers and readers of *Traveler* magazine to "sample" a destination via seminal experiences with food and wine tastings, photo gallery exhibitions, live photography presentations, and live music concerts featuring artists from around the globe

In addition to her publishing responsibilities for the magazine, Dawn has remained active in the travel industry. Since 1996, she has served as a member of the Travel Industry Association (TIA) board of directors, has been chair of the research committee for three consecutive years, is currently chair of the marketing committee, has held officers' positions for five years, and is currently the second vice chair of the organization. In 2009, Dawn became national chair of the TIA, the first magazine publisher ever to hold that post.

During her tenure as chair of the research committee, National Geographic Traveler successfully collaborated with the TIA research division to produce a landmark study, "Geo-Tourism," the first major piece of research to examine the awareness and travel habits of Americans with regard to sustainable tourism. An updated version of this study was introduced in October 2007 at the TIA Marketing Outlook Forum.

An active member of the Pacific Asia Tourism Association (PATA), Dawn is a member of the board of directors, the originator and first chair of the Sustainable Tourism Committee, and was recently elected to serve on the Industry Council with 50 members of government in the PATA region.

Dawn has also been a member of the board of advisors for the Prince of Wales' International Business Leaders Forum based in London. Through this association, she worked with a number of travel companies, such as Marriott, British Airways, and Mandarin Oriental, to form the International Travel Partnership in sustainable tourism initiatives.

Dawn began her career in publishing as an editorial intern at *Newsweek* magazine, working for the back-of-the-book departments such as "cinema" and "book reviews." A move to a public relations firm, Circulation Experti, enabled Dawn to use her writing skills and learn the PR business, which allowed her to break into the promotion and marketing side of the publishing business.

The proving ground for Dawn was *W* magazine, where she was first promotion manager and then director of marketing for four years. She then moved on to a similar position at the *Atlantic Monthly* and subsequently into ad sales at another title.

Dawn spent eight formative career years at the *New York Times* Magazine Group, where she worked her way up from a sales position at *Golf Digest* to sales management positions at *Tennis* and *McCall's* magazines.

Much of the success and growth at *Traveler* stem from the leadership role the magazine has assumed within its core industry, along with its solid positioning as the only consumer magazine published that addresses the practical needs of the frequent traveler by covering "all travel, all the time." The activities, commitment, and interest in travel have generated an audience of more than 7 million readers, millions of dollars in revenue for the magazine, increased its stature in the field, and provided access to very active experiential consumers.

In her off hours, Dawn enjoys photography, and hopes she will one day be discovered by the National Geographic Society. She enjoys gourmet cooking and is an avid magazine reader.

A graduate of Tufts University, where she majored in political science and international law, Dawn has maintained a keen interest in world affairs and is proficient in French and Spanish. She has been to many parts of Asia, the Caribbean, Europe, the South Pacific, and North America, both for pleasure and as part of her job responsibilities at *Traveler*.

THE FUTURE: WE ARE ALL IN THE TRAVEL BUSINESS

TRAVEL AND THE FUTURE OF COMMUNITY-BASED SUSTAINABLE TOURISM

I used to look at the future of travel in terms of what it would one day become instead of what it, as an industry, would have the power to do. By nature, I am an optimist. And like the industry I have been a part of for so long, I still feel that travel has the power to cure many of the ills we face as a society. But there is a clarion call that must be answered—and there is no better way to connect the "haves" with the "have-nots" than travel.

The global recession has made a negative impact on jobs everywhere. The travel industry—one of the world's biggest employers—has an opportunity to not only put people back to work but also create careers and real commerce that can economically sustain local communities.

Careers and commerce are not limited to jobs with big companies, or start-ups of businesses in major urban areas. People in far-flung locations have an opportunity to cash in on the recent awakening of traveler's need for authentic experiences. Consumers are looking for intimate experiences in travel.

Handmade, one-of-a-kind items as souvenirs, personal encounters such as meals cooked in homes or community centers are a couple of examples of the level of intimacy travelers seek—all of which can be translated into business that can be sustained by travel.

What's new is that economically developed nations like the United States will begin to offer an increasing number of opportunities to draw travelers into the smaller corners of this country. Many major travel destinations have begun to consider how to bring travelers beyond the bigger cities and attractions, deeper into the countries where the benefits of tourism can filter deeper into the communities.

India's very impressive rural tourism program crafted by the Ministry of Tourism and the UN Development Program is an example of what can and should be created in many places. Each of the villages in the program offers visitors a cultural, communal experience that includes food, handicrafts, local entertainment, and lodging. It affords travelers the experiences that make great memories and allows members of small communities to create commerce that will sustain them economically. The rural villages are easily reached from many of the major destinations and receive marketing support from the federal and local governments.

This method of commerce, along with micro-financing for small or individual development of travel businesses, is becoming the norm globally. It is one of the ways travel will help to sustain individual cultures, maintain living wages, and allow citizens to make valuable contributions to society in general.

Festivals and Events

Festivals and events are one of the fastest-growing segments of the tourism industry. Event management is emerging as a field, is becoming more professional, and is providing a new source of job opportunities. Events are creating offices and moving them to year-round operation. The International Special Events Society (ISES) has a career center. Visit www.ises.com and click on *Career Center*.

Sports Tourism

Sports are popular throughout the world, with many sports teams and enterprises becoming big businesses and offering job opportunities in the management and marketing areas.

Tourist Offices and Information Centers

Numerous jobs are available in tourist offices and information centers. Many chambers of commerce function as information centers and hire employees to provide this information. Many states operate welcome centers. Job titles found in state tourism offices are director, assistant director, deputy director, travel representative, economic development specialist, assistant director for travel promotion, statistical analyst, public information officer, assistant director for public relations, marketing coordinator, communications specialist, travel editor, media liaison, media specialist, photographer, administrative assistant, information specialist, media coordinator, manager of travel literature, writer, chief of news and information, marketing coordinator, market analyst, research analyst, economist, reference coordinator, secretary, package tour coordinator, and information clerk.

Convention and Visitors Bureaus and Destination Management Organizations

As more and more cities enter the convention and visitor industry, employment opportunities in this segment grow. Many cities are devoting public funds to build convention centers to compete in this growing market. Convention and visitors bureaus require CEOs, managers, assistant managers, research directors, information specialists, marketing managers, public relations staff, sales personnel, secretaries, and clerks. The Professional Convention Management Association (PCMA) maintains a career center where employers post jobs and job seekers receive access. Visit www.pcma.org/careers.htm.

Meeting Planners

A growing profession is meeting planning. Many associations and corporations are hiring people whose job responsibilities are to arrange, plan, and conduct meetings. Meeting Planners International maintains an easy-to-use career site called Career Connections On-line Job Resources. Visit www .mpiweb.org to learn the valuable resources they provide.

Convention Center, Arena, Stadium, and Public Facilities Management

The management of convention centers, exhibition halls and trade centers, arenas, stadiums, performing arts centers, theaters, and special-use venues provides career opportunities around the world. Facilities management has job opportunities in finance, operations, event management, concessions management, marketing, human resources, and box office management. A leading company in this field is SMG, which manages 77 arenas, 9 stadiums, 67 convention centers, 52 performing arts centers, and 17 other facilities. Visit www.smgworld.com/career_opportunities.aspx.

Gaming

One of the fastest-growing sectors is gaming. Today, one is hard-pressed to find a state where gambling is not allowed or a gaming proposal is not in front of the state legislature. From riverboats to Indian reservations to land-based casinos, new destinations are being created. Casinos provide job opportunities ranging from managers to marketers to mechanics to clerical and maintenance jobs.

Other Opportunities

A fairly comprehensive list of career opportunities has been presented. Others that do not fit the general categories listed are club management, museum management, heritage management, trade show and exhibit management, exhibit and meeting decorating, entertainment management, corporate travel departments, hotel representative companies, in-flight and trade magazines, and trade and professional associations.

CAREER PATHS IN TOURISM

In addition to considering one of the foregoing kinds of positions within a particular segment of the tourism sector, it is also useful to examine the various career paths that might be pursued. Because the tourism industry is so large and so diverse, it offers a broad range of challenging positions. Although each of these positions offers its own unique opportunities and demands, people will find that the experience gained from working in a range of jobs in different subsectors of tourism can strengthen their understanding of the industry as a whole. Depending on one's career objectives, this broader understanding of tourism can be especially valuable when applying for certain types of positions. Examples include those in destination management organizations and national or provincial/state tourism offices.

To offer employees opportunities for growth and development, educators and personnel managers attempt continually to develop the concept of career paths in tourism. A schematic model illustrating the concept is shown in Figure 3.1. The fundamental premise of this general model is that people can pursue a variety of reasonably well-defined alternative routes, first through the educational system and subsequently through the industry itself. Based on the training and experience gained, combined with high-quality performance, a person can pursue a career path starting at different levels, with the ultimate goal of achieving the position of senior executive. Although not everyone will have the ability

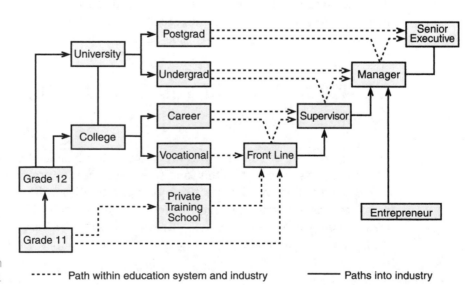

Figure 3.1 Career paths within the tourism industry.

------ Path within education system and industry   ——— Paths into industry or will necessarily want to pass through all levels of the model, Figure 3.1 does provide defined career paths for those who are interested. It also indicates what combination of training and experience is normally required to achieve various positions.

Although clearly an oversimplification, the career path model demonstrates that people may take a variety of routes in pursuing their careers at different levels within and across the various subsectors of tourism. The specific positions that will appeal to different people will, of course, vary according to their particular educational background and their occupational skills. The chosen career path will also reflect a person's values and interests. Just how the chosen occupation might reflect individual values and interest is shown in Figure 3.2. As indicated, front-line staff (entry level and operations) must like

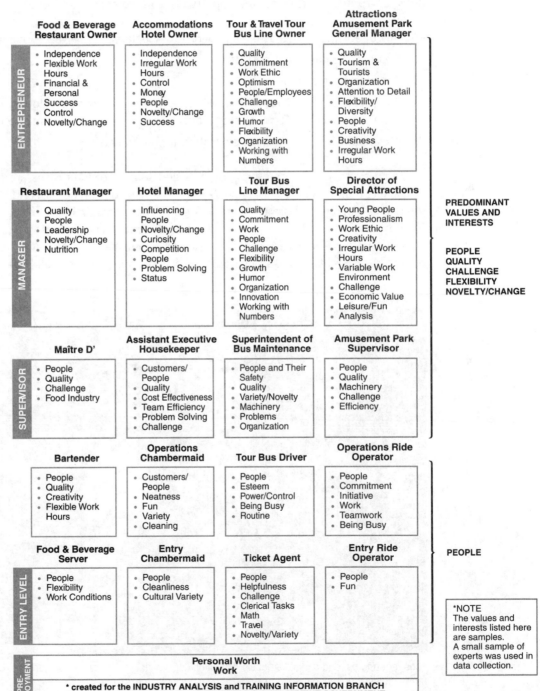

Figure 3.2 Career paths in tourism, sample occupations, values, and interests.

dealing with people and possess a strong interest in providing them with high-quality service. Supervisors, managers, and entrepreneurs must possess additional values and interests that enable them to face the challenges of change as they attempt to meet the needs of a demanding and ever-shifting marketplace.

INTERNSHIPS

One of the best ways to get the job you want is to have internship (cooperative education) experience. Internship opportunities abound in the tourism area. Most internship programs are designed to provide students the opportunity to accomplish five things:

1. Acquire valuable, hands-on experience to supplement their academic learning.
2. Learn potential practical skills.
3. Develop professionalism.
4. Interact with segments of the local business community and develop an appreciation for the daily operation and long-term strategic direction of a corporate or small business environment.
5. Develop a further understanding of their chosen field.

Some examples of internship programs and sources of internships are Marriott, Hyatt, Disney, Universal Studios, Starwood, and the World Travel and Tourism Council (WTTC). The Marriott Lodging Internship Program is designed to stimulate student interest in hotel management and a career with Marriott International. Through the program, students gain practical work experience necessary to pursue a management career in the hospitality industry. In addition, it provides Marriott with an opportunity to make sound evaluations of potential management candidates. Internship opportunities

Zoos, aquariums, and parks are popular tourist attractions that provide entry-level jobs for youth and many professional opportunities as well. Zoos, in particular, are highly sophisticated operations—often involving such initiatives as species protection through genetic research. As such, they require highly trained professionals who are in high demand worldwide. *Photo courtesy of Naples Zoo.*

are available in its Ritz Carlton Hotels, Marriott Hotels, Resorts, and Suites; Renaissance Hotels; Residence Inn; Courtyard; and TownePlace Suites brands and its time-share business, Marriott Vacation Club International. Visit www.marriott.com/careers/College.mi.

The Hyatt Hotels and Resorts Internship Program was created to generate student interest in hotel management and provide a venue for students to experience the culture of a hospitality leader. Internships also give Hyatt the opportunity to recognize potential managers and continue developing relationships throughout the academic year. Hyatt internships are offered in a variety of disciplines and vary by country, as described in the specific job descriptions of the available internship postings. Visit www.explorehyatt.jobs.

Disney Professional Internships are available in many disciplines at the *Walt Disney World*® Resort, *Disneyland*® Resort and Walt Disney Imagineering. Each of these unique areas of the global company offers students the ability to apply classroom studies while networking with Disney professionals, and gaining valuable experience. Visit www.disney.go.com/disneycareers/internships.

Universal Studios Orlando claims its internships add more excitement to your life and your résumé. It offers internships to help students gain valuable work experiences within their field of study at a world-class resort. Visit www.universalorlandojobs.com.

Starwood provides undergraduate students with the opportunity to grow their careers before graduation. When school is not in session, hundreds of students join properties in all departments to gain valuable experience with an industry leader. Students have an opportunity to experience the culture of Starwood, and one of the brands, which can help them determine if Starwood could be the right career fit for them upon graduation. Starwood gets to know the students, too. When it selects graduates to join its Management Training program, preference is given to those who have previously completed a successful Starwood externship or internship. Starwood Hotels and Resorts offers a unique range of brands: Sheraton, Westin, Four Points, W Hotels, St. Regis, The Luxury Collection, le Mériden, element, and Aloft with a presence in the world's most exciting destinations. Visit www.starwoodhotels.com/corporate/careers/recruiting/internships.html.

The WTTC internships place selected students at WTTC and provide them with the opportunity to gain experience in the tourism industry. Placements vary in length from three months to six months and consist of a variety of tasks that allow students to become familiar with WTTC work and, at the same time, play a valuable role in the day-to-day operations. A limited number of internship positions are available throughout the year. Applications are accepted on an ongoing basis for future positions. Candidates who wish to work in a dynamic and exciting team environment are encouraged to forward their cover letter and résumé to Ufi Ibrahim, chief operations officer, at: wttcvp@yahoo.co.uk.

These few examples provide a brief picture of the multitude of opportunities available. Get on the Internet! Opportunities are available all over the world. Visit www.goabroad.com and find some 367 organizations offering some 775 intern abroad programs.

OTHER SOURCES OF CAREER INFORMATION

Most of the career opportunities available in the travel field have been listed. It is hoped that this overview will provide you with a guide and point out that these industries are so large that they are worthy of much further study by themselves. In considering career opportunities, it is important to gather information before you invest a great deal of time looking for a job. The following are good references on tourism jobs:

- The Internet. A Google search of *tourism careers* will produce about 28.5 million hits.
- Eberts, Marjorie, Linda Brothers, and Ann Gisler. *Careers in Travel, Tourism, and Hospitality*. New York: McGraw-Hill, 2005.
- Rubin, Karen. *Inside Secrets to Finding a Career in Travel*. Indianapolis, IN: JIST Works, 2001.

One book on how to get a job is particularly recommended:

■ Bolles, Richard. *What Color Is Your Parachute? A Practical Manual for Job-Hunters and Career-Changers.* Berkeley, CA: Ten Speed Press, 2010.

The information provided in this chapter should be an important starting point for you. However, it is really just the tip of the iceberg. It is up to you to explore the subject further and to gain additional information. You need to learn not only about careers in tourism and travel-related fields but also about the task of marketing yourself—how to work up résumés and how to conduct yourself during interviews. General books on getting a job will help you in this task.

SUMMARY

A career in tourism offers many exciting and challenging employment opportunities. As indicated in Chapter 1, tourism is the largest industry in the world today. In the United States and throughout the rest of the world, the travel industry is expected to be a growth industry. The labor-intensive tourism industry has a need for motivated people of all ages and backgrounds. Those who prepare themselves, maintain high energy, have a talent for working with people, and are dedicated to high-quality service will find themselves climbing the career ladder to success. However, those who scan the industry with an innovative perspective to seek out a self-designed career ladder particularly suited to your own set of interests and skills will realize the greatest success and satisfaction.

❖ KEY CONCEPTS ❖

accommodations	food service	tourism education
airlines	gaming	tourism research
attractions	internships	tourist offices and information
bus companies	meeting planning	centers
career path	railroads	travel agencies
convention and visitors bureaus	recreation	travel communications
cruise lines	rental car companies	
employment forecasts	tour companies	

❖ INTERNET EXERCISES ❖

The Internet sites mentioned in this chapter plus some selected additional sites are listed for your convenience on the companion Web site for this book, www.wiley.com/college/goeldner.

ACTIVITY 1

Site Name: Hospitality Net

URL: www.hospitalitynet.org

Background Information: Hospitality Net is the leading hospitality industry resource on the Internet with

information on employment opportunities, events, industry news, links to other sites, and so on.

Exercises

1. What are the categories for the job opportunities listed on this Web site?

2. Choose a category and find a job that would be of interest to you. Describe the job, where it is located, and why it appeals to you.

ACTIVITY 2

Site Name: World Travel and Tourism Council

URL: www.wttc.org

Background Information: The World Travel and Tourism Council (WTTC) is the global business leaders' forum for travel and tourism. Its members are chief executives from all sectors of the travel and tourism industry, including accommodations, catering, cruises, entertainment, recreation, transportation, and travel-related services. Its central goal is to work with governments to realize the full economic impact of the world's largest generator of wealth and jobs: travel and tourism.

Exercise

1. What is the WTTC's vision on jobs in the travel and tourism industry for the next decade?

ACTIVITY 3

Site Name: Cool Works.com

URL: www.coolworks.com

Background Information: Cool Works® is about finding a seasonal job, internship, or career in some of the greatest places on earth. Ski resorts, ranches, theme parks, tour companies, and National Park jobs are featured.

Exercises

1. What internship opportunities are available on this site?
2. What volunteer programs are featured?
3. What position listing appeals to you?

❖ **QUESTIONS FOR REVIEW AND DISCUSSION** ❖

1. What is the growth potential for tourism jobs?
2. As a career in tourism, what position appeals to you at present?
3. What preparation will be needed for that position?
4. What are its probable rewards?
5. Identify the position's advancement opportunities.
6. Are your writing and speaking skills good enough to land a job?
7. What criteria would you use to choose a company for an interview?
8. How important is salary in your job choice?
9. Evaluate the job satisfaction in your chosen career.
10. What will tourism be like in the year 2020? 2030? What position might you visualize yourself to be in by that date?

 CASE PROBLEMS

1. Donnell C. is graduating from a four-year travel and tourism curriculum. She has had several job offers. What type of organization would afford her the broadest range of experiences? How important is her beginning salary?

2. Jim B. is a successful resort manager. He is visited one day by a very bright high school senior who is most interested in becoming a resort manager. What educational preparation advice might Jim offer?

PART 2 How Tourism Is Organized

The Dallas/Fort Worth Airport covers 17,500 acres. Purchasing facilities and an airport hotel can be seen in the center of the photograph. An automated shuttle train provides transportation to other terminals. *Photo courtesy of nuMedia Group, Inc.*

CHAPTER 4 ✢

World, National, Regional, and Other Organizations

LEARNING OBJECTIVES

- Understand the magnitude of world tourism in terms of the vast numbers of organizations that serve the needs of their diverse memberships.

- Recognize the variety of types and functions of tourism organizations.

- Know why states support official offices of tourism.

- Learn how national, regional, and trade organizations are structured and operated.

The Taj Mahal in Agra, India, is a favorite travel destination along the Asian Highway. The Asian Highway was initiated in 1958 and funded by the national governments in Asia. *Photo courtesy of the United Nations.*

INTRODUCTION

The complex organization of tourism involves literally thousands of units. This chapter focuses on some of the organizations that perform the catalyst, planning, development, and promotion functions within destinations. As Figure 4.1 stresses, all of these functions must be carried out with a high degree of cooperative interaction between the public and private sectors at all levels of the destination hierarchy. This destination hierarchy provides a geographical classification and sub-classification of the world. The world is divided into nations, which, in turn, commonly consist of regions, states/provinces, and urban centers (cities/municipalities).

In addition to a geographic classification, tourism organizations can also be classified by ownership, such as government, quasi-government, or private; by function or type of activity, such as regulators, suppliers, marketers, developers, consultants, researchers, educators, publishers, professional associations, trade organizations, and consumer organizations; by industry, such as transportation (air, bus, rail, auto, cruise), travel agents, tour wholesalers, lodging, attractions, and recreation; and by profit or nonprofit.

The purpose of Chapters 4 through 8 is to discuss the major types of tourist organizations and how they interrelate and operate, focusing on illustrative examples. The discussion begins with official international tourism groups in this chapter and ends with the private organizations and firms that make up the tourism industry, covered in Chapters 5, 6, 7, and 8.

INTERNATIONAL ORGANIZATIONS

The discussion first examines the nature and activities of the highly influential organizations representing the public and private sectors in tourism. These organizations provide both moral and functional leadership that coordinates and strengthens the visibility and effectiveness of tourism organizations that provide public-sector governance and private-sector functionality.

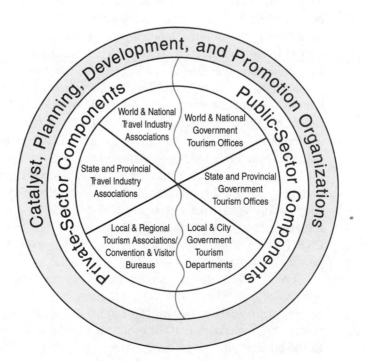

Figure 4.1   Tourism organizations.

United Nations World Tourism Organization

The United Nations World Tourism Organization (UNWTO) is the most widely recognized and the leading international organization in the field of travel and tourism today. It serves as a global forum for tourism policy issues provides moral leadership for the vast international tourism sector, and is a practical source of tourism know-how for its members. Its membership includes 154 countries, 7 territories, and more than 400 affiliate members representing local government, tourism associations, educational institutions, and private-sector companies, including airlines, hotel groups, and tour operators. With its headquarters in Madrid, UNWTO is a specialized agency of the United Nations (UN). UN specialized agency status entitles UNWTO to participate as a full member in the United Nations System Chief Executives Board for Coordination (CEB), which elaborates systemwide strategies in response to overall intergovernmental directives on economic cooperation and development. UNWTO's participation will enable it to highlight the role of tourism in support of socio-economic development and the achievement of the Millennium Development Goals.

The United Nations World Tourism Organization is an official specialized agency of the United Nations and has the objective of promoting and developing tourism worldwide. Shown here is the UN headquarters building in New York City.
Photo by Ron Nelson.

The specialized agencies function on an autonomous basis, with their own charter, budget, governing boards, staff, and publishing operations. They make annual or biennial reports to the Economic and Social Council. The General Assembly can examine their budgets and make recommendations; however, each specialized agency exercises final control over its operations.

Thus, UNWTO is vested by the United Nations with a central and decisive role in promoting the development of responsible, sustainable, and universally accessible tourism, with the aim of contributing to economic development, international understanding, peace, prosperity, and universal respect for and observance of human rights and fundamental freedoms. In pursuing this aim, UNWTO pays particular attention to the interests of the developing countries in the field of tourism.

The United Nations World Tourism Organization had its beginnings as the International Union of Official Tourist Publicity Organizations, set up in 1925 in The Hague. It was renamed the International Union for Official Tourism Organizations (IUOTO) after World War II and moved to Geneva. IUOTO was renamed the World Tourism Organization (WTO), and its first General Assembly was held in Madrid in May 1975. The Secretariat was installed in Madrid early the following year at the invitation of the Spanish government, which provides a building for the headquarters. In 1976, UNWTO became an executing agency of the United Nations Development Programme (UNDP); in 1977, a formal cooperation agreement was signed with the United Nations. In October 2003, UNWTO became a specialized agency of the United Nations and reaffirmed its leading role in international tourism. UNWTO is committed to the United Nations Millennium Development goals, geared toward reducing poverty and fostering sustainable development.

UNWTO is engaged in many activities. The transfer of tourism know-how to developing countries is a major task. Here, UNWTO contributes decades of experience in tourism to the sustainable development goals of nations throughout the world. UNWTO projects are based on the policy of sustainability, ensuring that the economic benefits of tourism development are not offset by damage to the environment or to local cultures.

The UNWTO works with the UNDP, which finances tourism planning projects and infrastructures, such as projects to improve transportation in southern Africa. *Photo courtesy of the United Nations.*

UNWTO is well known for its statistics and market research. Research has been one of UNWTO's most important contributions. Its work here has set international standards for tourism measurement and reporting, measured the impact of tourism on national economies, produced forecasts, examined trends, and made the results available in publications.

Human resource development is another UNWTO goal. UNWTO sets standards for tourism education. The UNWTO Education Council—made up of leading tourism education, training, and research institutions—drives the education program of work, which includes the accreditation program for tourism education institutions (TedQual) and the Graduate Tourism Aptitude Test (GTAT). These are examples of UNWTO's efforts to encourage standardization of curricula and to make degrees in tourism more internationally comparable. UNWTO also offers seminars, distance learning courses, and practicum courses for tourism officials from member countries.

UNWTO attempts to facilitate world travel through elimination or reduction of governmental measures for international travel, as well as standardization of requirements for passports, visas, and so forth. It works to improve the quality of tourism through trade liberalization, access for travelers with disabilities, safety and security, and technical standards. UNWTO also works to improve the promotional efforts of member governments through effective media relations and serves as a clearinghouse for international tourism information.

In addition to these global activities, UNWTO engages in regional activities. Each region of the world—Africa, the Americas, East Asia and the Pacific, Europe, the Middle East, and South Asia—receives special attention from that region's UNWTO representative. The representatives meet with top tourism officials from each of the countries in their region to analyze problems and help seek solutions, act as a liaison between tourism authorities and the UNDP to create specific development projects, organize national seminars of topics of particular relevance to an individual country, such as tourism promotion in Mexico or ecotourism in Kyrgyzstan, and hold regional conferences on problems that are shared by many countries so that members can exchange experiences and work toward common goals, such as safety and security in Eastern Europe or aviation and tourism policy in the Caribbean.

Key projects that UNWTO is currently working on are poverty alleviation and elimination through sustainable tourism, protecting children from sexual exploitation in tourism, crisis management, ecotourism, and safety and security. Visit the UNWTO Web site at www.unwto.org.

PROFILE

TALEB RIFAI
Secretary-General of
United Nations World
Tourism Organization
(UNWTO)

Taleb Rifai's background combines solid political experience and technical knowledge in the field of tourism, as well as experience in the work and functioning of international organizations. His background also provides him with extensive economic, business, and academic experience.

He was elected as secretary-general of the World Tourism Organization (UNWTO) at the United Nations General Assembly, Astana, Kazakhstan, in October 2009, after serving as secretary-general ad interim beginning March 1, 2009. His four-year term began on January 1, 2010.

Prior to assuming his current post, Rifai served as deputy secretary-general of the UNWTO from February 2006 to February 2009 and was assistant director-general of the International Labor Organization (ILO) for three consecutive years (January 2003 to February 2006). His responsibilities included the overall supervision and implementation of the International Labor Standards, as well as advising on labor markets and employment policies, particularly in the Middle East region.

Rifai comes to this position with an impressive background. He received his PhD in Urban Design and Regional Planning from the University of Pennsylvania in Philadelphia in 1983, his master's degree in Engineering and Architecture from the Illinois Institute of Technology (IIT) in Chicago in 1979, and his bachelor of science degree in Architectural Engineering from the University of Cairo in Egypt in 1973.

From 1973 to 1993, he was involved in research, teaching, and practicing architecture and urban design in Jordan and the United States. He was a professor of architecture at the University of Jordan in Amman and taught several courses in Philadelphia, Chicago, and MIT. As an architect, he won several international competitions and supervised numerous projects, particularly in the rehabilitation and renovation of old urban centers.

From 1993 to 1997, Rifai was actively involved in policy making and developing trade and investment strategies, initially in his capacity as director of Jordan's Economic Mission to Washington, D.C., promoting trade, investment, and economic relations between Jordan and the United States. In 1995, he became the director general of the newly established Investment Promotion Corporation (IPC), responsible for developing and implementing policies aimed at attracting foreign direct investment to Jordan.

He was appointed the CEO of Jordan's Cement Company, one of the country's largest public shareholding companies with more than 4,000 employees. As CEO, he successfully led and directed the first large-scale privatization and restructuring scheme in Jordan by bringing in the world-famous French cement company Lafarge in 1998. He continued to serve as CEO under the new Lafarge management.

From 1999 to 2003, he served in several ministerial portfolios in the government of Jordan, first as minister of planning and international cooperation in charge of Jordan's Development Agenda and bilateral and multilateral relationships with donors and agencies. He was subsequently appointed minister of information, in which capacity he was spokesman for the government of Jordan and in charge of communication and public media. During his tenure, he embarked on restructuring public media—in particular, the Jordan Television Network. In 2001, his portfolio was expanded to include the Ministry of Tourism and Antiquity.

During his term as head of the Ministry of Tourism and Antiquity, Rifai established Jordan's first Archaeological Park in the ancient city of Petra in collaboration with UNESCO and the World Bank. He also oversaw several large projects in Jerash, the Dead Sea, and Wadi Rum. As minister of tourism, he was the chairman of the Jordan Tourism Board, president of the Ammon School for Tourism and Hospitality, and chairman of the Executive Council of the UNWTO (elected in 2001).

Taleb Rifai, a Jordanian national born in 1949, has traveled and lectured extensively, and has received several distinguished decorations including one of Jordan's highest medals for public service, Al Kawkab, as well as several high-level decorations from France, Italy, and other countries.

Throughout his professional career, Rifai has been a *reformer* and a *consensus builder:* two important qualities in effecting *sustainable change.* His abilities to introduce fresh thinking and to work closely with people in order to ensure buy-in and to achieve enduring reforms are evident in all his endeavors—notably, restructuring the Jordan Television Network, privatizing the Jordan Cement Company, and introducing fresh thinking to the UNWTO.

WORDS ABOUT THE FUTURE

Tourism represents an estimated direct contribution of 5 percent of the world's GDP, accounting for as much as 30 percent of the world's exports of commercial services and around 6 to 7 percent of the total job market worldwide. As a field, tourism is growing rapidly.

In 2009, despite a global economic crisis posing significant challenges to the sector, 880 million people crossed international borders, with US$852 billion earned in tourism receipts. By 2020, an estimated 1.6 billion tourists will travel the globe annually, spending over US $2 trillion in the process. At the same time, domestic tourism, representing four times the volume of international travel, is also set to continue booming.

Along with this extraordinary growth have come continuous improvements in standards and quality, higher levels of competiveness and innovation, and a growing awareness and commitment to the principles of sustainability. As global awareness of the challenges to our climate grows, and travelers increasingly demand a greener travel experience, the sector is challenged to explore more and more ways to adopt environmentally sustainable policies.

The UNWTO Global Code of Ethics for Tourism envisages tourism as a right, equally open to all the world's inhabitants. The increasingly extensive participation in tourism is a positive phenomenon, generating wealth and employment, fostering development, and linking the world.

World Travel and Tourism Council

The World Travel and Tourism Council (WTTC) is the forum for global business leaders in travel and tourism. It comprises the presidents, chairs, and chief executive officers of 100 of the world's foremost companies. These include accommodation, catering, cruises, entertainment, recreation, transportation, and travel-related services. WTTC is the only body representing the private sector in all parts of the industry worldwide. Established in 1990, WTTC is led by a 19-member executive committee, which meets twice a year and reports to an annual meeting of all members. Day-to-day operations are carried out by the president and small staff based in London.

The mission of the council is to raise awareness of the economic and social contribution of travel and tourism and to work with governments on policies that unlock the industry's potential to create jobs and generate prosperity. Their vision of travel and tourism is that of a partnership among all stakeholders, delivering consistent results that match the needs of national economies, local and regional authorities, and local communities with those of business, based on: (1) governments recognizing travel and tourism as a top priority; (2) business balancing economics with people, culture, and the environment; and (3) a shared pursuit of long-term growth and prosperity.

The activities of the council can be summarized under three broad themes:

1. **Global activities.** WTTC addresses challenges and opportunities that affect all sectors of the global travel and tourism industry. It is empowered by its members to provide an effective voice for the industry in its dialogue with governments around the world. The council actively promotes public- and private-sector examples of best practices in tourism. A number of case studies from different parts of the world can be found on its Web site.

2. **Regional initiatives.** Regional initiatives are set up in countries and regions that have huge potential for travel and tourism development but lack the framework or resources to achieve growth. The objective of these initiatives is to translate WTTC's mission into action by working with governments, local leaders, and WTTC global members with a regional presence to identify and eliminate barriers to growth.

3. **Economic research.** WTTC now uses Oxford Economics and Accenture to undertake extensive research to determine travel and tourism's total size and contribution to world, regional, and national economies. The WTTC forecast is the primary vehicle used to convey the message that tourism is the world's largest industry, that it has been growing faster than most other industries, that it will continue to grow strongly, and that it can create jobs and increase gross domestic product (GDP). WTTC plans to continue publishing this forecast and enhance its methodology. In fact, it continues to increase the number of economic impact reports, and under the auspices of the UNWTO, WTTC has developed proposals for an international standard Satellite Accounting System. Its 2010 forecast covers 181 national economies and shows that the tourism industry currently generates 235.8 million jobs and contributes over 9.2 percent of global GDP. WTTC has

done more to create awareness of the economic importance of tourism than any other organization. Visit its Web site at www.wttc.org.

Skål International

Skål is a professional organization of tourism leaders around the world, promoting global tourism and friendship. Skål, founded as an international association in 1934, has approximately 20,000 members in 480 locations in 89 countries. Skål headquarters is in Torremolinos, Spain.

Skål International is an affiliate member of UNWTO and supports UNWTO's mission to promote the development of responsible, sustainable, and universally accessible tourism. Skål has adopted the Global Code of Ethics in tourism and is a sponsor of the Code of Conduct for the Protection of Children from sexual exploitation in tourism. Following the United Nations declaration of 2002 as the Year of Ecotourism and the Mountains, Skål launched the Ecotourism Awards to highlight and acknowledge best practices around the globe. Skål is a powerful force in the tourism industry to initiate change and encourage the conservation of the environment to promote tourism. Visit its Web site at www .skal.org.

International Air Transport Association

The **International Air Transport Association** (IATA) is the global organization for virtually all the international air carriers. Members number some 230 airlines, representing 93 percent of scheduled international air traffic. The principal function of IATA is to safely facilitate the movement of persons and goods from any point on the world air network to any other by any combination of routes. This can be accomplished by a single ticket bought at a single price in one currency and valid everywhere for the same amount and quality of service. The same principles apply to the movement of freight and mail.

Resolutions of IATA standardize not only tickets, but waybills, baggage checks, and other similar documents. These resolutions coordinate and unify handling and accounting procedures to permit rapid interline bookings and connections. They also create and maintain a stable pattern of international fares and rates. In effect, they permit the linking of many individual international airline routes into a single public service system.

While developing standards and procedures for the international airline industry to support interlining and enhance customer service continues to be a principal aim, IATA is involved in many other areas, such as industry support, the environment, consumer issues, regulatory monitoring, legal support, corporate communications, scheduling, facilitation, safety, security, and services.

IATA is a valuable information source on the world airline industry. Its annual publication, *World Air Transport Statistics*, is an authoritative source of international airline data. In addition, IATA makes passenger and freight forecasts. Its market research helps the industry develop its strategic and tactical marketing plans.

In summary, IATA's mission is to represent and serve the world airline industry. It serves four groups interested in the smooth operation of the world air transport system: (1) airlines, (2) the public, (3) governments, and (4) third parties, such as suppliers and travel and cargo agents. IATA works closely with the International Civil Aviation Organization. IATA's head office is in Montreal; its executive office is in Geneva, Switzerland; and it has regional offices around the world. The IATA Web site is at www.iata.org.

International Civil Aviation Organization

The International Civil Aviation Organization (ICAO), a UN specialized agency, is the global forum for civil aviation. The organization was established in 1944. ICAO works to achieve its vision of safe, secure, and sustainable development of civil aviation through cooperation of its member states. To implement this vision, the organization has established six strategic objectives for the period 2005 to 2010:

1. Enhance global civil aviation safety.
2. Enhance global civil aviation security.
3. Minimize the adverse effect of global civil aviation on the environment.
4. Enhance the efficiency of aviation operations.
5. Maintain the continuity of aviation operations.
6. Strengthen law governing international civil aviation.

Visit the ICAO Web site at www.icao.int.

International Institute for Peace Through Tourism

The International Institute for Peace Through Tourism (IIPT) is a not-for-profit organization dedicated to fostering and facilitating tourism initiatives that contribute to international understanding and cooperation, an improved quality of environment, the preservation of heritage, and through these initiatives, helping to bring about a peaceful and sustainable world.

It is based on a vision of the world's largest industry, travel and tourism—becoming the world's first global peace industry; and the belief that every traveler is potentially an "Ambassador for Peace."

A primary goal of IIPT is to mobilize the travel and tourism industry as a leading force for poverty reduction (see Chapter 10).

DEVELOPMENTAL ORGANIZATIONS (INTERNATIONAL AND NATIONAL)

Financing is always a major problem in tourism development. Large financial organizations are willing to make developmental loans. Examples include the World Bank (United States), International Finance Corporation (United States), the OPEC Fund for International Development (Austria), African Development Bank (Côte d'Ivoire), East African Development Bank (Uganda), Inter-American Development Bank (United States), Caribbean Development Bank (Barbados), Asian Development Bank (Philippines), European Investment Bank (Luxembourg), European Regional Development Fund (Belgium), European Bank for Reconstruction and Development (United Kingdom), Islamic Development Bank (Saudi Arabia), and the Arab Fund for Economic and Social Development (Kuwait). Examples of national organizations are FONATUR (Mexico) and Embratur (Brazil). Further sources include governments of countries that want additional hotel development or other supply components and are willing to make low-interest loans or grants or offer other financial inducements for such types of development.

Organization for Economic Cooperation and Development

The Organization for Economic Cooperation and Development (OECD) was set up under a convention, signed in Paris on December 14, 1960, that provides that the OECD shall promote policies designed to (1) achieve the highest sustainable economic growth and employment and a rising standard of living in member countries while maintaining financial stability and, thus, to contribute to the development of the world economy; (2) contribute to sound economic expansion in member as well as nonmember countries in the process of economic development; and (3) contribute to the expansion of world trade on a multilateral, nondiscriminatory basis in accordance with international obligations.

Members of OECD are Australia, Austria, Belgium, Canada, Chile, Czech Republic, Denmark, Finland, France, Germany, Greece, Hungary, Iceland, Ireland, Italy, Japan, Korea, Luxembourg, Mexico, the Netherlands, New Zealand, Norway, Poland, Portugal, Slovak Republic, Spain, Sweden, Switzerland, Turkey, the United Kingdom, and the United States. OECD's Tourism Committee acts as a forum of exchange for monitoring policies and structural changes affecting the development of international tourism. It encourages further liberalization of tourism activities, both within and outside the OECD area, and has undertaken the development of innovative statistics to improve the understanding of the role of tourism in the economy. Its recent study, *OECD Tourism Trends and Policies 2010*, provides a review of tourism trends and policies carried out by the OECD tourism committee, assesses the long-term evolution of tourism in the OECD area over the last two decades, and the impact of the global financial and economic crisis on the tourism industry. Also, for the first time it analyzes data and policy trends in 12 non-OECD countries, including large emerging economies such as Brazil, China, and India. Visit the OECD Web site at www.oecd.org.

REGIONAL INTERNATIONAL ORGANIZATIONS

In order to strengthen the competitive appeal of major regions in the world (such as Europe and the Asia Pacific), certain regions have established specialized research and/or promotional agencies, which provide the regions with an enhanced understanding of visitor markets and focus on the region as a tourist destination.

Pacific Asia Travel Association

Founded in Hawaii in 1951 to develop, promote, and facilitate travel to and among the destination areas in and bordering the Pacific Ocean, the Pacific Asia Travel Association (PATA) brings together governments, airline and steamship companies, hoteliers, tour operators, travel agents, and a wide range of other tourism-related organizations. Today, PATA is the global leader in Pacific Asian tourism. Members exchange ideas, seek solutions to problems, and participate in shaping the future of travel in Asia and the Pacific area. Membership totals more than 2,000 organizations worldwide. Since its founding, the association has become an important source of accurate, up-to-date information for its members in the fields of marketing, forecasting, development, information, education, sustainability, and other travel-related activities. PATA's activities and long-range plans are examined and adjusted each year at the association's annual conference.

The future of the tourism industry depends on protecting the region's environmental, heritage, and cultural resources. PATA develops industrywide initiatives and sponsors conservation conferences to ensure sustainable growth. The association also honors significant accomplishments in this arena under its Gold Awards program.

The work of the official PATA organization is greatly augmented by thousands of travel professionals who belong to a global network of PATA chapters. PATA's operational headquarters is in Bangkok, Thailand; the association's administrative headquarters is located in Oakland, California. Other offices are located in Sydney, Beijing, Dubai, and Frankfurt. Visit the association's Web site at www.pata.org.

Asia is one of the fastest-growing travel destinations in the world. Kuala Lumpur, the capital of Malaysia, is one of the many locations in Asia that can provide rewarding experiences for visitors from Western cultures. *Photo courtesy of the Malaysia Tourism Board.*

European Travel Commission

The **European Travel Commission** (ETC) is the strategic alliance that provides for the collaboration between national tourism organizations (NTOs) of 39 member countries. Founded in 1948, the ETC fills a unique role functioning as a "National Tourism Office of Europe." Its goal is to attract millions of potential and existing overseas customers from the major overseas markets to come to Europe. This is done through promotional campaigns and industry trade shows. The headquarters of the ETC is located in Brussels, Belgium. Visit its Web site at www .etc-corporate.org.

NATIONAL ORGANIZATIONS

Most countries feel it is essential to put in place a destination management organization (DMO) that is charged with monitoring and promoting the destination and coordinating its development in a way that requires an in-depth understanding of the destination and the major markets it seeks to attract.

Office of Travel and Tourism Industries

The U.S. Department of Commerce's **Office of Travel and Tourism Industries** (OTTI) serves as the National Tourism Office for the United States. It provides the primary source of international travel statistics, provides policy coordination and industry relations, and develops international promotion programs. OTTI was created in April 1996 when Congress defunded the U.S. Travel and Tourism Administration (USTTA), the national tourism office for the United States. USTTA was charged with developing tourism policy, promoting inbound travel and tourism from abroad, and collecting and reporting on international travel to and from the United States. USTTA was created in 1981 to replace the U.S. Travel Service, which was created in 1960. OTTI has a staff of 13, headed by an office director, who reports to the deputy assistant secretary for services. Services reports to an assistant secretary for manufacturing and services area of the International Trade Administration within the U.S. Department of Commerce. Commerce is one of the 15 major departments within the U.S. federal government. The primary functions of OTTI are:

- Management of the travel and tourism statistical system for assessing the economic contribution of the industry and providing the sole source for characteristic statistics on international travel to and from the United States
- Design and administration of export expansion activities

- Development and management of tourism policy, strategy, and advocacy
- Technical assistance for expanding this key export (international inbound tourism) and assisting in domestic economic development
- Working with the Corporation for Travel Promotion

Research

The OTTI oversees nine research programs that provide comprehensive, complementary information on international travelers to assist the industry to understand the dramatically changing international market:

1. **An international arrivals database obtained from the Department of Homeland Security (DHS).** It provides the only source for a count of overseas travelers to the United States (Note: "overseas" excludes Canada and Mexico).

2. **An international air traffic database also obtained from DHS.** It provides the only estimates of U.S. outbound travel as well as data on the U.S. flag and foreign flag total international air traffic to and from the United States by port and country.

3. **The Official Airlines Guide database.** This is used to provide the sample frame data on outbound flights from the United States.

4. **The Survey of International Air Travelers (or In-Flight Survey).** This is the major research program for the office. It is a contract in which OTTI administers the collection and dissemination of data on international travelers to and from the United States. Over 30 key traveler characteristics data are collected on international travelers on departing flights from the United States each month on over 80 U.S. and foreign flag carriers. Annually, between 60,000 and 95,000 surveys are collected and weighted to the corresponding travel populations of inbound and outbound travelers. This program provides the only comprehensive, comparable estimates of international destinations visited and the states and cities visited by overseas travelers to the United States.

5. **A Travel and Tourism Satellite Account (TTSA).** This is an economic tool to more accurately measure the impact of the travel and tourism industries on the U.S. economy. It also measures job creation and provides industry comparability by using the U.S. System of National Accounts, which is the basis for configuring the GDP. It is called a Satellite Account because it is derived from the U.S. national income accounts.

6. **International travel receipts and payments data.** OTTI staff work with the Bureau of Economic Analysis to develop estimates of the travel and passenger fare exports and imports for the United States and for over 30 countries.

7. **Canadian travel to the United States with data provided based on the Statistics Canada survey program.** Each year, OTTI issues state visitation estimates and traveler characteristics for this largest inbound arrival market for the country.

8. **A forecast for international travel to the United States developed with a private-sector firm.** The forecast projects the number and percentage increase of arrivals to the United States for 40 top inbound markets for the next several years, based on an econometric model.

9. **An Internet-based Travel Trade *Barometer* each quarter for several of the top inbound markets to the country.** The *Barometer* provides a short-term forecast on travel demand and market conditions in each of the participating countries.

The OTTI research staff also oversees the office Web site. The top-line results of the nine research programs' information are posted to the Web site. The office also issues *TInews* releases to inform subscribers of the latest developments in the international travel market. Information on the programs administered by the office, as well as content on each of the areas the office oversees, is provided on the site. To learn more, go to www.tinet.ita.doc.gov.

Advisory Board

The U.S. Travel and Tourism Advisory Board serves as the advisory body to the Department of Commerce on matters relating to the travel and tourism industry in the United States. The board advises the commerce secretary on government policies and programs that affect the U.S. travel and tourism industry, offers counsel on current and emerging issues, and provides a forum for discussing and proposing solutions to industry-related problems.

The U.S. Travel and Tourism Advisory board consists of up to 30 members appointed by the secretary of commerce. Members represent companies and organizations in the travel and tourism industry from a broad range of products and services, company sizes, and geographic locations. Members serve, at the pleasure of the secretary, from the date of appointment to the board until the date on which the board's charter terminates.

Export Assistance

The OTTI offers export assistance to American travel and tourism industry suppliers, from communities to individual establishments, through consultations using market analysis and intelligence. Working in conjunction with the promotional efforts of Commercial Service officers nationwide and around the globe, these services offer in-depth market conditions and industry knowledge to position a specific market to expand this vital export, encouraging more international travelers to visit the United States.

The focus of export assistance is outreach carried out through the tourism trade specialists and research analysts at OTTI. Outreach involves a concerted effort with convention and visitor bureaus to reach communities, trade associations to reach industry players, state tourism offices, and other federal agencies involved in tourism-related activities or products. A key partner in the effectiveness of export assistance efforts is the Commercial Service, both domestic and foreign, in the International Trade Administration. This covers more than 100 export assistance offices throughout the United States and more than 150 foreign Commercial Service offices in more than 80 countries throughout the world.

Policy

The OTTI plays an active role in domestic and international policy issues as they relate to the U.S. travel and tourism industry. From a domestic policy perspective, OTTI serves as the secretariat for the Tourism Policy Council. The Tourism Policy Council (TPC) is an interagency committee established by law for the purpose of ensuring that the nation's tourism interests are considered in federal decision making. Its major function is to coordinate national policies and programs relating to international travel and tourism, recreation, and national heritage resources that involve federal agencies. The TPC, originally established in 1981, was reauthorized by the U.S. National Tourism Organization Act of 1996 and began to hold meetings from that time. The TPC has been involved in visa policy issues, the new entry/exit requirements, opening China as a tourism destination for the United States, and numerous other government policy issues. The OTTI participates in the activities of global tourism development in multiple international intergovernmental organizations. Serving as the National Tourism Office for the U.S. government, the OTTI is the representative to the Asia Pacific Economic Cooperation (APEC) Tourism Working Group, Organization for Economic Cooperation and Development (OECD) Tourism Committee, and the United Nations World Tourism Organization. The list of the Tourism Policy Council members includes the following:

- Advisory Council on Historic Preservation
- Department of Agriculture
- Department of Commerce
- Department of Education
- Department of Health and Human Services
- Department of Homeland Security
- Department of Housing and Urban Development
- Department of Interior
- Department of Labor
- Department of State
- Department of Transportation
- Environmental Protection Agency
- Executive Office of the President
- Office of Management and Budget
- President's Committee on the Arts and the Humanities
- Small Business Administration
- U.S. Army Corps of Engineers

Other departments and agencies are requested to join in discussions as issues affect their organization.

Travel Promotion Act

The **Travel Promotion Act** was signed by President Barack Obama on March 4, 2010. The act will have significant operational, managerial, and funding impacts on the Department of Commerce. Specifically, the act:

- Establishes the Corporation for Travel Promotion, a nonprofit entity, to communicate U.S. entry policies and otherwise promote leisure, business, and scholarly travel to the United States.
- Authorizes the secretary of commerce, in consultation with the secretaries of state and homeland security, to appoint the corporation's board of directors, review and approve the corporation's annual objectives, and transmit the corporation's report to Congress.
- Funds the corporation from the collection of a fee assessed on travelers from visa waiver countries in the completion of a form under the DHS requirement for the Electronic System of Travel Authorization (ESTA). In year one, the corporation is to be funded from a drawdown of up to $10 million; in year two, the drawdown is up to $100 million with a 50 percent match by industry (80 percent of the match can be in-kind, 20 percent must be in cash); in years three, four, and five, the drawdown is up to $100 million with 100 percent industry match; and in year six and beyond, funding of the corporation would be by industry assessment only as the act sunsets in 2014.
- Establishes an Office of Travel Promotion within the Department of Commerce, to be headed by a director appointed by, and reporting to, the secretary who has significant travel and tourism industry experience. The office will serve as a liaison to the corporation and be responsible for a broad range of additional activities.

■ Additionally, authorizes a major expansion of the research programs currently administered by the International Trade Administration's Office of Travel and Tourism Industries.

Canadian Tourism Commission

The Canadian Tourism Commission (CTC) was created in 1995 to promote Canadian tourism in order to capitalize on one of the fastest-growing international industries. The CTC is dedicated to promoting the growth and profitability of the Canadian tourism industry by marketing Canada as a desirable travel destination and providing timely and accurate information to the Canadian tourism industry to assist in its decision making. The CTC is a unique public/private-sector partnership that provides an innovative approach to tourism: one that is industry led and market driven. The commission recognizes that the greatest source of tourism knowledge and expertise rests with the tourism industry itself. Therefore, the CTC designs, delivers, and funds marketing and research initiatives in partnership with provincial and regional tourism associations, government agencies, hoteliers, tour operators, airlines, and attractions managers. CTC has one of the best and most comprehensive tourism programs in the world and serves as a model that many other nations strive to equal. The CTC is headquartered in Vancouver, British Columbia, and maintains offices in nine key global markets. In India and Brazil, the CTC employs general services agents. Visit the CTC Web site at www.CanadaTourism.com.

Tourism Australia

On July 1, 2004, a new body, Tourism Australia, was created that brought together the Australian Tourist Commission, See Australia, the Bureau of Tourism Research, and the Tourism Forecasting Council, harnessing the skills and knowledge of these organizations under one umbrella. Two new business units, Tourism Events Australia and Tourism Research Australia, were also established to focus on industry and market needs. Tourism Research Australia incorporates a merger of the Bureau of Tourism Research and the Tourism Forecasting Council. Tourism Australia is now the federal government statutory authority responsible for international and domestic tourism marketing as well as the delivery of research and forecasts for the sector. The main objectives of Tourism Australia are to influence people to travel to and throughout Australia, help foster a sustainable tourism industry, and help increase the economic benefits to Australia from tourism. Tourism Australia is another outstanding national tourism organization and would be a good model for others to follow. Visit its Web site at www.tourismaustralia.com.

U.S. Federal Aviation Administration

Numerous responsibilities for efficient and safe air travel are assigned to the Federal Aviation Administration (FAA), which is illustrative of governmental regulating bodies. This U.S. government organization in the Department of Transportation formulates regulations and supervises or controls various aspects of airline and airport operations. Examples of these functions are air traffic control, air safety, flight standards, aviation engineering, airport administration districts, airways facilities, and certification of new aircraft. The FAA also examines and licenses pilots and flight engineers. Its Web site is www.faa.gov.

U.S. Department of Transportation

The mission of the U.S. Department of Transportation (DOT) is to serve the United States by ensuring a fast, safe, efficient, accessible, and convenient transportation system that meets our

The U.S. Federal Aviation Administration provides air traffic control, air safety, and other vital aviation regulation and services. Shown here is the FAA control tower and Concourse C at the Denver International Airport. *Photo courtesy of Denver International Airport.*

vital national interests and enhances the quality of life of the American people, today and into the future. DOT agencies are the Office of the Secretary of Transportation (OST), the previously mentioned Federal Aviation Administration (FAA), Federal Highway Administration (FHWA), Federal Motor Carrier Safety Administration (FMCSA), Federal Railroad Administration (FRA), Federal Transit Administration (FTA), Maritime Administration (MARAD), National Highway Traffic Safety Administration (NHTSA), Office of Inspector General (OIG), Pipeline and Hazardous Materials Safety Administration (PHMSA), Research and Innovative Technology Administration (RITA), Saint Lawrence Seaway Development Corporation (SLSDC), and the Surface Transportation Board (STB).

The Research and Innovative Technology Administration (RITA) deserves special mention as this agency houses the Bureau of Transportation Statistics (BTS), which provides a multitude of transportation statistics. Visit www.dot.gov. Also see Chapter 5, "Passenger Transportation."

U.S. Department of Homeland Security

The events of September 11, 2001, brought another government agency that impacts tourism, the Department of Homeland Security (DHS). One primary reason for the establishment of the DHS was to provide the unifying core for the vast national network of 22 organizations and institutions involved in efforts to secure the nation. The Transportation Security Administration (TSA) is responsible for protecting our nation's transportation systems and is the most visible at airports. TSA screening is no easy task since 730 million people travel on commercial aircraft each year and more than 700 million pieces of baggage are screened for explosives each year. A tourism position has been established in the DHS to represent the interests of the tourism industry and to work to meet security objectives while minimizing travel disruptions. Visit www.dhs.gov and www.tsa.gov.

U.S. Department of State

The U.S. Department of State plays an important role in international travel. The department issues passports to U.S. citizens and visas to foreign citizens. State Department policies have a worldwide impact. An example is the recent Western Hemisphere Travel Initiative (WHTI). The Intelligence Reform and Terrorism Prevention Act of 2004 required the Department of Homeland Security and Department of State to develop and implement a plan to require all travelers, U.S. citizens and foreign nationals alike, to present a passport or other document, or a combination of documents, that denote identity and citizenship when entering the United States. Congress amended portions of the act in 2006. The Western Hemisphere Travel Initiative implements this mandate.

On January 23, 2007, U.S. citizens traveling by air between the United States and Canada, Mexico, Central and South America, the Caribbean, and Bermuda were required to present a valid U.S. passport, Air NEXUS card, or U.S. Coast Guard Merchant Mariner Document. The same requirement for travel by land or sea took effect January 1, 2008.

The initiative has resulted in a tremendous demand for passports. Currently, 85.5 million Americans have a U.S. passport, approximately 28 percent of the population. This pales in comparison with Canada, where 40 percent of the population has a passport.

Travel warnings are another responsibility of the Department of State. Travel warnings are issued when the State Department recommends that Americans avoid certain countries. In addition, the department issues Consular Information Sheets for every country of the world with information on such matters as the health conditions, crime, entry requirements, currency, any areas of instability, and the location of the nearest U.S. embassy or consulate.

Other (U.S.) Government Agencies

Numerous other government agencies play an active role in tourism. The U.S. Customs Service monitors international travel, the U.S. Bureau of the Census compiles travel statistics and data, the Interstate Commerce Commission regulates bus transportation, the National Maritime Commission deals with ships, the National Park Service and the Forest Service provide and administer many scenic attractions and facilities, the Bureau of Land Management is involved in several tourism initiatives (such as Back Country Byways, Adventures in the Past, and Watchable Wildlife), the Bureau of Reclamation administers over 300 recreation areas in 17 western states, and the Federal Highway Administration is involved in the National Scenic Byways program, with the objective of increasing tourism while preserving the environment. Other agencies involved in tourism are the National Trust for Historic Preservation, National Marine Sanctuary Program, Tennessee Valley Authority, Army Corps of Engineers, Fish and Wildlife Service, and the Immigration and Naturalization Service.

United States Travel Association

The Washington, D.C.–based **United States Travel Association** (USTA) is the leading private tourism organization in the United States. It was formed January 1, 2009, with the merger of the Travel Industry Association (TIA) and the Travel Business Roundtable. The nonprofit association serves as the unifying organization for all components of the U.S. travel industry. The business of travel and tourism in America is served by more than one-half million different organizations that offer a wide range of services to the traveler.

Originally founded in 1941, U.S. Travel has grown from a small association of travel officials into a national nonprofit organization with a membership that now represents all components of the travel

PROFILE

ROGER DOW
President and CEO, U.S.
Travel Association (USTA).

R oger Dow is president and chief executive officer of the U.S. Travel Association, the national umbrella organization representing all segments of the $704 billion U.S. travel and tourism industry. It is headquartered in Washington, D.C., with an active presence in Europe, Asia, and Latin America.

The mission of U.S. Travel is to increase travel to and within the United States. It advocates the power of travel to leaders in government, provides authoritative travel research and analysis, and hosts annual signature events, including International Pow Wow, that support its mission. U.S. Travel also operates DiscoverAmerica.com, the Official Travel and Tourism Web site of the United States.

Dow was instrumental in leading an industrywide movement for creation of the Travel Promotion Act. This bipartisan legislation, signed into law by President Obama in March 2010, established a first-ever communications and promotion program aimed at increasing international travel to the United States.

He has served in his present position since 2005. Prior to joining U.S. Travel, Dow advanced through the ranks at Marriott International in a career that spanned 34 years, where he began as a summer lifeguard at the sixth Marriott hotel and rose to senior vice president, global and field sales, where he led Marriott's 10,000-person worldwide sales organization. His many accomplishments for the company included development of Marriott Rewards, the world's leading frequent traveler program.

Dow was recognized by his peers as the association executive of the year, an honor presented by *Association Trends* magazine that

reflected Dow's success in unifying the travel industry and greatly increasing its effectiveness on Capitol Hill. He has also been named to the Convention Industry Council's prestigious Hall of Leaders, was recognized by Meeting Professionals International (MPI) as one of the industry's top leaders, was selected by *MeetingNews* as one of the 25 most influential people in the meetings industry and has been honored by the American Society of Association Executives (ASAE) with its Academy of Leaders Award. In 2009, Dow was presented with an honorary degree from Johnson & Wales University (doctor of business administration in Hospitality Management).

Dow frequently speaks on leadership, sales, marketing, and management at conventions and corporate meetings. He has co-authored two books: *Turned On—Eight Vital Insights to Energize Your People, Customers and Profits* and *The Trust Imperative—The Competitive Advantage of Trust-Based Business Relationships.*

He serves, or has served, on the board of directors of ASAE, PCMA, ASAE Foundation, MPI Foundation (chairman), GWSAE, the Travel Institute, RE/MAX International, and on the Advisory Boards of Arizona State University's Center for Services Leadership and the University of Richmond Robins School of Business.

Dow served in the United States Army with the 101st Airborne Division in Vietnam, where he received the Bronze Star and other citations.

A native of New Jersey, he earned a bachelor of science degree from Seton Hall University, where he was senior class president, captain of the varsity wrestling team, and secretary of Tau Kappa Epsilon fraternity.

He was named TKE alumnus of the year for 1991 and was presented with the award by President Ronald Reagan.

Dow and his wife, Linda, reside in Potomac, Maryland.

WORDS FOR THE FUTURE

The passage of the Travel Promotion Act was a great step forward for the U.S. travel and tourism industry. By leveling the playing field, it enables the United States to be competitive in the world's tourism market. Not only will it help finally reverse the declines since 9/11 in overseas travel to the United States but the influx of new visitors will boost our economy, create new jobs, and improve international perceptions of our country.

My advice to destinations and suppliers is to be flexible, patient, creative and willing to embrace new ideas. The industry must think positively and continue to find ways to do more with less, and to be less provincial in our thinking. My last bit of advice is that as an industry, we need to be ever alert to any number of new challenges that may confront us. Recent events such as the meetings crisis, swine flu, and the oil spill have shown us that we can't afford to rest on our laurels.

industry: airlines, attractions, hotels and motels, travel agents, tour operators and brokers, convention and visitors bureaus, state government travel offices, area and regional tourism organizations, food service establishments, auto rental companies, intercity bus and rail lines, cruise lines, and other segments of what is known today as the travel industry.

U.S. Travel serves the industry through a number of programs that market and promote the U.S. travel experience, both abroad and at home: by furnishing research, publications, and reports for and about the industry as well as U.S. and international travelers; by providing strategic leadership for the industry in the U.S. business community and in matters of government at all levels; through its councils and committees that represent specific components of the industry; with its foundation, which finances research and scholarships in the area of travel and tourism; and through its nearly half-century-old awards program that honors achievements by both individuals and organizations within the travel and tourism industry.

The current mission of the U.S. Travel is to represent the whole of the U.S. travel industry to promote and facilitate increased travel to and within the United States. U.S. Travel has seven goals:

1. Promote a wider understanding of travel and tourism as a major industry that contributes to the economic, cultural, and social well being of the nation (visit www.poweroftravel.org).
2. Develop, coordinate, and implement the industry's umbrella marketing efforts to promote travel to and within the United States.
3. Pursue and influence policies, programs, and legislation that are responsive to the needs of the industry as a whole.
4. Improve domestic and international travelers' experience, including gaining access to, arriving in, traveling within, and departing the United States.
5. Enhance U.S. Travel's position as the authoritative source for travel industry information and research of the industry as a whole.
6. Promote travel industry cohesion and provide communication forums for industry leaders.
7. Leverage resources to develop and execute programs that benefit the travel industry, such as TravelCom, ESTO (Educational Seminar for Tourism Organizations), and the Travel Outlook Forum.

U.S. Travel's industry councils provide a unified voice for segments of the industry that enables them to address legislative issues of mutual concern, carry out educational programs unique to their industry components, and offer guidance in the development of U.S. Travel policies and programs. Each of the councils is described briefly.

The National Council of State Tourism Directors (NCSTD), formed in 1969, was the first of the national councils to be established under the umbrella of U.S. Travel. Its purpose is to provide a forum for state tourism directors to exchange ideas and information on matters common to state and territorial tourism offices and to develop unified positions on industry issues at the national level. Although there is great diversity among the states and territories in terms of specific needs and priorities, there are a number of common concerns in such areas as education, communication, marketing, research, and public affairs where NCSTD serves as a catalyst for developing programs that benefit all states and territories and, therefore, the entire U.S. travel industry.

The National Council of Destination Organizations (NCDO) was originally established in 1976 as the National Council of Area and Regional Tourism Organizations (CARTO). In 1999, as a result of a merger with the National Council of Urban Tourism Organizations (NCUTO), the NCDO was created. This council represents more than 400 U.S. Travel member destination marketing organizations whose concern is the promotion and facilitation of travel to and within that specific area or region. NCDO provides a forum and communications network for professionals from these organizations to address matters common to their specific areas of interest and to develop consensus positions on national issues.

The National Council of Attractions (NCA) was formed in 1976 to unify the widely diverse travel attractions segment within U.S. Travel, which includes historic, cultural, scientific, scenic, natural, themed, and entertainment attractions, as well as attraction-related service organizations. The NCA has more than 200 members.

U.S. Travel supports four major marketing programs:

1. **Discover America International Pow Wow.** This internationally acclaimed program brings together international tour operators and journalists from over 70 nations with U.S. travel suppliers, yielding the sale of more than $3.5 billion worth of U.S. travel product and invaluable media promotion of travel and tourism in America. See www.ustravel.org/events/international-pow-wow.

2. **The Marketing Outlook Forum.** This is an annual educational event that is an intensive two-day series of seminars preparing travel industry leaders to understand and deal with travel issues. It provides detailed projections concerning future travel patterns. See www.ustravel.org/events/marketing-outlook-forum.

3. **Discover America National Domestic Travel Marketing Program.** This ongoing, multifaceted, nationwide campaign is designed to encourage U.S. consumers to see more of their country through themed promotions, electronic travel information, and widespread use of the title logo, which reinforces the urge to see America. See www.ustravel.org/marketing/discover-america/discoveramerica-com.

4. **Discover America Pavilions.** This international marketing effort is spearheaded by the Discover America brand campaign. See www.ustravel.org/events/discover-america-pavilions.

Visit both the U.S. Travel and Discover America Web sites at www.ustravel.org and www.discoveramerica.com to explore these organizations in more detail.

REGIONAL ORGANIZATIONS

Regional tourism organizations have the goal of attracting tourists to their specific geographic region. There are several types of regional associations, such as multicountry, multistate, and multicounty. Examples range from PATA, which covers the Pacific region of the world, to groups such as Travel South USA, which promotes travel in the southern states, to the West Michigan Tourist Association, which promotes the West Michigan region from Northwest Indiana to the Straits of Mackinac, encompassing the entire half of the Lower Peninsula. Pennsylvania probably has more regional tourism organizations within its boundaries than any other state; its state tourism office supported 71 different agencies with regional marketing partnership grants or promotion assistance grants in 2009 to 2010.

STATE AND COMMUNITY ORGANIZATIONS

Because states/provinces are politically independent from their national governments and often possess highly unique market appeals, they usually establish an independent state/province tourism department to promote and coordinate development of the destinations. Similarly, larger cities having distinct tourism appeals will often put in place a DMO to promote and help develop tourism for the city/community. Often such community DMOs are highly effective as they benefit from high levels of commitment to the tourism cause of their community.

State governments have enacted many laws and regulations affecting tourism. Examples are organizations for promotion, transportation, food products, restaurant inspection, licensing boats, and many others. *Photo by South Dakota Tourism.*

State

Traditionally, states have promoted tourism as a tool for economic development. In most states, a tourism office has been established by statute and charged with the orderly growth and development of the travel and tourism industry in the state. State tourism offices conduct programs of information, advertising, publicity, and research relating to the recreational, scenic, historic, highway, and tourist attractions in the state at large.

Each of the 50 states has a government agency responsible for travel development and promotion. Most states have one agency responsible; however, Massachusetts has three entities. The Office of Travel and Tourism is complemented by the Massachusetts International Trade Council responsible for international tourism and the Massachusetts Convention Center Authority responsible for attracting conventions and events to the state. Texas has two entities devoting funds and resources to tourism development.

Hawaii and Alaska operate a little differently from other states in that the Hawaii Tourism Authority and the Alaska Department of Community and Economic Development contract out to private organizations the handling of the marketing and promotion responsibilities. The majority of states house their tourism offices in a department of economic development (or commerce).

Community

Most communities have also recognized the importance of tourism and have established convention and visitors bureaus. In many smaller communities, the chambers of commerce or resort associations perform this function. Larger cities now own the central convention facilities. A great deal of promotion and sales effort is then devoted to backing these facilities.

Community tourism offices appear to have a long history. The first tourism office in France was created in 1875, in the town of Gerardmer, followed by Grenoble in 1889. In the Netherlands, the first office (in Dutch, Vereniging voor Vreendenverkeer, abbreviated VVV) was founded in the small city of Valkenburg in the province of Limburg in 1885. It was meant to promote the city and to assist tourists. It is the predecessor of today's local tourist offices all over The Netherlands, which are still called VVV.

City Convention and Visitors Bureaus

A **convention and visitors bureau** is a not-for-profit umbrella organization that represents a city or urban area in the solicitation and servicing of all types of travelers to that city or area, whether they visit for business, pleasure, or both. It is also frequently called a destination management organization (DMO) or destination marketing organization. It is the single entity that brings together the interests of city government, trade and civic associations, and individual "travel suppliers"—hotels, motels, restaurants, attractions, local transportation—in building outside visitor traffic to the area.

Urban tourism is an increasingly important source of income and employment in most metropolitan areas, and therefore it warrants a coordinated and concerted effort to make it grow. This growth is best nurtured by the role a convention and visitors bureau can play in continually improving the scope and caliber of services the city provides to corporate and association meeting planners, to individual business travelers, and to leisure travelers.

The bureau is the city's liaison between potential visitors to the area and the businesses that will host them when they come. It acts as an information clearinghouse, convention management consultant, and promotional agency for the city and often as a catalyst for urban development and renewal.

Typical services offered to meeting planners include orientation to the city, a liaison between suppliers and meeting planners, and meeting management. The meetings and conventions market is huge. The Convention Industry Council estimates that meetings and conventions are a $263 billion-per-year industry (see Chapter 6).

Destination Marketing Association International

Most of the city convention and visitors bureaus belong to the Destination Marketing Association International (DMAI), 2025 M Street, NW, Suite 500, Washington, D.C. 20036. This group was founded in 1914 as the International Association of Convention Bureaus to promote sound professional practices in the solicitation and servicing of meetings and conventions. In 1974, the words "and Visitor" were added to IACB's name to reflect most bureaus' increasing involvement in the promotion of tourism. In August 2005, the organization changed its name to Destination Marketing Association International to clarify what members do (i.e., destination marketing).

Since its inception, the association has taken a strong position of leadership in the travel industry. The organization has more than 2,800 members in over 650 city destination management organizations in more than 30 countries. DMAI provides its members with numerous opportunities for professional dialogue and exchange of industry data on convention-holding organizations.

The DMAI Meeting Information Network (MINT) is the world's leading meetings and convention database, tracking historical and future records on more than 20,000 meeting profiles of associations and corporations. The database provides marketing and sales direction to thousands of convention and visitor bureaus, hotels and motels, and other convention industry suppliers. Visit www.empowermint.com.

To encourage exchange between its members, DMAI holds an annual convention, organizes annual educational seminars leading to certificates in sales or bureau operations, organizes topical workshops and seminars, makes regular studies of convention industry trends, maintains a consulting service, and provides its members with government and industry liaison services. Visit its Web site at www.destinationmarketing.org.

Tourists are provided with timely information and services at tourism information centers all over the world, such as this one in Torremolinos, Spain. *Photo courtesy of the author.*

EDUCATION AND EDUCATIONAL ORGANIZATIONS

Suppliers of the tourism product look to educational organizations as sources of talent for their industries. These include secondary schools, vocational schools, junior or community colleges, four-year colleges and universities, and trade association schools and institutes. Most high schools, which are known by various terms in different countries, offer curricula and subjects of value to travel firms. Examples are native and foreign languages, geography, history, writing, use of computers, secretarial skills, book-keeping, and food preparation. Many vocational schools produce entry-level employees for travel agencies, tour companies, airlines, accommodations, food service, and other organizations, and junior and community colleges offer education and training in various skills applicable to the travel industry.

Trade associations and professional societies are also active in education. Examples of these are the educational programs and home-study courses of the American Society of Travel Agents, the Travel Institute, the Educational Institute of the American Hotel and Lodging Association, the National Restaurant Association Educational Foundation, and, in Great Britain, the Institute of Travel and Tourism. Most public carriers, especially the airlines, provide rigorous training and educational programs for their employees, as well as for those working for travel agencies and tour companies. The International Labour Organization (a United Nations affiliate in Geneva, Switzerland) has conducted numerous types of training programs in tourism-related vocations. Similarly, the United Nations World Tourism Organization conducts courses for those in official tourism departments.

Four-year colleges and universities provide instruction in similar skills and management education. In keeping with the diversity of the industry, courses are offered in schools of business, schools of hotel and restaurant administration, colleges of natural resources, commercial recreation departments, sociology departments, geography departments, and anthropology departments. A number of schools offer graduate programs in travel and tourism. In addition to courses and educational programs, universities and colleges conduct a great deal of research, which is available to the industry.

The International Council on Hotel, Restaurant, and Institutional Education (ICHRIE) publishes a directory listing schools that offer two-year, four-year, and graduate study programs in North America and abroad. The publication, *Guide to College Programs in Hospitality, Tourism and Culinary Arts*, 9th edition, provides vital statistics on each program: student enrollment, program features, accreditation, admission and graduation requirements, and financial aid sources. It is available from ICHRIE in both CD-ROM format and hardbound (printed) copies. Visit www.chrie.org.

Finally, land-grant schools provide services through the Cooperative Extension Service, which operates in all 50 states. Educational services are available to managers of hotels, motels, restaurants, resorts, clubs, marinas, small service businesses, and similar enterprises from some state organizations. Short courses and conferences are sometimes held for managers of these businesses to make them more efficient and productive. These educational services are provided by the land-grant colleges and universities and by the Cooperative Extension Service, which is supported in part by the U.S. Department of Agriculture.

The Travel and Tourism Research Association (TTRA) has over 150 educational members. In addition, educators' sessions are held at the annual conference. The National Recreation and Park Association has a section called the Society of Park and Recreation Educators (SPRE). This group works on appropriate curriculum and features programs on education and research. Hotel and restaurant educators formed the International Council on Hotel, Restaurant, and Institutional Education (ICHRIE), which fosters improved teaching methods and aids in curriculum development for all educational levels, from high schools through four-year colleges and universities. The International Society of Travel and Tourism Educators (ISTTE) holds an annual conference and publishes a newsletter. The society strives to improve tourism teaching. Finally, there is the International Academy for the Study of Tourism, which seeks to improve tourism education and research.

SUMMARY

The United Nations World Tourism Organization represents governmental tourist interests and aids in world tourism development. Individual countries, states, and provinces have their own tourist promotion and development organizations that work to promote tourism in their area and coordinate tourism promotion with other groups. Most governments play a regulatory as well as a developmental role in tourism through such agencies as civil aeronautics boards, federal aviation administrations, customs offices, passport bureaus, and so on. Government agencies typically compile research statistics and gather data. Governments also operate tourist enterprises such as airlines, national parks, and sometimes hotels and campgrounds.

 KEY CONCEPTS

Canadian Tourism Commission
chambers of commerce
convention and visitors bureaus
Department of Homeland Security
Destination Marketing Association International
European Travel Commission
Federal Aviation Administration

International Air Transport Association
Office of Travel and Tourism Industries
Organization for Economic Cooperation and Development
Pacific Asia Travel Association
resort associations
state tourism offices
Tourism Australia

World Bank
United Nations World Tourism Organization
U.S. Department of Transportation
U.S. Travel Association
World Travel and Tourism Council

 INTERNET EXERCISES

The Internet sites mentioned in this chapter plus some selected additional sites are listed for your convenience on the companion Web site for this book, www.wiley.com/college/goeldner.

ACTIVITY 1

Site Name: United Nations World Tourism Organization

URL: unwto.org/en

Background Information: The United Nations World Tourism Organization is the leading international organization in the field of travel and tourism. It serves as a global forum for tourism policy issues and a practical source of tourism know-how.

Exercises

Explore the UNWTO Web site and find the following information.

1. How does the UNWTO communicate with its members and nonmembers?

2. As global competition in tourism becomes more intense, quality is the factor that can make the difference between success and failure. UNWTO's section on Quality and Trade in Tourism aims to help member destinations improve quality to become more competitive and ensure sustainable development. What are the basic components of UNWTO's quality program?

3. List five publications produced by the UNWTO and why they might be beneficial to a tourism professional.

ACTIVITY 2

Site Name: Pacific Asia Travel Association

URL: www.pata.org

Background Information: PATA was founded in 1951 to develop, promote, and facilitate travel to and among the destination areas in and bordering the Pacific Ocean and has become the leader of Asia Pacific travel and tourism.

Exercises

Explore the PATA Web site and find:

1. PATA's commitment to sustainable tourism.

2. The latest travel statistics showing inbound arrivals to the region.

✦ **QUESTIONS FOR REVIEW AND DISCUSSION** ✦

1. The United Nations World Tourism Organization (UNWTO) has made poverty alleviation through tourism one of its leading priorities. Do you believe this is feasible? What are the major problems you anticipate UNWTO will encounter in its efforts to develop and implement this priority?

2. If you were minister of tourism for Thailand, what types of assistance might you request from UNWTO? from PATA?

3. Tourism is the largest export industry in American Samoa. How might its minister of tourism's office be organized?

4. Do you feel that education should be one of the principal functions of any tourism organization? Why or why not?

5. If you were the president of a large international development bank such as FONATUR, what interest would you have in the World Travel and Tourism Council (WTTC)?

6. Speaking philosophically, why should a national government transportation department have any authority to regulate or control passenger fares or cargo rates?

7. Referring to question 6, should a private international organization such as the International Air Transport Association (IATA) have any authority to govern passenger airfares? If so, why?

8. Explain how the Organization for Economic Cooperation and Development (OECD), headquartered in Paris, could help develop tourism in its European member countries.

9. What main points would you expound on if you were supporting next year's Office of Travel and Tourism Industries (OTTI) budget on the floor of the U.S. House of Representatives?

10. Is there any need for a private national organization such as the U.S. Travel Association?

11. A state senator strongly opposes the budget for tourism promotion. "Let the hotels and transportation companies promote our state," he exclaims. "We need this money for better schools." As a member of the senate's tourism committee, what would your rebuttal be?

12. If you are a Canadian citizen, how do you feel about your tax dollars being spent on research jointly with the U.S. Tourism Industries Office?

13. Is there a relationship between the work of the Office of Travel and Tourism and the U.S. trade deficit?

14. In what ways does a city's convention and visitors bureau function? How is this organization usually financed?

15. As the manager of a fine resort lodge, what arguments would you use with your board of directors to obtain financial support for your local and regional tourism promotion organization?

16. If you, as manager of a hotel, had joined a tourist association and placed an ad in its publication, how would you ascertain if such investments were paying off?

❖ **CASE PROBLEMS** ❖

1. A popular tourist state has fallen on hard times. The state government can no longer provide adequate funds for its state park system. The governor has proposed a "group maintenance" policy for the parks. This means that all the parks in a given part of the state would be managed on a group basis. Eliminated would be all of the individual local park managers. Several million people visit these parks each year—an important part of the state's tourism. What might be some feasible solutions to the funding problems of the park system?

2. Two city council members are having an argument. A proposed budget item for tourist promotion for the coming fiscal year is being considered. One member endorses this item enthusiastically. The other states, "We don't benefit much from tourists' spending here because of the high leakage. I won't vote for this item; let's forget it." You are attending this meeting as a representative of the convention and visitor bureau. How would you respond? If you felt that your declarations were not very convincing, what research should be conducted immediately to strengthen your protourism position?

CHAPTER 5 ✥

Passenger Transportation

LEARNING OBJECTIVES

- Comprehend the importance of transportation in tourism.
- Understand the airline industry and its role in travel.
- Examine the domination of the automobile in travel.
- Learn about the role of rail and motorcoach travel.
- Study the cruise industry.

The jet plane and automobiles transformed the travel industry over 60 years ago. Now the increasingly modern, more fuel-efficient, and much quieter jets of today are but one component of a complex, highly integrated transportation system designed to meet the needs of a broad range of travelers on a cost-efficient basis. *Photo courtesy of PhotoDisc Inc.*

INTRODUCTION

Chapters 5, 6, 7, and 8 focus on the operating sectors of the tourism industry, starting with transportation. As shown in Figure 5.1, these sectors represent a critical segment of the tourism phenomenon shown in Figure 1.2. It is the operating sectors that deliver the tourism experience and tend to be viewed by the media, public, and visitors as the "tourism industry." It is the task of the operating sectors to develop and deliver tourism services and experiences with a spirit of hospitality so they will be enjoyable and truly memorable.

Turning our attention to the transportation sector, we find that since the beginning of time, people have been traveling by various modes, from on foot to riding in a supersonic aircraft. Tourism and *transportation* are inextricably linked—indeed, it is difficult to overstate the importance of **transportation** in tourism. As world tourism increases, additional demands will be placed on the transportation sectors (see Figure 5.2). Looking at the position occupied by the various modes of passenger transportation, one finds that air travel dominates long-distance and middle-distance tourism. The private automobile dominates for shorter trips and is the most popular means of travel for most domestic journeys. The automobile is also very important in regional and international tourism. Rail travel now plays a more limited role than it did in the past. However, this mode could increase its market share, especially in Europe and Asia. The development of high-speed trains will increase rail traffic.

Motorcoach transportation reaches many communities that are not served by any other public mode; but quantitatively, motorcoaches account for a very small percentage of vehicle miles. Cruises are becoming more popular and are the fastest-growing segment of tourism. However, this segment is still small quantitatively.

An increase in traffic due to world tourism growth puts pressure on transportation facilities, and this can have adverse effects. Situations in the world vary widely within regions, countries, states, and provinces. Also, variations exist among such areas. Even so, the problems seem to be the same all over the world. Those needing the urgent attention of policy makers are as follows:

1. **Congestion.** Serious congestion affects most passenger transportation modes, particularly on roads and at airports during peak periods. In major cities, there is the danger of reaching gridlock. Congestion means delays that are a serious waste of time and energy.

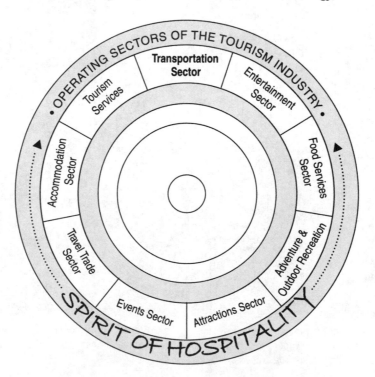

Figure 5.1 Operating sectors of the tourism industry: transportation.

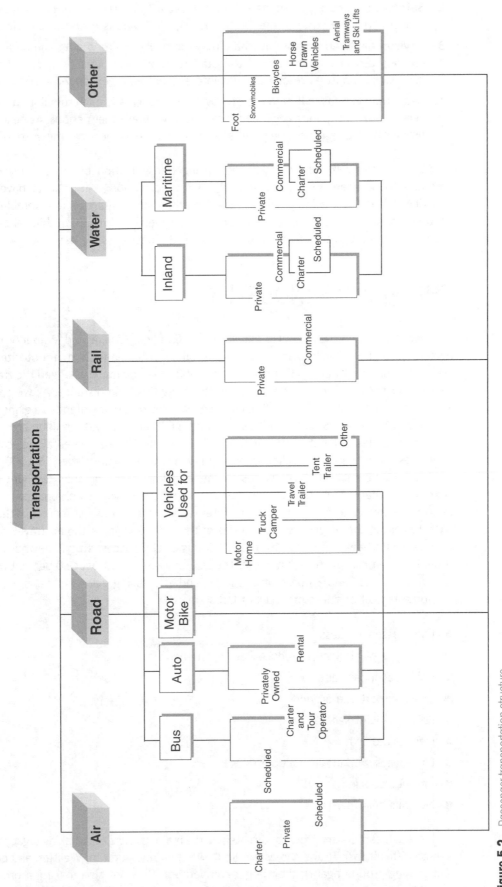

Figure 5.2 Passenger transportation structure.

2. **Safety and security.** Ensuring **safety and security** in transportation is a basic requirement for tourism. This was true before September 11, 2001, and is even more critical today.

3. **Environment.** An increase in traffic may harm the environment if an area does not have the carrying capacity for additional tourists. Transportation planning must take economic, social, cultural, and natural resources costs into account when expanded facilities are designed.

4. **Seasonality.** Seasonal patterns of travel demand create overcrowding at certain times. Conversely, low occupancies and load factors will occur at other periods. At peak travel periods, the problems of congestion, security, and the environment become much more severe.

All of these problems are challenges facing transportation planners. They have had and will continue to have an unfavorable impact on the perception that tourists have of their vacation experiences. Transportation problems have the potential to create an unfavorable image of a tourist destination. As the modes of transportation are reviewed in this chapter, think about how they can be developed and integrated to serve the tourist in the best possible manner.

THE AIRLINE INDUSTRY

On December 17, 1903, at Kitty Hawk, North Carolina, Orville and Wilbur Wright launched the aviation age when Orville made the first controlled, sustained flight in a motorized, heavier-than-air craft. Although that famous first flight lasted less than a minute, it changed the transportation world forever. Air travel has changed the way people view time and distance. As we celebrate more than 100 years of flight, we find the **airline industry** has grown from an infant to a giant. The world's airline industry numbers 1,715 airlines, 27,024 aircraft, 3,670 airports, 28.6 million scheduled departures a year, and carries 2.4 billion passengers a year. In the United States alone, commercial aviation generates more than $150 billion in annual revenue and employs over 550,000 people.[1]

A low-cost carrier (LCC) or low-cost airline—also known as a no-frills, discount, or budget airline—is an airline that offers generally low fares by eliminating many traditional passenger services. This concept, experienced first in the United States with Pacific Southwest Airlines in the early 1950s, gave birth to one of the biggest success stories of the last 20 years in the air travel industry. Southwest Airlines, which began service in 1971, is LCC's biggest U.S. success story. They have been a model that other low-cost carriers have emulated. The LCCs now represent over 30 percent of total air travel in the United States and 25 percent in Europe, and are making gains in Asia.

Some typical business practices of LCCs are:

- One passenger class
- One type of airplane to reduce fleet maintenance costs
- Using secondary airports
- Quick airport turnarounds
- Point-to-point service
- Unreserved seating
- Employees working in multiple roles
- Internet booking
- No frills, just low fares

Low-cost carriers are growing, threatening the major carriers and making legacy carrier profitability a more difficult task. Brand names like Southwest, JetBlue, AirTran, WestJet, and easyJet are growing and gaining ground against their larger competitors. They are also making a profit. They are being joined by new low-cost carriers in all parts of the world. Ryan Air and Spirit Airlines seem to be vying

A jet aircraft can carry hundreds of passengers in a minimum amount of time. Air travel is the most comfortable mode for mid- to long-distance trips. *Photo courtesy of Corbis Digital Stock.*

for the "ultra-low-fare" category. After eliminating reclining seats, window blinds, seat rest covers, and seat pockets, Ryan Air is making noises about charging passengers to use the toilets and selling standing room. Realistic or not, it is keeping the Ryan Air name in front of the public.

The bright spot in the global air industry is Asia and the Pacific. The dynamic economy of the region is making its own airlines profitable and helping carriers from outside the region with extensive Asia/Pacific operations. At present, the Orient is the world's number-one growth center for air travel.

The world's economy and the tourism industry need a healthy air transportation system. Without airline passengers, rental cars go unrented, hotel beds go unsold, and attractions go unvisited. The airlines have revolutionized long-haul travel, and the range and speed of jet travel have greatly expanded what tourists or business travelers could once accomplish with the equivalent time and funds at their disposal.

Today, for example, it is possible to fly around the globe in less time than it takes to drive across the United States. The system is also incredibly efficient: You need to make only one call to an airline or a travel agent or get on the Internet to purchase a ticket to your desired destination; then all you have to do is go to the airport and check your bags through to the final destination. The logistics that make it happen are complex, but the system works well. For example, the new United (together with United Express, Continental Express, and Continental Connection) operates a total of approximately 5,800 flights a day to 371 destinations throughout the Americas, Europe, and Asia (www.united.com).

Although the major advantage of air travel is speed, which results in more time for other activities, there are negative aspects for those who wish to travel by air. These include some people's fear of flying and a lack of geographic accessibility, since many communities in the country are not served by air transportation. An additional problem is the length of time spent getting to and from the airport. Frequently, this time exceeds that spent en route.

In the United States, the Air Transport Association classifies air carriers as major if they record over $1 billion in revenue annually. There are 20: ABX, AirTran Airways, Alaska Airlines, American Airlines, American Eagle, ATA, Atlas/Air, Comair, Continental Airlines, Delta Air Lines, ExpressJet, FedEx, Frontier, JetBlue, Mesa, SkyWest, Southwest Airlines, United Airlines, UPS Airlines, and US Airways. National carriers are those recording annual revenues of $100 million to $1 billion and include Air Transport International, Air Wisconsin Airlines, Allegiant, Aloha Airlines, Amerijet, Arrow Air, ASTAR Air Cargo, Continental Microensia, Evergreen International Airlines, Executive Airlines, Florida West,

TABLE 5.1 Top Nine U.S. Airlines by Passenger Revenue, 2009

Airline	Passenger Revenue ($000,000)
1 Delta	$18,522
2 American	15,037
3 United	11,910
4 Southwest	9,892
5 Continental	9,244
6 U.S. Airways	6,752
7 Jet Blue	2,928
8 Alaska	2,439
9 Air Tran	2,089

Source: Business Travel News.

Gemini Air Cargo, GoJet Airlines, Hawaiian Airlines, Horizon Air, Kalitta Air, Mesaba Airlines, Miami Air International, Midwest Airlines, North American Airlines, Omni Air International, Pinnacle Airlines, PSA Airlines, Southern Air, Spirit Airlines, Sun Country Airlines, USA 3000 Airlines, USA Jet, and World Airways. There are about a hundred regional airlines with annual revenues under $100 million.

The top nine U.S. airlines by passenger revenue are shown in Table 5.1. The table shows that Delta was the largest carrier in 2009 following its merger with Northwest. The United/Continental merger in 2010 has made United the current largest carrier in the United States by passenger revenue. See Table 5.1 and add the United and Continental figures together to see the scope of this merger.

It is interesting to compare Tables 5.1 and 5.2. Table 5.2 shows the top world airlines based on passenger revenue. Note that U.S. airlines occupy five of the top ten spots. This will change to four when the United-Continental merger is finally completed.

One of the best sources of data on the U.S. airline industry is an annual report published by the Air Transport Association of America, 1301 Pennsylvania Avenue NW, Suite 1100, Washington, D.C. 20004. The International Air Transport Association (see Chapter 4) makes forecasts and publishes financial and traffic statistics on the world airline industry. Its *World Air Transport Statistics* is in its fifty-fifth edition and is reported to be the single most timely and authoritative source of international airline data.

Air Transport World (ATW) publishes an annual World Airline Report that typically appears in its July issue. The report is available from *ATW* at (202) 659-8500 or www.atwonline.com. The comprehensive report covers the world's top 25 airlines, world airline financial statistics, Africa, Asia/Pacific, Canada, Europe, Latin America/Caribbean, Middle East, U.S. Majors, U.S. Nationals, U.S. Cargo Carriers, U.S. Regional/Specialty Carriers, and World Airline Fleets. *Air Transport World* is published monthly by Penton Media, Inc.

Another useful source of information on the airline industry is the U.S. Federal Aviation Administration. Consumer protection is the responsibility of the Department of Transportation.

Deregulation, Alliances, and Consolidation

Under deregulation, the airline industry has undergone dramatic change. It is hard to believe that 33 years have gone by since U.S. airline deregulation was passed in October 1978. Looking back, we can see that it has led to significant consolidation, hub systems, low airfares in competitive situations, and high airfares where competition is lacking.

The future foresees more concentration as consolidations and a wave of **alliances** have taken place and more are proposed. Alliances now involve the six largest carriers in the United States. International

TABLE 5.2 Top Twenty World Airlines by Passenger Revenue, 2009

Rank Airline	Passenger Revenue ($000,000)
1 Air France-KLM	$23,314
2 Lufthansa	22,598
3 Delta	18,522
4 American	15,037
5 United	11,910
6 British Airways	10,548
7 Southwest	9,892
8 Qantas	9,336
9 Continental	9,244
10 ANA	9,117
11 Emirates	8,981
12 Air Canada	8,099
13 Singapore	7,633
14 China Southern	7,322
15 U.S. Airways	6,752
16 Air China	6,245
17 Cathay Pacific	5,921
18 Thai Airways	5,599
19 Iberia	4,765
20 Korean Air	4,686

Source: Business Travel News.

alliances have been debated since KLM and Northwest linked in 1992. United has the Star Alliance (created in May 1997), which originally included Lufthansa, Air Canada, Thai Airways, and SAS. Since then, Star Alliance has added Adria Airways, Aegean Airlines, Air China, Air New Zealand, ANA, Asiana Airlines, Austrian, Blue 1, bmi British Midland, Brussels Airlines, Continental Airlines, Croatia Airlines, EGYPTAIR, LOT Polish Airlines, Shanghai Airlines, Singapore Airlines, South African Airways, Spanair, SWISS, TAM Airlines, TAP Portugal, Turkish Airlines, and U.S. Airways. Through membership in the Star Alliance, United provides connections to 11,160 destinations in 181 countries worldwide (www.staralliance.com).

SkyTeam is the global alliance partnering Aeroflot, Aeromexico, AirEuropa, Air France–KLM, Alitalia, China Southern, Czech Airlines, Delta, Kenya Airways, Korean Air, TAROM, and Vietnam Airlines. Through one of the world's most extensive hub networks, SkyTeam offers its passengers a worldwide system of more than 13,000 daily flights covering 898 destinations in 169 countries (www.skyteam.com).

American and British Airways have launched a global alliance with Cathay Pacific Airways, Finnair, Iberia, Japan Airlines, Lan, Malev, Mexicana, Qantas, and Royal Jordanian, and S7 Airlines called Oneworld (www.oneworld.com). They also plan to expand the grouping. There are other alliances and partners too numerous to mention, but the alliances cited indicate the high level of concentration present.

More alliances and more consolidations are the wave of the future in the airline industry as alliances continue to add new members, and merger talks take place, resulting in more consolidation. In September 2010, Southwest Airlines announced plans to acquire smaller rival AirTran in a $1.4 billion cash and stock deal that reflects the intensifying consolidation in the industry, expected to be finalized in 2011. WestJet Airlines and American Airlines have entered into an interline agreement, and it is expected that in time it will be expanded to a code-share agreement. West Jet plans three or four more code share agreements in 2011. Will alliances benefit the consumer through greater choice, more seamless travel, lower fares, greater convenience, and frequent-flyer miles? Or will consolidations and alliances create oligopoly and monopoly, higher fares, and a noncompetitive situation? Only time and government action will answer these questions. The expectation is that the consolidation and alliance trend will continue for several years unless regulatory agencies stop it. Authorities in both the United States and the European Union are analyzing how to deal with major airline alliances and consolidations. The decisions made will shape the future of airlines around the world.

❖ GLOBAL INSIGHT ❖

Open Skies

On June 24, 2010, representatives of the United States and the European Union (EU) and its 27 member states signed a "Second Stage" civil aviation agreement, providing for greater U.S.-EU cooperation on a wide range of aviation issues. The accord builds on the historic U.S.-EU "Open Skies" agreement that was signed in April 2007. The pro-consumer, pro-competitive agreement eliminated restrictions on air services between the United States and EU member states, allowing airlines from both sides to select routes and destinations based on consumer demand for both passenger and cargo services, without limitations on the number of U.S. or EU carriers that can fly or the number of flights they can operate. The Centre for Asia Pacific Aviation (CAPA), based in Sydney, Australia, predicts aviation liberalization will gain momentum in Asia. In Canada, air service liberalization is referred to as "blue skies." Canada is moving ahead with a number of agreements.

Open skies agreements set liberal ground rules for international aviation markets and minimize government intervention. Provisions apply to passenger, all-cargo, and combination air transportation and encompass both scheduled and charter services. There are eight key provisions:

1. **Free market competition.** No restrictions on international route rights, number of designated airlines, capacity, frequencies, or types of aircraft.

2. **Pricing determined by market forces.** A fare can be disallowed only if both governments concur—*double-disapproval pricing*—and only for certain, specified reasons intended to ensure competition.

3. **Doing business protections.** For example:

   ■ All carriers of both countries may establish sales offices in the other country, and convert earnings and remit them in hard currency promptly and without restrictions.

   ■ Carriers are free to provide their own ground-handling services—*self-handling*—or choose among competing providers. Airlines and cargo consolidators may arrange ground transport of air cargo and are guaranteed access to customs services.

   ■ User charges are nondiscriminatory and based on costs.

4. **Cooperative marketing arrangements.** Airlines may enter into code-sharing or leasing arrangements with airlines of either country, or with those of third countries, subject to usual regulations. An optional provision authorizes code-sharing between airlines and surface transportation companies.

5. **Provisions for consumer consultation and arbitration.** Model text includes procedures for resolving differences that arise under the agreement.

6. **Liberal charter arrangements.** Carriers may choose to operate under the charter regulations of either country.

7. **Safety and security.** Each government agrees to observe high standards of aviation safety and security, and to render assistance to the other in certain circumstances.

8. **Optional 7th freedom all-cargo rights.** Provides authority for an airline of one country to operate all-cargo services between the other country and a third country, via flights that are not linked to its homeland.

Open skies agreements can be either bilateral or multilateral. The United States has concluded more than 96 bilateral open skies agreements with countries from every region of the world and at every level of economic development. A list of these countries can be found on the U.S. Department of State Web site, www.state.gov.

DISCUSSION QUESTIONS

1. What are open skies agreements?

2. Are open skies agreements good for the airlines, the consumer, the country?

Growth

World and U.S. air transportation is expected to grow in the future. Growth, as in the past, will be tempered by war, diseases such as SARS, tsunamis, volcanic ash, and economic recessions; however, the long-term trend is growth even with these setbacks.

The U.S. Federal Aviation Administration's 20-year forecast for fiscal years 2010–2030 predicts domestic passenger enplanements will increase by 0.5 percent in 2010 and then grow an average of 2.5 percent per year through 2030 (Table 5.3). U.S. airlines, which carried 704 million passengers (passenger enplanements) in 2009, will carry one billion passengers a year by 2023 and 1.21 billion by

TABLE 5.3   U.S. Commercial Air Carriers[a] Total Scheduled U.S. Passenger Traffic

Fiscal Year	Revenue Passenger Enplanements (in millions)			Revenue Passenger Miles (in billions)		
	Domestic	International	System	Domestic	International	System
2010	634.1	73.4	707.4	551.5	220.7	772.2
2011	645.7	76.3	722.0	561.5	231.0	792.5
2012	667.7	79.7	747.3	585.5	242.7	828.2
2013	687.8	83.2	771.1	608.3	254.9	863.2
2014	705.5	86.9	792.4	629.1	267.6	896.7
2015	723.1	90.6	813.7	650.3	280.5	930.8
2016	740.6	94.3	834.9	671.1	293.8	964.9
2017	758.2	98.1	856.3	692.4	307.3	999.7
2018	777.4	102.2	879.6	715.4	321.6	1,037.0
2019	798.3	106.5	904.8	740.4	336.9	1,077.3
2020	821.4	111.1	932.6	767.8	353.2	1,120.9
2021	842.5	115.7	958.2	792.9	369.6	1,162.4
2022	863.3	120.5	983.7	818.1	386.4	1,204.4
2023	884.7	125.3	1,010.1	844.2	403.8	1,248.1
2024	906.4	130.3	1,036.7	870.8	422.0	1,292.8
2025	929.3	135.6	1,064.9	899.0	441.2	1,340.2
2026	952.4	141.1	1,093.5	927.0	461.1	1,388.1
2027	974.9	146.7	1,121.5	954.7	481.6	1,436.2
2028	997.9	152.4	1,150.3	983.2	502.8	1,486.0
2029	1,021.0	158.3	1,179.3	1,012.1	524.8	1,536.8
2030	1,045.5	164.5	1,210.0	1,042.6	547.9	1,590.6
Avg. Annual Growth						
2000–2009	−0.2%	2.9%	0.1%	0.8%	2.1%	1.1%
2009–2010	0.4%	0.9%	0.5%	0.4%	0.3%	0.3%
2010–2020	2.6%	4.2%	2.8%	3.4%	4.8%	3.8%
2009–2030	2.4%	4.0%	2.6%	3.1%	4.4%	3.5%

[a] Sum of U.S. Mainline and Regional Air Carriers.

Source: Federal Aviation Administration, U.S. Department of Transportation.

2030. Domestic and international enplanements are projected to grow 2.5 percent and 4.2 percent per year, respectively, during the next 20 years. Visit www.faa.gov and click on Aviation Forecasts for the most current information.

Air transport growth is an essential ingredient in tourism's future because the growth of tourism is linked to air transport performance. Without growth in airline passengers, there are fewer new customers to rent cars, stay in accommodations, and visit attractions.

Some Predictions

To accommodate future air travel growth, the current U.S. aging mid-twentieth century air traffic control system will have to be replaced with twenty-first century, satellite-based GPS-oriented smart technology to maximize the efficient movement of aircraft. A satellite-based system provided by the FAA is currently being used in Philadelphia, Pennsylvania. Called Automatic Dependent Surveillance-Broadcast (ADS-B), the system is a core technology under the Next Generation Air Transportation System (NextGen).

If current experiments are successful, radio-frequency identification (RFID) will greatly reduce lost bags. Is it possible for this technology to end lost bags? The price of fuel will drive new technology, leading to the development of alternative fuels and more fuel-efficient and environmentally friendly aircraft. Some are predicting that planes will fly mostly on biofuels in ten years.

There will continue to be an expansion of fees for unbundled services. Ancillary fees include fees for baggage, priority seating, food and beverages, and pillows.

Technology holds the potential to speed consumers through airport security because of advances in molecular diagnostics, facial recognition technology, iris identification, and nanosensors.

Some low-cost carriers will merge and start flying internationally across the Atlantic and the Pacific oceans.

Air Transport Association of America

The airline industry is supported by three major organizations. IATA and ICAO have already been discussed in Chapter 4 under international organizations; they are two key associations controlling air travel. The major U.S. organization is the Air Transport Association of America.

In 1936, 14 fledgling airlines met in Chicago to form the Air Transport Association (ATA) "to do all things tending to promote the betterment of airline business, and in general, to do everything in its power to best serve the interest and welfare of the members of this association and the public at large."

Today, from its headquarters in Washington, D.C., ATA is the nation's oldest and largest airline trade association. Its membership of seventeen U.S. and three associate (non-U.S.) airlines carry about 95 percent of the passenger and cargo traffic carried by scheduled U.S. airlines.

ATA is the meeting place where the airlines cooperate in noncompetitive areas to improve airline service, safety, and efficiency. The mission of ATA is to support and assist its member carriers by promoting aviation safety, advocating industry positions, conducting designated industrywide programs, and ensuring public understanding.

Thus, while the carriers are intensely competitive among themselves and with other forms of transportation in their individual promotion of airline service for the traveling and shipping public, they are equally intense in their mutual cooperation on matters of industrywide importance, such as safety, technological progress, and passenger service improvement.

Although ATA's agenda of issues continuously changes, its major priorities remain unchanged. They include the following:

- Assisting the airline industry in continuing to provide the world's safest system of transportation
- Advocating the modernization of the Federal Aviation Administration's air traffic control system, in order to improve service for airline customers and to benefit the environment

- Protecting airline passengers, crew members, aircraft and cargo, working collaboratively with the Department of Homeland Security and the Transportation Security Administration
- Seeking to prevent legislative and regulatory actions that would penalize airlines and their customers by imposing rate, route, service, or schedule controls on the industry
- Endeavoring to reduce the disproportionate share of taxes and fees paid by airlines and their customers at the federal, state, and local levels
- Improving the industry's ability to attract capital
- Helping to shape international aviation policy, to ensure that U.S. and foreign carriers can compete on equal terms

During its more than 75 years of existence, ATA has seen the airline industry grow from the small, pioneering companies of the 1930s into key players in the world's economy. ATA members continue to play a major role in shaping the future of air transportation.

ATA headquarters are located at 1301 Pennsylvania Avenue NW, Suite 1100, Washington, D.C. 20004; telephone (202) 626-4000; Web site at www.airlines.org.

THE RAIL INDUSTRY

Rail passenger transportation, once the major mode of travel in the United States, reached its peak volume in 1920. Major railroads have sought to rid themselves of the passenger business, and today the survival of service (other than commuter service) depends largely on Amtrak. In Canada, the situation has been similar, and future rail travel depends on VIA Rail Canada.

Outside North America, where passenger rail service is more extensive, rail transportation assumes a more important role. Ultramodern railway systems with high-speed trains operate in many countries, handling passenger traffic in an economical and efficient manner and providing an alternative to air travel. France and Japan are well known for their high-speed trains. The French

Amtrak's Acela Express exemplifies the latest technology in rail service. Passengers in the Northeast Corridor can enjoy high-speed rail service traveling at 150 miles per hour in modern comfort.
Copyright © 2001 Amtrak. Photo provided as a courtesy by Amtrak.

government has taken responsibility for rail infrastructure of the state-owned SNCF rail company. Japan continues to improve and expand its famous "bullet train." Some of the largest railways in the world are found in the former Soviet Union, India, and China.

Australia made a significant step forward in rail travel in February 2004 when the new 882 miles of tracks from Alice Springs to Darwin opened. Now, one can finally travel on the legendary Ghan Train across the country from Adelaide in the south to Darwin in the north.

Amtrak

Amtrak is the marketing name for the National Railroad Passenger Corporation, an operating railroad corporation, the controlling stock of which is owned by the U.S. government through the U.S. Department of Transportation. Amtrak's business is providing rail passenger transportation in the major intercity markets of the United States. The National Railroad Passenger Corporation was established by the Rail Passenger Service Act of 1970.

The corporation has a history of recurring operating losses and is dependent on subsidies from the federal government to operate the national passenger rail system and maintain the underlying infrastructure. These subsidies are usually received through annual appropriations. Amtrak's ability to continue operating in its current form is dependent on the continued receipt of subsidies from the federal government.

Amtrak operates a nationwide rail network, serving over 500 destinations in 46 states and 3 Canadian provinces on its 21,000-mile route system, Amtrak carried more than 27.1 million intercity passengers in fiscal 2009. Amtrak employs over 19,000 people. Its employees are represented by 14 different labor organizations.

In fiscal year 2009, Amtrak earned just over $2.35 billion in total revenue and incurred $3.5 billion in expenses. The annual federal appropriation on which Amtrak relies totaled $1.49 billion in fiscal year 2009, comprising $475 million in operating funds, $75 million for retroactive labor payments, and $940 million for capital investments, of which $285 million was for debt service. Amtrak states: "No country in the world operates a passenger rail system without some form of public support for capital costs and/or operating expenses."[2] The United States continues to make substantial investments in Amtrak and rail service.

The Passenger Rail Investment and Improvement Act of 2008 (ARRA) sets objectives for Amtrak in its role as America's passenger rail service provider. In recognition of the increased desire for passenger rail across the country, the law also gives states more control over the development and expansion of service. In addition, the ARRA of 2009 provided $1.3 billion for Amtrak to make or accelerate capital investments that would otherwise remain on backlog.

In January 2010, the White House announced the award of $8 billion in ARRA capital grants to 31 states for expansion and development of intercity and high-speed passenger rail, the cornerstone of President Obama's long-term vision to build and sustain a rejuvenated passenger rail network in the United States. Nearly 60 percent of the $8 billion awarded to the states will be invested in routes and services that are or will be part of Amtrak's system in the future.[3]

Amtrak was launched as an experiment to identify the importance of rail passenger service to a balanced national transportation system. A key for continued support of Amtrak in the mid-1970s was the dramatic impact of the oil embargo and recognition of the need for alternative forms of transportation.

In various transportation corridors, Amtrak is the dominant public carrier. Amtrak provides energy-efficient and environmentally friendly service in some of the nation's most densely populated, congested, and polluted rail corridors, including the Washington, D.C.–Boston Northeast Corridor and between San Diego and Los Angeles, San Francisco and Sacramento, St. Louis and Chicago, and Chicago and Detroit. Amtrak currently serves almost half of the combined air-rail market between the end points of New York and Washington, D.C.; when intermediate cities (such as Baltimore and Philadelphia) are included, Amtrak's share of the air-rail market rises to 70 percent.

Cable cars not only provide transportation, but they also deliver a unique tourist experience and are an essential part of a visit to San Francisco. Their charm continues to attract visitors from around the world. *Photo courtesy of PhotoDisc, Inc./Getty Images.*

Amtrak launched its Acela Express service between Boston and Washington, D.C., in December 2000 to serve the Northeast Corridor. Passengers can enjoy high-speed rail service traveling at 150 miles per hour in modern comfort. On average, the line is not as fast as high-speed rail lines in other countries. The Acela Express service promises to improve Amtrak's revenue stream. It will become the prototype for high-speed trains in the Pacific Northwest, the Midwest, and the South but is currently the only high-speed rail line in operation in the United States.

Because Amtrak is subsidized, suppliers of the other modes of transportation (especially bus) think that Amtrak is attracting its customers with taxpayer assistance.

High-Speed Rail

The countries that have trains currently operating at 125 to 185 miles per hour (mph) (200–300 kilometers per hour [km/h]) are Belgium, China, Finland, France, Germany, Italy, Japan, Portugal, South Korea, Spain, Taiwan, Turkey, the United Kingdom, and the United States. As constraints on the growth of highway and air travel systems build, high-speed rail has the potential to relieve congestion on other systems. High-speed trains have lower energy consumption per passenger mile than air or automobile modes of transportation. They can move passengers at speeds far faster than cars. Although they do not travel as fast as jet planes, they have advantages over air travel for relatively short distances (300 miles) because of the time required for the journey to the airport, checking in, going through security screening, and arriving in the city center. Japan and France have been major leaders in high-speed rail.

Japan

Japan was one of the first countries to develop modern high-speed railways. Many would credit Japan with being the inventor of the concept because in 1964, the country launched the famous Shinkansen (bullet train) with speeds of 132 mph (210 km/h). Many countries still have no trains running at this speed. Today, Japan has trains running at 186 mph (300 km/h) and the most heavily traveled network. Japan's speed record is 277 mph (443 km/h). Japan had the largest high-speed rail network in operation until China opened 3,750 miles (6000 km) in April 2007.

France and Europe

France is another leader in modern high-speed rail travel. The country holds the speed record of 357 mph (574.8 km/h) set April 13, 2007. France has the most developed high-speed network in Europe. Trains have been running daily in the country at 186 mph (300 km/h) speeds since 1989 and have encouraged construction of high-speed lines in Germany, Belgium, The Netherlands, the United Kingdom, and Spain.

Starting with the birth of France's TGV (Train à Grande Vitesse, or High-Speed Train) in 1981, the European train industry (led by Alstom in France and Siemens in Germany) has been on the forefront of high-speed innovation. Streamlined design, underfloor traction systems, and tilting technology have brought the European high-speed train up to these high speeds. The factor that limits the speed of trains now is the tracks on which they run and the different systems the countries have, which create problems at the borders.

China

The Shanghai Maglev Train has connected Shanghai and Pu Dong International Airport since March 2004. Imported from Germany, it has an operational speed of 268.7 mph (430 km/h). China has an aggressive high-speed rail program and in April 2007 opened several high-speed rail lines between major cities. These lines made China the country with the world's largest high-speed rail network, moving it from last place to first place in network size.

Train Travel as a Tourist Attraction

Trains can provide a romantic and intriguing way to spend a holiday. Top tourist trains such as the Palace on Wheels in India; Blue Train in South Africa; Glacier Express in Switzerland; Orient Express in France and Austria; Copper Canyon in Mexico; Rocky Mountaineer in Canada; Ghan in Australia; Royal Scotsman in Scotland; Trans Siberian Railway in Russia, Mongolia, and China; West Highland Railway in the United Kingdom; and Durango and Silverton Narrow Gauge Railroad in Colorado are just a few of the world-class train experience vacations.

THE MOTORCOACH INDUSTRY

The American Bus Association (ABA) reports that there are over 35,000 commercial motorcoaches in use for charters, tours, regular route service, and special operations in North America. The buses carry over 752 million passengers a year. Carriers involved in the regular-route part of the industry operate approximately 8,000 to 10,000 over-the-road intercity coaches. Buses perform a wide range of services, with half of industry mileage on scheduled intercity services, one-third on charters, and the rest on tours, private commutes, airport shuttles, and others.

In 2008, motorcoaches were driven about 1.8 billion miles, with the average bus traveling 51,868 miles. More than half of motorcoach passengers are students and senior citizens.

Intercity bus service is the most energy-efficient passenger transportation mode in the United States when compared to all others by measuring passenger miles per gallon. On average, the motorcoach industry provides 206.6 passenger miles per gallon of fuel, compared to the single-passenger automobile at 27.2 or transit bus at 31.4 passenger miles per gallon. The study titled *Updated Comparisons of Energy Use and Emissions from Different Transportation Modes,* produced by M.J. Bradley and Associates, also shows that motorcoaches produce the lowest carbon dioxide emissions per passenger mile of any of the 14 transportation modes analyzed.

The motorcoach industry is composed largely of small entrepreneurial businesses. There are over 3,500 companies, 90 percent of which have fewer than 25 buses. These entrepreneurial companies operate about 19,000 motorcoaches, account for almost 40 percent of the total industry mileage, and carry one in five passengers. More than half of motorcoach jobs are with small businesses employing fewer than 50 people. The industry employs 200,000 workers, not including jobs in the bus manufacturing and supplier sector. Clearly, motorcoach travel contributes significantly to tourism revenues in local communities. In Washington, D.C., alone, 23.4 percent of 21 million annual visitors arrive by motorcoach. If only half of those visitors came as part of an overnight tour, $424 million would flow into those local businesses.

Motorcoaches are also the intermodal glue in America's often-disjointed transportation system. Motorcoaches link passengers arriving and departing through airports, train stations, and seaports with their final home, work, and tourism destinations.

Regular/Route/Scheduled Bus Service

About 100 privately owned companies in the United States offer regular route bus service. Greyhound Lines, Inc., the only nationwide bus carrier for regular intercity route service, serves more than 2,300 destinations with 13,000 daily departures. Nearly 2.5 million passengers each year use Greyhound. Greyhound has three subsidiaries in the United States that are a part of the nationwide Greyhound network. They include: Valley Transit Company, serving the Texas–Mexico border; Crucero USA, serving southern California and Arizona into Mexico; and Americanos USA, serving points in Mexico from Texas and New Mexico. The company's Greyhound Travel Services unit offers charter packages for business, conventions, schools, and other groups.

In addition, Greyhound has interline partnerships with a number of independent bus lines across the United States. These bus companies provide complementary service to Greyhound Lines' existing schedules and link to many of the smaller towns in Greyhound Lines' national route system.

Amtrak passengers use Greyhound to make connections to cities not served by rail on Amtrak Thruway service, by purchasing a ticket for the bus connection from Amtrak in conjunction with the purchase of their rail ticket. If passengers desire, they may also buy a bus ticket directly from Greyhound.

For travel within Canada, Greyhound Canada carries millions of passengers across the country's provinces and territories each year. The company also provides Greyhound Courier Express package delivery service to its various Canadian locations.

For those within Mexico who wish to travel by Greyhound in the United States, Greyhound subsidiary Greyhound de Mexico can sell Greyhound tickets at one of more than a hundred agencies located throughout Mexico. The agencies also sell tickets for several Mexican bus companies, such as Estrella Blanca, which connect to Greyhound service at the United States–Mexico border cities. Greyhound is owed by First Group plc of Aberdeen, Scotland. Visit www.greyhound.com.

The Trailways Transportation System, a federation of independently owned bus companies that market intercity service under the Trailways name, covers a large portion of the United States. They serve over 1,000 destinations and carry over 16 million passengers a year. Other independent companies provide service on a regional basis and feed passengers into the Greyhound or Trailways systems, into the Amtrak rail system, and into airports. The approximate number of places in the United States served by intercity buses is 3,300. This compares to about 400 airports with scheduled airline service and to about 500 Amtrak stations.

The motorcoach industry is the most pervasive form of intercity public transportation in the world. Motorcoaches provide both scheduled and charter service. This motorcoach carried passengers from Alice Springs, Australia, to Ayers Rock. *Photo by the author.*

Charters and Tours

Both domestic and international travelers are heavy users of motorcoaches because coach travel gives them time to see and experience sights with a group of friends without having to deal with traffic and road maps. Sales of tours and charters continue to be popular all over the world. Because of the popularity of motorcoach tours, tour operators worldwide now conduct trips to myriad destinations and drive there safely in state-of-the-art-equipped vehicles at an economical price.

According to the American Bus Association, most of the bus companies provide charter service. The top three activities for bus charters are theater shows, gaming/casinos, and sightseeing. Sightseeing tours come in all shapes and sizes in the United States and around the world. Motorcoaches offer day excursions, short breaks, and long tours. Motorcoaches range in size from 19 to 85 seats so that all types of travel groups can be served to all types of destinations.

Group tours provide stress-free, worry-free travel. The consumer is in the hands of a capable driver and tour guide following an itinerary that provides lifelong experiences.

Trends

Do you expect to enjoy a full-length feature film on your next motorcoach trip? Or relax in a comfortable seat? If you think you can do these traveling only on an airline, think again. Leisure motorcoach travel is a popular way to see North America. The modern trip by motorcoach is nothing like you remember from your childhood days. Forget your preconceived ideas of crowded, stuffy buses. Today's luxury vehicles have WiFi, flat-screen DVDs, iPod® hook-ups, reclining seats, and air conditioning, and are among the safest and cleanest modes of transportation available. Charter luxury motorcoaches are more luxurious than flying on a commercial airline.

Motorcoach Organizations

The American Bus Association (ABA) is the national organization of the intercity bus industry and serves as the prime source of industry statistics. ABA represents approximately 1,000 motorcoach and tour companies in the United States and Canada. Its members operate charter, tour, regular route, airport express, special operations, and contract services (commuter, school, transit). Another 2,800 member organizations represent the travel and tourism industry and suppliers of bus products and services who work in partnership with the North American motorcoach industry. ABA is also home to the ABA Foundation, a nonprofit organization with an emphasis on scholarships, research, and continuing education. The American Bus Association's headquarters are located in downtown Washington, D.C.: 700 13th Street NW, Suite 575, Washington, D.C. 20005-5923; telephone (202) 842-1645; fax (202) 842-0850; e-mail abainfo@buses.org; its Web site is www.buses.org.

The United Motorcoach Association (UMA), founded as the United Bus Owners of America in 1971, is a trade association with more than 1,000 motorcoach company members and motorcoach industry manufacturers, suppliers, and vendors spread across North America. UMA member companies provide a broad variety of charter motorcoach services. Other member services include tours, schools, intercity transit, and shuttle or commuter lines. UMA serves the informational, legislative, regulatory, and business needs of its member companies. Within the membership, companies range from one and two vehicles to those with many hundreds of coaches, from small tour-specific companies to those performing intercity route service, charter operations, and tour operations on a coast-to-coast scale.

UMA's offices are located at 113 S. West Street, Alexandria, VA 22314-2824; telephone (800) 424-8262 or (703) 838-2929; e-mail info@uma.org; Web site www.uma.org.

THE AUTOMOBILE

Most of the travel in the world takes place in the **automobile**. In the United States, auto travel is an integral part of the travel industry with the vast majority—79 percent—of U.S. domestic person-trips taken by car, truck, camper/recreation vehicle, or rental car. Affordability, flexibility, convenience, and personal control make auto travel the most popular mode of transportation all over the world. Because passenger car registrations continue to increase worldwide, motor vehicles will continue to be the dominant mode of transportation for decades to come.

All studies show the automobile's dominance, whether the study is from the Air Transport Association, the Highway Administration, the Census Bureau, or U.S. Travel Association's research department. There is no doubt that the great bulk of intercity transportation of passengers is by automobile. Data also indicate that this has been constant for several decades. However, because of the great dominance of the automobile in travel, even a small shift in automobile travel to the common carriers can result in enormous increases in the carriers' business.

The interstate highway system significantly encouraged vacation travel and especially encouraged long-distance travel. It made automobile travel much faster and more comfortable. A major concern of tourism groups today is the maintenance of the highway network. There is growing evidence that the highway system is in need of substantial repair to prevent it from suffering further deterioration. A poor road system costs the individual driver, the bus operator, and other users additional funds in terms of increased fuel use and vehicle maintenance, and the knowledge that a highway is in poor condition may cause travelers to select another destination to avoid the problem.

On the whole, people's attitudes are very favorable toward travel by automobile. The key feature of the automobile is immediate accessibility and convenience. The automobile owner can leave from his or her own doorstep at any hour of the day or night and travel to a chosen destination. When two or more persons travel by automobile, the per-person cost of travel is more favorable than it is with the other transportation modes. Air is the primary competitor to the automobile when it comes to travel, especially for long trips. Travelers must weigh the advantages of air travel—the quality of service, speed, and comfort—against the automobile's advantages of price and accessibility.

Recreation Vehicles

The **recreation vehicle (RV)** segment deserves special mention because, according to the Recreation Vehicle Industry Association (RVIA), there are currently 8.3 million RVs on the road in the United States, enjoyed by some 30 million enthusiasts. One in twelve vehicle-owning households has an RV, with ownership predicted to increase to 8.5 million by the year 2011. RVers travel an average of 4,500 miles per year, spending 26 days in their vehicle. In Canada, estimates put privately owned RVs at 500,000 to 850,000. While the RV market has had its ups and downs because of events such as the energy crisis, the recession, and the Iraq war, the market for recreation vehicles is huge, with sales ranging from $8 billion to $14 billion a year.[4]

Slide-out technology, introduced during the mid-1990s, has now advanced to become available in living rooms, dining rooms, bedrooms, and kitchens. At the touch of a button, this mechanism lets a portion of the room and the objects in it, such as a couch, table, or refrigerator, slide outward up to about $3\frac{1}{2}$ feet. Slide-outs are available in a wide variety of RVs: motor homes, mini-motor-homes, travel trailers, fifth-wheel trailers, and even folding camping trailers. Electronics have also come to RV travel, with direct broadcast satellite systems, computer hookups, onboard global positioning systems (GPS), and rearview monitors now popular options.

The typical U.S. RV owner is 49 years old, is married, owns a home, and has an annual income of $68,000. A University of Michigan study indicates that intentions to purchase an RV are strongest among baby boomers. Nearly 9 percent of households headed by 35- to 54-year-olds own an RV, slightly exceeding the 8.6 percent ownership rates of those 55 years old and over.[5]

Of increasing economic significance is the steady rise in RV rentals. The Recreation Vehicle Rental Association (RVRA) reports that its members are experiencing significant growth, and strong demand has encouraged hundreds of businesses to enter the rental market, while others have expanded their operations. More than 400 national RV rental chain outlets and local RV dealerships offer state-of-the-art, late-model-year vehicles for rent.

Travel agencies around the world are responding to the demand by including RV rental information in their customer brochures. Also available from some rental dealers are comprehensive tour packages that include services such as airline and railway connections for fly/drive and rail/drive plans, one-way packages, off-season rates, vacation planning, guided escort tours, and campground discounts. The recent surge of foreign visitors has helped increase the RV rental market. Visitors from Japan, Australia, New Zealand, and the United Kingdom are major customers. An estimated half million overseas visitors a year rent RVs. Visit the Recreation Vehicle Industry Association Web site at www.rvia.org.

Highways and Scenic Byways

Automobile travel in the United States has received a boost from the **National Scenic Byways program**. The Intermodal Surface Transportation Efficiency Act of 1991 (ISTEA) established the Scenic Byways program, which provided $80 million over six years for carrying out eligible programs on designated scenic byways. According to the Federal Highway Administration, the United States has 4 million miles of roads, and approximately 51,500 have been designated as or are potential scenic byways. All 50 states have existing byways, with an average of nine routes per state. An ISTEA reauthorization bill, the Transportation Equity Act for the Twenty-first Century (TEA-21), became law on June 9, 1998, and ensured continuation of the National Scenic Byways program. The act called for $148 million for improvements to roads of scenic or historic value. TEA-21 provided 40 percent more funding for transportation than the 1991 law it replaced, authorizing a six-year expenditure of $216 billion. TEA-21 was reauthorized in 2005 as SAFETEA-LU (Safe, Accountable, Flexible and Efficient Transportation Equity Act—A Legacy for Users) with guaranteed funding for highways, highway safety, and public transportation totaling $244.1 billion. SAFETEA-LU represents the largest surface transportation investment in U.S. history.

The act authorizes a total of $175 million through 2009 for technical assistance and grants to states and Indian tribes to develop scenic byways programs and to implement projects on highways of outstanding scenic, historic, cultural, natural, recreational, and archaeological qualities designated as National Scenic Byways, All-American Roads, America's Byways, state scenic, or Indian tribe scenic byways. Additional spending authority totaling $13.5 million was provided to fund technical support and educational activities provided by the America's Byways Resource Center. In October 2009, U.S. Transportation Secretary Ray LaHood announced 42 new designations to the America's Byways collection, including five All-American Roads and 37 National Scenic Byways in 26 states. This increases the number of America's Byways to 151.

Rental Cars

An important aspect of automobile travel is the **rental car** industry, whose growth has been paralleling or exceeding the growth in air travel. While there is no question about the rental car business having heavy use by businesses, it also has substantial vacation use and frequent combination-trip use.

Air travel is critical to the car rental business as airport revenues account for much of overall car rentals in the United States. Hertz is the airport market leader with about 25 percent of the airport rental business.

According to *Business Travel News* (*BTN*) in its *2010 Business Travel Survey*, the rental car industry grosses around $25 billion. The major companies are Hertz, Enterprise, Avis, Budget, National, Alamo, Dollar Thrifty. Table 5.4 shows them ranked by their 2009 total revenue.

Recent years have witnessed a vast change in the ownership of the major rental car companies as consolidation has taken place. Enterprise now owns Alamo and National (and continues to operate these two brands under the Enterprise umbrella), while Avis has acquired Budget to form the Avis Budget group. It still operates the two brands as distinctive entities, with Avis targeting the premium business and leisure customer and Budget targeting the value-conscious renter. Dollar Thrifty has been courted by both Hertz and Avis Budget.

A customer-oriented transportation system requires that the interface between different modes of travel be facilitated. Technology is increasingly used to ensure fast and convenient service. *Photo courtesy of Budget Rent-A-Car Company.*

TABLE 5.4 U.S. Rental Car Companies, Ranked by Revenue, 2009

Car Company	Revenue ($000,000)
1 Enterprise	$12,100
2 Hertz	6,000
3 Avis	3,100
4 Budget	1,400
5 Dollar Thrifty	1,648

Source: Business Travel News.

Enterprise Rent-A-Car is one of the surprises in the rental car business. The privately held rental car firm has the largest revenue ($12.1 million) and one of the largest fleets of rental cars in the United States, with over 842,000. It was launched as an insurance replacement firm that supplies rental cars to people whose vehicles have been damaged or stolen or are undergoing mechanical repairs. In addition to this market segment, Enterprise has now gone global and serves all rental markets. However, airport locations are dominated by the big four brands: Hertz, Avis, Budget, and National. Enterprise delivers its cars to customers who phone for service.

Computerized navigation systems have come to rental cars and are predicted to be a growing attraction. Bookings over the Internet are increasing.

Many of the auto rental systems are international and have services in virtually every tourist destination area in the world. These companies arrange for the purchase, lease, or rental of automobiles domestically and abroad. Companies representative of this type of organization are American Rental System; Auto Europe; Europcar International; Hertz International, Ltd.; the Kemwel Group, Inc.; and Inter Rent.

Taxi and Limousine Service

Taxi and limousine service plays an exceedingly important part in tourism. Local transportation companies perform vital services for air, bus, rail, and cruise lines. Businesspersons and tourists alike

At many destinations, visitors begin their journey in a taxi. Cab drivers represent the "first ambassador" of a destination and thus are critically important to visitor satisfaction. *Photo courtesy of Corbis Digital Stock.*

would have a difficult time getting from place to place if these services were not available. Streetcars, trolleys, inclines, and aerial trams serve as a form of taxi service and are of a special interest to visitors in scenic tourist destination areas as a form of recreation and sightseeing.

The Taxicab, Limousine, and Paratransit Association (TLPA) in Kensington, Maryland, is the major taxicab association. TLPA has 1,100 members who are fleet owners operating thousands of passenger vehicles, including taxicabs, limousines, liveries, vans, airport shuttle fleets, and minibuses. The association sponsors an annual convention and trade show, is involved with political action, and publishes *Transportation Leader* quarterly.

The National Limousine Association, located in Marlton, New Jersey, was founded in 1985, has 2,000 members, and is made up of limousine owners and operators and limousine manufacturers and suppliers to the industry. It seeks to promote and advance industry professionalism, the common interests of members, and the use of limousines. It monitors legislation; sponsors seminars on safety, regulatory issues, and management; compiles statistics; and offers insurance plans.

Oil Companies

Oil companies the world over have a very important stake in automobile tourism and, thus, are organized in many ways to serve the wants and needs of travelers. In the United States, many of the major oil companies publish road maps as a touring service. Some companies have organized motor clubs, such as the Amoco Motor Club, which provides travel information and routing services for its members, among other services.

Automobile Clubs and Organizations

The American Automobile Association (AAA) is the world's largest single-membership travel group, with a membership of over 50 million people in the United States and Canada. This organization promotes travel in several different forms among its members, including auto travel as a primary form of transportation. It also operates worldwide travel services similar to those provided by a travel agency or tour company. The AAA Travel Agency also provides travel services for nonmembers and is, thus, competitive with other tour companies and retail travel agencies. This additional service gives the club a certain glamour and status in the community, and nonmembers who are brought into the club office through the travel service become prospective new members in the automobile club.

AAA provides emergency road service to members. It also provides insurance protection to motorists through its various state and city affiliate organizations (such as AAA Michigan), publishes travel maps and tour books, and has a national touring board as well as a national touring bureau staff. The principal function of the tour books is to describe the history, attractions, points of interest, and accommodations in hotels, resorts, and motels, and restaurants that have been inspected and approved by AAA field representatives. All accommodations listed have been selected on the basis of a satisfactory report submitted by the AAA field representative.

An organization of wider geographic membership is the World Touring and Automobile Organization, with headquarters in London, England. Other organizations of a similar nature are the International Road Federation of Washington, D.C.; the Pan American Highway Congress, Washington, D.C.; Inter-American Federation of Touring and Automobile Clubs, Buenos Aires; and the International Automobile Federation, with headquarters in Paris.

THE CRUISE INDUSTRY

Cruise Lines International Association (CLIA) states that cruising is currently the fastest-growing segment of the travel industry. It is experiencing a surge of growth in passengers, ships, and ship

Trams and cable cars can greatly enhance visitors' abilities to enjoy many different views of a destination. Here, the halfway point on the Palm Springs tram's journey from the 2,643-foot Valley Station to the 8,516-foot Mountain Station is reached when the two cars pass between towers two and three. At this point, the two cars are 34 feet apart. *Photo courtesy of the Palm Springs Aerial Tramway.*

passenger capacity. **Cruise lines** are expanding their fleets and adding new amenities and new ports of call. As with other sectors of travel suppliers, a great deal of consolidation is taking place.

Since 1990, the industry has had an average annual growth rate of about 7.2 percent. In 1990, 3.8 million passengers cruised; in 2009, a new record was set with 13.4 million passengers (see Table 5.5). The average length of a cruise in 2009 was 7.2 days. CLIA estimates that a record 14.4 million passengers will take a cruise in 2010. The increase in travelers choosing to cruise in 2010 is supported by the introduction of 12 new ships, adding 23,080 beds to the fleet. CLIA member lines have invested more than $21.5 billion in 26 new vessels that will enter service between 2010 and the end of 2012. This will be a capacity increase of 18 percent.

Although ships have been a means of transportation since early times, the cruise industry is young. Its purpose is really to provide a resort experience rather than point-to-point transportation. Though

TABLE 5.5 Annual Cruise Passenger Growth

Year	Actual (000s)		
	North America	Foreign	Worldwide
1990	3,496	278	3,774
1991	3,834	334	4,168
1992	4,023	362	4,385
1993	4,318	410	4,728
1994	4,314	486	4,800
1995	4,223	498	4,721
1996	4,477	493	4,970
1997	4,864	516	5,380
1998	5,243	625	5,868
1999	5,690	647	6,337
2000	6,546	668	7,214
2001	6,637	862	7,499
2002	7,472	1,176	8,648
2003	7,990	1,536	9,526
2004	8,870	1,590	10,460
2005	9,671	1,509	11,180
2006	10,078	1,928	12,006
2007	10,247	2,316	12,563
2008[a]	10,093	2,912	13,005
2009[b]	10,198	3,244	13,442

[a] estimated
[b] projected

Source: Cruise Lines International Association.

the modern-day cruise industry is barely 30 years old, it has established itself as an important component of the United States travel and tourism industry. According to a study by Business Research Economic Advisors (BREA), the North American cruise industry generated $40.2 billion in total economic activity in 2008. An estimated 357,700 American jobs were created.

Historically, most of the cruise companies have focused their marketing efforts on North American clientele. However, with a marked increase in recent years of European, South American, and Asian vacationers taking American-style cruises, cruise companies have begun to pay more attention to the international markets. Additionally, some of these cruise companies have positioned ships in Europe and Asia for seasonal operations, thereby creating greater awareness among European and Asian clientele.

The cruise industry's performance and satisfaction are the pacesetter for the rest of the travel industry. No other vacation category can touch a cruise for product satisfaction and repeat business.

Growth has affected not only passenger and ship capacity but the ports of embarkation as well.

Embarkation Ports

Ports within the state of Florida serve as home for the majority of the U.S.-based cruise industry. This is primarily due to the state's close proximity to the prime cruising waters of the Caribbean. Most of these cruises are 3, 4, or 7 days in length, though there are some voyages of 10 or 14 days. Miami currently claims the title "Cruise Capital of the World." Ports in Fort Lauderdale, Tampa, and Port Canaveral also play host to a number of cruise ships. Several ships operating Caribbean cruises are also based in New Orleans.

New York City and Boston are popular embarkation points for cruises to New England, Bermuda, and Canada's Maritime Provinces. On the West Coast of the United States, both Los Angeles and San Diego are home ports for cruises of three, four, or seven days to Mexico. San Francisco and Seattle are also popular ports. San Juan, Puerto Rico, a U.S. territory, has also become a popular port of embarkation for seven-day cruises to the southern Caribbean.

One of the most popular summertime cruising areas in recent years is Alaska's Inside Passage. These cruises are frequently combined with land excursions into Alaska's interior and the Yukon Territory. Most of these cruises depart from Vancouver, British Columbia, Canada.

Cruise Itineraries Cover the Globe

Though the islands of the Caribbean continue to be the leading year-round destination, CLIA member cruise lines service cruising areas around the world. The Mediterranean Sea plays host to an increasing number of cruise ships during the summer season, and CLIA reports that the industry continues to show an increased emphasis on European and Southeast Asia itineraries. In 2010, the Caribbean share was over 41 percent. The Mediterranean, Europe, Alaska, and Mexico followed the Caribbean in popularity. Today these destinations remain strong, but the trend is to visit destinations farther afield, with regions such as Asia, South America, and the South Pacific becoming hot destinations.

Security

The cruise industry's highest priority is to ensure the security and safety of its passengers and crew. CLIA works closely with the Department of Homeland Security (DHS), which now houses the U.S. Coast Guard, Customs and Border Protection, Bureau of Immigration and Customs Enforcement, and Transportation Security Administration. By working with these agencies, the industry ensures compliance with all U.S. and international maritime standards established to maintain shipboard security.

CLIA MEMBER LINES

AMA Waterways	MSC Cruises
American Cruise Lines	Norwegian Cruise Line
Avalon Waterways	Oceania Cruises
Azamara Club Cruises	Paul Gauguin Cruises
Carnival Cruise Lines	Pearl Seas Cruises
Celebrity Cruises	Princess Cruises
Costa Cruises	Regent Seven Seas Cruises
Crystal Cruises	Royal Caribbean International
Cunard Line	Seabourn Cruise Line
Disney Cruise Line	SeaDream Yacht Club
Holland America Line	Silversea Cruises
Hurtigruten (formerly Norwegian Coastal Voyage Inc.)	Uniworld River Cruises
	Windstar Cruises

Consolidation

The consolidation that has been taking place in the travel industry is rampant in the cruise sector as well. Carnival Corporation, the world's largest cruise company, recently acquired Princess Cruises, and already owned Cunard, Costa, Holland America, Windstar, and Seabourn. Royal Caribbean International (RCI) is the second-largest player and recently acquired Celebrity Cruises. Competition is fierce, with these two companies adding new passenger ships. Disney now is in the cruise business and is adding a new ship.

Although CLIA members (see box) represent over 90 percent of the North American cruise market and over 80 percent of the ships, the world cruise fleet is supplemented by freighter cruises, river cruises, yachts, ferries, and charters. About 80 freighters provide accommodations for a limited number of passengers, such as 6 to 12. Freighter cruises tend to last a long time, go to unknown parts, have schedules that can change rapidly, and are moderately priced. They appeal to the more adventurous traveler.

River Cruises

Along with ocean cruises, river cruising has experienced rapid growth over the past decade, especially in Europe, where the number of passengers has more than quadrupled.

In comparison with ocean cruises, river cruise ships tend to be smaller, carrying around 100 to 150 passengers, generally travel only by day, and have onshore visits to cities and sites of cultural or historical interest built into the itinerary. In many ways they are more like a tour than a cruise. River cruises have a definite competitive advantage over bus trips as there is no need to unpack and repack luggage at every stop. An advantage over ocean cruising is that there is no risk of seasickness. River cruise passengers can sightsee from the comfort of the ship, an appealing feature to older travelers, who are the principal market for river cruising. The rapid aging of Europe and North America populations over the next 20 years bodes well for the future growth of river cruising.

Popular river cruise destinations are in Egypt on the Nile, in China on the Yangtze, in Brazil on the Amazon, in Russia between St. Petersburg and Moscow, in the Ukraine on the Dnieper River, and in Europe on the Rhine, Danube, Main, Seine, Rhône, and Elbe, just to mention a few. Barge and canal trips are also popular in many places.

Viking is the world's largest river cruise line. Other major operators are AMA Waterways, Avalon Waterways, Croisi Europe, Globus/Cosmo, Grand Circle, INTRAV, Lüftner, Nicko Tours, Scylla, and Uniworld.

Cruise Lines International Association

Cruise Lines International Association, Inc. is a marketing and promotional trade organization made up of 25 of the major cruise lines serving North America, representing more than 200 ships (see box). CLIA was formed in 1975 out of a need for the cruise industry to develop a vehicle to promote the general concept of cruising. In 2006, it merged with the International Council of Cruise Lines (ICCL), a sister entity created in 1990 dedicated to participating in the regulatory and policy development process of the cruise industry. Today, CLIA exists to promote all measures that foster a safe, secure, and healthy cruise ship environment; educate; train its agent members; and promote and explain the value, desirability, and affordability of the cruise vacation experience.

When, in mid-1984, the Federal Maritime Commission consolidated other industry organizations into CLIA, it became the sole marketing organization of the cruise industry. CLIA represents 97 percent of the cruise industry; more than 14,000 travel agents are affiliated with CLIA and display the CLIA seal, which identifies them as authorities on cruise vacations. The CLIA headquarters is located at 910 SE 17th Street, Suite 400, Fort Lauderdale, FL 33316; telephone (754) 224-2200; fax (754) 224-2250; the Web site is www.cruising.org.

OTHER MODES OF TRANSPORTATION

Although tourists use planes, trains, motorcoaches, taxis, shuttle buses, boats, and cruise ships to arrive at destinations, other modes of transportation are also an integral part of tourism. One of the most important and easily overlooked is pedestrian travel, or walking. Tourists and locals alike depend on their feet as a primary mode of travel. Tourists are great walkers, covering many miles sightseeing or using their feet to arrive at an attraction, sidewalk café, or gelato stand. Thus, it is imperative that pedestrian environments and the surface where tourists walk and the areas in which they move are welcoming and safe. Tourism planners must make pedestrian travel part of their development plans.

The walking paths by the river in Brisbane, Australia, are an outstanding example of good planning benefiting both tourist and locals with an attractive, safe, integrated transportation scheme. In contrast, walking in Cairo, Egypt, or Kuala Lumpur, Malaysia, is a challenge.

In addition, walking tours around the world have proven popular, as evidenced by the many itineraries offered by such firms as Country Walkers, whose slogan is "Explore the world one step at a time."®

Cycling is another mode embraced by some travelers and tourist destinations. A number of companies feature biking tours. The Hoge Veluwe National Park in Holland is laced with paths for cars, bicycles, and walkers. There are more than 27 miles of paths specifically designed for bicycling. While most people visit the park for the Kroller-Muller Museum (famous for its Van Gogh paintings), the park also contains a magnificent sculpture garden, forests, and sand dunes. It is possible to cycle your way around the park, thanks to a thousand-plus fleet of free-to-use white bicycles. The fleet of bicycles reduces bus and auto traffic in the park and allows tourists a convenient way to see all the sights.

Trams, cable cars, gondolas, and ski lifts are all additional modes of transportation that are important to specific resorts and destinations. They facilitate the flow of tourists and in many cases bring them to places that would otherwise be inaccessible. Also, they can be tourist attractions themselves.

SUMMARY

Transportation services and facilities are an integral component of tourism. In fact, the success of practically all forms of travel depends on adequate transportation. Transportation services and facilities are the arteries through which the lifeblood of the travel industry flows. Travel by air dominates long- and middle-distance travel in the United States. But private automobiles carry the bulk (about 80 percent) of all travelers on short trips. Automobiles are also very important on long and international trips. Rental cars are popular, because they supplement air travel. Rail travel in the United States has declined substantially since the 1950s but is still important in commuting and longer-haul traffic. Motorcoach transportation is available in far more places than either air or rail, but it constitutes a rather small percentage of total vehicle miles. Vacationing on cruise ships has become the fastest-growing segment of the U.S. travel industry. New and refurbished cruise ships are appearing regularly.

Associations and groups of passenger carriers are important to their sectors' well-being and growth. Some of the most important are Air Transport Association of America; American Bus Association; United Motorcoach Association; American Automobile Association (affiliated with the Canadian Automobile Association); World Touring and Automobile Association; Recreation Vehicle Industry Association; Taxicab, Limousine, and Paratransit Association; National Limousine Association; and the Cruise Lines International Association.

Increases in almost all forms of tourism automatically boost passenger traffic, sometimes creating problems. Congestion can be especially bad on streets and roads and at airport terminals. Safety and security are basic requirements, and successful tourism depends on these factors. The environment will be affected by any form of transportation. Careful planning and increased awareness and preventive measures are needed to minimize such undesirable effects.

Long-term projections show increases in the demand for transportation. Increased taxes and fuel prices on this industry are having an adverse effect. It is hoped that these can be mitigated in time. Rail travel is increasing in Europe and Asia, where high-speed trains are being used.

 KEY CONCEPTS

airline industry	automobile	recreation vehicles
Air Transport Association	cruise lines	rental cars
alliances	motorcoaches	safety and security
American Automobile Association	National Scenic Byways program	taxi and limousine service
American Bus Association	oil companies	
Amtrak	rail transportation	

INTERNET EXERCISES

The Internet sites mentioned in this chapter plus some selected additional sites are listed for your convenience on the companion Web site for this book, www.wiley.com/college/goeldner.

ACTIVITY 1

Site Name: Cruise Lines International Association, Inc. (CLIA)

URL: www.cruising.org

Background Information: CLIA's primary objective is to help the over 14,000 CLIA-affiliated agencies become more successful at capitalizing on the booming and profitable cruise market. CLIA has 25 member lines, which represent 97 percent of the cruise industry.

Exercises

1. You are working for a travel agency and have a family in your office. You realize early in the conversation that the wife is very interested in a cruise but the husband has some definite reservations. After probing for several minutes, the husband identifies the following concerns and questions he has about cruises: (1) I will get bored and feel confined. (2) I am afraid I will get seasick. (3)

Cruises are only for rich people. (4) What can you do with kids on a ship? (5) What is there to do at night? How would you address these concerns/questions in order to sell this family a cruise?

2. Choose a cruise line and develop a summary of entertainment features the cruise line offers.

3. Choose a cruise line and identify what packages they offer for honeymooners and for families with children.

ACTIVITY 2

Site Name: Air Transport Association (ATA)

URL: www.airlines.org

Background Information: The Air Transport Association of America is the trade organization of principal U.S. airlines. ATA airline members and their affiliates transport more than 90 percent of all U.S. airline passenger and cargo traffic.

Exercises

1. What does the site say about airline safety?

2. What is the forecast for future air travel?

QUESTIONS FOR REVIEW AND DISCUSSION

1. Explain why air travel now dominates long- and middle-distance travel.

2. What were the main reasons that rail passenger transportation declined in the United States after 1920?

3. Identify the social and economic factors that would bring about a resurgence in motorcoach travel.

4. Describe the principal appeals of cruising.

5. Why is the cruise market expected to continue its extraordinary growth pattern?

6. What might be at least a partial solution to the problem of automobile congestion at major airports?

7. Similarly, make clear your ideas for alleviating flight arrival and departure congestion.

8. If you knew in advance that you would have a long drive through heavy traffic to reach the airport, followed by a wait in line for 30 minutes at the airline

departure desk, and 30 minutes at security, and that your plane would remain on the runway for 30 minutes before taking off, would you still make the pleasure trip?

9. Evaluate the importance of safety and security in all forms of travel. What is the safest mode of passenger transportation?

10. Taking each mode of transportation, what specifically can be done to minimize damage to the environment?

11. If you were vice president of marketing for an airline, what programs would you undertake to even out peaks and valleys in demand?

 CASE PROBLEMS

1. The Rotary Club program chairman has asked you to give a talk on the advantages of cruises. He has also hinted that club members might be interested in taking a group cruise with their spouses and children. What would you include in your talk?

2. Air transportation is truly a global industry. However, future growth in world demand is being impeded by many nations that have enacted various air regulations and restrictive laws. A beginning toward a "new world order" of global competition and interconnectedness has occurred. The first "open skies" agreement was established between the United States and The Netherlands. This agreement, dubbed Open Skies I, signals the beginning of open skies becoming global. The agreement abolishes all legal and diplomatic environments, as well as all other trade barriers, that impede airline efficiency. It also encourages competition. The Open Skies I accord completely deregulates air services between the two countries. Now such a pact has been agreed to between the United States and the European Union. How will this affect demand for travel on the world's airlines? Explain and give several examples.

ENDNOTES

1. International Air Transport Association and Air Transport Association of America annual reports, news releases, speeches, and Web sites.
2. Amtrak Annual Report, 2009, p. 9 and www.amtrak.com.
3. Amtrak Annual Report, 2009, p. 4.
4. RVIA, *Industry Profile 2009* (Reston, VA: RVIA, 2010), and the RVIA Web site.
5. Richard Curtain, *The RV Consumer Demographic Profile* (Reston, VA: RVIA, 2005) and the RVIA Web site, Frequently Asked Questions and Quick Facts Section.

CHAPTER 6

Hospitality and Related Services

- Study the lodging industry, its ancient origins, its associations, names of leading companies, and its vital role in the economy.

- Appreciate the immensity of the restaurant food service industry.

- Learn the current trends in resorts and timesharing modes of operation.

- Discover why meetings and conventions, as well as meeting planners, are so important to tourism.

There are numerous resorts on the Mexican coast, such as those found in Manzanillo. *Photo courtesy of Corbis Digital Stock.*

INTRODUCTION

As noted in Chapter 2, providing overnight accommodations for travelers goes back into antiquity; it is the world's oldest commercial business. Guest rooms were first part of private dwellings. Then came caravansaries and guest quarters provided in monasteries. Today, lodging and food service activities are enormous in economic importance. Many lodging places provide meeting rooms, convention facilities and services, restaurants, bars, entertainment, gift shops, gaming, health clubs, and other activities and facilities. Figure 6.1 extracts the operating sectors from Figure 1.2 and shows that accommodations and food services are critical sectors of the tourism industry. See Figure 6.2 for the structure of the accommodations industry. In this chapter, we examine this industry as well as the even larger food service business, meetings and conventions, and related services.

THE LODGING INDUSTRY

The United Nations World Tourism Organization (UNWTO) estimates that the world hotel room inventory grows by about 2.5 percent a year. Occupancy rates vary, but they average about 65 percent overall in a normal year. Such places as London, Beijing, New York, San Francisco, Hawaii, the Caribbean area, and the city of Las Vegas are noted for higher occupancy rates.

World hotel accommodations are heavily concentrated in Europe and North America, with Europe accounting for 44.7 percent of the world's room supply and the United States accounting for 27 percent, for a total of over 71 percent. Asia and the Pacific region account for 13.9 percent, Africa 3.1 percent, and the Middle East 1.5 percent. The most growth is taking place in the Asia-Pacific region.

According to the **American Hotel and Lodging Association** (AH&LA), the U.S. **lodging industry** (which includes hotels, motels, suites, and resort properties) recorded a profitable year in 2009. The industry grossed $16.0 billion in pretax profits in 2009, down considerably from $25.8 billion in 2008,

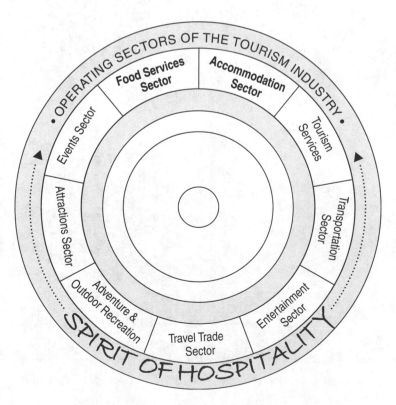

Figure 6.1 Operating sectors of the tourism industry: accommodation and food services.

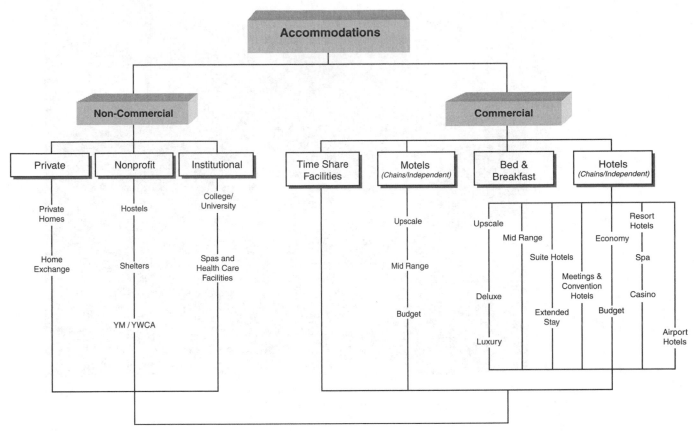

Figure 6.2 Accommodations structure.

which was already down from the previous record $26.6 billion in pretax profits in 2006, reflecting the harsh economic conditions of the global recession in 2008 and 2009.

The AH&LA 2010 Lodging Industry Profile shows the industry numbered 50,800 properties, 4.76 million rooms, $127.2 billion in sales, $16.0 billion in pretax profit, 54.7 percent average occupancy rate, and $53.50 revenue per available room (RevPAR, a combination of occupancy and average room rate). The average room rate was $97.85 in 2009, down from $106.84 in 2008.[1]

Who is the typical lodging customer? According to the AH&LA, 40 percent are business travelers and 60 percent are leisure travelers. The typical business room night is generated by a male (69 percent), age 35 to 54 (48 percent), employed in a professional or managerial position (53 percent), and earning an average yearly household income of $105,764. Typically, these guests travel alone (64 percent), make reservations (91 percent), and pay $123 per room night.

The typical leisure room night is generated by two adults (51 percent), ages 35 to 54 (40 percent), and earning an average yearly household income of $90,712. The typical leisure traveler also travels by auto (80 percent), makes reservations (87 percent), and pays $105 per room night.

For a hotel stay, 36 percent of all business travelers spend one night, 22 percent spend two nights, and 42 percent spend three or more nights. Of leisure travelers, 48 percent spend one night, 25 percent spend two nights, and 27 percent spend three or more nights.

The impact of international travelers on the hotel industry is considerable. In 2009, 18.5 million overseas travelers stayed in a hotel or motel. Their average length of stay in a hotel was 8.2 nights, with 1.7 people in the travel party. The main purposes of trips for overseas travelers who stayed in hotels and motels were leisure, recreation, and holiday at 61 percent, and business at 27 percent. These extremely mobile travelers visited 1.6 states while in the country. To move about the United States, they rented cars (33 percent), took taxis and limousines (48 percent), and traveled by air (27 percent).[2]

Elegance and comfort meet in this spacious double guest room at the Phoenician Resort in Scottsdale, Arizona, which also offers scenic views of the desert. *Photo courtesy of the Phoenician.*

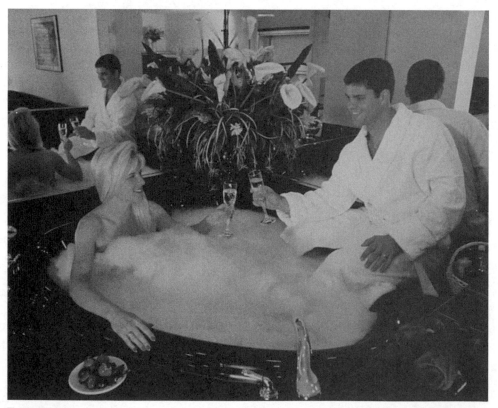

The hospitality industry creates many unique, pleasurable, and memorable experiences for the tourist. *Photo courtesy of Holiday Inn Family Suites Resort, Lake Buena Vista, Orlando, Florida.*

Technology has had a profound influence on the lodging industry in recent years. Over 90 percent of hotel companies have Web sites, and industry surveys show that business travelers want Internet access in their guest rooms. Many hotels are becoming wireless. Online expenditures for hotel bookings are increasing.

Self-service check-in and check-out continues to grow as self-service kiosks are multiplying. The kiosks are located in the lobby and allow the guests to check in or out of the hotel by simply swiping their credit card, eliminating the need to go to the front desk. The kiosks are similar to the ones used by the airlines. Major chains, such as Hyatt, Hilton, Marriott, Sheraton, and Fairmont, are installing kiosks that allow busy customers to check themselves in and get a key. According to kiosk maker NCR Corporation, a person who checks in at a kiosk can speed the process by 48 percent.

Smith Travel Research and AH&LA provide valuable information on the lodging industry. In addition to the annual lodging profile, AH&LA has Smith Travel Research do a comprehensive study of the industry periodically. The last AH&LA study was released in 2010 and looked at the size, scope, and emerging trends of the lodging industry and made comparisons with previous studies.

The lodging industry has increased their emphasis on market segmentation in recent years. Many of the big chains offer products at almost every price level: full-service luxury hotels, luxury all-suite hotels, resort hotels, moderately priced full-service hotels, moderately priced all-suites, moderately priced limited-service, and economy or budget motels. Hotels and motels are classified in a variety of ways. One of the most common is by location, such as resort, city center, airport, suburban, or highway.

Rank

There are a number of very large companies in the lodging industry, and many of the big chains are getting bigger. *Hotels* (published by Marketing and Technology Group, a Chicago-based business-to-business media company whose properties serve the global information needs of professionals in the food service and hospitality industries) compiles an annual listing of the world's 325 largest corporate hotel chains. The October 2010 issue reports the fortieth annual listing of lodging's giant companies. The concentration of the lodging industry is clearly demonstrated by the ranking of the top 25, which appears in Table 6.1. The ranking is based on the number of rooms. The top ten companies have 4.3 million rooms. *Hotels* reports that the InterContinental Hotel Group continues to head the list with a total room count of 646,679. Wyndham Hotel Group (formerly Cendant) was second with 597,674. Marriott International ranked third with 595,461 rooms. Hilton Hotels Corporation was fourth with 585,060, and Accor Hotels rounded out the top five with 499,456.

While 14 of the top 25 international franchised hotel chains are headquartered in the United States, the list is global. England has the top-ranked InterContinental Hotels Group; France has Accor, ranked fifth, and Groupe du Louvre, ranked twelfth; China has Jin Jiang International Hotels, ranked thirteenth, Home Inns and Hotels Management, ranked nineteenth, and GreenTree Inns and Hotel Management Group, Inc., ranked twenty-second; Germany has TUI AG Hotels and Resorts, ranked fourteenth; Belgium has the Rezidor Hotel Group, ranked fifteenth; and Spain has Sol Melia SA, ranked seventeenth, NH Hoteles SA, ranked twenty-first, and Barcelo Hotels and Resorts ranked twenty-fourth.

Trends

The trend in the lodging industry has been away from independently owned and operated properties toward chain and franchise affiliations, which get larger and larger. There are also referral groups or voluntary membership associations. Both independents and chains have found it profitable to join together to market their properties.

❖ GLOSSARY ❖

- **ADR (average daily rate).** A measure of the average rate paid for rooms sold, calculated by dividing room revenue by rooms sold (ADR = Room revenue/Rooms sold).

- **Food & beverage (F&B) revenue.** Revenues derived from the sale of food (including coffee, milk, tea, and soft drinks), beverages (including beer, wine, and liquors), banquet beverages and other F&B sources. Other F&B sources include meeting room rentals, audiovisual equipment rentals, cover or service charges or other revenues within the food and beverage department (includes banquet services charges).

- **Occupancy.** Occupancy is the percentage of available rooms that were sold during a specified period of time. Occupancy is calculated by dividing the number of rooms sold by rooms available (Occupancy = Rooms sold/Rooms available).

- **RevPAR (revenue per available room).** Revenue per available room (RevPAR) is the total guest room revenue divided by the total number of available rooms. RevPAR differs from ADR because RevPAR is affected by the amount of unoccupied available rooms, while ADR shows only the average rate of rooms actually sold (Occupancy × ADR = RevPAR).

- **Room revenue.** Total room revenue generated from the sale or rental of rooms.

- **Rooms available (room supply).** The number of rooms in a hotel or set of hotels multiplied by the number of days in a specified time period. Example: 100 available rooms in subject hotel × 31 days in the month = room supply of 3,100 for the month.

- **Rooms sold (room demand).** The number of rooms sold in a specified time period (excludes complimentary rooms).

- **Total revenue.** Revenue from all hotel operations, including rooms sold, F&B, parking, laundry, phone, miscellaneous, etc.

The trend toward consolidation and acquisition will continue because chains have the potential for improvement in productivity and because of the advantages that accrue to large size. Chains can most effectively use training programs, employee selection programs, major equipment with different layouts, prices, advertising, equipment, technology, marketing, and so on, and what works well in one property can be employed chainwide. One reason for the popularity of the referral groups is that members who are independent operators achieve the marketing benefits of chains without chain membership.

Franchising is also well known in the lodging industry and has made a rapid penetration into the marketplace. However, franchising generates mixed reports. Many managements believe that it is difficult to control the franchises and maintain the quality that the chain advertises and the standards that are supposed to be met. Thus, many chains are buying back franchises to ensure that management maintains the quality level desired. In other cases, firms are moving ahead rapidly with franchising because they can conserve cash and expand more rapidly by franchising. In addition, the franchisee, having invested his or her own capital, has great motivation to succeed.

Franchisees have the advantage that they receive a known "name," as well as the knowledge, advice, and assistance of a proven operator. Franchising also spreads the costs of promotion, advertising, and reservation systems over all outlets, making the unit cost much lower. If the franchiser has an excellent reputation and image, the franchisee benefits greatly. Most of the companies with franchise operations also operate company-owned units. Industry predictions are that as the industry grows and matures, there will be less franchising, which will give the chains more control over their properties and operations so that they can maintain the desired quality control. Increased competitiveness and improved properties will necessitate having the ability to make these improvements.

A trend in the lodging industry appears to be that more large properties will be operated under management contracts. Investors, such as insurance companies, frequently purchase hotel properties and turn them over to chains or independents to manage—a process that has advantages to both parties. The owner has the financial resources and the manager has the reputation and experience to manage the property profitably. Other trends are the increased use of central reservation systems, emphasis on service, and the use of yield management techniques.

TABLE 6.1   Top Twenty-Five Hotel Chains

Rank[a]	Company Headquarters	Rooms 2009	Hotels 2009
1	**InterContinental Hotels Group,** Windsor, England	646,679	4,438
2	**Wyndham Hotel Group,** Parsippany, New Jersey	597,674	7,114
3	**Marriott International,** Bethesda, Maryland	595,461	3,420
4	**Hilton Worldwide,** McLean, Virginia	585,060	3,530
5	**Accor Hospitality,** Paris, France	499,456	4,120
6	**Choice Hotels International,** Silver Spring, Maryland	487,410	6,021
7	**Best Western International,** Phoenix, Arizona	308,477	4,048
8	**Starwood Hotels & Resorts Worldwide,** White Plains, New York	298,522	992
9	**Carlson Hospitality Worldwide,** Minneapolis, Minnesota	159,756	1,058
10	**Hyatt Hotels Corp.,** Chicago, Illinois	122,317	424
11	**Westmount Hospitality Group,** Houston, Texas	113,771	803
12	**Groupe du Louvre,** Paris, France	91,409	1,097
13	**Jin Jiang International Hotels,** Shanghai, China	89,251	546
14	**TUI AG,** Hannover, Germany	83,728	297
15	**Rezidor Hotel Group,** Brussels, Belgium	83,200	389
16	**LQ Management,** Irving, Texas	78,945	766
17	**Sol Meliá SA,** Palma de Mallorca, Spain	76,887	305
18	**Extended Stay Hotels,** Spartanburg, South Carolina	76,384	686
19	**Home Inns & Motels Management,** Shanghai, China	71,671	616
20	**Vantage Hospitality Group,** Coral Springs, Florida	65,232	906
21	**NH Hoteles SA,** Madrid, Spain	61,317	401
22	**GreenTree Inns Hotel Management Group,** Shanghai, China	49,700	450
23	**Interstate Hotels & Resorts,** Arlington, Virginia	46,129	228
24	**Barcelo Hotels & Resorts,** Palma de Mallorca, Spain	45,939	181
25	**MGM Resorts International,** Las Vega, Nevada	45,701	16

[a]Rankings are based on total rooms.

Source: Hotels, October 2010.

Bed and Breakfasts, Guest Houses, Inns

Moving from the megacorporate chain to the **bed and breakfasts (B&Bs)**, guest houses, and inn establishments demonstrates the diversity in lodging accommodations and the fact that many small businesses make up much of the tourism industry. Those small business sectors of the lodging industry encompass a number of different types of operation. A B&B is a small lodging establishment that offers overnight accommodation and breakfast. Typically, B&Bs are private homes with fewer than 10 bedrooms available for commercial use and are family owned.

A guest house is a kind of lodging that is defined differently around the world. In some parts of the world, guest houses are similar to a hostel, bed and breakfast, or inn, whereas in other parts of the world (Caribbean) guest houses are a type of inexpensive hotel type lodging. In still others, they are private homes that have been converted for guest accommodation. In the United Kingdom, B&B and guest house enterprises are not significantly different.

One of the increasingly popular amenities offered by modern hotels is a fitness facility. These are provided in response to the changing lifestyles and demands of customers.
Photo courtesy of Hot Springs Lodge & Pool.

Country inns are owner-operated establishments providing lodging and meals (usually breakfast and dinner). They are usually larger, typically ten or more rooms, and offer a number of amenities. Many inns provide Internet, magazines, hot/cold beverages, games, fireplace, refrigerator, newspapers, telephone, cookies/cakes/candy/fruit, flowers, and televisions in common areas. In guest rooms, they might provide Internet, television, luxury bed/linens, branded toiletries, and robes.

The Professional Association of Innkeepers International (PAII) uses the terms B&B and inns interchangeably and state they are operated by innkeepers.

B&Bs in the United States began as inexpensive informal places to stay with shared baths and minimal amenities, but today many B&Bs have evolved into accommodations with high levels of comfort, service, and amenities. Thus, B&Bs provide both luxury and economy accommodations.

Insight into the characteristics and operation of B&Bs is provided by the trade association, the Professional Association of Innkeepers International (PAII), which hired Industry Insights to study the operations, marketing, and finances of B&Bs. The PAII study is the nation's (U.S.) only authoritative and comprehensive research report on the finances and operations of this segment of the hospitality industry. *PAII 2009-10 Industry Study* shows the B&B industry is $3.4 billion in size. The average B&B had six rooms, an average daily rate of $150.00, an average occupancy rate of 41 percent, and RevPAR of $58.00. The study found 29 percent were in rural locations, 23 percent were urban, 5 percent were suburban, and 43 were village; 87 percent were tourist destination/resort properties; 94 percent of rooms had a private bath; 5,700 square feet is the average size of a B&B; 36 percent have achieved an "historical designation" by a local, state or national historic preservation organization; 72 percent are run by owner couples; 79 percent of innkeepers live on premise; the average B&B offer free high-speed wireless Internet.[3]

B&Bs provide the best possible avenue for travelers of all ages and locations to experience firsthand the lifestyles in areas of the country previously unknown to guests. The B&B host can become an area's best ambassador. In many cases around the nation, the institution of a B&B has saved a historic property that might otherwise have been destroyed.

B&B reservation services inspect and approve B&B homes and inns, maintain ongoing quality control, and provide one-stop shopping for the traveler. They can provide the traveler with recourse in case of a problem. Reservation services are privately owned corporations, partnerships, or single proprietorships, each representing from 35 to hundreds of host homes and inns.

The Professional Association of Innkeepers International is the leading trade association representing owners of bed and breakfasts and country inns. PAII provides education, communications, public relations, networking, and research services to the industry. Visit the PAII Web site at www.innkeeping.org to learn about its latest studies. Austin, Texas–based BedandBreakfast.com, the largest international travel Web site in the B&B industry has partnered with PAII to help the organization grow and promote awareness that B&Bs are a "Better Way to Stay."

It is difficult to determine how many B&Bs and inns there are in the world. BedandBreakfast.com lists about 11,000 B&Bs in its worldwide database. It offers gift cards good at about 4,000 B&Bs in the United States and Canada. According to the Web site, "BedandBreakfast.com is owned and operated by HomeAway, Inc., the worldwide leader in online vacation rentals, representing more than 475,000 paid vacation rental home listings across 120 countries" (see www.bedandbreakfast.com/about/index.aspx and www.homeaway.com).

The site helps travelers find the ideal B&B or small inns through informative descriptions, photos, and more than 100,000 consumer reviews, and make confirmed reservations instantly at nearly 2,000 properties. The company also operates RezOvation, the industry leader in property management systems, online reservations, Web site design, and Internet marketing for the inn and B&B market.

PROFILE

MR. J. W. MARRIOTT
chairman and chief
executive officer,
Marriott
International, Inc.
Bethesda, Maryland

J. W. Marriott Jr. is chairman and chief executive officer of Marriott International, Inc., one of the world's largest lodging companies. His leadership spans more than 50 years, and he has taken Marriott from a family restaurant business to a global lodging company with more than 3,500 properties in 70 countries and territories.

Mr. Marriott's vision for the company is to be the world's lodging leader. It is grounded in his intense focus on taking care of the guest, extensive operational knowledge, the development of a highly skilled and diverse workforce, and offering the best portfolio of lodging brands in the industry. Under his leadership, Marriott continues to enjoy strong customer, owner, and franchise preference, steady growth, and profitability.

Known throughout the industry for his hands-on management style, Mr. Marriott has built a highly regarded culture that emphasizes the importance of Marriott's people and recognizes the value they bring to the organization. Marriott International's "spirit to serve" culture is based on a business philosophy originated more than 80 years ago by his parents, J. Willard and Alice S. Marriott: "Take care of the associate, and they'll take care of the guest." Today, approximately 300,000 Marriott associates are serving guests in Marriott managed and franchised properties throughout the world.

Marriott International is also well known as a great place to work and for its commitment to diversity, social responsibility, and community engagement. It has consistently been named to *Fortune's* lists of most admired companies, best places to work, and top companies for minorities.

At an early age, Mr. Marriott developed a passion for the business and worked in a variety of positions in the Hot Shoppes restaurant chain during his high school and college years. He joined the company full-time in 1956 and soon afterward, took over management of Marriott's first hotel. Mr. Marriott became executive vice president of the company, then its president, in 1964. He was elected chief executive officer in 1972, and chairman of the board in 1985.

Regarded as a lodging innovator, Mr. Marriott began shifting the company in the late 1970s from hotel ownership to property management and franchising. His strategic decision allowed the company to accelerate its growth and broaden its leadership position. That transformation culminated in the company's split into Marriott International, a hotel management and franchising company, headed by Mr. Marriott, and Host Marriott International, a hotel ownership company chaired by his younger brother, Richard Marriott.

Mr. Marriott has also worked to compile a family of 18 lodging brands that range from limited service to full-service luxury hotels that meet the needs of any traveler. Today, the company manages and franchises hotels and resorts under the Marriott, JW Marriott, The Ritz-Carlton, Renaissance, Residence Inn, Courtyard, Towne-Place Suites, Fairfield Inn, SpringHill Suites, and Bulgari brand names; develops and operates vacation ownership resorts under the Marriott Vacation Club, The Ritz-Carlton Destination Club, and Grand Residences by Marriott brands; licenses and manages whole-ownership residential brands, including The Ritz-Carlton Residences, JW Marriott Residences, and Marriott Residences; operates Marriott Executive Apartments; provides furnished corporate housing through its Marriott ExecuStay division; and operates conference centers.

Mr. Marriott serves on the board of The J. Willard & Alice S. Marriott Foundation. He is a member of the National Business Council and the executive committee of the World Travel & Tourism Council. Mr. Marriott served on the board of trustees of the National Geographic Society, as director of the United States Naval Academy Foundation, as chairman of the President's Export Council (PEC) and as a member of the Secure Borders Open Doors Advisory Committee (SBODAC) and the U.S. Travel and Tourism Advisory Board (TTAB). He also recently served as chairman of the Mayo Clinic Capital Campaign.

Mr. Marriott attended St. Albans School in Washington, D.C., earned a B.S. degree in banking and finance from the University of Utah and served as an officer in the U.S. Navy. He is an active member of The Church of Jesus Christ of Latter-day Saints. He is married to the former Donna Garff. They have 4 children and 15 grandchildren and 5 great grandchildren.

WORDS ABOUT THE FUTURE

In 2012, Marriott celebrates its 85th anniversary. We've come a long way from our origins as a nine-stool root beer stand in downtown Washington, D.C. Today, Marriott has more than 3,500 hotels in 70 countries. Approximately 300,000 people serve guests in Marriott managed and franchised properties throughout the world. Our associates—like our customers—come from every walk of life. They speak many languages, and bring the depth and uniqueness of their cultures to everything they do.

As the travel industry emerges from the worst economic downturn in my career, we anticipate a time of tremendous growth ahead. Marriott is more globally focused than ever before, as we open new hotels in exciting international markets like China, India, and Africa. Growing middle classes in those countries mean new travelers looking to explore the world.

I'm confident that the Travel Promotion Act will help attract more visitors to the United States by marketing "Brand America." We still have work to do to improve our visa and entry processes so that visitors have a positive experience. In the meantime, we need to let the world know that the United States is open for business, and we look forward to welcoming travelers to our shores.

Timeshare Resorts

A **timeshare** is a form of ownership or right to the use of a property, or the term used to describe such properties. Timeshare is also known as vacation ownership. These properties are typically resort condominium units, in which multiple parties hold rights to use the property. Each purchaser is allotted a period of time, typically one week and usually the same time every year, in which they may use the property. Many timeshare purchasers buy more than one week. Units may be on a part-ownership or "right to use" basis. There are also vacation ownership programs, which are based on point systems.

Deeded Timeshare Ownership

In a timeshare, you either own your vacation unit for the rest of your life, for the number of years spelled out in your purchase contract, or until you sell it. Your interest is legally considered real property. You purchase the right to use a specific unit at a specific time every year, and you may rent, sell, exchange, or bequeath your specific timeshare unit. You and the other timeshare owners collectively own the resort.

Owners share in the use and upkeep of the units and of the common grounds of the resort property. A homeowners' association usually handles management of the resort. Timeshare owners elect officers and control the expenses, the upkeep of the resort property, and the selection of the resort management company.

"Right to Use" Vacation Interval Option

In this option, a developer owns the resort, which is made up of condominiums or units. Each condo or unit is divided into intervals—either by weeks or the equivalent in points. You purchase the right to use an interval as the resort for a specific number of years—typically between 10 and 50 years. At some point the contract ends and all rights revert to the property owner. The interest you own is legally considered personal property. The specific unit you use at the resort may not be the same each year. In addition to the price for the right to use an interval, you pay an annual maintenance fee.

Within the "right to use" option several plans can affect your ability to use a unit:

- **Fixed or floating time.** In a fixed time option, you purchase the unit for use during a specific week of the year. In a floating time option, you use the unit within a certain season of the year, reserving the time you want in advance; confirmation typically is provided on a first-come, first-served basis.

- **Fractional ownership.** Rather than an annual week, you buy a large share of vacation ownership, such as 13 or 26 weeks.

- **Biennial ownership.** You use a resort unit every other year.

- **Lockoff or lockout.** You occupy a portion of the unit and offer the remaining space for rental or exchange. These units typically have two to three bedrooms and baths.

- **Points-based vacation plans.** You purchase a certain number of points, and exchange them for the right to use an interval at one or more resorts. In a points-based vacation plan (frequently called a vacation club), the number of points you need to use an interval varies according to the length of the stay, size of the unit, location of the resort, and when you want to use it.

A number of countries have limits on foreign property ownership, so right to use is a way to develop resorts. An example is Mexico. Over the years, resorts have added innovation and sophistication to the way owners can buy timeshare intervals. Just over half (51 percent) still offer a traditional weekly interval, while 49 percent offer some form of points-based product and 31 percent offer biennials. To further increase flexibility, many resorts make special programs available: 28 percent allow conversions from fixed intervals (the same week every year) to floating intervals (owners can select different weeks from year to year), 46 percent offer an upgrade program, 53 percent offer conversions from weekly intervals to points-based equivalents, and 71 percent offer a sample or trial membership.

In a majority of resorts today, your vacation ownership interest will include a deeded interest in real estate. Other timeshare programs do not include an interest in real property, but are structured more like a membership. How you actually use your timeshare vacation is generally not affected by the absence or presence of a real estate interest.

The timeshare concept is typically thought of as vacation lodging ownership at a destination resort; however, this form of lodging has created a variety of products sold on similar occupying concepts. Today, the concept has been applied to airplanes, automobiles, recreation vehicles, boats, cruise ships, campgrounds, luxury fractional properties, and private residence clubs.

Exchanging Timeshares

A major attraction of vacation ownership is the opportunity for owners to exchange their week, or interval, either independently or through exchange agencies, to stay at one of the thousands of other resorts worldwide. There are many exchange agencies with Group RCI and Interval International being the largest. Group RCI (formerly, Resort Condominiums International) is a division of Wyndham Worldwide. RCI was founded in 1974 as an exchange service for condominium owners and now serves its global community of more than 3 million timeshare owners with exchange vacations at more than 3,700 resorts in 101 countries through RCI's week-for-week and points-based timeshare exchange networks. Visit their Web site at www.rci.com. Interval International (II) has been serving the vacation ownership market for over 34 years. Interval has an exchange network of more than 2,500 resorts in over 75 nations. With offices in 14 countries, Interval services approximately 2 million members. Visit www.intervalworld.com. RCI and II charge a yearly membership fee and a fee for finding an exchange. Owners can also exchange their weeks or points through independent exchange companies. Also, owners may arrange a direct exchange. Several bulletin boards have been created to help timeshare owners meet others and swap. Timex is such a site; visit www.timex.to.

Industry Overview

The American Resort Development Association (ARDA) is the preeminent source of information about timesharing and vacation ownership. It conducts regular research studies on owners, economic impact, financial performance, and state of the industry through the ARDA International Foundation (AIF), which is the research arm of ARDA. Visit its Web site at www.arda.org.

ARDA's last worldwide report stated there are 5,425 resorts worldwide located in 95 countries. Figure 6.3 shows locations of timeshare resorts. North America has the most with 31 percent led by the United States, Europe hosts 25 percent led by Spain, Latin America, has 16 percent led by Mexico; and Asia has 14 percent led by Japan. Africa with 6 percent, the Caribbean with 5 percent, and the Pacific with 3 percent round out the locations.

For the United States ARDA reports there were 1,548 timeshare resorts in the United States in 2009, representing approximately 170,200 units for an average resort size of 110 units. Of these, 6 percent were studio units, 23 percent were one-bedrooms, 66 percent were two-bedrooms, and 6 percent had three bedrooms or more. There were 7.2 million intervals owned. Occupancy was strong at 79.7 percent. Florida, California, and South Carolina remain as the three states that have the most resorts, representing 39 percent of all U.S. timeshare resorts. The predominant resort category was a beach destination, reported by 31 percent of responding resorts. This was followed by country/lakes resorts (18 percent), and golf and ski resorts each at 10 percent.

Year 2009 sales volume totaled $6.3 billion, a sharp decrease of 35 percent from 2008 because of the economy and the lack of funding available from banks for consumer loans. The industry is currently recovering from the great recession. Although sales volume declined, the average cost per timeshare interval increased to $20,468, a modest 2 percent increase over 2008. For the first time in the industry's history, points-based products outsold traditional weeks. In 2009, timeshare resort occupancy remained strong at 79.7 percent, compared to the 54.7 percent hotel industry occupancy reported by Smith Travel Research.

The Profile of a Timeshare Owner

The average age of a timeshare owner is 48. Average household income is $94,933, 75 percent are married and 9 percent have a domestic partner. Baby boomers are the largest generation of timeshare

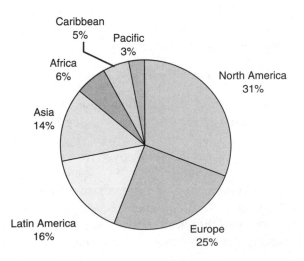

Figure 6.3 Locations of timeshare resorts.
Source: ARDA.

owners, 45 percent. On average, owners have owned the intervals for 8.26 years. They say beaches (52 percent), attractions/entertainment (48 percent), and shopping (39 percent) are the most appealing resort characteristics. The strongest motivators for purchasing were the certainty of quality accommodations (93 percent), saving on future vacation costs (90 percent), and credibility of the timeshare company (90 percent). Ownership experience is a positive 86 percent. On average, the total number of guests on a timeshare vacation is 3.71, including the owner.

The Future

Timesharing will continue to increase in the United States because major companies, such as Disney, Marriott, Hyatt, Four Seasons, Ramada, Accor, Starwood, and Hilton, have become involved and brought quality, luxury, and respectability to the industry. Timesharing has evolved into a mainstream vacation option. Today, timeshares are sold by some of the best names in the hotel industry and major hotel chains are gaining a large share of the market.

An example is Marriott. It entered the vacation ownership industry in 1984 and began redefining the timeshare industry. Incorporating the signature quality, service, and hospitality expertise of Marriott, a new product was created that offered the ownership of a first-class luxury villa and the flexibility to experience great vacation destinations around the world. Marriott Vacation Club International has successfully combined the benefits of property ownership, Marriott quality management, and fixed costs for a lifetime of vacations. Marriott has over 2,000 villas at beach and ski resorts across the country. Over the past years, Marriott has refined a low-key approach and sold vacation ownership intervals to nearly 400,000 owners.

Camping and Campgrounds

Camping has a long history in many countries including the United States. Millions of campsites are available to the tourist, both public and private. At one time camping meant roughing it and involved setting up a tent or sleeping under the stars. Today travelers can still do that, or more likely they will park a recreational vehicle, or rent cabins, cottages, or lodges. RV parks and campgrounds offer a wide variety of amenities, activities, and services for the comfort of their camping customers. Many campgrounds offer electricity, cable TV hookups, computer connections, wireless Internet service, hot showers, and laundry facilities. The National Association of RV Parks and Campgrounds is the national association representing over 3,700 parks and campgrounds in North America. The association is headquartered in Falls Church, Virginia. Visit its Web site at www.arvc.org.

Lodging Organizations

In 2010, AH&LA celebrated serving the hospitality industry for a century (1910–2010). Headquartered in Washington, D.C., AH&LA provides its 11,000 members with national advocacy on Capital Hill, public relations and image management, education, research and information, and other value-added services to provide bottom-line savings and ensure a positive business climate for the lodging industry. As the voice of the $134 billion lodging industry, AH&LA serves as a valuable resource for timely lodging news, statistics and expert comment.

In addition, AH&LA is partnered with 44 state associations to provide local representation and cost-saving benefits to members. Students are especially interested in AH&LA's Information Center that answers questions about the industry and its Education Foundation that awarded more than $550,000 in scholarships to about 370 promising students and lodging industry professionals in 2009.

AH&LA is a leader in hospitality education with its Educational Institute (EI). The Institute is a source for delivering quality hospitality education, training, and professional certification that serves the needs of hospitality schools and industries worldwide. EI provides materials for all levels of hospitality personnel via online learning, distance learning courses, videos, seminars, textbooks, and study guides. Visit the AH&LA Web site at www.ahla.com and the Institute Web site at www.ahlei.org.

The International Hotel and Restaurant Association (IH&RA), located in Geneva, Switzerland, is a global network for the hotel and restaurant industry in over 100 countries. It represents, protects, promotes, and informs its members. IH&RA research reports provide members with valuable information on the global hospitality industry, careers, taxes, and technology. Visit its Web site at www.ih-ra.com.

Lodging Information Sources

For more than 20 years, Smith Travel Research (STR) has been the recognized leader for lodging industry benchmarking and research. In 2008, STR combined its non–North American operations with the two international leaders in the benchmarking arena, Deloitte's HotelBenchmark and the Bench, both based in London, to form STR Global (STRG). STR continues serving the North American market, which it has been supporting since its foundation in 1985. STR Global brings the benefits of the well-known STAR reports to a truly global audience. STR and STR Global track supply and demand data for the hotel industry and provide valuable market share analysis for all major international hotel chains and brands. With tens of thousands of hotels, representing over 5 million hotel rooms, participating in its hotel performance surveys, it is the world's foremost source of historical hotel performance trends. STR's family of companies also includes Hotel NewsNow.com, RRC Associates, and STR Analytics. Visit its Web site at www.strglobal.com.

PKF Consulting is another information source. Its *Trends*® *in the Hotel Industry* is an annual compilation of unit-level hotel financial statements. Since 1936, PKF has collected year-end operating statements from thousands of hotels across the nation. From these statements, the firm extracts 200 specific revenue and expense items and then puts the data into a uniform format to ensure equitable benchmarking. The *Trends*® database is the oldest source of hotel financial information in the United States. Visit www.pkfc.com.

Ernst and Young examines key influences affecting the hospitality sector such as the global credit crunch, the scarcity of capital, green building, and shifting demographic trends. It publishes a *Global Hospitality and Leisure Outlook* and a *U.S. Lodging Report*. Visit www.ey.com. PricewaterhouseCoopers and the U.S. Census Bureau also provide lodging information.

THE FOOD SERVICE INDUSTRY

Early Food Services

Like the lodging industry, the food service industry is a very old business. Such service came out of the early inns and monasteries. In cities, small restaurants began serving simple dishes such as soups and breads. One such restaurant, *le restaurant divin* (the divine restorative), opened in Paris in 1765. (Like *tourist, restaurant* is a French word.) The famous English taverns provided food, drink, and lodging.

In the United States, the early ordinaries, taverns, and inns typically provided food and lodging. Good examples of these can be found in Colonial Williamsburg, Virginia. Politics and other concerns of the day were often discussed in such taverns.

With the development of stagecoaches, taverns began providing food and lodging along the early roads and in small communities. Some believe that these roadside taverns were really the beginnings of the American hotel industry. As cities grew, so did eating establishments. Some names of historic restaurants in the 1820s in New York City were Niblo's Garden, the Sans Souci, and Delmonico's.

French service was often used in these early restaurants. In French service, some kinds of entrées are prepared by the dining room captain right at the guests' table, sometimes using heat from a small

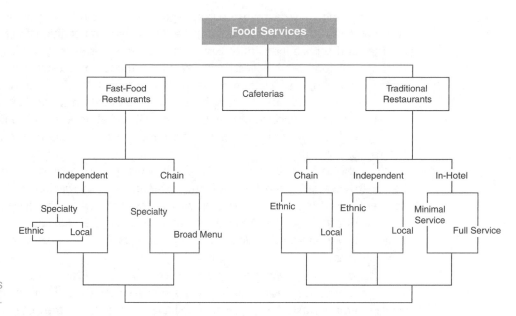

Figure 6.4 Food services structure.

burner, then serving from larger dishes onto the guest's plate. The kinds and amounts of each food item are chosen individually. By contrast, in Russian service, the entire plate, with predetermined portions, is served to each guest.

Menus can be of two types, à la carte and table d'hôte. The à la carte menu consists of a complete list of all the food items being offered on that day. The patron then chooses the individual items desired. In table d'hôte, a combination of items is chosen.

Eating and drinking places are big business. Although much of this activity is local, eating and drinking are favorite pastimes of travelers, and the food service industry would face difficult times without the tourist market. See Figure 6.4 for the structure of the food service industry.

The National Restaurant Association (NRA) projected that food industry sales for 2010 would total $580 billion and equal 4 percent of U.S. gross domestic product. This level is 2.5 percent over 2009 sales, which is an improvement over the 1.2 percent and 2.4 percent negative growth that the industry experienced in 2008 and 2009, respectively. The nation's 945,000 restaurants provide employment for 12.7 million people, over 9 percent of the U.S. workforce, making the industry the largest private-sector employer in the nation. For only the second time in nearly half a century, the restaurant industry lost jobs in 2009. Despite the losses, the industry still outperformed the national economy, and job growth resumed in 2010. By 2020, the industry is projected to employ 14 million people—an increase of 1.3 million jobs. The typical employee in a food service occupation is female, under 30 years of age, single, working part-time. The food service industry employs more minority managers than any other retail industry. Travelers contribute about $130 billion to food service sales each year, whether for a coffee shop breakfast, a dinner on an airline, a sandwich from a bus station vending machine, or a ten-course dinner on a cruise ship. Travelers, including foreign visitors, spend more money on food than anything else except transportation, and travelers account for about one-fourth of the total sales in the food service industry.[4]

Social media will become more critical to restaurant marketing. A good plan and solid understanding of these tools—including Facebook, Twitter, Yelp, and YouTube—can help operators mitigate the effects of economic environment. "Word of mouth" has moved online, and more consumers use the Web to browse menus, make reservations, and get recommendations from other diners. Restaurants' use of e-mail, Internet, and cell phone text messages in marketing efforts is also a growing trend.

Restaurant operators continue to step up their efforts to go green, investing in energy-efficient equipment and fixtures, using recyclable materials and reducing their water use. Green initiatives not only help manage costs, they can also drive traffic. Four of ten full service and 31 percent of quick-service operators plan to devote more resources to green initiatives in 2010 than they did in 2009, and four in ten consumers say they choose restaurants based on their conservation practices.

The food service industry consists of restaurants, travel food service, and vending and contract institutional food service. Local restaurants are made up of establishments that include fast-food units, coffee shops, specialty restaurants, family restaurants, cafeterias, and full-service restaurants with carefully orchestrated "atmosphere." Travel food service consists of food operations in hotels and motels, roadside service to automobile travelers, and all food service on airplanes, trains, and ships. Institutional food service in companies, hospitals, nursing homes, and so on is not considered part of the tourism industry.

Over the past two decades, the food and beverage business has grown at a phenomenal rate. This has been especially true for fast-food companies, with the franchising portion in the fast-food segment becoming the dominant growth sector. This remarkable increase has been gained at the expense of other food service operators and supermarkets. Franchisees control approximately three-fourths of the fast-food outlets, whose hamburgers, chickens, steaks, and pizzas dominate the fast-food business.

Fast-food chains have enjoyed great success in part because they limit their menus, which gives them greater purchasing power, less waste, more portion control, and, of importance to the consumer, lower operating costs. They are leaders in labor productivity in the restaurant industry. Most fast-food operations use disposable paper and plastic; the expense for these materials is more than offset by the savings resulting from not providing regular service and from not employing the personnel required to wash the dinner service. Fast-food operations also enjoy the advantages of specialization; they have become specialists in menu items, job simplification, and operating systems. Franchising has been used extensively in both the restaurant field and the lodging field as a means of achieving rapid growth. Using the franchisee's capital, the entrepreneur can get much more rapid penetration of the marketplace.

As noted earlier, franchise units account for approximately three-fourths of the growing fast-food portion of the industry. Advantages of franchising accrue to both sides. The franchisee gets the start-up help, advice from experienced management, buying power, advertising, and low unit costs from spreading fixed costs over large numbers of units. The franchisor has the advantage of a lower capital investment, rapid growth, and royalty income. The fast-food franchise operators have a great deal of concentration in their segment of the industry. The seven largest account for almost half of the fast-food units and almost half of the sales. Franchise firms are household words: McDonald's, KFC (Kentucky Fried Chicken), A&W, Wendy's, Dairy Queen, Burger King, Pizza Hut, Arby's, and Taco Bell.

Although the fast-food segment is the most rapidly growing segment, the high-quality segment of the restaurant industry must not be overlooked. Much of this business is based on customers seeking a special or different experience in dining out. Local entrepreneurs who emphasize special menus, varying atmospheres, and high-quality food and service have most effectively satisfied this demand. New concepts or trends include ethnic restaurants, especially those with an Asian or Mexican flavor; increased demand for health foods, fish, local produce, and regional dishes; and variety in portion sizes.

Menu Trends

The annual NRA survey of American Culinary Federation member chefs is a comprehensive culinary forecast and menu prediction report. In its latest report, *Chef Survey: What's Hot in 2010*, more than 1,800 professional chefs ranked 214 culinary items as a hot trend, yesterday's news, or perennial favorite on restaurant menus.

The top five trends are locally grown produce; locally sourced meats and seafood, sustainability as a culinary theme, mini-desserts, and local produced wine and beer. Rounding out the top ten list are nutritious kids' meals, half-portions/smaller portions for a smaller price, farm-branded ingredients, gluten-free/food allergy conscious meals, and sustainable seafood. Ethnic cuisines and flavors are also

Although the truly fine dining of the past is still available to travelers throughout the world, many now prefer the casual sophistication of high-quality food, served in unique, comfortable, outdoor environments. Here, visitors are enjoying a patio setting in the outdoors of New Smyrna, Florida. *Photo courtesy of the New Smyrna Beach Visitors Center.*

a hot menu trend, including regional ethnic cuisine and fusion cuisine. Consumers are interested in trying French, Spanish, Japanese (other than sushi), Thai, Cajun/Creole, soul food, and sushi.

Yesterday's news were such items as boxed wine, ostrich/emu, sea urchin, organ meats, offal, bottled water, energy drinks, and flavored/enhanced water. Some perennial favorites were omelets, pasta, potatoes/french fries, cucumber, crème brulée, soup, California wines, traditional cocktails, nuts, and avocado.

The Culinary Tourist

Although food and beverages have always been a part of the tourism experience, culinary tourism is a relatively new niche and has come into its own in the last decade. Today, one can find Web sites on culinary tourism, the subject on regional, state, and national tourism conferences, and books on culinary tourism. The International Culinary Tourism Association (ICTA) defines culinary tourism as the pursuit of unique and memorable culinary experiences of all kinds, often while traveling, but one can also be a culinary tourist at home. Wikipedia defines culinary tourism or food tourism as experiencing the food of the country, region, or area, and it is now considered a vital component of the tourism experience. Dining out is common among tourists and food can be the major driver in deciding when and where to travel. Food is also considered a part of cultural tourism and is linked to agritourism. Wine tourism, whiskey tourism, and beer tourism are all part of culinary tourism.

Lucy Long, professor at Bowling Green State University, is credited with coining the term in her 1998 book *Culinary Tourism*. She defines culinary tourism as exploratory eating—individuals exploring foods new to them as well as using foods to explore new cultures and ways of being. It is about groups using food "to sell" their histories and to construct marketable and publicly attractive identities, and it is about individuals satisfying curiosity.[5] She noted that culinary tourism encompasses history, nutrition, culinary arts, hospitality, psychology, and sociology.

ICTA states that culinary tourism includes culinary experiences of all kinds. It is much more than just tasting and eating. It encompasses cooking schools, cookbook and kitchen gadgets stores, wine tasting tours, culinary tours and tour leaders, festivals and events, culinary media, guidebooks, caterers, wineries, breweries, distilleries, food growers and manufacturers, culinary attractions, and more.

The food industry has always known that food, wine, and other culinary experiences are not only an important ingredient in travel but also a powerful motivation to travel. A U.S. Travel Association study reports 25 percent of leisure travelers say food is a vital factor when choosing a destination. Travelers are stating that food is a key aspect of the travel experience and that they believe experiencing a country's food is essential to understanding its culture.

Notable food attractions are the Octoberfest in Munich, Germany; the whiskey trail in Scotland; the wine trail in Napa, California; the slow food movement's biennial Terra Madre and Salore del Gusto festival in Turin, Italy; Harrods Food Hall in London, England; St. Moritz Gourmet Festival in St. Moritz, Switzerland; and Tsukiji Fish Market in Tokyo, Japan.

Restaurant Organizations

The National Restaurant Association (NRA) is the most important trade association in the food service field. For more than 90 years, NRA has represented, educated, and promoted the restaurant industry. It works closely with a network of 53 state restaurant associations and has established the National Restaurant Association Education Foundation to further the education of tomorrow's restaurant industry professionals. The Foundation also provides scholarships.

The members of NRA come from every corner of the restaurant/hospitality industry. Restaurant members come from chef-owned restaurants, family restaurant chains, quick-service franchises, contract food-service organizations, suppliers, distributors, and consultants, plus student and faculty members who are part of the industry's educational community.

Initiatives, programs, and services provided members are (1) advocacy and representation building and sustaining positive public opinion and a favorable political environment; (2) tools and solutions to help grow revenues, increase profitability, and develop employees; (3) education and networking; and (4) responsible stewardship providing leadership. NRA is located at 1200 Seventeenth Street NW, Washington, D.C. 20036; telephone (202) 331-5900; Web site www .restaurant.org.

MEETINGS INDUSTRY

Because of the growth in the meeting and conventions area, it is an area of interest to students of tourism. With the growth of more corporate and association meetings, there is a need for more meeting planners, meeting consultants, and suppliers of goods and services to meeting planners. The meetings industry often includes significant elements of hospitality, such as lodging and food service—plus additional elements that make the meetings industry a challenging and rewarding option for people interested in a career in tourism.

Meeting Planners

Professional meeting planners are involved with such tasks as selecting sites, negotiating hotel contracts, negotiating with airlines, writing contracts, planning food and beverage, preparing signage, managing traffic flow, planning audiovisual, performing site logistics, planning educational meetings and seminars, developing incentive meetings, negotiating with foreign countries and hotels for incentive travel, budgeting, promotion, public relations, and planning special events and postmeeting tours. Meeting planners are found in corporations, special-interest associations, educational institutions, trade shows, and government.

Several organizations serve the meetings industry. The largest is Meeting Professionals International (MPI). MPI helps their members by providing human connections to knowledge and ideas, relationships, and marketplaces. Their vision is to build a rich global meeting industry community. MPI membership is 24,000 belonging to 71 chapters and clubs worldwide. Visit www.mpiweb.org.

The Professional Convention Management Association (PCMA) represents more than 6,000 meeting professionals from 17 chapters in the United States, Canada, and Mexico. Members include planner professionals, suppliers, faculty and students. Professionals are individuals who are responsible for the development, organization, site selection and management of meetings, conventions, exhibits, and seminars. Suppliers are individuals whose organization provides products and services related to meetings, conventions, exhibits, and seminars. Visit www.pcma.org.

The Society of Corporate Meeting Professionals (SCMP) was founded over 30 years ago to serve as a vehicle for corporate meeting professionals to interact with their peers, to gain advanced knowledge, and to develop enhanced professional skills. This unique partnership among the membership of corporate planners, hotel/convention center/CVB service professionals, independent planners, and students provides an atmosphere to achieve a high level of professional excellence. Visit www.scmp.org.

This couple enjoying a break at the Lake Powell Java City Coffee shop represents the increasingly popular upscale role of coffee in the daily life of students and young professionals. Sparked by the widespread popularity of the Starbucks chain, many other shops have also realized considerable success. Great opportunity exists for young entrepreneurs in tourism to seize and profit from the "next wave" of consumer preferences. *Photo courtesy of Lake Powell Resorts and Marinas.*

The Society of Government Meeting Professionals (SGMP) is a national association for individuals involved in planning government meetings and for the companies who provide facilities or services to those planners. Their membership includes employees of federal, state, and local governments, as well as contract meeting planners, who manage government meetings on a full- or part-time basis. Its mission is to enhance the knowledge and expertise of government meeting professionals. Visit www.sgmp.org.

Meetings and Conventions

By any name—whether it be conference, convention, meeting, trade show, exhibition, symposium, or seminar—this market is huge. It is crucial to the health of many communities and their hotel, restaurant, transportation, and audiovisual businesses. Most large cities have a convention center dedicated to hosting meetings because of the enormous economic impact. This sector is frequently given the acronym MICE, which stands for **meetings, incentives, conventions, and exhibitions**. The components seem to be easily understood except for the "I." *Incentives* can be powerful motivators for employee performance and travel is a prime reward incentive. Consequently, incentive tourism is providing travel rewards to employees who meet or exceed targets or quotas or excel in job performance. Unlike the other components of MICE, which have a professional or educational purpose, incentive tourism is a reward and usually conducted purely for entertainment (see Chapter 7, "Incentive Travel Firms").

MICE refers to the type of tourism in which small and large groups, usually planned and promoted in advance, are brought together for a particular purpose. The term is widely used, especially in Asia, as a description of the industry. Others such as the Convention Industry Council (CIC) use the term "meetings industry" to describe this sector. The meetings industry is huge and booms when the economy is growing and retrenches when economic growth slows. CIC conducts an economic impact study every five years to show the strength of the industry. The 2005 study of the economic impact of the meetings, conventions, exhibition, and incentive travel industry was released in September 2005. It showed the meetings industry is a 365-day-a-year business that operates in communities, large and small, across the country. Taken as a whole, it generated $122.31 billion in total direct spending in 2004, making it the twenty-ninth largest contributor to the gross domestic product. The industry's spending and tax revenue ripples through every sector of the local economy, from restaurants and transportation to retail stores and other services, while supporting 1.7 million jobs in the United States.

In April 2010, CIC launched a new study to update the impact. The study, *The Economic Significance of Meetings to the U.S. Economy,* was conducted by PriceWaterhouseCoopers. It was released by the Convention Industry Council on February 17, 2011 revealing that the U.S. meetings industry creates $263 billion in direct spending, supports 1.7 million direct jobs, results in $14.3 billion in federal tax revenue, and $11.3 billion in state and local tax revenue. The study considered 1.8 million meetings held in the U.S. during 2009 that met the UNWTO definition of a gathering of 10 or more participants for a minimum of four hours in a contracted venue. The total economic output of these 1.8 million meetings including direct spending and multiplier effects equals $907 billion in total U.S. economic activity, 6.3 million U.S. jobs, $458 billion contribution to GDP, $64 billion federal tax revenue, and $46 billion state and local tax revenue. Detailed results, a press release, an executive summary, and more about the study can be found at www.meetingsmeanbusiness.com.[6]

In discussing the meetings industry, the CIC deserves special mention. CIC is a nonprofit federation of 31 leading U.S. and international organizations in the MICE industry. CIC's member organizations are a "who's who" of the industry, and they represent more than 103,500 individuals and 19,500 firms and properties involved in the meetings, conventions, and exhibitions industry. CIC facilitates the exchange of information, develops programs to promote professionalism with the industry, and educates the public on its profound economic impact. A list of CIC

The Champagne Pool in New Zealand provides visitors with the opportunity to see minerals depositing as hot water flows out of the pool and across the flats. *Photo courtesy of Digital Vision.*

Experiencing culture through food is important for many travelers. *Photo courtesy of Sandestin Golf and Beach Resort and photographer Allison Yii.*

Going off the beaten path to see more of the surrounding environment is one way to enhance one's experience. *Photo courtesy of Florida EcoSafaris at Forever Florida.*

The decorated legs of Cuna Indian women in Panama are a unique fashion statement that tourists encounter and can even take on themselves during their travels. *Photo courtesy of Flat Earth.*

Adventure hiking can be an exciting and scenic vacation experience with family and friends. *Photo courtesy of ImageState.*

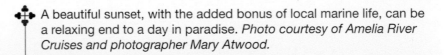

A beautiful sunset, with the added bonus of local marine life, can be a relaxing end to a day in paradise. *Photo courtesy of Amelia River Cruises and photographer Mary Atwood.*

The city of Tel Aviv, Israel's largest metropolis and cultural center, overlooks the Mediterranean with seafront skyscrapers visible from a distance. *Photo courtesy of PhotoDisc, Inc./Getty Images.*

Catching a glimpse of the Serengeti Blue Wildebeests on the East African Savannas is a sight few who have seen will forget. *Photo courtesy of Image100 Ltd.*

Whale watching is a popular excursion along some coastal regions. *Photo courtesy of photographer Nathan Horn, used by permission of Nathan Horn and Sea Kayak Adventures, Inc.*

Considered one of the greatest outdoor museums in Turkey, the elegant Library of Celsus in Ephesus draws tourists from around the world to behold the ancient ruins of its colossal galleries and statue-adorned facades. *Photo courtesy of Corbis Digital Stock.*

Restaurants can use their natural surroundings to enhance guest experiences. *Photo courtesy of Sandestin Golf and Beach Resort and photographer Allison Yii.*

A bright arrangement of colored spices on display in an Indian marketplace in Mysore is representative of the country's vibrant and colorful culture. *Photo courtesy of Flat Earth.*

The Houses of Parliament, a luxurious model of British gothic architecture located on the banks of the River Thames, is open to the public for visitor tours of its main galleries. *Photo courtesy of Peter Adams/ Digital Vision.*

Some people enjoy the opportunity to spend time in their natural surroundings and enjoy activities such as fishing on an autumn day. *Photo courtesy of Wisconsin Department of Tourism.*

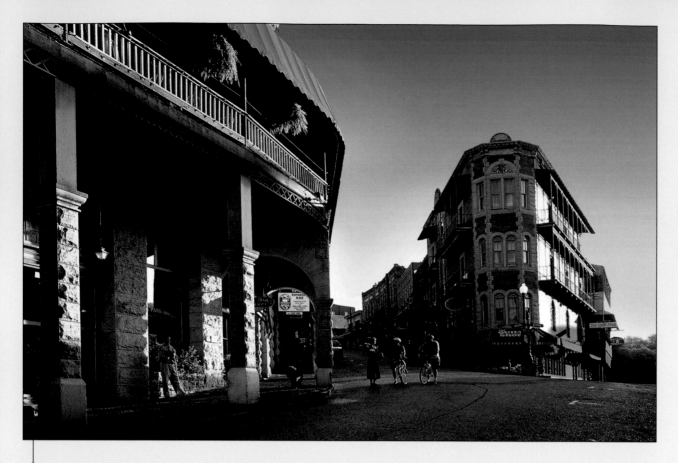

✛ The charm of a small town, such as Eureka Springs, Arkansas, can draw many day trippers and weekenders. *Photo courtesy of Arkansas Department of Parks and Tourism.*

✛ A golf resort is a destination for both the golfer and nongolfer. *Photo courtesy of the Ballantyne Hotel and Lodge.*

No trip to Sydney is complete without a tour of the Opera House, one of the world's most daring and beautiful examples of twentieth-century architecture. *Photo courtesy of Digital Vision.*

Tourists are drawn to this breathtaking view in The Garden of the Gods Park in Colorado Springs, Colorado. *Photo courtesy of The Broadmoor.*

There's often as much to see underground as above. *Photo courtesy of Springfield, Missouri Convention & Visitors Bureau.*

The chance to feel alone in the world appeals to many travelers. *Photo courtesy of Arkansas Department of Parks and Tourism.*

✤ Part of the UNESCO World Heritage Site, the temple of Abu Simbel is among the finest tourist attractions in Egypt with its rich history and ancient architecture. *Photo courtesy of Corbis Digital Stock.*

✤ The serene waters of Patagonia's Lagos De Los Tres are beautifully complemented by a glimmering sun-bathed Mt. Fitzroy in the background. *Photo courtesy of Digital Vision.*

✥ This bird's-eye view of the Australian Great Barrier Reef is a spectacular sight to see. *Photo courtesy of Corbis Digital Stock.*

✥ Tiers of small white houses in Santorini, one of the most popular tourist destinations in Greece, hug the edges of the island's cliffs that tower above the deep blue Aegean Sea. *Photo courtesy of Corbis Digital Stock.*

✤ The Colosseum, Rome's historic amphitheater and once battleground for the gladiators, attracts millions of visitors every year to experience its colossal columns and arcades. *Photo courtesy of Corbis Digital Stock.*

✤ The rugged beauty and haunting mystery of Stonehenge cause visitors to give pause and consider their place as a grain of sand in the hourglass of time. *Photo courtesy of Peter Adams/Digital Vision.*

The Great Wall of China stretches into the horizon, undeterred by the most formidable topographical obstacles. *Photo courtesy of Corbis Digital Stock.*

Tourists are often drawn to the serenity and calm of Japanese temples and gardens. *Photo courtesy of Corbis Digital Stock.*

A gorgeous trademark of Berlin, and once a symbol for the division of the East and West, the Brandenburg Gate today stands as a magnificent gateway that both locals and tourists can enjoy the freedom to walk through and admire. *Photo courtesy of ImageState.*

When touring Venice, Italy, visitors can see Piazza San Marco from their gondolas. *Photo courtesy of Corbis Digital Stock.*

The majestic beauty of the waterfall at Yosemite National Park in California is a travel motivator. *Photo courtesy of PhotoDisc/Getty Images.*

✛ This tranquil silhouette view of an Istanbulian mosque at dusk can be an awe-inspiring sight for tourists of all religious backgrounds. *Photo courtesy of ImageState.*

✛ The tallest mountain in Japan, Mount Fuji has inspired nature lovers and artists from all around the world to behold its picturesque snow-capped peaks and elegant slopes. *Photo courtesy of PhotoDisc, Inc.*

members follows and illustrates the scope of the industry and the information they can provide on their sector:

- Alliance of Meeting Management Consultants (AMMC)
- AMC Institute, *formerly IAAMC*
- American Hotel & Lodging Association (AH&LA)
- American Society of Association Executives and the Center (ASAE & The Center)
- Association for Convention Operations Management (ACOM)
- Association of Collegiate Conference and Events Directors-International (ACCED-I)
- Association of Destination Management Executives (ADME)
- Center for Exhibition Industry Research (CEIR)
- Council of Engineering and Scientific Society Executives (CESSE)
- Destination Marketing Association International (DMAI); *formerly IACVB*
- Exhibition Services & Contractors Association (ESCA)
- Financial and Insurance Conference Planners (FICP); *formerly ICPA*
- Green Meetings Industry Council (GMIC)
- Healthcare Convention and Exhibitors Association (HCEA)
- Hospitality Sales and Marketing Association International (HSMAI)
- International Association of Venue Managers (IAVM)
- International Association of Conference Centers (IACC)
- International Association of Exhibitions and Events (IAEE); *formerly IAEM*
- International Association of Professional Congress Organisers (IAPCO)
- International Association of Speakers Bureaus (IASB)
- International Congress and Convention Association (ICCA)
- International Special Events Society (ISES)
- Meeting Professionals International (MPI)
- National Association of Catering Executives (NACE)
- National Coalition of Black Meeting Planners (NCBMP)
- National Speakers Association (NSA)
- Professional Convention Management Association (PCMA)
- Religious Conference Management Association (RCMA)
- Society of Government Meeting Professionals (SGMP)
- Society of Incentive & Travel Executives (SITE)
- U.S. Travel Association (U.S. Travel)

Visit its Web site at www.conventionindustry.org.

Although domestic conferences provide the greatest source of business for most convention sites, international conventions, conferences, and congresses are also a very attractive segment of the market. In addition, they are often the largest and highest-profile conferences attracting massive media coverage. Examples are the biannual congress of the United Nations World Tourism Organization and the annual Davos (Switzerland) conference of the World Economic Forum—which each year is characterized by major statements by world political and economic leaders.

In addition, smaller but even higher-profile international gatherings can greatly enhance international awareness of the host venue. In this case, the meeting of the "G20" heads of government of the

Facilities such as those shown are in great demand to meet the needs of the growing association and corporate meetings market. The small meetings market has important economic impacts. *Photo courtesy of The Broadmoor.*

leading 20 economic nations of the world, while relatively small in terms of number of direct participants, is one of the most widely covered events on the meeting and convention calendar.

The International Congress and Convention Association (ICCA) seeks to gather and disseminate information regarding international meetings of its membership. The ICCA represents the main specialists in handling, transportation, and accommodation for international events. It comprises more than 900 member corporations and organizations in 85 countries worldwide.

The ICCA assists members in identifying business leads, primarily by means of the association's online database, which provides a historical overview of past association meetings as well as a means to search for possible future meetings. The ICCA also produces rankings of the overseas countries and cities that host, or seek to host, meetings organized by international associations that take place on a regular basis, and that rotate between a minimum of three countries. The 2010 database, which contains data on 2009, provided the rankings shown in Table 6.2.

As has been the case since 2004, the United States and Germany are the number one and two countries, respectively, measured by the number of international meetings organized in 2009. Spain remains third. Italy jumps from sixth to fourth place, and the United Kingdom remains fifth. China-P.R. and Austria (which shares tenth place with The Netherlands) are newcomers in the top ten.

For the fifth year in a row, Vienna is the most popular city. Barcelona jumped from third to second place, and Paris, which shared first place with Vienna in 2008, is now third. The only newcomer in the top 20 is Madrid, at thirteenth place. Visit www.iccaworld.org.

There will probably be an oversupply of convention meeting facilities in the United States as the number of convention centers continues to grow. Many U.S. cities are building new convention centers or expanding their existing centers. Even though the United States leads the world in

TABLE 6.2   ICCA Country and City Ranking Measured by Number of Meetings Organized in 2009

Number of Meetings per Country			Number of Meetings per City		
Ranking	Country	# Meetings	Ranking	City	# Meetings
1	USA	595	1	Vienna	160
2	Germany	458	2	Barcelona	135
3	Spain	360	3	Paris	131
4	Italy	350	4	Berlin	129
5	United Kingdom	345	5	Singapore	119
6	France	341	6	Copenhagen	103
7	Brazil	293	7	Stockholm	102
8	Japan	257	8	Amsterdam	98
9	China-P.R.	245	9	Lisbon	98
10	Austria	236	10	Beijing	96
	Netherlands	236	11	Buenos Aires	90
12	Switzerland	214	12	Seoul	90
13	Canada	213	13	Budapest	87
14	Sweden	184	14	Madrid	87
15	Republic of Korea	176	15	Prague	86
16	Australia	169	16	London	83
17	Portugal	168	17	Istanbul	80
18	Denmark	151	18	Sao Paulo	79
19	Argentina	145	19	Bangkok	76
20	Belgium	130	20	Athens	75

Source: International Congress and Convention Association.

The meetings and conventions business is important to local economies. *Photo courtesy of The Greater Minneapolis Convention & Visitors Association © Bob Perzel.*

conventions, in terms of both numbers of attendees and the amount of exhibit and meeting space, the growth in facilities is outpacing the demand.

MISCELLANEOUS SERVICES

Many other organizations provide essential services to tourism. Examples are hospitals and medical services; police services; sanitary trash pickup and disposal services; laundry services; construction services; retail stores such as department stores, drugstores, and clothing stores; advertising agencies; marketing consultants; newspapers (including tourist newspapers and special travel editions); travel writers; television stations; and magazines.

SUMMARY

Lodging and food services are major essential supply components of tourism. These services date back to antiquity. World hotel room inventory is growing about 2.5 percent yearly. Room occupancy averages about 65 percent. But such data vary considerably. The 1980s saw considerable overbuilding and losses, especially in North America. However, in the late 1990s, record profitability was achieved. In the new century, lodging has been profitable but has suffered from the events of 9/11, war, terrorism, and SARS, and economic recession. About 70 percent of the world's lodging establishments are located in Europe and North America. There is a trend toward more franchising, chain or system ownership, and growth in bed-and-breakfast lodging.

Resort and timesharing arrangements are also increasing worldwide. There are thousands of timeshare resorts worldwide. The American Hotel and Lodging Association is the leading lodging trade association in the United States, but many others are active in North America and elsewhere. Eating and drinking places are big business. In the United States, this industry is expected to gross $580 billion in 2010 and employ over 12.7 million persons, making the industry the largest private-sector employer in the nation. The National Restaurant Association is the industry's most important trade association.

Meetings and conventions constitute a major reason for business travel and have a huge economic impact. Expenditure on these stimulates all segments of tourism.

The profession of meeting planner is an important and growing one. Those attending meetings and conventions expect a rewarding experience. Thus, expert planning is critical to the success of such events. Meeting planners provide all arrangements necessary for a successful meeting, from transportation services to special events. They are particularly adept at negotiating elements needed for the meeting. Some corporations, associations, government agencies, and others have created their own meeting-planning department, with their own employees handling this important function.

❖ **KEY CONCEPTS** ❖

American Hotel and Lodging
   Association
bed and breakfasts (B&Bs)
culinary tourism
fast-food companies

food service industry
franchising
largest hotel companies
lodging industry
meeting planners

meetings, incentives, conventions,
   and exhibitions
National Restaurant Association
timeshare
trends in the lodging industry

❖ **INTERNET EXERCISES** ❖

The Internet sites mentioned in this chapter plus some selected additional sites are listed for your convenience on the companion Web site for this book, www.wiley.com/college/goeldner.

ACTIVITY 1

Site Name: The National Restaurant Association (NRA)

URL: www.restaurant.org

Background Information: The NRA provides information on consumer studies, trends in restaurants, and press releases that identify trends and issues confronting the industry.

Exercises

1. Choose a state or region in the United States and describe the potential for growth in the restaurant industry for that state/region.

2. What impact do you think travel has on the growth of the restaurant industry in the state/region selected? Why?

ACTIVITY 2

Site Name: International Congress and Convention Association

URL: www.iccaworld.org

Background Information: ICCA is the global community for the meetings industry.

Exercise

1. Determine the types of information you can find in ICCA Statistics Reports.

2. Describe the educational activities provided by ICCA.

❖ **QUESTIONS FOR REVIEW AND DISCUSSION** ❖

1. Why are the world's lodging businesses growing at the rate of about 2.5 percent per year in normal economic times?

2. Identify the reasons why Las Vegas has a high hotel occupancy.

3. Explain the current trend in the United States for slow expansion in the construction of new lodging places.

4. What is culinary tourism?

5. What reasons have brought about the concentration of lodging businesses in Europe and North America?

6. Why have chain and brand-identification hotels and motels continued to expand worldwide versus independent properties?

7. Define franchising. What are the trends and benefits of such groupings? Give examples.

8. List services provided to its members by the American Hotel and Lodging Association. Are state hotel and motel associations affiliated?

9. Similarly, what services do members obtain from the National Restaurant Association?

10. Explain timesharing. Describe its advantages over owning one's own resort property.

11. What factors influence attendance at meetings and conventions?

12. Would you be interested in a career as a professional meeting planner? If so, where would you find out more about this field?

❖ **CASE PROBLEMS** ❖

1. You are the food and beverage manager of a resort hotel located in an interesting historical destination similar to Colonial Williamsburg, Virginia. Recently, you decided that all the guest servers in the dining room should wear authentic costumes typical of those when the area was at its peak as an early trading center. Some of the staff object to this plan, saying that it is a silly idea and also that the costumes look like they might be uncomfortable. What would your reaction be?

2. Angelo V. and his son Leonard are co-owners of a fine-quality 150-seat table-service restaurant. Leonard has been gradually acquiring more authority and responsibility for management. However, recently he and his father have had some sharp disagreements relating to becoming members of their state's restaurant association and the National Restaurant Association. Angelo feels that membership would be a waste of money. If you were Leonard, what would your arguments in favor be?

ENDNOTES

1. American Hotel and Lodging Association, *2010 Lodging Industry Profile* (Washington, DC: AH&LA, 2010) and www.ahla.com.
2. Ibid.
3. Professional Association of Innkeepers International, *Industry Study of Innkeeping Operations and Finance, 2009-2010 edition* (Haddon Heights, NJ: PAII, 2010) and www.innkeeping.org.
4. Hudson Riehle, *2011 Restaurant Industry Forecast* (Washington DC: National Restaurant Association, 2010) and www.restaurant.org.
5. Lucy Long, "A Folkloristic Perspective on Eating and Otherness," in *Culinary Tourism* (Lexington: University of Kentucky Press, 2004).
6. PriceWaterhouseCoopers, *The Economic Significance of Meetings to the U.S. Economy* (Alexandria, VA: Convention Industry Council, 2011) and www.meetingsmeanbusiness.com.

Organizations in the Distribution Process

- Become familiar with tourism distribution system organizations and their functions.

- Understand travel agents and their role in the distribution system.

- Consider the growing impact of the Internet on the distribution system.

- Examine the role of the tour wholesaler.

- Recognize that travel suppliers can use a combination of all channels of distribution.

The ruins of the Colosseum in Rome hold visitors spellbound; they see the pomp of emperors, the spectacle of gladiators and lions, as well as the shards of a great empire. It is probably the finest surviving example of ancient Roman architectural engineering. Tour operators and travel agents send thousands of tourists to visit each year. The Colosseum has been named one of the new seven wonders of the world. *Photo courtesy of Corbis Digital Stock.*

INTRODUCTION

The tourism *channel of distribution* is an operating structure, system, or linkage of various combinations of organizations through which a producer of travel products describes, sells, or confirms travel arrangements to the buyer. For example, it would be impractical for a cruise line to have a sales office in every market city of 5,000 or more people. The most efficient method is to market through more than 15,000 retail travel agencies in the United States and pay them a commission for every cruise sold. The cruises could also be sold through such intermediaries as tour wholesalers (who would include a cruise in a package vacation), through corporate travel offices, via the Internet, or by an association such as an automobile club. Thus, the cruise line uses a combination of distribution channel organizations to sell cruises. Figure 7.1 extracts the operating sectors from Figure 1.2 and shows that travel trade is one of the important sectors of the tourism industry. Tourism distribution channels are similar to those of other basic industries such as agriculture or manufacturing (see Figure 7.2). Their products flow to the ultimate consumer through wholesalers, distributors, and middlemen. Although there are similarities with other industries, the tourism distribution system is unique. Tourism produces mainly services that are intangible. There is no physical product that can be held in inventory to flow from one sales intermediary to another. Instead, the "product" is, for example, a hotel room that is available on a certain day, which is very temporal. If the room is not sold, that revenue is lost forever.

The travel industry landscape is constantly changing, and nowhere is this more true than in travel distribution. Powered by advances in technology and the growth of e-commerce, social media, and smart phones, travel distribution has changed dramatically. The impact on travel agents and consumers brought about by the Internet and technology are examined in this chapter.

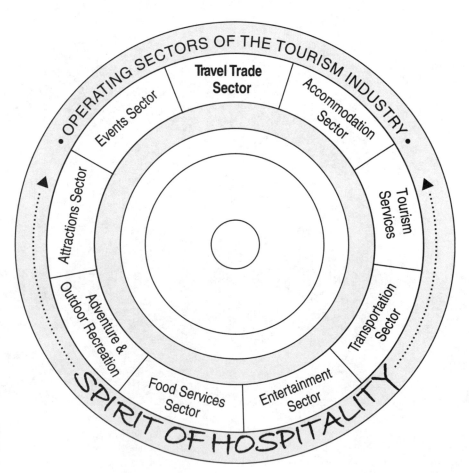

Figure 7.1 Operating sectors of the tourism industry: travel trade.

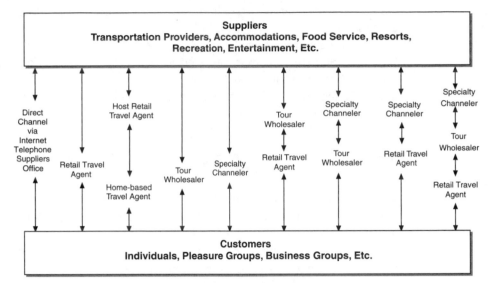

Figure 7.2 Tourism distribution channels.

TRAVEL AGENTS

Travel, whether for business or pleasure, requires arrangements. The traveler usually faces a variety of choices regarding transportation and accommodations; and if the trip is for pleasure, there are a variety of choices regarding destinations, attractions, and activities. The traveler may gather information on prices, value, schedules, characteristics of the destination, and available activities directly, investing a considerable amount of time on the Internet, or possibly money on long-distance telephone calls, to complete the trip arrangements. Alternatively, the traveler may use the services of a retail travel agency, obtaining all these arrangements for a fee.

What Is a Travel Agent?

A **travel agency** is a middleman—a business or person selling the travel industry's individual parts or a combination of the parts to the consumer. In marketing terms, a travel agent is an agent middleman, acting on behalf of the client, making arrangements with suppliers of travel (airlines, hotels, tour operators) and receiving a commission from the suppliers and/or a fee from the client.

In legal terms, a travel agency is an agent of the principal—specifically, transportation companies. The agency operates as a legally appointed agent, representing the principal in a certain geographic area. The agency functions as a broker (bringing buyer and seller together) for the other suppliers, such as hotels, car rentals, ground operators, and tour companies.

A travel agent is thus an expert, knowledgeable in schedules, routing, lodging, currency, prices, regulations, destinations, and all other aspects of travel and travel opportunities. In short, the travel agent is a specialist and counselor who saves the client both time and money. This travel agent still exists today, but in smaller numbers than in the past. Increasingly, they are being replaced by online travel agencies (OTAs), which provide information and let the consumer make the booking. These include companies such as Expedia, Travelocity, Orbitz, Priceline, and Hotwire, for example. Finally, there are home-based travel agents working with hosts.

Airlines Reporting Corporation

When talking about travel agents, it is necessary to talk about the Airlines Reporting Corporation (ARC) because travel agents are accredited by ARC, endorsed by the International Airlines

Travel Agency Network (IATAN), or appointed by Cruise Lines International Association (CLIA) to do business.

ARC is the premier provider of financial settlement solutions and data and analytical services for the travel industry. Airlines, travel agencies, corporate travel departments, railroads, and other travel suppliers process more than $80 billion annually through ARC's world-class settlement system, making it the financial backbone of travel distribution. ARC is an airline-owned company. The ARC Web site is www.arccorp.com.

The Changing World of the Travel Agent

Although the travel industry has struggled through tough times in the twenty-first century because of 9/11 (that is, September 11, 2001) fears of severe acute respiratory syndrome (SARS) in 2003, the global recession of 2008 and 2009, and concerns regarding terrorism and war throughout the decade, the long-term expectation for all travel sectors—except travel agents, is recovery and growth. The travel agent sector reached its peak in numbers in September 1997 with 33,775 ARC-accredited retail agency locations. As of July 2010, there were 15,335 ARC-accredited retail agency locations. Agents sold over $80 billion worth of air travel in 2009.[1]

After decades of offering travel agents a standard commission of 10 percent or more, air carriers in the United States stopped paying base commissions to travel agents in 2002. These changes in the commission system driven by the airlines altered the distribution system fundamentally. Agents were no longer paid to process transactions, and the airlines lost a huge sales force that was not paid until a sale was made.

To offset the loss of commissions, agents developed new sources of income. The most readily available source was service fees. Today, travel agencies charge fees for their services. In addition to charging fees, many agents have also turned to selling more cruises and tour packages and shifted to an emphasis on leisure travel.

A second major factor in the decline in travel agents is the Internet, which has affected travel purchase behavior. The Internet has changed the way much commerce is conducted. Many businesses

Travel agents work with clients, saving them time and money with a personal touch. Using the latest computer reservation technologies, travel agents are able to access the most up-to-date information.
Photo by the author.

use the Internet as a way to bypass product and service intermediaries and deal directly with consumers. The airlines have been a leader in aggressively using e-commerce.

In 1995, low-fare carrier Southwest Airlines was the first to provide customers with schedule and fare information on the Internet. This marked a significant departure for the air industry, which had been limited almost exclusively to central reservation systems (CRSs) for the electronic distribution of information. The Internet and e-tickets became a natural combination as airlines added online booking in 1996. At first, airline booking site development was slower than that of the leading online travel agents, Expedia and Travelocity. Soon, airlines realized they could reduce distribution costs and have direct contact with consumers. The major carriers built powerful Web sites where passengers could make reservations, review frequent-flyer accounts, and check on the status of flights. As a result, airline online bookings increased, as did the depth of information airlines were able to collect on customers. Such information gave the airlines a marketing advantage in creating direct relationships with consumers. The relatively low cost of e-mail marketing enabled the airlines to contact customers more frequently and less expensively than through the mail.

The low-cost carriers in the United States and around the world have been leaders in the use of the Internet and will continue to do so to keep their distribution costs low. The major carriers have followed, aggressively promoting direct booking on their Web sites.

In parallel with airline Web site development, online travel agencies invested large sums to improve their sites and presence. Since 1995, a number of online booking and fare search sites have appeared (and disappeared), disseminating almost unlimited information on any possible destination and thus creating more interest in travel. Consumers search for information and book online to make travel the most successful commercial sector on the Internet. Surveys show the public perceives that the lowest airfares are on the Internet. As the Internet's "easier and less expensive" reputation grows, air market share will continue to shift away from traditional travel agents and be booked directly.

The Internet has become the distribution channel of choice for the airlines, and they are aggressively pushing sales on their own sites. Airlines have grown their share of direct online distribution from less than 3 percent of passenger revenue in 1999 to more than 30 percent today. Traditional travel agents will continue to compete for sales with airlines sites and online agencies.

Although this explains some major reasons why there has been a decrease in the number of travel agents, they have not gone away and are still a major distribution channel for travel. They will maintain that position as long as they continue to deliver valuable service and save clients time and money. Skilled travel agents are still the best choice for complex travel arrangements.

The Travel Agent versus the Internet

The Internet is no longer an emerging channel, but a major channel—a juggernaut—with half of travel in the United States now booked online. Consumers have a choice. They can make their own bookings on the Internet, or they can use the services of the travel agent and they are choosing the Internet. For simple, easy-to-make transactions and attractive travel opportunities, the Internet is a powerful tool. It can increase the scope and reach of a consumer's efforts and allow a person to check hundreds of options or research destinations in depth. But to make the Internet work effectively, a person has to understand where to look and what questions to ask; otherwise, hours can be wasted surfing the Web. This is where a travel agent can save clients a lot of time and effort.

Because of the expertise of travel agents, many customers may save time and achieve savings that more than cover the cost of service fees. Agents have superior knowledge of the industry and are aware of various alternatives that provide lower fares that the average consumer is unaware of. Agents are more likely to know enough to check alternative airports and departure times. Agents can search the Internet as well as their CRS for low fares, and they typically have specialized Web search tools that make searching more efficient. Perhaps the greatest advantage is that once a booking is made, travel agents continue to manage the customer's travel, serving as an alert system, troubleshooter, and customer advocate when supplier problems occur. The Internet can be a valuable resource, but it cannot replace a human being who will provide personalized service to help a client and offer a number of alternatives.

Traditional travel agents have an advantage over Internet sites because they know their clients and how to serve and please them. For example, they know or have the opportunity to know when their birthdays are, their anniversaries, their travel patterns and history, their limitations of time and budget. Their database allows them to suggest a trip to celebrate an anniversary. The personal touch can be a real competitive advantage for traditional travel agents.

The market segment looking for these benefits will continue to use the traditional travel agent while the price-sensitive consumer will go online because the Internet can provide multiple comparisons and it enjoys the perception that the lowest price can be found on the Internet. Currently, the Internet is winning the marketplace battle.

Dimension of the Travel Agency Business

Data are available on travel agencies from American Society of Travel Agents (ASTA), and some highlights from their 2010 travel agency profile are shown on the following pages. Another good source of travel agent information is to look at the studies produced by *Travel Weekly*. Their PowerList published in 2010 shows that 2009 was the year that online travel agency Expedia replaced American Express as the largest seller of travel. In addition to its annual PowerList, the ASTA's annual *Consumer Trends* and *Preview* issues contain valuable information.

Top Ten Agencies

Table 7.1 shows the top ten travel agencies by sales volume. All ten recorded over $1 billion in sales, and their total sales volume was $121.5 billion. Missing is Travelocity which did not provide *Travel Weekly* with sales figures. It is estimated that Travelocity would be ranked seventh had sales figures been reported, as it does close to $10 billion.

Numbers

For years, it was easy to track the number of travel agents because the Airlines Reporting Corporation (ARC) provided an accurate count of the travel agent market. However, since travel agencies became less reliant on selling airline tickets, ARC accreditation no longer gives a true picture of market size. The travel agency market is now made up of ARC and non-ARC sellers of travel. As of July 2010, there were

TABLE 7.1   Top Ten Travel Agencies

Rank	Company	2009 Sales
1	Expedia	$21.8 billion
2	American Express	21.5 billion
3	Carlson Wangonlit Travel	21.4 billion
4	Hogg Robinson Group (HRG)	16.0 billion
5	BCD Travel	14.6 billion
6	Orbitz Worldwide	10.1 billion
7	Priceline.com	9.3 billion
8	AAA Travel	3.2 billion
9	Flight Centre USA	1.9 billion
10	Travel Leaders Group	1.7 billion

Source: Travel Weekly, June 28, 2010.

15,335 ARC-accredited retail agency locations. The number of non-ARC sellers, including home-based agents, has not been quantified, but is in the thousands. The average ASTA travel agency was established in 1985, has been in business for 25 years, and has been an ASTA member for 18 years.[2]

Agency Size

The average ASTA agency has 8 full-time employees, 3 part-time employees, and 12 independent contractors. Although there are large agencies that do billions of dollars in sales, most agencies tend to be small businesses. The vast majority of agencies operate with one or two employees. Almost half of agencies do not have part-time employees or independent contractors.[3]

Agency Location and Business Model

The largest percentage of ASTA agencies is located in one retail location open to walk-ins and with multiple employees (41 percent). Home-based agencies with multiple employees total 16 percent, home-based with one employee 11 percent, multioffice locations 11 percent, one-office location with multiple employees 10 percent, retail location open to walk-ins with one employee 5 percent, and independent agent with host agency affiliation 3 percent.[4]

Business Practices

The phone continues to be the number-one way for agents to conduct business. Agents report they conduct an average of 52 percent of total business over the phone, customers visiting the office account for an average of 20 percent, and the Internet accounts for 28 percent. The trend is for phone communications to drop while the Internet use increases. E-mail has also become an indispensable means of communication. The vast majority of travel agencies now charge service fees on airlines reservations. A typical charge for an airline ticket would be $37.

Most agencies (79 percent) belong to a consortia and/or franchise such as Vacation.com, Travelsavers, Carlson Wagonlit, Ensemble, American Express, and Virtuoso.

ASTA respondents reported 70 percent use an ARC identification number. IATA and CLIA identification numbers were the next two most cited numbers, with 67 percent and 50 percent, respectively. Only 4 percent have taken advantage of ARC's new VTC (Verified Travel Consultant option).

ASTA agencies report that leisure products account for about 78 percent of total sales. Corporate sales make up just under one-quarter of total sales. The percent of share of international sales has increased over the last six years and caught up with domestic sales in 2009 with a 50–50 split. In 2010, international sales are expected to total 55 percent and domestic, 45 percent. A trend is specialization. Agencies are specializing in leisure products and/or destinations.[5]

Types of Travel Arrangements Made

Table 7.2 shows travel agency sales by travel sector for selected years and indicates the trend away from air travel arrangements. ASTA projected that 2010 air sales would fall to 24 percent of sales, while cruise sales would grow to 26 percent and tour packages would be 20 percent. Much smaller proportions of the total sales are attributable to lodging, car rentals, and miscellaneous arrangements; these activities account for 22 percent of sales.

Independent and Home-Based Travel Sellers

Another large part of the decrease in ARC agents is people going independent and being home-based. Independents are the growing segment of the industry. This is a trend not only in travel distribution but also in other fields where it is possible to work from home by going into business for oneself. In the

TABLE 7.2 Agency Sales by Travel Sector[6]

	2002 % Share	2003 % Share	2005 % Share	2006 % Share	2007 % Share	2008 % Share	2009[a] % Share	2010[b] % Share	10/02 % Change
Tour Packages	27%	29%	30%	30%	31%	37%	35%	29%	6%
Airline	34	32	29	27	26	24	24	24	−29%
Cruise	22	22	24	24	25	20	25	26	18%
Hotel	8	9	9	8	10	13	9	10	23%
Car Rental	5	5	5	4	4	3	4	4	−20%
Other	4	4	4	7	4	3	4	8	111%

[a]2009 sales by segment data is revised from last years projections.
[b]2010 sales by segment data is projected.

Source: ASTA.

travel industry, technology has turned just about any location such as a home into a sophisticated office from which business can be conducted.

As independents started writing a considerable amount of business, suppliers that were once skeptical of working with independents have become increasingly eager for their business. This once-maligned and misunderstood marketing force that was once shunned by suppliers is now sought after by agencies and suppliers alike. Although no figures are available on the number of agents who are either home-based or working in host agencies as independent contractors, organizations that serve them give an indication of growth and importance. The National Association of Career Travel Agents (NACTA) serves this group. NACTA is the national trade association for independent travel agents, home-based travel agents, cruise-oriented agents, outside sales travel agents, and traditional ARC-appointed travel agencies that provide services and support to such professionals. NACTA is an affiliate of the American Society of Travel Agents. Visit the NACTA Web site at www.nacta.com.

A resource for these agents is the Home Based Travel Agent Network, www.hbtanetwork.com. The Travel Agent Resource Center, Travel Affiliate Resource Center, and Cruise Agent Link have all been consolidated into this site to create the most current and complete online resource for home-based agents. The Home Based Travel Agent Community is a social network for travel professionals, and more than 6,891 members share information and experiences on this site.

In 2010, the travel agency industry survives in a form that would have been unrecognizable a decade or two ago. Successful agencies have shown a flexibility and adaptability to compete in a changing world.

The Future of Travel Agents

One of the problems of being an intermediary (wholesaler or retailer) is that someone is always trying to eliminate you. So-called experts have been predicting for years that *intermediaries* would disappear—that with the current level of education, technology, and communication, consumers could conduct business directly with suppliers, and middlemen would gradually disappear because they were no longer needed. The experts have been wrong; intermediaries are doing more dollar business than ever before, while at the same time there has been an increase in direct selling.

Because of the Internet, commission caps, commission cuts, commission eliminations, and the changing world of travel, popular questions being raised today are: Will there be a travel agent in the future? Will travel agents survive the elimination of airline commissions? Will the Internet result in the demise of the travel agent? Ever since the Internet gave consumers the ability to plan and book their own travel, there has been speculation surrounding the viability of the traditional travel agent. Numerous articles have suggested the downfall of the travel agent channel of distribution.

Travel agents love sending clients on cruise vacations because they come back as satisfied customers. Cruise vacations have one of the highest satisfaction ratings of all vacation types. *Photo courtesy of Carnival Cruise Lines.*

Despite the many predictions that the travel agent would disappear, the species is alive and will continue to adapt to the changing marketplace and survive as long as they offer a service that is valued by clients. There will be further consolidation driven by the economics of this business.

It is also increasingly clear that agents will morph into sellers of more leisure travel services. Furthermore, their product mix will grow to favor more "complex" and "high-risk" transactions, such as bookings for tours, cruises, honeymoons, and all-inclusives, as the Internet becomes the preferred choice for "simple" and "low-risk" transactions, such as point-to-point airline tickets or a hotel room for two nights. Agents will continue to be the preferred choice of many affluent and international travelers because of the complexity associated with planning travel outside of the United States.

Travel Agency Organizations

The American Society of Travel Agents is the largest association of travel and tourism professionals in the world, with 20,000 members located in over 140 countries. Established in 1931, ASTA continues to serve the best interests of the travel industry and the traveling public. ASTA's purposes are:

■ To promote and encourage travel among people of all nations
■ To promote the image and encourage the use of professional travel agents worldwide
■ To promote and represent the views and interests of travel agents to all levels of government and industry
■ To promote professional and ethical conduct in the travel agency industry worldwide
■ To serve as an information resource for the industry worldwide

■ To promote consumer protection and safety for the traveling public
■ To conduct educational programs for members on subjects related to the travel industry
■ To encourage environmentally sound tourism worldwide

To be an active ASTA member, a travel agency must be currently accredited with the Airline Reporting Corporation or endorsed by the International Airlines Travel Agent Network. All ASTA members agree to comply with the society's Principles of Professional Conduct and Ethics. Visit the ASTA Web site at www.astanet.com.

A smaller organization of travel agents is the Association of Retail Travel Agents (ARTA). They are the voice of the small and independent travel agents. The purpose of this organization is similar to that of ASTA, but ARTA does not supply the range of services provided to the members of ASTA. Although ARTA addresses many travel agency issues at different levels, its two primary activities are to provide education and training to its members and to lobby on their behalf. Visit its Web site at www.artaonline.com.

For specialized travel agencies that sell only cruises, there is the National Association of Cruise Oriented Agencies (NACOA). This group provides promotional and management assistance to its members. On a global scale, travel agent organizations include the United Federation of Travel Agents' Associations and the World Association of Travel Agencies.

Particularly in the British Commonwealth and in the United States, there are travel agents' organizations whose purpose is to raise business and professional competency and to award certification. In the United States, The Travel Institute, formerly the Institute of Certified Travel Agents (ICTA), provides an educational and certification program leading to the designation CTC (Certified Travel Counselor), CTA (Certified Travel Associate), and Certified Travel Industry Executive (CTIE). The Travel Institute has developed unique destination specialist courses, which cover destinations such as Alaska, Caribbean, France, India, Mexico, South Pacific, and Southern Europe. In addition, it has developed Lifestyle Specialists programs such as accessible travel, adventure travel, gay and lesbian travel, luxury travel, skiing, spa travel, and sustainable travel. With ASTA, it developed the Travel Agent Proficiency Test (TAP).

Travel agents love to send their clients to relaxing and idyllic settings such as the Abaco Beach Resort and Boat Harbour in Abaco, Bahamas. *Photo courtesy of Abaco Beach Resort and Boat Harbour.*

Global Distribution Systems

The term *global distribution system* (GDS) is used to describe the large and sophisticated electronic travel reservation systems in use throughout the world. There are currently three major GDS companies in operation: Amadeus, Sabre, and Travelport GDS, which includes Galileo and Worldspan. They are frequently called the legacy GDSs. There are other smaller GDS systems, such as Abacus with a focus on Asia/Pacific and KIV Systems with a focus on Latin America, but these big three are the most used systems accounting for the majority of global bookings. Today, they are independently owned companies capable of handling tens of millions of transactions a day for every aspect of the travel services industry.

It all started in the late 1950s and early 1960s, when airlines created their own proprietary automated reservation systems to manage booking air travel. By the 1970s, American Airlines' SABRE system, TWA's PARS system, Eastern Airlines' SYSTEM ONE system, United Airlines' APOLLO system, and Delta Airlines' DATAS II system evolved to become the most popular systems in use. In the late 1970s and early 1980s, the airlines expanded their systems to provide service to multiple airlines and began installing their reservation systems directly in travel agent offices to provide convenient and efficient access for travel agents.

Since then, the reservations systems have evolved beyond just air travel reservations to become the big three independently owned companies covering all aspects of travel. They are no longer regulated in the United States, but remain subject to government regulations in Canada and the European Union. Amadeus evolved from Eastern Airlines System One, Sabre from American Airlines, Galileo from United's Apollo, and Worldspan from Delta, Northwest, and TWA systems. Numerous smaller companies have also been formed to compete. Many are aimed at geographic, industry, or language niches inadequately served by the big three. The Interactive Travel Services Association (www.interactivetravel.org) calls these smaller systems Limited Travel Distributors (LTDs). An example is rezStream (www.rezstream.com), who is developing GDS alternatives.

The world's GDS companies have created new trends in travel distribution. Relying on state-of-the-art technology, GDSs provide their travel partners with comprehensive services ranging from the simplest round-trip air ticket to complex global itineraries encompassing air, lodging, ground transportation, tours and packages, entertainment, cruises, insurance, and more. They deliver a worldwide distribution network. GDS systems have multiyear contracts with thousands of travel agents to provide access to the broad range of travel offerings they cover. They also have multiyear contracts with hundreds of airlines to manage reservations. They continue to handle about 80 percent of transactions.

GDSs are responsible for some of the most important innovations in the travel industry, including electronic ticketing, travel e-commerce, graphic seat selection, lowest-fare search capability, and the ability for agents and travelers to view, on one screen, public, private/negotiated, consolidator, and Web fares.

GDSs Sabre and Amadeus are working on the electronic miscellaneous document (EMD) technology that will enable fees for airline ancillary services, such as baggage fees, to be paid through GDSs.

Online travel is an e-commerce success story. Online travel companies offer consumers access to travel and tourism options and furnish suppliers with opportunities to distribute their products widely and at low cost. Online travel agencies such as Expedia, Travelocity, Orbitz, Hotwire, Priceline, ebookers, Site 59, Cheap Tickets, and Opodo use the GDS systems; some are owned by the GDS systems.

The GDS companies and online travel companies continue to evolve along with technology. Continuous change is forecast for these elements of the distribution system.

THE INTERNET

In today's marketplace it is necessary to talk about the juggernaut *Internet* as a channel of distribution. It makes direct selling from the supplier to the consumer more possible than ever before. In travel, there have always been direct sales, from suppliers to consumers, via suppliers' offices or the telephone. Telephone sales received a huge boost with the advent of 800 numbers, and at the time, 800 numbers were considered to be state-of-the-art technology. We have witnessed the coming of computers, central reservation systems, faxes, smart cards, videos, CD-ROMS, DVDs, and the impact they have had on the travel distribution process. Today, the Internet has become the major channel of distribution for travel and continues to grow. The Web gives consumers the information and power to plan and book their own travel. It also gives travel agents and tour operators the opportunity to have their own sites and greatly expands their reach. The Web gives suppliers (airlines, hotels, rental car companies, cruise lines, attractions, etc.) a direct sales channel that can reduce distribution costs by having the consumer do the booking, thereby eliminating travel agency commissions and computer reservation system fees. The Internet is both an information source and a transaction source. Consequently, the Internet continues to evolve as a new marketing medium. It has the advantage that it can be used by virtually everyone in the tourism industry, from the largest operator to the smallest. The airline giants and lodging giants have excellent Web sites, as do smaller-scale businesses such as bed and breakfasts, dude ranches, ski areas, tour operators, travel agents, tourism organizations, and even restaurants. These travel suppliers have a new promotional and distribution tool to work with and one that promises cost savings.

Today, the Internet is not only used by suppliers for destination information and booking all aspects of travel, but has become a powerful social medium. Users are now a major force on the Web. The term Web 2.0 refers to a change in how the Web is used, which is now user-centered. The term **Tourism 2.0** is the use of Web 2.0 applications in the tourist industry. The key features are the user-generated content, where users express opinions about their preferences and social networking. In planning trips, consumers not only consult destination Web site, but visit social sites, check travel blogs, look for user recommendations, examine opinions, and enjoy photos and videos. Once they travel, they share their own experiences on the Internet. For example, they might rate the hotels where they have stayed on Tripadvisor, publish their photos on Flickr, upload their videos on YouTube, and share their experiences on Facebook and Twitter. The Web gives "word-of-mouth recommendations" new meaning and impacts e-commerce. Social media are providing new ways for suppliers to connect with their markets.

Electronic Commerce

The term **e-commerce** refers to the selling of goods and services via the Internet. Many studies indicate that travel is now the king of Internet sales. Because of the importance of e-commerce, the U.S. Travel Association, PhoCusWright, Forrester Research, and Jupiter Research all conduct studies on a regular basis that show online travel sales are increasing and are expected to continue to grow.

Creating growth are suppliers' Web sites and Internet booking services such as Expedia, Travelocity, Orbitz, GetThere.com, Vacation.com, Cheap Tickets, Cruises Only, Priceline, American Express, and Travel Web, which are full-service megasites. Although most airlines and other travel suppliers have sophisticated Web sites for their own schedules and fares, these sites rarely show comparison rates. Consumers may find it easier to use services of travel aggregators such as Kayak, Farechase, Booking Buddy, Mobissimo, Cheap Flights, Dohop, Momando, Skyscanner, and Ixigo to find helpful travel information and a comparison of fares and schedules among different airlines and other travel suppliers.

Small to medium-size firms are using the global reach of the Web. It serves as a great equalizer for small firms because travelers around the globe can seek out a small hotel or B&B just as easily as a five-star property. A small hotel in Amsterdam, unlisted in guidebooks, reported that 80 percent of its U.S. reservations came from the Web.

The easiest prediction of all to make is that Internet technology and growth will continue, as will the number of people who buy and sell on the Internet. This channel does have some limitations.

Limitations

Despite its great sales volume, the Internet has limitations. It is high tech, but it is not high touch. It produces an overwhelming amount of information—in many cases, more than the consumer can digest. It is a challenge to hold the user's attention long enough to deliver your message. A key to Web success is keeping information current, which is a formidable task. Nothing is worse than seeing outdated information on the Web. Speed and ease of use still need to be improved. Pop-up ads are also annoying. Consumers have two major concerns about the Web. One is their right to privacy, and the other is the security of the site.

The Future

In the ever-changing technological environment, it is essential that all components of the tourism industry, whether large or small, public or private, have the best intelligence on which to base decisions. One of the ways to do that is to tap the Internet as an information source. The day has come when a large segment of the market communicates and transacts business on the Internet as routinely as talking on the phone.

Speaking of the phone, it is beginning to show great promise to be a powerful force in travel. Peter Yesawich, CEO of Ypartnership, reports that three out of ten cell phones in the United States are smart phones with Internet connectivity. Travelers are using them to search for the latest information on flight schedules and delays, comparison shop airfares and hotel rates, view virtual visitor guides, and book air travel and lodging. Apple's iPhone has a travel portal application that is a travel booking portal for flights, hotels, vehicles, and events. Travelers also use their BlackBerry to check flights.

Google is poised to be a greater force in travel distribution with its acquisition of the flight information company ITA Software, the leading provider of flight information from airlines to travel Web sites. Google will use the acquisition to create an interface to make it easier for people to search for flights on Google, which already provides a lot of travel information. The acquisition gives Google the potential to become the predominant online company for travel search. A Google press release states the acquisition will benefit passengers, airlines, and online travel agencies by making it easier for users to comparison shop for flights and airfares and by driving more potential customers to airlines' and online travel agencies' Web sites. Google will not be setting airfare prices and has no plans to sell airline tickets to consumers.

Another way is to think beyond the Internet. How soon will the Internet be old technology? Will the mobile phone become the dominant Internet platform? How soon will consumers be able to book travel from all sorts of devices, such as their television set or an appliance we do not know about yet in a networked home? Voice-recognition systems are improving, and the price of hardware and software required to support them is declining. How soon will they become a part of the automated system? The smart agent or digital robot is a computer application that can complete specific tasks without human intervention. Will this application become commonplace?

CONSOLIDATORS

Consolidators are travel agencies that sell airline tickets at sizable discounts. They specialize in this area and have contracts with one or more airlines to distribute discount tickets. Airlines work with consolidators to help fill what would otherwise be empty seats.

Some consolidators act strictly as wholesalers, selling their tickets only through other travel agencies. Others also sell directly to the public, usually at higher-than-wholesale prices. Thus, they function as both a wholesaler and a retailer.

Travel agents are booking more adventure travel, which is a fast-growing segment of the tourism industry. Outdoor participation activities such as rafting and kayaking are popular. *Photo courtesy of Tuolumne County Visitors Bureau.*

Discount agencies sell consolidator tickets or other discounted travel services to the public. Some act as their own consolidators, while others buy from wholesale consolidators. It is now relatively easy to find a discounter that sells consolidator tickets. Consumer travel publications list consolidators, and consumers can also buy consolidator tickets from most full-service travel agencies.

THE TOUR WHOLESALER

The **tour wholesaler** (also called tour operator) puts together a tour and all of its components and sells the tour through his or her own company, through retail outlets, and/or through approved retail travel agencies. Wholesalers can offer vacation packages to the traveling public at prices lower than an individual traveler can arrange because wholesalers can buy services such as transportation, hotel rooms, sightseeing services, airport transfers, and meals in large quantities at discounted prices.

Tour wholesaling became an important segment of the U.S. travel industry after World War II. It has expanded substantially since the 1960s, largely because air carriers wanted to fill the increasing numbers of aircraft seats. The tour wholesale business consists primarily of planning, preparing, and marketing a vacation tour, including making reservations and consolidating transportation and ground services into a tour assembled for a departure date to a specific destination. Tours are then sold to the public through retail outlets such as travel agents and airline ticket offices.

The number of independent tour operators has grown dramatically over the past decade and now numbers over 2,000. A large portion of the business, however, is concentrated in the hands of a small number of large operators.

Independent tour wholesalers provide significant revenue to transportation and ground service suppliers. They also provide the retailer and the public with a wide selection of tours to a large number of destinations at varying costs, for varying durations, and in various seasons. Furthermore, they supply advance notice and increased assurance of future passenger volumes to suppliers.

The independent tour wholesaler's business is characterized by relative ease of entry, high velocity of cash flow, low return on sales, and the potential for high return on equity because the investment necessary to start such a business is small.

ROBIN TAUCK
owner/past president and CEO of
Tauck Inc., founder of Robin Tauck
& Partners, and board officer of
Tauck Foundation, Fairfield County,
Connecticut, www.robintauck.com

Founded in 1925, Tauck World Discovery is a leading escorted tour operator that offers more than 100 upscale land, cruise, riverboat, and safari itineraries in more than 80 countries worldwide. A family-owned and operated company, Tauck was launched as Tauck Tours in 1925 by Arthur Tauck, Sr. From 1997 to 2008, his granddaughter Robin Tauck served as company president, CEO, and a board officer.

During her 30-year career at Tauck, Robin held a number of positions and led new growth initiatives, most notably expansions into 80 countries and seven continents, "Tauck at Sea" luxury small ship cruising, European river cruising, Tauck Bridges family programs, and premier events.

A proponent of one-to-one marketing to upscale clients, Robin fostered Tauck's customer-focused direction and brand loyalty efforts, including strategic agent partnerships and the development of "E-Tauck" initiatives. She also chaired the company's executive group, led its strategic planning efforts, and instituted brand steering and "World of Giving" advisory boards.

In 2000, Robin began Tauck's "World of Giving" corporate social responsibility philanthropic "giving back" efforts and new *volun-tourism* (over 15,000 participants), and dozens of heritage grants. Robin led Tauck's support of the U.S. National Parks, and those efforts were recognized in 2006 with the nation's highest honor, the "Preserve America Presidential Award," in an Oval Office ceremony with the President George W. Bush and First Lady Laura Bush. Tauck's support of the National Parks has also been honored with the U.S. Interior Department's 2005 "Take Pride In America Award" and TIA's 2004 "Public & Community Service Odyssey Award."

In 2008, Robin made a transition from her three-decade career with Tauck management to that of major shareholder. She is involved with high-level industry issues and also formed a new venture, Robin Tauck & Partners LLC, to align leaders within the specialty segments of global travel arena with a focus on public–private partnerships.

Robin is a board member on the prestigious World Travel and Tourism Council (WTTC) of London, which represents 100 of the top CEO's owners and chairmen in travel and tourism. She has also served on several boards and affiliations, including US/ICOMOS, Save America's Treasures, and USTA in Washington, D.C.

On multiple occasions, Robin has been named one of the "Most Powerful Women in Travel" by *Travel Agent* magazine.

Robin is focusing her advocacy and expertise externally, serving as a representative of the U.S. travel industry for public–private partnerships in protecting global sites and building economic development through tourism. She continues to be a family member spokesperson for Tauck Inc. Additionally, as a spokesperson for sustainable travel, she is often asked to speak at nonindustry events, sharing the message of the "Power of Travel," which is now the number-one income source (GDP) for many developing countries.

WORDS FOR THE FUTURE

This is an exciting time for our industry, with a bright future! People are traveling in record numbers. As the world reaches a record population of 7 billion, it is remarkable that by 2015, an estimated 1.5 billion people will be recorded as international arrivals (crossing borders)—and such figures do not include the burgeoning domestic travel market. Just imagine the future . . . .

Such mobility on a global scale is unprecedented and provides enormous opportunity—for bringing people together in understanding, for prospering in business and economies, for developing education, and for improving and furthering the interests and the welfare of society-at-large. Indeed, many lesser developed nations now report up to 60 percent of their GDP directly related to travel and tourism—moving from agriculture, mining, seafood, and other traditional sectors. I believe this is the most promising industry at one of the most promising times in the history of the world. Yet it also comes with responsibility, which is a new opportunity in and of itself.

For example, the climate challenge and its related effects are now described as "the largest challenge this industry will likely face for the next 40 years" according to UNWTO and WTTC leadership groups who attended the Copenhagen Climate Conference with 148 nations. Currently, travel and tourism accounts for only 5 percent of global emissions, yet it is a large, visible, responsible, and ethical industry with a new bold plan. Concurrently, the opportunity for cultural heritage development, appreciation for and development of environmental protection, and even the UN Millennium goals of the eradication of poverty and other international priorities, are all possible with this new phenomenon referred to as the *power of travel*.

New-generation thinking and "voice" as well as vastly expanding technology and social media are bringing together people in ways unimaginable in the past—transforming an ability to collaborate and .connect; to learn about each others' lives and to build a better world through understanding, participation, and action. Global travel no longer imbues an image of sightseeing journeys for the privileged, but rather, a way of life for the masses with unforeseen benefits in education, health, happiness, and prosperity.

It is noteworthy, that the continual upward trend of leisure travel has proven tenuous yet steady and resilient, despite a myriad of threats including significant global recessions, political turmoil and revolutions, major terrorist events, environmental concerns, and other challenges of our recent time. In my lifetime and career in travel, I have personally worked and led through nearly 30 crises of differing proportions that affected the travel industry as a whole, and I have seen this industry rebound and get stronger through each and every challenge. And the travelers keep traveling.

Heritage travel remains a primary reason for visiting new destinations, and travelers are seeking authentic experiences that celebrate and reveal local culture. Clearly, the growth in tourism in less-developed countries (LDCs, where populations earn less than $5/day) is improving the lives of the people. This is a service industry in which entry-level service jobs are easily developed, and these opportunities occur virtually across the globe.

Going forward, our industry needs to focus on making sure that travel is sustainable. We need to ensure that visiting the sites we care so much about preserves them for future generations and doesn't hasten their destruction. We need to preserve and support the native cultures indigenous to these amazing places, and we need to travel more efficiently in order to minimize our impact on the environment.

Travel and tourism is on an exciting path of promise on many levels, and this is one of the best times to join the travel industry. In many ways, the most exciting part of the future will fall to future travel industry professionals—like you. I'm an optimist in every way, and I wish you a fulfilling journey.

rtauck@robintauck.com

Tour wholesaling businesses are usually one of four kinds: (1) the independent tour wholesaler, (2) the airline working in close cooperation with a tour wholesaling business, (3) the retail travel agent who packages tours for its clients, and (4) the operator of motorcoach tours. These four entities, along with incentive travel companies and travel clubs, make up the industry.

Figure 7.3 illustrates the position of the tour wholesaler in the basic structure of the travel industry. The public or the consumer is the driving force and can purchase travel services from a retail travel agent or directly from the suppliers of travel services: the airlines, hotels, and other providers of destination services. The tour wholesaler's role is that of consolidating the services of airlines and other

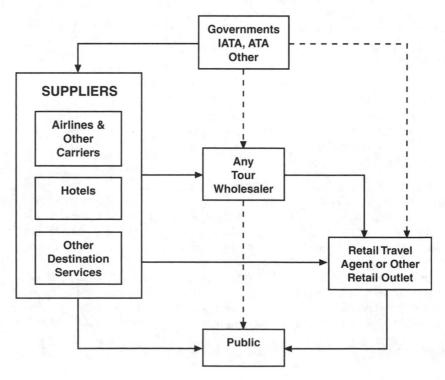

Figure 7.3 Basic structure of the U.S. travel industry.
Source: Tour Wholesaler Industry Study, Touche, Ross & Co.

carriers with the ground services needed into one package, which can be sold through travel agents to the consuming public.

Tour operators have not been immune to the effects of online packaging and have been working to keep pace with this distribution channel. The Internet is ideally suited to feature their tours and destinations and the Web has become a major sales channel for them.

TOUR WHOLESALER ORGANIZATIONS

The National Tour Association **(NTA)** is an association for travel professionals who have a keen interest in the packaged travel sector for the industry. Promoting partnering and networking among its members, the association brings together those who package travel with suppliers and destinations who represent the various components of a trip. NTA focuses on the development, promotion, and increased use of tour operator packaged travel. They also serve as a consumer advocate through their code of ethics, stringent membership requirements, and education.

The association provides marketing assistance, educational programs, governmental representation, and communications for its membership, and it annually produces the NTA Convention and Tour and Travel Exchange. This event is one of the largest travel industry gatherings held in North America, offering members the opportunity to conduct intensive business sessions and attend education seminars that increase professionalism in the industry. The association also produces the Grass Roots Symposium, Montage, and Contact. These events provide members with additional opportunities each year to network and participate in educational programs.

NTA requires its members to adhere to a strict code of ethics that ensures proper business activity between individual members for the ultimate good of the traveling public. The association acts as the primary advocate for consumers of the group tour product in North America and works to promote consumer awareness of that vacation alternative. NTA provides the traveling public protection through their Consumer Protection Plan. Visit its Web site at www.ntaonline.com.

The United States Tour Operators Association (USTOA) represents the tour operators industry. They are composed of companies whose tours and packages encompass the entire globe and who conduct business in the United States. The goals of USTOA are to ensure consumer protection and education; to inform the travel industry, government agencies, and the public about tour operators' activities and objectives; to maintain a high level of professionalism within the industry; and to facilitate travel on a worldwide basis. USTOA's members must subscribe to the organization's strict code of ethics. Members are required to represent all information pertaining to tours, to maintain a high level of professionalism, and to state clearly all costs and facilities in advertising and promotional materials. Visit its Web site at www.ustoa.com.

Most tour operators and wholesalers belong to the American Society of Travel Agents. Many also belong to the various promotional groups, such as the Pacific Asia Travel Association (PATA), the Caribbean Tourism Organization (CTO), and USTA (U.S. Travel Association).

SIGHTSEEING AND RECEPTIVE SERVICE AGENCIES

Local or short tours are conducted by sightseeing companies, and many of them are organized into American Sightseeing International and Gray Line. These organizations aid sightseeing companies by providing local sightseeing services and competent personnel. Many sightseeing tour companies are also affiliated with the organizations already mentioned.

Receptive operators are located across the country and handle inbound package tour business. Receptive operators advise international tour operators about which itineraries and travel experiences will work best for their clients. Once the best itinerary has been determined the receptive operator will organize the countless details to make the client's trip successful. They typically meet the needs of any

Touring the mountains of Queenstown, New Zealand, from a jet boat never fails to overwhelm visitors with the majesty of the surroundings and the thrill of coming close to rocks. *Photo courtesy of PhotoDisc, Inc.*

size group and can arrange everything from transfers, currency exchange, interpreters, accommodations, attractions, meals, entertainment, and transportation. They have local personal knowledge of the best and most reliable motor coach companies, hotels, restaurants, attractions, and other suppliers who will ensure a successful travel experience. The receptive agent serves as a mediator in negotiating deposit and payment deadlines that are acceptable to the supplier and the international tour operator.

Although mainly serving inbound groups from abroad, some receptive service operators also service other markets and groups such as special interest and technical groups, special events, fraternal organizations, people with handicaps, senior groups, and student groups.

The Receptive Services Association of America (RSAA) serves this group of travel professionals. RSAA's mission is helping receptive operators serve international tour companies through partnerships with North American suppliers. Visit its Web site at www.rsana.com.

❖ GLOBAL INSIGHT ❖

Trade Fairs and Shows

Special entities in the promotion and distribution of travel are fairs, exchanges, shows, exhibitions, and markets. The entities bring buyers and sellers together at venues where billions of dollars of business is transacted.

ITB BERLIN

The biggest of these entities is ITB Berlin, which takes place in March every year. ITB is, without doubt, the largest travel trade show in the world. The exhibitors at the ITB come from all sectors of the international travel and tourism industry and include government tourism offices, national and regional tourism organizations, tour operators, hotels, airline carriers, insurance companies, communication and information systems, travel agencies, publishing, and dot-com companies. ITB also has consumer days where consumers are allowed in to see what the world's travel industry has to offer. In 2010, more than 11,000 organizations from 180 countries exhibited using 160,000 square yards of exhibition area. Seminars, symposia, workshops, and working groups also take place at ITB. Visit ITB's Web site at www.fair.itb-berlin.de. In 2008, a new ITB Trade Show, ITB Asia, was launched and is now held annually in Singapore.

WORLD TRAVEL MARKET

The World Travel Market (WTM) held annually in London each November is the world's second largest travel trade show. WTM is a four-day travel industry event that brings together worldwide buyers and sellers from every sector of the industry. It provides a unique opportunity for the global travel trade industry to meet, network, negotiate, conduct business, and learn about the latest developments in the travel industry. Over 45,500 travel industry professionals representing 187 countries participated in WTM in 2009. Visit its Web site at www.wtmlondon.com.

POW WOW

In the United States, the major trade show is USTA's International Pow Wow. It provides a venue to bring U.S. suppliers together with tour operators and buyers from around the world. Pow Wow moves from city to city. In 2010, it was held in Orlando, Florida. It will be held in San Francisco, California, in 2011; Los Angeles, California, in 2012, and Las Vegas, Nevada, in 2013. See www.ustravel.org/events/international-pow-wow.

DISCUSSION QUESTIONS

1. What is the largest tourism trade fair in the world?

2. What are the advantages of participating in trade fairs and shows?

SPECIALTY CHANNELERS

Specialty intermediaries include such organizations as incentive travel firms, business meeting and convention planners, corporate travel offices, association executives, hotel representatives, travel consultants, trade shows, and supplier sales offices. Although specialty intermediaries are a small force in distribution compared to travel agencies, they have considerable power to influence when, where, and how people travel. Such groups can represent either buyers or sellers, receiving either a commission or a salary from their employer. Specialty intermediaries are experts in their particular aspect of travel. As tourism becomes more specialized, these types of channelers will become increasingly important.

Incentive Travel Firms

Incentive travel has been enjoying significant growth because travel rewards are one of the most powerful motivators for increased employee performance. Companies can reward distributors, customers, and their employees. In the United States, there are about 500 incentive travel firms selling their professional services of designing, promoting, and accomplishing incentive travel programs for buyers. They have a national trade association, the Society of Incentive Travel Executives (SITE).

Corporate Travel Departments

Just as many corporations have chosen to set up their own meeting planning departments, many also have travel sections. Growth in this area took place when the airline industry was deregulated in the late 1970s. Such in-house corporate travel departments try to contain travel and entertainment costs by getting the best prices on travel. They typically provide the same services as those of travel agencies serving the corporate market.

Hotel Sales Representative Firms

Some companies specialize in representing hotels, motels, resorts, and destination areas. This type of firm provides an alternative to a property hiring its own sales force and is an economical way to be represented in foreign markets. Hotel sales representatives are also active in the convention and meetings field.

Tour operators plan and organize all elements of a trip. Viewing wild animals in their natural habitat is the mainstay of African safari tours. *Photo courtesy of PhotoDisc/Getty Images.*

Automated Distribution

Using telephone lines, the satellite ticket printer (STP) enables a travel agency to print tickets electronically in an office of a corporation that the agency serves, thus eliminating the cost of delivering tickets. If this corporation wishes to use a particular agency's expertise, automated distribution allows it to do so, regardless of the distance involved. Also, the corporation's travel expenses can be summarized into one periodic account—a beneficial arrangement.

CHOOSING CHANNELS

Any marketing executive must decide which combination of distribution channels would be most productive. One of his or her most important tasks is choosing channels, which involves—researching and identifying distribution possibilities. Then, the particular travel product can be integrated into the distributor's operation. Some channels are very evident, such as the Internet, travel agencies, and tour operators. However, depending on the individual product, additional distributors such as tour companies, specialty channelers, incentive travel firms, corporate travel departments, hotel sales reps, and associations, can be very sales effective. Often, associations have huge numbers of members, which make them particularly good avenues for increasing sales. Suppliers will typically use multiple channels of distribution.

SUMMARY

Tourism channels of distribution are organizational links in a travel product producer's system of describing, selling, and confirming travel arrangements to the buyer. Such channels are needed because it is impractical for any supplier to own sales outlets in every market city. It is much more feasible and productive to distribute the product through, for example, 15,000 retail travel agencies or online travel agencies. There are specialty channelers of many kinds.

The Internet is a force in the sale of travel today. It will continue to grow in importance in the future and have additional impacts on the travel distribution system. Travel distribution channels are similar to those used in other industries. But tourism products are intangible. They cannot be stored and sold another time. An airplane seat, if not occupied on a given trip, is revenue lost forever.

 KEY CONCEPTS

American Society of Travel Agents	hotel sales representatives	specialty intermediaries
automated distribution	incentive travel firms	Tourism 2.0
choosing channels	intermediaries	tour wholesalers
consolidators	Internet	trade fairs & shows
corporate travel departments	ITB Berlin	travel agencies
distribution channels	National Tour Association	United States Tour Operators
e-commerce	online travel agencies	Association
home-based travel seller	receptive service agencies	

 INTERNET EXERCISES

The Internet sites mentioned in this chapter plus some selected additional sites are listed for your convenience on the companion Web site for this book, www.wiley.com/college/goeldner.

ACTIVITY 1

Site Name: Expedia Travel

URL: www.expedia.com

Background Information: This site features comprehensive destination information, timely and relevant travel news, expert advice, the lowdown on deals, and much more.

Site Name: Travelocity

URL: www.travelocity.com

Background Information: Travelocity, powered by the Sabre system, provides reservations capabilities for over 420 airlines, 40,000 hotels, and more than 50 car rental companies.

Site Name: Orbitz

URL: www.orbitz.com

Background Information: Orbitz is another online agency. It is a major competitor to Expedia and Travelocity.

Exercises

1. Describe the features of these three sites.
2. Identify their role in the tourism distribution system.

Site Name: National Tour Association

URL: www.ntaonline.com

Background Information: The National Tour Association is an association for travel professionals who have a keen interest in the packaged travel sector of the industry. Their mission is to provide unsurpassed value for the global packaged travel industry.

Exercises

1. Go to the site and find the definition of "packaged travel."
2. Find the number and composition of members of the National Tour Association.
3. Outline the membership benefits.

❖ **QUESTIONS FOR REVIEW AND DISCUSSION** ❖

1. As a producer of travel products, why not just sell your services directly to the consumer?
2. Why has the Internet become the most important tourism distribution channel?
3. Give some examples of marketing aids that a supplier might provide to a travel agency.
4. Some counselors are not really good salespersons. As manager of your agency, what skill-building program would you inaugurate?
5. You are marketing director for a cruise line operating truly luxurious ships. It has superb service and cuisine. How would you proceed to identify the most promising distributors?
6. What do receptive services operators do?
7. As the president of a newly formed tour company, you must now decide if your tours are to be marketed through retail travel agencies or whether you should try to sell them directly to the consumer. Identify the advantages and disadvantages of each alternative. Would it be wise to do both? Discuss.
8. Why should an independently owned and operated travel agency become affiliated with one of the consortia, cooperatives, or franchise groups?
9. What do you see as the future of the travel agent?
10. List the advantages of a tour company becoming a member of USTOA.
11. What do travel aggregators do?
12. A fairly large manufacturer of specialty electric products is located in your city. What steps would you take to sell this company on an incentive travel plan?
13. What do you see as the strength and weaknesses of a home-based travel agency? What is their future?

❖ **CASE PROBLEMS** ❖

1. Joan S. and her husband are planning a vacation to a destination about which they know very little. They have seen an exciting ad for this area in a travel magazine. They respond to the ad, and subsequently they receive a group of fascinating brochures describing all the attractions, accommodations, shops, climate, and other allures. In the same magazine they saw an ad for an airline that serves this destination, including Web site information for reservations. Should they make their own reservations or should they seek the help of a travel agency?

2. A professor recently walked into a travel agency—his first visit there—and asked for a specific cruise brochure. The travel agent rose from her desk, found the promotional piece requested, and handed it to him. The professor thanked her and then asked, "How is the

travel business these days?" She replied, "Business and corporate are OK but vacation travel is way off because of the economy." She then sat down, looked into her CRS screen, and said, "Have a nice day." Can you believe such a scenario? What should the conversation have been?

3. A prominent national columnist recently advised his readers that they should bypass their local travel agencies and obtain their cruise vacations directly from the suppliers by phone or Internet. This recommendation was intended to save the public money because, he explained, ship lines pay commissions to travel agencies whenever a sale is made. What's wrong with such advice?

4. An international tour company partnership is owned by Bill and Jane W. Bill is a rather deliberate, cautious type; Jane tends to be more aggressive and promotional in her day-to-day business relationships. The company's volume of business has declined somewhat during the past two years. Considering the decline, the couple recently had an extended discussion as to possible steps that might increase tour sales. Jane finally proposed that they should contact some of the largest travel agency cooperatives, also known as co-ops, consortia, franchisers, joint marketing organizations, stockholder licensee groups, and individual and corporate-owned chains. Jane thought that perhaps if their company could become a so-called preferred supplier to one or several of these groups, they would then increase their business considerably. Almost all of their tours are sold through retail travel agencies. Bill listened to this suggestion and then said, "I doubt that this idea would do us any good. The co-op movement is not well established, and a lot of agencies are not members at all." Who's right? Why? Explain your position.

ENDNOTES

1. Airline Reporting Corporation, *Sales and Documents* (Arlington, VA: ARC, 2010) and www.arccorp.com.
2. American Society of Travel Agents, *ASTA Agency Profile* (Alexandria, VA: ASTA, 2010) and www.asta.org.
3. Ibid.
4. Ibid.
5. Ibid.
6. Ibid.

CHAPTER 8 ✛

Attractions, Entertainment, Recreation, and Other Tourist Draws

LEARNING OBJECTIVES

- Examine the attractions sphere.
- Look at the role of theme parks.
- Understand the gaming industry.

- Describe public and commercial recreation facilities.
- Recognize shopping as a travel attraction.

Preserved castles, mansions, and gardens are a popular tourist attraction throughout Europe. Shown here is Egeskov Castle in Funen, Denmark. *Photo courtesy of Corbis Digital Stock.*

INTRODUCTION

One can make the argument that attractions are the reason people travel. If so, attractions are the most important component in the tourism system—and a case could be made that because of their importance in the tourism system, they should be covered in Chapter 1 rather than Chapter 8. There is no doubt that attractions are the main motivators for travel. Without attractions drawing tourists to destinations, there would be little need for all other tourism services such as transportation, lodging, food, distribution, and so on. However, as important as attractions are in motivating the tourist to travel, the attraction frequently receives the smallest portion of the tourist's expenditure. An example is the ski resort that sells only the lift ticket providing uphill transportation. This expenditure is the smallest of the travel experience, with the most expenditures going for air transportation, lodging, and food.

The list of attractions is extensive, and in many cases it is a combination of attractions that brings the tourist to a destination area. The opportunities for sightseeing, shopping, entertainment, gaming, culture, and recreation play an important role in determining the competitiveness of a destination. Figure 8.1 extracts the operating sectors from Figure 1.2 and shows that attractions, events, adventure and outdoor recreation, and entertainment are important supply components.

ATTRACTIONS

Attractions can be classified in a number of ways (see Figure 8.2). One of the categories that first comes to mind is theme or amusement parks. The roots of these attractions go back to medieval Europe, when pleasure gardens were created. These gardens were the forerunner of today's parks, featuring rides, fireworks, dancing, and games. Today, theme parks are high-profile attractions made famous by Disney, Universal Studios, Busch Gardens, and others. They represent multimillion-dollar investments.

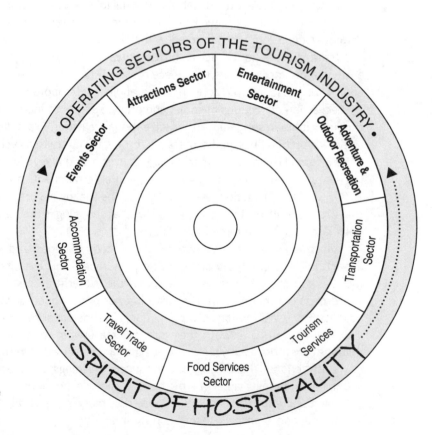

Figure 8.1 Operating sectors of the tourism industry: attractions, events, adventure, and entertainment.

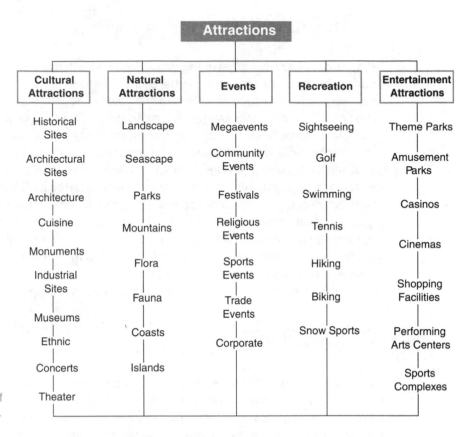

Figure 8.2 Overview of attractions.

Natural attractions are the "mainsprings" that drive many people to travel. The great national parks of the United States and other countries, such as those in Canada, India, Australia, and Japan, are examples. National forests in the United States attract millions of recreationists. State parks exist in many areas that have tourist appeal. The same is true for botanical, zoological, mountain, and seaside parks. Thus, these natural wonders lure travelers to enjoy the natural beauty, recreation, and inspiration that they provide.

Heritage attractions (such as historic sites) and prehistoric and archaeological sites (such as the ancient monuments of Egypt, Greece, Israel, Turkey, Indonesia, India, Mexico, and Peru) also have appeal for those inspired to learn more about contemporary and long-vanished civilizations.

Recreation attractions maintain and provide access to indoor and outdoor facilities where people can participate in sports and other recreational activities. Examples include swimming pools, bowling alleys, ice skating rinks, golf courses, ski resorts, hiking trails, bicycle paths, and marinas. Times Square in New York, Fisherman's Wharf in San Francisco, and Navy Pier in Chicago combine the appeal of a large city with shopping, dining, culture, and entertainment to attract millions of visitors each year.

Commercial attractions are retail operations dealing in gifts, handcrafted goods, art, and souvenirs that attract tourists. Recent surveys show that shopping is the number-one activity participated in by both domestic and international visitors.

Industrial attractions cannot be overlooked. Wineries and breweries have long been tourist attractions. Factory tours are growing in number, and manufacturers have developed elaborate facilities to handle tourists. An example is the Waterford Crystal Factory in Ireland, which houses a world-class crystal museum. The vast oil sands mining operations in Northern Alberta, Canada, now attracts many visitors for both professional and personal reasons.

Great modern cities with their cultural treasures of many sorts provide powerful attractions to millions of visitors each year. Sightseeing tours are provided in most cities, giving easy access to the city's attractions. Theaters, museums, special buildings, zoos, aquariums, cultural events, festivals, shopping, and dining are some of the appealing destinations.

Entertainment has become a powerful magnet. Musical entertainment has put Nashville, Tennessee, and Branson, Missouri, on the map.

The Attractions Industry

The attractions industry consists of fixed-location amusement parks and attractions in the United States and other countries. They are primarily private businesses, although there are a number of publicly operated facilities. Amusement parks and attractions in the United States generate over $11.5 billion in annual revenues. Approximately 500,000 people are employed year round/seasonally by the industry in the United States, and over 300 million people visited amusement parks and attractions, according to the International Association of Amusement Parks and Attractions (IAAPA).

The attractions industry is dominated by Disneyland and Walt Disney World, which have been two of the most successful attractions ever developed. However, while theme parks are a major tourist attraction, there are more than 10,000 natural scenic, historic, cultural, and entertainment attractions that appeal to travelers in the United States. Attractions include not only theme parks but also the entertainment park, amusement park, animal park, water park, museum, scenic railway, historic village, preserved mansion, scenic cruise, natural wonder, restaurant, music festival, industry exhibit, cave, theater, historic farm, scenic overlook, resort complex, historic site, botanical garden, arboretum, plantation, hall of fame, water show, zoo, sports complex, cultural center, state park, national park, county park, outdoor theater, Native American reservation, and transportation exhibit.

Theme Parks

The theme park business has enjoyed spectacular expansion since the opening of Disneyland in 1955 in Anaheim, California. This theme park changed the local amusement park business considerably because it expanded the concept of amusement parks from simply rides and carnival barkers to include shows, shops, and restaurants in theme settings with immaculate cleanliness, promising adventure, history, science fiction, and fantasy.

The success of Disneyland brought Walt Disney World, the largest and grandest theme park in the world, with Magic Kingdom as the focal point of the resort complex. The Magic Kingdom attracts over 17.2 million visitors annually (see Table 8.1). The Orlando site also has a 500-acre conservation project for the preservation of fauna and wildlife, including 1,700 animals from 250 species (Animal Kingdom); Epcot, which is divided into Future World, an experimental prototype community of tomorrow, and the World Showcase, where several nations feature exhibits of their country's attractions and culture; Disney Hollywood Studios, with rides, behind-the-scenes movie experiences, and shows; and Downtown Disney, with a wide variety of entertainment, shopping, and dining (see disneyworld.disney.go.com).

Table 8.1 shows the top 25 theme parks in the world ranked by attendance. Disney dominates, holding the first 8 positions, plus 2 more for a total of 10 of the top parks. The United States has 13 parks, Japan 4, South Korea 2, Hong Kong 2, France 1, Germany 1, The Netherlands 1, and Denmark 1 in the top 25.

As would be expected, the success of the Disney theme parks brought imitators and large corporations to the business. In addition to those listed in Table 8.1, other prominent theme parks in the United States are Knott's Berry Farm in Buena Park, California; Kings Island in Mason, Ohio; Cedar Point in Sandusky, Ohio; Busch Gardens Europe in Williamsburg, Virginia; Hershey Park in Hershey, Pennsylvania; Legoland in Carlsbad, California; and Six Flags Park in Jackson, New Jersey, Valencia, California, and Gurnee, Illinois.

Global park attendance figures prepared by TEA (Themed Entertainment Association), in association with AECOM (formerly Economic Research Associates), are published in *Park World* (www.parkworld-online.com). The information is also available in pdf format on the TEA and AECOM Web sites at www.teaconnect.org and www.aecom.com./economics. Attendance numbers are provided for the top 25 theme parks worldwide, top 20 parks in North America, top 20 parks in Europe, top 20 water parks worldwide, top 15 parks in Asia, top 10 parks in Latin America, and top 10 chains worldwide. Visit those sites for the latest information.

TABLE 8.1 Top 25 Global Theme Parks

Rank	Theme Park and Location	Attendance (in millions)
1	**The Magic Kingdom at Walt Disney World**, *Lake Buena Vista, Florida*	17.2[a]
2	**Disneyland**, *Anaheim, California*	15.9
3	**Tokyo Disneyland**, *Tokyo, Japan*	13.6
4	**Disneyland Park**, *Marne-de-Vallee, France*	12.7
5	**Tokyo Disney Sea**, *Tokyo, Japan*	12.0
6	**Epcot at Walt Disney World**, *Lake Buena Vista, Florida*	11.0
7	**Disney's Hollywood Studios at Walt Disney World**, *Lake Buena Vista, Florida*	9.7
8	**Disney's Animal Kingdom at Walt Disney World**, *Lake Buena Vista, Florida*	9.6
9	**Universal Studios**, *Osaka, Japan*	8.0
10	**Everland**, *Gyeonggi-Do, South Korea*	6.2
11	**Disney's California Adventure**, *Anaheim, California*	6.1
12	**Seaworld Florida**, *Orlando, Florida*	5.8
13	**Universal Studios**, *Orlando, Florida*	5.5
14	**Ocean Park**, *Hong Kong*	4.8
15	**Nagashima Spa Land**, *Kuwana, Japan*	4.7
16	**Islands of Adventure at Universal Orlando**, *Orlando, Florida*	4.6
17	**Hong Kong Disneyland**, *Hong Kong*	4.6
18	**Yokohama Hakkeijima Spa Paradise**, *Yokohama, Japan*	4.5
19	**Universal Studios Hollywood**, *Universal City, California*	4.3
20	**Lotte World**, *Seoul, South Korea*	4.2
21	**Europa Park**, *Rust, Germany*	4.2
22	**Seaworld California**, *San Diego, California*	4.2
23	**Busch Gardens Tampa Bay**, *Tampa Bay, Florida*	4.1
24	**De Efteling**, *Kaatsheuvel, Netherlands*	4.0
25	**Tivoli Gardens**, *Copenhagen, Denmark*	3.8

[a] Note: Attendance figures are estimates, based on company information, annual reports, published information and from reliable TEA/EACOM industry and tourism sources. Percent changes for 2009 for certain parks are based on adjusted/updated figures for 2008, thus not directly comparable to published TEA/EACOM list for 2008/07.

Source: TEA/AECOM.

The United States' major theme parks are concentrated in Florida and California. Disney has projects in both states, and the Orlando area has the largest number of theme parks and attractions in any single location. This concentration is likely to continue, because new attractions or expansions are still taking place in the area. The latest is the magic of the Harry Potter books and movies; Universal Orlando held the Grand Opening of the Wizarding World of Harry Potter on June 18, 2010.

The U.S. Travel Association reports theme and amusement park trips are likely to be family vacations, as they are much more likely than the average trip to include children under age 19 (55 percent versus 24 percent). These trips also include longer overnight stays (5.3 nights) compared to the average U.S. trip (4.1 nights). One-fourth (25 percent) of theme park trips last seven nights or more. In addition, overnight trips including a theme park are more likely than the average U.S. trip to include a stay in a hotel/motel/bed and breakfast (67 percent versus 55 percent) or a condo/timeshare (9 percent versus 4 percent).

Theme park travelers are more likely than average to fly to their destination (19 percent versus 16 percent) and rent a car once they arrive (8 percent versus 5 percent). These travelers also engage in

America's first theme park, Knott's Berry Farm, has 150 acres of rides, live shows, and family adventures celebrating the lure and lore of the West. Snoopy is part of the magic at Knott's. Camp Snoopy is the official six-acre home of the Peanuts gang. Photo courtesy of Knott's Berry Farm. Snoopy ℝ 1958 United Features Syndicate, Inc.

many other activities while on theme park trips. For example, many theme park trips also include shopping (40 percent), visits to historical places or museums (20 percent), and visits to the beach (20 percent).

Theme parks are popular all over the world. New parks and expanded parks are appearing in the United States, Latin America, Europe, Middle East, and Asia. For example, Asia is one of the amusement industry's prime markets, as it is home to 9 of the 20 most visited theme parks in the world. Dubai is constructing a $20 billion "Dubailand" theme park. The mixed-use theme park spread over 3 billion square feet is located 10 minutes from Dubai International Airport and 60 minutes from Abu Dhabi. The development will include 45 mega projects having seven themes: (1) theme parks, (2) culture and art, (3) science and planetariums, (4) sports and sports academies, (5) well-being and health, (6) shopping, and (7) resorts and hotels. It is touted as the world's most ambitious tourism, leisure, and entertainment project, designed to catalyze the position of Dubai as an international hub of family tourism.

Theme parks have found that in order to grow attendance and revenue, they have to add new attractions on a regular basis. The industry is constantly making annual improvements that range from fresh paint, to multimillion-dollar rides, to entire new parks.

Sea World of San Antonio permits children to have a close, personal encounter with the park's dolphins. *Photo courtesy of the San Antonio Convention & Visitor Bureau (SACVB)/Sea World San Antonio.*

❖ GLOBAL INSIGHT ❖

Theme Park Trivia

- A European invention: "Amusement parks" and "theme parks" are often regarded as typically American; however, amusement parks were first created in the "Old World."

- The world's oldest operating amusement park is Bakken in Klampenborg, Denmark, which dates to 1583. The oldest continually operating amusement park in the United States is Lake Compounce in Bristol, Connecticut, which opened in 1846.

- Many people believe that America's fascination with amusement parks began with the opening of the Cyclone roller coaster at Coney Island, New York, in 1927. Originally costing only $175,000 to construct, the coaster still operates at Astroland amusement park in New York.

- Rides are the number-one reason that Americans visit amusement parks, according to an IAAPA survey. Of the many rides available, 46 percent of people say that their favorite ride is the roller coaster.

- The oldest operating Ferris wheel is located in Europe at The Prater, Vienna, Austria. It was built in 1897.

- The largest amusement park, by acreage, is Walt Disney World in Lake Buena Vista, Florida, which encompasses 47 square miles.

- According to an IAAPA survey, 94 percent of people who visit amusement parks have a favorite amusement park food. Of those surveyed, 28 percent prefer funnel cake, 17 percent prefer ice cream, 14 percent prefer pizza, 13 percent prefer hot dogs, and 12 percent prefer cotton candy.

Source: International Association of Amusement Parks and Attractions.

DISCUSSION QUESTIONS

1. What is your favorite ride at a theme park? Why do 46 percent of visitors say that the roller coaster is their favorite ride?

2. Why are theme parks attractive destinations?

3. Can you think of an idea for a new type of theme park?

International Association of Amusement Parks and Attractions

The world's largest amusement park and attractions association is the International Association of Amusement Parks and Attractions (IAAPA). The association, founded in 1918, has over 4,000 members in 93 countries. It represents and serves operators of amusement parks, tourist attractions, water parks, miniature golf courses, family entertainment centers, zoos, aquariums, museums, science centers, resorts, casinos, and manufacturers and suppliers of amusement equipment and services. The association conducts research, compiles statistics, and publishes *FunWorld* and an annual *International Directory and Buyer's Guide*. It holds an annual convention and worldwide expos. Located in Alexandria, Virginia, IAAPA can be reached at (703) 836-4800 or www.iaapa.org.

GAMING

The U.S. gaming-entertainment industry has seen tremendous change over the last decade. As recently as 1988, only two states—Nevada and New Jersey—permitted casino gaming, but now, in 2011, with Indian gaming included, 29 states have some type of casino gaming. Today, only two states—Hawaii and Utah—have no legalized gaming whatsoever.

Gambling, or the gaming industry, has become a major force in the tourism industry. The gaming industry has grown from a narrow Nevada base with limited acceptance in the financial and public sector to a recognized growth industry. Although gaming has always been a popular form of recreation, it has also been controversial.

Gaming as a recreational pursuit is becoming more popular, especially in the United States. It is often combined with other types of entertainment, such as nightclub shows and sports activities. *Photo courtesy of Carnival Cruise Lines.*

There is no question that gaming generates travel. Nevada has been the leader in gambling, which has made tourism the leading industry in the state. Las Vegas has long been considered as the casino capital of the world; however, today it has been surpassed in gaming revenue by Macau Special Administrative Region, China. It is interesting to note the differences in the types of tourists and their modes of transportation when comparing Las Vegas and Atlantic City. Las Vegas attracts destination visitors from long distances who fly or drive, while Atlantic City is located in a densely populated area and attracts nearby residents (those within 150 miles). Atlantic City has successfully promoted short-duration motorcoach tours to increase its numbers. It is also now successfully promoting itself as a destination area.

Today, according to the American Gaming Association (AGA), the gaming industry is a $92.3 billion business that employs, directly and indirectly, more than one million men and women. This includes all forms of gaming, including commercial casinos, card rooms, Indian casinos, legal bookmaking, charitable organizations, the pari-mutuel industry (e.g., horse racing, greyhound racing, and jai alai), and lotteries.

The fact is that people enjoy gaming as an entertainment option in their lives. According to a 2010 AGA survey, 81 percent of the American people view casino entertainment as acceptable for themselves or others. In 2009, there were 61.7 million visitors to casinos, or 28 percent of the U.S. population age 21 and older. As acceptance has grown, millions of Americans also understand the capital investment, tourism, public revenues, and employment impacts of casino gaming. According to the same survey, 61 percent of Americans see casino gaming as an important part of the community's entertainment and tourism offering.

In 1993, the casino industry reached a milestone when more Americans went to casinos than visited major league baseball parks. Today, more Americans visit casinos than zoos, aquariums, and wildlife parks. This entertainment trend is continuing as more and more people visit casinos.

The employment opportunities provided by the gaming-entertainment industry deserve special attention. In 2009, the U.S. commercial casino industry created 328,377 direct industry employees, who earned $13.1 billion in wages, contributed $5.5 billion in direct gaming taxes, and earned $30.7 billion in gross gaming revenue. Table 8.2 shows the top 20 U.S. casino markets by revenue and illustrates the importance of Las Vegas and Atlantic City.

TABLE 8.2 Top 20 U.S. Casino Markets by Annual Revenue

Rank	Casino Market	2009 Annual Revenues (USD in millions)[a]
1	Las Vegas Strip, NV	$5,550.0
2	Atlantic City, NJ	3,943.0
3	Chicagoland, IN/IL	2,092.0
4	Connecticut	1,448.0
5	Detroit, MI	1,339.0
6	St. Louis, MO/IL	1,050.0
7	Tunica/Lula, MS	997.0
8	Biloxi, MS	833.5
9	Shreveport, LA	779.7
10	Boulder Strip, NV	774.3
11	Kansas City, MO *(includes St. Joseph)*	758.0
12	Reno/Sparks, NV	715.2
13	Lawrenceburg/Rising Sun/Belterra, IN	691.2
14	Lake Charles, LA	662.6
15	New Orleans, LA	653.1
16	Black Hawk/Central City, CO	596.3
17	Yonkers, NY	540.5
18	Downtown Las Vegas, NV	523.8
19	Laughlin, NV	492.5
20	Council Bluffs, IA	430.7

[a]Gross revenue is earnings taken before taxes, salaries, and expenses are paid—the equivalent of sales, not profit.

Source: The Innovation Group and the American Gaming Association.

In deciding whether to add casino gaming to a community or to the mix of gaming already in existence, it is important that voters and their elected representatives have the correct information and statistics so that their decision, either pro or con, is an informed one. The National Gambling Impact Study Commission (NGISC), signed into law in August 1996 to conduct a comprehensive study of the social and economic impacts of gaming in the United States, released its report in 1999. The final report concluded the following: "As it has grown, [gambling] has become more than simply an entertainment past-time: the gambling industry has emerged as an economic mainstay in many communities and plays an increasingly prominent role in state and even regional economies."[1]

Indian reservation gaming in the United States became a growth industry when the U.S. Supreme Court in 1987 recognized Indian people's right to run gaming. It ruled that states had no authority to regulate gaming on Indian land if such gaming is permitted outside the reservation for any other purpose. Congress established the legal basis for this right when it passed the Indian Gaming Regulatory Act (IGRA) in 1988. The National Indian Gaming Association reports that 233 Indian tribes in 28 states use Indian gaming to create new jobs, fund essential government services, and rebuild communities. In 2008, tribal governments generated $25.9 billion in gross gaming revenue; $3.2 billion in gross revenue from related hospitality and entertainment services; created 636,000 jobs (direct and indirect); contributed $8.0 billion in federal taxes and revenue savings, $2.5 billion state taxes, and over $100 million in payments to local governments. Nationally, charities gained $150 million in contributions from gaming tribes. Across the United States, 231 tribes in the lower 48 states and two Alaska Native villages operate 411 Indian gaming facilities, including casino operations, bingo halls, travel plazas, and pull-tab operations. The IGRA mandates that tribal governments, not individuals, can have gaming operations. Thus, the entire proceeds of the industry go back to fund tribal government programs. Indian tribes are using gaming revenues to build houses, schools, roads, and sewer and water systems; to fund the health care and education of their people; and to develop a strong, diverse economic base for the future.

The Mashantucket Pequot Tribal Nation operates the Foxwoods Resort Casino, Connecticut, which is the largest casino in the United States. Foxwoods comprises six casinos that offer 6,200 slot machines and 380 tables for 17 types of table games, and the world's largest bingo hall.

Gaming is available in many parts of the world as well as on cruise ships. Well-known areas for casino gambling include Monaco, the Caribbean, London, Nice, Macau, and Rio de Janeiro.

As new casinos go up in Las Vegas, Atlantic City, New Orleans, Colorado, the Mississippi River, South Dakota, Indian reservations, and the Bahamas, one sees the impact of gaming on tourism and the local economy. Given the current growth in gaming, it is safe to predict that gaming will continue to play a role in tourism and economic development.

Gaming Organizations

The American Gaming Association (AGA) was formed in June 1995 after President Bill Clinton proposed a 4 percent gross receipts tax on the gaming industry. Realizing that this would have monumental repercussions, casino industry leaders decided that it was time to form an association to represent them on Capitol Hill. Although the bill did not materialize, the AGA thrived and today has more than 100 member companies. Since the AGA's opening, when the first 14 members consisted exclusively of casino companies and gaming equipment manufacturers, the diversity of the association's members has expanded to include financial and professional services, suppliers and vendors, state associations, and publications.

The AGA's primary goal is to create a better understanding of gaming entertainment by bringing the facts about the industry to the general public, elected officials, other decision makers, and the media through education and advocacy. Its Web site is a one-stop resource for information about the casino entertainment industry. Visit www.americangaming.org.

The National Indian Gaming Association (NIGA) operates as a clearinghouse and educational, legislative, and public policy resource for tribes, policy makers, and the public on Indian gaming issues and tribal community development. NIGA has statistics and economic studies on Indian gaming. It is located in Washington, D.C.; telephone (202) 546-7711; fax (202) 546-1755; e-mail info@indian gaming.org; Web site www.indiangaming.org.

RECREATION

Recreation is a diverse industry, representing more than $400 billion in expenditures each year. The industry generates millions of jobs in the manufacturing, sales, and service sectors. Nearly 50 percent of Americans describe themselves as "outdoor people." They enjoy a wide variety of activities to keep fit, to add excitement to their lives, to have fun with family and friends, to pursue solitary activities, and to experience nature firsthand.

The draw of recreation opportunities throughout the United States is one factor in the rise of domestic travel, as well as in the increase in international visits to the United States. Outdoor adventure travel is gaining in popularity, and travel professionals have better access to information on recreational travel options than they used to. People are seeking higher-quality services and amenities.

Illustrative of the range of businesses within the recreation industry are recreation vehicle (RV) manufacturers and dealers, boat manufacturers and dealers, full-line recreation product manufacturers, park concessionaires, campground owners, resorts, enthusiast groups, snowmobile manufacturers, recreation publications, motorcoach operators, bicycling interests, and others.

The top outdoor recreation adventure activity in the United States is overnight vacation camping, with 48.6 million participants. This family is enjoying a Wisconsin campground in a tent trailer. *Photo courtesy of Wisconsin Department of Tourism.*

Companies manufacturing recreation products tend to be large. For example, the manufacturing of new RVs is a $14 billion-per-year industry, according to the Recreation Vehicle Dealers Association (see Chapter 5).

The **Recreation Vehicle Industry Association** (RVIA), located in Reston, Virginia, is a primary source of shipment statistics, market research, and technical data. The association also supplies campground directories and publications covering RV maintenance, trip preparation, and safety issues (www.rvia.org).

In contrast to the large companies involved in manufacturing RVs, boats, pools, mountain bikes, skis, and so on, the private service sector is made up primarily of small businesses, ranging from campgrounds, to marinas, to wilderness guides. There is also the public sector, providing services through the National Park Service, Forest Service, and state and local agencies.

Parks

Both private and government enterprises operate various kinds of *parks*, including amusement parks. National parks are often very important parts of a nation's or state's tourism. In some countries (such as certain countries in Africa), national parks are the primary attractions. Typical are Kenya, Rwanda, Uganda, Tanzania, Botswana, and South Africa.

National and State Parks

The U.S. National Park System is one of the country's greatest tourist attractions, appealing to both domestic and international visitors. U.S. National Parks host over 285 million visitors a year. A recreation visit is the entry of one person for any part of a day on lands or waters administered by the **National Park Service** (NPS) for recreation purposes. The NPS administers 393 national parks, plus hundreds of other recreation areas, preserves, natural landmarks, battlefields, historical sites,

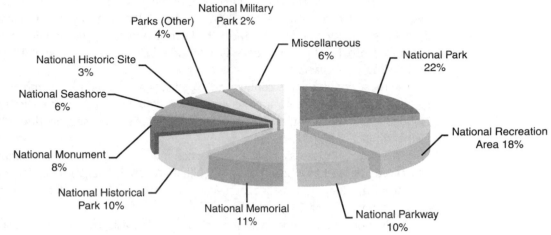

Figure 8.3 Percent of Recreation Visits by Type of Unit in 2009.
Source: National Park Service, Statistical Abstract 2009 (Denver, CO: NPS, 2010).

lakeshores, monuments, memorials, seashores, and parkways, which encompass more than 84 million acres of land and another 4.5 million acres of water. Figure 8.3 shows the percent of recreation visits by type of unit for 2009. The Blue Ridge Parkway (at 15.9 million visits) continued as the most visited unit of the system, and Great Smoky Mountains National Park continued as the most visited national park (at 9.5 million). Table 8.3 shows the Top 20 National Park Units by number of visits. The Top 20 total 43.9 percent of all visits.

TABLE 8.3 Top 20 National Park Units for Recreation Visits in 2009

Park	Rank	Visitors	% of Total
Blue Ridge Parkway	1	15,936,316	5.58%
Golden Gate National Recreation Area	2	15,036,372	5.27%
Great Smoky Mountains National Park	3	9,491,437	3.32%
Gateway National Recreation Area	4	9,010,522	3.16%
Lake Mead National Recreation Area	5	7,668,689	2.69%
George Washington Memorial Parkway	6	6,938,309	2.43%
Natchez Trace Parkway	7	5,934,363	2.08%
Lincoln Memorial	8	5,255,570	1.84%
Delaware Water Gap National Recreation Area	9	5,213,030	1.83%
Vietnam Veterans Memorial	10	4,437,771	1.55%
Grand Canyon National Park	11	4,348,068	1.52%
Cape Cod National Seashore	12	4,311,949	1.51%
San Francisco Maritime National Historical Park	13	4,152,497	1.45%
Gulf Islands National Seashore	14	4,132,674	1.45%
World War II Memorial	15	4,118,528	1.44%
Castle Clinton National Monument	16	4,080,152	1.43%
Independence National Historical Park	17	3,967,694	1.39%
Statue of Liberty National Memorial Monument	18	3,829,483	1.34%
Chesapeake & Ohio Canal National Historical Park	19	3,751,681	1.31%
Yosemite National Park	20	3,737,472	1.31%
			43.9%

Source: National Park Service, Statistical Abstract 2009 (Denver, CO: NPS, 2010).

Overnight stays in the concession lodges of the parks totaled 3.4 million, while campgrounds saw over 3.2 million overnight guests in 2009. Another 1.3 million stayed in a concession campground, and 2.1 million were RV campers. Another 1.8 million visitors spent the night in a park backcountry site that they hiked into. Most park visitors stay in facilities in "gateway communities" outside park boundaries or are simply day users.[2]

The most popular parks continue to experience a crowded peak summer season. In contrast, the spring and fall are excellent times to visit the well-known areas, and there are a great many units of the National Park System that are still underutilized. See the section titled "Matching Supply with Demand" in Chapter 12.

Visitors to NPS areas have a large economic impact on the surrounding communities with estimated direct sales in 2009 of $11.89 billion. An additional $3.69 billion was generated indirectly from tourism expenditures, for a total economic impact of $15.58 billion. This spending by NPS visitors helped generate over 247,000 jobs.[3]

The National Park Service publishes information on visits to national park areas in its annual report, *National Park Statistical Abstract.* It also publishes biannually *The National Parks Index,* which contains brief descriptions, with acreages, of each area administered by the NPS.

In the United States, many individual states operate park systems, some of the most outstanding being in New York, California, Tennessee, Oregon, Indiana, Kentucky, Florida, and Michigan. The National Association of State Park Directors (NASPD) compiles statistics for state parks. There are 6,624 state parks totaling over 13 million acres and 5,875 trails encompassing over 41,725 miles of trails. State parks received over 725 million visitors with 91.5 percent being daytime users. The parks employ 20,603 full-time personnel and 53,898 total personnel, including part-time and seasonal staff. Visit www.naspd.org.

Parks are also operated by other units of government, such as county or park districts like the Huron-Clinton Metropolitan Authority of the greater Detroit area in southeastern Michigan. This system has six parks within easy access of residents of the Detroit metropolitan area. Counties, townships, and cities also operate parks and often campgrounds as parts of parks.

"Horseback riding in the Adirondacks." The relaxed smiles on this couple convey a feeling of enjoyment from the very special experience. Although not everyone enjoys this form of recreation, those who do get a view of the countryside available to few others. *Photo courtesy of The Adirondack Regional Tourism Council.*

National Forests

The annual number of visits to national forests total over 192 million. Part of the U.S. Department of Agriculture, the U.S. Forest Service maintains 193 million acres in the National Forest System, with 155 national forests and 20 grasslands in 44 states, Puerto Rico, and the Virgin Islands. Especially popular activities are hiking, camping, hunting, fishing, canoeing, and skiing.

The U.S. Forest Service reports that its developed recreation sites include 4,677 campgrounds, over 140 swimming areas, 1,496 picnic grounds; 1,222 boating sites, and 135 alpine ski areas. Other tourism assets are 4,418 miles of wild and scenic rivers, 136 scenic byways, 143,346 miles of trails, 277,000 heritage sites, and 403 wilderness areas (see www.fs.fed.us).

Other Public Recreational Lands

The Bureau of Land Management (BLM) oversees more than 245 million acres of public land located primarily in 12 western states. The BLM has nearly 2400 day-use and 16,698 family camp units on 50,000 acres. It also has 3,179 miles of designated backcountry byways, 62,768 miles of roads suitable for highway vehicles, 90.8 acres open to off-highway vehicles, 54.4 million more acres open to limited off highway vehicular use, and 19,000 miles of trails for motorized vehicles. The most popular recreational activities on BLM lands are camping and motorized travel.

The U.S. Corps of Engineers (COE) is the nation's largest provider of outdoor recreation, operating more than 2,500 recreation areas at 463 projects (mostly lakes) and leasing an additional 1,800 sites to state or local park and recreation authorities or private interests. The COE hosts about 368 million visits a year at its lakes, beaches, and other areas. They estimate that 25 million Americans visit a COE project at least once a year. Some of the recreation facilities provided on the 12 million acres include some 90,000 campsites, 35,000 picnic areas, 3,500 boat launching ramps, 826 swimming areas, and 4,200 miles of hiking trails.

The U.S. Fish and Wildlife Service (FWS) manages over 97 million acres of fish and wildlife habitats and provides recreation opportunities. According to the FWS, participants in hunting, fishing, bird-watching, and other wildlife-related recreation spend $120 billion annually enjoying these activities.

Adventure Travel

It is the resources provided by the National Park Service, the Forest Service, Bureau of Land Management, Corp of Engineers, and the Fish and Wildlife Service that make adventure travel so popular and feasible in the United States.

Many outdoor recreation activities are sports related and have been classified in the adventure travel area. The National Sporting Goods Association (NSGA) conducts an annual study of sports participation by Americans seven years of age and older. NSGA reports that the top outdoor recreation adventure activities were overnight vacation camping (50.9 million participants), bicycle riding (38.1 million), fishing (32.9 million), hiking (34.0 million), hunting with firearms (18.8 million), backpacking/wilderness camping (12.7 million), alpine skiing (7.0 million), off-road mountain biking (8.4 million), waterskiing (5.2 million), hunting with a bow and arrow (6.2 million), snowboarding (6.2 million), and cross-country skiing (1.7 million).[4]

A recent George Washington University study (2010), which was conducted in partnership with the Adventure Travel Trade Association and Xola Consulting, estimated that consumers spent more than $89 billion (excluding airfare and gear/clothing purchases) worldwide on adventure travel in 2009. The study shows that adventure tourism is a sizable market with the potential for economic growth. The

After a hike to Hanging Lake, visitors are rewarded with not only the beauty of the site but also interpretive information that greatly improves their understanding of the destination, thus enhancing the visitor experience. *Photo courtesy of Glenwood Springs Chamber Resort Association, Colorado.*

study found adventure travelers tend to be affluent and well-educated. They are also typically environmentally and culturally aware consumers.[5]

The NSGA is the world's largest sporting goods trade association, representing more than 22,000 retail outlets and 3,000 product manufacturers, suppliers, and sales agents. It is located at 1601 Feehanville Drive, Suite 300, Mount Prospect, IL 60056; telephone (800) 815-5422; fax (847) 391-9827; e-mail info@nsga.org; Web site: www.nsga.org.

Another source of outdoor recreation information is the American Recreation Coalition (ARC). It conducts research on a regular basis, organizes national conferences, and disseminates information on recreational needs, satisfaction, and initiatives. ARC monitors legislative proposals that influence recreation and works with government agencies. ARC is located at 1225 New York Avenue, N.W., Suite 450, Washington, D.C. 20005; telephone (202) 682-9530; fax (202) 682-9529; Web site: www.funoutdoors.com.

Winter Sports

Snow and winter sports tourism is an important component of the world tourism industry and is a key element for a better quality of life in many countries. Of the modern winter sports activities, skiing/snowboarding is by far the most popular. In the United States, almost 500 ski resorts were operating in the 2010–2011 season. Skier/snowboarder visits are one of the key performance indicators (KPIs) in the U.S. ski industry. On a nationwide basis, the number of visits has been relatively flat for the last decade, hovering around 55–60 million. The 2009–2010 season recorded 59.7 million visits, the second best season ever. In spite of continued pressures from a weak economy and without the catalyst of an exceptional snow year, skier/snowboarder visits this season increased by 4.2 percent, only 1.2 percent below the all-time record of 60.5 million visits achieved in 2007–2008. A skier/snowboarder visit represents one person visiting a ski area for all or any part of a day or night and includes full-day, half-day, night, and complimentary, adult, child, season, and any other ticket types that give one the use of an area's facility. Snowboarding has been the growth portion of the ski industry, representing more than 30 percent of the total visits.

Another trend is the emphasis on the multidimensional aspects of the snow resort experience. Today, ski areas appeal to all on-snow participants whether they are downhill skiers, snowboarders, telemarkers, cross-country skiers, snowshoers, or tubers. Vail Resorts has created Adventure Ridge, which is an example of this trend. This facility, located at the top of Vail Mountain, in Colorado, offers snowshoeing, tubing, ice skating, laser tag, snowmobile tours, and four dining experiences until 10 P.M. every night.

Over the years, the U.S. ski industry has grown and evolved just like other industries. Consolidations continue to take place, and ski resorts have developed into major destination resorts. Today, two companies have emerged at the forefront to consolidate ski areas under corporate banners. Large operations have become even larger. The big two are Vail Resorts, Inc., and Intrawest Corporation.

Ownership consolidation will lead to more innovative development and marketing. We will see more emphasis on real estate with core village developments that feature shopping, attractions, conference facilities, and other amenities that create a year-round destination resort. On the marketing scene, we will see interchangeable lift tickets, frequent-skier programs, ski discount cards good at multiple resorts, and increased promotion. Increased size presents the opportunity to use media more effectively, especially television.

The National Ski Areas Association (NSAA) is the trade association for ski area owners and operators. It represents 329 alpine resorts that account for more than 90 percent of the skier/snowboarder visits nationwide. Additionally, it has over 329 supplier members who provide equipment, goods, and services to the mountain resort industry. For more information, visit www.nsaa.org.

Historic Sites

Historic sites have always been popular attractions for both domestic and international travelers. A report on historic/cultural travelers shows that more than 81 percent of adults (118 million) who traveled were considered historic/cultural travelers. Although travelers tend to engage in multiple activities when they travel, 30 percent of the historic/cultural travelers said these activities were the primary motive for the trip.

The National Park Service maintains an estimated 66,757 historic sites, as noted in the National Register of Historic Places. Approximately 15 percent of these properties are historic districts, and about 1,015,434 historic properties are located within the sites.

The National Trust for Historic Preservation provides leadership, education, and advocacy to save America's diverse historic places and revitalize communities. It owns and manages 29 historic sites that are open to the public and attract over 800,000 visitors a year. Travel programs include National Trust Study Tours, which plans, operates, and markets more than 50 domestic and international tours a year to members, and the Historic Hotels of America program. The National Trust is a nonprofit organization chartered by Congress in 1949 and has over 270,000 members. Located in Washington, D.C., it can be reached by telephone (800-315-6847) and via its Web site (www.preservationnation.org).

Zoos, Rain Forests, and Aquariums

The menageries and aviaries of China, Egypt, and Rome were famous in ancient times. Today, zoological parks and aquariums continue to be popular attractions. A recent development in the United States has been the creation of indoor rain forests. Notable are the Lied Jungle in the Henry Doorly Zoo in Omaha, Nebraska, and the RainForest within the Cleveland, Ohio, Metroparks Zoo. The Lied Jungle is the world's largest indoor rain forest, with its $15 million cost financed by the Lied Foundation. It recreates rain forests as found in Asia, Africa, and South America. The rain forest occupies 1.5 acres under one roof. It contains 2,000 species of tropical plants and 517 animal species, and it attracts more than 1.3 million visitors annually. This has become the biggest tourist attraction in Nebraska. Artificial Rain forests are popular in other parts of the world, such as the rain forest in the Melbourne Museum in Australia.

LIVE ENTERTAINMENT

Another powerful tourism magnet is live entertainment. Live performance is often the main attraction for a vacation trip. It includes such things as theater, music concerts, and circuses. In addition, live performers are often additional draws to other tourist attractions such as theme parks or festivals.

The Deadheads who followed the Grateful Dead concert tour are a prime example of fans who base their travel decisions on where the live entertainment will be. Another is people traveling to Nashville, Tennessee, to hear country-and-western music at the Grand Ole Opry. Branson, Missouri, has put itself on the map as a music entertainment center and is now challenging Nashville. One of the centerpieces of the famous "I Love New York" advertising campaign was going to a Broadway play or musical. A theater tour to London is a powerful vacation lure. Large numbers of performing arts tours are offered.

Entertainment has risen to a new level in the vacation decision-making process. There is a growing influence of entertainment on vacation travel choices. Today, the traveling public wants to have fun, to be entertained, to enjoy fantasy, and to escape from the realities of everyday life. Think about these facts: The top two North American vacation destinations—Walt Disney World and Las Vegas—are built around the appeal of entertainment. The growing cruise market features entertainment. Disney features "edutainment" (combining education and entertainment). The growing influence of entertainment and the marriage of gaming, live entertainment, themed resorts, and theme parks are creating new careers in entertainment management.

The development of super-entertainment complexes is a trend in the tourism industry. It is happening not only in Las Vegas and Atlantic City but also in other markets. Las Vegas mega-resorts appeal to the family vacation market as well as to gamblers. It is interesting to note that Las Vegas has most of the largest hotels in the world, and the majority are not only hotels but attractions and entertainment centers as well. The Luxor, New York New York, Excalibur, Paris Las Vegas, Bellagio, Mandalay Bay, Venetian, and Treasure Island are all examples of themed resort hotels.

FESTIVALS AND EVENTS

Among the fastest-growing segments of tourism in the world are festivals and events. Countries and cities compete vigorously for mega-events such as the Olympics, World Cup, and World's Fairs. Festivals and events are pervasive around the globe. Societies are always holding some kind of an event, whether it is a fair, festival, market, parade, celebration, anniversary, sports event, or a charitable endeavor.

Festivals and events are an important part of the tourism industry. They can serve as a powerful tool to attract tourists during the off-season and to create an image and awareness for an area.

Sponsorships have become an essential ingredient in festivals and events. Most events, whether local, national, or international, would have a difficult time existing without them. Sponsors provide funds or "in-kind" contributions to promoters of events. Sponsorships have become big business today and involve the right to use logos and identify with the event.

Volunteers are one of the key factors in the success of events. The International Festivals and Events Association (IFEA) reports that the average weekend attendance at an event is approximately 222,000. It takes hard work and support from community volunteers to ensure that a festival or event

Weddings are special events that have considerable economic impact. Many resort properties specialize in wedding planning offering unique activities, superb food and beverages, and outstanding resort experiences. *Photo courtesy of Amelia Island Convention & Visitors Bureau.*

runs smoothly. With the average weekend event requiring up to 2,000 volunteers, most events would not be able to take place without them.

There is a movement toward professional management of events and year-round operation of event offices. Event management is emerging as a field, becoming more professional, and providing a new source of job opportunities. As the number of events has grown and expanded in size and complexity, the number of staff and volunteers has mushroomed. This has given rise to professional associations, books, formal education, and training programs. Classes are offered in event management in a number of tourism programs around the globe. George Washington University in Washington, D.C., offers a certificate program and a sequence in their master's degree program in event management.

Donald Getz, of the University of Calgary, wrote a book titled *Festivals, Special Events, and Tourism.* He states that festivals and events appeal to a very broad audience. However, elements of these or specific themes can be effectively targeted to desired tourist market segments. Festivals and events also have the ability to spread tourism geographically and seasonally. Special events allow a region or community to celebrate its uniqueness, promote itself, develop local pride, and enhance its economic well-being.

Events produce sizable economic and tourism benefits. For example, SunFest, an annual festival in Florida, has a year-round staff of nine and a budget of $3 million. SunFest generates an economic impact of approximately $21.5 million in the local community. The National Western Stock Show held in Denver each January for 16 days has a permanent staff of about 50 year-round employees who plan, organize, and market the event. During the stock show, this grows to 950 employees. They serve some 2,000 animals and over 600,000 people attending the event. Considering both direct and indirect effects, it is estimated that the event provides a hefty $123 million boost to the Denver economy.

Even small communities can stage such events. Many local festivals originally designed to entertain local residents have grown to attract visitors from many miles away. Smaller communities that do not have convention bureaus and meeting space can turn to event tourism to seek tourism dollars by producing arts and craft shows, historical reenactments, music festivals, film festivals, food festivals, and the like. Consequently, events have shown tremendous growth as small and medium-size towns seek tourism dollars through short-term events. IFEA estimates that every year there are between 50,000 and 60,000 half-day to one-day events and 5,000 or more festivals of two days or longer.

IFEA has provided cutting-edge professional development and fundraising ideas for the special events industry for 55 years. Through publications, seminars, annual conventions, trade shows, and ongoing networking, IFEA is advancing festivals and events throughout the world. More than 2,000 professionals are currently members. IFEA is located in Boise, Idaho; telephone (208) 433-0950; fax (208) 433-9812; Web site www.ifea.com.

SPORTING EVENTS

The world of sports has grown up along with tourism over the past 50 years—to the point where certain sporting mega-events are catalysts for creating substantial amounts of travel and tourism. In North America (and the United States in particular, where sports and entertainment are an integral part of daily life), baseball's World Series has been the forerunner of the sports-driven hallmark event. It has served as a catalyst for extensive amounts of travel on the part of spectator fans, media professionals, and supporting technicians. More recently, the National Football League's Super Bowl provides a preeminent annual stimulus for travel activity throughout the country. At the international level, the Summer Olympic Games, whose media dominance every four years has historically made it the world's premier sporting event, now threatens being overshadowed by the World Cup of Football/ Soccer, another mega-hallmark-event that is also held every four years—but one that is much less elitist. As such, it draws attention from a much wider spectrum of the world population. It follows that its travel implications are also, in all likelihood, greater than the Olympics, although, to our knowledge this reality has not yet been formally documented.

In addition to these famous events there are also countless other sporting events such as the Commonwealth Games, Pan American Games, All Africa Games, and Asian Games that also create much travel. Sports such as football, basketball, baseball, soccer, volleyball, tennis, golf, lacrosse, rugby, skiing, swimming, diving, track and field, and many others are being played by both men and women. They are played at many levels: professional, college, semi-pro, high school, and amateur leagues. When one thinks of all the sporting activities that take place in the world and the fans that they attract, it is clear these events are a powerful, broadly based force for travel.

SHOPPING

Shopping is an important part of any tourist's activities. Shopping leads as the number one or two activity while traveling for both domestic and international travelers. U.S. Travel Association reports that shopping continues to be one of the most popular of common activities for U.S. travelers, along with dining. The Office of Travel and Tourism Industries in the U.S. Department of Commerce reports that shopping is the top leisure activity participated in by overseas travelers; 86.6 percent shopped in the United States as part of their vacation activities.

An example of shopping's importance is the Bayside Marketplace. Launched by the Rouse Company in April 1987, the Bayside Marketplace has attracted more than 120 million visitors from South Florida and around the world. The Greater Miami Convention and Visitors Bureau has repeatedly identified Bayside as Miami–Dade County's number-one visitor attraction, and *Florida Trend* magazine recently named Bayside as the fifth-most-visited attraction in the state of Florida.

Bayside has nearly 140 shops offering a variety of merchandise in both the North and South Pavilions and Pier 5 Marketplace. In addition, Hard Rock Café and nine additional full-service restaurants offer everything from Italian to Caribbean, Spanish, Nicaraguan, Cuban, and American

Shopping leads as the number-one activity while traveling. Vacation shopping is one of the features of Old Town in Kissimmee, Florida. *Photo courtesy of Old Town.*

cuisine. For visitors on the run, the International Food Court offers 20 fast-food eateries. Bayside is also the only entertainment venue in the city offering free concerts every day of the year.

The **Mall of America** in Bloomington, Minnesota, is the largest mall in the United States in terms of retail space. Excursion motorcoach tours in Minnesota and nearby states now feature packages with Mall of America as their destination. This mall is particularly attractive to children because it features Lego's gigantic space station, dinosaurs, a medieval castle, and other intricate creations. They can also enjoy Knott's Camp Snoopy and plenty of rides. There are 14 theaters in the Upper East Side entertainment district, plus a comedy club, sports bars, and a variety of nightclubs.

While shopping at the **West Edmonton Mall** in Alberta, Canada, one can view sharks from a submarine, live a Roman fantasy, or soak in a bubble-filled spa near a volcano. This mall is the largest in the world. It even contains a full-scale replica of Columbus's ship *Santa Maria,* roulette wheels, the Ice Palace, and, of course, hundreds of stores, plus some theme parks. It is Alberta's number-one attraction, drawing in 21 million visitors a year. The world-famous Banff National Park, Alberta, Canada, draws about 4 million visitors a year.

Factory **outlet shopping malls** have become major attractions for U.S. and international travelers. There are approximately 325 outlet centers scattered over the United States, occupying more than 50 million square feet of space. Over 13,000 stores are open in factory outlets. An example of an outlet shopping mall is Sawgrass Mills, the 2.3-million-square-foot complex in Sunrise, Florida. It is the largest outlet mall in the United States combining retail and entertainment and is second only to Walt Disney World as the most popular tourist attraction in the state, according to the Mills Corporation (now Simon Property Group), which developed it. Over 25 million people annually tramp through the mile-long stretch of stores, from Bed Bath & Beyond to the Ann Taylor Loft; about 7 million shoppers come from abroad.

To make shopping as convenient as possible, many resorts and hotels provide shops featuring gift items, particularly local handicrafts and artwork. In the shopping areas of each community that caters successfully to tourists, there are high-quality gift and souvenir shops featuring items of particular interest to visitors. Chain hotel and motel companies have also organized gift shops as part of their operations. Airports have virtually become shopping centers.

SUMMARY

The businesses and organizations that provide attractions, recreation, entertainment, shopping, and others are major parts of tourism. For example, trips just for entertainment constitute about one-fourth of all travel in the United States. Tourists engage in many activities—a wealth of opportunities.

Theme parks, such as Disneyland and Universal Studios, also attract millions each year. Most of these are showing a steady rise in patronage. Gaming or gambling is also a growing industry. It has now been legalized in states other than Nevada and New Jersey, and attendance continues to rise. Parks come in all sizes and types. They serve both local and visitor recreational needs. National parks are very popular and of particular interest to both domestic and international visitors. National forests are also very popular. Zoos, rain forests, and aquariums, usually located in parks, attract locals as well as millions of tourists. A new development is the re-creation of tropical rain forests within zoological parks. An outstanding example is the Lied Jungle in Omaha, Nebraska.

Shopping continues to be a major attraction. Spectacular malls, such as the Mall of America in Minnesota and the West Edmonton Mall in Alberta, Canada, have become tourist destinations. They contain an amazing variety of recreational facilities as well as hundreds of shops. Festivals and events are attractions of great and growing importance. Mega-events such as the Olympics are sought-after awards to a city. Local festivals typically attract a wider audience once they become better publicized.

 KEY CONCEPTS

activities	live entertainment	recreation
aquariums	Mall of America	Recreation Vehicle Industry
attractions	national forests	Association
events	National Park Service	shopping
festivals	Olympic Games	theme park
gambling or gaming industry	outlet shopping malls	West Edmonton Mall
International Association of	parks	zoological parks
Amusement Parks and Attractions	rain forests	

 INTERNET EXERCISES

The Internet sites mentioned in this chapter plus some selected additional sites are listed for your convenience on the companion Web site for this book, www.wiley.com/college/goeldner.

ACTIVITY 1

Site Name: Walt Disney World

URL: www.disneyworld.disney.go.com

Background Information: Everything you need to plan your Walt Disney World Resort vacation is at this site.

You can use this site to make all your Disney arrangements.

Site Name: Guide to Theme Parks

URL: themeparks.about.com

Background Information: Provides links to theme parks and amusement parks worldwide.

Site Name: Recreation.gov

URL: www.recreation.gov

Background Information: Recreation.gov is a one-stop resource for information about recreation on federal lands. The site offers information from all of the federal land management agencies and allows tourists to search for recreation sites by state, by agency, or by recreational activity.

Site Name: National Park Service

URL: www.nps.gov

Background Information: On August 25, 1916, President Woodrow Wilson signed the act creating the National Park Service, a new federal bureau in the Department of the Interior. The fundamental purpose of the National Park Service is to conserve the scenery, natural and historic objects, and wildlife in the parks, as well as to provide for the enjoyment of the national parks in such manner that they remain unimpaired for the enjoyment of future generations.

Exercises

1. What role do the above sites play in the tourism industry? How do these sites encourage people to travel?

2. Choose a commercial destination and a government-sponsored destination from these sites and describe how they differ. To whom would these sites appeal?

ACTIVITY 2

Site Name: International Association of Amusement Parks and Attractions

URL: www.iaapa.org

Background Information: Founded in 1918, IAAPA is the largest international trade association for permanently situated amusement facilities worldwide.

Exercises

1. What types of career opportunities exist in the amusement industry?

2. What is the show ambassador program?

 QUESTIONS FOR REVIEW AND DISCUSSION ❖

1. Give some of the main reasons that attractions and entertainment places are enjoying growing popularity.

2. How important are these factors as pleasure travel motivators?

3. If you were planning a destination-type resort, how much attention would you give to its recreation and entertainment features?

4. Why have theme parks changed the amusement park business so drastically?

5. Identify the principal appealing features of theme parks. Explain their growth trends.

6. What are the directions being taken in the U.S. gambling industry?

7. Is the ownership of recreational vehicles a passing fad?

8. Where are the most famous national parks located? Select various countries.

9. Should the spectacular shopping malls include a director of tourism?

10. Suppose that your firm was considering building a new theater or attraction in Branson, Missouri. Where would you seek information and data? What kind of data would be needed?

11. List the advantages to local people who sponsor a festival that subsequently becomes attractive to a wider market.

12. Evaluate the national forests as recreational resources.

 CASE PROBLEM

1. Many of the states in the United States are experiencing budget problems. A number of legislatures are considering legalizing gaming (gambling). Some states have already done so. As a state representative, you have decided to introduce legislation legalizing gaming to bolster your state's budget. What would be your arguments supporting this bill? What opposition would you expect?

ENDNOTES

1. NGISC, *The National Gambling Impact Study Commission Report* (Washington DC: NGISC, 1999) and govinfo.library.unt.edu/ngisc.
2. National Park Service, *Statistical Abstract 2009* (Denver,CO: NPS, 2010).
3. Daniel Stynes, *Economic Benefits to Local Communities from National Park Visitation and Payroll, 2009* (Fort Collins, CO: National Park Service, January 2011) and www.nature.nps.gov/stats.
4. National Sporting Goods Association, *Sports Participation in 2009* (Mt. Prospect, IL: NSGA, 2010).
5. Adventure Travel Trade Association, *Adventure Travel Market Report* (Seattle: ATTA, 2010) and www.adventuretravel.biz.

 **PART 3** # Understanding Travel Behavior

Travelers passing through an airport.
Photo courtesy of PhotoDisc, Inc.

CHAPTER 9

Motivation for Pleasure Travel[1]

LEARNING OBJECTIVES

- Adopt a professional approach to motivation and recognize differences in other people's motives.

- Appreciate the range of ideas on travel motivation, including historical accounts and psychological theories.

- Be aware of contemporary research practices in tourism that integrate motive and destination feature assessments.

- Be familiar with conceptual approaches to tourist motivation and recognize that there is continual development and enhancement of ideas in this field.

Special thanks go to Philip L. Pearce, James Cook University, Queensland, Australia who prepared this chapter.

Internationally recognized tourism icons are a powerful draw to any destination fortunate enough to have inherited or created one. The Eiffel Tower in Paris, France, is one of the world's most instantly recognizable icons. Constructed for the 1889 World's Fair, the Eiffel Tower is a must-see structure for all visitors to France. A photo taken beside the tower is a lifelong treasure for many tourists. The challenge for all destinations is to find "the stroke of genius" that will uniquely associate the icon with the destination—and that will, for any number of reasons, make it internationally popular. *Photo courtesy of ImageState.*

INTRODUCTION

To be successful, tourism practitioners must understand consumer motivation. History offers a glimpse of behaviors to study. Even the supposedly spiritually motivated medieval pilgrims were sometimes wont to yield to temptations during the long journey! So, although crusaders' motivations might have been spiritual, they often succumbed to the desire for immediate gratification. Thus, from ancient times until now, astute operators have understood the importance of psychology in tourism. Such travel motivation studies include consumer motivation, decision making, product satisfaction, overall desirability of holiday experiences, pleasure in the vacation environment, and interaction with the local inhabitants. In short, tourists travel for many reasons, including spirituality, social status, escape, and cultural enrichment. Maslow's hierarchy of needs provides insight into ways in which a trip may satisfy disparate needs. If these concepts are studied within a context, they can provide insight into how visitors select activities and experiences to suit their personal psychological and motivational profiles.

A FOCUS ON CUSTOMERS

Students and analysts of tourist behavior face a particular problem when attempting to assess tourist **motivation**. Many individuals with an enthusiasm for traveling and holidays are able to articulate their own motivation. The problem lies in then assuming that other people are also motivated by these same forces. This chapter introduces a range of ideas, concepts, and studies on pleasure travel motivation. Readers are encouraged to develop a professional view of motivation, constantly being mindful that other travelers might not be driven by the same social, cultural, and biological needs as themselves.

A professional understanding of the consumer is at the core of successful business practice in the tourist industry. If the various facets of the tourism, travel, and hospitality world can meet the needs of the consumer, then some chance of business success is possible, provided other financial and managerial inputs are appropriate. Thus, if a theme park can meet the needs of its customers, if a wilderness lodge can provide the kind of accommodation its users expect, and if an adventure tour operator can organize an exciting whitewater rafting trip, then there is a basis for a successful tourism business. When consumer expectations are met or exceeded by the tourism operations, one can expect repeat business and positive word-of-mouth advertising, as well as the ability to maintain or even increase the current level of charging for the existing tourism service. Clearly, consumers matter to tourism businesses.

The general issue of understanding consumer needs falls within the area of the **psychology** of tourists' behavior. This study area is concerned with what motivates tourists, how they make decisions, what tourists think of the products they buy, how much they enjoy and learn during their holiday experiences, how they interact with the local people and environment, and how satisfied they are with their holidays.

Asking the Question

The study of travel motivation is the fundamental starting point in studying the psychology of tourist behavior. The question is often expressed simply as: Why do tourists travel? One of the lessons of social science research is to learn to ask good questions—that is, questions that are stimulating and challenging to our understanding of the world but that can be answered with enough specificity and information to enhance our understanding. "Why do tourists travel?" is not a good question. Instead, we need to ask why certain groups of people choose certain holiday experiences, because this more specific question focuses attention on the similarities and differences among groups of people and the kinds of experiences they seek. It should be noted that we are emphasizing people's desire for certain experiences and we are not assuming that destinations such as Las Vegas or central Africa offer only one kind of experience to fulfill travelers' motives. It can be argued that destinations offer many kinds of holiday experiences; to assume that areas as diverse as resort cities or countries are going to attract just one group of visitors with a certain narrow range of motivations would be simplistic. The title of this chapter is "Motivation for Pleasure Travel," an obvious indication of the focus of attention, but it is worth noting that rich research and practical opportunities exist to develop our understanding of the motivation of business, sports, and other travel groups.[2]

Background

Three main sources of ideas assist in answering questions concerning travel motivation. Historical and literary accounts of travel and travelers provide one such source. Additionally, the discipline of psychology and its long history of trying to understand and explain human behavior is a rich vein of writing for travel motivation. And finally, the current practices of tourism industry researchers, particularly those involved in surveying visitors, offer some additional insights concerning how we might approach travel motivation.

History and Literature

Historians provide a range of accounts concerning why travelers have set about their journeys over the centuries. Casson[3] and Wolfe[4] point out that the wealthier members of Athenian and Roman society owned summer resorts and used to holiday there to avoid the heat of the cities and indulge in a social life characterized by much eating and drinking. The stability of the Roman world permitted its citizens to interest themselves in some long-distant travel; Anthony reports that visiting the Egyptian monuments and collecting souvenirs from these sites were well-accepted and socially prestigious practices.[5] If motives such as escape, social interaction, and social comparison were popular in Roman times, then the emergence of the pilgrimage in the Middle Ages can be seen as adding a serious travel motive to our historical perspective. The original pilgrimages were essentially journeys to sacred places undertaken because of religious motives. Travelers sought the assistance or bounty of their god and journeyed long distances to revere the deity. Rowling has noted that later in the Middle Ages, revelry

Don't you wish! This vacationer appears to be appreciating euphoria—the kind of optimal experience we all hope to have when on holidays. Clearly some in-depth motivational research is in order here—to discover this destination's secret of success in filling visitors needs. *Photo courtesy of Wisconsin Department of Tourism.*

and feasting became important accompaniments to the journey and "licentious living" among the pilgrims was not unknown.[6] The legacy of the pilgrimage for understanding modern traveler motivation is not insignificant. The pilgrimage elevated the importance of travel as an activity in one's life and created the idea that certain key sites or attractions were of long-lasting spiritual benefit to the sojourner. Good times and spiritual times were, however, often linked.

The seriousness of travel was further enhanced by the Grand Tour, an activity intended principally as a training ground for the young and wealthy members of the English courts in Tudor times. By the end of the eighteenth century, the Grand Tour had gained favor as an ideal finishing school for a youth's education, a theme consistent with the analysis of much contemporary youth travel.[7]

The effects of industrialization, urbanization, and improved transportation possibilities brought travel to the middle classes in the mid-nineteenth century, and strong elements of social status and class consciousness characterize the fashions of the railway and spa resorts of nineteenth-century Europe.[8] One of the first tourism scholars, Pimlott, writing in 1947, noted, "In the present century holidays have become a cult. . . . For many they are the principal objects for life—saved and planned for during the rest of the year and enjoyed in retrospect when they are over."[9]

Tourism is now, of course, a worldwide phenomenon with enormous differentiation in its available environments, host cultures, and types of visitors. Nevertheless, some of the chief motivations noted in this brief historical review—such as travel for escape, cultural curiosity, spirituality, education, and social status—must be accounted for in any summary of contemporary travel.

Much of the contemporary travel scene is eloquently described by literary figures and professional travel writers. Their accounts of travel motivation, both of themselves and of others, are subjective rather than professional but can also be considered as a background for our understanding. The noted American writer John Steinbeck conceived of travel as an "itch," a disease or pseudomedical condition, "the travel bug," which periodically drove him to "be someplace else." Additionally, the theme of traveling to discover oneself has a long literary tradition and is present in the early works of Ovid, Chaucer, Spenser, and Tennyson as well as in twentieth-century fiction, including works by Kerouac, Forster, Lawrence, Hemingway, and Conrad. The professional travel writers of the last two decades, such as Paul Theroux, Jan Morris, and Eric Newby, have also emphasized discovery and curiosity in their analysis of the motives of travelers.

The rich tapestry of ideas about travel motivation from historical accounts and literary sources can be supplemented by theories of motivation from the discipline of psychology.

The Contribution of Psychological Theory

Psychology, as a separate area of inquiry, is often considered as originating in 1879 with the creation of the first laboratory for the scientific study of behavior by Wilhelm Wundt in Germany. In their own journey studying human behavior, psychology writers and researchers have frequently addressed the topic of human motivation. The scope of this research is impressive, as it embraces both detailed studies of human physiology and the nervous system as well as broad approaches with a more sociological and anthropological orientation.

Many well-known theories in psychology have a strong motivation component. In many instances the discussion or study of motivation is a part of a broader theory directed at understanding human personality or, more simply, what makes individuals different. A summary of some major theories in psychology that have been concerned in part with the topic of motivation is presented in Table 9.1. It must be noted that these psychology researchers and thinkers were not considering travel motivation directly when formulating these approaches. Nevertheless, the third column of the table lists a number of human needs and motives that might be usefully applied to the question of why certain groups of travelers seek particular kinds of holiday experiences.

A direct application of these psychological theories for tourist motivation adds some new motives to the list obtained from the historical and literary review. In particular, motives such as personal control, love, sex, competence, tension reduction, arousal, achievement, acceptance, self-development, respect, curiosity, security, understanding, and self-actualization can be identified.

The beauty of an unspoiled natural landscape is a strong travel motivator. These boys are on a rock overlooking Victoria Falls in Zimbabwe, one of southern Africa's most famous natural attractions. *Photo courtesy of Zimbabwe Tourism Authority.*

Current Market Research Practices

An understanding of travel motivation can also be approached by examining the kinds of motivation questions asked in surveys of travelers. Basic passport questions that are standardized around the world include only broad categories of motivation and are limited to such distinctions as "Are you traveling for business reasons, for holiday, to visit friends and relatives, for a convention, or for other reasons?"

More specific market research questions are typified in the studies of "travel benefits" or the rewards of travel. It can be argued that these travel benefits or rewards can be seen as the outcomes or satisfactions linked to tourists' motives for traveling.

In a typical study of travel benefits, Loker and Perdue studied visitors to North Carolina and factor-analyzed 12 benefit statements as a part of a survey of summer travelers to that state.[10] Using the two statistical sorting procedures of factor analysis and cluster analysis, the researchers argued that there were six segments of the market receiving different kinds of benefits from their holidays:

1. Those who emphasized excitement and escape
2. Pure adrenaline/excitement seekers
3. A family- and friends-oriented group
4. Naturalists (those who enjoyed natural surroundings)
5. A group who emphasized the value of escape by itself
6. A group who enjoyed all benefits

This kind of research, which has been repeated by several other scholars with slightly different benefit groups emerging for different settings, represents a summary of travel satisfaction for a particular destination. It is, thus, not a pure or clean analysis of travel motivation but helps us to understand the importance of travel motivation in tourism studies by emphasizing that for travel motivation analysis to be useful and meaningful it must be put in a context. Thus, while the list of

TABLE 9.1 Human Motives and Needs in Psychology Theory and Research[a]

Theorist/Researcher	Theoretical Approach	Motives or Needs Emphasized
Sigmund Freud	Psychoanalytic theory	Need for sex, need for aggression; emphasis on unconscious needs
Carl Jung	Psychoanalytic approach	Need for arousal, need to create and self-actualize
Alfred Adler	Modified psychoanalytic	Need for competence, need for mastery to overcome incompetence
Harry Stack Sullivan	Modified psychoanalytic	Need for acceptance and love
Karen Horney	Modified psychoanalytic	Need to control anxiety, need for love and security
Clark Hull	Learning theory	Need to reduce tension
Gordon Allport	Trait theory	Need to repeat intrinsically satisfying behaviors
Albert Bandura, David McClelland, John Atkinson	Social learning theory, social approaches	Need for self-efficacy or personal mastery; need for achievement
Carl Rogers	Humanistic	Need for self-development
Abraham Maslow	Humanistic	Hierarchy of needs from physiological needs, to safety needs, to love and relationship needs, to self-esteem, to self-actualization
D. E. Berlyne	Cognitive approaches	Need to satisfy curiosity, seek mental stimulation
Rom Harré	Ethogenic (social and philosophical)	Need to earn respect and avoid contempt of others
Stanley Cohen and Laurie Taylor	Sociological theory	Need to escape, need for excitement and meaning
George Kelly	Personal construct theory	Need to predict and explain the world
Mihaly Csikszentmihalyi	Humanistic approach	Need for peak experiences

[a]For clarity, the terms motives and needs are used together in this summary table. Some writers prefer to see needs as more physiologically based and motives as more socially oriented.

motives from psychology theories and the history/literature of travel provide a rich source of potential motives, an understanding of travel motivation makes sense only in a particular context—that is, when people are describing why they might seek certain holiday experiences.

Frequently, market survey companies or firms provide potential travelers with lists of items that the researchers believe are relevant to the question of why people travel to particular destinations. In reviewing this kind of work, Echtner and Ritchie list 34 *attributes* used in 14 key studies of destination image.[11] Of these 34 attributes, 24 were used in at least three studies. These lists are often a mixture of attributes of the destination and select motives of the traveler. An example of such a list is provided in Table 9.2. The items in the table were derived from the Pleasure Travel Market Survey, a major survey

TABLE 9.2 Trip-Driven Attributes for Australian Outbound Travelers (Bold items represent statements corresponding to motives. Items not in bold are destination characteristics.)

Item	Mean Importance Rating[a]
Going to places I haven't visited before	**3.26**
Outstanding scenery	3.16
Meeting new and different people	**3.11**
Opportunities to increase one's knowledge	**3.10**
Interesting rural countryside	3.10
Destinations that provide value for my holiday money	3.01
Personal safety	**3.01**
Arts and cultural attractions	2.98

(continued)

TABLE 9.2 (*Continued*)

Item	Mean Importance Rating
Public transportation such as airlines	2.97
Experiencing new and different lifestyles	**2.97**
Having fun, being entertained	**2.92**
Standards of hygiene and cleanliness	2.89
Visiting friends and relatives	**2.86**
Historical, archaeological, or military sites, buildings, and places	2.85
Just relaxing	**2.85**
Escaping from the ordinary	**2.85**
Being together as a family	**2.84**
Inexpensive travel to the country	2.79
The best deal I could get	2.78
Availability of pretrip/in-country tourist information	2.78
Being able to communicate in English	2.72
Inexpensive travel within the country	2.71
Nice weather	2.69
Trying new food	**2.67**
Shopping	2.66
Ease of obtaining visa	2.61
Visits to appreciate natural ecological sites (forests, wetlands, etc.)	2.59
Talking about the trip after I returned home	**2.55**
Meeting people with similar interests	**2.55**
Getting a change from a busy job	**2.47**
Unique or different native cultural groups such as Eskimo and Indian	2.45
Ease of exchanging the currency	2.40
Getting away from the demands of home	2.36
Finding thrills and excitement	2.33
Exotic atmosphere	2.30
Unique or different immigrant culture	2.27
Ease of driving on my own	2.25
Advertised low-cost excursions	2.24
Environmental quality of the air, water, and soil	2.24
Indulging in luxury	**2.20**
Visiting places where my family came from	2.19
Activities for the whole family	2.16
Going places my friends have not been	1.97
Being able to communicate in the foreign language	1.96
Outdoor activity	1.92
Experiencing a simpler lifestyle	**1.91**
Doing nothing at all	**1.83**
Exercise and fitness opportunities	1.55
Roughing it	**1.50**

[a]4 = very important; 1 = not at all important.

Most parents are motivated to provide their children with wholesome and memorable vacation experiences. This lakeside campsite is one popular example of where and how parents create an opportunity for lasting memories for everyone in the family. *Photo courtesy of IT Stock Free.*

conducted by United States and Canadian tourism authorities throughout the 1980s and 1990s. The survey contains a list of travel philosophies (parallel to travel motives) and trip-driven attributes (destination features). The travel motivation items are represented in bold.

Although such lists of motives and destination features mixed together are common in studies trying to explain the appeal of places, they have some limitations. In particular, the lists may not be comprehensive; they may reflect the biases of the researchers; they may not explore the relative importance of the various features or reasons for visiting and incorrectly assume that all reasons are equally important (although the data in Table 9.2 do indicate importance). Additionally, the way in which the attributes are interrelated is not often considered. For example, the characteristics of "seclusion" and "exciting nightlife" might be mutually exclusive.

THE NEED FOR A THEORY

This review of travel motivation has stressed that three sources of information can provide a listing of motives concerning why people travel. The list of potential travel motivations is a long one and includes a range of needs from excitement and arousal to self-development and personal growth. Additionally, the brief review of contemporary market research practice concerning destination image indicated that there were further lists of destination features that might be thought of as a mix of travel motives and destination characteristics.

Theories or models in social science research typically summarize or reorganize knowledge in an area. Occasionally, a theory will provide a new perspective and foster prediction or specifications of future directions for human action and research. The area of tourist motivation requires a theoretical approach. The lists of motives need to be summarized, connections need to be made with other areas of inquiry such as destination image studies, and our current understanding needs to be challenged and enhanced. Pearce has outlined seven features that are necessary for a good theory of tourist motivation.[12] These are listed in Table 9.3.

TABLE 9.3 Requirements of a Sound Theory of Tourist Motivation

Element	Explanation
1. The role of the theory	Must be able to integrate existing tourist needs, reorganize the needs, and provide a new orientation for future research.
2. The ownership and appeal of the theory	Must be appealing to specialist researchers, useful in tourism industry settings, and credible to marketers and consumers.
3. Ease of communication	Must be relatively easy to explain to potential users and be universal (not country-specific) in its application.
4. Ability to measure travel motivation	Must be amenable to empirical study. The ideas can be translated into questions and responses for assessment purposes.
5. A multimotive versus single-trait approach	Must consider the view that travelers may seek to satisfy several needs at once. Must be able to model the pattern of traveler needs, not just consider one need.
6. A dynamic versus snapshot approach	Must recognize that both individuals and societies change over time. Must be able to consider or model the changes that take place continuously in tourism.
7. The roles of extrinsic and intrinsic	Must be able to consider that travelers are variously motivated by intrinsic, self-satisfying goals and at other times are motivated by extrinsic, socially controlled rewards (e.g., others' opinions).

One starting point in the conceptual approaches to motivation is the work of Stanley Plog.[13] This work, often uncritically accepted as the major approach to tourist motivation, stressed that travelers could be categorized on a psychocentric (nonadventurous, inward-looking) to allocentric (adventurous, outward-looking) scale. Plog claimed the U.S. population was normally distributed along a continuum between these two extreme types. The approach was historically important in providing one organizing theory of travel motivation. It does not, however, fulfill many of the criteria listed in Table 9.3 and was notably deficient, at least initially, in terms of offering only a single-trait, static, and extrinsic account of tourist motivation. In the 1991 version of the approach, a second dimension, energy versus lethargy, was added to the psychocentric-allocentric dimension, thus developing a four-part categorization scheme. Nevertheless, the approach is still limited because of its North American bias, and it does not consider the issues of multimotive behavior, nor does it provide measurement details or consider the dynamic nature of motives in the travelers' life span.

Some new emerging theories of tourist and leisure motivation fulfill more of the criteria described in Table 9.3. In particular, the intrinsic-motivation—optimal-arousal perspective of Iso-Ahola[14] and the travel needs model of Pearce both added new perspectives to the tourist-motivation field.[15]

Iso-Ahola argues that tourist and leisure behavior takes place within a framework of optimal arousal and incongruity. That is, while individuals seek different levels of stimulation, they share the need to avoid either overstimulation (mental and physical exhaustion) or boredom (too little stimulation). Leisure needs change during the life span and across places and social company. He advises researchers to keep the motivation questions for leisure close to the actual participation in time and emphasizes the importance of participants' feelings of self-determination and competence to ensure satisfaction.

The **travel-needs model** articulated by Pearce and coworkers is more explicitly concerned with tourists and their motives rather than with leisure, which is the focus of Iso-Ahola's work. The travel-needs model argues that people have a career in their travel behavior that reflects a hierarchy of their travel motives. A travel career is similar to a work career: People may start at different levels, they are likely to change their levels during their life cycle, and they can be inhibited in their travel career by money, health, and other people.

The steps or levels on the travel-needs or career model were likened to a ladder, and this concept was built on Abraham Maslow's hierarchy of needs.[16] By expanding and extending the range of specific needs at each ladder level that fit with Maslow's original formulation, Pearce achieved a comprehensive and rich catalog of the many different psychological needs and motives noted earlier in this chapter (see Figure 9.1). The earliest version of the travel-needs ladder retained Maslow's ideas that lower levels on the ladder have to be satisfied before the individual moves to higher levels of the ladder. In this approach, travelers concerned with developing and extending their relationships while traveling will also have needs in terms of safety and physiological level factors but may not yet be particularly concerned with self-esteem and self-development needs. Recent and ongoing revisions to this model place less emphasis on the strict hierarchy of needs and more on changing patterns of motives. Importantly, the travel-needs ladder approach emphasizes that people have a range of motives for seeking out holiday experiences. For example, a visitor to Canada who attends the Calgary Stampede might be motivated to do so by the pleasant, safe setting; to entertain a child and develop family experiences of togetherness; and to add to knowledge about Canadian culture. That is, several levels of a travel-needs pattern work together for a rich multimotive picture of travel motivation. This flexibility and variability recognizes that motivation may change over time and across situations so that the same individual visiting Great Britain might emphasize cultural understanding and curiosity motives more than relationship and family-development motives.

In the travel-needs model, destinations are seen as settings where vastly different holiday experiences are possible. Thus, travelers' motives influence what they seek from a destination, and destinations will vary in their capacity to provide a range of holiday experiences. In short, travelers do not visit a place with standard objective destination features but instead journey to a location where they select activities and holiday experiences from those on offer to suit their personal psychological and motivational profile.

Traveling on a train with family members is a satisfying holiday experience. *Copyright © 2001 Amtrak. Photo provided as a courtesy by Amtrak.*

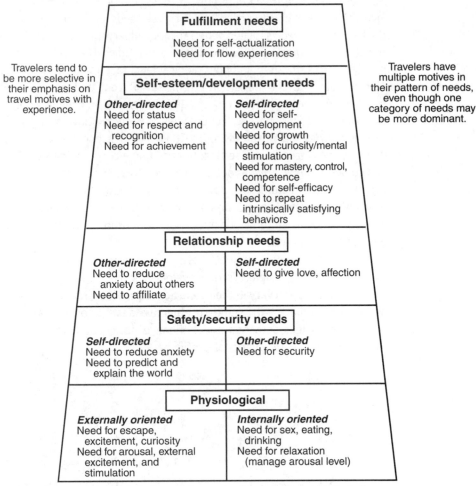

Travelers tend to be more selective in their emphasis on travel motives with experience.

Travelers have multiple motives in their pattern of needs, even though one category of needs may be more dominant.

Fulfillment needs

Need for self-actualization
Need for flow experiences

Self-esteem/development needs

Other-directed
Need for status
Need for respect and recognition
Need for achievement

Self-directed
Need for self-development
Need for growth
Need for curiosity/mental stimulation
Need for mastery, control, competence
Need for self-efficacy
Need to repeat intrinsically satisfying behaviors

Relationship needs

Other-directed
Need to reduce anxiety about others
Need to affiliate

Self-directed
Need to give love, affection

Safety/security needs

Self-directed
Need to reduce anxiety
Need to predict and explain the world

Other-directed
Need for security

Physiological

Externally oriented
Need for escape, excitement, curiosity
Need for arousal, external excitement, and stimulation

Internally oriented
Need for sex, eating, drinking
Need for relaxation (manage arousal level)

A "spine" or "core" of needs for nearly all travelers seems to include relationships, curiosity, and relaxation.

Figure 9.1 Travel-career needs.

The travel-needs model was formulated so that a dynamic, multimotive account of travel behavior could serve our understanding of tourism. It acts as a blueprint for the assessment of tourist motives and requires individual tailoring to specific situations. That is, the context or setting helps frame the way in which the travel-needs ladder questions are asked. Pearce and Dermott, working in a theme-park setting, were able to use the travel-needs ladder to explain the motives of different consumers for that setting.[17] This individual tailoring is done by taking sections of the travel-needs ladder (e.g., the physiological level and the need for stimulation) and asking questions about the importance of rides and adventure activities in the theme park. Similarly, questions about the importance of going with friends were asked. In this way, a full range of theme-park motives is determined by linking travel motivation to other tourism studies.

THE DEVELOPMENT OF MOTIVATION MODELS

The proposals for travel motivation put forward by Plog, Iso-Ahola, and Pearce (and other researchers not listed in full in this chapter) are not static or "finished" products of social science research. The model developed by Plog in 1973 was updated in 1991 and is undoubtedly undergoing further modification in the tourism consultancy world, where it is principally used. Similarly, Ryan provided a commentary on the travel-needs ladder of Pearce, arguing that there was not yet solid evidence that the "ladder" component of the model was appropriate.[18] It is important for the tourism student to understand the value of this kind of academic revision. Some commentary and criticisms of a theory or approach do not necessarily mean all of it is wrong or, more simply, that academics disagree. Instead, it is more useful to see the comments as a part of a constructive process. For example, the travel-career ladder model is currently being enhanced by referring to the system as travel-career patterns, an approach that retains the multimotive focus but that accounts for some recent findings that inexperienced travelers emphasize all motives whereas experienced travelers are more selective in their ratings of motivation statements. Further, initial work suggests that a core spine of motives (curiosity, relationships, relaxation) exists in everyone's motivation, and extensions to this core vary with experience. Tourism students have a rich opportunity to participate in the development of ideas in this field in graduate study as researchers develop this area of tourism analysis in the next decade.

SUMMARY

This chapter has argued that a theory of tourist motivation such as the travel-needs approach helps summarize existing statements and ideas about the motives of travelers. It can also be useful in answering the questions:

- Why do certain groups of travelers seek particular holiday experiences?
- Why do certain groups of travelers travel to destination X?

The chapter has stressed that these questions will not have one simple answer, but rather that different groups of individuals will place different weightings on a structured set of answers, producing shifting patterns of motivation. For example, young teenagers emphasize the motives of stimulation and relationships in visiting theme parks, while young couples emphasize developing relationships and the need for relaxation. For other travelers—for example, those exploring exotic locations and participating in more diverse forms of tourism—a wider range of motives including self-development, mastery, curiosity, escape, and self-fulfillment will be involved.[19]

Travel motivation studies can be the basis of many consumer analyses in tourism. A good motivational profile of visitors should be of assistance in understanding how well the destination characteristics fit the needs of the travelers. The key to linking travel motivation studies to other tourism studies such as destination choice lies in analyzing the activities offered by the destination and the activities that fulfill the travelers' motives. Thus, if visitors strongly motivated by the need to enhance their understanding of art and history visit well-managed, high-quality cultural attractions, then satisfaction is likely. A mismatch can also occur, such as the unfortunate visitor to a tropical island who is seeking peace and quiet but is instead assaulted by a tourism product that is set up for those seeking a party lifestyle—that is, stimulation, excitement, and new relationships. As tourism grows into an increasingly sophisticated consumer industry, the value of understanding the needs of travelers will increase and the motivation of tourists will become a driving part of all tourism studies.

❖ **KEY CONCEPTS** ❖

consumers	motivation	self-development needs
destination attributes	needs	self-esteem needs
discipline of psychology	physiological needs	tourism experience
Grand Tour	psychological theories	travel motivation
history	relationship needs	travel-needs model
Maslow	safety/security needs	

❖ **INTERNET EXERCISES** ❖

The Internet sites mentioned in this chapter plus some selected additional sites are listed for your convenience on the companion Web site for this book, www.wiley.com/college/goeldner.

ACTIVITY 1

Site Name: Seniors Search

URL: www.seniorssearch.com

Background Information: A search directory exclusively for the over-50 age group.

Site Name: Accessible Journeys

URL: www.disabilitytravel.com

Background Information: Since 1985, Disability Travel has been designing accessible holidays and escorting groups on vacations exclusively for slow walkers, wheelchair travelers, and their families and friends.

Site Name: Kids Go Too

URL: www.kidsgotootravel.com

Background Information: Kids Go Too provides you with specific and meaningful information on lodging, activities, and restaurants that are perfectly suited to a unique and exciting vacation that is fun and satisfying to every member of the family.

Site Name: Eurocamp

URL: www.eurocamp.com

Background Information: Visit this Web site to find out more about self-drive camping holidays in Europe. You can search their campsite and regional databases.

Exercise

1. Choose at least two of the Web sites indicated above. Describe how they use travel psychology to motivate people to travel who may have barriers to travel.

ACTIVITY 2

Site Name: The Travel Psychologist

URL: www.michaelbrein.com

Background Information: Dr. Michael Brein is the "Travel Psychologist." He is an avid world traveler as well as the author, publisher, and lecturer on travel subjects. The site has short essays on Travel Psychology 101, 102, 103, 104, and 105, plus frequently asked questions.

Exercises

1. What are the seven points Dr. Brein makes in Psychology 101?

2. What is the psychology of travel?

❖ **QUESTIONS FOR REVIEW AND DISCUSSION** ❖

1. Why is it important for tourism people to have a good understanding of travel motivation?

2. Explain the relationship of customer (tourist) satisfaction and travel motivation.

3. The author states that the question "Why do tourists travel?" is not a good starting point for research on this subject. Comment.

4. "Why do certain groups of people choose certain holiday experiences?" is a much better question. Why?

5. Identify five motivations for travel of Europeans during Roman times, the Middle Ages, and Tudor times. Do such motivations exist today?

6. How important are the motives of discovery and curiosity?

7. Are your travel benefits or rewards linked closely to your travel motives? Elucidate.

8. Provide a few examples of how a person's travel needs change over a life span.

9. Why is it important to understand motivations regarding the "total tourism experience" rather than simply motivations for the "tourist's trip?"

10. Give an example of travel experience overstimulation (mental or physical exhaustion or both). Similarly, give an example of boredom (too little stimulation).

11. Consider Pearce's five-level travel-needs ladder and provide some examples of externally and internally oriented physiological needs. Why are these needs at the bottom of the ladder?

12. Referring to the preceding question, provide similar representations of safety/security needs, relationship needs, self-esteem/development needs, and fulfillment needs.

13. Is travel becoming a human need?

14. Assume that you are employed by a nature (ecotour) company and are planning a new tour to a newly established national park. Describe several ingredients of such a tour that meet most of these needs, as shown in question 11.

15. How could a resort hotel's activities or social director help guests with their fulfillment needs? Give several cases in point.

16. Below is a short list of travel motivations. Suggest a travel experience or product that would match each motivation.

    a. Rest/relaxation

    b. Unspoiled natural environment enjoyment

    c. Interesting countryside and wildlife study opportunities

    d. Lots of nightlife and entertainment

    e. Adventure activities

    f. Good shopping and browsing

17. How important are a variety of available experiences at a destination?

 CASE PROBLEMS

1. You have been promoted to director of training of the Cruise Lines International Association. Reviewing the listed travel motivations in question 16, which would you select for a group of travel marketing sales seminars that will be sponsored by CLIA? (Attending would be travel agents and tour company reps.)

2. Referring to the preceding problem, after selecting the motivations, what kinds of instructional materials and teaching methods would you employ? Why?

3. Your first assignment after joining a tour company staff is to design a tour that would appeal to young singles. Obviously, you must create a tour that would probably motivate a market sufficiently large for your company to make a profit on it. Identify the motivation(s) selected, then describe briefly your tour concept and the specific marketing elements you would feature in its promotion to reach this very promising market.

4. Pleasure travel motivation is often added to a business trip, such as attending a convention. Give an example of such a combination. Identify the principal motivations involved. How would you sell this idea to the convention planning committee?

5. The holiday season is approaching. Jeff R. is trying to compose a direct-mail promotion letter to be sent to each person on his travel agency's mailing list. He's convinced that giving a gift of travel would be very appealing to many of his clients. What key phrases should he embody in this letter to motivate such giving?

ENDNOTES

1. This chapter was prepared by Philip L. Pearce, Tourism Program, James Cook University, Queensland, Australia.

2. G. Moscardo, P. Pearce, A. Morrison, D. Green, and J. T. O'Leary, "Developing a Typology for Understanding Visiting Friends and Relatives Markets," *Journal of Travel Research,* vol. 38, no. 3 (February 2000), pp. 251–259.

3. L. Casson, *Travel in the Ancient World* (London: Allen and Unwin, 1974).

4. R. I. Wolfe, "Recreational Travel: The New Migration," *Geographical Bulletin,* vol. 2 (1967), pp. 159–167.

5. I. Anthony, *Verulamium* (Hanley, UK: Wood Mitchell, 1973).

6. M. Rowling, *Everyday Life of Medieval Travellers* (London: B. T. Batsford, 1971).

7. C. Hibbert, *The Grand Tour* (London: Weidenfeld and Nicolson, 1969).

8. E. Swinglehurst, *The Romantic Journey* (London: Pica Editions, 1974).

9. J. A. R. Pimlott, *The Englishman's Holiday* (London: Faber & Faber, 1947).

10. L. E. Loker and R. Perdue, "A Benefit-Based Segmentation of a Nonresident Summer Travel Market," *Journal of Travel Research,* vol. 31, no. 1 (1992), pp. 30–35.

11. Echtner, Charlotte M. and J. R. Brent Ritchie. "The Meaning and Measurement of Destination Image." *Journal of Tourism Studies,* vol. 2, no. 2 pp. 2-12, (1991).

12. P. L. Pearce, "*Fundamentals of Tourist Motivation.*" In D. G. Pearce and R. W. Butler (eds.) *Fundamentals of Tourist Motivation* (London: Routledge, 1992), pp. 113–134.

13. S. Plog, "*Understanding Psychographics in Tourism Research.*" In J. R. B. Ritchie and C. Goeldner (eds.), *Travel, Tourism, and Hospitality Research* (New York: John Wiley & Sons, 1987), pp. 203–214.

Also S. Plog, "Why Destination Areas Rise and Fall in Popularity," *Cornell Hotel and Restaurant Quarterly* (1974), pp. 55–58; and S. Plog, *Leisure Travel: Making it a Growth Market . . . Again!* (New York: John Wiley & Sons, 1991).

14. S. Iso-Ahola, "Toward a Social Psychological Theory of Tourism Motivation: A Rejoinder," *Annals of Tourism Research,* vol. 9, no. 2 (1982), pp. 256–262.

15. P. L. Pearce, *"Fundamentals of Tourist Motivation."* In D. G. Pearce and R. W. Butler (eds.) *Fundamentals of Tourist Motivation* (London: Routledge, 1992), pp. 113–134; and P. L. Pearce, *The Ulysses Factor: Evaluating Visitors in Tourist Settings* (New York: Springer-Verlag, 1988).

16. A. H. Maslow, *Motivation and Personality,* 2nd ed. (New York: Harper & Row, 1970).

17. P. Pearce and B. Dermott, *Dreamworld Report.* Department of Tourism, James Cook Univerisity of North Queensland, 1991.

18. C. Ryan, "The Travel Career Ladder: An Appraisal," *Annals of Tourism Research,* vol. *25,* no. 4 (October 1998), pp. 936–957.

19. K. Fielding, P. L. Pearce, and K. Hughes, "Climbing Ayers Rock: Relating Motivation, Time Perception, and Enjoyment." *Journal of Tourism Studies,* vol. 3, no. 2, pp. 49–57, (1992).

CHAPTER 10

Cultural and International Tourism for Life's Enrichment

LEARNING OBJECTIVES

- Recognize that travel experiences are the best way to learn about other cultures.

- Identify the cultural factors in tourism.

- Appreciate the rewards of participation in life-seeing tourism.

- Become aware of the most effective promotional measures involving an area's cultural resources.

- Realize the importance of cultural attractions to any area promoting itself as a tourist destination.

- Evaluate the contributions that international tourism can make toward world peace.

The Hermitage Museum in St. Petersburg, Russia. *Photo courtesy of Corbis Digital Stock.*

INTRODUCTION

The highest purpose of tourism is to become better acquainted with people in other places and countries, because this furthers the understanding and appreciation that builds a better world for all. International travel also involves the exchange of knowledge and ideas, another worthy objective. Travel raises levels of human experience, recognition, and achievements in many areas of learning, research, and artistic activity. Tourism goes beyond dependable transportation and comfortable hotels; it necessitates enhancing all the avenues through which a country presents itself. They include educational, cultural, media, science, and meeting/congress activities. To increase accessibility, cultural institutions need to adapt to meet visitors' needs, sometimes providing multilingual guides and signage. Tourists can then more easily choose the purposeful activities that will match their interests.

Travel experiences vary according to the varieties of humankind and their geographical distribution. To classify destinations so that a systematic discussion of tourism motivation can be undertaken, Valene L. Smith has identified six categories of tourism: (1) ethnic tourism, (2) cultural tourism, (3) historical tourism, (4) environmental tourism, (5) recreational tourism, and (6) business tourism. Obviously, destinations can, and usually do, provide more than one type of tourism experience.[1]

IMPORTANCE

Although **culture** is only one factor that determines the overall attractiveness of a tourism region (see Figure 10.1, Stage 1), it is a very rich and diverse one. The elements of a society's culture are a complex reflection of the way its people live, work, and play (Figure 10.1, Stage 2).

Cultural tourism covers all aspects of travel whereby people learn about each other's ways of life and thought. The National Trust for Historic Preservation provides another widely used definition: "*Cultural and heritage tourism is traveling to experience the places and activities that authentically represent the stories and people of the past and present. It includes historic, cultural and natural resources.*"[2] Tourism is, thus, an important means of promoting cultural relations and international cooperation. Conversely, development of cultural factors within a nation is a means of enhancing resources to attract visitors. In many countries, tourism can be linked with a "cultural relations" policy. It is used to promote not only knowledge and understanding but also a favorable image of the nation among foreigners in the travel market.

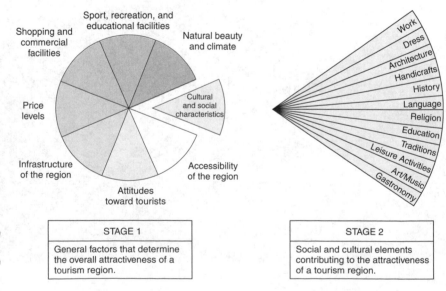

Figure 10.1 Cultural variables influencing the attractiveness of a tourism region.
Source: J. R. Brent Ritchie and Michel Zins, "Culture as Determinant of the Attractiveness of a Tourism Region," *Annals of Tourism Research* (April–June 1978), p. 256.

STAGE 1
General factors that determine the overall attractiveness of a tourism region.

STAGE 2
Social and cultural elements contributing to the attractiveness of a tourism region.

The channels through which a country presents itself to tourists can be considered its cultural factors. These are the entertainment, food, drink, hospitality, art, architecture, theater, festivals, manufactured and handcrafted products of a country, and all other characteristics of a nation's way of life.

Successful tourism is not simply a matter of having better transportation and hotels but of adding a particular national flavor in keeping with traditional ways of life and projecting a favorable image of the benefits to tourists of such goods and services. A nation's cultural attractions must be presented intelligently and creatively. In this age of uniformity, there is a risk that the products of one nation can become almost indistinguishable from those of another. Consequently, there is a great need for encouraging cultural diversity. Improved techniques of architectural design and artistic presentation can be used to create an expression of originality in every part of the world.

Taken in their narrower sense, cultural factors in tourism play a dominant role chiefly in activities that are specifically intended to promote the transmission or sharing of knowledge and ideas. Consider the following factors:

1. Libraries, museums, exhibitions
2. Musical, dramatic, or film performances
3. Radio and television programs, recordings
4. Study tours or short courses
5. Schools and universities for longer-term study and research
6. Scientific and archaeological expeditions, schools at sea
7. Joint production of films
8. Conferences, congresses, meetings, seminars

In addition, many activities that are not educational or cultural in a narrow sense provide opportunities for peoples of different nations to get to know each other.

A 2009 study titled Cultural and Heritage Tourism Study by Mandala Research shows continued and strong interest in travelers' desire to experience cultural, arts, historic, and heritage activities. The study reports that a remarkable 78 percent of all U.S. leisure travelers participate in cultural and/or heritage activities while traveling, totaling 118.3 million adults each year.[3]

The study demonstrates that cultural tourists are some of the best when it comes to economic impact as they spend more than other types of travelers. They average $994 per trip compared to $611 for all U.S. tourists. This spending translates to a contribution of more than $192 billion annually to the U.S. economy, making cultural/heritage travelers a lucrative market for destinations and attractions.

The study was conducted for the U.S. Department of Commerce, U.S. Cultural Heritage Tourism Marketing Council, and sponsored by Heritage Travel, Inc. It found cultural/heritage travelers are more frequent travelers, reporting an average of 5.01 leisure trips a year versus noncultural travelers 3.98 trips. Cultural heritage travelers engage in a variety of activities on their trips. The 2009 Mandala Research Study identified the top cultural and heritage activities as:[4]

1. Visiting historic site (66%)
2. Participating in historical reenactments (64%)
3. Visiting art museums/galleries (54%)
4. Attending an art/craft fair or festival (45%)
5. Attending a professional dance or performance (44%)
6. Visiting state/national parks (41%)
7. Shopping in museum stores (32%)
8. Exploring urban neighborhoods (30%)

According to the 2009 study, cultural and heritage travelers are also interested in culinary activities such as sampling local food and wines, attending food and wine festivals, visiting farmers markets, shopping for gourmet foods, and seeking out unique dining experiences.[5]

LIFE-SEEING TOURISM

Traditionally, a person "sees the high points" of a given location and thus feels that he or she has "seen" this area. However, there is a growing belief among tourism specialists that such an approach,

This Witch Museum in Salem, Massachusetts, is a somewhat unusual cultural attraction. This distinctiveness is exactly what tourism destination managers are seeking. Not only is it interesting and motivating, but it also serves to create a unique image, which other destinations often find difficult to replicate. *Photo courtesy of Tina Jordan/Salem Witch Museum.*

although traditionally valid, is by no means the best approach. Purposeful activities that match the travelers' interests are becoming more commonly accepted and recognized. (In popular tourist areas, such arrangements may have to be limited to the off-season periods of the year.) For example, a physician on a vacation might be interested in talking with local physicians and viewing interesting or progressive medical installations or facilities. He or she might wish to participate in a symposium or some type of educational endeavor there or have lunch with a group of physicians interested in the same particular specialty or in public health or medical practices in general. This visitor may also wish to visit the home of a well-known physician to exchange ideas.

Suggestions made by the travel agent and the means provided to make such experiences come about are of growing importance to successful tourism. Any place that wishes to become a successful tourist destination must have a greater range of activities for visitors than the traditional recreational activities such as lying on the beach or patronizing a nightclub or visiting popular tourist attractions.

Axel Dessau, former director of the Danish Tourist Board, is credited with this concept of life-seeing tourism. In Denmark, for example, the visitor is met by a graduate student or other person who is technically familiar with the field of interest that a visitor may have. This guide then arranges for purposeful visits in a schedule suited to the visitor.

The plan is usually set up on a half-day basis, with the visitor spending afternoons visiting tourist highlights, shopping, and pursuing other traditional recreational activities. The mornings would be devoted to visiting organizations and establishments with programs planned by a special expert guide. A travel agent can make these arrangements.

For example, the visitor might be interested in reviewing social problems and city government. The expert guide would make arrangements for the visitor to visit city planning offices, schools, social welfare establishments, and rehabilitation centers; to attend meetings or seminars at which problems of this nature are discussed; and to participate in other opportunities to learn firsthand what is happening in his or her field in Denmark.

Another aspect of life-seeing tourism is the opportunity to have social intercourse with families. These families host the visitor or the visitor's family in the evening after dinner for

Experiencing new cultures, along with their architecture, food, and dress, is a strong travel motivation. This mosque in the Arab community of Singapore presents striking architecture. Photo by the author.

conversation and sociability. Or the visitor can stay in a private home—an excellent way in which to become acquainted with the culture and lifestyle of persons in a different locality. In the Bahamas, visitors can discover the island group's people and culture in a very personal way through its People-to-People program (see Global Insights). This stimulating and exciting program is organized by the Ministry of Tourism. It matches Bahamian volunteers with visitors having similar professions or interests. The Bahamian host or host family may choose to take guests to a local theater performance or a Sunday church service or may invite them to a home-cooked Bahamian dinner. A wide variety of other activities may be included, depending on the interests of the visitor(s). Such opportunities substantially increase visitor appreciation and understanding of the culture they are visiting, and often bring about lasting friendships.

Other organizations are the People to People Ambassador Program and People to People International that have programs for both students and adults. Visit www.peopletopeople.com and www.ptpi.org.

❖ GLOBAL INSIGHT ❖

Bahamas People-to-People Program

A leader in providing a local experience to thousands of foreign visitors is the islands of the Bahamas. The People-to-People program established by the Ministry of Tourism has created lasting friendships between visitors and locals since its inception more than 19 years ago. It has provided an opportunity for visitors to learn hands-on the culture of the island by interacting with the Bahamians themselves.

The program matches guests with more than 1,500 Bahamian volunteers of similar ages and interests for a day or evening activity, which could include boating, fishing, shopping at the local outdoor market, attending a local school or church service, enjoying back-street tours, or, more often, visiting Bahamians in

their homes for a traditional meal of peas 'n' rice, fried fish, and guava duff.

Since the start of People-to-People, the idea has expanded its outreach program offerings, moving beyond Nassau and Grand Bahama Island to the out islands of Eleuthra, Exuma, San Salvador, Bimini, and Abaco. It has created branches geared toward visiting students and convention attendees. Tourists gain an informed view of the local culture as well as gain an insight into the distinctive cultures each island offers.

DISCUSSION QUESTIONS

1. Why did the Bahamas adopt a People-to-People program?

2. What are some of the rewards of international travel?

THE ROMANCE OF PLEASURE TRAVEL

Perhaps the strongest of all individual travel motivations is simply that of satisfying a need for pleasure. Travel has the unique quality of being able to satisfy this desire to an extremely high degree. Not all trips are pleasurable, but some are more pleasurable than anticipated. The planning and anticipation period prior to the trip can be as enjoyable as the trip itself. Discussing prospects of the trip with friends and pursuing research, educational, and shopping activities relating to the trip and the area to be visited are important parts of the total pleasure travel experience. In the formulation of marketing programs and advertising, in particular, the pleasurable aspects of the trip need to be emphasized. The prospective traveler should be told how much fun it is to go to the popular, as well as some of the more uncommon, destinations.

The romance of the trip is also a strong motivation, particularly in relation to honeymoon travel and for those who are thrilled with the romantic aspects of seeing, experiencing, and enjoying the culture of strange and attractive places. Thus, the romance and pleasure of the trip are primary attributes of the travel experience and need to be emphasized far more than they have been in the past. Sharing experiences with members of the family or friends is another integral part of the enjoyment of the trip. A trip can become a fine medium through which additional pleasure, appreciation, and romance are experienced.

DEVELOPMENTAL AND PROMOTIONAL MEASURES

Measures taken to develop and promote the cultural elements in tourism through special activities can be considered from several different points of view.

Development of Methods and Techniques

The examples just listed involve specialized methods, techniques, and skills, all of which can be developed in their own right, without any direct reference to the promotion of tourism. Theaters, libraries, museums, and other such national institutions are not usually created with tourism in mind, but they are a great asset in attracting the interest of visitors. Museums and monuments, especially, are among the expected features of a tourist itinerary. These and other activities that can assist in the development of tourism may also be desirable elements in the cultural development of the nation. The methods and techniques associated with each of the examples listed constitute a whole field of specialized knowledge. As in most other fields of expert knowledge, information and ideas can be acquired from abroad and adapted to national situations.

Even when the necessary facilities exist, it may be desirable to adapt them to the needs of tourism. Special courses will often have to be created for foreigners. Multilingual guides must be trained. Captions and instructions in museums and cinemas should be provided in at least two languages. Special arrangements may be made for tourists to be given free or inexpensive access to institutions of interest to them. Life-seeing arrangements can also be made.

Improvement in Educational and Cultural Content of Tourism

There is always room for improvement in what a tourist may learn abroad. This applies chiefly to books, pamphlets, films, and all types of illustrated information material. The services of experts are greatly needed in such matters, not only in assembling material on the history or geography of a country, but also in the attractive and accurate presentation of the material in several languages.

Heritage interpretation as an academic discipline can be very useful in tourism. Courses can be developed to enable local citizens to become authentic interpreters of their area's cultural, historical, and natural heritage. Achievement of such knowledge builds a person's ability to become a fully

The Terra Cotta Warriors and Horses at the Qin Shi Huang's Mausoleum, Lintong County, Shaanxi province, are an important archaeological excavation that attracts many tourists. *Photo courtesy of Corbis Digital Stock.*

qualified interpreter. One example might be a 40-hour course titled "Tourism: Keeper of the Culture." Those who successfully complete the course would be fully aware of their area's resources and, thus, would be capable of providing guide services or other services in which their knowledge can be useful. All forms of tourism, from group to individual, can in various ways benefit from the assistance of such informed, enthusiastic individuals.

Such an educational effort, when publicized, also creates a new self-awareness and pride in the community and a resulting improvement in the quality of life. Local art events, for example, can be organized to be attractive to the community and tourists alike. "Heritage Trails" or "Cultural Highways" can be designated. "Art in the Park" and festivals with various cultural themes help show off the area's resources and help to lengthen the season or fill in low spots in visitor demand. From the tourist's standpoint, engaging in such culturally oriented activities builds a heightened appreciation and respect for the qualities and abilities of the hosts.

Concentration of Activities around Important Themes

In recent years, much has been done to link tourist-related activities with themes or events of widespread interest, as in the case of festivals that bring together a variety of dramatic, musical, or cinema performances. An example is the successful Winter Carnival in Quebec, Canada. Another way is to focus attention on large exhibitions or fairs. Events such as these give an opportunity for the combined sponsorship of many different types of activity. International congresses or meetings can be held at the same time as the exhibitions or festivals. Youth festivals or jamborees can take place to coincide with important sporting events or large conventions.

Another way of stimulating interest is through **twinning**, whereby towns, communities, or regions in different countries establish relations with each other and send delegations to events arranged by their partners. Special attractions such as Epcot at Walt Disney World in Florida bring together in one location large-scale cultural exhibits and entertainment of several countries. Another example is the Polynesian Cultural Center in Hawaii. A map of the center is shown in Figure 10.2.

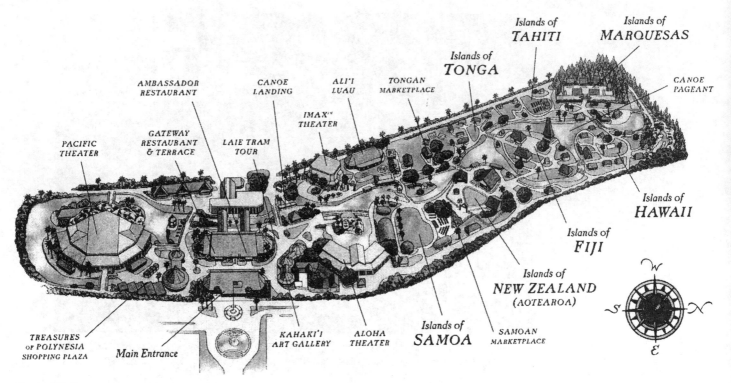

Figure 10.2 Polynesian Cultural Center, Hawaii. There are many different villages at the Polynesian Cultural Center. Each is a combination of buildings, gardens, activities, and people as you would find them if you were to travel to the various island groups represented. *Photo courtesy of Polynesian Cultural Center.*

Uses of Mass Media

Mass media are always important in the development of tourism. Whether for use outside a country as a means of attracting tourists or to inform and entertain them after their arrival, high-quality products created by journalists, film producers, and artists can fill a great need. Many countries have some who already specialize in the field of tourism whose services can be used to advantage. The Society of American Travel Writers is one professional group dedicated to good travel journalism.

Development of Out-of-Season Tourism

Educational and cultural activities are particularly well adapted to out-of-season tourism development. International meetings and study courses do not depend on good weather and entertainment. Often, their sponsors are glad to take advantage of off-season rates in hotels. Efforts should, therefore, be made to develop facilities and publicity to attract suitable activities and events. Theater tours are a good example.

ANTHROPOGRAPHY (GEOGRAPHY OF HUMANKIND)

Anthropography is defined as the branch of anthropology that describes the varieties of humankind and its geographical distribution. One of the most important motivations for travel is interest in the culture of other peoples. The Mexicans are not like the Swiss, and the Balinese are not like the Eskimos. Our natural curiosity about our world and its peoples constitutes one of the most powerful travel-motivating influences. A travel agent or other travel counselor must be familiar with the basic differences in culture among the peoples of the world, where accessible examples of such cultures are located, and which of these cultures (or groups of cultures) would be most interesting to a particular would-be traveler.

Most of the earth's 6.9 billion people are concentrated in a limited number of geographical areas. These population concentrations provide attractions in themselves. On the other hand, areas of the earth that are largely empty—such as Canada, parts of the western United States, Siberia, western China, Australia, most of Africa, and much of South America—have appeal because of the absence of humans. The landscape, with its towns and villages and rural (and perhaps nomadic) cultures, provides interesting contrasts to urban centers. Visits to primitive cultures are enriching and exciting travel experiences. In the United States, such cultural groups as the Amish in Pennsylvania or the American Indian have tourist appeal.

TYPES OF DESTINATIONS AS TRAVEL EXPERIENCES

The spatial and characteristic diversity among destinations has become so great that it is important to classify destinations so that a systematic discussion of tourism psychology and motivation can be undertaken. One way to do this is to build on Valene L. Smith's identification of several types of tourism.[6] That is, a classification of destinations can be developed on the basis of the types of travel experience provided at the various destinations.

Smith identified six categories of tourism:

1. **Ethnic tourism** is travel for the purpose of observing the cultural expressions and lifestyles of truly exotic peoples. Such tourism is exemplified by travel to Panama to study the San Blas Indians or to India to observe the isolated hill tribes of Assam. Typical destination activities would include visiting native homes, attending dances and ceremonies, and possibly participating in religious rituals.

2. **Cultural tourism** is travel to experience and, in some cases, participate in a vanishing lifestyle that lies within human memory (see Figure 10.3). The picturesque setting or "local color" in the destination area is the main attraction. Destination activities typically include meals in rustic inns, costume festivals, folk dance performances, and arts and crafts demonstrations in "old-style" fashion. Visits to Colonial Williamsburg, Virginia, and Greenfield Village in Dearborn, Michigan, or to Mystic Seaport, Connecticut, are examples of cultural tourism.

3. **Historical tourism** is the museum-cathedral tour that stresses the glories of the past—Rome, Egypt, and Greece. Civil War sites in the United States such as Gettysburg, Pennsylvania, and Chancellorsville, Virginia, are other examples. Guided tours of monuments, visits to churches and cathedrals, and sound and light performances that encapsulate the lifestyle of important events of a bygone era are favored destination activities. Such tourism is facilitated because the attractions are either in or are readily accessible from large cities. Typically, such attractions seem particularly adaptable to organized mass tourism.

4. **Environmental tourism** is similar to ethnic tourism, drawing tourists to remote areas. But the emphasis here is on natural and environmental attractions rather than ethnic ones. Travel for the purposes of "getting back to nature" and to appreciate (or become sensitive to) people-land relationships falls in this category. Environmental tourism is primarily geographic and includes such destinations and natural wonders as the Galápagos, Antarctica, Victoria Falls, Niagara Falls, the Grand Canyon, and Yellowstone National Park. Typical destination activities include photography, hiking, mountain climbing, canoeing, and camping.

5. **Recreational tourism** centers on participation in sports, curative spas, sunbathing, and social contacts in a relaxed environment. Such areas often promote sand, sea, and sex through beautiful color photographs that make you want to be there on the ski slopes, on palm-fringed beaches, on championship golf courses, or on tennis courts. Such promotion is designed to attract tourists

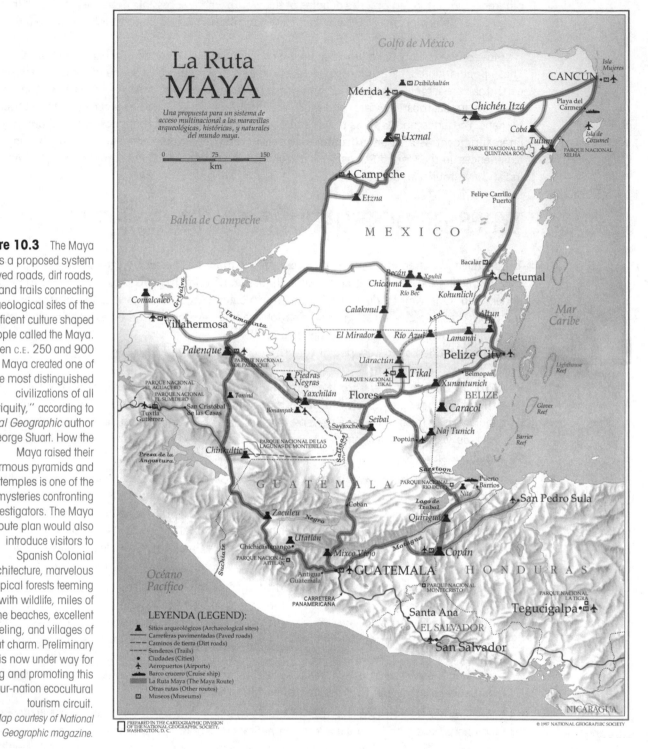

Figure 10.3 The Maya Route is a proposed system of paved roads, dirt roads, and trails connecting archaeological sites of the magnificent culture shaped by people called the Maya. Between C.E. 250 and 900 ``the Maya created one of the most distinguished civilizations of all antiquity,'' according to *National Geographic* author George Stuart. How the Maya raised their enormous pyramids and stone temples is one of the many mysteries confronting investigators. The Maya Route plan would also introduce visitors to Spanish Colonial architecture, marvelous tropical forests teeming with wildlife, miles of pristine beaches, excellent snorkeling, and villages of great charm. Preliminary work is now under way for creating and promoting this four-nation ecocultural tourism circuit. *Map courtesy of National Geographic magazine.*

whose essential purpose is to relax. Las Vegas epitomizes another type of recreational travel—gambling, spectacular floor shows, and away-from-home freedom.

6. **Business tourism** as characterized by conventions, meetings, and seminars is another important form of travel. (The United Nations includes the business traveler in its definition of a tourist.) Business travel is frequently combined with one or more of the types of tourism already identified.

Art museums are an attraction of choice for many visitors. Here, the Fort Lauderdale Museum of Art possesses a sculpture that appears to be drawing the undivided attention of this visitor. *Photo courtesy of The Greater Fort Lauderdale Convention and Visitors Bureau.*

This classification system is by no means unassailable. Destination areas can, and in most cases do, provide more than one type of tourism experience. For example, Las Vegas, which essentially provides recreational tourism, is also a popular convention destination. Resorts in Hawaii provide recreational, environmental, and cultural tourism, depending on what types of activities the tourist desires. A tourist vacationing in India, in addition to recreational tourism on one of the spectacular beaches in that country, has the opportunity for ethnic tourist experiences. Visits can be made to the villages to observe the lifestyles of remote populations. Conversely, a tourist can select from myriad destinations that provide the same basic type of tourism. For instance, a tourist with an interest in historical tourism may travel to any country that has historical appeal.

OTHER TOURIST APPEALS

Other representative expressions of a people provide powerful attractions for travel. Art, music, architecture, engineering achievements, and many other areas of activity have tourist appeal.

Fine Arts

Such *cultural* media as painting, sculpture, graphic arts, architecture, and landscape architecture constitute an important motivation for travel—visiting **fine arts**. As a specific example, recall the beauty of art forms such as cloisonné or scroll paintings.

A recent trend in resort hotel operations has been the display of local art and craft objects within the hotel or in the immediate vicinity so that the guests may become acquainted with the art of the local people. These objects may be for sale and thus become valued souvenirs. Art festivals often

Feeding the Flamingos by Louis Comfort Tiffany is just one of the works of art that visitors can view at the Charles Hosmer Morse Museum of American Art in Winter Park, Florida. *From the collection of the Charles Hosmer Morse Museum of American Art, Winter Park, Florida.*

include various types of fine arts together with other cultural expressions to make them more broadly appealing. There are many examples of these, such as the Edinburgh Festival in Scotland. This festival features not only displays of art but also other forms of craftwork, music, pageants, ceremonial military formations, and other cultural attractions.

Music and Dance

The expression and resources of a country's **music** are among its most appealing and enjoyable aspects. In fact, in some countries or states the music is a major source of enjoyment and satisfaction to visitors. Hawaii, Mexico, Haiti, Spain, various sections of the continental United States, and the Balkans are examples.

Resort hotels, particularly, can bring to the guests opportunities for enjoyment of local music at its best. Evening entertainment programs, concerts, recordings, and sound reproduction systems all aid in presenting this aspect of the art of the country. Community concerts, parades, and welcoming ceremonies are appreciated by visitors. DVDs, CDs, and digital or tape recordings that the visitor can purchase provide another effective means of keeping in touch with the culture of a particular area.

Ethnic dancing is another exciting and appealing aspect of a country's culture. The color, costumes, music, setting, and skill of forms and execution add to the appeal. Almost all countries have native or ethnic dancing. Local shows, nightclubs, and community programs present additional opportunities.

Notable examples of dance as a cultural expression are those of Polynesian dancers, the Ballet Folklorico of Mexico, the Russian ballet, folk dances of the Eastern European countries, dances of many African nations, Thai dancing, the Kabuki dancers of Japan, and Philippine country dancing.

Handicraft

To satisfy tourists, gifts and souvenirs offered for sale should be *handcrafted* or manufactured in the country or region where the purchase is made. There is much dissatisfaction in purchasing a craft article that you later discover was made in another country thousands of miles away. There is no substitute for genuineness. If the locally produced article is useful and appealing, it should be made available in conveniently located shops. A visit to shops where **handicraft** products for sale are actually being made is another effective form of guest entertainment.

Ancient Malaysian craftsmen lovingly carved and painted temple statuary that commands our respect and admiration. *Photo courtesy of Corbis Digital Stock.*

The hills and "hollers" of the southern Appalachian Mountains have long been known as a source of quality, traditional handmade crafts. Here Kevin Riddle creates chairs and hayforks using only hand tools. *Photo by Tom Myers/Copyright © Kevin Riddle.*

Industry and Business

The *industrial* aspects of an area provide important motivation for travel. A large proportion of travelers, particularly international travelers, are intellectually curious about the economy of any state or country. They are interested in the country's industry, commerce, manufactured products, and economic base.

Souvenirs that bring back memories of a travel experience can be a lifelong treasure. Those based on authentic craftsmanship from a local artisan can be especially valuable. *Photo courtesy of the Malaysia Tourism Board.*

Industry tours are a good way to develop an interest in the culture of the area and provide a potential market for the product being made. Tourist organizations should encourage tours to factories or processing plants when such visits are appropriate and pleasant experiences. Lists of such industrial installations can be maintained by tourist promotional organizations, chambers of commerce, resort hotels, motels, restaurants, or other establishments or service organizations where tourist contacts are made.

Industrialists from one country are often interested in the industry of another. Group tours can be organized for manufacturers of a particular product who visit another country to see how the manufacture of that or a similar product is accomplished. Such visits are mutually beneficial because each country's representatives learn from the others.

Chambers of commerce or other business or industrial groups often conduct tours to become acquainted with markets and processors in other countries in an effort to develop more interest in their products and to increase sales in various market areas. Business establishments, particularly retail stores, are of considerable interest to visitors. Excellent examples are shopping centers near resort areas, where a wide variety of stores are concentrated so that the visitor can readily find the products or services desired.

Shopping is one of the most important elements in tourism. Attractiveness, cleanliness, courtesy, and variety of products are among the most significant elements of the success of any shopping area. In fact, much goodwill can be created by courteous and devoted store clerks who assist the visitor in finding just what is being sought. Probably the world's most notable example of businesses that cater to the tourist is in Hong Kong, where shopping and business activity are most likely the most important aspects of any visitor's experience.

Agriculture

The **agriculture** of an area may be of interest to visitors. The type of farming conducted—livestock, poultry, dairy, crops, vineyards and wine production, fresh fruits and vegetables—is an interesting aspect of the culture. Farmers markets such as the well-known Los Angeles Farmers Market or roadside stands that offer local agriculture products are also an important part of tourist services in many areas. This is particularly true of stands selling fresh fruits, vegetables, honey, wine, cider and other drinks, and products from nearby farms readily enjoyed by the traveler.

Exemplary agricultural systems provide a point of interest for farm groups who may wish to visit a particular industry from another part of the country. Denmark, with its outstanding pork industry, is of great interest to hog farmers in many parts of the world. The country's world famous breweries are undoubtedly of greater interest to most visitors.

Agritourism is especially popular at harvest time. Tourists get an extra sense of satisfaction picking out their own pumpkin at the farm. Other agritourism opportunities allow tourists to pick fruits and vegetables, ride horses, taste wine, and enjoy other experiences. Photo courtesy of Wisconsin Department of Tourism.

Local tours should include agricultural developments and services so that visitors can see the agricultural products and operations within the country and perhaps try some of the products. On a one-day tour of Oahu in Hawaii, visitors have a chance to sample field-ripened pineapple at a stand adjacent to a great pineapple plantation. State and country fairs and livestock shows also have interesting tourist attractions. Other examples are cheese tours in Austria and Holland; wine tours in many parts of the world; the Peach Festival in Grand Junction, Colorado; and the fresh food farm tour on the Mornington Peninsula, Australia.

Education

Citizens of one country are often concerned with **education** systems of another. The college and university campuses of any country provide important attractions to tourists. Many of these are beautifully landscaped and attractively situated for a pleasant and enlightening visit. Well-known universities in England such as Oxford or Cambridge are in themselves important tourist attractions.

The operation of high schools and grade schools as well as private schools and other types of vocational training institutions are features of the culture of the area that can be utilized to a considerable degree as attractions for visitors. International education centers provide still another dimension of the relationship between tourism and education. Many universities conduct adult education programs within the university's continuing education service. Such educational opportunities attract learners from other areas within their own country or from many countries around the world. This provides an incentive for travel. International conferences of business and industrial groups as well as scientific and educational organizations are often held on the campuses of colleges, universities, or other educational institutions.

Outstanding examples of this type of operation are two adult education centers, the Kellogg Center at Michigan State University and the East-West Center at the University of Hawaii. These centers attract thousands of adults each year for continuing education courses, conferences, and meetings of an educational nature. "Elderhostel" educational programs for senior citizens are held at many colleges and universities around the world. These are short programs embracing a wide range of subject matter.

Literature and Language

The literary achievements of a state or country, though having more limited appeal than some cultural aspects, still constitute a significant element of travel motivation. Books, magazines, newspapers, booklets, pamphlets, and other printed literary works are among the most important expressions of the culture of the country. Interestingly, the availability or absence of certain **literature** is indicative of the political system of the area. Consider the restriction on distribution of literature from various areas of the world practiced by some countries.

Libraries are favorite cultural institutions for the visitor. Many have well-appointed reading lounges and comfortable, attractive surroundings. Particularly on rainy days, the visitor can enjoy reading about the history, culture, arts, and folkways of the host area. Often guest entertainment programs will feature the reading of poetry or the discussion of various books or other literary works as a cultural enrichment opportunity for visitors.

A well-educated person is likely to speak or at least have studied more than one **language**. Interest in the language of another nation or state is a motivating force for travel. This is particularly true of students traveling to a particular area to practice the language and to become better acquainted with its colloquial usage.

Travel-study programs are particularly valuable learning experiences. Receiving instruction in a foreign language abroad might well be integrated into any comprehensive travel-study

A good way for a traveler to sample local foods and learn about local culture is to visit farmers markets where they will find the best local food and products available. Farmers markets are an important part of the growing agritourism market. Photo courtesy of Fernandina Farmers Market.

curriculum. Language study institutes flourish all over the world. They can be private or associated with universities. Some examples of the latter are the University of Geneva, Switzerland; the University of Grenoble, France; and the University of California at Berkeley in the United States. Study abroad programs for college students provide excellent opportunities to learn a different language. Such programs are becoming a more common part of the university experience in the United States, Europe, and elsewhere. Many universities have cooperating agreements that allow students to attend universities in another country for the same cost as their "home" university, including the transfer of scholarship funds and university credits. Elderhostel learning opportunities for senior citizens provide another example of travel-study programs in which a foreign language can be pursued.

Most travelers like to learn at least some of the language to use while they are in a foreign country. Usually this is in the form of expressions related to ordering food in a restaurant or in talking with hotel or other tourism employees. Classes in language could be included in an entertainment or activities program within a tourist area.

Science

The **scientific activities** of a country constitute an interest to visitors, particularly those in technical industries, education, or scientific research. Organizations responsible for tourist promotion can serve the scientific community by offering facilities for the exchange of scientific information, organization of scientific seminars, visits to scientific installations, and other activities that provide access to scientific information by visitors.

The most popular scientific appeals include museums of science and industry, planetariums, and visits to unusual scientific installations such as atomic power plants and space exploration centers. Zoos and aquariums are also popular. An outstanding example is the Kennedy Space Center in northeastern Florida. This installation attracts substantial numbers of visitors each year and provides educational and scientific knowledge for even the most unsophisticated visitor. Another is the Smithsonian National Air and Space Museum in Washington, D.C. The European Nuclear Research Centre (EFRN) in Geneva, Switzerland with its world-class atomic particle accelerator is also becoming of major international interest.

Government

Systems of **government** vary throughout the world. Persons interested in political science and government find visits to centers of government, such as capitals, particularly valuable and highly motivating. Whenever a person visits another area, he or she is made aware of the type of government system in effect and notes the differences between this and the home country.

Persons interested in politics and the ways in which other countries and areas solve their political problems represent another part of the market. Lawmakers often visit another state or country to observe the procedures developed to solve social or economic problems.

A visit to Washington, D.C. can show visitors the lawmaking process in the House of Representatives and in the Senate. Hearings on various proposed regulations or statutes are often open to visitors. As the center of the government of the United States, this city provides educational opportunities in many areas to both American and foreign travelers. Today many buildings in Washington, D.C. and other government centers require advance clearance to visit, as security has been greatly increased.

Religion

Another major motivation for travel through all of recorded history is the **religious pilgrimage**. As noted in Chapter 2, pilgrimages are one of the oldest reasons for travel. Many inns and taverns were

Paris is indeed blessed with tourism icons. In addition to the Eiffel Tower, the Gothic Notre Dame cathedral is one of the most outstanding and most significant examples of the Roman Catholic religion's impact on architecture in all of Europe. In 1768, geographers decided that all distances in France would be measured from Notre Dame. Thus, Notre Dame was, and in many ways, still is the center of France. *Photo courtesy of Corbis Digital Stock.*

developed to support pilgrimage travelers. Probably the best-known pilgrimages are to Mecca. Large numbers of people go to the headquarters of their church organizations and to areas well known in their religious literature. Often these are group trips—for example, a group of Protestants visiting magnificent churches and headquarters of various church denominations in different parts of the world. Similarly, missionaries travel with a religious mission. The large amount of travel to Israel is in part based on religious motivation, as are travels to the Catholic centers at Vatican City within Rome; Oberammergau, in Bavaria, Germany; Lourdes, France; and Mexico City, Mexico. Visits to prominent houses of worship of all forms of religious doctrine are an important motivation for travel. Notre Dame cathedral in Paris, Saint Peter's Basilica in Rome, and the Great Mosque at Mecca are examples.

Food and Drink

Food and drink of a country are among its most important cultural expressions. The tourist enjoys native foods, particularly items of a local or ethnic nature. When traveling, trying out local dishes is part of the fun.

Restaurants and hotels can make a favorable impression on the tourist if they feature local dishes and also perhaps an explanation on the menu about what the dish consists of and how it is prepared. Of particular appeal is the restaurant in which the atmosphere complements the type of food being served, such as seafood restaurants on the wharf.

The purchase of local food and drink is another source of tourist revenue. Advertising messages that include reference to local food are highly effective. The tourist considers eating and drinking important aspects of a vacation. How these foods and drinks are prepared and presented are of great importance. Among the happiest memories may be the experience of dining in a particularly attractive or unusual eating place where local foods were prepared and served. Encouragement from tourist organizations for restaurants and hotels to feature local food is highly recommended.

History and Prehistory

The cultural heritage of an area is expressed in its historical resources (see Figure 10.3). Some tourist destination areas are devoted to history, such as the Mackinaw City area of northern Michigan; St. Augustine, Florida; the Alamo and San Juan Mission in San Antonio, Texas; old gold-mining tours in many western states; Machu Picchu in Peru; and the spectacular archaeological find at Xian in east-central China.

The preservation of **history** and the quality and management of museums is of utmost importance for successful tourism. Becoming familiar with the history and **prehistory** (archaeology) of an area can be one of the most compelling of all travel motivations. One of the principal weaknesses observed in historical museums is that the explanations of the exhibits are provided in only one language. This is a serious limitation to many tourists' enjoyment of such historical exhibits.

The Clinton Library in Little Rock, Arkansas, is one of a series of presidential libraries to honor past presidents. Because of the extent of text and visual documents, each library has become a significant attraction for tourists from all over the world. *Photo courtesy of Cranford Johnson Robinson Woods, Little Rock, Arkansas.*

The hours of operation of historical points of interest and museums are significant and should be arranged to provide access for visitors at convenient times. Admittance fees to museums and points of historical interest should be kept as low as possible to encourage maximum attendance. Promotion is necessary, and tourist contact organizations such as chambers of commerce, tourist information offices, hotels, resorts, restaurants, and other businesses should have available literature that describes the point of interest, hours, admittance fees, special events, and any other information needed by the tourist to visit this historical attraction.

Some notable examples of museums include the Istanbul Archaeology Museum, the National Museum of Anthropology at Mexico City, the American Museum of Natural History of New York City, the various branches of the British Museum in London, the Hermitage in St. Petersburg, and the various museums of the Smithsonian in Washington, D.C.

Other types of historical preservation are national historic parks and monuments and national parks with a history or prehistory theme, such as Mesa Verde National Park, Colorado. Another type is the "living history" farms in Iowa and Illinois.

Among the most outstanding innovations in the presentation of history are the "sound-and-light" programs found mainly in Europe, the Mediterranean countries, and Mexico. A series of loudspeakers, broadcasting recorded voices in several languages with sound effects, tell the history of an unusually significant structure or place. Varying lights intensify the effect and focus the attention of the audience on various parts of the location.

At the Forum in Rome, Italy, the history of Rome is presented at night in half a dozen languages. Visitors can hear the voices of the emperors and the crackling flames as Rome burns. At the pyramids of Teotihuacán, about 30 miles northeast of Mexico City, famous actors relate the history of the area in another sound-and-light presentation given in Spanish- and English-language versions. Egypt offers similar programs at its ancient monuments.

TOURISM AND PEACE

Tourism is believed to have a positive effect on world peace. When people travel from place to place with a sincere desire to learn more about their global neighbors, knowledge and understanding grow. Then, at least a start has been made in improving world communication, which seems so important in building bridges of mutual appreciation, respect, and friendship.

Tourism: A Vital Force for Peace

Since its founding in 1986, the International Institute for Peace Through Tourism (IIPT) has sponsored a series of global conferences, summits, round tables, and seminars that seek to "build a culture of peace through tourism." In October 1988, the inaugural conference on the theme "Tourism: A Vital Force for Peace" was held in Vancouver, British Columbia, Canada. Some 500 delegates from 65 countries attended. The purpose of the conference was to explore ways in which the world's hundreds of millions of international travelers could, by increasing interests, improving attitudes, and engaging in various social and other activities, contribute to better mutual understanding and appreciation—an important contribution toward world peace.

The conference provided a forum to examine tourism and its many dimensions as a force for peace. It brought recognition that tourism has the potential to be the largest peacetime movement in the history of humankind because tourism involves people: their culture, economy, traditions, heritage, and religion. Tourism provides the contacts that make understanding possible among peoples and cultures. The conference clearly demonstrated that tourism has the potential to make the world a better place in which to live.

Travel Experiences

- **The "Get Away from It All" Relaxation Experience** The typical "sun, sand, and sea" or other type of holiday experience vacation where visitors are seeking a period of rest and renewal.

- **The Exploration Experience** The experience in which the visitor is seeking to expand his or her visitation horizons. The newness of the experience depends on the individual. For novice travelers, virtually any different locale may be "new." For the experienced traveler, it may be difficult to find new travel horizons.

- **The Adventure Experience** In these experiences, the visitor is seeking the so-called adrenaline high that may come from whitewater rafting, heli-skiing, jungle exploration, mountaineering, Antarctic expeditions, or even visitation to insecure, war-torn areas.

- **The Social Experience** These experiences provide an opportunity for the visitor either to share the travel experience with old friends or to make new ones. To some extent, the actual destination may be unimportant.

- **The Family Travel Experience** The family travel experience is a special subset of the social travel experience in which the social network involved is very special to the visitor—especially in relation to the stage of the family cycle for the visitor. Clearly, "young" families are seeking quite different experiences from more mature families. Nevertheless, underlying the motivation to visit a destination is the desire to create and retain a very special experience for the given stage of the family life cycle.

- **The Educational or Learning Experience** This type of travel experience has grown in significance lately and often reflects the desire of a more mature, more sophisticated travelers to enhance their depth of understanding of a destination, its culture, or some special characteristic it may possess.

- **The "Quick Getaway" Experience** This is again a subset of a broader type of experience, the "Get Away from It All" relaxation experience. In this case, however, the emphasis is more on the getting away from it all than on total relaxation and renewal. These experiences are often as short as a weekend and may not be that distant from the individual's place of residence.

- **The VFR (Visit Friends and Relatives) Experience** For many, the VFR experience is by far the most valued, and may be the only type of experience they seek for most of their lifetime. For a destination manager, the challenge is to discuss how the destination in question can benefit most from this popular form of travel.

- **The "Return to a Single Destination" Experience** As Stanley C. Plog, contributor to the *Cornell Hotel and Restaurant Administration Quarterly*, pointed out many years ago, a certain segment of the travel market eschews all the glamour of international travel and simply wishes to return to a "comfortable" destination repeatedly. This comfortable destination may be a privately owned recreation facility, or it may be a public destination site to which the visitor has become attached for a whole range of reasons.

- **The Special Event Experience** Many destinations have come to appreciate the appeal that a special event may have in attracting visitors who might otherwise have little or no interest in visiting the destination. Destinations that host such one-time mega-events as the Olympic Games or World Cup Finals can increase visitation both during the event and following it as a result of their enhanced awareness, reputation, and image. Alternatively, the successful repeat event, such as the Boston Marathon, Oberammergau, the Master's Golf Tournament, the New Orleans Mardi Gras, the Calgary Stampede, and the Super Bowl, attract what are often one-time visitors. This market, however, is large, and it can be a major source of reputation and of visitation as part of total destination marketing strategy.

- **The Participation Event Experience** In contrast to events that draw visitors to observe the event, other events can draw visitors who are seeking to participate actively in the event or who wish to watch a close friend or family member perform in the event. Examples include amateur sporting events (softball, hockey, soccer, football, races), music festivals, beauty festivals, and children's festivals.

- **The Nature-Based Experience** As the concern for and interest in the environment has grown, the appeal of destinations that provide the opportunity for visitors to "commune with nature" is also growing in significance. Destinations that contain areas such as national parks are often viewed as the epitome of the nature-based experience. Here the opportunity to explore environmentally sensitive yet protected regions and to view wildlife in close proximity is becoming increasingly valued.

- **The Spiritual Experience** Destinations that for historical reasons have a particular spiritual attraction to individuals around the world have a special advantage in their ability to provide a spiritual experience. Cities such as Mecca and Rome, which are the seats of major religions, as well as those that are the home to recognized religious structures, can focus on their ability to provide spiritually related experiences. But not all spiritual experiences are related to traditional religions. Other destinations, such as Nepal, have over time gained a special spiritual reputation in many parts.

■ **The Entertainment Experience** While broad in concept, a destination may focus on the provision of various types of entertainment as the basis of its primary market appeal. London, New York, Las Vegas, Nashville, and Branson, Missouri, have become classic examples of the providers of entertainment experiences, but they are certainly not alone. The essence of this experience is the opportunity for the destination visitor to observe performances that are either well known in themselves or presented by well-known "stars." To the extent that a destination can develop a critical mass of these entertainment experiences, it can position itself as an entertainment-based destination.

■ **The Attractions Experience** Certain attractions can become so well known that they can provide the basis of the appeal of an entire destination and indeed may almost become the totality of the destination (see Chapter 8). Disney World in Florida is undoubtedly the classic example of an attraction that many families feel they must "experience" at least once in the lifetime of the family. Indeed, this attraction experience has become so pervasive that it forms the foundation for most of the tourism industry in the city of Orlando, Florida. It has proven popular in other parts of the world with Disney parks being developed in Japan, France, and Hong Kong.

■ **The "Take a Chance" Experience** More commonly referred to as gaming or gambling, the "take a chance" experience is designed to appeal to those whose adrenaline is stimulated by the risk taking associated with a broad range of games of chance. Many well-known destinations owe their origin and often their continuing existence to the legalization of activities that 50 years ago were considered both illegal and immoral. Times have changed, so much that just about every destination wants to add a gaming component to its array of attractions. In the meantime, Las Vegas, Atlantic City, and Monte Carlo continue to maintain their pinnacle positions as providers of this type of experience. The first two, located in North America, combine gaming with entertainment. In contrast, Monte Carlo's European location emphasizes class and eliteness in appealing to a select market segment.

■ **The "No Holds Barred" Experience** This experience often has names that are much less socially acceptable. "Sex tourism" was in the past a popular but disguised travel experience that the World Tourism Organization and some governments have now explicitly declared undesirable and even illegal. For many years Club Méditerranée (Club Med) implied that visitors to certain of its many resorts around the globe could expect a vacation free of normal social constraints. The piles of broken glass around nightspots in Spanish seaside resorts following all-night festivities gives evidence to behaviors not normally engaged in by many of their U.K. (and other) guests. Since their inception in the eighteenth century, Mardi Gras in New Orleans and Carnival in Rio de Janeiro have attracted both residents and visitors seeking experiences in very specific segments of the market.

■ **The "Get to Know Your Global Friends" Experience** This type of experience represents what many feel tourism should be all about: visitation experiences that encourage the visitor to get to know members of the host destination. There are many ways to attempt to achieve this goal, but Ireland has been offering an approach that many consider to be par excellence. For years, the Irish Tourist Board has worked with residents to develop a comprehensive network of homes that are willing to welcome visitors from around the world to visit not only the house but also, to a certain degree, household members. While admittedly (and necessarily) having multiple dimensions that can be difficult to manage in terms of quality control, it is a "risk" that many visitors consider very worthwhile. Visit the Web site at www.irishfarmholidays.com.

■ **The "Understand the Real World" Experience** While some may interpret this kind of experience as a version of the adventure experience, it depends on the travelers. This experience implies visitation to a destination in which the traveler is not artificially protected from some of the realities of living that many of the world's residents experience every day. Visits to many regions of Africa, India, China, and Asia in which the visitor does not stay in high-quality hotels, eats the food of the common people, and travels using the local modes of transportation are not for everyone, but they can provide memorable lifetime experiences for those in good physical condition with the right mind-set.

■ **The "Volunteer" Experience** A "volunteer" experience is a service-based experience where one helps the host country build a house or church, for example. It is an interactive experience between hosts and visitors in which tourists, for various reasons, volunteer in an organized way to undertake holidays that might involve aiding or alleviating the material poverty of some groups in society, the restoration of certain environments, or research into aspects of society or environment.

DISCUSSION QUESTIONS

1. What travel experiences have you enjoyed?

2. What experience would you most like to enjoy on your next vacation? Why?

One of the outcomes of the conference was distribution of the following.

Credo of the Peaceful Traveler
Grateful for the opportunity to travel and experience the world and because peace begins with the individual, I affirm my personal responsibility and commitment to:

■ Journey with an open mind and gentle heart.

■ Accept with grace and gratitude the diversity I encounter.

■ Revere and protect the natural environment that sustains all life.

■ Appreciate all cultures I discover.

■ Respect and thank my hosts for their welcome.

■ Offer my hand in friendship to everyone I meet.

■ Support travel services that share these views and act upon them.

■ By my spirit, words, and actions, encourage others to travel the world in peace.

Subsequently, two more conferences have been held in Montreal, Quebec, Canada, in 1994, and in Glasgow, Scotland, in 1999. The first Global Summit on Peace Through Tourism was held in Amman, Jordan, in 2000. Refer to the declaration that emanated from the Jordan conference.

Amman Declaration on Peace Through Tourism
We the representatives and participants at the Global Summit on Peace Through Tourism, assembled in Amman, Jordan, from 8–11 November 2000 . . . . . . **recognize** that travel and tourism is a worldwide social and cultural phenomenon, engaging people of all nations as hosts and guests, and as such is one of humanity's truly global activities.

. . . and that travel and tourism is one of the world's largest and fastest growing industries, creating one in eleven jobs, contributing to international and regional economic growth, bridging disparities between developed and developing countries, and bringing prosperity which fosters peace.

. . . . and that peace is an essential precondition for travel and tourism and all aspects of human growth and development.

. . . and the development of tourism as a global vehicle for promoting understanding, trust and goodwill among peoples of the world requires an appropriate political and economic framework.

. . . Do hereby **declare** our commitment to building a Culture of Peace Through Tourism, and support for the following principles:

1. That tourism is a fundamental human activity engaging social, cultural, religious, economic, educational, environmental, and political values and responsibilities.

2. That the right of people to travel is a fundamental human right which should be exercised without undue restriction including the facilitation of travel for those with disabilities and special needs.

3. That community livelihood should be enhanced and local cohesion encouraged and that all peoples and communities be recognized as being manifestations of a heritage.

4. That human differences be respected and cultural diversity celebrated as a precious human asset and that peaceful relationships among all people be promoted and nurtured through sustainable tourism.

5. That historical monuments and landmarks be protected and where necessary restored and rehabilitated and made accessible to everyone as valuable assets for humanity and legacies for future generations.

6. That the preservation and wise use of the environment, and ecological balance, are essential to the future of tourism, and that ancient wisdoms of Indigenous Peoples and care for the Earth be acknowledged and respected.

7. That the global reach of the tourist industry be utilized in promoting "dialogues on peace" and in bridging the have and have-not societies of the various regions of the world.

. . . and **acknowledge** the legacy of His Majesty The Late King Hussein of Jordan in laying the foundations of peace in the region and for his effort to make the Hashemite Kingdom of Jordan "a land of peace" and a place of welcome for the peaceful traveler; the commitment of His Majesty King

Abdullah II to strengthen and expand King Hussein's Legacy of peace; and to the Government and people of Jordan, for their hospitality and support and their generous contributions to the success of the conference.

. . . and **commend** the IIPT for giving scope to the vision of peace through tourism and for its untiring effort toward that end, and to the title sponsor and other sponsors and contributors, for advancing the cause of Peace through Tourism.

. . . and **welcome** the declaration by the United Nations of the International Year for the Culture of Peace (2000) and the International Decade for a Culture of Peace and Non-Violence for the Children of the World (2001–2010).

. . . and **commit** ourselves to the realization of the goals and objectives as enshrined in the United Nations Declaration of Program of Action on a Culture of Peace through our activities and initiatives.

Adopted at Amman November 11, 2000
May Peace prevail on Earth

Conferences on "Peace Through Tourism" continue to be offered at destinations around the world and address critical tourism issues such as peace, culture, environment, poverty reduction, and sustainable tourism. These have included a number of African and Regional conferences from 2001–2011.

The IIPT is a nonprofit organization dedicated to fostering and facilitating tourism initiatives that contribute to international understanding and cooperation, an improved quality of environment, the preservation of heritage, and through these initiatives, helping to bring about a peaceful and sustainable world. It is based on a vision of the world's largest industry, travel and tourism, becoming the world's first global peace industry and the belief that every traveler is potentially an ambassador for peace. Visit the IIPT Web site at www.iipt.org.

A Philosophy of Tourism and Peace

Great leaders in many fields have extolled the social benefits to humanity that result from travel. Travel is one of the noblest human occupations. In 550 B.C.E. the famous Greek statesman Solon recommended that we travel "in order to see." To see is to increase understanding and appreciation of other peoples, other cultures, and other lands. Jason, leader of the Argonauts—those incessant sailors in Greek mythology who were searching for the Golden Fleece—said, "The essential thing is not to live, the essential thing is to navigate."

Marco Polo became a prince of merchants, papal envoy, governor of a Chinese city, favorite of Kublai Khan, master of exotic languages, war correspondent, and the first travel writer. His book describing his adventures, written in 1298 C.E., established the first bond between East and West. Polo was wonderstruck at splendors that he saw and of which he heard. During the Renaissance, his book was the chief and almost the sole Western source of information on the East.

This brief dip into history and mythology has but one purpose: to emphasize that travel—and written accounts of it in later years—has often done more to create bonds and mutual understanding between various peoples of the world than any other single force throughout civilization's long existence.

There's no better way in which to gain a panoramic view of civilization than making a trip around the world. Being a guest for dinner is probably the best way to sense the unity that exists among peoples throughout the world. Here, people joined by blood or friendly spirit gather to break bread under the same roof. A few examples might include a dinner with a Japanese family, marveling at the swift movement of chopsticks gracefully picking rice from small snow-white porcelain bowls. Or a meal with Thais in the floating markets of Bangkok, where sampans loaded with pyramids of tropical fruits, vegetables, and fish ply the klongs (canals) in search of buyers. With Arabs in Tunisia, it may be having a delicious lunch in the shade of a tent out on the Sahara desert, in a landscape of stark, wild beauty, enriched by the lively warm hospitality of these friendly people.

Whatever happens in any home—be it a modest wooden house furnished with straw mats and rice-paper windows in Kyoto, a solemn British mansion on Victoria Hill, a mud hut on the banks of the Nile, a Cape Cod bungalow, or a Rio de Janeiro apartment—being born, living, eating, drinking, resting, and dying are the same the world over. These similarities reflect the basic unity of people. This unity is really well understood by people but, alas, is too often forgotten by nations and their rulers and leaders.

There are many ways in which a traveling family can meet and become acquainted with families in other lands. One of the best known of these plans is the "people-to-people" programs. Arrangements can be made by a travel agent through a local contractor, say, in Copenhagen, to provide a program of social contacts and other activities to enrich the visitor's acquaintanceship and understanding of the Danish people. Arrangements can be made to stay in a private home or to attend a seminar or similar program. Such opportunities can be and are operating in hundreds of places, in many parts of the world. A greater awareness of such possibilities and more widespread use of this type of program would increase understanding, friendship, and appreciation of other people.

A tourist standing on the balcony of a $100- to $200-per-day hotel room looking at the passersby below obtains little real knowledge of the people in the country being visited. However, if opportunities are readily available for social contacts with locals of that country, increased understanding and appreciation for the people of that area will take place.

Can tourism contribute to peace? If understanding and increased appreciation for other people's way of life, mores, culture, and language make us more a part of a world community, then the answer must be yes. This is especially so if at least casual acquaintance can be made with residents of the host country. Tourism provides a vehicle whereby people from one area become acquainted with people of another. Efforts to build that acquaintance will contribute to understanding, and understanding is at least the first step in creating and maintaining friendly national relationships.

Countries whose leaders understand and encourage tourism are making an effort to improve the personal relationship between their citizens and those of other countries. Although economic considerations may be uppermost, the importance of social contacts is also recognized.

Tourism flourishes in a climate of peace and prosperity. Political unrest, terrorism, wars, depressions, recessions, and civil strife discourage tourism.

In Malaysia, visitors can observe local carvers creating works of art. Such opportunities for interaction increase understanding and awareness. *Photo courtesy of the Malaysia Tourism Board.*

Tourism, if properly planned, organized, and managed, can bring understanding, appreciation, prosperity, and a better life to all who are involved. Let it grow and its positive effects increase. Tourism, if not a passport to peace, is at least a worthy effort toward building peace. Wherever and whenever visitor and host meet and greet each other with mutual appreciation, respect, and friendship, a movement toward peace has been made.

The following statement, from a Holiday Inn publication, reflects the goals of tourism:

> In today's shrinking world, neighbors are across the ocean, down the continent, and in every corner of the world. Time is different. So is dress, language, even food. But for all to live as neighbors, mankind must understand each other.
>
> Understanding is impossible without communication. That which is unknown often seems forbidding, even wrong. People must learn other ways of life besides their own.
>
> Only travel and communication closes this gap of knowledge. By world tourism it is possible to discover distant neighbors, how they live and think as human beings.
>
> World tourism and understanding go hand in hand. For travel is the way to knowledge. So let everyone do his part, traveling about the earth, keeping his mind and heart open. And the world will become a better place for all.

SUMMARY

The cultural expressions of a people are of great interest to most travelers. These include fine arts, music and dance, handicrafts, food and drink, industry and business, agriculture, education, literature and language, science, government, religion, history, and prehistory. Tourists' experiences are enriched when they make a sincere effort to become better acquainted with local people.

Any country or area that seeks to attract tourists must plan and develop facilities and promote programs that invite access to such cultural expressions. A useful concept is "life-seeing tourism," a structured local program that arranges evening visits to local homes by tourists or, alternatively, a plan whereby interested tourists are accommodated for a few days in local homes.

Cultural interpretation in any area that hosts foreign tourists requires bilingual provisions. These include foreign language ability by guides, bilingual signs, labels, and literature.

Examination of the interrelationships of the cultural backgrounds of visitors and cultural expressions of the host society as provided by this chapter should provide useful guidance to hosts.

Because tourism can lead to better understanding among people, it has the potential to contribute to a more peaceful and better world.

✧ **KEY CONCEPTS** ✧

agriculture	environmental tourism	literature
anthropography	fine arts	music
appreciation	food and drink	recreational tourism
business tourism	government	religious pilgrimage
cultural attractions	handicraft	scientific activities
cultural tourism	heritage interpretation	twinning
culture	historical tourism	understanding
education	industry tours	world peace
ethnic dancing	language	
ethnic tourism	life-seeing tourism	

INTERNET EXERCISES

The Internet sites mentioned in this chapter plus some selected additional sites are listed for your convenience on the companion Web site for this book, www.wiley.com/college/goeldner.

ACTIVITY 1

Site Name: National Geographic Society

URL: www.nationalgeographic.com

Background Information: The National Geographic Society is propelled by new concerns: the alarming lack of geographic knowledge among our nation's young people and the pressing need to protect the planet's natural resources. The Society continues to develop new and exciting vehicles for broadening its reach and enhancing its ability to get people in touch with the world around them.

Exercise

1. Visit the National Geographic Society and search its database for two destinations you think would have a cultural tourism attraction. Collect data on these destinations and design an advertisement that would appeal to individuals who have cultural tourism in mind.

ACTIVITY 2

Site Name: International Institute for Peace Through Tourism

URL: www.iipt.org

Background Information: IIPT is a nonprofit organization dedicated to fostering tourism initiatives that contribute to international understanding and cooperation, an improved quality of environment, and the preservation of heritage. Through these initiatives, IIPT helps bring about a peaceful and sustainable world.

Exercises

1. Does tourism have a role in building bridges of understanding between countries, civilizations, cultures, and religions?

2. What can IIPT do to reduce poverty?

QUESTIONS FOR REVIEW AND DISCUSSION

1. Evaluate culture as a travel motivator.

2. What do you see as the appeal of cultural similarities and cultural differences as motivation to travel to various destinations?

3. Give an example of a cultural experience that would be most satisfying to a visitor in a country much different from his or her own.

4. Create a life-seeing tourism program in your community.

5. What type of life-seeing experience would you particularly enjoy?

6. How much cultural difference can most tourists tolerate? Give examples of "too much."

7. Identify some of the rewards that international travel can bring to a perceptive, sensitive traveler.

8. For what reasons did the minister of tourism for the Bahamas promote its People-to-People program?

9. Referring to question 8, identify some other countries where a similar program would be equally successful.

10. A philosopher states that culture is what we know. Research changes our viewpoint. Thus, new discoveries make us change. Do you agree?

11. Does your community possess some distinctive cultural attraction?

12. In what way can world peace be enhanced by tourism?

CASE PROBLEMS

1. An attractive lakeside community of 5,000 persons is presently a popular tourist center, primarily because of its appeal to sports enthusiasts and its proximity to a magnificent state park. However, tourist expenditures are low, principally because of the lack of entertainment in the community. The movie theater closed three years ago, and there is virtually no entertainment except that to be found in a couple of beer taverns. The town and surrounding countryside are rich in history, but the only museum is a small one in the front part of a bar. How could a museum and other entertainment be provided?

2. As the director of an area tourism organization, you have been approached by a fine arts group to consider the feasibility of promoting a Shakespearean festival in your community similar to the long-established festival at Stratford, Ontario, Canada. What factors would you consider in evaluating this request, and how would you work with your state and national tourism organizations to determine how this cultural event could be publicized?

ENDNOTES

1. Valene L. Smith, *Host and Guests* (Philadelphia: University of Pennsylvania Press, 1997), pp. 2-31
2. National Trust for Historic Preservation, www.preservationnation.org/issues/heritage-tourism.
3. Mandala Research, *The Cultural and Heritage Travel Study* (Alexandria, VA: Mandala Research LLC, 2009) and www.culturalheritagetourism.org/resources/research.htm.
4. Ibid.
5. Ibid.
6. Smith, *Hosts and Guests*, pp. 2-3.

CHAPTER 11

Sociology of Tourism

LEARNING OBJECTIVES

- Appreciate the inordinate social impact that travel experiences make on the individual, the family or group, and society as a whole—especially the host society.

- Recognize that a country's indigenous population may resent the presence of visitors, especially in large numbers. Also recognize that the influence of these visitors may be

considered detrimental, both socially and economically.

- Discover that travel patterns change with changing life characteristics and social class.

- Become familiar with the concept of social tourism and its importance in various countries.

It is the uniqueness of travel experiences that have an impact on people. Although playing chess might not be all that unique, it is not very often that a family will play the game using giant pieces such as those found at the North Carolina Botanical Garden in Chapel Hill. Checkmate! *Photo courtesy of Chapel Hill/Orange County Visitors Bureau.*

INTRODUCTION

Sociology is the science of society, social institutions, and social relationships. Visitors to a community or area create social relationships that typically differ greatly from the affiliations among the indigenous population. In this chapter, we identify and evaluate tourist–host relationships and prescribe methods of managing these to create significant advantages for both groups. The ultimate effects of travel experiences on the population in areas of origin, as well as in places of destination, should determine to what extent societies encourage or discourage tourism.

EFFECTS ON THE INDIVIDUAL

Someone who travels, particularly to a strange location, often finds an environment that is unfamiliar, not only geographically but also personally, socially, and culturally. Thus, the traveler faces problems for which a solution must be found if the trip is to be fully enjoyable and rewarding. Travelers must manage their resources of money and time in situations much different from those at home. They also must manage their social interactions and social relations to obtain sustenance, shelter, and other needs and possibly to find companionship. Determining the extent of the cultural distance, they may wish to maintain results in decisions as to just how unfamiliar the traveler wants his or her environment away from home base to be. People who travel do so with different degrees of contact with the new cultures in which they may find themselves. Life-seeing tourism, for example, is a structured method for those who wish deeper immersion in local ways of life to acquire such enrichment. Some travelers prefer a more selective contact experience, such as might be arranged by a tour company. Tours designed around cultural subjects and experiences such as an anthropological study tour or participation in an arts and crafts festival are examples. Regardless of the degree of local participation, the individual traveler must at least superficially study the country to be visited and reach some level of decision on how these problems in environmental differences are to be resolved. Advance preparation is an intelligent approach. The effects of travel experiences are profound—on the host society as well as on the traveler, particularly because travel experiences often are among the most outstanding memories in the traveler's life.

EFFECTS ON THE FAMILY

As a **family** is growing and the children are maturing, the trips taken as a family are highlights of any year. The excitement of preparation and anticipation and the actual travel experience are memorable occasions of family life. Travels with a measure of adventure are likely to be the most memorable. Family travel may also be educational. The more purposeful and educational a trip becomes, the more beneficial it is. Study before taking the trip and expert travel counseling greatly add to a maximization of the trip's benefits.

EFFECTS ON SOCIETY

Travel has a significant influence on national understanding and appreciation of other people. Government policies in progressive and enlightened nations encourage travel, particularly domestic travel, as a means of acquainting citizens with other parts of their country and building appreciation for the homeland.

The presence of visitors in a country affects the living patterns of indigenous peoples. The way visitors conduct themselves and their personal relationships with citizens of the host country often has a profound effect on the mode of life and attitudes of local people. Probably the most pronounced

Family vacations, as we have seen, are a mainstay of tourism as beaches and sun are mainstays of family vacations. Here we observe the traditional family sharing of sun and sand. *Photo courtesy of Panama City Beach Convention and Visitors Bureau.*

effects of this phenomenon are noted when visitors from North America or Europe travel in an emerging country that has a primitive culture or a culture characterized by a low (economic) standard of living and an unsophisticated population. The visitor is influenced by the contrast in culture. Generally, however, this brings about an increased appreciation for qualities of life in the society visited that may not be present at home.

A favorable situation exists when visitors and residents of the host country mingle socially and become better acquainted. This greatly increases the awareness of one another's character and qualities, building appreciation and respect in both groups.

Tourism: Security and Crime

Unfortunately, tourists can be easy prey for criminals. Tourists do not know about dangerous areas or local situations in which they might be very vulnerable to violent crimes. They become easy marks for robbers and other offenders because they are readily identified and are usually not very well equipped to ward off an attack.

Sometimes popular tourist attractions such as parks or beaches are within walking distance from hotel areas. However, a walking tour from the hotel may bring the tourist into a high-crime area lying directly in the path taken to reach this attraction. If such high-crime areas exist, active efforts must be made to inform visitors and guests. Hotels and others that publish maps of walking tours should route such tours into safe areas only. Also, they should warn guests of the danger that could arise if the visitor undertakes certain activities.

Crimes against tourists result in bad publicity and create a negative image in the minds of prospective visitors. Thus, tour companies tend to avoid destinations that have the reputation for crimes against tourists. Eventually, no matter how much effort is applied to publicize the area's benefits and visitor rewards, failure to minimize crime will result in decreasing popularity and destination failure.

Pizam, Reichel, and Shieh found that tourism expenditures had a negligible effect on crime.[1] However, they suggested that tourism could be considered a potential determinant of crime, negatively affecting the quality of the environment. The tourist industry cannot be held responsible for the occurrence of crime. But one must be aware that tourists are a potential target of crime. Protecting them from offenders is essential to the survival and growth of the industry.

Resentments

Resentment by local people **toward tourists** can be generated by the apparent gap in economic circumstances, behavioral patterns, appearance, and economic effects. Such resentment of visitors is not uncommon in areas where there is conflict of interests because of tourists. For example, in North America, local people may resent visiting sports enthusiasts because they are "shooting our deer" or "catching our fish." The demand by tourists for goods may also tend to increase prices and cause bad feelings.

Another form of resentment can result in a feeling of inferiority among indigenous groups because of unfavorable contrasts with foreign visitors. Local persons employed in the service industries catering to visitors may be better paid and, thus, exhibit feelings of superiority toward their less fortunate fellow citizens. This creates a poor attitude toward the entire visitor industry.

Financial dislocations can also occur. While a tourist may give a young bellhop a dollar tip for delivering bags, the bellhop's father may be working out in the fields as a farm laborer for a total daily wage of only a dollar or two.

As a rule, both hosts and guests in any society can learn from one another. Beneficial social contact and planned visits to observe local life and culture do much to build appreciation for the indigenous culture. At the same time, the visitors' interest in indigenous ways of life increases the local people's respect for the visitors and gives them a feeling of pride in their own accomplishments. Tourism often facilitates a transition from rigid authoritarian social structure to one that is more sensitive to the individual's needs. When societies are "closed" from outside influences, they tend to become rigid. By encouraging visitors, this policy is changed to a more moderate one, for the benefit of hosts and guests. The preservation of wildlife sanctuaries and parks as well as national monuments and other cultural resources is often encouraged when tourism begins to be a force in the society.

Nothing hits the spot like an ice cream cone when on a family vacation. *Photo courtesy of Wisconsin Department of Tourism.*

One-to-one interaction between hosts and guests can break down stereotypes, or the act of categorizing groups of people based on a single dimension. By "labeling" people, often erroneously, individualism is lost. When a visitor gets to know people personally and is aware of their problems, hopes, and ways in which they are making life more pleasant, this visitor becomes much more sensitive to the universality of humankind. It is much easier to distrust and dislike indistinguishable groups of people than to distrust and dislike individuals one has come to know personally.

Some problems are often rooted in economic problems, such as unemployment or underemployment. The economic contributions of tourism can help to moderate such social difficulties. Nine negative social effects on a host society have been identified:

1. Introduction of undesirable activities, such as gambling, prostitution, drunkenness, and other excesses
2. The so-called demonstration effect of local people wanting the same luxuries and imported goods as those indulged in by tourists
3. Racial tension, particularly where there are very obvious racial differences between tourists and their hosts
4. Development of a servile attitude on the part of tourist business employees
5. Trinketization of crafts and art to produce volumes of souvenirs for the tourist trade
6. Standardization of employee roles such as the international waiter—the same type of person in every country
7. Loss of cultural pride, if the culture is viewed by the visitor as a quaint custom or as entertainment
8. Too-rapid change in local ways of life because of being overwhelmed by too many tourists
9. Disproportionate numbers of workers in low-paid, menial jobs characteristic of much hotel and restaurant employment

Many, if not all, of these negative effects can be moderated or eliminated by intelligent planning and progressive management methods. Tourism can be developed in ways that will not impose such a heavy social cost. Strict control of land use by *zoning* and building codes, enlightened policies on the part of the minister of tourism or similar official organization, and proper phasing of supply components, such as infrastructure and superstructure, to match supply with demand for orderly development are some of the measures needed. Education and good public relations programs can accomplish much. Enforcing proper standards of quality in the marketing of local arts and crafts can actually enhance and "rescue" such skills from oblivion. As cited in the book *Hosts and Guests*,[2] the creative skills of America's Indians of the Southwest were kept alive, enhanced, encouraged, and ultimately expanded to provide tourists with authentic Indian rugs and turquoise jewelry particularly, but other crafts as well. Fred Harvey, founder of the Fred Harvey Company, is credited with encouraging Indians to continue these attractive crafts so that he could market them in his hotels, restaurants, and gift shops.

Changing Population and Travel Interests

People change, group attitudes change, and populations change. All these factors affect travel interests. Travel interests also change. Some countries grow in travel popularity; others wane. World events tend to focus public attention on particular countries or regions of the world. Examples are the emergence of Japan and Korea as travel destinations following World War II and the Korean War, and interest in visiting the Caribbean area, as well as Israel, Spain, Morocco, and east Africa. Currently, travel to China and Australia is of great interest. There is an old saying among travel promoters that "mass follows class." This has been proven beyond a doubt. Travel-page publicity concerning prominent persons visiting a particular area inevitably produces a growth of interest in the area and subsequent increases in demand for travel to such well-publicized places.

The growth of communication systems, particularly network and cable television, has broadened the scope of people's interests in other lands and other peoples. To be able to see, as well as hear, has a powerful impact on the viewer's mind and provides acquaintanceship with conditions in another country, and this viewer may develop a desire for a visit. As communications resources grow, awareness and interest also grow.

LIFE CHARACTERISTICS AND TRAVEL

Rising standards of living, changes in the population age composition, the increasing levels of educational attainment, better communication, increased social consciousness of people relating to the welfare and activities of other people throughout the world, and the psychological shrinking of the world by the jet plane have combined to produce an interest among nations in all other nations.

Travel Patterns Related to Age

With age (late seventies and upward), the traveler may become more passive. Family **travel patterns** are associated with life stages of the family. The presence of young children tends to reduce the number of trips taken, whereas married couples with no children are among the best travel prospects. As the children mature, however, families increase their travel activities, and families with children between the ages of 15 and 17 have a much higher family travel pattern than do those with younger children. As the children grow up and leave home, the married couple (again without children) renews interest in travel. Also, couples in this life stage are more likely to have more discretionary income and are financially able to afford more travel. Persons living in urban centers are more travel inclined than are those in rural areas.

Senior Citizen Market

A major trend is the growth of the over-65 senior citizen market and the semi-senior citizen market—that is, those over 55 years old. Many have dubbed this the mature market, senior market, retirement market, or elderly market. Others look at it as the 50-plus market because 50 is the age for membership in AARP (formerly the American Association of Retired Persons).

Whatever this market is called, it is an important and growing market. The over-65 group totaled 25.5 million in 1980, 31.2 million in 1990, and 34.8 million in 2000. Because of the small number of births during the Great Depression, the group will grow more slowly to 39.7 million in 2010. After that, it is expected to grow rapidly to 70.3 million in 2030 as the baby boomers reach this age (see Figure 11.1).

In Millions

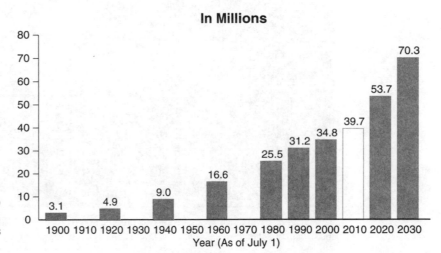

Figure 11.1 Number of persons 65 and over, 1900–2030.
Source: U.S. Bureau of the Census and AARP.

This massive growth of seniors is worldwide. The segment has been targeted both domestically and internationally by tourism managers because they have a lifestyle that is experienced, discerning, and likes to travel. In addition, they have the freedom to travel, are more active and healthy than previous generations, are media and Internet aware, and have discretionary income. They will continue to become a more important market group.

Income

Buying power is another factor for the tourism manager to consider. People must have buying power to create a market. There is no question that a large and increasing percentage of the population today has sufficient **discretionary income** to finance business and pleasure travel, although some families may be limited to inexpensive trips. The frequency of travel and the magnitude of travel expenditures increase rapidly as income increases. All travel surveys, whether conducted by the Census Bureau, the U.S. Travel Association, market research firms, or the media, show a direct relationship between family income and the incidence of travel. The greater the income, the more likely a household will travel. The affluent spend more on just about everything, but spending on travel is particularly strong. The value placed on time increases with household income, which is one of the reasons air travel attracts the higher-income consumer.

How the travel dollar is spent obviously depends on income. When the income of the population is divided into fifths, less than 33 percent of the lowest fifth report an expenditure for travel, whereas 85 percent of those in the top fifth report a travel expenditure. Almost half of all consumer spending for vacation and pleasure trips comes from households in the top fifth of the income scale. The affluent spend more on lodging, all-expense-paid tours, food, and shopping, but transportation expenditures are a smaller share of their total travel outlays than with those at the bottom of the income scale— 32 percent versus 43 percent. This results from the fact that it is more difficult to economize on transportation than on food, lodging, and miscellaneous expenses.[3]

If current long-term trends continue, the U.S. population will become wealthier. However, the recession put a dent in the current trend. The Bureau of Census reports that real median household

To reflect the travel patterns of different age groups, some cruise lines offer special cruises and trips for those with specific interests. *Photo courtesy of Carnival Cruise Lines.*

income in the United States fell between the 2008 and 2009 American Community Survey, decreasing by 2.9 percent from $51,726 to $50,221. An exceedingly important factor in household income is dual wage earners. The increase in the number of women who work outside the home has been dramatic and has boosted household income. The U.S. Department of Labor estimates that 59.2 percent of wives worked in 2009, compared with less than 45 percent in 1975. Married-couple families with both parents employed were just over 51 percent in 2008. As incomes increase, it bodes well for travel, but with husbands and wives both working, it may be more difficult to find time for travel and vacation. It is believed that this is one of the reasons for the trend toward shorter and more frequent vacations.[4]

Travel expenditures historically have been income elastic; consequently, as per capita real incomes continue to rise, consumers should spend an increasing proportion of their incomes on travel. Besides making more trips in the future, increasing numbers of consumers can be expected to choose air travel over other modes of travel. Income and education are closely correlated.

Education

Another factor deserving attention from tourism managers is education, because it tends to broaden people's interests and, thus, stimulate travel. People with college educations take more pleasure trips than do those with high school educations, and those with high school educations take more trips than do those with grade school educations. Educators are forecasting continued increases in the average educational level, which would result in a continued positive impact on pleasure travel.

Studies uniformly show that well-educated individuals account for the most travel and the most dollars spent for vacation and pleasure trips. Only about 50 percent of the homes where the household head did not earn a high school diploma report an expenditure for vacation trips. Where the head holds a high school diploma, about 65 percent report vacation expenditures; where the head has some college, 75 percent spend on vacations; and where the head has a degree, 85 percent report vacation expenditures. Income accompanies education as an important factor. In the approximately 35 percent of the homes where the head of the household has had some college, approximately 55 percent of the expenditures for vacation travel are made. Where the head has more than four years of college, vacation expenditures run two to three times the U.S. average. There appears to be no question that increased education levels heighten the propensity to travel, and with expanding higher education levels within the population, air travel should also expand.

The nation's educational level continues to rise. Fifty years ago, a high school diploma was nearly as rare a credential as a four-year college degree is today. In 2005, the proportion of the U.S. population having finished high school and the percentage of those receiving bachelor's degrees remained at an all-time high. A large majority of the population, 85.2 percent, graduated from high school and 27.2 percent earned a bachelor's degree. In 1960, only 9.7 percent of men and 5.8 percent of women had completed college. Today, the majority of college students (56.6 percent) are women.[5] Education is closely correlated with income and occupation, so the rising level of education should help to increase the demand for travel.

Gay and Lesbian Tourism

A growing market that is getting a lot of attention is the gay and lesbian market. Lesbian, gay, bisexual, and transgender (LGBT) tourism is a highly profitable segment. It is also referred to as **pink tourism**. Gay tourism has moved from being almost invisible to something that is studied by academics for its social impact and counted by tourism suppliers for its considerable dollar impact. In 2010, ITB Berlin, the world's largest trade fair, introduced Gay and Lesbian Travel in its own hall as a

Can a family have more fun than to swim and play in a hot springs pool? The experience can be the highlight of a family vacation. *Photo Courtesy of Glenwood Springs Chamber Resort Association, Colorado.*

new segment of the trade fair and provided a workshop on the subject. The Gay and Lesbian Pavilion presented the International Gay and Lesbian Travel Association (IGLTA), members, and individual exhibitors to this market from all over the world. Books such as *Gay Tourism Culture and Context*, *Pink Tourism: Holidays of Gay Men and Lesbians*, and *Gay and Lesbian Tourism: The Essential Guide to Marketing* provide insight on this travel segment.

For the past 15 years, Community Marketing, Inc. (CMI) has been conducting an annual gay and lesbian tourism study. Its comprehensive study covers such factors as booking patterns, pride events, top travel brands, top destinations, and estimates of LGBT travelers' economic impact. The economic impact estimate is $63 billion for the United States alone. Their research shows that gay men and lesbians travel more, spend more, and have the largest amount of disposable income. Visit www .CommunityMarketingInc.com.

The LGBT market is served by travel agencies, tour operators, suppliers, and associations. The previously mentioned IGLTA is an excellent source to find LGBT travel businesses and destinations. Its resources provide information on welcoming hotels, cities, countries, travel agents, and tour operators around the world. Visit www.iglta.org. Other sites are www.gaytravel.org, www.RainbowTourism.com, and www.outeverywhere.com.

Travel for People with Disabilities

In the United States alone, there are about 50 million people with disabilities—more than twice the total population of Australia.[6] This group constitutes an excellent potential market for travel if the facilities and arrangements are suitable for their use and enjoyment. Woodside and Etzel made a study of the degree to which physical and mental conditions restricted travel activities by households and how households with one or more handicapped persons were likely to adjust their vacation travel behavior.[7]

Findings in Table 11.1 indicate that many of the physical or mental conditions that limit travel (such as heart condition or diabetes) are unobservable by other travelers or by employees of tourist facilities. But this high percentage of disabled persons creates a substantial potential for emergency situations,

TABLE 11.1 Physical or Mental Conditions Limiting Travel

Condition	Number of Conditions	Percentage of Respondents
Heart condition	20	33
Crutches	6	10
Old age	5	8
Wheelchair	3	5
Stroke victim	3	5
Recent major surgery	3	5
Diabetes	3	5
Leg braces	2	3
Blindness	2	3
Other[a]	15	23
	62	100
		(n = 60)

[a]For example, phobia of mountains, mental retardation, pregnancy, bad leg, dizziness, sprained back, flu, and stomach virus.

and the planning and management of travel equipment and facilities must aim for a major reduction or elimination of such possibilities.

The effect of the presence of disabled persons in a family on lengths of stay is summarized in Table 11.2. The number of nights away from home differed considerably between those traveling with persons with a disability and those traveling without persons with a disability.

Many households reported little difficulty in using accommodations, because of careful planning before making the trip. The majority of difficulties encountered seemed to be at recreational facilities.

In a later study, Burnett and Baker found that people with disabilities represent the largest and fastest-growing market segment. These consumers, while not wealthy, have adequate resources to travel several times per year, especially for the purpose of vacations, family visits, and medical care. It is necessary to recognize that as is the case with any consumer group, much is to be learned if the

TABLE 11.2 Number of Nights Away from Home (as a Percentage of Total)

Nights	Travel Parties	
	With Persons with Disabilities, %	Without Persons with Disabilities, %
1–3	37	42
4–6	24	31
7–9	15	15
10–12	5	5
13–15	7	3
16 or more	12	4
Number of respondents	60	530

group is considered as being made up of segments rather than being homogeneous. Historically, individuals with disabilities have been categorized by either their medical conditions or their level of self-sufficiency. Severe, moderate, or minor are the common disability classifications. Of the three subgroups, the more severe the mobility disability, the more special attention is needed. The severely disabled are seeking a quiet and peaceful destination that allows them to be independent and that provides easy access. Travel suppliers should know that the moderately and severely disabled use only two modes of transportation: car or van and air. Mobility-disabled consumers are very loyal to destination hotels, motels, and resorts that are sensitive to their needs while not being patronizing.[8]

For additional information and statistics on people with disabilities, contact the American Association of People with Disabilities (AAPD) www.aapd.com and the Cornell University Rehabilitation Research and Training Center on Disability Demographics and Statistics, www.disabilitystatistics.org.

Americans with Disabilities Act

Substantial improvements have been made by the tourist industry to serve this segment of the market over the years. Activity accelerated with the enactment of the Americans with Disabilities Act (ADA) on July 26, 1990. ADA contains five titles, or sections: Employment, Public Services, Public Accommodations and Services Operated by Private Entities, Telecommunications, and Miscellaneous Provisions. Included in these titles are mandates for accessible public transit and complementary paratransit; accessible intercity (Amtrak) and commuter rail; accessible stations; accessible public accommodation (private entities), including inns, hotels, motels, restaurants, bars, theaters, concert halls, auditoriums, convention centers, all kinds of stores, service establishments, offices, terminals and depots, museums, libraries, galleries, schools, and so on; and telecommunications relay services for hearing- and speech-impaired persons.

Although the act is not specifically a travel law, travel agencies, lodging establishments, motorcoach operators, museums, and restaurants fall into the broad category of public accommodations that are required to make their facilities accessible to disabled persons. As the U.S. Justice Department and Transportation Department issue final regulations and firms comply, easier travel for the disabled will result.

The American with Disabilities Act (ADA) now makes it easier for handicapped persons to enjoy travel. *Photo courtesy of Image Source/Getty Images.*

The Society for Accessible Travel and Hospitality

The Society of Accessible Travel and Hospitality (SATH), founded in 1976 as the Society for Advancement of Travel for the Handicapped, is an educational, nonprofit membership organization whose mission is to raise awareness of the needs of all travelers with disabilities, remove physical and attitudinal barriers to free access, and expand travel opportunities in the United States and abroad. Members include travel professionals, consumers with disabilities, and other individuals and corporations who support this mission.

SATH has a well-established record in representing the interests of persons with disabilities. SATH participated in the writing of the regulations for the Americans with Disabilities Act and the Air Carriers Access Act, as well as Resolutions 700 and 1700 of the International Air Transport Association. A Code of Conduct toward travelers with disabilities written by SATH was adopted by the World Tourism Organization in 1991. SATH has also lobbied for legislative change in the European Community and assisted numerous governments to develop national access guidelines.

To raise awareness and provide detailed training on how to serve and market to travelers with disabilities, SATH organizes conferences and provides speakers and panels for other industry associations such as American Society of Travel Agents, National Tourism Association, International Institute for Peace Through Tourism, and Travel Industry Association of America. SATH has sponsored the World Congress for Travelers with Disabilities and the Mature since 1977. It also sponsors Travelers with Disabilities Awareness Week, created in 1990 by SATH founder Murray Vidockler, CTC, to commemorate the ADA.

Since its inception, SATH has served as a clearinghouse for access information. SATH's travel magazine, *Open World*, features inspiring articles by travelers with disabilities and updates on destinations, cruises, Web sites, legislation, and more. The SATH Web site (www.sath.org) is geared to consumers.

EMERGENCE OF GROUP TRAVEL PATTERNS

Group travel involves a group combining both transportation and ground services into tours. Chapter 7 discusses retail travel agents and tour wholesalers who organize group tours (group inclusive tours or GITs) that they sell to travelers. Travel clubs, incentive travel companies, airlines, cruise lines, educational institutions, religious groups, and associations are examples of other organizations developing group travel arrangements.

Travel Clubs

Travel clubs are groups of people, sometimes with a common interest (if only in travel), who have formed travel organizations for their mutual benefit. For example, some purchase an aircraft and then arrange trips for their members. Others join international membership clubs such as Club Méditerranée, which owns resort properties in many countries and provides package-type holidays at usually modest cost.

Low-Priced Group Travel

Many tour companies cater to common-interest groups, such as the members of a religious group or professional or work group. A tour is arranged, often at reasonable cost, and is promoted to members of the group.

Public Carrier Group Rates and Arrangements

Airlines and other public carriers make special rates available for groups; a common number is 10 or 15 at discounted rates. A free ticket is issued to the group's escort or leader. Chartering all or part of a public transportation vehicle, aircraft, or ship is also a special effort on the part of the carrier to accommodate travel groups.

Special hobbies and interests such as fishing provide a strong motivation for travel. These two fishermen are clearly taking pride in the results of their efforts. According to the National Sporting Goods Association, fishing is enjoyed by 40.6 million people annually. *Photo courtesy of Wisconsin Department of Tourism.*

Incentive Tours

One of the fastest-growing group arrangements is that of incentive tours provided by a company to members who are successful in achieving some objective, usually a sales goal. Spouses are often included on these tours. At the destination, the group is sometimes asked to review new products and receive some company indoctrination.

Special-Interest Tours

Special-interest group travel is another segment growing in importance. Tours are arranged for those interested in agriculture, archaeology, architecture, art, bird-watching, business, castles and palaces, ethnic studies, fall foliage, festivals, fishing, flower arranging, gardening, gems and minerals, golf, health and wellness, history, hunting, industry, literature, music, nature, opera, photography, professional interests, psychic research, safaris, skiing, scuba diving, social studies, sports, study, theater, and wine, to name a few examples. Social and fraternal organizations also are traveling more in groups. Some private clubs are taking group trips. Some are extensive trips around the world or trips lasting up to 60 days. Women's groups, social groups, youth groups, alumni, and professional societies commonly take extended trips together as a group. Preconvention and postconvention trips are also popular.

SOCIAL (SUBSIDIZED) TOURISM

Although there is as yet no agreed definition of social tourism, there has been considerable study of the question. W. Hunziker at the Second Congress of Social Tourism held at Vienna and Salzburg in 1959 proposed the following definition: "Social tourism is a type of tourism practiced by low

Dark Tourism

Dark tourism is a rather perverse view of the world in the eyes of many. Based on the defining book by John Lennon and Malcolm Foley,[9] the term *dark tourism* refers to the "attraction of death and disaster"—or more specifically perhaps, those sites where death and disaster have occurred and that attract tourists. Auschwitz, the German death camp, is probably the most infamous of all dark tourism sites. Despite its reputation, Dachau, near Munich, is the most important in terms of visitation, with more than 900,000 visitors per year.

Both Auschwitz and Dachau have spawned a number of memorial sites associated with Nazism and the Jewish Holocaust. While many sites are located behind the former Iron Curtain, there is a growing effort by the Jewish community and others to build parallel memorials in many other countries. Just as the Holocaust museums are highly popular in tourism terms, they are followed closely by remnants of the Berlin Wall and, more recently, Ground Zero in New York.

The definition of dark tourism may also be expanded to include sites where killing wars are currently being conducted. Iraq and Afghanistan are such examples, where both worldwide media and the truly adventurous tourists are drawn to the "action." Lesser-known dark attractions include sites where hangings or executions are to occur, are occurring, or have occurred.

As emphasized by the Tourism Society, the area of dark tourism has become a fascinating and important subject for research regarding its implications for the tourism industry and its fundamental relationships within the cultural condition of society as a whole. Despite this elevation to academic status, dark tourism must still be viewed as perverse by nature.

DISCUSSION QUESTIONS

1. What is dark tourism?

2. Why has dark tourism been growing in sites and popularity?

income groups, and which is rendered possible and facilitated by entirely separate and therefore easily recognizable services." Another definition, that of M. Andre Poplimont, is as follows: "Social tourism is a type of tourism practiced by those who would not be able to meet the cost without social intervention, that is, without the assistance of an association to which the individual belongs."

From these definitions and from the reports of the three International Congresses on Social Tourism, it is clear that certain elements may be described. First is the idea of "limited means." Second, social tourism is subsidized by the states, local authorities, employers, trade unions, clubs, or other associations to which the worker belongs. Third, it involves travel outside the normal place of residence, preferably to a different environment that is usually within the tourist's own country or sometimes to a country nearby.

Holidays with Pay

Paid holidays are now established all over the world, and in most countries a minimum duration (one, two, or three weeks) is specified either by law or by collective agreement. Some, however, consider this institution only a first stage, and they believe that attention should now be turned to the way in which these holidays are used. Great subjects of discussion by twenty-first-century sociologists are: (1) the use of the increased leisure time now available to workers, and (2) the cultural and educational development that such leisure time makes possible.

Large numbers of workers are obliged to spend their holidays at home, partly because of their lack of means or tourist experience and partly because of lack of information, transport difficulties, or shortage of suitable accommodation. Organized social tourism, if efficiently managed, can overcome most of these problems: finance through subsidies and savings schemes, experience and information through contacts elsewhere in the country concerned or abroad, transportation through package deals with carriers, and accommodation through contracts with resorts. Thus, organizations can bring tourism within the reach of many who would otherwise be unable to travel. There will be some, however, who for reasons of age, health, family responsibility, or disinclination are unwilling to join in such holidays even when all arrangements are made for them.

Determination of Needs

Some countries carry out research in this field. In Belgium, almost 60 percent of the respondents to an inquiry preferred a continuous stay to moving from place to place, but this preference was more marked among older people than among younger ones. In the Netherlands, another inquiry revealed that about a million holidaymakers preferred not to rely on the hospitality of relatives if other facilities within their means were provided. It was evident that existing facilities of this kind were inadequate.

It was also found that the tendency to take holidays away from home was increasing and that more attention should be given to the educational and cultural aspects of tourism. Studies in France and Italy have found orders of preference among the countryside, the seaside, the mountains, health resorts, and other places; and in Sweden and Italy, inquiries have been carried out into the types of accommodations favored.

Examples of Social Tourism

Leysin, in Switzerland, is one of the best-known examples of holiday centers for social tourism. Originally a famous health resort, advances in medicine meant that its clientele would gradually diminish; but with the cooperation of certain organizations, including the Caisse Suisse de Voyage, the resort was adapted to attract a new type of tourist. A small golf course, a swimming pool, tennis courts, and arrangements for skiing were established, and sanatoria and hotels were converted to meet the new demands. A publicity campaign was begun, and in its first year, over two thousand tourists arrived and spent more than fifty thousand bed-nights in the resort. Camping and staying at hostels are popular with younger tourists and also with families. In recent years, there has been a considerable development of recreation vehicle (RV) camps, particularly in Great Britain. Camping has the advantage of being one of the least expensive forms of holiday and makes possible more mobility. Financial aid is given to camps by the state in France and other countries. In Greece, camps are operated by some large industrial firms for the benefit of their employees, and in most countries, they are run by camping clubs and youth associations.

In 1999, the French government set up an official state-funded agency to help French tourist resorts fill vacant beds with up to one thousand unemployed or otherwise struggling citizens. Supporters claim that the right to leisure is as important a human value as the right to housing, education, and medical care.

Provision of Information

In the development of social tourism, other problems arise, but these are largely common to tourism in general. The provision of information, however, deserves brief mention here, because many of the beneficiaries of social tourism will have little knowledge of the special attractions of different resorts. In some countries, government authorities, trade unions, national tourist organizations, and other bodies have given attention to this question. In the United States, for example, there are tourist information offices in the large cities, and publications are issued advising workers how they can spend their holidays. In Canada, bulletins are sent to the trade union offices and other organizations.

To date, most progress has been made in domestic tourism only; and although many workers are already traveling abroad, there is great opportunity for joint action between the official travel organizations of different states. Proposals have been made in some regions regarding how best to promote foreign travel by lower-income groups, and the Argentine national tourist organization has invited corresponding bodies in other South American states to arrange programs on a reciprocal basis.

SUMMARY OF THE PRINCIPAL SOCIAL EFFECTS OF TOURISM

1. The vacation and special business trips a person takes are often among life's most vivid memories.
2. For families, vacation trips taken together are among the highlights of the year's activities.
3. The presence of visitors in a particular area can affect the living patterns of local people. The extent to which a local population is affected depends on the diversity of the mixing groups, including factors such as obvious differences in wealth, habits, appearance, and behavior.
4. On a national basis, people of a particular country can have their lives changed by tourism, particularly if there are large numbers of tourists in proportion to the indigenous population. Visitors may influence ways of dressing, consumption patterns, desire for products used by tourists, sexual freedoms, and a broadening outlook on the world.
5. For both hosts and guests, the most satisfying relationships are formed when they can meet and interact socially at a gathering such as a reception, a tea, or a cultural event; in "people-to-people" programs (home visitation); or in life-seeing tourism (a structured learning-leisure program).
6. Tourism's effects on crime are negligible, but tourists can become easy victims of crime. Hosts must help them avoid dangerous places and areas.
7. Resentment of visitors by local (indigenous) people can occur. There may be conflicts over the use (or abuse) of local facilities and resources. Consumer prices may rise during the "tourist season."
8. Extensive tourism development can bring about undesirable social effects such as increased prostitution, gambling, drunkenness, rowdyism, unwanted noise, congestion, and other excesses.
9. Domestic and international tourism increases for people in a country that has a rising standard of living, a population age distribution favoring young adults or young marrieds with no children, and an increasing population of older, affluent adults.
10. People living in cities are more interested in travel than those living in small towns or rural areas.
11. Wealthy people and those in higher social classes are greatly inclined to travel.
12. Increase in the educational level in a population brings about an increase in travel.
13. Catering to people with disabilities substantially increases markets.
14. Group travel and tours are popular ways to travel.
15. Social tourism is a form of travel wherein the cost is subsidized by the traveler's trade union, government, public carrier, hotel, or association.
16. Travelers thus assisted are in low-income groups or older age groups, or they are workers in organizations authorized to receive such subsidies or vacation bonuses.

THE INTERNATIONAL TOURIST

International travel largely emanates from countries with a comparatively high standard of living, with high rates of economic growth, and with social systems characterized by declining inequality of incomes and a sizable urban population. In addition, these international travelers come from countries where large-scale industry and commerce comprise the foundations of the economy and where the communications and information environment is dominated by the mass media. The international market is largely made up of middle-income people, including the more prosperous minority of the working class, who normally live in large cities and earn their living in managerial, professional, white-collar, supervisory, and skilled occupations.

There are four extremes relating to the travel preferences of international tourists: (1) complete relaxation to constant activity, (2) traveling close to one's home environment to a totally strange environment, (3) complete dependence on group travel to traveling alone, and (4) order to disorder. These extremes are not completely separate, and most travelers may have any number of combinations on any given trip. For example, a traveler may take a peaceful river cruise and then enjoy a strenuous swim.

Relaxation versus Activity

Historically, the first wave of mass international travel occurred at a time when there was a sharp differentiation between work and leisure and when the workweek for most people, including the middle class, was long and exhausting. Under these circumstances, it was not surprising that the demand concentrated on holidays that offered relaxation, recuperation, and rest. Essentially, they provided an opportunity for winding down and getting fit for the next 49 weeks of arduous activity. Since then, the balance between work and leisure has shifted sharply in favor of the latter. Usually the weekend is free, and the annual holiday leave for some workers has been lengthened. In other words, over the past decades, people have become used to greater slices of leisure time. Relaxation is possible throughout the year, and there is less need to use a holiday exclusively for this purpose.

With the arrival of year-round leisure, there seems to be a surfeit of opportunities for relaxation, so that increasingly people have started to use their nonholiday leisure time to acquire and exercise new activity skills: sailing, climbing, biking, sports, horseback riding. It is reasonable to forecast that the balance between leisure and work will continue to move in the direction of leisure and that the relative demand for activity-oriented travel will increase.

A great deal of international travel is conducted to experience the novel. A striking example is the well-known floating market in Bangkok. *Photo courtesy of Corbis Digital Stock.*

Familiarity versus Novelty

Most people, when they make their first venture abroad, tend to seek familiarity rather than novelty: people speaking the visitors' language, providing the meals and beverages they are accustomed to, using the same traffic conventions, and so on. Having found a destination where he or she feels at home, this sort of tourist, at least for the first few ventures abroad, will be a "repeater," going back time and again to the same place. Not until more experience is gained will the traveler want to get away from a normal environment—to mix with people who speak differently, eat differently, and dress differently.

In the Western world, the general change in social conditions seems to be in the direction of speeding up the readiness for novelty. Where previously the social climate and rigid structure of society had reinforced a negative attitude to change, we now find increasingly a positive attitude to change. People accept and seek innovation in industry, education, family life, the arts, social relationships, and the like.

In particular, in countries with high living standards, manufacturers faced with quickly saturated markets concentrate on developing new products and encouraging the consumer to show greater psychological flexibility. More and more markets are dependent on the systematic organization of rapid change in fashion to sustain and expand. With the blurring of class differences and rising standards of living, travel demand will likely reflect this climate and express fragmentation of the total market as people move away from the traditional resorts to a succession of new places.

Dependence versus Autonomy

A widely accepted analysis of modern industrial society is based on the concept of alienation in work. Briefly, this view states that most people are inevitably employed in work that, though perhaps well paid, is not intrinsically rewarding and satisfying and that from this frustration results in, among other things, a general sense of powerlessness, a withdrawal from political and social activities, and the pursuit of status symbols. In the field of leisure, this work alienation should lead to a demand for passive, time-killing holidays or for holidays where the main gratification is the achievement of easily recognized status. Fundamental absence of significance in work, in other words, would lead to holidays during which the same sense of powerlessness and dependence would prevail—organized holiday camps, organized package trips, mass entertainment, and so forth.

In fact, very little empirical research has substantiated this description of an industrialized society. Indeed, the data available suggest the contrary—that many industrial workers, backed by strong trade unions and state-created full employment, feel that as workers, they wield considerable power. Certainly industry and social organization is moving in the direction of providing work that is intrinsically rewarding and satisfying, which should enhance life for today's workers, leading to a sense of personal autonomy in all aspects of their lives, including their leisure time. They are likely to seek holidays during which they feel independent and in control of what they do and how they do it. One would expect that for some time ahead, economic and social circumstances should generate a greater proportion of autonomous participants in the total demand for travel.

Order versus Disorder

Until recently in most Western societies, the training of children has been based on control and conformity, defined and enforced by an all-embracing circle of adult authority figures: parents, teachers, police officers, clergy, employers, civil authorities. With such a background, it is not surprising that most tourists sought holidays that reinforced this indoctrination: set meals at fixed times, guidebooks that told them the "right" places to visit, and resorts where their fellow tourists were tidy, well behaved, "properly" dressed, and so on. They avoided situations where their sense of orderliness might be embarrassed or offended.

More recently, child-rearing practices have changed in the direction of greater permissiveness, and the traditional incarnations of authority have lost much of their Victorian impressiveness. The newer generation of tourists no longer feels inhibited about what to wear and how to behave when on holiday; differences of others, opportunities for unplanned action, and freedom from institutionalized regulations are distinctive characteristics of the contemporary traveler.

Summing up, then, one would predict that because of deep and persisting social and economic changes in modern Western society, the demand for travel will be based less on the goals of relaxation, familiarity, dependence, and order and increasingly on activity, novelty, autonomy, and informality. One should not, of course, ignore the fact that, since international travel is a rapidly growing market, each year's total consumers will always include a minority who value familiarity, dependency, and order.

BARRIERS TO TRAVEL

While travel has become a popular social phenomenon, there are a number of reasons why people do not travel extensively or do not travel at all. The reasons, products of psychological analysis, are not meant to be ultimate answers as to why people travel where they do. We can, however, look at the more concrete reasons why those studied did not go on a trip during a certain period of time. For most of these studies, barriers to travel fall into six broad categories:

1. **Cost.** Consumers operate within monetary constraints, and travel must compete with other allocations of funds. Saying that travel is too expensive is an indirect way of saying that travel is not important, but, even allowing this interpretation, costs are a principal reason for staying home.

2. **Lack of time.** Many people cannot leave their businesses, jobs, or professions for vacation purposes.

3. **Health limitations.** Poor health and physical limitations keep many persons at home. Also, the fear of contracting AIDS, severe acute respiratory syndrome (SARS), malaria, Norwalk flu, bird flu, Legionnaire's disease, food poisoning, and so on keeps people from traveling. For many, health has become a major tourism safety issue.

4. **Family stage.** Parents of young children often do not travel because of family obligations and inconveniences in traveling with children. Widows and singles sometimes do not travel because of the lack of a traveling companion.

5. **Lack of interest.** Unawareness of travel destinations that would bring pleasurable satisfaction is a major barrier.

6. **Fear and safety.** Things unknown are often feared, and in travel, much is often not familiar to the would-be traveler. Wars, unrest, and negative publicity about an area will create doubt and fear in the mind of the prospective traveler. Terrorism has reared its ugly head in the last decade and is a deterrent to travel.

When motivation to travel is sufficiently powerful, the barriers may be overcome, but these forces may still influence means of travel and destinations selected.

Although travelers may be able to overcome the first four variables listed, tourism marketers need to modify the fifth barrier—lack of interest. This is a challenge for tourism marketing managers. To illustrate just how widespread this barrier is, the following approach was taken where the cost barrier was eliminated. The respondents were asked this incomplete sentence: "Mr. and Mrs. Brown were offered an expense-free tour of the United States, but they didn't want to go because . . . " Forty-two percent of the respondents said that the Browns wanted to go on the trip but couldn't because of job reasons, poor health, age, or responsibilities for children. However, 26 percent indicated that the Browns did not want to go on the trip at all; they would rather stay home, or they did not like to travel, or they were afraid to travel. It is evident that in spite of widespread desires to travel, some people would rather stay home. For others, a weak desire to travel is compounded by nervousness or fear of what the experience might bring. Such a reluctance to travel runs counter to the tide, but this segment is too large a group to be overlooked. With the proper motivational tools, a significant percentage of this untapped group of potential travelers might be convinced that there are places or things of interest outside the world in which they now exist.

When analyzing some of the psychological reasons contributing to the lack of interest in travel, at least some are related to conflicts between exploration and safety needs. A person's home is safe and is a place thoroughly known, and he or she is not required to maintain a facade there. On the other hand, the familiarity of home can also produce boredom and the need to explore. A person is, thus, possessed of two very strong drives, *safety* and *exploration*, and he or she needs to reduce this conflict.

One way to do this is by traveling in areas that the person knows well. He or she may go to the same cottage at the same lake with the same people that he or she has known for years. This meets the safety needs because the person enjoys a new experience in a comfortable (safe-feeling) environment. At the same time, it meets the exploration need because the person leaves home and travels to a different place, albeit a familiar one.

SUMMARY

Sociologists are interested in tourism because travel profoundly affects individuals and families who travel, inducing behavioral changes. The new insights, understandings, and appreciations that travel brings are enlightening and educational.

A person who travels to a strange environment encounters problems that must be resolved. How well the traveler solves these problems will largely determine the degree of the trip's success. In planning a trip, the traveler must decide how much cultural distance (from the home environment) he or she desires. Tourists differ greatly in this regard.

In this chapter we have described various social phenomena related to mass tourism. Included are social tourism, international travel behavior extremes, and barriers to travel. Your understanding of these can help to provide a basis for determining tourist volume policy. Consideration must be given to the likely influence that masses of tourists will have on their hosts. Furthermore, applying the procedures explained in this chapter should minimize the negative sociological influences and enhance the positive effects of large numbers of tourists on their host society. Although tourism expenditures have a negligible effect on crime, tourists are potential targets for crime. It is essential that they be protected as much as possible.

✧ **KEY CONCEPTS** ✧

crimes against tourists	negative social effects on host society	standardization
cultural distance	people with disabilities	travel patterns
discretionary income	resentment toward tourists	travel preferences of international tourists
effects of travel experiences	social tourism	
group travel	sociology	trinketization

✧ **INTERNET EXERCISES** ✧

The Internet sites mentioned in this chapter plus some selected additional sites are listed for your convenience on the companion Web site for this book, www.wiley.com/college/goeldner.

ACTIVITY 1

Site Name: Open Doors Organization

URL: www.opendoorsnfp.org

Background Information: The Open Doors Organization (ODO) was founded in 2000 for the purpose of creating a society in which all persons with disabilities have the same consumer opportunities as those without. It aspires to teach businesses to succeed in the disability market, while simultaneously empowering the disability community.

Exercises

1. What corporate programs are offered?

2. What community programs are offered?

3. What youth programs are offered?

ACTIVITY 2

Site Name: International Organization of Social Tourism (OITS)

URL: http://www.bits-int.org/en/

Background Information: OITS is an international non-profit association whose aim is to promote access to tourism for all, and more particularly, for low income population groups.

Exercise

1. What are the origins of social tourism?

2. What is the Calypso project?

❖ **QUESTIONS FOR REVIEW AND DISCUSSION** ❖

1. As a manager of a resort hotel popular with families, what social and/or educational activities would you offer your guests?

2. You have decided to take a trip to a country whose culture is very much different from your own. Would you participate in a group tour or go alone? Why?

3. Would a child's learning experience during a trip to another part of his or her country be comparable to school learning for that period of time? In what ways might parents maximize the educational benefits of such a trip?

4. With the ever-growing aging population in developing countries, how will changing demographics worldwide impact the travel industry?

5. Discuss the effects of television news coverage of global and national events on tourism.

6. Give some examples of how tourism suppliers accommodate handicapped travelers. How important is this segment of the market?

7. Is there a potential for increased social tourism in your country?

8. How might the four extremes relating to the preferences of present-day international tourists affect a resort hotel's social and recreational program? Give some specific examples.

9. How do your travel interests differ from those of your parents? From those of your grandparents?

10. Do you feel governments have a responsibility to encourage and support social tourism?

❖ **CASE PROBLEMS** ❖

1. Alfred K. is a widower, 67 years old. He has not had an opportunity to travel much, but now as a retiree, he has the time and money to take extensive trips. As a travel counselor, what kinds of travel products would you recommend?

2. Sadie W. is president of her church missionary society. She has observed that many visitors to her fairly small city in England are interested in the local history. Her church is a magnificent cathedral, the construction of which began in the year 1083. Mrs. W. and her colleagues believe that missionary work begins at home. By what methods could her group reach and become acquainted with the cathedral visitors?

3. A U.S. group tour conductor wishes to maximize the mutual social benefits of a trip to an underdeveloped country. Describe possible kinds of social contacts that would be beneficial to the hosts and to the members of the tour group.

4. A popular beach resort hotel is located in a tropical country that, unfortunately, has a high crime rate. One section of the city nearby has some South Seas–atmosphere gambling casinos. Many guests would like to visit them. How might the hotel's staff control this situation?

5. Nadia P. is minister of tourism for a small West African country. This country has become a very popular winter destination for Scandinavians. The tourists seem to be mainly interested in the beaches, which are among the finest in the world. However, it is customary for these visitors to wear very scanty clothing, especially when swimming. In fact, nude swimming is occasionally practiced. About 90 percent of the indigenous population of the host country are Muslims. The appearance and sometimes behavior of the visitors, especially when shopping and otherwise contacting local citizens, often seem improper to their hosts. Tourism is increasing each year. The economic benefits are considerable and are very much needed. However, the social problem is becoming more acute. What should Ms. P. do about this?

ENDNOTES

1. Abraham Pizam, Arie Reichel, and Chia Fian Shieh, "Tourism and Crime: Is There a Relationship?" *Journal of Travel Research,* vol. 20, no. 3 (Winter 1982), pp. 7–10.
2. Valene L. Smith (ed.), Hosts and Guests (Philadelphia: University of Pennsylvania Press, 1977), p. 176.

3. Fabian Linden, "The Business of Vacation Traveling," *Across the Board,* vol. 27, no. 4 (April 1980), pp. 72–75.

4. Amanda Noss, Household Income for States: 2008 and 2009, *American Community Survey Briefs* (Washington DC: U.S. Census Bureau, September 2010).

5. U.S. Bureau of the Census, *Statistical Abstract of the United States: 2009,* 128th ed. (Washington, D.C.: U.S. Government Printing Office, 2008).

6. John J. Burnett and Heather B. Baker, "Assessing the Travel-Related Behaviors of the Mobility-Disabled Consumer," *Journal of Travel Research,* vol. 40, no. 1 (August 2001), pp. 4–11.

7. Arch G. Woodside and Michael J. Etzel, "Impact of Physical and Mental Handicaps on Vacation Travel Behavior," *Journal of Travel Research,* vol. 18, no. 3 (Winter 1980), pp. 9–11.

8. Burnett and Baker, pp. 6–11.

9. John Lennon and Malcolm Foley, *Dark Tourism: The Attraction of Death and Disaster* (London: Continuum International Publishing Group, 2000), p. 40.

PART 4

Tourism Supply, Demand, Policy, Planning, and Development

Hotel facilities built to accommodate visitors to Ayers Rock (seen in distance), one of Australia's most famous landmarks. *Photo courtesy of the author.*

CHAPTER 12

Tourism Components and Supply

LEARNING OBJECTIVES

- Know the major supply components that any tourist area must possess.
- Be able to use the mathematical formula to calculate the number of guest rooms needed for the estimated future demand.
- Develop the ability to perform a task analysis in order to match supply components with anticipated demand.
- Discover methods of adjusting supply components in accordance with fluctuating demand levels.

Spain has an ample supply of tourist attractions. One of the best is the Alhambra in Granada. Shown here is just one of the spectacular buildings in the Alhambra, which is the most visited monument in Spain receiving some 3.2 million visitors a year. *Photo courtesy of the author.*

INTRODUCTION

Considering that tourism is a composite of activities, services, and industries that deliver a travel experience, it is important to identify and categorize its supply components. The quality and quantity of these determine tourism's success in any area.

In Chapter 1 (Figure 1.2) you observed that tourism was a complex phenomenon—the composite of activities, policies, services, and industries involving many players that deliver the travel experience. The purpose of this chapter is to look at just one segment of the tourism phenomenon by examining the physical supply side of tourism. It is important for a tourist area to identify and categorize its supply components and compare them with the competition because the quality and quantity of supply components are a critical factor in determining tourism's success. Figure 12.1 extracts the supply components from Figure 1.2 and provides the basis for discussion in this chapter. However, it is important to recognize that no segment operates in a vacuum and that supply is interrelated to all other aspects of tourism. It must be matched with demand (see Chapter 13). It is also an important part of policy considerations (see Chapter 15).

SUPPLY COMPONENTS

Tourism supply components are classified into four broad categories for discussion in this chapter.

1. **Natural resources and environment.** This category constitutes the fundamental measure of supply—the natural resources that any area has available for the use and enjoyment of visitors.

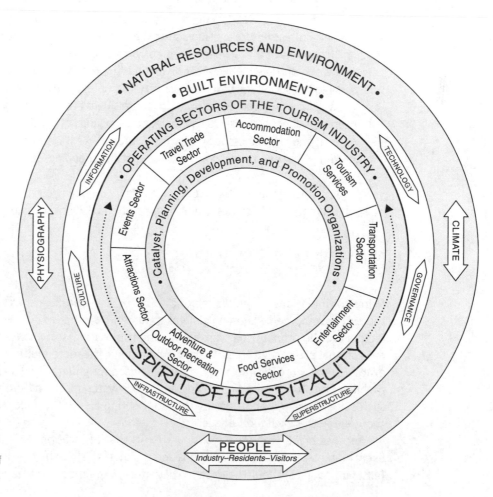

Figure 12.1 Components of tourism supply.

Basic elements in this category include air and climate, physiography of the region, landforms, terrain, flora, fauna, bodies of water, beaches, natural beauty, and water supply for drinking, sanitation, and similar uses.

2. **Built environment.** This includes the infrastructure and superstructure discussed in Chapter 1. This component has been developed within or upon the natural environment. One of the most basic elements of the built environment is the infrastructure of the region, which consists of all underground and surface developmental construction, such as water supply systems, sewage disposal systems, gas lines, electrical lines, drainage systems, roads, communications networks, and many commercial facilities. The tourism superstructure includes facilities constructed primarily to support visitation and visitor activities. Primary examples are airports, railroads, roads, drives, parking lots, parks, marinas and dock facilities, bus and train station facilities, resorts, hotels, motels, restaurants, shopping centers, places of entertainment, museums, stores, and similar structures. For the most part, the operating sectors of the industry are part of the built environment and provide much of the superstructure or facilitate access to the physical supply.

3. **Operating sectors.** The operating sectors of the tourism industry represent what many of the general public perceive as "tourism." First and foremost, the transportation sector, comprising airlines, cruise lines, motorcoach companies, taxis, limousines, automobiles, aerial tramways, and so on, typify the movement of people in travel (see Chapter 5). Because nothing happens until someone plans to leaves home, transportation is a critical component. Without transportation, the tourist would be unable to reach and enjoy the natural and built environment. Tourists need a place to stay and be fed, so the accommodation sector and the food service sector are important supply components (see Chapter 6). Attractions are the reason people travel. Without attractions (see Chapter 8) drawing tourists to destinations, there would be little need for all other tourism services such as transportation, lodging, food, distribution, and so on.

4. **Spirit of hospitality and cultural resources.** Pervading all of the foregoing physical elements of the built infrastructure and superstructures is the social foundation of the destination—its culture, which consists of the language, food, customs, and religions of the residents of the region, as well as their work- and leisure-related behaviors. It is the people and the cultural wealth of an area that make possible the successful hosting of tourists. Examples are the tourist business employees' welcoming aloha spirit in Hawaii, the attitude of the residents toward visitors, courtesy, friendliness, sincere interest, willingness to serve and to get better acquainted with visitors, and other manifestations of warmth and friendliness. In addition, the cultural resources of any area are included here: fine arts, literature, history, music, dramatic art, dancing, shopping, sports, and other activities.

A wide range of tourist resources is created by combining cultural resources. Such examples would be sports events and facilities, traditional or national festivals, games, and pageants.

NATURAL RESOURCES

Many combinations of factors relating to natural resources can create environments attractive to tourism development. Thus, no general statements can be formulated. Probably the most noticeable factors are the pronounced seasonal variations of temperature zones and the changes in demand for recreational use of such areas. To even out demand, the more multiple-use possibilities, the better. For example, it is more desirable that an area be used for golf, riding, fishing, hunting, snow skiing, snow-mobiling, mushroom hunting, sailing and other water sports, nature study, and artistic appreciation such as painting and photography than for hunting alone. The wider the appeal throughout the year, the greater the likelihood of success.

Another highly important consideration is that of location. As a rule, the closer an area is to its likely markets, the more desirable it is and the more likely to have a high demand. User-oriented areas (e.g., golf courses) should be close to their users. By contrast, an area of superb natural beauty, such as

Delicate Arch in Arches National Park, Utah, is an example of how the beauty of natural resources attract tourists. *Photo courtesy of the Utah Travel Council.*

a U.S. national park, could be several thousand miles from major market areas and yet have very satisfactory levels of demand.

Productivity of the natural resources of the area for tourism is a function of the application of labor and management. The amounts and proportions of these inputs will determine the quality and quantity of the output. The terrain, vegetation, and beaches of the natural resources will be affected by the intensity of use. Taking such concentrations of use under consideration and planning accordingly for permanent aesthetic appreciation will help to maintain the quality of the natural resources for the enjoyment of present and future users.

The quality of the natural resources must be maintained to sustain tourism demand. Proper levels of quality must be considered when planning, and the maintenance of quality standards after construction is completed is absolutely necessary for continued satisfaction of the visitor. In fact, tourism is very sensitive to the quality of recreational use of natural resources, and unless high standards are maintained, a decrease in demand will inevitably result. Thus, ecological and environmental considerations are vital.

BUILT ENVIRONMENT

Another supply component is the **built environment** that has been created by humans. It includes the infrastructure and superstructure of the destination.

Infrastructure and Superstructure

The ground and service installations described as infrastructure are of paramount importance to successful tourism. These installations must be adequate. For example, the diameters of the pipes in various utility systems should be ample for any future increase in use. Electrical installations, water supply systems, communications installations, waste disposal, and similar service facilities should be planned with a long-term viewpoint so that they can accommodate future expansion. Airport runways should be built to adequate standards for use by the newest group of jets so that future costly modifications will not be necessary.

Hotel or lodging structures are among the most important parts of the superstructure. The goal should be to produce an architectural design and quality of construction that will result in a distinctive permanent environment. A boxlike hotel typical of any modern city is not considered appropriate for a seaside resort dominated by palms and other tropical vegetation, nor is it likely to attract tourists.

A tourist is often more attracted by a facility designed in conformance with local architecture as a part of the local landscape than by the modernistic hotel that might be found at home. Attention must be given to this subject because people often travel to immerse themselves in an environment totally different from their own. Modern amenities such as air-conditioning, central heating, and plumbing, however, should be used in buildings otherwise characteristic of a particular region.

Interior design should also be stimulating and attractive. Lodging structures need local decor and atmosphere as well as comfort. To minimize the expense of obsolescence, high-quality materials and furnishings and first-rate maintenance are necessary. Infrastructure is expensive and requires considerable time to construct.

Auto Traveler Services

In developed countries, automobile transportation is most common. As the economy of a country develops, the usual pattern progresses from walking, to using horses or other working animals, to bicycles, to motorcycles, and finally to small and then larger automobiles, augmented by public

An example of the built environment is the Pepsi Center in Denver, Colorado. This sports and entertainment venue illustrates how corporate sponsorship has become important in the marketplace.
Photo by Randy Brown; courtesy of the Denver Metro Convention and Visitors Bureau.

The provision of information to visitors is one of the primary responsibilities of a destination management organization (DMO). Here the DMO information center for the town of Manitou Springs is fulfilled by the local chamber of commerce. *Photo courtesy of Manitou Springs Chamber of Commerce and Visitors Bureau.*

transport. Roads should be hard, all-weather surfaced, properly graded and drained, and built to international standards for safe use. Small, inadequate roads will only have to be torn up and replaced with better and more adequate systems.

Auxiliary services, such as gasoline stations, roadside eating facilities, motels, roadside parks, roadside picnic facilities, rest parks that have toilet facilities, scenic turnouts, marked points of interest within easy access of the road, and auto repair and service facilities, are all needed for successful auto tourism. The number and spacing of essential services depend on the nature of the area, but a spacing of about one hour's driving distance is recommended.

Roadside Parks

Auto tourists use and enjoy roadside parks, picnic tables, rest areas, scenic turnouts, and similar roadside facilities. These facilities are sometimes abused by inconsiderate motorists who litter the area with their trash. Thus, the rule "If you can't maintain it, don't build it" is a cardinal principle of tourism development, and regular maintenance to keep the park in an orderly condition is essential. If the parks are not properly maintained, the tourist is disappointed and the investment in the park is largely wasted.

Some states provide deluxe roadside parks with a fine information building, free refreshments, tourist hosts and hostesses, and restrooms. These parks are equipped with supplies of folders, maps, pictures, and other amenities for a refreshing, informative stop.

OPERATING SECTORS

It is the operating sectors that deliver the tourism experience and tend to be viewed by the media, public, and visitors as the "tourism industry." It is the task of the operating sectors to develop and deliver tourism services and experiences with a spirit of hospitality so they will be memorable.

Accommodations

For successful tourism, accommodations must be available in sufficient quantity to match the demand of the travelers who arrive at the destination. Given access to the destination, accommodations should precede any other type of development; their importance cannot be overemphasized.

Lodging facilities vary tremendously in their physical facilities, level of maintenance and cleanliness, and services provided. Unless all of these factors are at satisfactory levels, tourism cannot succeed. The lodging must provide the physical facilities, price ranges, locations, and services that meet the expectations, wants, and needs of the travelers. Should the quality of facilities and services drop, demand will fall off—a serious blow to the tourism industry in the area.

Supply of Accommodations

Lodging comes in many forms aimed at satisfying the needs of the market. The range of supply in the marketplace is vast. From the tourist's standpoint, the primary type is the destination resort hotel situated in attractive surroundings and usually accompanied by a large mix of services, including entertainment and recreational activities for the travelers and vacationer. Another major type is the commercial hotel, usually a downtown structure, located conveniently for the business traveler and vacationer. However, while important, these types are just the beginning of the supply picture. We also have boutique, all-suite, extended stay, conference, convention, motel, condominium, timeshare, bed and breakfast, inn, gite (a French home available for rent), cabin, cottage, hostel, pension, farm stay, campground, apartment, and tent accommodation to mention a number. We also have cruise ships that have become floating resorts. Many resorts are designed especially to accommodate special activities such as gaming, golf, tennis, skiing, and spas. There are also unique accommodations such as the seasonal ice hotels in Canada, Sweden, and Finland.

The demand for accommodations varies according to the price that guests are willing to pay, services required, and similar considerations. Consequently, we have luxury, upscale, mid-price, economy, and budget market price segments to appeal to travelers.

In the United States, Smith Travel Research (STR) defines these as follows:

- Luxury—highest 15 percent average room rates
- Upscale—next highest 15 percent average room rates
- Mid-price—next 30 percent average room rates
- Economy—next 20 percent average room rates
- Budget—lowest 20 percent average room rates

Because consumers seek different levels of service, there are full-service accommodations that offer restaurants, lounge facilities, meeting space, bell service, and room service. These are typically mid-price, upscale, or luxury hotels. Competing with them are limited-service hotels that have rooms-only operations or offer very few other services or amenities. These operations are in the economy or budget grouping. Many successful tourism areas have no multistoried, expensive, contemporary-looking hotels. For example, bungalow-type accommodations constructed with native materials, built to modern standards of comfort and safety, and kept immaculately clean are acceptable to a large segment of the market.

Condominiums

Individual buyers of condominium units typically use the apartment for their own enjoyment, or they rent it to tourists for all or part of the year. This form of accommodation has become increasingly important in ski and beach destinations, and in some resort areas it constitutes considerable

The personal greeting of guests conveys a feeling of warmth and professionalism at the Sheraton New York Hotel and Towers. *Photo courtesy of Sheraton Hotels of New York.*

competition to the resort hotels. Real estate management firms often manage such apartments or groups of condos within a building or complex and thus serve as agents for the owners. They rent the condos as managers of the group, charging a fee for this service to the absent owner. Such arrangements can be made through a local travel agent in the prospective traveler's home city. The agent will book the reservation through the real estate management firm.

Timesharing

Timesharing is a technique for the multiple ownership and/or use of resort and recreational properties. Timesharing has been applied to hotels, motels, condominiums, townhouses, single-family detached homes, campgrounds, and even boats and yachts. It involves both new construction and conversion of existing structures, along with properties devoted solely to timesharing and projects that integrate timesharing and nontimesharing properties. While most programs may be classified as either ownership or nonownership (right to use), there are wide variations in program and legal format.

The attraction of timesharing is simple: It permits purchasers to own or have occupancy rights at a resort accommodation for a period of time each year for a fraction of the purchasing price of the entire unit. Timeshare owners pay for exactly what they plan on using, and when they leave they don't have to think about where they'll be vacationing next year. Another option or advantage of timesharing is the exchange program. The exchange system affords vacation flexibility by allowing owners to trade or swap their timeshares for other locations and times. Finally, a well-designed timeshare program can be a hedge against inflation in resort accommodations.

The benefits of timesharing are substantially borne out by the high degree of consumer satisfaction it has achieved. In a survey of approximately 10,000 timeshare buyers, conducted by the National Timesharing Council, 86.3 percent of the respondents said they were "very satisfied" or "satisfied" with their purchase. About 40 percent indicated that they were interested in purchasing additional timeshares. Additional information on timesharing is available from the American Resort Development Association, www.arda.org. Also see the discussion in Chapter 6.

The supply of accommodations varies tremendously from luxury properties to hostels. This luxury property is the Ritz-Carlton, Tamuda Bay, Morocco. *Photo courtesy of destination design firm WATG.*

Hotel Classification

Hotels are classified using a number of different systems. Then, too, many tourist countries have no classification system whatsoever. Many in the industry prefer the five-star rating system, which grades hotels according to specific criteria (usually by the national tourist organization) from the highest (five stars) to the most modest accommodations (one star) suitable for travelers. Countries such as Spain also classify nonhotel accommodations, such as pensions. Criteria used for star ratings are public rooms, bathrooms, climatization, telephone, bar, dining rooms, and other characteristics. The Burj Al Arab hotel in Dubai, United Arab Emirates, consistently voted the world's most luxurious hotel, claims it is a seven-star property.

Other classifications are deluxe, superior, and good; or superdeluxe, and first-class reasonable. Still another classification is A, B, C, D, or E. Because many classification schemes are confusing or not useful, a uniform worldwide classification truly indicative of the grades of hotels in any country would be a real plus to tourism. Of course, differences in general standards of development in various countries would be understood. A five-star hotel in a highly developed country would likely be more deluxe than would a five-star hotel in a less developed area.

Types of Transportation

All factors concerning **transportation** should be considered in developing tourism, beginning with taxis, limousines, and bus service from the place of lodging to the departure terminals. Such services must be adequate and economical.

Air

As described in Chapter 5, the airline industry dominates public intercity transportation systems, capturing over 92 percent of the common-carrier passenger mile market. Thus, planners looking to improve tourism must evaluate the adequacy of air transportation. Flight frequencies as well as

The Ginza Station of the modern Tokyo Subway System provides the ideal way to travel around the city.
Photo courtesy of Corbis Digital Stock.

size and type of aircraft are important. Air service from important origins for tourists is, of course, essential.

Airport facilities must be adequate. Major problems frequently encountered are the accessibility to the airport, aircraft slots availability, and the passenger loading-unloading parking space sequence. Newly built airports seem to have solved these to a considerable degree and have also reduced walking distances because of design improvements. There is also frequent shuttle bus service for interline passengers.

Airboats are a popular means of transportation in the Florida Everglades and the Louisiana Bayou, where they are used for fishing, bowfishing, hunting, and tourism in marshy shallow areas. A standard engine with a submerged propeller would not work. Here, tourists are enjoying a tour in the Everglades.
Photo courtesy of Everglades Alligator Farm.

Motorcoach

Motorcoaches intended for tour use should have large windows, air-conditioning, comfortable seats, and restroom facilities. Springs or other suspension systems in the coaches should be designed so that the joggling of passengers is kept to a minimum or eliminated. Multilingual guide service or multilingual tape recording facilities with earphones for each passenger are useful in communities or on tours where an interpretation of the points of interest is desirable.

Personnel assigned to buses should be selected for suitable temperament, courtesy, and spirit of hospitality. For example, if a bus is staffed by a driver and an interpreter, the interpreter can assist passengers on and off the bus as well as inform them of local environment, particularly attractions of interest. Interpreters or guides should be trained and educated for this duty. Too often, the interpretation of points of interest is superficial (and inaccurate). A program of certification for guides should be conducted by a special school or provided in the curriculum of an institution of higher learning. In such a program, competent instructors should educate potential guides in the history, archaeology, ethnology, culture, and economic system of the area in which the tour is being conducted. Competency in the various languages commonly encountered with tourists is also an essential qualification.

Ship and Boat

Water travel is a major part of tourism and contributes considerably to the development of travel on land and by air. Forms of water travel include ocean cruise ships, river cruises, passenger travel on freighters, ferryboats, river sternwheeler, chartered boats and yachts, houseboats, and smaller family boats and canoes.

Cruise ships and other large vessels need convenient piers and good land-air transportation connections for their passengers. Smaller boats need docks and loading-unloading ramps for easy accessibility to water. Charter boat operators must have reliable weather forecasting and ready availability of needed supplies and repair services. Where rental canoes are popular, delivery and pickup services are often necessary, as are campgrounds in wilderness areas where canoeists can stay overnight. Persons owning their own boats appreciate good public-access points for launching.

Rail

Travelers worldwide often prefer rail travel, particularly because of its safety record and the convenience and comfort of viewing the scenery from an air-conditioned car. Also, the frequent schedules of trains in many countries appeal to travelers. The recent advent of high-speed trains further enhances their appeal. Some trains have stewards or hosts, which travelers seem to appreciate.

Adequate taxi, limousine, or bus service from the railroad station to hotels and downtown points is essential. Such transportation service must be frequent enough to get the traveler to the destination promptly. Conversely, the traveler should be able to get to the railroad station in ample time to make connections with the train.

Taxis

Adequate taxi and limousine services are essential in a tourist area. Ideally, taxis should have removable and washable seat covers so the car always presents a clean appearance to the passenger. Also, to make the best impression, the taxi driver should dismount from the driver's seat and open the door for the passenger. He or she also should assist in stowing the luggage in the trunk or elsewhere in the cab and be courteous at all times.

Taxi drivers who are multilingual are highly desirable and, in fact, essential if tourism is to be an important element of the economy of the location. Training taxi drivers in foreign languages should be no more difficult than training tourist guides or front-desk clerks. Where taxi drivers have no foreign language ability, hotels may provide written directions for the tourist to give to the driver concerning the destination and the return to the hotel at the end of the excursion.

Rail allows travelers the opportunity to view scenery as they travel in a comfortable atmosphere.
Copyright © 2001 Amtrak. Photo provided as a courtesy by Amtrak.

SPIRIT OF HOSPITALITY AND CULTURAL RESOURCES

The development of **hospitality resources** is perhaps the most important factor in tourism. The finest physical facilities will be worthless if the tourist feels unwelcome. For example, we suggest having a welcoming sign and a special reception area for visitors at airports and other entry points. A favorable attitude toward the visitor can be created through programs of public information and propaganda and initial welcoming (often by local volunteers). In this regard, public relations and publicity designed to convince local citizens of the importance of tourism are helpful. Courses at tourist hospitality schools for all persons who have direct contact with visitors are useful. In these schools, store clerks, gasoline station attendants, hotel clerks, and other persons who are directly in contact with the visitor are given indoctrination on the importance of tourism to their community and are taught the location of important points of interest. Other parts of the program include the importance of appearance and good grooming, greeting of visitors, providing information, and being helpful, gracious, friendly, and cooperative.

Cultural programs such as "Meet the Danes" (home visitation arrangements) help greatly in this respect. Adequate training of personnel by tourist hospitality businesses can also create the desired hospitable attitude.

Activities Tourists Enjoy Most

One of the most important functions of a tourism promotion organization is to ascertain what activities visitors would enjoy while in their destination. When substantial data are accumulated, the findings should be reported to those who accommodate and entertain. Thus, they are guided into more successful methods and programs. Table 12.1 shows some of tourists' favorite things.

The best method of obtaining this information is by interviewing both the visitors and their hosts using scientific sampling methods. Careful recording and thorough analysis of these data will result in findings of real value. When those responsible for attracting and hosting visitors provide the requested entertainment activities, the community will likely be a preferred destination area. There is no better advertising than a satisfied visitor (see Chapter 18 on research).

Shopping

Shopping is an important tourist activity and thus an essential element in tourism supply because it affects the success of the tourist destination area. The most important single element in shopping is

TABLE 12.1 Tourists' Favorite Things: What European-Bound Travelers Plan to Do

Activity	Percent Citing It
Dining at restaurants	86.2
Shopping	76.9
Visiting a historical site	67.5
Visiting a small town	53.6
Sightseeing in a city	51.8
Touring the countryside	47.0
Visiting an art gallery/museum	40.1
Visiting a cultural heritage site	38.3
Visiting a nightclub/dancing	21.4
Taking a guided tour	21.0
Attending a concert/play	20.2
Visiting an ethnic heritage site	13.3
Participating in water sports/sunbathing	10.7
Visiting an amusement park	8.1
Visiting a national park	6.7
Taking a cruise	6.4
Camping/hiking	4.9
Playing golf/tennis	4.9
Visiting a casino	4.8
Attending a sports event	3.8
Skiing	2.9
Participating in an ecological excursion	2.5
Hunting/fishing	1.4

Source: Travel Weekly, European Travel Commission, and Tourism Industries, U.S. Department of Commerce.

The growing popularity of "heritage tourism" has created a desire to preserve and enjoy early railway equipment. *Photo courtesy of Utah Travel Council.*

the authenticity of the products offered for sale as they relate to the local area. A product that is supposedly a "native handicraft" should be that. If it is an import, the purchaser may be disappointed if he or she expected an authentic, locally made item.

Tourists who are shopping are particularly interested in handicraft items that are typical or indigenous to the particular locale or region. Of course, they are also interested in essential items such as toothpaste, but our discussion here is confined to purchases that tourists make as souvenirs or special gifts.

Tourists can be encouraged to spend more money on shopping if displays are high quality, imaginative, and attractive. Hotels are excellent places for shops, and if these shops are exquisitely furnished and stocked, the tourist is attracted to the shop and is more likely to make purchases.

Native Marketplaces

Another shopping experience concerns the local market or so-called native marketplace. Such areas are rich in ethnicity and have much local color. They are popular with visitors, even though the visitor may not understand the language and may have trouble making a purchase. Although many persons in native shopping places do not understand any foreign languages, the sign language of bargaining is fairly universal.

Shopkeepers and Clerks

Shopkeepers and clerks themselves should be amiable and courteous. Furthermore, the shopkeeper should not be so anxious to close a sale that the tourist is pressured. A tourist who is courteously served in a store and who makes a good purchase will tell friends back home. Thus, future business can be developed in this way. Salespeople should also take the time to explain the value of the item and relate something of its history that would be otherwise unknown to the purchaser. Of course, this information should be accurate and truthful.

Salespersons must have sufficient language ability to conduct conversations with the visitors. The most common language is English, but a knowledge of other languages that are commonly spoken by tourists who visit a particular area is a necessary qualification of clerks who serve these visitors. Salespersons must be patient and understanding and try to help the prospective purchaser cheerfully at all times.

Prices and Unethical Practices

One of the most important considerations in shopping is the pricing of the goods. Probably resented more than any other single factor of tourism is higher prices for tourists than for local residents.

Tourism shopping is not always for designer products on Rodeo Drive in Beverly Hills. Tourists also derive great enjoyment from exploring the wares of basic stores that are reminiscent of America's past. Here, a small community food and souvenir store in North Carolina allows the visitor to interact with local residents. *Photo courtesy of Chapel Hill/Orange County Visitors Bureau.*

Because many shoppers compare prices from one store to another, prices should be as consistent as possible and in line with costs. If the shopkeeper resorts to unethical methods of selling, such as deception, selling imitation goods or products of inferior quality, refusing to exchange damaged goods, or shortchanging or shortweighting, the seller is hurting the tourist trade and should be prosecuted by local authorities.

Entertainment, Recreation, and Other Activities

The recreation and other activities engaged in by tourists at their destination are a major supply component of tourism. Thus, considerable thought and effort should be devoted to the type of activities that visitors are likely to enjoy.

Entertainment

The most satisfying entertainment for visitors is that which is native to the area. In any country, there are expressions of the culture in the music, dance, drama, poetry, literature, motion pictures, television, ceremonies, festivals, exhibits, shows, meetings, food and beverage services, and tours (or local excursions) that portray the best the area has to offer.

Not all forms of entertainment can be successfully described or illustrated in tourist promotional literature. One of the best ways to bring these entertainment opportunities to the attention of the visitor is with a social director whose desk is in the lobby of hotels, resorts, and other forms of accommodation so that the visitor can readily find out what is going on and make arrangements to attend. In European hotels, this desk is traditionally staffed by the concierge, who provides an amazing amount of information concerning all types of entertainment and activities available. An appropriate substitute is a knowledgeable person at the front desk to provide information concerning recreation and entertainment.

Bulletin board displays or posters and verbal announcements of outstanding events made in the dining room or other areas where guests gather can also provide entertainment information. A local newspaper that features articles concerning everyday as well as special entertainment events and opportunities is a valuable method of distributing information. These newspapers or bulletins are provided in popular vacation destination areas such as Miami Beach and Honolulu, but the idea is not widespread. In metropolitan centers, a weekly magazine is normally provided to hotel guests to give current information on entertainment, recreational, and cultural opportunities in the city. The Internet is another information source as hotel Web sites feature and provide links to local attractions and entertainment. For example see www.marriott.com/hotels/local-things-to-do/sfocd-courtyard-san-francisco-downtown/.

Special Events

Entertainment can be provided very effectively as a special promotional event to attract visitors during an off-season. One of the best examples of this is Aloha Festivals, which was inaugurated in Hawaii as Aloha Week in the mid-1940s to bolster tourist traffic in the fall. This festival is enthusiastically supported by local tourism interests and is very successful in attracting tourists. Musicians, dancers, exhibits, floral displays, and special programs are assembled and give the visitor an unusual opportunity to enjoy the beauty and excitement of cultural expression that this state offers. Once created, such events become annual and typically grow in visitors and importance. Expositions and festivals are very attractive to visitors and deserve adequate promotion.

Museums and Art Galleries

Museums and art galleries are another major attraction for tourists. They provide some of the highlights in many of the world's most important tourist destinations, such as New York; Washington, D.C.; Chicago; Paris; London; Madrid; Rome; Singapore; Tokyo; Buenos Aires; Mexico City; and many others. The quality and magnitude of these institutions are an important consideration for attracting and satisfying tourists.

Speaking of icons, this Kansas museum is the home of one of America's best. "The Tin Man" from the classic movie Wizard of Oz is recognized by movie goers worldwide and by many others. Outside of its iconic status, the larger-than-life-size version of the Tin Man is a great attraction for children of all ages.
Photo by John Noltner; courtesy of Kansas Department of Commerce.

Sports

Golf and sports—such as tennis, surfing, swimming, mountain climbing, skiing, hunting, fishing, hiking, prospecting, or any other outdoor sports activity—require properly publicized facilities and services. Guides, equipment, charter boats, and other services needed to enjoy these sports must be readily available at fair prices. Convenience and accessibility are key factors in this type of entertainment.

MATCHING SUPPLY WITH DEMAND

Providing an ample tourism supply to meet anticipated demand is a challenge for the tourism planner or manager. Supply functions are always constrained by demand. The following formula can be used to calculate the number of hotel rooms (or other types of lodging) required:

$$\text{Room demand/night(100\% occupancy)} = \frac{\text{No. tourists} \times \% \text{ Staying in hotels} \times \text{Average stay}}{365 \times \text{Average number of persons per room}}$$

$$R = \frac{T \times P \times L}{S \times N}$$

where

R = room demand per night, at 100 percent occupancy

T = number of tourists

P = percentage staying in hotels

L = average length of stay

S = number of days per year open for business

N = average number of persons per room (obtained from hoteliers); total number of guest nights divided by the number of guests, during any period of time

O = hotel occupancy used for estimating; for 70 percent occupancy, divide number of rooms needed at 100 percent occupancy by 70 percent

Illustration of application of the formula:

T = 1,560,000 visitors

P = 98% staying in hotels

L = 9 days

S = 365 days per year open for business

N = 1.69 persons per room

O = 70% occupancy

$$R = \frac{(1,560,000 \times 0.98 \times 9)}{(365 \times 1.69)} = \frac{(13,759,200)}{(616.85)} = 22,306 \text{ (rooms needed at 100\% occupancy)}$$

$$= \frac{22,306}{0.70} \text{ (as more rooms will be needed at 70\% occupancy than at 100\%)}$$

$$= 31,866 \text{ rooms needed}$$

The fact that more rooms will be needed at 70 percent occupancy than at 100 percent occupancy may be confusing to some—although mathematically it is clear that dividing 22,306 by 1.0 will result in a smaller number than when 22,306 is divided by 0.70. The situation that creates this is that, if rooms are not full (as in 70 percent occupancy), a greater number of rooms will be required to house a given number of guests (such as 22,306). However, while they might like to, hotels cannot afford to build room numbers to a level that assumes 100 percent occupancy, since this is unrealistic, given that worldwide hotel occupancy fluctuates around 65 percent.

Infrastructure factors in supply will be determined largely by the number of guest rooms as well as restaurants, stores, and similar installations. Infrastructure appropriate to the size of the development is an engineering problem and is readily ascertained as the plans are developed. Transportation equipment is generally supplied by commercial firms as well as publicly owned or quasi-public transportation facilities and services.

Regarding hospitality resources, the recruiting and training of staff for the various elements of supply is a critical one. The traveler generally enjoys being served by unsophisticated local persons who have had proper training and possess a hospitable attitude. Such persons may be recruited through government and private employment agencies as well as through direct advertisement to the public. Newly hired employees must be indoctrinated in the importance of tourism, how it affects their own personal welfare as well as that of their community, the importance of proper service to the visitors, and how their economic welfare is closely related to their performance.

Museums, art exhibits, festivals, craft shows, and similar cultural resources are usually created by community cooperation and the willing assistance of talented people. A chamber of commerce or tourism body is the best mechanism for organizing the creation of these hospitality resources.

Task Analysis

The procedure used in matching supply with demand is called a **task analysis**. Suggested steps are as follows:

1. Identification of the present demand
   a. By mode of transportation and by seasons of the year
   b. For various forms of tourism such as activities, attendance at attractions, and similar categories
   c. For special events such as conventions, celebrations, fairs
   d. Group and tour visitors
   e. Family and individual visitors
   f. Business visitors

2. A quantitative and qualitative inventory of the existing supply

3. The adequacy of present supply with present demand
   a. Natural resources
   b. Infrastructure
   c. Transportation and equipment
   d. Hospitality and cultural resources

4. Examination of present markets and the socioeconomic trends
   a. Geographic market segmentation and orientation
   b. Demographic market segmentation and orientation
      i. Population age, sex, occupation, family life stages, income, and similar data
      ii. Leisure time and work patterns
   c. Psychographic market segmentation
      i. Motivations, interests, hobbies, employment orientation, skills, professional interests
      ii. Propensity to travel, responsiveness to advertising

5. Forecast of tourism demand
   a. Computer systems simulation method
   b. Trend analysis
   c. Simple regression—linear least squares
   d. Multiple regression—linear least squares
   e. Executive judgment or Delphi method

6. Matching supply with anticipated demand
   a. If adequate, no further action necessary
   b. If inadequate, inauguration of planning and development procedures

To perform the task analysis, certain skills are required, with statistical research techniques employed to identify and quantify the current demand. Suggestions for doing this are provided in Chapter 13.

When making a quantitative and qualitative inventory of the existing supply, the aid of specialists and experts is usually needed. For example, the adequacy of the current supply in relation to current demand requires the work of tourism specialists such as travel agents, tour company and hotel executives, tourism promotion people, ground operators (companies that provide baggage transfers, taxi services, local tours, and similar services), shopkeepers, and perhaps a sample of the tourists themselves.

Examining the current markets and the socioeconomic trends that will affect future markets requires specialized market research activities. These should include determination of market characteristics, development of market potentials, market share analysis, sales analysis, competitive destination studies, potentials of the existing and possibly new markets, short-range forecasting, and studies of travel business trends. A number of sophisticated techniques are now available. The engagement of a reputable market research firm is one way to obtain this information.

Forecasting tourism demand is a perilous business. However, a well-structured statistical analysis, coupled with executive judgment, is most likely the best approach to this difficult problem. See Chapter 13 for several methods for accomplishing this.

Finally, matching supply with the anticipated demand must be done by knowledgeable planners. A tourism development plan within the master plan is recommended. Supply items are essentially rigid. They are elaborate and expensive and, thus, cannot be expanded rapidly. An exception would be transportation equipment. Additional planes, buses, train cars, or automobiles could be assembled quite rapidly to meet an unusually high demand situation.

Peaks and Valleys

The foregoing discussion dealt with matching supply and demand in a long-run context. Another important consideration is that of fluctuations in demand in the short run (**seasonality**) and the resulting **peaks and valleys of demand** This is a vexing problem.

The reason for this is simply that tourism is a service, and services cannot be placed in inventory. If a 400-room hotel rents (sells) 350 rooms on a particular night, it cannot place the other 50 rooms in inventory for sale the following night. Regardless of how many rooms went unoccupied in the past, a 400-room property can rent no more than 400 rooms on any given night. By way of contrast, consider the case of some tangible good, say, television sets. If some television sets are not sold in one month, the storekeeper can keep them in inventory and sell them the next month. Of course, the storage charges, interest payments, and other expenses incurred in inventorying a particular item reduce the item's economic value. But in tourism, the economic value of unsold items, such as the 50 hotel rooms mentioned, is exactly zero.

Thus, it should be clear that while, in most cases, firms selling tangible goods can deal with demand fluctuation through the inventory process, this option is not available to firms providing travel services. In the travel industry, an effort must be made to reduce seasonal fluctuations as much as possible. Because of the high economic cost involved, no effort should be spared in attempting to limit the amount of seasonal variations in demand. Nor can the problem be dealt with by simply selecting an appropriate supply level. The following charts illustrate various supply situations associated with fluctuating demand levels.

Suppose that the demand for a particular destination exhibits the seasonal pattern depicted in Figure 12.2a. If no action is taken to "level off" the demand, then three possible levels of supply can be considered. In Figure 12.2b, the level of supply is provided so that demand in the peak season is fully satisfied. This implies that tourists coming to the destination in the peak season will be accommodated comfortably and without overcrowding. However, during the slack season, the destination will suffer from extremely low occupancy levels, with obvious implications for profitability. If, on the other hand, the supply is set at a low level (Figure 12.2c), the facilities during the peak season will be overcrowded enough to detract from the tourist experience. Visitor satisfaction will be at a low level, and the future of such a resort area will be doubtful. Last, if supply is set in between the level of demand during the peak season and the off-season (Figure 12.2d), the problems are somewhat mitigated. Nevertheless, low

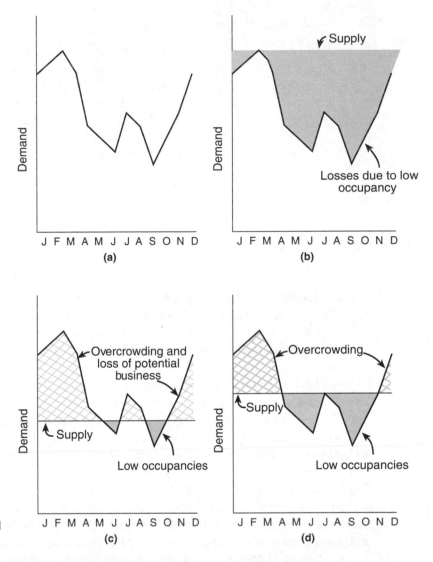

Figure 12.2 Fluctuating demand levels and supply.

occupancy will result during low demand periods, and overcrowding will result in peak periods; neither is desirable. To maximize customer satisfaction and to utilize the facilities year-round, some action must be taken. Two strategies for dealing with this situation are as follows:

1. **Multiple use.** This involves supplementing peak-season attractions of a destination with other attractions that would create demand for travel to that destination during off-season periods. In effect, the peak season for the destination is extended. Examples of such efforts abound. In Michigan, for example, the current demand for off-season travel (during the fall, winter, and spring) has been successfully increased and sustained at much higher levels than in the past. While Michigan was once viewed primarily as a summer destination, the development and promotion of winter sports in resort areas, foliage tours, and superb salmon fishing in the fall and spring have created new markets for these off-season periods. Festivals, special celebrations, conventions, and sports activities sponsored and promoted during off-seasons are other examples of multiple-use strategies.

2. **Price differential.** This technique, in contrast with the multiple-use strategy, creates new markets for the off-season periods by employing price differentials as a strong tool to shift demand away from the peak season in favor of the off-season. Florida and destinations in the Caribbean have used this strategy rather effectively. The prices in these destinations during the off-seasons are considerably less than during the peak seasons. In addition, the development of promotional fares by airlines and other carriers, along with the expansion of the number, timing, and variety of price-

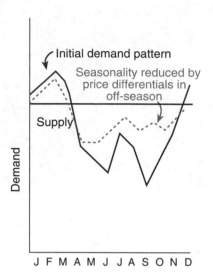

Figure 12.3 Reducing seasonality through price differentials.

discounted tours, have helped to stimulate demand in the off-season. Increased efficiency and effectiveness of promotional campaigns and better marketing also tend to offset the traditional seasonal patterns of demand. Yield management techniques used in the airline and lodging industries are very effective in using price differentials to match supply and demand.

In addition to these strategies implemented by destination areas, some trends in the employment and leisure patterns of Western societies contribute further to the leveling of demand between off-seasons and peak seasons. The staggering of holidays, the increasing popularity of three-day weekends with a holiday on Friday or Monday, and the splitting of vacations between various seasons of the year all lend themselves to leveling the demand for travel. Once the demand is evened out, the destination is then able to maximize customer satisfaction during the peak season and during the off-season. Also, facilities are utilized at a considerably higher level than previously. The importance of boosting off-season demand and, therefore, the utilization level is further underscored by the fact that in most tourist service businesses, fixed costs are quite high in relation to operating costs. This implies that increasing total yearly revenue, even modestly, produces proportionally larger profits. There may be some softening of demand during the peak season due to those who might switch to the off-season because of the lower prices (see Figure 12.3). However, this is believed to be minimal. When off-season demand is boosted by the multiple-use strategy, peak-season demand is unaffected. Therefore, overall demand for the entire year will be substantially higher (see Figure 12.4).

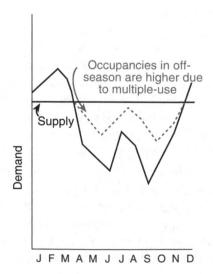

Figure 12.4 Reducing seasonality through multiple use.

SUMMARY

Certain broad classifications of supply components must be provided by any area that is attractive to tourists. The components consist of natural resources, the built environment, operating sectors, and the spirit of hospitality and cultural resources. These factors may be combined in many ways to create the environment, facilities, and services that the planners hope will attract and please the customers.

Creation of supply components necessarily involves financing—a critical element. Ideally, all the supply components perfectly match the demand at any given time. However, this is unrealistic. Too much supply means unused facilities, which is uneconomic. Too little supply results in overcrowding with resultant depreciation of the vacation experience or lost sales, which could have contributed significantly to the bottom line profits. A moderate supply level is recommended.

Supply can be matched with demand using a mathematical formula. When confronted with a supply problem, the proper level of supply to meet the anticipated demand can be estimated by using the formula provided in this chapter. The process is refined and completed by a six-step task analysis.

❖ KEY CONCEPTS ❖

accommodations
built environment
cultural resources
entertainment and recreation
   activities
hospitality resources

infrastructure
multiple use
natural resources
peaks and valleys of demand
price differentials
seasonality

shopping
superstructure
supply components
task analysis
timesharing
transportation

❖ INTERNET EXERCISES ❖

The Internet sites mentioned in this chapter plus some selected additional sites are listed for your convenience on the companion Web site for this book, www.wiley.com/college/goeldner.

ACTIVITY 1

Site Name: Fodor's Travel Publications

URL: www.fodors.com

Background Information: Fodor's Travel Publications, a subsidiary of Random House, is the largest publisher of English-language travel information in the world. Fodor's now publishes more than 300 books on destinations around the world.

Exercise

1. Using the four major supply components your textbook indicates that any tourist area must possess, discuss how

the Fodor's Web site addresses each of these areas for the potential tourist.

ACTIVITY 2

Site Name: Lonely Planet Online

URL: www.lonelyplanet.com

Background Information: Lonely Planet publishes some of the world's best guidebooks for independent travelers. Its books are known worldwide for reliable, insightful travel information, maps, photos, and background historical and cultural information.

Exercise

1. Choose a destination or use one provided by the instructor. How does this site address the four components of travel for the potential tourist to this destination?

❖ QUESTION FOR REVIEW AND DISCUSSION ❖

1. In planning supply components for a development in an entirely new area, which one of the four components should be considered first? Last? Why?

2. When a gorgeous new resort is opened for business, are the attractive physical facilities more important than the quality and training of the staff?

3. As a resort hotel manager, do you believe your guests need to be educated about environmental protection? Do you need to educate your staff?

4. In a poor, developing country, a world-class hotel uses about half of the community's water supply. This requires rationing of water by the local people, which creates resentment. Suggest a partial solution to this problem.

5. For new developments, should the access roads be supplied by a government agency, the developer, or both? If both, who should supply what?

6. What might be appropriate costumes and uniforms for waiters and waitresses in various localities?

7. The sports director of a large resort hotel has been instructed to upgrade the hotel's physical fitness program. Provide some suggestions as to how this might be done.

8. Is changing the prices of hotel rooms, meals, and entertainment the best way to mitigate fluctuating levels of demand? Are there nonprice methods? Could combinations of methods be used?

❖ CASE PROBLEMS ❖

1. To maintain and hopefully enhance the appeal and quality of its area's natural resources, the city council has decided that it needs to enact protective laws to help ensure its future tourism success. What specific laws and regulations might these be?

2. Resort City is anxious to attract more tourists. The chamber of commerce has been successful in attracting several new tourist firms to the community. These firms plan to develop new hotels, lodges, shops, and restaurants. However, an influential member of the chamber of commerce expresses the viewpoint that the community should enact some strict zoning and building code laws before these construction

projects get under way. The prospective developers and many other members of the chamber disagree. What do you think should be done to resolve this situation, and why?

3. A destination tourism organization (DMO) is seeking ways in which to improve the proficiency of accommodations booking. It is exploring the possibility of installing a computer-based accommodations information system. This system provides data comparisons between similar operations considering size, location, and countrywide averages. What do you see as advantages for implementing such a system? How might the system be implemented in your destination?

CHAPTER 13

Measuring and Forecasting Demand

LEARNING OBJECTIVES

- Understand the concept of demand and its application and importance in tourism development planning.

- Understand the factors determining the magnitude and fluctuations of demand.

- Become able to apply various methods to measure and forecast demand.

Travelers enjoy the speed of the Très Grand Vitesse (TGV) train to Paris. *Photo courtesy of Corbis Digital Stock.*

INTRODUCTION

E conomists define demand as a schedule of the amount of any product or service that people are willing and able to buy at each specific price in a set of possible prices during some specified period of time. Thus, there exists at any one time a definite relationship between the market price and the quantity demanded.

WHY DEMAND IS IMPORTANT

The amount of demand for travel to a particular destination is of great concern to anyone involved in tourism. Vital demand data include: (1) how many visitors arrived, (2) by what means of transportation, (3) how long they stayed and in what type of accommodations, and (4) how much money was spent. There are various measures of demand; some are much easier to obtain and are usually of more general interest than are others. Techniques also exist for making forecasts of future demand. Such estimates are of great interest to anyone planning future tourism developments. The availability of financing will depend largely on reliable forecasts of the future gross sales or revenues from the project to determine if the proposal will be financially feasible.

Marketing and sales promotion programs are, of course, aimed at increasing demand. Sometimes this effort focuses on increasing demand at certain times of the year or to a particular market. But the basic purpose is the same: to increase demand.

DEMAND TO A DESTINATION

In somewhat more specific terms, the demand for travel to a particular destination will be a function of the person's **propensity** to travel and the reciprocal of the **resistance** of the link between origin and destination areas. Thus,

$$D = f(\text{propensity, resistance})$$

where D is demand.

Propensity can be thought of as a person's predisposition to travel—in other words, how willing the person is to travel, what types of travel experiences he or she prefers, and what types of destinations are considered. A person's propensity to travel will, quite obviously, be determined largely by his or her psychographic profile and travel motivation, as discussed in previous chapters. In addition, a person's socioeconomic status will have an important bearing on propensity. It follows that to estimate a person's propensity to travel, we must understand both psychographic and demographic variables concerning the person. Propensity is *directly* related to demand.

Resistance, on the other hand, relates to the relative attractiveness of various destinations. This factor is, in turn, a function of several other variables, such as economic distance, cultural distance, the cost of tourist services at destination, the quality of service at destination, effectiveness of advertising and promotion, and seasonality. Resistance is inversely related to demand.

Economic Distance

Economic distance relates to the time and cost involved in traveling from the origin to the destination area and back. The higher the economic distance, the higher the resistance for that destination and, consequently, the lower the demand. It follows, conversely, that between any origin and destination point, if the travel time or travel cost can be reduced, demand will increase. Many excellent examples of this are available, such as the introduction of the jet plane in 1959 and the introduction of the wide-bodied jets in the late 1960s. Jet planes first cut travel time between California and Hawaii, for example, from 12 hours to 5 hours, and demand grew dramatically. A similar surge in demand was experienced with the introduction of the wide-bodied planes for transatlantic flights. The introduction of these planes cut the travel cost by almost 50 percent between the United States and most countries on the European continent.

Cultural Distance

Cultural distance refers to the extent to which the culture of the area from which the tourist originates differs from the culture of the host region. In general, the greater the cultural distance, the greater will be the resistance. In some cases, however, the relationship might be the opposite. For example, the higher the cultural distance between particular origin and destination areas, the more an allocentric person may wish to travel to that destination, to experience this extreme difference.

Cost of Services

The higher the **cost of services** at a destination, the higher the resistance to travel to that destination will be and, therefore, the lower the demand. This variable captures the familiar inverse relationship between the price of a good or service and demand for it.

Quality of Service

Clearly, the higher the **quality of service** at a destination, the lower the resistance will be for travel to that destination. Although the relationship between quality of service and demand is straight-forward enough, a difficulty arises in the interpretation and evaluation of *quality*. Evaluation of

Many tourists seek familiarity while others seek adventure. Up for adventure? Try a zipline safari for a thrilling new experience. Because there is a strong demand, ziplines are becoming a popular tourist attraction around the world. *Photo courtesy of Florida EcoSafaris at Forever Florida.*

quality is a highly personal matter, and what is high quality to one tourist is not necessarily high quality to another. Also, if a tourist does not have previous travel experience at a destination, can he or she accurately judge the quality of services there? In such a case, the tourist must select a destination based on what the quality of service is *perceived* to be. Often, due to misleading advertisements or inaccurate input from others, the tourist's perception of the quality of service may not be realized at the destination. Such a situation has serious implications for establishing a repeat clientele, which is an important ingredient for success in the tourist business. Consequently, a destination area must be meticulous in projecting an accurate image.

Seasonality

The effect of seasonality on demand is quite apparent. The relative attractiveness of a given destination will depend on the time of year for which a vacation is planned. For a ski resort, for example, the demand will be at the highest level during the winter months. Resistance is at a minimum in this season.

The following illustrates the relationship between propensity, resistance, and demand, in terms of these variables as just described.

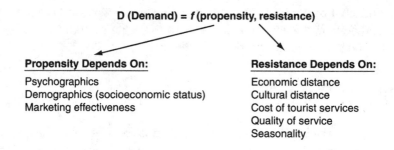

D (Demand) = *f* (propensity, resistance)

Propensity Depends On:	**Resistance Depends On:**
Psychographics	Economic distance
Demographics (socioeconomic status)	Cultural distance
Marketing effectiveness	Cost of tourist services
	Quality of service
	Seasonality

MEASURING DEMAND

Demand is strongly affected and limited by the supply. If the supply aspects are not taken into consideration when using demand figures, planners might be led into the false assumption that in a particular area, the supply should be increased to meet the demand when, in actuality, the increased supply may be needed much more elsewhere.

There are several measures of actual demand:

1. Visitor arrivals
2. Visitor-days or visitor-nights
3. Amount spent

Visitor Arrivals

Simply counting the number of people who arrive at a destination is a measure of demand, although not a particularly adequate one. However, when visitors arrive by ship or aircraft, for example, to an island, quite accurate data are obtainable. Those who are en route to another destination should not be included in the arrival data. Visitor arrivals are the easiest type of data to obtain, especially if public transportation is the principal mode used. Regular reporting of visitor arrivals is of value in

Tourists seek out famous sights such as the Leaning Tower of Pisa in Italy and create visitor-days and visitor-nights, which are a convenient way of measuring travel demand. *Photo courtesy of Corbis Digital Stock.*

measuring broad changes in demand. Variation in the number of arrivals month by month is quite significant because it indicates the rise and fall of demand during the course of a year.

Arrival data become more of a problem if a large proportion of visitors arrive by private automobile on many major highways. In this case, a sampling method is employed, sometimes involving a tourist information center. Those stopping at the center are asked to fill out a card with data about their trip. The total number of visitors is then estimated, based on the sample obtained.

Visitors coming through seaports should be classified according to the United Nations' definition of tourists and excursionists. Excursionists remain in an area for less than 24 hours, whereas tourists stay 24 hours or longer. Arrival statistics should not include those who enter the country illegally, air travelers who do not leave the airport transit area, or analogous cases.

Visitor-Days or Visitor-Nights

Data on **visitor-days** and **visitor-nights** are much more valuable to tourism planners than are data on the number of arrivals. To calculate the former, the number of visitors is multiplied by their average length of stay. Public park planners and beach managers are interested in visitor-day figures. Hotel and other accommodations people want data on visitor-nights. When such data are obtained, it is not difficult to make an estimate of the likely expenditures made per visitor per day or night. But these expenditure figures are at best only estimates and need to be used carefully. Data on visitor-days and visitor-nights are of great benefit to planners who work on public facilities for tourists, such as utility systems, parking, and recreation areas. Similarly, private developers planning new hotels or other accommodations or services want and need visitor-night information. Thus, visitor-days and/or visitor-nights are the most practical data to obtain and are useful to tourism people.

$$D = \text{No. of visitors} \times \text{Avg. no. of days or nights at destination}$$

Amount Spent

Amount spent is the most meaningful measure of demand, if it is determined accurately. However, it is the *most* difficult measure to obtain. Statistics of this type tend to be hidden or partially forgotten by the visitor. Thus, they are not as accurate as desired. However, to members of legislatures and the public, total tourist expenditures are the most easily understood and the most impressive.

The most common method of estimating tourist expenditures is to multiply visitor-days or visitor-nights by the average per-day or per-night expenditure. Thus,

$$D(\$) = \text{No. of visitor-days or visitor-nights} \times \text{Avg. expenditures per day/night}$$

Total expenditures in an area consist of the visitor-day and visitor-night total expenditures over a specified period of time.

Measuring Tourism Expenditures through Tax Collections

Many states have a sales and use tax on consumer items. These tax collections provide a statistical base for calculating tourist expenditures. Suppose that a state has a 4 percent use tax on hotel and motel rooms. If we know what percentage of the average tourist dollar is spent for lodging, we could make an estimate of how much is spent on lodging and total expenditures, as illustrated in the following hypothetical example:

Rooms tax collections = $5 million

Rooms use tax rate = 4 percent

Total lodging spending = $5 million ÷ 0.04 = $125 million

Lodging expenditures = 25 percent of total spending

Total expenditures = $125 million ÷ 0.25 = $500 million (visitor-nights)

Estimated spending of those not using commercial lodging + Visitor-day spending = $600 million

Total $D(\$) = \$500$ million + $600 million = $1.1 billion

Research in Measuring Demand

Considerable interest exists in improving methods of measuring current demand. Tourism is a labor-intensive service industry. As such, it is looked upon by state governments as a promising business to relieve unemployment. But one of the main problems is to determine its current financial dimensions.

Official tourism organizations are typically charged with the responsibility of undertaking research to measure economic impact and current demand. In this task they are assisted greatly by the U.S. Travel Association (USTA). Details on research are provided in Chapter 18. The next research task is to make an estimate of what the future demand might be should certain steps be taken by the destination area.

PROJECTION METHODOLOGY

Several statistical methods or econometric analyses can be used to project demand. All require a degree of statistical or mathematical sophistication, familiarity with computers, and a clear understanding of the purpose (and limitations) of such projections. Listed are several such methods with brief explanations. For a more complete review, see the references for this chapter at the end of the book.

Trend Analysis Method

The trend analysis method involves the interpretation of historical demand data. For instance, if a record of the number of tourist arrivals in an area on an annual basis is available, then demand for future years can be projected using this information. The first step is to plot the available data on a graph: time (in years) against the tourist arrivals. Once this has been done, a linear trend can be established that best captures the changes in demand levels in the past. Demand projections for future years can now be made by extending the trend line up to the relevant year and reading the demand estimate off the graph. Figure 13.1 illustrates this procedure. The points represent the levels of demand for the six-year period for which data are available.

Projecting restaurant sales was an easy task until the great recession of 2008–2009 caused sales to decline after 16 years of steady increases. Such changes make forecasting more difficult, but trend analysis is still a useful tool for making projections. Tourists enjoy food in many settings. Here, tourists are dining in the lovely Golf Club restaurant with excellent food and views. *Photo courtesy of The Broadmoor.*

A linear trend in demand levels can then be determined (say, line *AB*). If a demand projection for year 10 were needed, the trend line *AB* can be extended to a point such as *C*. Finally, the projected demand level in year 10 can be determined to be approximately 180,000 arrivals, as shown in Figure 13.1.

The advantage of using trend analysis is that the data needed are rather basic and easy to obtain. Only one data series is required: visitor arrivals, or some other measure of demand on a quarterly or on an annual basis for the past few years. In addition, the method is simple and does not require a great deal of mathematical sophistication. Characteristically, however, the simplicity of the model is to a large extent a trade-off for the usefulness of the results. For instance, the future demand estimates obtained in this manner should be interpreted with a great deal of caution. There are several reasons

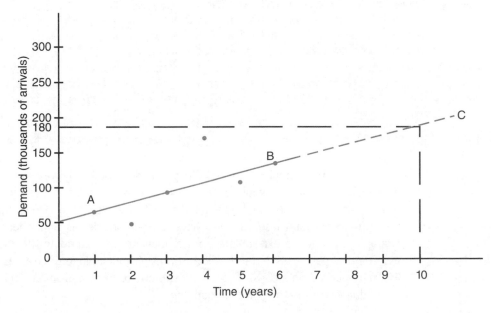

Figure 13.1 Trend analysis.

SUZANNE COOK
President, Suzanne Cook Consulting,
LLC and Senior Advisor, U.S. Travel
Association

For more than three decades, Suzanne Cook served as the senior vice president of research for the U.S. Travel Association, the industry's leading "umbrella" trade association, providing economic and marketing research and analysis to benefit its members and support industry efforts involving promotion and advocacy. The comprehensive program she developed and directed includes the Travel Economic Impact Model, the only national model that provides consistent and comparable estimates of both domestic and international travel's economic impact at the national, state, and local levels. She was also instrumental in the creation of several consumer research programs designed to monitor the size, characteristics, and growth of existing and emerging travel markets on an ongoing basis, such as TravelHorizons™, a quarterly, forward-looking survey conducted in conjunction with the Ypartnership. She was also the principle architect of travelgreen.org, the primary source for information on sustainability efforts within the travel community, and some of our industry's best efforts, developed in partnership with American Express.

Suzanne now serves as senior advisor to the association related to its research and strategic initiatives. She continues to author the monthly e-newsletter *U.S. Travel Outlook*, which monitors ongoing travel industry performance; synthesizes relevant economic, social, and consumer trends that can affect travel; and provides regular forecasts and qualitative analysis about the future of U.S. travel. She also serves as general manager of U.S. Travel's Marketing Outlook Forum, the industry's leading strategic forecasting conference, is a frequent speaker at industry conferences, and has been cited frequently in leading national media. Suzanne has also been appointed senior executive associate with the Consumer Insights and Brand Strategy Group of the Ypartnership, a leading marketing service company serving the travel industry. In addition, she has established her own company, Suzanne Cook Consulting, LLC, specializing in research, strategic planning, and presentations for destinations and travel corporations.

Prior to joining the U.S. Travel Association, Suzanne held the position of senior project director for the Arbitron Company, a major broadcasting research firm. She is an adjunct faculty member at The George Washington University, where she received her doctor of philosophy degree in social psychology, and has taught graduate level courses in research methods and statistics in Washington, D.C., abroad, and online. She also served as president and chairman of the board of the International Travel and Tourism Research Association (TTRA), and is currently the chairman of the board of governors for the Alexandria, Virginia, Convention & Visitors Association. *Travel Agent* magazine named Suzanne as one of the most powerful women in the travel industry. She is the recipient of TTRA's highest and most prestigious award, The Lifetime Achievement Award, as well as the Access to Freedom Award given by the Society for Accessible Travel & Hospitality.

WORDS ABOUT THE FUTURE

The future belongs to those who best understand and serve the current needs of their customers, while also being attentive to major demographic, social, economic, political, environmental, technological, global and other trends that are likely to affect our industry and customers in the future. This requires a rigorous approach to research, built on appropriate theoretical underpinnings, familiarity with the knowledge base of other relevant research, and great attention to the reliability and validity of the research methods used. It also requires curiosity and creativity—a focus on developments in the world around us and the trends as they evolve, as well as the ability to extrapolate these trends so as to gain new insight into the most likely scenarios for the future.

for this. First, trend analysis does not "explain" demand in any way. In other words, if demand changes from year to year, we would expect this to be because of changes in the components of demand (propensity and resistance, as discussed earlier in this chapter). Trend analysis does not acknowledge the influence that these variables have on demand levels and, therefore, cannot explain why it changed. Second, to *extrapolate* from a linear trend (extending the trend line AB to point C) is to assume that past growth trends will continue without change. Such an assumption is tentative at best. Estimates based on a constant growth rate tend to become very unrealistic in rather short periods of time, due to the nature of compounding.

TABLE 13.1 Demand and Income Data

Year	Number of Tourist Per Arrivals (thousands)	Capita Income of Tourists (dollars)
1	75	$6,300
2	90	7,200
3	100	7,000
4	105	7,400
5	95	6,800
6	110	7,500
7	105	7,500
8	100	7,200
9	110	7,600
10	120	7,900

Simple Regression: Linear Least Squares Method

In simple regression, information on demand levels for past years is plotted against one important determinant of demand, say, income or prices. Then, through the application of a statistical technique called least squares regression, a straight line is used to "explain" the relationship between demand and the particular variable being considered (such as income levels of tourists). Consider, for example, the hypothetical data in Table 13.1 for demand levels for ten years and the income levels of tourists for these same years.

By plotting the pairs of arrivals and income data on a graph, we obtain a relationship between income and travel demand, illustrated in Figure 13.2. The points represent the annual observations, and the line *AB* represents the line of "best fit." It is obtained by the least squares method. We can now obtain demand projections from this method based on what we expect income levels to be in the future. Suppose we wish to estimate demand for year 15. In this year, income is projected to be $8,300 per capita. As shown in the figure, the estimate of demand for this income level is 128,000.

Because income is a major determinant of demand, simple regression "explains" demand to some extent. It is superior to trend analysis for this reason. Besides, the methodology is still relatively simple and can be presented visually. Data needed for this method are relatively easy to collect, when compared to the data needs of the two following projection methods.

Multiple Regression: Linear Least Squares Method

The major drawback of simple regression is that only one variable can be considered at a time. In reality, demand is affected by all the factors that influence propensity and resistance, as discussed earlier. It may not be feasible to include all these variables at one time, but it is certainly practical to isolate a few that are particularly relevant to determining demand and deal with these in one model. Multiple regression is one way to do this. It is essentially the same as simple regression, except that now more than one variable can be used to explain demand. Through a mathematical formula, a relationship is established between demand and the variables that we have chosen to consider in the model. For example, suppose that we had data on the prices of tourist services at a destination in addition to the incomes of the tourists. We could then regress demand on these two variables (income

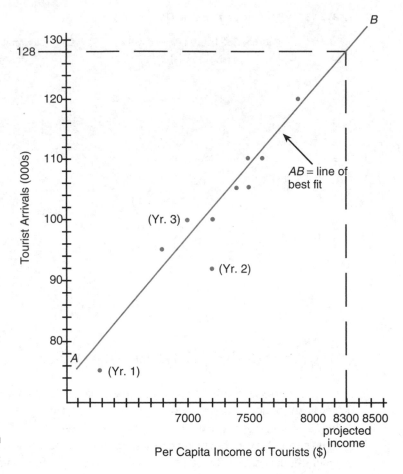

Figure 13.2 Relationship between income and travel demand.

and prices) and obtain a mathematical relationship between them. To estimate future demand, projected income and price levels for the relevant year can simply be substituted into the mathematical formula. The resulting estimate of demand will be more reliable than will one obtained by the simple regression method, because the former incorporates the *combined* effect of income and price on demand.

Indeed, the analysis is not restricted to these two variables alone. Conceptually, any number of variables can be used to explain and predict demand levels. But there are some practical limitations. As the number of "explanatory" variables increases, the calculations become increasingly complex. In addition, the costs involved in collecting the additional data and solving the mathematics of the technique are considerable. In some instances, the incremental reliability of the estimates may not justify these expenses, because estimates are after all only estimates and are not certain to materialize—no matter how comprehensively they may be calculated.

In addition to the expense involved, another drawback of multiple regression is that the relationships cannot be depicted graphically, as the results of the two earlier methods can be. The reason is, of course, that we get into multidimensional planes. Up to three dimensions can be depicted visually, but beyond that it becomes impossible.

Computer Simulations and Models

Another projection method is to build a computer model that will simulate tourist demand. Typically, the demand for tourism to a particular area is a function of factors such as levels of income of tourists, the cost of travel from the tourists' homes to the destination, price levels, competition, currency

Cruise travel is forecasted to continue to be the fastest-growing sector of the travel industry. This forecast is based on survey research, past trends, demographics, customer satisfaction, marketing efforts, and new ships joining the fleet. *Photo by Andy Newman; courtesy of Carnival Cruise Lines.*

exchange rates, and distance or journey time. These relationships are usually identified using multiple regression, as already discussed.

Computer simulation models include a complex set of equations that will usually combine both the trend-line extrapolation methods and the regression-technique models into a more comprehensive systems simulation. Relationships between many variables are specified through interrelated equations. Simulation models rely on historical data for input and model calibration. Once a model gives reasonably accurate distributions for past years, it can be used to predict probable future distributions.

Simulation models require specially trained personnel with a high degree of technical expertise to set up original model and data processing programs. Knowledge of time-series, cross-sectional, and causal relationships and change processes is required. Also, powerful computing resources and high data precision are necessary. These are serious problems that have to be faced by any tourism organization that might consider using this approach. Simulation forecasting is best suited for a problem that is complex with known and quantifiable relationships and some feedback effects. It is also suitable for long forecast horizons.

Executive Judgment (Delphi) Method

Mathematical and statistical models are most useful and often produce accurate results. However, the combined experience of tourism executives is also valuable. The Delphi method, in essence, consists of a systematic survey of such experts. A series of questions is asked, and then the results, as a consensus, are reached. An example of the **executive judgment** method is the United Nations World Tourism Organization (UNWTO) Panel of Tourism Experts, where 250-plus experts contribute information on tourism trends.

Mathematical statistical tools cannot incorporate the influences of variables not explicitly included in the model. For example, under multiple regression, income and travel prices were the only two variables used to predict demand. However, other factors, such as the political situation, fuel situation, changes in taste, amounts of leisure, and the effectiveness of promotion campaigns, obviously have an impact on demand levels. By the Delphi method, the combined effects of all such factors are carefully considered from the base of the executive's experience. For estimating tourism demand, then, a combination of various mathematical statistical methods and the **Delphi method** is believed to produce the most reliable demand estimates in any given situation. Of course, to implement this combination of methods is costly and time consuming—and as such, requires a full commitment.

❖ GLOBAL INSIGHT ❖

Tourism Forecasts

There are several places to turn for tourism forecasts. One of the best is the World Travel and Tourism Council (WTTC) Web site (www.wttc.org), where you will click on Economic Data Search. This will allow you to access forecasts for the current year and ten years out for 13 regions and 181 countries without charge. WTTC and its research partner, Oxford Economics (OE), use a sophisticated combination of macroeconomic research and forecasts, national accounting data, travel and tourism variables, and econometric modeling to product forecasts covering concepts of travel and tourism demand, gross domestic product, and employment.

Another source is UNWTO's *Tourism: 2020 Vision*, a long-term forecast that covers the development of tourism for the first 20 years of this century. It is a quantitative forecast covering a 25-year period, with 1995 as the base year and forecasts for 2010 and 2020. They also publish *Tourism Indicators*, which cover international tourist arrivals and receipts that are useful for making forecasts. Visit www.unwto.org.

For tourism forecasts for the United States, one needs to turn to the U.S. Travel Association (USTA). USTA has instituted several major industry forecast programs for travel volume and trends. These include the Marketing Outlook Forum proceedings *Domestic Outlook for Travel and Tourism*, and the *International Outlook for Travel and Tourism*. Its travel forecast predicts total travel expenditures in the United States will reach $862.7 billion in 2012. Visit www.ustravel.org.

For Asia-Pacific tourism forecasts, contact the Pacific Asia Travel Association (PATA) and purchase their *Asia Pacific Tourism*

Forecasts 2010–2012. PATA forecasts are published annually and provide a comprehensive numeric insight into the patterns of growth in the region. Visit www.pata.org.

The Canadian Tourism Commission's Research and Statistics section provides an outlook on travel volumes for the upcoming travel season. It also tracks trends and maintain statistics and figures that are useful in preparing forecasts. Its Web site is www.CanadaTourism.com.

Tourism Australia has established the Tourism Forecasting Committee (TFC). The TFC is an independent body charged with providing present and potential tourism investors, industry, and government(s) with consensus forecasts of activity for the international, domestic, and outbound tourism sectors. The resources for the TFC are provided by Tourism Australia. Its forecast prepared in June 2010 of inbound arrivals sees an increase of 4.9 percent in 2011, and then with growth easing will average 3.9 percent a year over the 10-year period to 2019. Visit www.tourismaustralia.com.

These examples reflect the importance of forecasting demand as an essential tool of tourism planning and are indicative of the types of effort that many national tourism offices engage in.

DISCUSSION QUESTIONS

1. Why is it important to forecast tourism expenditures? Tourism arrivals?

2. What is the best source of tourism forecasts?

SUMMARY

Demand, without doubt, is the fundamental measure of any area's success in attracting visitors. All planning activities are ultimately intended to increase or control demand. Marketing programs are aimed at increasing demand, sometimes at certain periods during the year, and/or to attract particularly identified market segments.

Understanding demand requires a knowledge of its definition, what demand comprises, what affects the levels of demand, and how future demand can be identified and estimated. Thus, use of demand data is essential in any tourist business situation.

Development of a destination area, whether by public authority, private developers, or both, requires demand data that are as accurate as possible. Providing such data is one of the most important responsibilities of an official tourism organization. Similar data are provided by research organizations and consulting firms, usually when commissioned to make feasibility studies. Any development proposal must have ample estimates of expected demand before any financing can be committed.

Becoming familiar with methods of measuring or estimating present and future demand, as described in this chapter, should enable you to produce such data. With the current high cost of land and construction, reasonably accurate demand statistics are of paramount importance.

❖ **KEY CONCEPTS** ❖

amount spent	executive judgment (Delphi method)	seasonality
computer simulation	least squares regression	simple regression
cost of services	multiple regression	tax collections
cultural distance	propensity	trend analysis
demand	quality of service	visitor arrivals
demand projections	resistance	visitor-days
economic distance	sales and use tax	visitor-nights

❖ **INTERNET EXERCISES** ❖

The Internet sites mentioned in this chapter plus some selected additional sites are listed for your convenience on the companion Web site for this book, www.wiley.com/college/goeldner.

ACTIVITY 1

Site Name: Office of Travel and Tourism Industries

URL: www.tinet.ita.doc.gov

Background Information: The Office of Travel and Tourism Industries functions as the U.S. federal tourism office. Its core responsibility is to collect, analyze, and disseminate international travel and tourism statistics for the U.S. Travel and Tourism Statistical System.

Exercise

1. What statistical data are available at this Web site that would help a tourism professional determine the demand for travel and tourism?

ACTIVITY 2

Site Name: Hong Kong Tourism Demand Forecasting System

URL: www.tourismforecasting.net/hktdfs

Background Information: This Web site is a part of the research project "Developing a Tourism Demand Forecasting System for Hong Kong." The project also sponsors the Tourism Forecasting Special Interest Group of the International Institute of Forecasters (www.forecasters.org).

Exercises

1. Go to 'project details' on the Web site and find the four specific objectives of the project.

2. What is the current time period forecasts are being made for?

❖ **QUESTIONS FOR REVIEW AND DISCUSSION** ❖

1. Why are demand data so important? Give examples. By whom are demand data used?

2. Explain why resistance to make a trip is inversely related to demand. Are there situations with which you are familiar? Explain.

3. Describe in detail the three factors that determine propensity to travel. Create an example using all three of these major elements.

4. What determines the degree of resistance to travel experiences? Considering the five factors described in this chapter, give an example involving: (1) an irresistible travel offer, and (2) a seasonal travel product.

5. Using the three measures of demand presented, describe a situation in which each one of these would be the most meaningful.

6. A state tourism director wants to convince the legislature to increase the promotion budget for the next fiscal year. What measure of demand should be used? How might these data be obtained?

7. How much faith should be placed in mathematical models of demand projection? What characteristics of input data affect the degree of reliability?

8. A national lodging chain is planning expansion. What are the best methods for estimating future demand?

9. How valuable is trend analysis?

10. What is the Delphi method?

❖ **CASE PROBLEMS** ❖

1. Assume that the federal government has imposed an increase in the gasoline tax of 50 cents per gallon, effective in three months. How might a motel franchise headquarters organization estimate the effect on demand that this new tax would have for their member motels, which are located in all parts of the country? How could a restaurant chain organization operating turnpike food services make such an estimate? How could a regional airline?

2. Byron C. is director of development for a major hotel systems firm. His company has formulated a new concept in resort-type overnight and longer-stay accommodations. The new suites will possess an exciting array of electronic entertainment features, including a large screen, stereo sound, movies, and DVDs. Understandably, these suites are quite expensive to build. Thus, reasonably accurate demand forecasts are essential. Byron C. has tentatively selected your city as a location for the first of these new suite concepts. As executive vice president of your city's convention and visitors bureau, what method would you use to assist Mr. C. in making these crucial demand estimates?

Tourism's Economic Impact

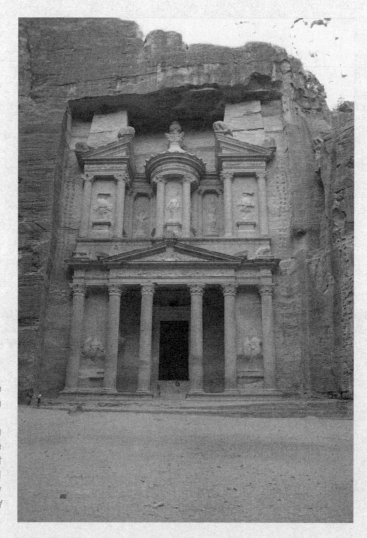

Petra is without doubt Jordan's most valuable treasure and greatest tourism attraction—an economic anchor of tourism. Petra is a vast, unique city, carved into sheer rock. When Petra was designated a UNESCO World Heritage Site in 1985, it was described as "one of the most precious cultural properties of man's cultural heritage." It has been named one of the new seven wonders of the world. *Photo courtesy of Angus McIntyre, 1995.*

INTRODUCTION

Tourism is a powerful economic force providing employment, foreign exchange, income, and tax revenue. The generators of economic impact for a city, a state, a province, a country, or a destination area are visitors, their expenditures, and the multiplier effect. The economic impact of tourism spending is a function of the numbers of domestic and international visitors and their expenditures (see Chapter 1). Because of the economic importance of tourism, the United Nations World Tourism Organization (UNWTO) maintains statistics by region and country on tourism arrivals (visitors) and both tourism expenditures (what a country spends) and receipts (what a country receives from visitor expenditures). Tourism destinations are becoming increasingly competitive as more and more destinations look at tourism to become the new economic generator replacing declining activity in agriculture, mining, and manufacturing.

As noted by the members of the International Academy for the Study of Tourism (IAST) who recently, with a special issue of the *Journal of Travel Research*, presented their insights on "The Global Economic Crisis and Tourism." IAST noted specifically, "The Global Financial Crisis (GFC) has seen financial, business, and consumer confidence sink to almost record low levels. Tourism spending has experienced greater falls than other consumer spending, affecting outbound, inbound, and domestic tourism flows and with that, the economic contribution of tourism to destinations worldwide. Declining asset prices and wealth have affected the ability of firms to fund debt and invest. Credit availability and the derisking of bank balance sheets have also stifled tourism investments with consequent impacts on employment in the industry."[1] The detailed nature of the decline in tourism arrivals and receipts in 2009 throughout the world is shown in Tables 14.1 and 14.2, respectively.

TOURISM'S ECONOMIC IMPACT: AN INTERNATIONAL PERSPECTIVE

Reflecting the impacts of the global financial crisis of 2008 and 2009, international tourist arrivals declined by 4.2 percent in 2009 to $880 million (Table 14.1). International tourism receipts reached US$852 billion (611 billion euros) in 2009, corresponding to a decrease in real terms of 5.7 percent on 2008 (Table 14.2), which shows that receipts were not very much more affected by the crisis than arrivals.[2]

In 2009, there were only slight changes in the ranking of the first ten destinations by international tourist arrivals and receipts. France continues to lead the ranking of the world's major tourism destinations in terms of arrivals and ranks third in receipts. The United States ranks first in receipts and

TABLE 14.1 International Tourist Arrivals

	Arrivals (million)		Change Rate (%)	Market Share (%)
	2008	**2009**	**2009[a]/2008**	**2009**
World	919.0	880.0	−4.2	100.0
Africa	44.3	45.6	2.9	5.6
Americas	140.9	140.1	−4.6	15.9
Asia and the Pacific	184.0	181.6	−1.3	20.6
Europe	482.6	460.0	−5.7	52.2
Middle East	56.0	453.2	−4.9	6.0

[a]Data as collected in UNWTO database, June 2010.

Source: UNWTO World Tourism Barometer, United Nations World Tourism Organization, June 2010.

TABLE 14.2 International Tourist Receipts

	$US (Billion)		Change Rate Local Currencies (%)	Market Share (%)	Receipts per Arrival ($US)
	2008	**2009**	**2009[a]/2008**	**2009**	**2009**
World	$942.0	$852.0	−5.7	100.0	$970
Europe	473.7	413.3	−6.5	52.2	900
Asia and the Pacific	208.9	203.2	−0.9	20.6	1,120
Americas	187.6	166.2	−9.8	15.9	1,180
Africa	30.0	28.7	−4.0	5.2	630
Middle East	41.5	41.8	−3.7	6.0	790

[a]Data as collected in UNWTO database, June 2010.

Source: UNWTO World Tourism Barometer, United Nations World Tourism Organization, June 2010.

second in arrivals. Spain maintains its position as the second biggest earner worldwide and the first in Europe, and ranks third in arrivals. China and Italy rank fourth and fifth, respectively, in arrivals, and in reverse order for receipts.

Europe is the main tourist receiving region (Table 14.1), followed by Asia and the Pacific, and the Americas. In 2009, Europe accounted for more than 52 percent of the arrivals, Asia and the Pacific 20.6 percent, and the Americas 15.9 percent. However, all regions except Africa saw a decline in arrivals. The decline is from −5.7 percent for Europe, to −4.9 for the Middle East, and −4.6 for the Americas, while Africa grew by a modest 2.9 percent.[3]

Table 14.2 shows international tourism receipts by region in U.S. dollars for 2009. An analysis of the data in Table 14.2 shows that international receipts declined by $90 billion, for a 5.7 percent decrease. Every region recorded a decrease in receipts in U.S. dollars. Europe again led with $413.3 billion for a 52.2 percent share.

Asia and the Pacific leaped into second place with receipts of $203.2 billion for a 20.6 percent market share, with the Americas falling to third with receipts of $166.2 billion for a 15.9 percent market share. The Middle East recorded receipts of $41.8 billion for a 6.0 percent share, and Africa recorded receipts of $28.7 billion for a 5.2 percent share.

Receipts per arrival averaged $970. The Americas averaged the highest receipts per arrival at $1,180, followed by Asia and the Pacific with an average of $1,120, Europe with $900, the Middle East with $790, and Africa with $630.

The data in Tables 14.1 and 14.2 are preliminary data and, as with most statistical data, will undergo revision as time passes and the database is updated and improved. Go to the UNWTO Web site www.unwto.org to get the latest data.

Expectations for 2010 and Beyond

Prospects for the future appear to be positive. Travel statistics indicate tourism is resilient and overcomes negative factors relatively quickly. Although oil prices, the economy, and terrorism are always causes for concern, tourism appears to be on target to achieve 2020 forecasts.

Tourism 2020 Vision is the United Nations World Tourism Organization's long-term forecast and assessment of the development of tourism through the first 20 years of the new millennium. An essential outcome of *Tourism 2020 Vision* are quantitative forecasts covering a 25-year period, with 1995 as the base year and forecasts for 2000, 2010, and 2020.[4]

UNWTO's *Tourism 2020 Vision* forecasts that international arrivals are expected to reach over 1.56 billion by the year 2020. Of these worldwide arrivals in 2020, 1.18 billion will be intraregional and 377 million will be long-haul travelers.

Hot Springs, Fairy Caves, the Colorado River, a ski resort, dude ranches, and easy access via Interstate 70 provide Glenwood Springs, Colorado, with a vibrant tourism economy. *Photo courtesy of Hot Springs Lodge and Pool.*

The estimates of total tourist arrivals by region show that by 2020, the top three receiving regions will be Europe (717 million tourists), East Asia and the Pacific (397 million), and the Americas (282 million), followed by Africa, the Middle East, and South Asia. East Asia and the Pacific, South Asia, the Middle East, and Africa are forecasted to record growth at rates of over 5 percent, compared to the world average of 4.1 percent. The more mature regions of Europe and the Americas are anticipated to show lower-than-average growth rates.

Europe will maintain the highest share of world arrivals, although there will be a decline from 60 percent in 1995 to 46 percent in 2020. By 2010, the Americas will lose its number-two position to the East Asia and Pacific region, which will receive 25 percent of world arrivals in 2020, with the Americas decreasing from 19 percent in 1995 to 18 percent in 2020.

Long-haul travel worldwide will grow faster, at 5.4 percent per year over the period 1995 to 2020, than intraregional travel, at 3.8 percent. Consequently, the ratio between intraregional and long-haul travel will shift from around 82:18 in 1995 to close to 76:24 in 2020.[5]

COMPARING INTERNATIONAL AND DOMESTIC EXPENDITURES

Despite the glamour of international tourism (that is, tourists traveling outside of their country of residence), for many (if not most) countries, domestic tourism (tourists traveling in their country of residence) is more important. As shown in Table 14.2, the UNWTO estimated (based on preliminary figures) that international travel involved receipts of US$852 billion in 2009. In contrast, the World Travel and Tourism Council estimated that in 2007, both international and domestic travel together generated about US$1,851.2 billion. As can be seen from these estimates of the magnitude of international and domestic travel, the latter is much greater than the former. This fact surprises many people who primarily think of tourism as being exotic, international travel.

Employment

The World Travel and Tourism Council estimates that in 2010, employment in the total (direct and indirect) travel and tourism economy was 235,785,000 jobs, or 9.1 percent of total employment, which is 1

Antoni Gaudí's most ambitious and still under-construction architectural marvel, La Sagrada Familia—or the Holy Family Church—is a favorite landmark amongst visitors touring the city of Barcelona. *Photo courtesy of PhotoDisc, Inc./Getty Images.*

Tourists from around the world are driven to the warmth and relaxation that the gorgeous aqua waters and beaches of the Caribbean provide all year round. *Photo courtesy of Digital Vision.*

Tourists are drawn to marketplaces, such as this Tokyo outdoor market, to shop for local food ingredients and interesting souvenirs. *Photo courtesy of Corbis Digital Stock.*

◆ Considered one of the top technology capitals of the world, Tokyo boasts an impressively lit cityscape and is home to numerous unique and state-of-the-art venues—an experience that visitors would not want to miss. *Photo courtesy of PhotoDisc, Inc./Getty Images.*

◆ Safari vacations to the Serengeti can be an enriching experience of a lifetime, allowing visitors to encounter nature at its most raw and untampered state. *Photo courtesy of PhotoDisc, Inc./Getty Images.*

The towering glaciers adorning the calm waters of Prince William Sound in Alaska are truly an ethereal sight to behold. *Photo courtesy of Digital Vision.*

Architectural beauty, history, and pop culture intertwine to lure tourists at every season to visit L'Arc de Triomphe, which stands majestically in the busy center of the Place Charles de Gaulle in Paris. *Photo courtesy of Corbis Digital Stock.*

One small path can lead to the beauty of an ocean expanse. *Photo courtesy of photographer Erin Whittle and the Wilmington/Cape Fear Coast CVB.*

The Byzantine-inspired white stone domes of the Sacré Coeur Basilica, located at the very top of hilly Montmartre, can be seen towering over what many locals consider the best and most dazzling panoramic view of Paris. *Photo courtesy of ImageState.*

The spectacle of an airshow is awe inspiring. *Photo courtesy of Lumberton Visitors Bureau, Lumberton, NC. Visit www.lumberton-nc.com.*

 A romantic air surrounds the Schloss Neuschwanstein Castle as it stands proudly against the breathtaking backdrop of the Bavarian Alps in Fussen, Germany. *Photo courtesy of Corbis Digital Stock.*

Native tour guides row visitors on rafts along the beautiful calm waters of the Martha Brae River in Jamaica. *Photo courtesy of Digital Vision.*

The hot springs famous to Yellowstone National Park are an always intriguing tourist site for all ages to experience the natural wonders of the Earth. *Photo courtesy of Corbis Digital Stock.*

The exhilaration and adrenaline-rush one can only gain from skiing through stunning snowcapped mountains, such as those in Matterhorn, Switzerland, lure visitors from around the world to test the peaks. *Photo courtesy of Corbis Digital Stock.*

The Geysers in New Zealand allow for a fun and exciting natural attraction for tourists to marvel at the amazing features of the land. *Photo courtesy of ImageState.*

Visitors to other countries may encounter exciting, traditional celebrations on their travels, much like this street celebration in Singapore, for a new and enriching cultural experience. *Photo courtesy of PhotoDisc, Inc./Getty Images.*

Tourists are drawn to the center of Beijing to witness the Forbidden City's astounding collection of ancient Chinese buildings dating back to the Ming Dynasty. *Photo courtesy of Corbis Digital Stock.*

The Glacial Channel in South Island, New Zealand, is an awe-inspiring natural sight to witness. *Photo courtesy of Digital Vision.*

Alaskan waters boast a wide range of whale inhabitance, making it a coveted whale-watching destination for tourists who wish to catch a glimpse of these remarkable mammals before their migration periods. *Photo courtesy of Purestock.*

The historic Victoria Railway Station in Bombay is one of India's busiest railway stations, and is a great starting point for tourists who wish to undertake the city's rapidly growing transportation system. *Photo courtesy of Corbis Digital Stock.*

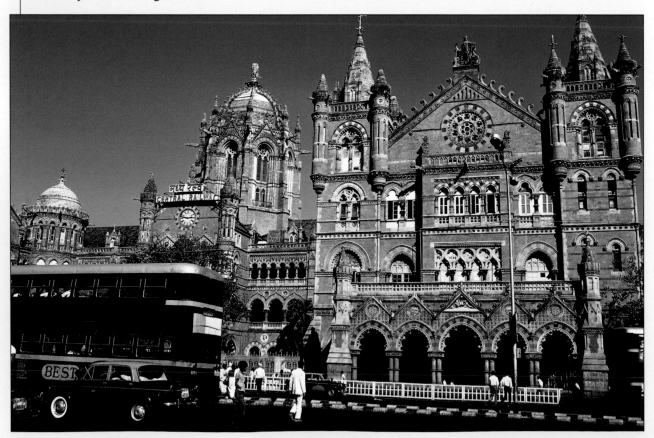

An aquarium such as the North Carolina Aquarium at Fort Fisher provides a glimpse into the underwater world. *Photo courtesy of the North Carolina Aquarium at Fort Fisher.*

Hot air ballooning is a unique experience that can attract tourists' attentions. *Photo courtesy of New Mexico Tourism Department.*

Two kimono-clad female students play the Koto, a Japanese string instrument, in Hawai'i—a popular tourist location where Japanese traditions contribute largely to the evolving Hawaiian culture. *Photo courtesy of PhotoDisc, Inc.*

A visit to a horse race for many can be a once-in-a-lifetime experience. *Photo courtesy of Arkansas Department of Parks and Tourism.*

✥ From this expansive view of Antigua's capital city of St. John's, the baroque towers of St. John's Cathedral can be seen raised high above the city infrastructure. *Photo courtesy of Digital Vision.*

✥ A tourist boat carries visitors along the River Li, one of the largest and most scenic rivers in China. *Photo courtesy of Flat Earth.*

✥ Tourists are driven to the Badlands National Park of South Dakota to witness the colorful and multifaceted canyons and hills chiseled down by millions of years' worth of weather and erosion. *Photo courtesy of PhotoDisc/Getty Images.*

Visitors can get a taste of renaissance when visiting Egeskov Castle in Denmark, which is considered one of Europe's best-preserved moat island castles. *Photo courtesy of Digital Vision.*

The intricately designed red clay buildings of Morocco are a striking view for visitors to absorb and appreciate. *Photo courtesy of Corbis Digital Stock.*

✤ Interactive history experiences bring the past to the present and are wonderful learning environments for people of all ages. *Photo courtesy of Conner Prairie Interactive History Park.*

✤ Rookeries of penguins settle on patches of ice amongst other wildlife in the glacial waters of the Antarctic. *Photo courtesy of Digital Vision.*

The expansive beauty of the Grand Canyon gives tourists an appreciation for the natural world that surrounds them. *Photo courtesy of Robert Glusic/PhotoDisc/Getty Images.*

TABLE 14.3 Impact of Travel on U.S. Economy

Travel Expenditures ($ billions)										
	2000	**2001**	**2002**	**2003**	**2004**	**2005**	**2006**	**2007**	**2008**	**2009**
Direct Expenditures	$585.8	$555.7	$544.9	$560.1	$606.9	$653.7	$695.7	$738.0	$772.5	$704.4
Domestic	503.4	483.8	478.3	495.8	532.4	572.0	610.0	641.3	662.4	610.2
International[a]	82.4	71.9	66.6	64.3	74.5	81.7	85.7	96.7	110.1	94.2

[a]*Not including international passenger fares.*

Source: U.S. Travel Association, U.S. Department of Commerce Office of Travel and Tourism Industries.

Travel-Generated Employment (Thousands)										
	2000	**2001**	**2002**	**2003**	**2004**	**2005**	**2006**	**2007**	**2008**	**2009**
Direct Travel-Generated Employment	7,779.7	7,673.1	7,440.5	7,336.0	7,452.7	7,508.8	7,550.5	7,699.6[a]	7,705.9	7,393.6
Domestic	6,788.4	6,728.6	6,561.6	6,521.2	6,569.3	6,613.9	6,657.0	6,728.5	6,709.2	6,510.0
International	991.3	944.5	878.9	814.8	883.4	894.9	893.5	971.4	996.8	883.6

Source: U.S. Travel Association, U.S. Department of Commerce Office of Travel and Tourism Industries.

in every 12.3 jobs. By 2020, this should grow to 303,019,000 jobs, 9.2 percent of total employment or 1 in every 10.9 jobs. The 81,913,000 direct travel and tourism industry jobs accounted for 2.5 percent of total employment in 2008 and are forecast to rise to 104,740,000 jobs or 2.8 percent of the total by 2020.[6]

As noted above, tourism provides both direct and indirect employment. Firms such as hotels, restaurants, airlines, cruise lines, and resorts provide direct employment because their employees are in contact with tourists and provide the tourist experience. Employees of firms providing goods and services to the direct employment firms, such as aircraft manufacturers, construction firms, tourism consultants, and restaurant suppliers, create indirect employment.

The impact of this can be illustrated using a U.S. example. In 2010, the U.S. Travel Association (USTA) published its annual study, *Tourism Works for America*, which contains estimates of travel-generated employment in the United States. As shown in Table 14.3, in 2009 tourism directly generated a total of about 7.4 million jobs in the U.S. economy. An examination of Table 14.3 also reveals that in 2009, 6.5 of the 7.4 million direct jobs were due to domestic tourism, with 883,600 generated by international travel. Thus, while international visitors to the U.S. account for only 3 percent of total U.S. travel, they represent as much as 13 percent of the U.S. travel-related spending.

Visitors to the U.S. overall spend more than domestic travelers on their travels, on average $2,200 when they visit. And travel and tourism is the largest services sector export of the entire U.S. economy. It accounts for 8 percent of all U.S. exports (and 25 percent of services sector exports) and continues to make an outsized contribution to growth in trade, according to the U.S. Department of Commerce.

In 2009, the United States was visited by 54.9 million international travelers, down 5.3 percent from the previous year. Declines are attributed to the adverse effects of a troubled world economy and challenges in U.S. entry procedures facing inbound travelers. Growth is expected in 2010 (up 2.9 percent) and in each subsequent year through 2013.

Travelers from outside U.S. borders visiting for leisure and business purposes are frequently segmented into two groups: those from Canada and Mexico (the two largest generators of inbound travel) and long-haul travelers from overseas markets.

Canada is the number-one source market for travel to the United States, accounting for 33 percent (18.0 million visitors) of all international travel to the United States in 2009. Visitors from Mexico are the second largest source of inbound travel, 24 percent of international travel in 2009 (13.2 million).

Visits from Canadian and Mexican travelers were a bright a spot in inbound travel over the past decade, up 23 percent from 2000, or 5.9 million more North American visitors.

❖ **GLOBAL INSIGHT** ❖

Travel Advisories

Since an important role of every country's government is to help protect their citizens, many countries issue "travel advisories," "travel warnings, "travel advice," or "consular information sheets." Whatever the specific name, this information is intended to provide information on the safety and security conditions, entry requirements, and more for countries worldwide.

Canadian "Travel Reports & Warnings" can be found on the Web site (www.voyage.gc.ca). Essentially, Canada identifies nine levels of concern, with appropriate warnings to travelers. The United Kingdom Foreign and Commonwealth Office (FCO, www.fco.gov.uk/en/travel-and-living-abroad/) issues travel advice notices in four categories:

1. Countries the FCO advises against all travel to

2. Countries the FCO advises against all travel to parts of

3. Countries the FCO advises against all but essential travel to

4. Countries the FCO advises against all but essential travel to parts of

In the United States, travel warnings are issued when the State Department decides, based on all relevant information, to recommend that Americans avoid travel to a certain country. Countries where avoidance of travel is recommended will have travel warnings as well as consular information sheets.

Although travel advisories are generally regarded as positive, they frequently raise objections on the part of travel destinations that believe they have been unnecessarily identified—thus, unfairly restricting visitation by both leisure and business travelers and creating a negative economic impact.

DISCUSSION QUESTIONS

1. What is the economic impact of travel advisories?

2. Are travel advisories or warnings fair?

Visitors from these two countries had a combined average spending of about $790 on their U.S. trips (not including international passenger fares). The overseas travel segment represented less than half of all international arrivals (43%) to the United States in 2009, yet accounted for 80 percent of total international traveler receipts in the United States. Overseas travel is also referred to as *long-haul,* meaning it is international travel outside of a respective origin region. Overseas visitors stay longer and spend more when they visit the United States than other travelers, on average more than 16 nights with spending in excess of $4,000.[7]

The complexity of accurately measuring the vast economic impacts of the tourism industry has created a movement to link tourism expenditure accounting with that used for the national system of accounting in most countries. Earlier attempts to include tourism in the standard industry classification (SIC) codes proved unsuccessful because of the diversity and overlapping nature of many tourism expenditures. In order to overcome these difficulties, a system of tourism satellite accounting has been proposed and implemented. The Tourism Satellite Account (TSA) is discussed later in the chapter.

OPTIMIZATION

Economics is concerned with the attainment of an *optimum* return from the use of scarce resources. Whether it is a person seeking psychological benefit from travel, or a business interested in providing tourists goods and services at a profit, or a host community government viewing tourism in terms of the economic benefits resulting from tourist expenditures, the principle is the same. In economic terms, optimization occurs when agents seek to allocate the limited supply of tourism resources (both physical and financial) in the best possible way to meet the demands of tourists. The demands are the result of their physical/functional needs (which, as a rule, are limited) and their psychological wants (which can be virtually unlimited).

Optimizing the tourist experience is both a managerial and a personal challenge. In this instance, the hotel guests appear to be optimizing at the personal level. *Photo courtesy of Gaylord Opryland.*

As such, the problem that economics attempts to solve is how to achieve an economical optimal allocation of scarce tourism resources when facing the constantly shifting demand (generated by physical needs and psychological wants) for these resources.

Goals

As indicated, at least three major goals can be identified in tourism:

1. Maximize the quality of psychological experience for tourists.
2. Maximize profits for firms providing goods and services to tourists.
3. Maximize the direct (primary) and indirect (secondary) benefits of tourist expenditures on a community or region.

These goals are often compatible; maximizing psychological experience creates happy clientele, which causes them to return, to spend money, and to make everyone in the industry and the region satisfied. In certain situations, they can also be incompatible.

A short-run profit-maximizing goal might cause the development of facilities beyond the capacity of the site, thus leading to overuse and a decline in psychological enjoyment. Extreme emphasis on tourism as an element in economic development might have the same result. There can also be clashes between the use of resources for tourism and for other kinds of development.

Constraints

The second half of the optimizing situation is occupied by those factors that place obstacles in the way of goal attainment. We assume that it is desirable to have unlimited amounts of psychological enjoyment, profits, and local economic impacts. But that is not possible because something always gets in the way. Tourism, being extremely broad and diverse, must deal with a large number of constraints. To make an analysis of relationships, it will be necessary to classify them.

Demand

Every firm providing goods and services to tourists is constrained by the demand functions of its customers. These relate quantity purchased to price, wealth, and income.

Supply of Attractive Resources

Possibly one of the most important constraints faced by the industry as a whole is the limited amount of resources available for tourist enjoyment. This is particularly true when geographic distribution of these sites is considered. Some areas are simply better attractions for tourists than others are.

Technical and Environmental Constraints

Each particular site or situation has certain technical and environmental constraints. They involve such things as the relationship between sewage effluent disposal and the environment, numbers of fish and numbers of fishermen, number of people who can walk in a given area without causing unacceptable damage, number of elephants supportable on a wildlife range, impact on lions' behavior of tourists observing them from a car, number of campsites possible in a given area without harming the environment, and so on.

Time Constraints

The amount of vacation time available limits what the vacationer can do. The length of the tourist season influences profitability of tourist-oriented businesses and the impact of tourist expenditures on the local economy.

Indivisibilities

Many times it is necessary to deal either with all of something or with nothing. It is not possible to fly half an airplane, even though the seats are only half filled. It may not be profitable to build a hotel under a given size. A road has to be built all the way from one point to another.

Legal Constraints

Several types of legal constraints affect tourism. Activities of the government tourist bureau might be one. Laws concerning environmental problems could be another. Zoning and building codes influence the construction of facilities. Laws concerning contractual relations may limit activities.

Self-Imposed Constraints

Conflicting goals need to be reconciled, which leads to self-imposed constraints. The conflicts may arise within a firm or among firms, government agencies, and so on, that are seeking to develop a particular area or concept.

Lack of Knowledge

Many activities are limited because little is known about particular situations. Businesspeople are used to living with a certain amount of uncertainty, but there are inevitable limits to the amount they are willing to countenance. Ignorance influences governmental operations as well.

Limits on Supportive Resources

There are always limits to the amount of money, managerial talent, workers, construction materials, social capital, and so on. And these, in turn, limit chances to provide psychological enjoyment, take advantage of profit-making opportunities, or develop local attractions. Many times these individual constraints interact, creating compound constraints on given activities.

Optimizing the Experience

Maximization of the tourist experience is subject to a number of constraints and is manifested in the demand function. Demand for tourist experience is peculiar in the sense that the product being purchased is not easy to identify directly and is frequently purchased sight unseen.

The tourist is particularly constrained by time and budget. To optimize the experience, it is necessary to determine the combination of destinations preferred and then the possibilities within the money and time constraints. This explains some of the popularity of package tours, where both time and cost can be known in advance. There are some exceptions. Retired persons and young people often have time but limited resources. A few people have neither constraint.

Optimizing Returns to Businesses

Because goods and services provided to tourists are really inputs to the process of producing the experience, demand for them is derived from demand for tourism as a whole. Some goods and services are complementary, and their demand is interrelated in a positive fashion. Others are substitutes and are characterized by limited area competition.

Packaged tours have the characteristic of putting all parts and services together, so they become complementary. Competition occurs among tours. Tour operators can maximize profits by selling tours of different value and costs, in order to cater to as many people as possible along the demand curve. The number of people to be accommodated can be determined from the marginal cost of the tour and the marginal revenue to be derived from a given price level.

Goods and services sold to tourists are subject to severe peaking in demand. That is, the heaviest tourist season is usually limited. During that period, demand is intense and must be met with facilities that are excess in the off-season. This means that investment necessary to provide the excess capacity must be paid for from revenues received during the peak period. During off-peak periods, only variable cost is of interest, but because demand is low, some capacity will not be utilized.

As owners of the facilities, firms are concerned with providing adequate long-run capacity and with choosing those investments that will give optimum returns. In the tourist industry, a number of interrelationships must be considered. Sometimes low benefit-cost investments are made so that higher-yielding investments can succeed. Consequently, it is not always true that investors choose the highest-yielding opportunities.

Generally, it is considered the long-run goal of the firm to remove constraints on operations. But tourism has a number of constraints to expansion. These include demand for the tourist experience and environmental constraints.

Optimizing for the Local Economy

Tourism affects a region during periods of intense investment activity and afterward when the investments are producing. The effects depend on linkages among economic units. Money spent for investment will go to construction and a few other industrial sectors. These will have links to economic units varying from households to manufacturing plants. Money spent by tourists will also be introduced through a few sectors that will also be linked to the economy.

The multiplier effects in both cases depend on the strength of the linkages. The multiplier reflects the amount of new economic activity generated as basic income circulates through the economy. Some sectors have strong links to other sectors in an economy and a large multiplier effect. Others have weak links and small multipliers. It is possible to have a thriving tourist industry and abject poverty in the local populace if there are no links. For example, linkages will be strong and the income multiplier high if the year-round resorts in a particular destination area hire all local labor; buy their flowers, fruit, vegetables, and poultry products from local farmers; hire local entertainers; and buy furnishings for guest rooms from local manufacturers. Linkages would be weak if most of these goods and services were imported from another state or country.

Tourism Exports and Imports

The host region is defined loosely as a county, a state, or a nation, depending on the level at which the problem is being considered. For a county-level government, the income of the county is of primary interest. A state government would perceive the maximization of the combined income of the entire state to be its objective, and so on.

Regardless of which definition of host region is being considered, expenditures in this area by tourists coming from another region represent injections into the area's economy.

Japanese tourists traveling to the United States presumably earned their income in Japan. When spending money in the United States as tourists, they are "injecting" money into our economy that wasn't here before. As such, expenditures by foreigners in this country (for travel purposes) represent tourism exports for the United States. This may be somewhat confusing because we are accustomed to thinking of something leaving the country as an export. When we export computers or cars, for example, these commodities are sent out of the United States. In the example of the Japanese tourists, the tourists are coming into this country. So how is it an export? There seems to be a contradiction in terminology. As the astute student would note, however, when tourists come into this country, they are purchasing travel experiences. When they leave, they take these experiences back with them. Thus, we have exported travel experiences, which are, after all, what tourism is all about.

Figure 14.1 clarifies this concept. When U.S. tourists travel to Japan and spend money there, this becomes a tourism import to the U.S. economy. Japanese money spent in the United States is a

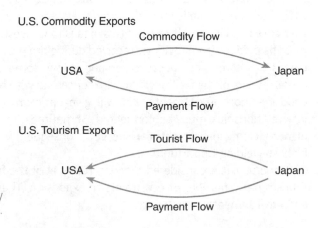

Figure 14.1 Economic comparison: Commodity flow and tourist flows.

tourism import for the Japanese economy. In tourism exports, the flows of tourists and payments are in the same direction, whereas in commodity exports, the two flows are in opposite directions. Therein lies the confusion. However, if one were to look at the *direction of payment flow* to determine what is an export, there is no contradiction between the two cases. When payment flows into the United States, something has been exported—travel experiences, for instance, or commodities. Both payment flows are in the same direction.

Balance-of-Payments Effects

Tourism is one of the world's largest international industries. As such, it has a noticeable impact on the **balance of payments** of many nations. We have heard much about the balance-of-payments problems of the United States, and, indeed, tourism imports do affect the balance of payments and economic conditions generally. We define tourism imports as those expenditures made by American tourists in foreign countries. An easy way to remember this is to ask, "Who got the money?" If, for example, Great Britain received American funds, it makes no difference whether an American bought some English china or an American tourist visited England.

Our balance-of-payments situation directly affects the gross domestic product (GDP) of the United States (Y). The formula is

$$Y = C + I + G + (X - M)$$

where

Y = gross domestic product
C = consumer expenditures
I = investments
G = government expenditures
X = exports
M = imports

By looking at the formula, we can see that if imports (M) exceed exports (X), then the difference ($X - M$) will be a negative number, and Y will thus be smaller. Thus, it is advantageous to the U.S. economy to attract more visitor spending in the United States. These "tourism exports" are like credits and help the U.S. economy. It is economically better to have foreign visitors come to the United States than it is to have U.S. citizens travel abroad. However, this should be tempered with the realization that the situation is not entirely positive or negative.

Expenditures by U.S. tourists abroad make possible purchasing power in those countries to buy American-made products. For example, most airlines of the world use U.S.-made equipment. Purchase of these aircraft, parts, supplies, repair services, and so forth makes an important contribution to the export trade of the United States; thus, we cannot charge the U.S. international traveler with a total negative balance of payments. The purpose of the foregoing discussion is simply to point out the relationships.

Tourism exports become very desirable as far as the gross domestic product and the prosperity of the country are concerned. Efforts on the part of national tourism offices to attract foreign visitors have a great impact on the balance-of-payments situation. Business firms that serve the foreign visitor, provide desired services, and stimulate sales materially help our national economy. However, during periods when the U.S. dollar is high against foreign currencies, a dampening effect occurs on our tourism exports because this situation is seen as unfavorable by prospective foreign visitors. Conversely, if the dollar is low, more foreign tourists will visit the United States. This increases our tourism exports, improves our balance of payments, and raises the GDP. These same relationships of comparable currency values exist between any country that exports tourism and the countries of its tourists' origin.

In 1998, the value of the Canadian dollar was low in comparison to the U.S. dollar and illustrated this principle. The number of Americans visiting Canada to take advantage of the exchange rate increased

Houseboating on Lake Powell, Glen Canyon National Recreation Area, is a major attraction in Utah and delivers a significant economic impact for the region. *Photo courtesy of Lake Powell Resorts and Marinas.*

dramatically. This contributed positively to Canada's balance of payments. Today, the Canadian dollar is strong, so more Canadians are visiting the United States, contributing positively to the U.S. balance of payments.

Investment Stimulation

The tourist industry has a unique structure. It is characterized by and, in fact, is an agglomeration of a large number of very small units, covering a variety of different service trades—the small restaurants, motels, guest houses, laundries, arts and crafts shops, and others. Thus, investment in infrastructure and sometimes expensive superstructure by the government stimulates investment in numerous smaller businesses. Because of the small size of these businesses, capital requirements are relatively low and investment generally proceeds at a rapid pace. In this respect, too, governments view tourism rather favorably. The initial investment in tourism brings forth a large investment in supporting and tertiary industries. This also includes large investments in major hotels, restaurants, shopping centers, marinas, airports, and so on.

Tourism Increases Tax Revenue

Tourists must pay taxes like most other people. Because they come from other regions or countries, their expenditures represent an increased tax base for the host government. In addition to the usual sales tax, tourists sometimes pay taxes in less direct ways. Airport taxes, exit fees, customs duty, and charges assessed for granting visas are just a few examples of commonly used methods of taxing tourists. The wisdom of imposing such special taxes on tourists is questionable, because it merely serves to reduce demand. In some countries, for instance, the room rate at a hotel can be different for tourists (generally higher) than for residents. This is a questionable practice, because it leaves tourists with a feeling that they have been "taken." Apart from these special cases, the usual taxes collected from both tourists and residents increase because of tourism expenditures.

Is tourism, then, a panacea for all the economic woes of a region or country? It has been claimed that tourism increases incomes, employment, investment, tax revenues, and so forth, so it might indeed appear to be one. However, constraints limit the extent to which governments can maximize the benefit from these aspects of tourism. These constraints are of two types: social and economic. The social constraints have already been discussed. The economic constraints are in the form of potential economic costs that the tourism industry may impose. These merit further scrutiny to gain a better understanding of the government's optimization problem.

Inflationary Pressure

Tourists inject money (earned elsewhere) into the destination economy. Although this increases the income of the region (as discussed earlier), it also might cause inflationary pressures. Tourists typically have a higher expenditure capability than the residents do—either because tourists have higher incomes or because they have saved for the trip and are inclined to "splurge" while on vacation. Hence, they are able to somewhat bid up the prices of such commodities as food, transportation, and arts and crafts. This causes inflationary pressures, which can be detrimental to the economic welfare of residents of the host community. This is particularly true when inflation affects the prices of essentials such as food, clothing, transportation, and housing. Land prices have been known to escalate rapidly in tourist destination areas. The prices that foreigners are willing to pay for vacation homes in the area can decrease the demand for first homes by residents—or as presently in the United States, help correct past excesses.

✦ GLOBAL INSIGHT ✦

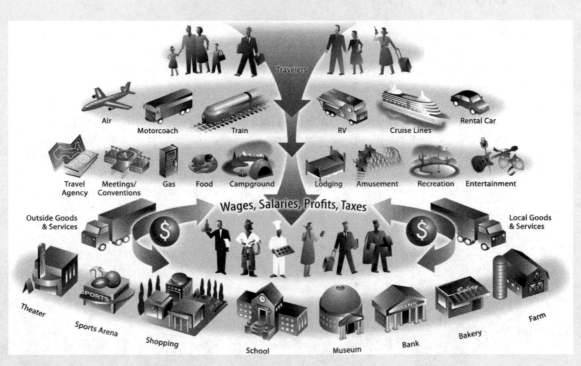

The Power of Travel. *Source: TIA*

DISCUSSION QUESTIONS

1. How does the tourism multiplier work?

2. Discuss how tourism dollars flow in your home community.

Lundberg notes that as the tourist industry developed in an area, land prices rose sharply.[8] In a particular underdeveloped area, the amount of investment in land constituted just 1 percent of the total investment for a hotel project. By contrast, this ratio increased to 20 percent in an area where tourism was already overdeveloped. With such increases in land prices, it can be expected that local residents (with their lower incomes) are effectively "chased out" of the housing market in a tourism-developing section.

ECONOMIC MULTIPLIERS

Direct Effect

In addition to the **direct impacts** of tourism expenditures on an area, there are also **indirect impacts**. The indirect or multiplier impact comes into play as visitor spending circulates and recirculates. The direct effects are the easiest to understand because they result from the visitor spending money in tourist enterprises and providing a living for the owners and managers and creating jobs for employees.

Indirect Effect

This visitor expenditure gives rise to an income that, in turn, leads to a chain of expenditure-income-expenditure, and so on, until leakages bring the chain to a halt. Consequently, the impact of the initial income derived from the tourist's expenditure is usually greater than the initial income, because subsequent rounds of spending are related to it. For example, a skier purchases a lift ticket for $60. This money received by the ski area will be used to pay the wages of the lift operators. The lift operator spends the money on groceries; the grocer uses the money to pay part of his rent to the local landlady; the landlady uses it to pay for her dry cleaning; the dry cleaner spends it in a restaurant for a dinner; the restaurant owner spends it for steaks shipped in from Kansas City; and the cycle stops as the money is lost to the local economy. This last transaction is known as **leakage** from the economy. The combination of the direct and indirect effects of an expenditure pattern determines the impact. In a

Shopping is one of the top tourist activities and good for the local economy. The money spent by tourists circulates and recirculates, creating an economic multiplier. *Photo courtesy of Glenwood Hot Springs Sport Shop in Glenwood Springs, Colorado.*

typical situation, not all of the income generated in each round of expenditure is respent. Some portion tends to be saved, and some portion tends to be spent outside the local economy. The greater the proportion of income spent locally, the greater will be the multiplier.

The degree to which a local area is able to retain tourist income depends on how self-sufficient the local economy is. If the local economy is able to produce the goods and services tourists buy, the greater will be the multiplier effect. The more goods that have to be imported from outside the region, the smaller the multiplier will be.

From the discussion, it is clear that when a tourist's spending injects funds into the economy of a host area, an economic effect occurs that is a specified number of times what was originally spent. Initially, this effect is thought of as an income multiplier, as tourist expenditures become income directly and indirectly to local people. However, there are additional economic phenomena. Increased spending necessitates more jobs, which results in an employment multiplier. Because money changes hands a number of times during a year, there is a transactions multiplier. This is of particular interest to governmental tax officials where sales taxes are imposed. As business grows in a tourist destination area, more infrastructure and superstructure are constructed. This results in a capital multiplier. Examples are provided here of how an employment multiplier and an income multiplier were determined.

Employment Multiplier

The employment multiplier varies from region to region depending on its economic base. In a study titled *Recreation as an Industry,* by Robert R. Nathan Associates, county employment multipliers calculated for the Appalachian region provide a good illustration of what typical multipliers are and how they work.[9]

The multipliers estimated in this study were based on county employment data. They represent the approximate measure of the direct and indirect employment associated with each addition of direct employment to the export sector of a county. Multipliers were estimated for 375 counties and three independent cities. The smallest multiplier was 1.13, and the highest was 2.63. Thus, the county with the smallest multiplier value would provide other employment opportunities for approximately 0.13 person for each person directly employed in servicing export demand, and the county with the highest multiplier value would provide other employment opportunities for approximately 1.63 persons for each person directly employed in servicing export demand. In general, county employment multipliers vary directly with the population or total employment size of the counties: As county population size grows, so does the multiplier value. This relationship is as might be expected, insofar as import leakages would tend to be less where diversity of occupations is greater, and diversity is positively associated with county population or total employment.

Income Multiplier

Jobs mean income, which stimulates the economy of the area in which the development occurs. How much stimulation occurs depends on several factors. The management of a hotel, for example, takes two actions with the revenue earned: It spends parts of the money on goods and services, and it saves part of such funds. Economists refer to such actions as marginal propensity to consume (MPC) and marginal propensity to save (MPS)—removing funds from the local economy. Such removal of these marginal (extra) funds can be made in two ways: (1) they can be saved and not loaned to another spender, or (2) they can be used to purchase imports. In either case, so doing removes the funds and thus does not stimulate the local economy.

Economic research is needed in a tourist destination area to determine what these income relationships are. If the results of such economic research were made available, many beneficial results might be possible. For example, governmental bodies might be more inclined to appropriate

TABLE 14.4   Formula for the Multiplier

$$\text{Multiplier} = \frac{1}{1 - MPC}$$

where

M = marginal (extra)

P = propensity (inclination)

C = consume (spending, MPC)

S = savings (money out of circulation, MPS)

Suppose $1,000 of tourist expenditure and an MPC of $\frac{1}{2}$. Then

$1,000.00
+
$500.00 $\frac{1}{2} \times 1,000$
+
250.00 $(\frac{1}{2})^2 \times 1,000$
+
125.00 $(\frac{1}{2})^3 \times 1,000$
+
62.50 $(\frac{1}{2})^4 \times 1,000$
+
31.25 $(\frac{1}{2})^5 \times 1,000$
+
15.63 $(\frac{1}{2})^6 \times 1,000$
+
7.81 $(\frac{1}{2})^7 \times 1,000$
. . .
$2,000.00 (approx.)

$$\text{Multiply}: \frac{1}{1 - \frac{1}{2}} \times \$1,000, \text{ or } 2 \times \$1,000 = \$2,000$$

Thus, the original $1,000 of tourist expenditure becomes $2,000 of income to the community.

additional funds for tourism promotion to their areas if they knew more about the income that was generated by tourist expenditures. Also, improved and added developments of facilities to serve tourists might be more forthcoming if prospective investors could have more factual data upon which to base decisions.

To understand the multiplier, we must first make some approximation as to what portion of the tourist dollars received in a community is spent (consumed) and what portion is saved (leakage). To illustrate this, suppose that we had a total of $1,000 of tourist spending in a community and that there was an MPC of 0.5. The expenditure pattern might go through seven transactions in a year. These are illustrated in Table 14.4. The other formula for the multiplier is 1/MPS. This is a simpler formula, because it is the reciprocal of the marginal propensity to save. If the marginal propensity to save were 0.34, the multiplier would be 3. This is shown in Table 14.5.

Leakage, as defined, is a combination of savings and imports. If we spend the money outside our country for imports, obviously it does not stimulate the economy locally. If it is put into some form of savings that are not loaned to another spender within a year, it has the same effect as imports—not stimulating the economy. Thus, to get the maximum benefits economically from tourist expenditures, we should introduce as much of the tourist funds as possible into the local economy for goods and services rather than save the proceeds or buy a large amount of imports.

TABLE 14.5 "Leakage"

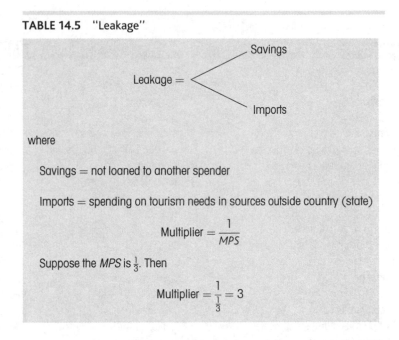

$$\text{Leakage} = \begin{cases} \text{Savings} \\ \text{Imports} \end{cases}$$

where

Savings = not loaned to another spender

Imports = spending on tourism needs in sources outside country (state)

$$\text{Multiplier} = \frac{1}{MPS}$$

Suppose the *MPS* is $\frac{1}{3}$. Then

$$\text{Multiplier} = \frac{1}{\frac{1}{3}} = 3$$

Here, also, more economic research is needed. Some studies have indicated that the multiplier might be as high as 3.0 in some areas, but economic research in other localities indicates that it may be more typically lower than this.

Economic Benefits Widely Distributed

Using a conceptual approach, you should realize that tourism is characterized by the existence of a large number of very small businesses that support and are ancillary to the industry. The receipts from tourism quickly filter down to an extremely broad cross section of the population, so that the entire community shares the economic benefits. Table 14.6, based on a partially hypothetical example, illustrates how quickly tourism receipts seep through the economy and the diversity of the businesses that benefit from tourism. As the table indicates, the tourism dollar is shared by more than 70 distinguishable types of enterprises in just two rounds of spending.

Structural Changes

In countries that primarily rely on a single industry, such as agriculture, the introduction of tourism has often led to a decrease in the agricultural base of the country. Agriculture is an extremely low-productivity industry in the developing countries. The promise of much higher wages in the tourism industry draws people away from farming. Agricultural output declines as a result, just when the demand for food increases because of the influx of tourists. The inflationary pressure on food prices is further aggravated and can lead to considerable social upheaval. In the mid-1970s, some Caribbean countries experienced a wave of protests and even direct attacks on tourists, as the resident population expressed its dissatisfaction over rising prices.

Another major implication of the structural change is that instead of diversifying its economic base, the country's tourism sector merely "cannibalizes" other major economic sectors. Diversity is the foundation of economic stability. When one sector (or industry) experiences a slump, another sector booms, thus reducing the probability of a severe depression and, indeed, reducing its impact if a

316 ❖ Chapter 14 Tourism's Economic Impact

TABLE 14.6 Distribution of Tourism Expenditures

Visitors Spend for	Travel Industry Spends for	Ultimate Beneficiaries	
Lodging	Wages and salaries	Accountants	Government
Food	Tips, gratuities	Advertising and public	Education
Beverages	Payroll taxes	relations	Health
Entertainment	Commissions	Appliance stores	Roads and railroads
Clothing, etc.	Music and entertainment	Architects	Utilities
Gifts and souvenirs	Administrative and general expenses	Arts and crafts producers	Development and others
Photography	Legal and professional services	Attorneys	Greengrocers
Personal care	Purchases of food, beverages, etc.	Automobile agencies	Grocery stores
Drugs and cosmetics	Purchases of goods sold	Bakers	Financiers
Internal transportation	Purchases of materials and supplies	Banks	Furniture stores
Tours and sight-seeing	Repairs and maintenance	Beach accessories	Importers
Miscellaneous	Advertising, promotion, and publicity	Butchers	Insurance agencies
	Utilities—electricity, gas, water, etc.	Carpenters	Landlords
	Transportation	Cashiers	Laundries
	Licenses	Charities	Manufacturing agents
	Insurance premiums	Chemists	Managers
	Rental of premises and equipment	Clerks	Motion picture theaters
	Interest and principal payments of	Clothing stores	Newspapers, radio, etc.
	borrowed funds	Clubs	Nightclubs
	Income and other taxes	Confectioners	Office equipment suppliers
	Replacement of capital assets	Contractors	Painters
	Return to investors	Cooks	Pastoralists
		Cultural organizations	Plumbers
		Dairies	Porters
		Dentists	Printers, sign painters
		Department stores	Publishers
		Doctors	Real estate brokers and
		Dry cleaning establishments	developers
		Electricians	Resorts
		Engineers	Restaurants
		Farmers	Room maids
		Fishermen	Shareholders
		Freight forwarders	Sporting events
		Garages and auto repairs	Transportation
		Gardeners	Travel brokers
		Gas stations	Taxi, limo services
		Gift shops	Unions
			Wholesale establishments

Source: Pannell Kerr Forster and Belt Collins and Associates.

depression does occur. Thus, tourism, instead of diversifying an economy, sometimes replaces agriculture as a "subsistence" sector.

Dependence on Tourism

Permitting tourism to become the subsistence industry is not desirable, for a number of reasons. First, tourism is, by its very nature, subject to considerable seasonality.

Although seasonal fluctuations in demand can sometimes be reduced, they cannot be eliminated. Thus, when tourism is the primary industry in an area, the off-season periods inevitably result in

Seasonal fluctuations in tourism result in an uneven source of revenue. During the winter months, skiers enjoy powder snow and make a significant contribution to the Colorado economy. Here, skiers and snowboarders have just arrived on Amtrak and are headed for Sunlight Mountain Resort and Ski Area.
Photo courtesy of Glenwood Springs Chamber Resort Association, Colorado.

serious unemployment problems. Such areas find that the seasonal character of tourism leaves severe economic and social effects on the host region.

Another very important reason relates to the source of demand for tourism. The demand for tourism depends largely on the income and the tastes of tourists, both of which are beyond the control of the host region. When the American economy goes through a slump, demand for travel to a foreign destination by Americans will fall off. A destination area can do precious little, in this case, to increase the level of demand. If the tastes of the people in the tourist-generating area change—that is, they decide to travel to a new destination—tourism in the old area will decline, causing economic and social problems. Again, the destination can do little or nothing to avoid this. In fact, as Plog[10] points out, there is reason to believe that such a decline in an area's popularity may be largely inevitable. Quite clearly, then, tourism should not be allowed to grow to an extent that the destination area becomes totally dependent on it.

In other words, total dependence on a single industrial sector is undesirable. If it cannot be avoided, then dependence on domestic agriculture is in many ways preferable to dependence on tourism. The country has presumably adapted itself economically and socially to dependence on agriculture over several centuries. The demand for agricultural output is also unlikely to suffer from a secular decline, because people must eat. Also, it is the residents, not foreigners as in tourism, who directly benefit from agricultural production.

Investment Priorities

Sometimes governments of developing countries take an overly optimistic view of tourism. They undertake aggressive investment programs to develop tourism, assigning it top priority in their development plans. In extreme cases, such an approach can lead to the neglect of more fundamental investment needs of the country. For example, funds can be channeled into tourism development at the cost of education, health, and other social services—aspects of the social well-being of the population that should be of primary concern for a developing country. Not

TABLE 14.7 Relationships between Price Elasticity and Total Revenue (TR)

	Elastic Demand ($|\epsilon p| > 1$)	Unitary Elasticity ($|\epsilon p| = 1$)	Inelasticity Demand ($|\epsilon p| < 1$)
Price rises	*TR* falls	No change	*TR* rises
Price falls	*TR* rises	No change	*TR* falls

only is undue glamorization of tourism unwise because it usurps this position, but such a strategy only speeds up the process of dependence on tourism, which, as discussed earlier, can be itself undesirable. Moreover, investment in tourism at the cost of health and education programs also slows down the rate at which the local population is assimilated into the modern market economy of the country. Under certain circumstances, it may actually retard development rather than enhance it.

The conclusion is that although tourism has tremendous potential as a tool in economic development, it is no panacea. Governments should attempt to optimize (not maximize) the benefits that tourism provides, being ever mindful of the costs that it can impose. It should be noted also that the probability and the intensity of the economic costs of tourism are greater for developing nations (or regions) than for wealthy ones. Wealthy nations, by definition, possess robust economies that can more easily absorb the cost of tourism. Typically, such economies are well diversified, and government investment programs are not so central to development efforts.

The social benefits and costs of tourism should be viewed similarly. Although the host community seeks to maximize the benefits, it must weigh these against the social costs. The social costs are likewise higher in both probability and magnitude when tourism is being considered for development in an area that still possesses a traditional social structure.

Quantity Demanded and Price Elasticity

For some products, even a large change in price over a certain range of the demand curve results in only a small change in quantity demanded. In this case, demand is not very responsive to price (Table 14.7). For other products, or for the same product over a different range of prices, a relatively small change in price elicits a much larger relative change in quantity demanded. Demand can be classified as inelastic or elastic on the basis of the relative responsiveness of quantity demanded to changes in price. Specifically, price elasticity of demand may be defined as the percentage change in demand resulting from a given percentage change in price. Most tourism products are price elastic. During 1992, when U.S. airlines began offering half fares, the number of air travelers increased to record-high levels.

Income Elasticity of Demand

As income rises, more travel is demanded at any given price. Thus, the relationship between income and demand is positive. The responsiveness of demand to changes in income is called income elasticity of demand. It is defined as the percentage change in quantity demanded in response to a given percentage change in income, price remaining unchanged.

TOURISM SATELLITE ACCOUNTS

As can be seen from the beginning of this chapter, tourism makes a major economic contribution to the world economy. Despite this economic significance, tourism managers have for some time been met with complaints such as, "All the hype about tourism's contribution to economic growth and job creation is a gross exaggeration." Also, members of the industry itself want to be sure that the economic impact figures are indeed accurate so that they can better plan their investments and improve their productivity and performance.

In an attempt to ensure the accuracy and reliability of the measures of tourism's economic impact, the United Nations World Tourism Organization in collaboration with the World Travel and Tourism Council (WTTC) and with the support of the Canadian Tourism Commission (CTC), have undertaken to develop a tourism accounting system that is not only rigorous but also consistent with the national accounts of every country. This system has been named tourism satellite account.

What Is a Tourism Satellite Account?

A **tourism satellite account** (TSA) is a system developed by the United Nations to measure the size of economic sectors that are not defined as industries in national accounts. Tourism, for example, is an amalgam of industries such as transportation, accommodation, food and beverage services, recreation, and entertainment and travel agencies.

Tourism is a unique phenomenon, as it is defined by the consumption of the visitor. Visitors buy goods and services associated with both tourism and nontourism alike. The key from a measurement standpoint is to associate their purchases to the total supply of these goods and services within a country.

The TSA is a new statistical instrument designed to measure these goods and services according to international standards of concepts, classifications, and definitions that will allow for valid comparisons with other industries and eventually from country to country and between groups of countries. Such measures will also be comparable with other internationally recognized economic statistics.

In addition, a TSA possesses the following characteristics:

- Provides credible data on the impact of tourism and the associated employment
- Is a standard framework for organizing statistical data on tourism
- Is a new international standard endorsed by the UN Statistical Commission
- Is a powerful instrument for designing economic policies related to tourism development
- Provides data on tourism's impact on a nation's balance of payments
- Provides information on tourism human resource characteristics

Although it may be obvious, it is useful to stress why a TSA is needed. In brief, there is an acute shortage of information on the increasing role of tourism in national economies worldwide—hence, the need for reliable data relative to the importance and magnitude of tourism, using the same concepts, definitions, and measurement approaches as other industries. With the TSA, governments, entrepreneurs, and citizens will be better equipped for designing public policies and business strategies for tourism and for evaluating their effectiveness and efficiency.

Development of a TSA framework has been fueled by the recognition that its implementation will serve to increase and improve knowledge of tourism's importance relative to overall economic activity in a given country. It will also provide an instrument for designing more efficient policies relating to tourism and its employment aspects, and it will create awareness among the various players directly and indirectly involved with tourism of the economic importance of this activity, and by extension its role in all the industries involved in the production of goods and services demanded by visitors.

The Nature of a TSA

A TSA is characterized by the manner in which it seeks to balance measures of tourism demand against supply. Tourism measurements, in order to be credible and comparable with other industries in a country's economy, must follow concepts and definitions consistent with internationally accepted macroeconomic guidelines, such as the System of National Accounts.

The fundamental structure of the TSA therefore relies on the balance existing within an economy between, on one hand, the demand for goods and services generated by visitors and by other consumers and, on the other hand, the overall supply of these goods and services. The idea is to analyze in detail all aspects of demand for goods and services that are associated with tourism within the economy, and to measure the relationship with the supply of such goods and services within the same economy. More specifically, a TSA measures:

- Tourism's contribution to gross domestic product (GDP)
- Tourism's ranking compared to other economic sectors
- The number of jobs created by tourism in an economy
- The amount of tourism investment
- Tax revenues generated by tourism industries
- Tourism consumption
- Tourism's impact on a nation's balance of payments
- Characteristics of tourism human resources

Because of its comprehensive nature, a TSA provides decision makers with a valuable tool for planning and policy making. In particular, it provides them with reliable data of tourism's impact on the economy and employment. As well, it permits the measurement of both domestic and nonresident tourism—and the employment associated with each. A TSA, however, can do much more. Following are some examples.

A TSA can provide information on how much tourism is worth to the national economy, and how it compares to other industries and other countries. By demonstrating and using the size of tourism, tourism officials and private-sector businesses will have more influence on policy makers at all levels of government. As well, it can make clear which industries benefit from tourism and by how much—in particular, industries not traditionally associated with tourism. For instance, business enterprises can identify the role tourism plays in their success and develop business strategies accordingly.

A TSA is able to provide information regarding how much tax revenue is generated by tourism. This information is useful in convincing municipal, provincial, or federal levels of government to invest further in tourism. In addition, it provides data on visitor demand and how this demand is met by domestic supply. A TSA enables the establishment of a tourism economic impact model, which can be used to estimate the effect on the economy and on employment of various tourism expenditure shocks. Such an impact model provides a better understanding of tourism employment and where each industry ranks compared to other tourism industries.

It should be emphasized that the ongoing development of TSAs as national promotion tools has been a process dating back to at least 1993. The most recent focus of this development was a major international TSA conference held in Vancouver, Canada, in 2001. This and other conferences have brought together the following organizations: United Nations World Tourism Organization (UNWTO), World Travel and Tourism Council (WTTC), Organization for Economic Cooperation and Development (OECD), United Nations (UN), Eurostat, and a number of government statistical agencies, national tourism administrators, and central banks.

This collaboration demonstrates the general principle that in order to develop a national TSA, it is essential to involve a number of key actors within a country. The most significant of these are:

- National statistical offices, national tourism administrations (NTAs), central banks, and associations of national tourism enterprises
- Information-producing units such as tourism enterprises and establishments, and other public departments

- Users of the tourism information that is generated, the NTAs themselves, the units responsible for preparing the national accounts, and the balance of payments, and others
- The participation and collaboration of tourism enterprises and, more specifically, their corresponding national associations

Sources of Data Used in a TSA

Canada, as an Example

The data used in the calculation of a TSA in Canada come from a diverse number of surveys produced by Statistics Canada. The preparation of tourism demand estimates involve several surveys that record information on tourism consumption of Canadians traveling in and outside Canada and nonresidents traveling to Canada:

- Canadian Travel Survey
- International Travel Survey of Canadian Residents
- Canadian Resident Questionnaire for same-day automobile travel between the United States and Canada
- United States Resident Questionnaire for same-day automobile travel between the United States and Canada
- Government Travel Survey of U.S. visitors to Canada
- Government Travel Survey of visitors to Canada

Much of the information for the supply-side estimates are drawn from the worksheets used in the making of the input-output tables by industry, commodity, and employment of the System of National Accounts. Data from reference publications, and relevant business surveys and administrative data, are used to obtain as much detail as possible on revenues generated from the sale of tourism commodities.

In conclusion, a TSA recognizes that tourism is not an industry in the traditional sense—that is, identified in the System of National Accounts—because industries are classified according to the goods and services they produce (e.g., forestry), while tourism is a consumption-based concept that depends on the status of the customer. Furthermore, tourists buy many of the same products as other consumers, including items not normally associated with tourism—clothes, groceries—while Canadians at home buy tourism goods and services for nontourism reasons—restaurant meals, postcards, recreational services.

The TSA brings together these diverse aspects of tourism by providing a tourism dimension to the framework of the System of National Accounts. It makes it possible to separate and examine the demand and supply sides of tourism within an integrated system that describes the production and demand aspects of the whole economy.

The recognition of these factors has led to the situation where more than ten countries have a TSA and more than 30 are in the process of developing a TSA. These include Austria, Canada, Chile, the Dominican Republic, France, Mexico, New Zealand, Norway, Singapore, Sweden, the United States, Spain, and Italy.

SUMMARY

Domestic and international tourism are major economic strengths to many of the world's countries, states, cities, and rural areas. Thus, those who live there are affected by the economic results of tourist spending. This chapter explained why these resulting effects vary greatly and what brings about a large measure of benefits or possible detriments to a community. The main economic phenomena described are various multipliers, balance of payments, investments, tax consideration, employment, economic impact generators, travel expenditures, dependence on tourism, price and income elasticity as related to buying travel experiences, and optimization. The chapter also discussed a new method of measuring tourism economic impact, satellite accounting.

Many people do not understand or appreciate the economics of tourism. The following list summarizes the principal economic effects:

1. Expenditures by foreign visitors in one's country become exports (mainly of services). The economic effects are the same as those derived from exporting tangible goods. If there is a favorable exchange rate (foreign currency buying appreciably more of one's own country's currency), the country that has the devalued currency will experience a higher demand for visitor services than before devaluation.

2. If citizens of one country spend money in foreign countries, these expenditures become imports for the tourists' originating country.

3. Sums of the values of national exports and imports are used when calculating a nation's balance of payments. A positive balance results when exports exceed imports, thus increasing a nation's gross national product (GNP).

4. Tourism developments typically require large investments of capital. Thus, local economies where the developments take place are stimulated by such investments.

5. Tourists pay various kinds of taxes directly and indirectly while visiting an area. Thus, tax revenues are increased for all levels of government.

6. Because tourists usually spend more per day at a destination than they do while at home, these extra expenditures may cause inflationary pressures and rising prices for consumer goods in the destination area.

7. Tourism expenditures injected into the economy produce an income multiplier for local people. This is because of the diversity of expenditures made by those receiving tourist payments. Tourist receipts are used to buy a wide variety of goods and services over a year's time. The money turnover creates additional local income.

8. The amount of income multiplication, however, will depend on how much leakage takes place. Leakages are a combination of (1) imported goods and services purchased by tourism suppliers, and (2) savings made of tourist receipts not loaned to another spender within one year of receipt. Thus, the more tourist goods that are supplied locally, the higher will be the multiplier.

9. Income multiplication caused by tourist expenditures necessitates hiring more people. Thus, they also affect an employment multiplier.

10. As increased spending produces more financial transactions, they create a transactions multiplier. These are of particular interest to governments that have a sales or value-added tax on such transactions.

11. As a tourist area grows, more capital is invested in new facilities. This results in a capital multiplier.

12. It is an unwise policy for a society to place too much dependency on tourism as a subsistence industry.

13. Although tourism often has an excellent potential in economic development, it is not a panacea for economic ills. Its economic benefits should be optimized rather than maximized.

14. We believe that tourism products are mainly price elastic, meaning that as prices rise, the quantity demanded tends to drop.

15. In general, we believe that tourism is income elastic. This means that as family income rises, or a particular market's income rises, and tourism prices do not rise proportionally, the demand for travel to that particular area will increase.

KEY CONCEPTS

balance of payments	imports	multiplier effects
demand	income elasticity	optimization
direct impacts	income multiplier	price elasticity
economic impact	indirect impacts	taxes
employment multiplier	inflationary pressures	tourism satellite account
exports	leakage	

INTERNET EXERCISES

The Internet sites mentioned in this chapter plus some selected additional sites are listed for your convenience on the companion Web site for this book, www.wiley.com/college/goeldner.

ACTIVITY 1

Site Name: World Travel and Tourism Council

URL: www.wttc.org

Background Information: The World Travel and Tourism Council (WTTC) is the global business leaders forum for travel and tourism. Its central goal is to work with governments to realize the full economic impact of the world's largest generator of wealth and jobs—travel and tourism.

Exercises

1. Review the economic research for a particular region selected by either you or your instructor. What are the economic forecasts for that region?

2. What are the overall tourism forecasts worldwide?

3. What do the statistical data reveal about the United States?

4. What are the regional statistics for the region where you live?

5. What are the employment projections?

ACTIVITY 2

Site Name: Asia-Pacific Economic Cooperation (APEC)

URL: www.apec.org

Background Information: APEC is the forum for facilitating economic growth, cooperation, trade, and investment in the Asia-Pacific region.

Exercises

1. How many members does APEC have?

2. What percent of world population, world GDP, and world trade do APEC member economies account for?

3. Under member economies, what key economic indicators are listed?

QUESTIONS FOR REVIEW AND DISCUSSION

1. What is meant by optimization?

2. Discuss how an airline executive might use tourism economics relating to passenger load-factors, ticket prices, discounts, frequent-flyer programs, joint fares, and flight frequencies.

3. Selecting one form of public transportation, enumerate the economic constraints that affect this business.

4. A full-service restaurant is considering having an elaborate buffet dinner three nights a week. What constraints are likely to bear on this consideration?

5. Define tourism exports and imports in terms of national economies.

6. Explain how international tourism could assist in reducing the current sizable U.S. trade deficit. How could it increase the deficit?

7. Give several reasons why a hotel's purchasing director should be familiar with the income multiplier phenomenon.

8. Trace how tourist expenditures in a community provide financial support to the public library.

9. Enumerate various methods by which a tourist-dependent community can at least partially overcome seasonality of tourism demand.

10. Why is a tourism satellite account considered to be the best way to measure tourism's impact on the economy?

✤ **CASE PROBLEMS** ✤

1. Mr. and Mrs. Henry B. are considering taking their first trip abroad. Deciding to buy a group tour, they find that some countries in which they are interested seem to offer a much better value than do others. Assuming that the ingredients of the tours being considered are very similar, what factors are likely to account for this price difference?

2. A western U.S. state is quite popular with tourists, hosting about 6 million visitors per year. The state's director of sales and use taxes has recently advised the governor that a special 5 percent hotel and motel rooms tax should be added to the present 4 percent use tax, making a 9 percent total rooms tax. Currently, the state's budget is in the red. Thus, an increase in revenue is badly needed. What economic advice should the governor seek?

ENDNOTES

1. Sheldon, Pauline and Larry Dwyer, "The Global Financial Crisis and Tourism: Perspectives of the Academy." *Journal of Travel Research,* vol. 49, no. 1, p. 3.
2. *UNWTO World Tourism Barometer,* vol. 8, no. 2, June 2010. Madrid: United Nations World Tourism Organization.
3. Ibid.
4. *Tourism 2020 Vision* (2000). Madrid: United Nations World Tourism Organization—see Web site: http://www.unwto.org/facts/eng/vision.htm.
5. Ibid.
6. *Travel & Tourism Economic Impact: Executive Summary 2010.* London, UK: World Travel and Tourism Council—Web site:
   http://www.wttc.org/bin/pdf/original_pdf_file/2010_exec_summary_final.pdf.
7. *Travel and Tourism Works for America 2010–2011.* Washington, DC.
8. Donald E. Lundberg, "Caribbean Tourism," *Cornell Hotel and Restaurant Administration Quarterly,* vol. 14, no. 4 (February 1974), pp. 30–45.
9. Robert R. Nathan Associates and Resource Planning Associates, *Recreation as an Industry* (Washington, DC: Author, 1966), p. 57.
10. Stanley C. Plog, "Why Destination Areas Rise and Fall in Popularity," *Cornell Hotel and Restaurant Administration Quarterly,* vol. 14, no. 4 (February 1974), pp. 55–58.

CHAPTER 15

Tourism Policy: Structure, Content, and Process

LEARNING OBJECTIVES

- Demonstrate the critical importance of tourism policy to the competitiveness and sustainability of a tourism destination.

- Outline the structure and content of a typical policy framework for a tourism destination.

- Describe a process for the formulation of a destination tourism policy.

- Understand the need for a destination crisis management policy.

Developing new tourism destinations and successfully maintaining existing ones require a policy that combines competitiveness and sustainability. No trip to Sydney is complete without a tour of the Opera House, one the world's most daring and beautiful examples of twentieth-century architecture. *Photo courtesy of Corbis Digital Stock.*

INTRODUCTION

This chapter addresses an important dimension of tourism—one that is being increasingly recognized for the impact it can have on the long-term success of a tourism destination. Although the concept of "master planning" has been around for some time, the need for high-level strategic planning involving the explicit definition of major policies reflecting an ongoing consensus among all the stakeholders within a tourism destination is the outgrowth of social changes in which all citizens are demanding a greater level of participation in the formulation of policies and programs and in development that affects their daily lives.

Tourism has not escaped the pressure of this social change. As a consequence, this chapter plays several important roles in enhancing our understanding of tourism in future years. It also discusses two other global forces that all tourism destinations must now face: (1) the growing competition from both established and emerging destinations, and (2) the pressure to maintain the ecological integrity of regions affected by tourism. These two pressures together have led to the overall need to strive to build competitive and sustainable destinations (see Figure 15.1).

The impacts of September 11, 2001, the disasters in New Orleans (Katrina, 2005 and the oil spill of 2011), as well as the subsequent earthquakes in Haiti, New Zealand, and Japan (2011), illustrate the underlying significance to tourism of carefully formulating effective policies well in advance of unanticipated events. They also demonstrate the high degree of interdependence between tourism policy and a broad range of national and local policies. Some of the most obvious examples include policies regarding airline security, immigration and visitation, money laundering, and emergency health procedures. An area that has been neglected in the past may now receive greater attention.

The chapter starts by defining tourism policy and its overall purpose. It then demonstrates the broad scope of stakeholders who are affected by tourism policy, whether good or bad. Subsequent discussion focuses on the specific functions of tourism policy and describes the many areas that must be addressed by a comprehensive tourism policy.

TOURISM POLICY: A DEFINITION

Tourism policy can be defined as a set of regulations, rules, guidelines, directives, and development/promotion objectives and strategies that provide a framework within which the collective and

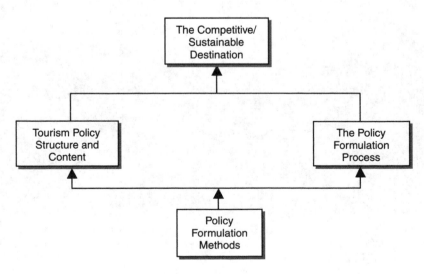

Figure 15.1 The competitive/sustainable tourist destination: A managerial framework.

- ■ Residents of the ``host'' destination
- ■ Local/municipal/regional/provincial/national governments
- ■ Local/regional/national environmental groups
- ■ Local visitors/excursionists
- ■ Remote visitors/tourists
- ■ Tourism industry sectors:
  - ☐ Accommodation
  - ☐ Attractions
  - ☐ Adventure and outdoor recreation
  - ☐ Entertainment
  - ☐ Events
  - ☐ Food services
  - ☐ Tourism visitor services
  - ☐ Transportation
  - ☐ Travel trade
- ■ Destination management organization (DMO)
- ■ Culture/heritage groups
- ■ Social/health/education groups

Figure 15.2 Examples of the many stakeholders in tourism within a given destination/region.

individual decisions directly affecting long-term tourism development and the daily activities within a destination are taken.

The Purpose of Tourism Policy

A tourism destination hosts visitors in order to provide its stakeholders (see Figure 15.2) with a broad range of economic and social benefits, most typically employment and income. This employment and income allow stakeholders to reside in and to enjoy the quality of the region. Tourism policy seeks to ensure that visitors are hosted in a way that maximizes the benefits to stakeholders while minimizing the negative effects, costs, and impacts associated with ensuring the success of the destination. In effect, tourism policy seeks to provide a framework within which the destination can provide high-quality visitor experiences that are profitable to destination stakeholders while ensuring that the destination is not compromised in terms of its environmental, social, and cultural integrity.

Why Is Tourism Policy Important?

The area of tourism policy is often overlooked in terms of its importance in ensuring the success of a tourism destination. Perhaps its most important role is to ensure that a given destination has a clear idea as to where it is going or what it is seeking to become in the long term. In parallel, it must strive to create a climate in which collaboration among the many stakeholders in tourism is both supported and facilitated. In more specific terms, tourism policy fulfills six functions:

1. It defines the rules of the game—the terms under which tourism operators must function.
2. It sets out activities and behaviors that are acceptable for visitors.
3. It provides a common direction and guidance for all tourism stakeholders within a destination.
4. It facilitates consensus around specific strategies and objectives for a given destination.

Very few attractions are as striking as the North American pronghorn antelope. Developing policies to promote tourism while ensuring the protection of wildlife demands commitment on the part of planners and sensitivity on the part of tourists. *Photo courtesy of Wyoming Division of Tourism.*

5. It provides a framework for public/private discussions on the role and contributions of the tourism sector to the economy and to society in general.

6. It allows tourism to interface more effectively with other sectors of the economy.

In light of the foregoing, it is important to keep in mind that tourism policy affects the extent to which all the day-to-day operational activities of tourism—such as marketing, event development, attraction operations, and visitor reception programs—are successful. As such, it is not just a theoretical concept; it has very real implications in day-to-day practice.

Areas Addressed by Tourism Policy

In general terms, a formal tourism policy for a given destination will address (at the national level) such areas as:

- The roles of tourism within the overall socioeconomic development of the destination region
- The type of destination that will most effectively fulfill the desired roles
- Taxation—types and levels
- Financing for the tourism sector—sources and terms
- The nature and direction of product development and maintenance
- Transportation access and infrastructure
- Regulatory practices (e.g., airlines, travel agencies)
- Environmental practices and restrictions
- Industry image, credibility
- Community relationships
- Human resources and labor supply
- Union and labor legislation
- Technology
- Marketing practices
- Foreign travel rules

THE FOCUS OF TOURISM POLICY: THE COMPETITIVE/SUSTAINABLE DESTINATION

In a complex world of many jurisdictions, it is important to explicitly identify the geographic area to which a tourism policy applies. We refer to the "generic" entity in question as the *tourism destination*. A tourism destination, in its simplest terms, is a particular geographic region within which the visitor enjoys various types of travel experiences.

Prior to the national transportation policy creating the interstate highway system, many family summer vacations were enjoyed traveling on the legendary Route 66, which has been immortalized by song and television. *Photo by Robert Holmes; courtesy of the California Division of Tourism.*

Types and Levels of Tourism Destinations

Tourism destinations are most commonly defined in formal terms by recognized political jurisdictions such as the following, listed from broadest to most local:

1. A nation or country
2. A macroregion, consisting of several countries (e.g., Europe) or other groupings that either transcend national borders (e.g., the European Riviera) or reflect economic trade zones (e.g., NAFTA [North American Free Trade Agreement] and the Americas)
3. A province or state within a country
4. A localized region within a country, such as western Canada or the U.S. Northwest or Southeast
5. A city or town
6. A unique locale, such as a national park, a historic site, or a memorial that is in itself sufficiently significant to attract visitors. (Substantive and readily identifiable institutions such as Walt Disney World in Orlando, the Hermitage in St. Petersburg, and St. Peter's Basilica in Rome might, in themselves, exert sufficient drawing power to be classified as destinations.)

THE MAJOR PARAMETERS OF TOURISM DESTINATION MANAGEMENT

Although the task of **tourism destination management** (TDM) is a complex, multidimensional challenge, when all the rhetoric is stripped away, there are two primary parameters that must be satisfied if the destination is to be successful. These are *competitiveness* and *sustainability*. Either alone is not sufficient; they are both essential and mutually supportive.

The competitiveness of a destination refers to its ability to compete effectively and profitably in the tourism marketplace. Sustainability pertains to the ability of a destination to maintain the quality of its physical, social, cultural, and environmental resources while it competes in the marketplace. A major concern in this regard is to avoid the false appearance of economic profitability, a profitability that is derived from the subtle, often invisible (in the short run) depletion of the destination's *natural capital.* Conversely, sustainability may be viewed as encouraging "natural capital investment"—that is, refraining from current consumption in order to protect the environment, and the restoration of natural stocks (those that are renewable), thus ensuring the availability of such resources for future consumption.[1]

We can see that, when viewed in the above light, successful TDM involves traditional economic/business management skills balanced with environmental management capabilities (Figure 15.3). The economic business skills required are those related to effective resource development and deployment. They include strategic planning for destination development (see Chapter 16), the marketing of the destination (see Chapter 19), the management of the human resources necessary to deliver quality visitor experiences, the management of the financial resources/investment required to support

COMPETITIVENESS (Resource Deployment) Business/Economic Management Skill	SUSTAINABILITY (Resource Stewardship) Environmental Management Capabilities
Marketing	Waste Management
Financial Management	Water Quality Management
Operations Management	Air Quality Management
Human Resources Management	Wildlife Management
Information Management	Forest/Plant Management
Organization Management	Visitor Management
Strategic Planning	Resident/Community Management
Project Development	Commemorative Integrity
Management	Recycling
	Site Protection

Information Management	
Destination Monitoring	Destination Research

Figure 15.3 Some elements of successful total tourism destination management (TTDM). Thomas Prugh et al., *National Capital and Human Economic Survival* (Solomons, MD: ISEEE Press, 1995).

development, and the ability to develop the organizational capacity to coordinate and ensure the delivery of essential services.

The environmental management capabilities are those that are critical to effective destination stewardship. Traditionally, these have included the knowledge and skills essential for ensuring the protection of air and water, forest and plants, and wildlife management.

More recently, the concept of stewardship has been expanded to encompass management practices designed to both maintain and enhance the commemorative, social, and cultural integrity of the destination. It also involves the ability to effectively manage the human presence within the boundaries of the destination. This human presence has two main components: visitor management and resident/community management.

Finally, the tasks of resource deployment and resource stewardship are linked by the shared need for a **tourism destination management information system** (TDMIS) to support policy formulation, strategic planning, day-to-day decision making, and overall performance evaluations. Information management has, in turn, two major components. The monitoring component provides stakeholders, and particularly the destination management organization, with an ongoing assessment of destination performance across a broad range of indicator variables. These indicator variables should be carefully chosen so as to be representative of the overall health of the destination in terms of both competitiveness and sustainability. Monitoring also includes an environmental scan component that seeks to identify unusual or emerging trends and forces that have the potential to significantly affect the competitiveness or sustainability of a destination.

The research component of the TDMIS is normally structured to play several distinct roles. One of these is to provide research for **policy formulation**. Policy research is characterized by analysis of the overall destination situation. It is undertaken with a view to providing information that assists in developing well-defined but broad guidelines that serve to establish priorities to direct the activities of the destination.[2]

More specifically, policy research seeks to gather and interpret macrolevel data related to present values and the evolution of trends of major economic, social, technological, and political factors that bear on the success of the destination.

A Model of the Competitive/Sustainable Destination

Regardless of the size or scope of a destination, it is useful to view it from a holistic perspective in which the structure and management processes are explicitly defined and examined. One framework that attempts to do this has been developed by Ritchie and Crouch.[3] From the standpoint of this model, the purpose of tourism policy is to ensure a common, agreed-upon purpose for tourism and to establish the broad parameters for planning and coordinating the efforts of all tourism stakeholders, those whose well-being relates in some way to the success of tourism in the destination. This model is shown and described in detail in Chapter 16.

Warning: Tourism Destinations and Tourism Policy Do Not Exist in a Vacuum

In all of the foregoing discussions, it needs to be kept in mind that tourism policies are but part of the social, economic, and political policies that govern and direct the functioning of the overall society within which tourism exists and functions.

In brief, a number of more general policies (regulations, rules, directives, objectives, strategies) are controlled by governments, as well as other industry sectors and organizations. These policies may have a significant effect on the success of tourism and tourism destinations:

- Passports and visas
- Taxation—affects costs and thus profitability
- Interest rate policy—affects costs and thus profitability
- Bilateral air agreements—determine foreign visitor access
- Environmental policy—limits growth and access to attractive but sensitive areas
- Customs and immigration policy—can facilitate or hinder international visitation
- Communications policy—can restrict use of certain advertising media

The White House tourism conference in the United States was a major tourism event where policy recommendations were made and are still being implemented. *Photo courtesy of © PhotoDisc, Inc./Getty Images.*

- Minimum wage policy—can affect labor markets
- Welfare policy—can influence nature and behavior of workforce
- Education policy—can affect quality of workforce
- Cultural policy—can affect preservation and promotion of national heritage
- Foreign investment policy/regulations—can affect availability of investment capital
- Local zoning policy/bylaws—can restrict or encourage tourism facility development
- National/provincial/local policy pertaining to funding support for major public facilities (e.g., stadiums, convention centers, museums, parks)—can drastically affect destination attractiveness
- Infrastructure policy—can make destination safer for visitors, or restrict resident travel to foreign destinations
- Currency/exchange-rate policies—directly affect destination cost competitiveness
- Legal system—determines consumer/visitor protection legislation (e.g., liability for failing to deliver advertised facilities/tours/experiences)

To summarize, a whole range of social, economic, legal, and technological policies greatly affects the appeal, attractiveness, competitiveness, and sustainability of a tourism destination. Some are under the control of the tourism sector (such as visitor satisfaction, guarantee policy, truth-in-advertising policy), but most are not. Thus, the challenge facing tourism managers is to try to influence global policies where they can, and adapt to them as effectively as possible where they cannot.

The Many Influences on Tourism Policy

As stressed earlier, tourism does not exist in a vacuum. It can function smoothly only if it shares, cooperates, and dialogues effectively with many other sectors of society and of the economy (Figure 15.4). Many of these sectors have little understanding of, or explicit interest in, tourism in the region—unless, of course, visitor activity somehow appears to detract from the functioning or

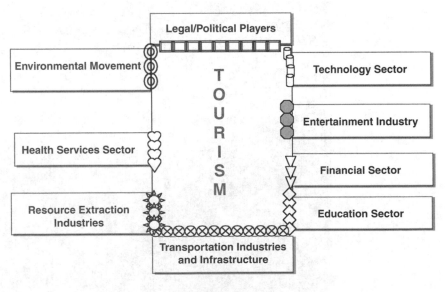

Figure 15.4 Tourism: Some of its multiple interfaces with other sectors of the economy and society.

well-being of another sector. Conflicts between tourism and other sectors most commonly arise when there is competition for a shared resource base (e.g., the extractive industries), where there is a common need for specific individuals or types of individuals (e.g., entertainment, technology, education), or where there may exist a divergence of philosophical views (e.g., the environment, transportation sectors).

Each of these interfaces can pose either a threat or an opportunity for tourism. The environmental sector and the extractive industries have traditionally viewed tourism as a competing force; the technology, entertainment, and transportation sectors most often perceive tourism as an ally or business opportunity.

In order to discuss and to present its case effectively at each interface, the tourism sector must be as capable, as well trained, and as well prepared as the professionals of any specific sector at any

❖ GLOBAL INSIGHT ❖

Policy Impacts

The Role of Passports and Visas as Policy Instruments in International Travel

The United States serves as an excellent example of how government policy impacts tourism. Since September 11, 2001, the United States has experienced a decline in overseas travel. As the global travel market continues its expansion, the U.S. share is shrinking. The U.S. Travel Association reports the consequences are profound. Overseas travel to the United States has fallen 9 percent from 2000 to 2009 despite the weak dollar that made the United States a travel bargain. The failure of the United States over the last decade to keep pace with the growth in international long-haul travel worldwide has cost the U.S. economy 68.3 million lost visitors, $509 billion in lost spending, and 441,000 in lost jobs.[1]

There are a variety of reasons why overseas travelers are choosing not to visit the United States in past numbers. However, one factor stands out: the perception that foreign travelers are no longer welcome because of the lengthy visa process and the often-confusing and claustrophobic entry process. Some visitors say that the United States has the world's worst entry process.

Visitors who are required to obtain a visa to travel to the United States must go through a personal interview at the visa-issuing post, which has taken as long as three months and required a long trip to an embassy. The process includes enrolling in US-VISIT, having two index fingers scanned by an inkless device, and having a digital photograph taken. The process is repeated when the person enters the country to make sure it is the same person who was issued the visa. The U.S. Travel Association is working with the State Department and the Department of Homeland Security to achieve more friendly entry policy while maintaining security.

Passports and visas were initially developed as a means by which countries could better control the entry and exit of foreign

nationals from their soil. In addition to the use of passports to control entry and exit, visas provide the host country with a greater degree of detailed information about the individual seeking to enter the country.

Over time, however, many countries started to view visas as a means to raise foreign funds. Although this distorts the true purpose of the visa, countries requiring them steadily became more dependent on the income they provided. The requirement for visas has declined in most countries wishing to facilitate international travel.

Following is a list of the cost of visas for a few selected countries. The costs are the 2010 prices (in U.S. dollars) for visas for a single-visit tourist visa (for persons holding a valid passport).

Brazil	$ 140
China	$ 130
India	$ 73
Russia	$ 160
Thailand	$ 35
Vietnam	$ 100
United States	$ 140

In addition to visa charges, a number of countries have imposed entrance or exit fees. These costs, while typically small, are an impediment to travel.

DISCUSSION QUESTIONS

1. What is the purpose of passports and visas?

2. How can government policies on passports and visas encourage travel? Discourage travel?

given point in time. Otherwise, tourism risks being undermined and weakened. Consequently, it may miss a critical market opportunity or may fail to establish an innovative alliance or partnership. All too often, tourism's lack of sophistication and preparedness has resulted in government decisions and policies that significantly weaken its ability to compete, or to do so more profitably. In certain cases, the tourism sector has never been aware of the extent to which it has been disadvantaged by its naïveté or by a failure to proactively and adequately prepare its case. This can be particularly disastrous in public forums where both the issue at hand and the industry's long-term credibility can be lost.

The Multidisciplinary Nature of Tourism and Tourism Policy

As explained in Chapter 1, tourism is, by its very nature, a multidisciplinary phenomenon (see Figure 1.3). The tourism experience is impacted by a range of economic, psychological, societal, technological, legal, and political forces.[4,5] It follows that, in order to formulate policies that accommodate or address these multiple forces, those involved must appreciate the complexities of each discipline and their interactions in any given situation. The disciplines of psychology, economics, sociology, and law are but some of the disciplines that can enhance our understanding of international marketing. The environmental sciences, political science, and the behavioral sciences are essential to the formulation of national park policy that defines the levels and types of tourism that are appropriate and desirable.

Essential Characteristics of Tourism Policy

In addition to the **multidisciplinary nature of tourism policy**, it also possesses nine other essential characteristics:

1. It must focus on macrolevel policies—that is, be concerned with societal views of the direction that tourism development should take at the subnational, national, and even transnational level.
2. It must be designed to formulate policies having a long-term perspective.
3. It must concentrate on how critical and limited resources can best respond to perceived needs and opportunities in a changing environment.
4. It must recognize the intellectual nature of the process of policy formulation. Thus, it must incorporate tacit knowledge and personal experience as important sources of information, in addition to more conventional methods of research and study.
5. It must encourage and stimulate organized creativity so as to avoid policies based on stereotyped or outmoded perceptions.
6. It must be constructed to permit and facilitate a continuing dynamic social process requiring inputs from multiple sources.
7. It must break down the traditional boundaries between industry sectors in tourism.
8. It must relate policies of the tourism subsystem to those of the total socioeconomic system of a nation or region of which it is a part.
9. It must acknowledge the destination roles of both competition and cooperation and seek to identify situations where each is appropriate. The judicious application of either or both in tourism policy has given rise to use of the term **coopetition**.[6]

TOURISM POLICY: STRUCTURE, CONTENT, AND PROCESS

In discussing tourism policy, it is helpful to clearly distinguish among the overall structure of a policy and the specific policy content found within that structure. In the same vein, readers must distinguish between: (1) the static concepts of policy structure and content, and (2) the dynamic concept of policy formulation. Structure and context define the "what" of tourism policy; the process of policy formulation describes the "how" of defining the structure of a destination's policy and determining the content of policy found within that structure. In tourism, the process, or the "how," provides the following:

- An overview of the different stages or steps involved in the policy formulation process
- A review of the various possible methodologies that might be used within, or across, the stages of policy formulation

The Structure of Tourism Policy

Although no single model can define the **structure of tourism policy**, Figure 15.5 provides one framework for tourism policy (i.e., a set of guidelines for successful destination development and operations).

Total System and Tourism Macropolicy

Macropolicy, or what some have referred to as *megapolicy,* involves determination of the premises, assumptions, and main guidelines to be followed by specific policies. It is a kind of master policy, clearly distinct from detailed discrete policies.[7] In this regard, tourism policy is viewed as being directly based on and derived from the policies that direct the total socioeconomic system of the nation or region in which the tourism subsystem is located. In fact, it is the general content of these

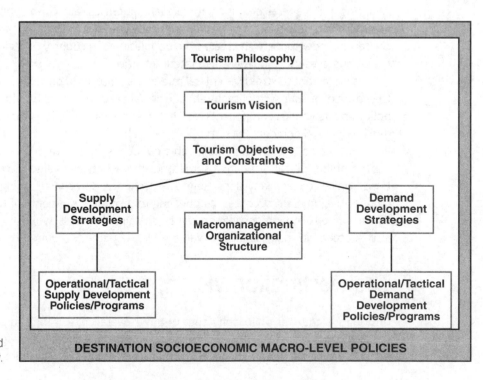

Figure 15.5 The structure and composition of tourism policy.

State governments are an important seat of tourism policy formation. Shown here is the state capitol building in Richmond, Virginia. *Photo courtesy of Washington, D.C., and the Capital Region.*

total system policies that provides much of the basis upon which to derive the tourism philosophy of the destination region in question.

Tourism Philosophy

An explicit tourism philosophy is an essential foundation on which to develop a coherent policy. In general, a philosophy may be defined as a system for guiding life—a body of principles of conduct, beliefs, or traditions—or the broad general principles of a particular subject or field of activity. Adapting this general definition for present purposes, a tourism philosophy may be defined as a general principle or set of *principles* that indicates the beliefs and values of members of a society concerning how tourism shall serve the population of a country or region, and that acts as a guide for evaluating the utility of tourism-related activities.

It is important to stress the critical role that the values of destination residents exert in determining the context of tourism policy. In effect, the values of residents provide the foundation on which the policy and its various components rest. In the end, tourism policies that do not reflect the values of the destination stakeholders, or hosts, will inevitably fail to gain ongoing popular or political support. Policies that do not maintain long-term political support are doomed to failure.

The philosophical distinction sometimes made between value-driven and market-driven destinations, while conceptually appealing, is, in practice, somewhat ambiguous. No destination can be competitive unless it succeeds in appealing to profitable segments of the market over the long term. By the same token, no destination can be sustainable unless, while it generates economic rewards, it also succeeds in maintaining the value-driven legitimacy required by a democratic society.

The Destination Vision

Although a tourism philosophy sets out the overall nature of tourism in a destination, it is the **destination vision** that provides the more functional and more inspirational portrait of the ideal future that the destination hopes to bring about in some defined future (usually 5, 10, 20, or 50 years).

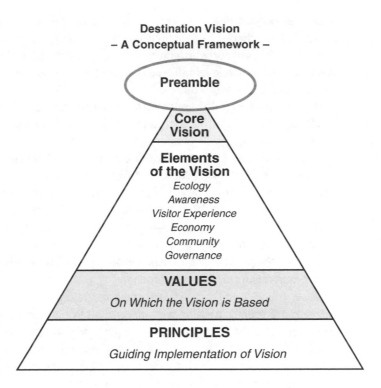

Figure 15.6 Destination vision framework.
Source: Ritchie 1996.

Visions can take many different forms. Some are very concise (similar to a corporate mission statement—which, in contrast, provides a succinct expression of the organization's purpose for existence); others are much more extensive and idealistic. Typically, however, a destination vision is structured as shown in Figure 15.6.

The preamble section of a vision sets the tone and provides the context and rationale for the vision being developed. The core vision, as the name implies, attempts to capture the overall essence of the ideal future for the destination in question. The values component of the vision statement seeks to provide an understanding of the deeply held enduring beliefs of the stakeholders formulating the vision. It is these values that effectively drive—or provide a foundation—for the vision statements that are enunciated by individuals. One cannot understand or appreciate a vision without understanding and appreciating the values on which it is based.

The elements of the vision are the means by which the essence or idealism of the vision (the core vision) is linked to the reality of the destination. In effect, they provide the means by which operational components of the vision can be defined. The nature of these components depends on the specific destination in question. In the example in Figure 15.6, the core vision for a Canadian national park gave rise to six vision elements.

Finally, once the core vision and its elements have been agreed upon, it is frequently useful to provide a statement of principles designed to provide guidance as to how the vision and its elements should be interpreted and implemented.

Crafting versus Formulating a Strategic Vision

The preparation of a destination vision is a stimulating, intellectual process that often attracts and should involve the relevant stakeholders of a destination. There is, however, a significant difference between formulating and crafting the vision. Policy formulation is a term reflecting a traditional approach to strategic planning that can be described as prescriptive in orientation. This terminology implies that strategy formulation is a process of conceptual design, of formal planning, and of analytical **positioning**. The essence of this model is that it is by nature structured, logical, and somewhat mechanical. It emphasizes that strategy formulation should be a controlled, conscious process of thought for which ultimate responsibility lies with the chief executive officer of the entity involved in strategy development. The outcome of this process is a simple, unique, and explicit "best" strategy for a given situation.

At the other end of the spectrum is what Mintzberg defines as the crafting of strategy. Under this conceptualization, crafting a strategy is a dynamic, evolving process in which strategies take form as a result of learning over a period of time, as opposed to being formulated at a fixed point in time. Mintzberg emphasizes that the crafting of strategy reflects an ongoing iterative process of thinking and acting—and then thinking some more. One idea leads to another until a new pattern forms. As such, strategies can form as well as be formulated. A strategy can emerge in response to an evolving situation, or it can be brought about deliberately, through a process of formulation followed by implementation. Crafting strategy requires dedication, experience, involvement with the material, the personal touch, mastery of detail, a sense of harmony, and integration.[8]

In brief, the process of **strategic visioning**—or simply *visioning*—like the crafting of strategy, is seen as a dynamic, interactive phenomenon.[9]

After the visioning process is complete, the organization will take that information and come up with a more specific mission statement to also help guide the organization. A mission statement is a short, formal, written statement of the purpose and aim of an organization or company. It has a more immediate tone than the vision statement. The vision statement defines what the organization aspires to be while the mission statement defines what the organization is. It provides the context within which the organization's strategies are formulated.

Tourism Objectives and Constraints

Component three of a tourism policy consists of a statement of the objectives of the tourism system. **Tourism objectives** are defined as operational statement(s) of the specific results sought by the tourism system within a given time frame. The objectives of the tourism system should possess a number of important characteristics. First, because the objectives are formulated in light of the tourism vision, their achievement should clearly contribute to the fulfillment of this vision. Second, in order that the objectives can be qualified as operational, it is essential that managers are able to measure the extent to which desired results have or have not been attained. This implies that we must have some explicit means of quantifying appropriate performance standards. Third, we must ensure that the measures selected with respect to each objective are indeed valid indicators of the desired results; that is, they must measure what we truly want to achieve. Fourth, in the common situation where the tourism system has multiple objectives, it is advisable to indicate an order or priority among objectives. This indication of relative importance provides a basis for decision making should different strategies or programs for achieving the objective be in conflict. Fifth, the objectives must be related to a given time period as is directly stated in the above definition. Finally, the objectives that are stated must be reasonable. Although they should serve to offer a real challenge, goals that are virtually impossible to attain quickly become a negative rather than a positive source of motivation.

One further remark concerning the formal statement of objectives is in order. Objectives identify those events or results that we wish to bring about. The word *objective* implies that the results are positive entities, such as a certain number of visitors, but this is not necessarily so. In fact, the managers of a tourism system may seek goals with respect to what they do not want to happen as a consequence of their activities. Examples include the avoidance of environmental and cultural pollution. These types of results could be stated as specific objectives of the tourism system. While very important, their essentially negative nature provides little incentive for management action. An alternative and more satisfactory manner of dealing with effects that one wishes to avoid is to express them in the form of **tourism constraints**. A common approach to formally stating constraints on system activities is to specify, where possible, the maximum level of each undesirable outcome (e.g., pollution) that can be tolerated as a result of tourism activity. Even where it is difficult to quantify the tolerable levels of undesirable outcomes, constraints can be formulated so as to at least provide explicit indications as to the type of outcomes to be minimized or avoided.

THE PROCESS OF TOURISM POLICY FORMULATION

Discussion to this point in the chapter has focused on the structure and content of tourism policy. In this section, attention is directed toward understanding the process by which the structure and content of policy, as presented in Figure 15.5, may be developed. This process is conceptualized as containing distinct stages grouped into four main phases (Figure 15.7). These phases are identified as the definitional phase, the analytical phase, the operational phase, and the implementation phase.

Definitional Phase

The definitional phase of tourism policy formulation is concerned with the development of explicit statements that define the content and direction of the overall tourism system in question. As shown in Figure 15.7, these statements deal with four different topics. The definition of the destination tourism system represents the critical first step in the process of policy formulation.

Figure 1.2 in Chapter 1 provides one model that might be useful as the basic framework for defining a tourism system. It views the tourism system as being constructed of two major components, namely, the operating sectors and the planning/catalyst organizations. These, in turn, contain various subcomponents that form the basis for identifying and classifying the individual organizations and actors (the stakeholders) that make up a given tourism system. It is essential that each region develop such a model that is generally accepted by the policy makers concerned. Once agreed to, this model should become a constant frame of reference for discussion and decision making.

The remaining three components of the definitional phase (Figure 15.7) involve the explication of a tourism philosophy, the formulation of a destination vision, and the determination of tourism objectives and constraints for the destination. Previous discussion has described the content of these policy components.

Definitional Phase	Analytical Phase	Operational Phase	Implementation Phase
Definition of tourism destination system	Internal Analysis ☐ Review of existing policies and programs	Identification of strategic conclusions	Implementation of strategy for destination of development, promotion, and stewardship
Explication of a tourism philosophy	☐ Resource audit ☐ Strategic impact analysis	Implications of conclusions for supply and demand development	Allocation of responsibilities for recommendation implementation
Crafting of a destination vision	External Analysis ☐ Macrolevel analysis of current and future demand	Policy/program recommendations	Identification of sources of funding to support competitive initiatives and stewardship programs
Objectives and constraints	☐ Microlevel analysis of current and future demand and behaviors		Specification of timing for recommendation implementation
	☐ Review of competitive and supportive tourism development and promotion policies		Monitoring and evaluation of the results

Figure 15.7 The process of tourism policy, strategy formulation, and implementation.

Analytical Phase

The analytical phase of tourism policy development, while perhaps less stressful than the previous one from a managerial standpoint, involves considerably greater amounts of effort. The definitional phase requires fundamental, value-based decisions concerning the nature and direction of tourism development in a region. The analytical phase accepts these decisions as a given and proceeds to carry out the extensive collection and assessment of information needed to identify and assess the desirability of alternative means of attaining the destination vision and to achieve the goals defined by the vision.

The overall process of analysis is best viewed as being composed of two major subprocesses: (1) an internal or supply-oriented analysis, and (2) an external or demand-oriented analysis.

The *internal/supply analysis* consists of a thorough review and analysis (frequently termed an *audit*) of two major elements. The first element relates to existing policies and programs for the development of the various components of tourism supply. These *policies/programs must be critically reviewed* to determine the extent to which they are both consistent with and effective in developing the type of tourism facilities and services that are likely to achieve the goals of the region, given the nature of demand facing that region. As can be quickly seen, this statement implies a direct interaction between the supply analysis and the demand analysis. In effect, the analytical phase involves parallel, iterative forms of analysis that must constantly be related one to the other.

A second element of the supply analysis is termed a resource audit. A resource audit is a comprehensive cataloguing of the quantity and distribution of tourism facilities and services within the tourism system. Such information is basic to an understanding of the current state of affairs of supply development. Second, the resource audit should provide some assessment of the quality of existing facilities and services. Again, the execution of the audit to assess the adequacy of the quantity, distribution, and quality of supply can only be meaningful if it is eventually related to the analysis of demand. There are no absolute measures of desirability in terms of supply; *only those that relate to a given demand at a given point in time for a given market segment are relevant.*

The third form of internal analysis is a *strategic impact analysis*. This analysis seeks to provide policy makers with well-defined benchmarks as to the extent to which tourism is currently impacting the destination in economic, ecological, social, and cultural terms. Economic benchmarks have traditionally been the most requested forms of impact analysis because both managers and politicians seek to measure and understand both the level of tourism receipts and the incomes and employment they create.

The *external/demand analysis* is composed of three distinct types of analytical activity. The first involves *macrolevel analysis* of data that describes and defines the overall nature and structure of current tourism demand as well as those markets having a potential for future demand. This form of analysis relies heavily on aggregate statistics measuring the flows of tourists and travel-related expenditures within a region; it must not, however, limit itself to such historical data. In addition, macrolevel analysis must be future-oriented and attempt to constantly monitor the environment in order to identify shifts or trends in social, political, or technological factors that might significantly affect the region's success in its field of tourism.

The second type of external/demand analysis is termed *microlevel analysis*. Here, rather than focusing on aggregate trends in tourism demand, attention is directed toward gaining an understanding of the motivations and behavior of the different segments of the total tourism market. The purpose of gaining this understanding is to provide those responsible for supply development with the information needed to design facilities and services that will appeal most to each of the various demand segments. In addition, such data facilitates the task of those responsible for the promotion of existing facilities and services.

The final component of external/demand analysis involves a review and evaluation of competitive and supportive tourism development and promotion policies and programs. *Competitive analysis* is a common form of managerial investigation. In this case, it is designed to produce a clear picture concerning the identity, strength, and strategies of those tourism destinations most likely to be appealing to the same segments of demand as those of interest to the tourism region in question. Such information is essential if a region is to effectively counter the efforts of such competitors from the standpoint of both supply development and demand modification.

Operational Phase

Once the various types of analysis have been carried out, policy makers must move to develop specific strategies and action plans that can be implemented. As shown in Figure 15.7, this operational phase is envisaged to contain three conceptually different types of activity; in reality, these different activities are executed almost simultaneously.

The identification of strategic conclusions flows directly out of the analytical phase, and its goal is to synthesize the large amounts of information obtained into a limited number of major conclusions. In addition to specifying the major findings from each type of internal and external analysis, this process also must attempt to provide conclusions that assess the impact of the trade-offs that inevitably are made when attempting to match supply and demand.

The strategic conclusions themselves may be viewed as reasonably factual information; that is, they are the result of a logical process of analysis that would give rise to generally similar findings irrespective of the investigator. In contrast, the drawing of "implications of the conclusions for supply-and-demand development strategies" involves a high degree of judgment on the part of the individuals involved. The goal of this process is to attempt to assess the significance of each conclusion for tourism in the region. Although the actual conclusions may be clear, the implications of these facts for the kind of policies and programs needed to deal with them involves a considerable level of interpretive skills derived from both experience and a creative mind.

The subsequent stage of the policy formulation process is the identification of specific "policy/program recommendations for supply/demand development." For our purposes, this rather complex

The presentation of national treasures is an integral part of tourism policy. In this photo, the great Buddha in Taiwan is but one of the kinds of treasure that policy formulation in tourism must address.
Photo courtesy of Corbis Digital Stock.

❖ GLOBAL INSIGHT ❖

Ethics

The "Responsible Tourist and Traveler" is a short, practical guide to make trips an enriching experience. The advice is based on the *Global Code of Ethics for Tourism* developed and published by the United Nations World Tourism Organization (UNWTO). This publication should be required reading for tourism policy makers, and they should incorporate the ethical principles into policy.

Visit www.unwto.org/en and click on Global Code of Ethics, then click on full text to review the entire code (eight pages).

The Responsible Tourist and Traveler

Travel and tourism should be planned and practiced as a means of individual and collective fulfillment. When practiced with an open mind, it is an irreplaceable factor of self-education and mutual tolerance and for learning about the legitimate differences between peoples and cultures and their diversity.

Everyone has a role to play creating responsible travel and tourism. Governments, business, and communities must do all they can, but as a guest, you can support this in many ways to make a difference:

1. **Open your mind to other cultures and traditions.** This will transform your experience; you will earn respect and be more readily welcomed by local people. Be tolerant and respect diversity—observe social and cultural traditions and practices.

2. **Respect human rights.** Exploitation in any form conflicts with the fundamental aims of tourism. The sexual exploitation of children is a crime punishable in the destination or at the offender's home country.

3. **Help preserve natural environments.** Protect wildlife and habitats and do not purchase products made from endangered plants or animals.

4. **Respect cultural resources.** Activities should be conducted with respect for the artistic, archaeological, and cultural heritage.

5. **Your trip can contribute to economic and social development.** Purchase local handicrafts and products to support the local economy using the principles of fair trade. Bargaining for goods should reflect an understanding of a fair wage.

6. **Inform yourself about the destination's current health situation and access to emergency and consular services prior to departure and be assured that your health and personal security will not be compromised.** Make sure that your specific requirements (diet, accessibility, medical care) can be fulfilled before you decide to travel this destination.

7. **Learn as much as possible about your destination and take time to understand the customs, norms, and traditions.** Avoid behavior that could offend the local population.

8. **Familiarize yourself with the laws so that you do not commit any act considered criminal by the law of the country visited.** Refrain from all trafficking in illicit drugs, arms, antiques, protected species, and products or substances that are dangerous or prohibited by national regulations.

DISCUSSION QUESTIONS

1. How does a responsible tourist behave?

2. Why is the UNWTO a leader in promoting tourism ethics?

---

activity has been oversimplified; in reality, a range of policy options would normally be developed in an attempt to respond to alternative implications or alternative scenarios. Some judgment would then be exercised as to which implications or scenarios are most likely to occur. Policy/program recommendations most appropriate to the most likely scenario events would probably, although not necessarily, be adopted.

Implementation Phase

Finally, for a destination tourism policy to truly succeed, it is essential to include an **implementation strategy**. At a minimum, such a strategy must: (1) identify the individual groups or organizations that will assume responsibility for each major dimension of the policy realization, (2) establish initial estimates of the financial requirements, and (3) provide preliminary timelines for the launching of all major facilities, events, and programs that support the destination vision. The specifics of implementation are the object of tourism planning. These specifics are examined in detail in Chapter 16.

TRANSLATING POLICY INTO REALITY

It must be emphasized that once overall supply-and-demand development strategies have been enunciated and appropriate organizational structures put in place, these strategies must be translated into specific policies and programs of an operational nature. At this level, the management process becomes one of detailed planning and implementation of the many tasks necessary to provide the individual tourist with the satisfying, yet challenging experience that he or she is seeking. Although detailed discussion of tourism planning is beyond the scope of this chapter, the need to effectively translate strategic ideas into real-world actions cannot be too strongly stressed. Without effective execution, even the most brilliant policies will prove of little value.

An example illustrating the need to translate policy into reality is crisis management. Today, every tourism organization needs crisis management policies and plans that work. A discussion of crisis management follows.

FORMULATING POLICY TO DEAL WITH CRISES

Despite the best efforts to formulate tourism policies that support destination development, to plan and execute the development of an attractive tourism destination, and to effectively manage a tourism destination, sometimes the unthinkable happens.

The September 11, 2001, terrorist bombing of the twin towers in New York and the Pentagon in Washington, D.C.; the 2002 bombing of a tourist-filled nightclub in Bali, Indonesia; the 2004 bombing of the commuter trains in Madrid, Spain; the 2003 failure of the electrical grid in eastern North America all created sudden disruptions in the normally smooth functioning of tourism. Other less sudden but more widespread happenings such as the Iraq war, the 2003 outbreaks of SARS (severe acute respiratory syndrome) in China and Canada, the outbreak of foot-and-mouth disease in the United Kingdom, the forest fires in the western United States, the tsunamis in Indonesia (2004) and Japan (2011), and especially the major economic recession of 2008–2009 all affected people's desire and ability to travel, and thus the well-being of tourism destinations around the world.

Although these crises were not all directly related to the tourism sector, their widespread repercussions created situations that seriously affected or interfered with people's willingness to travel, or the smooth functioning of the tourism system. They were thus the root cause of crises that tourism managers needed to understand or to take account of in their ongoing management of tourism destinations.

Types of Crisis-Causing Events

In an effort to help improve our formal understanding of the nature of *crisis management* related to both unthinkable happenings and major events having global repercussions, Mitroff and Anagnos divide crisis-causing events into seven general types and/or categories of risk:

1. Economic crises, such as labor strikes, labor shortage, market crashes, major declines in stock prices, and fluctuations or declines in major earnings

2. Informational crises, such as a loss of proprietary and confidential information, tampering with computer records, or the loss of key computer information that relates to customers and suppliers

3. Physical crises, such as loss of key equipment, plants, and material suppliers; breakdowns of key equipment and industrial plants; loss of key facilities; and major plant disruptions

4. Human resource crises, such as loss of key executives, loss of key personnel, increased absenteeism, increased vandalism, an increased number of accidents, and a rise in workplace violence

5. Reputation crises, such as slander, gossip, rumors, damage to corporate reputation, and tampering with corporate logos

6. Crises resulting from psychopathic acts, such as product tampering, kidnapping, hostage taking, terrorism, and workplace violence

7. Natural disasters, such as earthquakes, fires, floods, explosions, typhoons, and hurricanes[10]

They further stress that, although the major categories of crises share many similarities, there can be substantial differences in the impact they have on an organization.

More specifically, a crisis brought about by a natural disaster will probably affect a destination very differently from one caused by the loss of a key executive. Given this reality, Mitroff and Anagnos suggest that the best management approach is to develop policies to prepare for at least one crisis in each of the categories. Unfortunately, they note that the majority of organizations do much less, in that they tend to consider at most one or two categories. For example, most companies prepare for natural disasters. Organizations that do broaden their preparations for crises other than natural disasters often do so only for "core" or "normal" disasters that are specific to their particular industry.

Dealing with Crises

The best method of crisis management is preparation before a crisis occurs—first implementing an effort to prevent the crisis from occurring at all, and then developing the ability to react immediately and effectively should an outbreak or incident arise. This means a disaster (crisis) plan must be developed.

Good crisis management requires policies to deal with each stage of a crisis situation if a destination is to prevent or minimize a crisis. First, one needs detection policies. This requires a monitoring system of the macroenvironment to make sure one is detecting problems and anticipating tomorrow rather than reacting to yesterday. The second requirement is for prevention or minimization policies. This involves such areas as legislation, law enforcement, security devices, and safety and security training for employees. The third need is for readiness policies that require leadership for crisis coordination, emergency response, assistance for families, internal and external communications, information dissemination, and media relations. Fourth, response policies, which include effective emergency response and answering the public call for information, should be put in place. Telling the truth is a vital crisis management policy. Finally, recovery policies to enable a return to normalcy are a high priority. These include the rebuilding process, information dissemination, publicity, public relations, and marketing.

The concern of the United Nations World Tourism Organization (UNWTO) about crises resulted in its creating the UNWTO Recovery Committee. This committee has published *Crisis Guidelines for the Tourism Industry,* which offers a one-step reference document suggesting specific actions to take before, during, and immediately after a crisis to get tourists returning to a destination as quickly as possible. The publication is available on UNWTO's Web site (www.unwto.org).

SUMMARY

This chapter points out that: (1) tourism policy is needed for destinations at all levels and for all types of political jurisdictions; (2) in all cases, competitiveness and sustainability must be the primary goal of policy; and (3) the effective pursuit of each of these goals requires a different set of skills and capabilities. With this background firmly in place, the chapter then fulfills one additional role.

This role is to provide a framework describing the structure and composition of a formal tourism policy. The primary components discussed are the philosophy for tourism and the formulation of a long-term vision for the destination. This vision provides important guidance for the definition of specific objectives for a tourism destination, as well as for identifying any constraints that must be observed as tourism is developed. These objectives, in turn, provide a basis for formulating long-term development strategies for the region. Next, the chapter focuses on the process of policy formulation, which includes the definitional phase, the analytical phase, the operational phase, and the implementation phase. The chapter concludes with an example discussing crisis management.

 KEY CONCEPTS ❖

competitive destinations
content of tourism policy
coopetition
core vision
crafting a vision
destination positioning
destination vision
elements of the vision
implementation strategy

multidisciplinary nature of tourism
    policy
policy formulation
positioning
preamble section
resource audit
strategic visioning
structure of tourism policy
sustainable destinations

total system policies
tourism constraints
tourism destination management
tourism destination management
    information system
tourism objective
tourism policy

  INTERNET EXERCISES ❖

The Internet sites mentioned in this chapter plus some selected additional sites are listed for your convenience on the companion Web site for this book, www.wiley.com/college/goeldner.

ACTIVITY 1

Site Name: Tourism Policy in Turkey

URL: www.turizm.net/economy/touris~1.htm

Background Information: In 1983, the government of Turkey amended its tourism policy to encourage Turkish and foreign investment companies to participate more effectively in the development of Turkey's tourism sector.

Exercise

1. Compare the Turkish tourism policy with the elements of a good tourism policy as described in the textbook. What similarities and differences can you find?

ACTIVITY 2

Site Name: Western States Tourism Policy Council (WSTPC)

URL: www.wstpc.org

Background Information: The mission of the Western States Tourism Policy Council is to foster and encourage a positive environment for travel and tourism by serving as a forum to identify, research, analyze, and advocate travel and tourism related issues of public policy and opinion in the western United States.

Exercises

1. Using information from the site, list the objectives of WSTPC.

2. Identify the policy position papers published by WSTPC.

❖ **QUESTIONS FOR REVIEW AND DISCUSSION** ❖

1. What is a tourism policy, and why is it important for a tourism destination to have a formal policy?

2. Why might a major stakeholder not wish to participate in the policy process?

3. How might tourism policy differ from countries, states/provinces, and cities? Why might it differ?

4. How would you identify and choose the stakeholders who should be involved in the formulation of a tourism policy for a region? Is there anyone whom you feel should be excluded from the process?

5. What are the implications of no involvement in policy formulation by a major stakeholder?

6. What is the difference between a tourism policy and a tourism strategy?

7. Who should be in charge of policy formulation?

8. What are the most important interfaces of tourism policy; that is, which other sectors of the economy and society need to be aware of tourism policy or might have a significant impact on the success of tourism policy?

9. What do you see as the major barriers to successful policy formulation for tourism?

10. Must there be total consensus by all stakeholders on the content of a region's tourism policy? If not, how would you determine if there was adequate support for the different components of a policy?

11. How frequently should the policy formulation process take place for a destination? Why?

12. Why is a vision especially important for policy formulation? How long into the future should a vision attempt to define an ideal future?

13. Implementation of policy recommendations is often a problem. What do you see as the major barriers to the implementation of policy? Why do they exist? How might these barriers be overcome?

14. Why are ethics important?

15. Can good tourism policy help alleviate poverty?

16. How do government policies on passports and visas impact tourism?

❖ **CASE PROBLEM** ❖

As the newly named president and CEO of Tourism Banff, the Destination Management Organization for the world-famous iconic tourism community location in Banff National Park (BNP), and Canada's first and most famous national park, you have been asked to formulate a tourism development and promotion policy which balances the needs of residents of the small community of 6,700 permanent residents and the over 5 million annual visitors to BNP.

In formulating the requested policy, keep in mind that the town of Banff is located in a National Park, how would you balance the rights and responsibilities of:

a. permanent residents of the community;

b. visitors living in the nearby city of Calgary; and

c. visitors from the rest of Canada?

How would you decide which kind of tourism activities you would both allow and encourage within the National Park?

In formulating a vision for the future of the National Park community/destination, whom would you involve in the visioning process?

ENDNOTES

1. Oxford Economics, *The Lost Decade: The High Costs of America's Failure to Compete for International Travel* (Washington, DC: U.S. Travel Association, 2010).

2. J. R. Brent Ritchie and C. R. Goeldner (eds.), *Travel, Tourism, and Hospitality Research: A Handbook for Managers and Researchers*, 2nd ed. (New York: John Wiley & Sons, 1994).

3. J. R. Brent Ritchie and Geoffrey I. Crouch, *The Competitive Destination: A Sustainable Tourism Perspective* (Oxfordshire, UK: CABI Publishing, 2003).

4. J. Jafari and J. R. Brent Ritchie, "Toward a Framework for Tourism Education: Problems and Prospect," *Annals of Tourism Research,* vol. 8, no. 1 (1981), pp. 13–34.

5. C. Echtner and T. B. Jamal, "The Disciplinary Dilemma of Tourism Studies," *Annals of Tourism Research,* vol. 24, no. 4 (October 1997), pp. 868–883.

6. David L. Edgell and R. Todd Haenisch, *Coopetition: Global Tourism beyond the Millennium* (Kansas City: International Policy Publishing, 1995), p. 2.

7. Y. Dror, *Design for Policy Sciences* (New York: American Elsevier, 1971).

8. H. Mintzberg, "Crafting Strategy," *Harvard Business Review* (July–August 1987), pp. 66–75.

9. F. Westley and H. Mintzberg, "Visionary Leadership and Strategic Management," *Strategic Management Journal,* vol. 10 (1989), pp. 17–32.

10. I. I. Mitroff and G. Anagnos, *Managing Crises before They Happen: What Every Executive and Manager Needs to Know about Crisis Management* (New York: Amacom, 2001).

CHAPTER 16

Tourism Planning, Development, and Social Considerations

LEARNING OBJECTIVES

- Identify the factors that determine the success of a tourism destination.
- Relate tourism planning to tourism policy.
- Discover what the goals of tourism development should be.
- Recognize that some serious barriers to tourism development must be overcome if a desired growth is to occur.

- Learn the political and economic aspects of development, including those related to developing countries.
- Appreciate the importance of architectural design and concern for heritage preservation, local handicrafts, and use of indigenous materials in creating tourist facilities.

Good planning is necessary for a luxury resort to come together and work for management, guests, and the surrounding community. *Photo courtesy of the Phoenician.*

INTRODUCTION

Planning follows the **policy formulation** process described in Chapter 15. Tourism planners and managers need to use this process as a framework for the planning and development of a destination. Good policy and sound planning must be conducted to ensure that a destination will be both competitive and sustainable. This chapter presents a model for destination competitiveness and sustainability, the need for tourism policy and planning to be integrated, steps in the planning process, and development issues.

PLANNING FOR A COMPETITIVE/SUSTAINABLE DESTINATION

Good tourism planning must be based on a sound understanding of those factors that fundamentally determine the success of a tourism destination. One framework that graphically identifies these factors is given in Figure 16.1. As shown, the framework includes nine major components, each of which contains a number of subcomponents:

1. **The core resources and attractors:** The fundamental reasons why prospective visitors choose one destination over another. These factors fall into seven categories: physiography and climate, culture and history, market ties, mix of activities, special events, entertainment, and the tourism superstructure.

2. **Supporting factors and resources:** Whereas the core resources and attractors of a destination constitute the primary motivations for inbound tourism, the supporting factors and resources, as the term implies, provide a functional foundation that facilitates tourism and enhances its contribution to destination well-being. These factors are physical infrastructure, accessibility, resident/industry hospitality, the entrepreneurial efforts of tourism operators, political support for tourism, and facilitating resources such as a trained and welcoming customs/immigration staff.

3. **Qualifying and amplifying determinants:** The potential success of a destination is conditioned or limited by a number of factors. This group of factors might alternatively be labeled **situational conditioners** because their impact on the success of a tourism destination are to define its scale, limit, or potential. One particularly important factor that is increasingly limiting a destination's ability to compete is the perceived degree of security that exists at the destination. Historically, the safety/security of a destination was largely taken for granted. Today, however, such is not the case; crime and terrorism are factors that have become very real in many destinations. Every destination must undertake to ensure that it provides the visitor with safety and security across a broad range of both health and personal security dimensions. These qualifiers and amplifiers moderate or magnify destination success by filtering the influence of the other core groups of factors. Although they might be so important as to represent a ceiling to tourism demand or potential, they are largely beyond the control of the tourism sector alone.

4. **Destination policy, planning, and development:** Unfortunately, not all destinations have a formal tourism policy. However, a strategic or policy-driven framework for the planning and development of a destination, with particular economic, social, and other societal goals as the intended outcome, can help ensure that the tourism development that does occur promotes a successful and sustainable destination while meeting the quality-of-life aspirations of those who reside in the destination. This core component comprises eight subcomponents: a formal *definition* of the tourism system; an explication of a *philosophy* of tourism—or how tourism

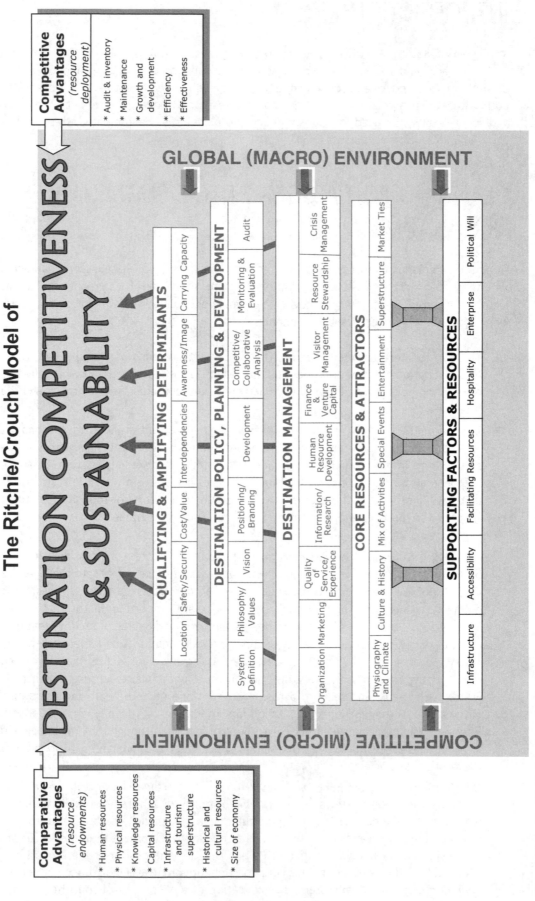

Figure 16.1 The Ritchie/Crouch model of destination competitiveness and sustainability.

should serve the community; a *vision*, which flows from the philosophy and is a formal statement describing the ideal future state of the tourism destination some 20, 50, or 100 years into the future; a *positioning/branding strategy* defining how the destination should be perceived relative to competitors; a detailed *development* plan; a *competitive/collaborative analysis* providing an evaluation of how the destination relates to and compares with other destinations and the international tourism system; the *monitoring and evaluation* of policies, programs, and their outcome; and finally, all the foregoing brought together into a rigorous *destination audit*, which identifies the destination's strengths, weaknesses, problems, challenges, and opportunities.

5. **Destination management:** This component of the model focuses on the activities that implement the policy and planning framework on a daily, operational basis. These nine activities involve effective *organization, marketing* of the destination, ensuring a high-quality *visitor experience*, gathering and disseminating *information, human resource development*, obtaining *adequate financing* and venture capital, effective *visitor management,* ongoing resource *stewardship,* and being prepared to *manage unexpected crises.*

6, 7. **Comparative versus competitive advantage:** An important characteristic of this model is the distinction it makes between comparative and competitive advantages of destinations. The former refers to the resources with which the destination is endowed and that enhance its chances of success, while the latter refers to the effectiveness with which a destination's resources are utilized or deployed, thus enhancing its relative probability of success relative to competing destinations.

8, 9. **Global (macro) versus competitive (micro) environment:** A final important dimension of the Ritchie/Crouch (R/C) framework is the distinction it makes between the impact of macro- versus microforces on destination success. *Global/macroforces* refer to the vast array of phenomena that broadly affect all human activities, and that are therefore not specific to the travel and tourism industry in their effect. By comparison, the *competitive or microenvironment* is part of the tourism system, and the forces it contains concern the actions and activities of entities in the tourism system that directly affect the goals of each member of the system, whether they be individual tourism firms or the collection of organizations that constitute a destination.

THE NATURE OF TOURISM PLANNING

Tourism planning seeks to provide a detailed, "on-the-ground" outline as to how each of the factors affecting the success of a tourism destination should be developed. Good tourism planning goes far beyond schemes to maximize profit. Although profitable development brings positive economic and social benefits to the community, it also carries inevitable drawbacks. Therefore, developers must incorporate ways to enhance human welfare and happiness. These include insistence on high-quality architectural, landscape, and environmental design; planning for transportation; and energy conservation and education.

If such diverse goals are to be achieved, planners must implement a model that will guide their thinking by incorporating each aspect (including various political aspects) into a master plan. These include zoning, road maintenance, water and sewage treatment systems, and promotional expenses. An official body, financed through tourist earnings, is useful in keeping abreast of socioeconomic activities in the industry as well as dealing with other problems such as stabilizing prices, forecasting demand, keeping an inventory of potential national tourist resources, and arranging publicity campaigns. Resort development also necessitates working out financial arrangements that will not only enable the developer to take out loans for construction but also to be granted reduced or forgiven taxes for a period of time in order to improve the venture's financial success.

RELATING TOURISM PLANNING TO TOURISM POLICY

The previous chapter provides an understanding of the role of tourism policy in providing a set of guidelines for the development and promotion of a tourism destination. It also describes the structure and content of a formal tourism policy, as well as the process of policy formulation.

Because tourism policy formulation and tourism planning are directly related to each other, it is important to distinguish between the two, to identify their similarities and their differences in a tourism context. Their similarities are:

1. They both deal with the future development of a tourism destination or region.
2. They both emphasize the strategic dimensions of managerial action, although planning must also address a number of tactical concerns.

Their differences are:

1. Policy formulation is definitely "big picture," while much of planning is characterized by an attention to detail.
2. Policy formulation is a creative, intellectual process, while planning is generally a more constrained practical exercise.
3. Policy, particularly its visioning component, has a very long-term strategic emphasis, while planning tends to be more restrictive in its time horizon. A one-year planning cycle is not uncommon, although three- to five-year plans are a possibility. In contrast, destination visions may have a 5-, 10-, 50-, or even 100-year time horizon.
4. Policy formulation must allow as-yet-unseen circumstances and technologies to be considered. In contrast, planning tends to assume current conditions and technologies, with some allowances for predictable (i.e., evolutionary) change.
5. Policy formulation tends to emphasize a systematic determination of "what" should be done in long-term tourism development, while planning tends to emphasize the "how" for the achievement of specific destination goals.

The reader should keep these distinctions in mind when reviewing the rest of this chapter. Although policy formulation and planning appear to have certain commonalties, they are, in effect, quite distinct processes. Failure to acknowledge this reality has been quite limiting in the past.

It should be noted that the definitions and distinctions related to policy, strategy, goals, objectives, and planning are ongoing sources of debate in the management literature. Different scholars and managers frequently debate the exact meaning of these terminologies. Although the debate is not inconsequential, it should not stand in the way of creative thinking or managerial action.

Integrating Policy and Planning

Although policy formulation and destination planning are different types of processes, they must nevertheless be seen as integrated components of an ongoing process of destination management. This need is reflected in Table 16.1. In examining Table 16.1, keep in mind that the ultimate goal of the **planning process** is to identify the exact nature and timing of the specific actions and activities that must be carried out in efforts to ensure that all the factors that influence destination success (see Figure 16.1) are made as effective as possible. To reiterate, policy provides the guidelines for the development of tourism facilities, events, and programs, while planning stipulates the details and timing of the specific actions/activities to develop each component, subcomponent, and element of the R/C model of destination competitiveness/success. It is essential that both policy and planning processes be fully integrated so as to avoid both waste and duplication.

TABLE 16.1 Tourism Planning: An Integrated Approach

Planning Activity	Organizational Development	Community Involvement	Tourism Product Development	Tourism Product Marketing
		Where Are We Today?		
1. Gather information.	Evaluate existing group composition. Identify potential representatives that could or should be involved.	Identify both tourism and nontourism interests that may be affected by the proposed tourism development. Determine key issues and concerns of the various stakeholders.	Conduct an inventory and assessment of the area's tourism resources, services, and infrastructure. Estimate existing levels of use and carrying capacity.	Profile the existing markets in terms of geographic origin, demographics, family life cycle, spending patterns, needs, and interests.
		Where Do We Want to Go?		
2. Identify community values.	Tourism organization members express community values by answering questions related to quality of life now and in the future.	Community representatives express their values by answering questions related to quality of life now and in the future.	Values expressed by the tourism organization and community representatives begin to form the foundation upon which future tourism development and resource allocation decisions will be based.	Values expressed by the tourism organization and community representatives begin to form the foundation upon which future tourism marketing decisions will be based.
3. Create a vision.	Tourism organization members create an image of how the community should look, feel, and be, now and in the future.	Community representatives create an image of how the community should look, feel, and be, now and in the future.	The descriptive "story" about future development and quality of life in the community further strengthens the foundation and guides tourism development and resource allocation decisions.	The descriptive "story" about future development and quality of life in the community further strengthens the foundation and guides tourism marketing decisions.
4. Identify concerns and opportunities.	Tourism organization members brainstorm a list of concerns and opportunities that the group or community may be facing. Similar ideas are combined and narrowed down to reflect (1) those related to tourism, and (2) those the tourism organization *should* handle.	Community representatives brainstorm a list of concerns and opportunities the community may be facing. Similar ideas are combined and narrowed down to reflect (1) those related to tourism and (2) those that can be addressed by the tourism organization or through tourism initiatives.	The major concerns and opportunities will provide direction for tourism development initiatives. Ideas expressed should be revisited as more concrete plans for developing or enhancing tourism attractions, services, and infrastructure are being considered.	The major concerns and opportunities will provide direction for tourism development initiatives. Ideas expressed should be revisited as more concrete plans for marketing tourism resources and services are being considered.
5. Develop a mission.	Tourism organization members articulate their purpose for existing and determine who they are serving. It is important to recognize not only the visitor; but also community needs during this activity.	The tourism organization's mission serves as a vehicle to inform the community about the group's purpose for existing.	The mission, along with the values, vision, concerns, and opportunities help guide the tourism development effort.	The mission, along with the values, vision, concerns, and opportunities help guide the tourism marketing effort.
6. Develop goals.	Based on the tourism organization's values, vision, concerns, opportunities, and mission, goals relative to the structure and administration of the organization are developed.	Goals related to community education and involvement in the tourism development effort are developed. Most likely, goals will center on ways to involve the public in the planning process.	Based on the expressed values, vision, concerns, opportunities, and mission, goals for the physical development and/or enhancement of tourism resources, traveler services, and infrastructure are developed.	Based on the plans for tourism product development and/or enhancement, goals for tourism marketing are developed.

How Are We Going to Get There?

	Organizational	Community education and involvement	Tourism product development	Tourism marketing
7. Develop objectives.	Tourism organization members develop action-oriented statements that propose how to achieve each *organizational* goal. The number of objectives for each goal will vary depending on the group's stage of development and available human, physical, and financial resources.	Tourism organization members develop action-oriented statements that propose how to achieve each *community education and involvement* goal. The number of objectives for each goal will vary depending on the community's level of interest and involvement in the tourism initiatives, and the available human, physical, and financial resources.	Tourism organization members develop action-oriented statements that propose how to achieve each *tourism product development* goal. The number of objectives for each goal will vary, depending on the community's stage of development, the quantity and quality of existing tourism resources, services, and infrastructure, and available human, physical, and financial resources.	Tourism organization members develop action-oriented statements that propose how to achieve each *tourism product marketing* goal. The number of objectives for each goal will vary depending on the quantity and quality of existing tourism marketing activities and available human, physical, and financial resources.
8. Develop actions.	Tourism organization members define strategies and tactics that outline specifically how each *organizational development* objective will be achieved. This includes exploring funding and technical assistance alternatives, identifying timelines, and assigning tasks.	Tourism organization members define strategies and tactics that outline specifically how each *community education and involvement* objective will be achieved. This includes exploring funding and technical assistance alternatives, identifying timelines, and assigning tasks.	Tourism organization members define strategies and tactics that outline specifically how each *tourism product development* objective will be achieved. This includes exploring funding and technical assistance alternatives, identifying timelines, and assigning tasks.	Tourism organization members define strategies and tactics that outline specifically how each *tourism marketing* objective will be achieved. This includes exploring funding and technical assistance alternatives, identifying timelines, and assigning tasks.

How Did We Do?

	Organizational	Community education and involvement	Tourism product development	Tourism marketing
9. Evaluate progress.	Organization members conduct a periodic review of the organization's activities and progress. A report is written and copies submitted to appropriate governing bodies, funding agencies, and the general public.	Organization members conduct a periodic review of key public involvement activities. A report is written and copies submitted to appropriate governing bodies, funding agencies, and the general public.	Organization members conduct a periodic review of tourism product development and implementation activities and progress. A report is written and copies submitted to appropriate governing bodies, funding agencies, and the general public.	Organization members conduct a periodic review of tourism product marketing activities and progress. A report is written and copies submitted to appropriate governing bodies, funding agencies, and the general public.
10. Update and modify plan.	Based on new information or changing circumstances, revisions to the organizational development plan are made.	Based on new information or changing circumstances, revisions to the plan for community involvement are made.	Based on new information or changing circumstances, revisions to the plan for tourism product development are made.	Based on new information or changing circumstances, revisions to the plan for tourism marketing are made.

Source: Jonelle Nuckolls and Patrick Long, *Organizing Resources for Tourism in Rural Areas* (Boulder, CO: University of Colorado, 1993).

WHY TOURISM PLANNING IS NECESSARY

The decision to develop tourism or expand present tourism development in a community, a region, or a country must be studied carefully. The socioeconomic benefits from tourism are powerful. Tourism development looks attractive to both developed and underdeveloped countries with the right preconditions—some combination of natural, scenic, historical, archaeological, cultural, and climate attractions. Tourism is a growth industry, and while that growth may show some slowing in the short run, the long-run prospects are good. The expected continued growth is based on continually rising per capita incomes, lower travel costs, increased leisure time, and changes in consumers' tastes and preferences toward travel, recreation, and leisure goods and services. Many advocates regard tourism as a panacea for solving an area's development problems. This view is unrealistic because benefits may be accompanied by detrimental consequences. A review of some advantages and disadvantages from Chapter 1 arising from tourism development will indicate why careful planning is necessary. There are a dozen major arguments for tourism:

1. Provides employment opportunities, both skilled and unskilled, because it is a labor-intensive industry
2. Generates a supply of needed foreign exchange
3. Increases incomes
4. Creates increased gross domestic product
5. Requires the development of an infrastructure that will also help stimulate local commerce and industry
6. Justifies environmental protection and improvement
7. Increases governmental revenues
8. Helps to diversify the economy
9. Creates a favorable worldwide image for the destination
10. Facilitates the process of modernization by education of youth and society and changing values
11. Provides tourist and recreational facilities that may be used by a local population who could not otherwise afford to develop facilities
12. Gives foreigners an opportunity to be favorably impressed by a little-known country or region

Nine disadvantages of tourism are that it:

1. Develops excess demand
2. Creates leakages so great that economic benefits might not accrue
3. Diverts funds from more promising forms of economic development
4. Creates social problems from income differences, social differences, introduction of prostitution, gambling, crime, and so on
5. Degrades the natural physical environment
6. Degrades the cultural environment
7. Poses the difficulties of seasonality
8. Increases vulnerability to economic and political changes
9. Adds to inflation of land values and the price of local goods and services

Consequently, tourism is not always a panacea. On the contrary, overdevelopment can generate soil and water pollution and even people pollution, if there are too many visitors at the same place at the same time. Consider automobile and bus traffic congestion, inadequate parking, hotels dwarfing the scale of historic districts, and the displacement of the local community-serving businesses by tourist-serving firms, leading to degradation, rather than improvement, of the quality of life.

Tropical island resorts require good planning to integrate facilities and protect the environment.
Photo courtesy of the Abaco Beach Resort and Boat Harbour.

Furthermore, too many visitors can have a harmful impact on life in the host country and on the visitors themselves. A beautiful landscape can suffer through thoughtless and unwise land development and construction methods. And customers and crafts can be vulgarized by over-emphasis on quantity and cheapness. These responsibilities cannot really be blamed on tourism, but rather on overcommercialization. Tourism is one of the world's greatest and most significant social and economic forces. But government officials and businesspeople must weigh the economic benefits against the possible future degradation of human and natural resources.

Tourism development must be guided by carefully planned policy, a policy built not on balance sheets and profit and loss statements alone, but on the ideals and principles of human welfare and happiness. Social problems cannot be solved without a strong and growing economy that tourism can help to create. Sound development policy can have the happy result of a growing tourist business, along with the preservation of the natural and cultural resources that attracted the visitors in the first place.

Planning is critical to having sustainable development and protecting the environment. For that reason, the next chapter has been devoted to tourism and the environment to expand the discussion on how to have development and, hopefully, both protect and enhance the environment.

Viewed comprehensively, the relationship between tourism and the community, state, regions, and countries requires consideration of many difficult issues: the quality of architecture, landscape, and environmental design; environmental reclamation and amenity; natural conservation; land-use management; financial strategies for long-term economic development; employment; transportation; energy conservation; education, information, and interpretation systems; and more.

These are the reasons why sound tourism planning is essential. Planning can ensure that tourist development has the ability to realize the advantages of tourism and reduce the disadvantages.

THE PLANNING PROCESS

Proper planning of the physical, legal, promotional, financial, economic, market, management, social, and environmental aspects will help to deliver the benefits of tourism development—and it can be carried out much more effectively when fully integrated with the process of policy formulation.

Good planning defines the desired result and works in a systematic manner to achieve success. The following steps briefly describe a logical sequence:

1. **Define the system.** What are its scale, size, market, character, and purpose? Formulate objectives. Without a set of objectives, the development concept has no direction. The objectives must be comprehensive and specific and should include a timetable for completion.

2. **Gather data.** Fact finding, or research, provides basic data that are essential to developing the plan. Examples of data gathering are preparing a fact book, making market surveys, undertaking site and infrastructure surveys, and analyzing existing facilities and competition.

3. **Analyze and interpret.** Once collected, the many fragments of information must be interpreted so the facts gathered will have meaning. This step produces a set of conclusions and recommendations that leads to making or conceptualizing a preliminary plan.

4. **Create the preliminary plan.** Based on the previous steps, alternatives are considered and alternative physical solutions are drawn up and tested. Frequently, scale models are developed to illustrate the land-use plans; sketches are prepared to show the image the development will project; financial plans are drafted from the market information, site surveys, and the layout plan to show the investment needed in each phase of the project and the cash flow expected; and legal requirements are met.

5. **Approve the plan.** The parties involved can now look at plans, drawings, scale models, estimates of costs, and estimates of profits and know what will be involved and what the chances for success or failure will be. While a great deal of money may have been spent up to this point, the sum is a relatively small amount compared to the expenditures that will be required once the plan is approved and master planning and implementation begin.

6. **Create the final plan.** This phase typically includes a definition of land use; plans for infrastructure facilities such as roads, airports, bike paths, horse trails, pedestrian walkways, sewage, water, and utilities; architectural standards; landscape plans; zoning and other land-use regulations; and economic analysis, market analysis, and financial programming.

7. **Implement the plan.** Implementation carries out the plan and creates an operational tourism development. It also follows up and evaluates. Good planning provides mechanisms that give continuing feedback on the tourism project and the levels of consumer satisfaction achieved.

Good planning should eliminate problems and provide user satisfaction. The final user is the judge in determining how successful the planning process has been.

Denver International Airport exemplifies good planning for traveler convenience. The modern terminal building has separate drop-off levels for passengers arriving in private and commercial vehicles, close-in parking, and trains to shuttle passengers from the terminal to three concourses. *Photo courtesy of Denver International Airport.*

Designed to be unobtrusive, the Hotel Bora Bora does not overwhelm its surroundings. It feels like a genuine Tahitian village with a South Seas atmosphere. In keeping with the use of indigenous materials and styles, the 80 thatched-roof bungalows form a villagelike grouping of informal, open-air structures. Incorporating regional influences, the design of the Hotel Bora Bora affords great economy in both construction and operation. *Photo courtesy of WATG.*

Figure 16.2 provides a graphical summary of the above tourism planning and development process and illustrates the increasingly detailed nature of the process as we move from stage to stage. The advantage of utilizing such a model is that it requires the planner to view the total picture and guides the thinking process. Although no model can depict all interrelated facts of a planning process or eliminate all guesswork, such a model deserves inclusion in the initial phases of planning as a tool that helps to order, coordinate, and control the process.

Table 16.1 shows an integrated approach to planning. Again, it serves as a guide to asking the right questions and making sure that the process is complete. It also illustrates that there are a number of approaches to tourism planning. There is no single magic approach.

GOALS OF TOURISM DEVELOPMENT

Tourism planners should aim for five **goals of tourism development**:

1. Providing a framework for raising the living standard of the people through the economic benefits of tourism

2. Developing an infrastructure and providing recreation facilities for visitors and residents alike

3. Ensuring types of development within visitor centers and resorts that are appropriate to the purposes of those areas

STAGE 1	STAGE 2	STAGE 3	STAGE 4	STAGE 5	STAGE 6	STAGE 7
Define the System	**Gather Necessary Data**	**Analyze & Interpret Data**	**Create Preliminary Plan**	**Approve the Plan**	**Create the Final Plan**	**Implement the Plan**
In doing so, ensure that the definitions for the policy formulation and destination planning are consistent.	Again, much of the data used for policy formulation may be helpful for the planning process. However, additional and much more detailed data will be required for the planning process.	In doing so, it is useful to relate data to the specific facilities, events, activities, and programs that impact on the factors that determine/influence destination success.	The plan should start to make clear the detailed nature of the facilities, events, activities, and programs that will deliver the unique high-quality destination experience that will enhance the competitiveness of the destination within strategic market segments.	It is critical to ensure that where approval is required no relevant stakeholders are overlooked.	At this stage, the level of detail becomes increasingly rigorous and directly related to the specific geography, legislation, financing, and timing of the "real world."	This stage allocates responsibility for development actions to specific individuals and organizations, defines the exact timing of these actions, and establishes contingencies for unexpected occurrences. This stage also monitors, follows up, and evaluates.

Figure 16.2 An overview of the tourism planning process.

4. Establishing a development program consistent with the cultural, social, and economic philosophy of the government and the people of the host country or area

5. Optimizing visitor satisfaction

OBSTACLES TO DEVELOPMENT OF SUPPLY

Obstacles to development can be external (outside the destination) or internal (in the destination). External obstacles are those which originate from outside the destination—such as political disagreements with the government of a major foreign market. Internal obstacles are, logically then, those which originate within the destination. The most common perhaps is resident opposition to a particular type of tourism development, such as a casino. The first obstacle to overcome in turning potential supply into actual supply is the lack or inadequacy of transportation and access routes to the tourist nucleus or center. It is, of course, not enough to get there. The tourist should also be induced to stay. To this end, another basic obstacle to the development of actual supply should be overcome: the lack or shortage of accommodation.

Tourists inevitably require a series of goods and services. Some may be found on the spot and may be economically flexible enough to adapt to the fluctuations of demand. The infrastructure capacity must meet maximum demand. Financing can be a major obstacle. Finally, we cannot overlook the need for sufficiently trained and hospitable personnel.

Internal obstacles found within the destination area can be corrected or eliminated by direct, voluntary means. The obstacles may occur in incoming as well as outgoing or internal tourism.

As tourism in all its forms absorbs consumer goods, prices in this field tend to be extremely sensitive to movements in the prices of goods. A rise in prices due to tourism has the same effect as a decrease in the income of the potential tourist. Consequently, when considering costs and

WATG

WATG has been *designing destinations for over 60 years*—places that delight their visitors and satisfy their owners, too. The work of WATG spans more than 160 countries and territories and is highly acclaimed for excellence in design and creativity.

The *firm's policy* is to respect the unique environment and cultural heritage of each host country, region or community, and to make a positive contribution to the lives and culture of that area. Our mission, "designing destinations that lift the spirit."

Having designed more hospitality projects than any other firm in the world, WATG has had the privilege of assisting preeminent owners, developers, operators and governments on six continents. No two places, no two clients, no two projects are alike. Yet they all succeed in achieving these critical balances: the needs of clients and the expectations of visitors, the wishes of the local community and the preferences of the international marketplace, the desire for design innovation, and the reality of economic restraints.

From offices in Honolulu, Irvine, Seattle, Orlando, London, Singapore, and various project site offices, WATG offers strategy, planning, architecture, interior design, and landscape architecture services. A talented and multicultural staff of over 300 professionals specializes in hospitality, leisure, and entertainment projects. As an industry leader with over a half-century of experience, WATG has been involved in the successful completion of over 250 hotel projects totaling more than 90,000 new guestrooms, and another 12,000 guestrooms are currently under construction.

WATG's client list includes almost every major international, national, and regional operator/owner, including: Conrad, Equatorial, Fairmont, Four Seasons, Grecotel, Hilton, Hyatt. Inter-Continental, Jumeirah, Kempinski, Kerzner International, Mandarin Oriental Hotel Group, Marriott, MGM Resorts International, Mövenpick, Okura, Peninsula, Radisson, Ramada, The Ritz-Carlton Hotel Company, RockResorts, Rosewood, Savoy Group of Hotels, Shangri-La, Shilla, Starwood (Le Meridien, Sheraton, St. Regis, W Hotels, Westin), Steigenberger Hotel Group, Swissotel, Viceroy, Waldorf-Astoria, Wynn Resorts, and many others.

In addition to designing hotels and resorts, WATG has been internationally acclaimed for creativity and bottom-line success of projects that include:

- casinos and cruise ships

- convention centers and conference facilities

- golf resorts and clubhouses

- marinas/waterfront developments

- master planned resort and recreational communities

- mixed-use developments

- residential: apartments, extended stay, assisted-living, custom homes

- restaurants and clubs

- retail, dining, and entertainment venues

- spas, sports clubs, and wellness centers

- theme parks, water parks, and themed environments

- vacation ownership/timeshare resorts and private residence clubs

Regardless of the project type or location, WATG offers clients *a cost-effective system for expediting the development process* and producing award-winning designs that consistently rank among the top in the world by the most discerning travelers. For further information about WATG, visit watg.com.

The firm is best known for such internationally acclaimed projects as King George II Palace, Athens, Greece; Atlantis Paradise Island, Bahamas; The Palace of the Lost City, Sun City, South Africa; Claridge's Hotel, London; Mövenpick Dead Sea Resort, Jordan; Grand Hyatt Kauai, Hawaii, USA; Regency Casino, Thessaloniki, Greece; Hotel Bora Bora, French Polynesia; Viceroy, Anguilla; St. Regis, Singapore; The Ritz-Carlton, Bali; and the Four Seasons in Maui, Mauritius, Mexico City, and Tokyo.

WATG has evidence that good design can improve clients' top and bottom line. In research conducted over a 20-year period by Smith Travel Research, it was revealed that WATG-designed hotels command more than a $50 premium in RevPAR (revenue per available room) for the hotels' owners and operators.

A word about the future. WATG does not follow trends, the firm sets them. That is why WATG is currently designing destinations not just on the earth, but above and below it too. Works in progress include a space resort, an undersea hotel, a city at sea, and an airship hotel. WATG is the number-one destination design firm in the world, according to surveys by *Hotel Design* and *Hotel & Motel Management* magazines. *Hospitality Design* magazine's recent survey of architecture and interior design firms ranked WATG's corporate culture among the top in the country: best career development, best firm philosophy, best client list, best list of projects, and most innovative.

planning a holiday, the tourist will choose to go—if the value is the same—where money goes the farthest.

Another major obstacle is the attitude of government and business leaders in the destination area. If this leadership is resistant or even passive toward tourism, development will lag.

POLITICAL ASPECTS OF TOURISM DEVELOPMENT

Like any significant element of an area's economy, **political aspects** can and often do have major influences on the creation, operation, and survival of tourism projects. Many examples can be cited. One is the land-use regulations (zoning) for commercial or public tourism developments, which can be emotionally and politically sensitive topics. Another is the degree of involvement of governmental agencies in creating and maintaining tourism infrastructure. A third is the type and extent of publicity, advertising, and other promotional efforts.

Land Use (Zoning)

Zoning ordinances specify the legal types of land use. But the final determination of the land use and the administration of the zoning ordinances are typically assigned to a publicly employed zoning administrator and a politically appointed or elected zoning board. Thus, the government decides how land is to be used, and it also rules on any request for changes in the zoning districts or rezoning to accommodate a nonconforming proposed development.

Attitudes of these public bodies toward tourism development will be influenced by the general public's perception of the desirability of a specific development. Creating a favorable public image is the responsibility of the developer and the managers of all tourism supply components. The public tourism promotion organization bears responsibility as well. If the public feels that tourism is desirable, rational zoning regulations and administration should result. Furthermore, if principles of tourism planning and development, as presented in this chapter, are faithfully implemented, the result should be well-planned projects. These will be accepted in the community as welcome sources of employment and tax revenues.

Creation and Maintenance of Infrastructure

Any tourism development will need infrastructure. Whether this is provided by government agencies or the private developer, or both, is basically a political question. What troubles many local people is that their taxes are spent in part to provide roads, water systems, sewers, airports, marinas, parks, and other infrastructure that they perceive as benefiting mainly tourism. Is this fair or desirable from their point of view? Those having a common concern in tourism must realize that it is their responsibility to convince the public that such expenditures by government are desirable and do benefit the local economy. One way to achieve this understanding is through an intelligent lobbying effort. Another approach is to address service clubs, social organizations, and school groups. A third method shows how much money was spent by tourists or convention delegates.

Maintenance policies are also a vital factor in successful tourism development. Any element of infrastructure, once created, needs maintenance. The level of this maintenance can greatly affect successful tourism. An example is the promptness and adequacy of snow removal from public roads servicing ski resorts. Another is the quality and adequacy of public water and sewage systems. Many other examples could be given. Political influence to obtain good maintenance can be brought to bear by hotel and motel associations, chambers of commerce, convention and visitors bureaus, and promotion groups. Such efforts can be very effective, because public service agencies tend to be receptive if the demands are frequent and forceful.

Government and private industry must interact cooperatively if tourism development is to be successful. Political friction can develop when government officials think that private industry should do more to help itself and businesspeople believe that the government should do more to assist them. A knowledgeable outside consulting firm can study the situation and make recommendations in the best interests of both factions.

Promotional Efforts

Publicly funded promotional programs are an essential part of the industry. However, the level or degree of participation in such publicity is largely a political process. To convince lawmakers and local political decision makers of the desirability of tourism, organizations representing tourism need to produce accurate data on the economic impact of tourism spending. An "investment" concept is the preferred way to view government programs. Pointing out industry diversification in the economy is another good approach. Other benefits cited could be employment, income multipliers, additional investments, and preservation and enhancement of local industries, crafts, and the arts, as well as building local pride and recognition.

Lobbying efforts need to be convincing and persistent. Organizations representing tourism must have both moral and monetary support in sufficient measure to bring about successful political influence. Nothing succeeds like success. If tourism booms, the politicians can well take pride in their important contribution. We repeat: As in all other aspects of the tourist business, cooperation pays!

❖ GLOBAL INSIGHT ❖

Security

To meet the needs of today's world, it is essential that tourism planners and managers put the safety and security factor into their designs and tourism development plans. Here, Dr. Peter E. Tarlow, president of Tourism and More, author of "Tourism Tidbits" and the book *Event Risk Management and Safety*, and world-renowned travel safety and security expert, shares a few tidbits of advice that he has communicated to planners around the world.

1. **It is only ten years since September 11, 2001.** Too many travel professionals function, however, as if that day were a one-time event or had never occurred. It is foolish to believe that the emotional scars of terrorism have healed. Furthermore, terrorism is more of a chronic disease than a war. It is a disease that at times may go into remission, but it is not going away. The tourism industry will continue to be one of its prime targets.

2. **Do not expect 100 percent security/safety.** Security and safety are goals but never total realities. All too many of us have come to believe that our governments can handle every eventuality; they cannot. Instead, the tourism industry must do its best to provide realistic assessments of each situation.

3. **Pay your security people top dollar.** In the twentieth century, tourism professionals tended to see security as an add-on, or a required extra. In the twenty-first century, tourism security has become a major marketing tool. Customers want to see security and they want to know that those who are providing security are well-trained professionals. This professionalization of the profession comes about through good training, good wages, and strict standards. For example those communities who have "Tourism-Oriented Policing Services units" (TOPS) are going to be well ahead of their competition in attracting meetings and conventions.

4. **Do a tourism security inventory.** Know what are your security strengths and weaknesses. For example, a good community security inventory examines everything from airport safety to who has access to a guest's room. Such an inventory should look not only at issues of terrorism but also at issues of crime, and how these crimes can be prevented. Furthermore, examine your personnel strengths and liabilities as well as your equipment and physical strengths and weaknesses.

5. **Do not only focus on terrorism.** Terrorism today is a hot topic, but there is a higher probability that visitors will be touched by an act of crime than by an act of terrorism. Know which crimes are most likely to impact visitors to your community. Then develop a plan that coordinates security professionals, law enforcement, the political establishment, and the tourism industry. Remember that a poorly trained police force can almost overnight destroy a well-thought-out marketing program.

6. **Be current.** What reality dictated two or three months ago might not be true tomorrow. Good security means taking the time to reassess situations and to change policies based on the latest data.

7. **Have a recovery plan.** Although the best form of good crisis management is good risk management, crises and tragedies will occur. Furthermore, in an age of terrorism, an event in one part of the world can impact many other parts of the world. That means that in a worldwide industry, such as tourism, individual companies and even countries often are not totally in control of their destinies. Because it is impossible to tell when the next "event" may strike, tourism professionals must have a full list of contingency plans available. While these plans should not be written in stone, it is always easier to change a plan than it is to write a plan during an emergency.

8. **The best security comes from places with good service.** If your employees do not care about good service, then they are indicating that they do not care about the welfare of their guests. Up the level of your service and make it fun. Travel for many people simply is not fun anymore. The word *travel* is derived from the French word *travil,* meaning "work." The more work travel becomes, the less people are going to want to travel. Long airport lines, the need to remove articles of clothing, the tearing apart of briefcases and suitcases, delayed planes, and no food or currently no liquids makes travel (especially air travel) much more of a hassle than a pleasure. Help your customer and guests to recover through extra thoughtful service. Encourage hotels to develop "stress-down" meals, to provide extras from a smile to special bathroom sundries. Encourage attractions to have special "thanks for traveling" days. In other words, do everything possible to put the fun back in travel. The bottom line is that during times of stress people need our smiles.

Dr. Peter Tarlow can be reached by e-mail at tourism@bihs.net.

DISCUSSION QUESTIONS

1. What is a tourism security inventory?

2. How important is it for tourism enterprises to work with local police and fire departments?

DEVELOPMENT OF TOURIST POTENTIAL

Official Tourism Body

A tourism body or organization (referred to as the destination management organization, or DMO) should be created to keep abreast of socioeconomic developments in the various market countries or areas to provide a reasonably early forecast of the size, type, and structure of probable tourism demand. It would be equally useful to have a report on developments in the tourist industry of supplying centers or areas and on activities and projects undertaken to promote development.

Because tourism is such a complex phenomenon, distinct ministerial departments are responsible for finding solutions to developmental problems.

The stabilization of general and tourist prices should be a constant objective, because rising prices automatically reduce the volume of demand. Land speculation should be discouraged.

The inventory of potential national tourist resources (parks, attractions, recreational facilities, and so on) should be kept up to date and extended so that these resources may be duly incorporated into actual tourist trade in accordance with quantity and quality forecasts of demand.

Tax pressures that directly affect operating costs also influence prices. Because of the export value of tourism, a fiscal policy similar to that applied to the conventional or classical export trade should be devised.

Publicity campaigns should be organized and implemented every year according to the forecasts. These should be to the point, detailed, and constructive, and should zero in on socioeconomic developments and activities in the market. Financing to cover this activity should be obtained from annual tourist earnings and other identifiable funds at a rate of not less than 1 percent and perhaps not more than 4 percent of total earnings. Customs facilities should be as lenient and hospitable as possible while ensuring control and maintenance of order and avoiding fraud or other crimes.

For their own benefit, host countries should make the tourists' sojourn as agreeable as possible. But proof that tourists have the financial means to cover the costs of their stay may be desirable.

The seasonal nature of mass tourism causes congestion in the use of services required by tourists. On the one hand, some services, such as accommodation, cannot adapt easily to seasonal fluctuation. On the other hand, some, such as transportation and communications, can adapt. Government provision of public services is important for development—and these too can be adapted to seasonal fluctuations.

Transportation

Because of the role of transportation in tourist development, the following measures are recommended:

1. Conduct continual, detailed study of transport used for tourism with a view toward planning necessary improvements and extensions.

2. Establish a national or international plan of roads relevant to tourism, building new roads if necessary, improving those in a deficient state, and improving road sign systems. Such activities should be included in the general road plans with priorities according to economic necessity and the significance of road transport in tourism.

3. Improve rail transport (where needed) for travelers on lines between the boundary and the main tourist centers and regions as well as short-distance services in these regions of maximum tourist influx.

4. Improve road frontier posts, extending their capacity to ensure smoother crossings, organizing easier movement of in- and outgoing tourist flows. Crossing the frontier is always either the prologue or the epilogue to any journey between countries and is therefore important for the favorable impression the tourist will gain or retain.

5. Provide adequate airport services and installations to meet demand. The rapid progress of technology in air transport makes reasonable forecasts possible.

6. Plan for ports and marinas equipped for tourism.

7. Extend car services (with and without drivers) for tourists who arrive by air or sea.

Accommodations

Accommodations must be properly placed in the regional plan. Hotels are permanent structures and grace the landscape for a long time. Planning considerations are vital. Figure 16.3 shows a specific site development plan.

One of the first considerations to be made by any planning body should be where hotels will be located. This can be accomplished by using zoning laws. Hotels are commonly allowed in "commercial" zones. Also to be decided is the number of hotel rooms needed in relation to the anticipated demand. Next to be considered is a provision for expansion of hotels as demand increases.

One consideration in hotel planning is intelligent spacing of hotels in a given area. Hotels spaced too close together tend to have a mutual value-reducing effect. Views are cut off or inhibited, and structures are lowered in value.

Also important is the ratio of the number of persons on the beach to the number of rooms in the hotel. Research in the Department of Natural Resources of the state of Michigan indicates that the optimum capacity of an average-size ocean or Great Lakes beach is approximately 1,000 persons for

Transportation is an important component of tourism planning. Union Station in Washington, D.C., is an outstanding example of good planning. This beautiful facility accommodates rail service, metro service, dining, and shopping in a pleasant atmosphere. *Photo courtesy of Washington, D.C., and the Capital Region, U.S.A.*

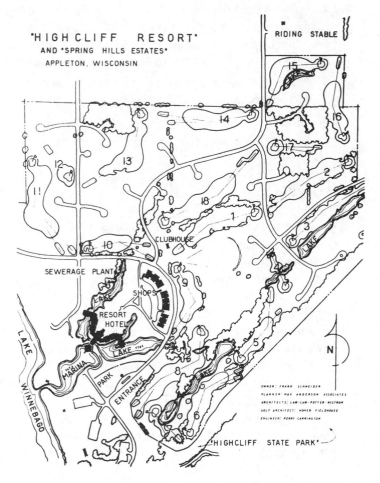

Figure 16.3 Example of "planning for private tourism development adjacent to a state park." Note integration of infrastructure and recreational facilities.
Source: Recreational Land Development, Wisconsin Department of Natural Resources, Division of Resource Development, Bureau of Recreation.

each 400 lineal feet of beach. Typically, about 50 percent of those vacationers in a resort or beach area will actually be on the beach, and of this group, 25 percent will be in the water and 75 percent will be on the beach.

Another consideration is the topography. In rolling or hilly country, more accommodations can be placed close together without a feeling of interference with one another than in a flat area. Also, the type of vegetative cover affects the density of the accommodations. A heavy, thick cover tends to obscure the view, and more accommodations can be successfully placed in a limited area than if the vegetation is sparse or absent entirely (see Figure 16.4).

Clustering accommodations in reasonably close proximity, surrounded by extensive natural areas, is recognized as superior planning, as opposed to spreading out accommodations over a wide area. The beauty of the natural environment can be more fully appreciated in such an arrangement.

Before any investment in hotels and similar lodging facilities is made, the traveling and vacation habits of the prospective guests should be studied to tailor the facilities to their requirements and desires. This is extremely important and conforms to the "market orientation" concept in which major decisions on investment begin with an understanding of the desires of the potential customers. Another factor is the harmony required between the various elements of the travel plan, the local environment, and infrastructure.

Finally, when resort development is to be limited (and it usually is), it is best to select the most desirable location and create a hotel of real distinction at this site. Then, later, if proper planning and promotion have been accomplished, expansion to other nearby sites can be achieved. Distinctive design of other hotel sites will encourage the visitor to enjoy the variety, architectural appeals, and other satisfactions inherent in each resort hotel.

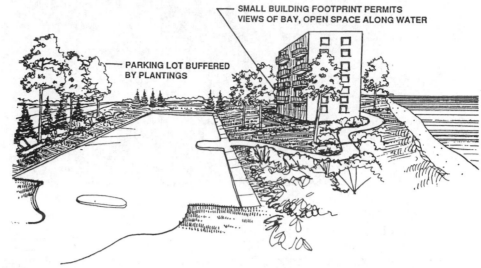

SMALL BUILDING FOOTPRINT PERMITS
VIEWS OF BAY, OPEN SPACE ALONG WATER

PARKING LOT BUFFERED
BY PLANTINGS

Figure 16.4 ``Better approach" planning principles of ``buffering and minimizing building site space to open scenic views."
Source: Grand Traverse Bay Region Development Guidelines.

Financing

Possible procedures for financing construction include a mortgage guarantee plan and direct loans from a variety of sources.

Mortgage Guarantee Plan

Under a mortgage guarantee plan, the government would guarantee mortgage loans up to 80 percent of the approved and appraised value of the land, building, furnishings, and equipment when the resort is completed. The approved mortgage would carry interest at prevailing mortgage rates and would require a schedule of amortization for the full retirement of the loan in not more than approximately 30 years.

A guarantee fund would be established that at all times would be maintained at 20 percent of the total outstanding principal amount of mortgages guaranteed under this plan. The guarantee fund would be managed by trustees who would make any payments of interest and principal certified to them by the agency in charge of the mortgage loan plan. This agency would supervise the status of all approved loans and would investigate the facts and situations whenever it might become necessary to rely on the guarantee fund to make the required interest and amortization payments. In such cases, an assignment of assets and income would be taken from the resort in default, which would have to be made up from subsequent earnings before any other use could be made of it.

Under this plan, the investor in the resort project would secure a mortgage loan from a lending institution or issue bonds or mortgage certificates to one or more sources of the borrowed capital. With the guarantee of payments of interest and principal and the existence of the guarantee fund for that purpose, mortgage loans under this plan should be attractive to lending institutions and other sources of borrowed capital.

With an approved resort development project and a guaranteed mortgage loan equivalent to 80 percent of the total financing required for land, building, furniture, and equipment, 20 percent of the cost could be invested as equity risk capital. The ability to finance on this basis would provide incentive to those directly interested in the business, as well as other investors, to participate in new resort development projects.

Hotel accommodations should be planned to blend in and enhance the surrounding environment so tourists will want to visit. The Loretto Inn, Sante Fe, New Mexico, sits at the end of the Santa Fe Trail and blends in with its surroundings. *Photo courtesy of Corbis Digital Stock.*

Financing Procedures

A group interested in building a resort must convince the local city, regional, or national authorities that the resort should be built. The next step is to obtain a suitable site designated for construction under a previously completed tourist development plan for the area. A third-party feasibility study should be undertaken.

To indicate that this group is seriously interested in building a resort, architects, engineers, consultants, and other specialists should be contacted during the planning phase. The organization that is to operate the resort should be the same group that builds the hotel. An important planning ingredient is the recommendation of experienced resort managers concerning design and layout of the project.

The next step is to obtain construction capital either from local sources or from government or foreign sources. Also, capital must be secured for equipment, supplies, and services, including opening expenses and pre–break-even expenses. Government aid in obtaining imported supplies and equipment is often necessary.

Governmental consideration should be given for reduction or elimination of taxes for an adequate length of time to help ensure the financial success of the resort venture. Elimination of import duties on materials needed to build and run resorts is also desirable.

SUMMARY

This chapter opens with the presentation of a model that identifies and explains those factors that fundamentally determine the competitiveness, sustainability, and success of tourism destinations. It then examines the nature and necessity of tourism planning and development, as well as the distinct characteristics of each process. Subsequently, discussion focuses on the importance of relating policy to planning with a view to achieving a meaningful integration of the two processes.

The quality of tourism planning and development will determine the ultimate success and longevity of any destination area. Thus, time, effort, and resources devoted to planning are essential investments.

Thoughtful planners have formulated the goals for tourism development, and these should be guiding principles everywhere. Obstacles must be overcome by sound planning augmented by political means, if growth is desired. This is often accomplished by the official tourism body. Tourism development should be a part of the overall regional or urban land-use development plan.

Tourism developments almost always involve both government and private developers. Each sector can best contribute certain parts of a project. Government typically provides the infrastructure, such as roads, water supply, sewers, public transportation terminals, and parks. Private developers supply superstructure, such as hotels, restaurants, recreation facilities, and shopping areas.

Government can also help considerably in making financing available. The private sector must deem an investment in a tourist facility attractive from the standpoint of financial return and risk before funds will be committed.

❖ **KEY CONCEPTS** ❖

architectural standards
destination management
  organization
goals of tourism development
infrastructure

land use
obstacles to development
planning process
policy formulation
political aspects

preservation
situational conditioners
transportation
zoning

❖ **INTERNET EXERCISES** ❖

The Internet sites mentioned in this chapter plus some selected additional sites are listed for your convenience on the companion Web site for this book, www.wiley.com/ college/goeldner.

ACTIVITY 1

Site Name: The International Ecotourism Society (TIES)

URL: www.ecotourism.org

Background Information: The International Ecotourism Society identifies key issues in the field of ecotourism that require international attention each year.

Exercise

1. What criteria do the International Ecotourism Society use to determine which issues to address?

ACTIVITY 2

Site Name: Alaska Wilderness Recreation and Tourism Association (AWRTA)

URL: www.awrta.org

Background Information: The Alaska Wilderness Recreation and Tourism Association is a nonprofit trade association that promotes the recognition and protection of Alaska's wilderness.

Exercises

1. What guidelines has AWRTA established for businesses to follow when planning for tourism?

2. What planning issues are currently being addressed by AWRTA?

ACTIVITY 3

Site Name: Cyburbia

URL: www.cyburbia.org

Background Information: Cyburbia contains a comprehensive directory of Internet resources relevant to planning, architecture, urbanism, and other topics related to the built environment. Cyburbia also contains information regarding architecture- and planning-related mailing lists and Usenet newsgroups, and it hosts interactive message areas.

Exercise

1. Surf this Web site and identify current issues facing the tourism industry. How do these issues coincide with those discussed in the textbook?

❖ **QUESTIONS FOR REVIEW AND DISCUSSION** ❖

1. What are the factors that determine the success of a tourism destination that the tourism manager can control?

2. What is destination competitiveness?

3. Basically, what is the purpose of planning?

4. Discuss the importance of transportation to tourism development.

5. Discuss the most important factors that would influence the success of a newly built resort.

6. Why is tourism developmental planning so necessary?

7. What are some of the most significant relationships between a large-size resort development and its nearby community?

8. Referring to the previous question, if the community is a rather small one, should any input be solicited from residents of the community before major remodeling or new construction is undertaken?

9. What goals should guide the land-use plan of a small lakeshore village that is popular with summer visitors?

10. Provide some descriptions of the importance of infrastructure to the following: ski resort, summer campground, fishing pier, public marina, shopping center, and resort apartment condominium project.

11. From planning to completed project, name the principal individuals and organizations that would be involved.

12. Do you agree with the statement that if a community's government and business leaders are resistant or passive toward tourism, development will lag?

13. Currently, heritage preservation is a popular trend. Is it a desirable one?

14. Would you encourage tourism development if your community and area were already very prosperous?

15. Enumerate various kinds of environmental pollution that unwise developments can create.

16. How could greater emphasis be placed on the importance of a development process in which meticulous attention is given to the environment to create a harmonious combination of natural assets and human-made facilities?

❖ **CASE PROBLEMS** ❖

1. A real estate developer, aware of a growing demand for a lakeshore resort condominium, planned for 126 apartments plus a 56-slip marina. After he submitted his plan, the township planning board informed him that only one apartment and one boat slip would be allowed for each hundred feet of lakeshore. Because he did not own that much lakeshore, plans were redrawn to construct the planned development back from the lakeshore. Access to the lake would be provided via a canal, using one of the lakeshore lots—a "keyhole" plan. This proposal was also rejected. The developer then sued the township board to force approval. What should the court or judge decide?

2. You have accepted a United Nations Development Program assignment in tourism to a small Central American country. Your first task is to make financial calculations concerning the economic feasibility for a resort development. What factors do you consider when beginning this process? Assuming your findings result in a favorable conclusion, what would your next step be?

3. Hotels built in a boxlike manner are cheaper to construct and maintain than those with more elaborate designs. Hotel companies normally aim to maximize profits. Thus, should all hotels be built in that manner?

CHAPTER 17

Tourism and the Environment

LEARNING OBJECTIVES

- Understand the fundamental nature of sustainable development and sustainable tourism.

- Identify guiding principles for achieving sustainable tourism.

- Review the policy aims of an agenda for sustainable tourism.

- Examine the major challenges facing achievement of sustainable tourism.

- Identify the new realities of tourism in an era of global climate change.

- Examine policies and measures to mitigate tourism-induced climate change.

- Examine the concept of ecotourism and its role in sustainable tourism.

The cliffs that make up the Dorsey Heritage Coast are a popular natural attraction in England. *Photo courtesy of the British Tourist Authority.*

INTRODUCTION

As tourism moves farther into the twenty-first century, both the destination and the enterprise will have to make the environment a priority. Because tourism is now the world's largest industry, the environment is taking center stage in tourism development. Tourism is not only a powerful economic force but a factor in the physical environment as well. Because more attention will be paid to the environment in the future, projects that are economically feasible but not environmentally desirable will remain unbuilt. The environment is the core of the tourism product. Profitability in tourism depends on maintaining the attractiveness of the destination people want to see and experience.

Tourism has the power to enhance the environment, to provide funds for conservation, to preserve culture and history, to set sustainable use limits, and to protect natural attractions. It also has the power to destroy. If tourism is not properly planned and implemented, it can destroy vegetation, create overcrowding, litter trekking areas, pollute beaches, result in overbuilding, eliminate open space, create sewage problems, cause housing problems, and ignore the needs and structure of the host community.

It is being recognized that tourism must preserve and protect the environment and natural attractions so that people will continue to travel, and must set use limits so that sites will be truly sustainable. The problem is how to do this. Concepts such sustainable development, sustainable tourism, carrying capacity, climate change, nature tourism, and ecotourism have been proposed and are examined in this chapter. Throughout the discussion, we constantly keep in mind the industry's obligation to be environmentally responsible.

DOES TOURISM THREATEN THE ENVIRONMENT? THE UNEP/UNWTO POSITION

Before addressing how tourism can best respond to the negative impacts on the environment, it is useful to obtain a clear understanding of the fundamental goal in this regard; namely, the achievement of a tourism system which is sustainable over the long term.

The Nature of Sustainable Development[1]

The most commonly used definition of sustainable development is still that given in the report of the World Commission on Environment and Development (1987).[2] That is, sustainable development is "*a process to meet the needs of the present without compromising the ability of future generations to meet their own needs.*"

Sustainable development is, therefore, about creating a better life for all people in ways that will be as viable in the future as they are at present. In other words, sustainable development is based on principles of sound husbandry of the world's resources, and on equity in the way those resources are used and in the way in which the benefits obtained from them are distributed.

The concept has evolved since the 1987 definition, notably through Agenda 21, the plan of action that emerged from the UN Conference on Environment and Development (Rio, 1992), and the plan of implementation from the World Summit on Sustainable Development (Johannesburg, 2002). Three dimensions or pillars of sustainable development are now recognized and underlined. These are:

- *Economic sustainability,* which means generating prosperity at different levels of society and addressing the cost effectiveness of all economic activity. Crucially, it is about the viability of enterprises and activities and their ability to be maintained in the long term.

The beach at Coral Bay in Cyprus has been awarded the Blue Flag, an exclusive eco-label awarded to more than 3,450 beaches and marinas across Europe, Africa, New Zealand, Brazil, Canada, and the Caribbean. The Blue Flag Campaign is owned and run by the independent, nonprofit organization Foundation for Environmental Education (FEE). *Courtesy of International Blue Flag Coordination.*

- *Social sustainability*, which means respecting human rights and equal opportunities for all in society. It requires an equitable distribution of benefits, with a focus on alleviating poverty. There is an emphasis on local communities, maintaining and strengthening their life support systems, recognizing and respecting different cultures, and avoiding any form of exploitation.

- *Environmental sustainability*, which means conserving and managing resources, especially those that are not renewable or are precious in terms of life support. It requires action to minimize pollution of air, land and water, and to conserve biological diversity and natural heritage.

It is important to appreciate that these three pillars are in many ways interdependent and can be both mutually reinforcing or in competition. Delivering sustainable development means striking a balance between them.

Making All Tourism More Sustainable

Some commentators and institutions have implied that **sustainable tourism** is a particular kind of tourism appealing to a market niche that is sensitive to environmental and social impacts, serviced by particular types of products and operators, and usually—in contrast with high-volume tourism—implying small in scale. This is a dangerous misapprehension. It must be clear that the term *sustainable tourism*—meaning tourism that is based on the principles of sustainable development—refers to a fundamental objective: to make *all* tourism more sustainable. The term should be used to refer to a *condition* of tourism, not a *type* of tourism. Well-managed, high-volume tourism can, and ought to be, just as sustainable as small-scale, dispersed special-interest tourism.

The World Tourism Organization's Definition of Sustainable Tourism

"Sustainable tourism development guidelines and management practices are applicable to all forms of tourism in all types of destinations, including mass tourism and the various niche tourism segments. Sustainability principles refer to the environmental, economic and sociocultural aspects of tourism development, and a suitable balance must be established among these three dimensions to guarantee its long-term sustainability."[3]

Thus, sustainable tourism should:

1. Make optimal use of environmental resources that constitute a key element in tourism development, maintaining essential ecological processes and helping to conserve natural resources and biodiversity.

2. Respect the **sociocultural authenticity** of host communities, conserve their built and living cultural heritage and traditional values, and contribute to intercultural understanding and tolerance.

3. Ensure viable, long-term economic operations, providing socioeconomic benefits to all stakeholders that are fairly distributed, including stable employment and income-earning opportunities and social services to host communities, and contributing to poverty alleviation.

4. Sustainable tourism development requires the informed participation of all relevant stakeholders, as well as strong political leadership to ensure wide participation and consensus building. Achieving sustainable tourism is a continuous process and it requires constant monitoring of impacts, introducing the necessary preventive and/or corrective measures whenever necessary.

5. Sustainable tourism should also maintain a high level of tourist satisfaction and ensure a meaningful experience to the tourists, raising their awareness about sustainability issues and promoting sustainable tourism practices amongst them.

Tourism and Sustainable Development: A Special Relationship

Tourism is in a special position in the contribution it can make to **sustainable development** and the challenges it presents. First, this is because of the dynamism and growth of the sector, and the major contribution that it makes to the economies of many countries and local destinations. Second, it is because tourism is an activity that involves a special relationship between consumers (visitors), the industry, the environment, and local communities.

This special relationship arises because, unlike most other sectors, the consumer of tourism (the tourist) travels to the producer and the product. This leads to three important and unique aspects of the relationship between tourism and sustainable development:

An auto-free Yosemite? Yosemite National park has recently proposed a bold new plan: Eliminate the cars! The plan seeks to restore habitat, dismantle facilities, remove roads, and eliminate private vehicles from the crowded Yosemite Valley. If the plan is implemented, we may see the day when the couple shown above—walking in relative tranquility—will be much more common. *Courtesy of Tuolumne County Visitors Bureau. Photo by Terri Meltz.*

■ *Interaction:* The nature of tourism, as a service industry that is based on delivering an experience of new places, means that it involves a considerable amount of interaction, both direct and indirect, between visitors, host communities, and their local environments.

■ *Awareness:* Tourism makes people (visitors and hosts) become far more conscious of environmental issues and differences between nations and cultures. This can affect attitudes and concerns for sustainability issues not only while traveling but throughout people's lives.

■ *Dependency:* Much of tourism is based on visitors seeking to experience intact and clean environments, attractive natural areas, authentic historic and cultural traditions, and welcoming hosts with whom they have a good relationship. The industry depends on these attributes being in place.

This close and direct relationship creates a sensitive situation, whereby tourism can be both very damaging but also very positive for sustainable development.

Some Guiding Principles and Approaches for Achieving Sustainability

The development and implementation of policies for sustainable tourism should be based on a number of overarching principles and approaches. Some of these are inherent to the principles of sustainability while others have been identified over time by those working in the field of tourism. These guiding concepts and principles are presented here.

Setting the Course for Sustainable Tourism

Take a Holistic View

Planning and development of tourism should not take place in isolation. Tourism should be considered as part of the sustainable development of communities, and the destination as a whole, alongside other activities. Its impact on other sectors, in terms of competing resource use and mutual support, should be considered. A *holistic approach* also takes account of all impacts and relationships within the tourism sector itself, and considers how all public policies might affect or be affected by tourism.

Pursue Multi-Stakeholder Engagement

Sustainable tourism is about local control, but also about working together. All those implicated by tourism should have an opportunity to influence its development and management.

Plan for the Long Term

Short-term approaches should be avoided and the long-term view encouraged, with resources committed accordingly. Where possible, actions should be self-sustaining.

Address Both Global and Local Impacts

Impacts on the local environment and communities are often apparent, and therefore it will be easier to gain support for policies that address them. However, the sustainable development of tourism should pay equal attention to global impacts, especially with respect to pollution from tourism (such as greenhouse gas emissions) and the use of nonrenewable resources. Such global impacts also have a direct effect on tourism itself (e.g., climate change).

Promote Sustainable Consumption

Sustainability is not just about the supply side. Equal consideration should be given to influencing the pattern and impact of consumption. This means influencing the volume and nature of tourism demand—that is, the choices made by tourists.

Equate Sustainability and Quality

It should be increasingly accepted that a quality tourism destination or product is one that addresses the full range of sustainability issues rather than simply concentrating on visitor satisfaction. Indeed, tourists should themselves be encouraged to think in these terms—a place that cares for the environment and its workforce is more likely also to care for them.

Formulating a Development Plan

Reflect All Impacts in Costs—Polluter Pays Principle

Under the polluter pays principle it is the perpetrator of environmental impacts who bears the responsibility for all costs incurred in delivering the tourism experience.

Minimize Risk Taking—Precautionary Principle

Careful risk assessment is an important component of sustainable tourism development. Where there is limited evidence about the possible impact of a development or action, a cautious approach should be adopted. The precautionary principle means putting in place measures to avoid damage before it occurs rather than trying to repair it afterward.

Take a Life-Cycle Perspective

Life-cycle assessment means taking full account of impacts over the entire life of a product or service, including initial resources used, siting and design, development and construction, all inputs to its operation, and disposal and after-use implications.

Consider Functional Alternatives

Consideration should be given to whether the same function can be performed and the same result achieved by doing things in a way that has more positive and less negative impacts on resources.

Respect Limits

The readiness and ability to limit the amount of tourism development or the volume of tourist flows in a destination or site are central to the concept of sustainable tourism. Limiting factors may be ecological resilience, resource capacity, community concerns, visitor satisfaction, and so on. Sound research can determine the carrying capacity of a destination or site. Carrying capacity is defined as the maximum amount of development, use, growth, or change that a site or destination can endure without an unacceptable alteration in the physical environment, the community's social fabric, and/or the local economy, and without an unacceptable decline in the quality of experience gained by the visitor.

Managing the Destination on an Ongoing Basis

Adapt to Changing Conditions

Adaptive response and management is an important aspect of sustainable development. Tourism is sensitive to external conditions in terms of its performance and the level of its impact.

Undertake Continuous Monitoring Using Indicators

Sound management of tourism requires continuous monitoring to measure changes in impact over time, so that adjustments to policies and actions can be made. Monitoring should be carried out using specific measures on the core indicators of sustainable tourism (see Table 17.1).

These indicators focus on what managers need to know most to reduce their risk of inadvertently making decisions that damage the natural and cultural environments on which the tourism industry depends. These include measures of:

- The general relationship between tourism and the environment
- The effects of environmental factors on tourism
- The impacts of the tourism industry on the environment

In effect, indicators seek to identify specific cause–effect relationships between tourism and the environment. Through their measurement and use, managers can more effectively do the following:

- Identify emerging issues, allowing prevention or mitigation
- Identify impacts, allowing action before they cause problems
- Support sustainable tourism development, identifying limits and opportunities
- Promote management accountability, developing responsible decision making built on knowledge

Two types of indicators are of value to tourism managers:

1. Core indicators of sustainable tourism have been developed for general application to all destinations.
2. *Destination-specific indicators* are applicable to particular ecosystems or types of tourism.

Destination-specific indicators fall into two categories: ecosystem specific- and site-specific. *Supplementary ecosystem-specific indicators* apply to particular ecosystems (e.g., coastal areas, parks and protected areas, or mountainous regions). *Site-specific indicators* are developed uniquely for the particular site. These indicators reflect important factors of the site that might not be adequately covered by the core and supplementary ecosystem-specific indicator sets but are nonetheless needed for management of the particular site.

Examples of such indices that were developed by an expert task force for the United Nations World Tourism Organization are given in Table 17.1. By identifying desirable levels of each indicator for a

TABLE 17.1 Core Indicators of Sustainable Tourism

Indicator	Specific Measures
Site protection	Category of site protection according to IUCN[a] index
Stress	Tourist numbers visiting site (per annum/peak month)
Use intensity	Intensity of use in peak period (persons/hectare)
Social impact	Ratio of tourists to locals (peak period and over time)
Development control	Existence of environmental review procedure or formal controls over development of site and use densities
Waste management	Percentage of sewage from site receiving treatment (additional indicators may include structural limits of other infrastructural capacity on-site, such as water supply)
Planning process	Existence of organized regional plan for tourist destination region (including tourism component)
Critical ecosystems	Number of rare/endangered species
Consumer satisfaction	Level of satisfaction by visitors (questionnaire-based)
Local satisfaction	Level of satisfaction by locals (questionnaire-based)
Tourism contribution to local economy	Proportion of total economic activity generated by tourism only
Composite Indices[b]	**Specific Measures**
Carrying capacity	Composite early-warning measure of key factors affecting the ability of the site to support different levels of tourism
Site stress	Composite measure of levels of impact on the site (its natural and cultural attributes due to tourism and other sector cumulative stresses)
Attractivity	Qualitative measure of those site attributes that make it attractive to tourism and can change over time

[a]IUCN, International Union for the Conservation of Nature and Natural Resources.
[b]The composite indices are largely composed of site-specific variables. Consequently, the identification and evaluation of the indicators composing these indices require on-site direction from an appropriately trained and experienced observer. In the future, based on the experiences in designing composite indicators for specific sites, it may be possible to derive these indices in a more systematic fashion. See the case studies for Villa Gesell and Peninsula Valdes for application of these indices.

Source: United Nations World Tourism Organization.

particular destination or site and then working toward meeting these ideals, managers can put in place a process that will ensure sustainability to the greatest extent possible.

It should be noted in reviewing these sets of indicators that they do not address environments or ecological goals alone. There are also indicators that seek to ensure desirable levels of visitor satisfaction and local resident satisfaction, as well as satisfactory levels of contributions to the local economy. The use of the indicators helps ensure the economic means to support sustainable ecotourism as well as public (and thus political) support for tourism with a destination.

Ensure Necessary Changes Are Implemented

Failure to make changes that have been identified by the monitoring process as necessary to maintain a sustainable tourism destination can undo years of effort and investment.

Setting an Agenda for Sustainable Tourism

An agenda for sustainable tourism sets out the major aims that destination managers seek to achieve. This agenda needs to embrace two, interrelated, elements of the sustainability of tourism:

1. The ability of tourism to continue as an activity in the future, ensuring that the conditions are right for this
2. The ability of society and the environment to absorb and benefit from the impacts of tourism in a sustainable way

Based on these two elements, an agenda for **sustainable tourism** can be articulated as a set of 12 aims that address economic, social, and environmental impacts. The agenda formulated in this way can then be used as a framework to develop policies for more sustainable tourism that recognize the directions in which tourism policy can exert an influence:

- Minimizing the negative impacts of tourism on society and the environment
- Maximizing tourism's positive and creative contribution to local economies, the conservation of natural and cultural heritage, and the quality of life of hosts and visitors

The 12 aims for an agenda for sustainable tourism are (see Figure 17.1):

1. **Economic viability:** Ensure the viability and competitiveness of tourism destinations and enterprises, so that they are able to continue to prosper and deliver benefits in the long term.
2. **Local prosperity:** Maximize the contribution of tourism to the economic prosperity of the host destination, including the proportion of visitor spending that is retained locally.
3. **Employment quality:** Strengthen the number and quality of local jobs created and supported by tourism, including the level of pay, conditions of service and availability to all without discrimination by gender, race, disability or in other ways.
4. **Social equity:** Seek a widespread and fair distribution of economic and social benefits from tourism throughout the recipient community, including improving opportunities, income and services available to the poor.
5. **Visitor fulfillment:** Provide a safe, satisfying, and fulfilling experience for visitors, available to all without discrimination by gender, race, or disability or in other ways.

6. **Local control:** Engage and empower local communities in planning and decision making about the management and future development of tourism in their area, in consultation with other stakeholders.

7. **Community well-being:** Maintain and strengthen the quality of life in local communities, including social structures and access to resources, amenities and life support systems, avoiding any form of social degradation or exploitation.

8. **Cultural richness:** Respect and enhance the historic heritage, authentic culture, traditions and distinctiveness of host communities.

9. **Physical integrity:** Maintain and enhance the quality of landscapes, both urban and rural, and avoid the physical and visual degradation of the environment.

10. **Biological diversity:** Support the conservation of natural areas, habitats and wildlife, and minimize damage to them.

11. **Resource efficiency:** Minimize the use of scarce and nonrenewable resources in the development and operation of tourism facilities and services.

12. **Environmental purity:** Minimize the pollution of air, water, and land and the generation of waste by tourism enterprises and visitors.

The reader should note that the order in which these 12 aims are listed does not imply any order of priority. Each one is equally important. Many of the aims relate to a combination of environmental, economic, and social issues and impacts, as illustrated by Figure 17.1.

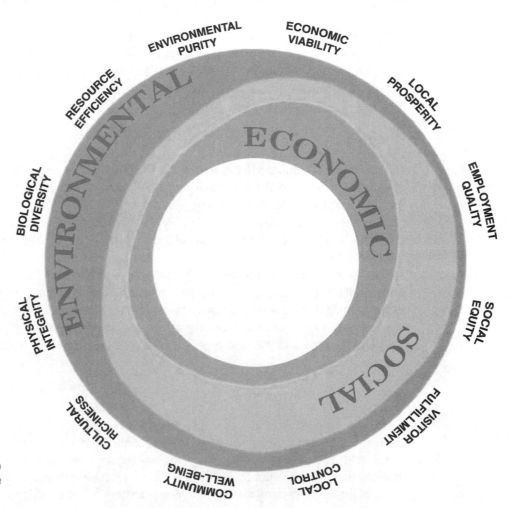

Figure 17.1 Relationship between the 12 aims and the 3 pillars of sustainability.

Sustainable Development and Tourism: Some Critical Implementation Issues

We have examined the steps involved in implementing a sustainable tourism program as well as certain related implementation issues. Five such stages are presented for discussion.

Defining the Relevant Population/Community

We now focus on the question of "sustainable development for whom?" As professionals in the field, we need to know if we are to take a global, macroperspective in our discussions of tourism and sustainable development, or whether we should restrict our thinking to a more local focus. While recognizing that there is a need for global thinking, we also need to recognize that we might need to restrict the allocation of our energies to those jurisdictions where we have the power to act and to make a difference.

In any event, the principle being enunciated here is that, as professionals, we need to define our sphere of interest and action. The impacts and populations of relevance might be quite different for each sphere, and, consequently, so might be our likely actions.

Defining the Values That Underlie Sustainable Development

Regardless of the way in which the values of a society are determined, they will ultimately determine the policies that emerge with regard to sustainable development. Whether these policies are the result of compromise or consensus is the concern of the political entity involved. In the end, however, the political process and the power of different political units will determine the level and form that sustainability will take. Those of us in the tourism sector have traditionally ignored this reality, and we are weaker for it. Thus, once the members of the relevant population/community have been defined, it is important to identify the values that underlie the kind of tourism they wish to develop for the destination.

Defining the Dimensions of Sustainability

The concept of sustainability is relevant in practical terms only when we define what is to be sustained. From a tourism perspective, discussions on sustainability may pertain to the environment, cultural identity, economic well-being, or social stability. Individuals responsible for, or interested in, each of these areas taken separately may very legitimately focus on their area of concern and attempt to achieve sustainability in relation to some acceptable ongoing carrying capacity of the destination.

However, from an overall destination management perspective, the task becomes much more complex. Here, the challenge becomes one of attempting to balance the sustainability of economic, cultural, social, and environmental systems. Although one hopes for compatibility in the pursuit of sustainability within and across these systems, this is not always possible. Often, the reason for such incompatibility is a divergence of the values from which the goal of sustainability is being pursued.

Defining the Time Horizon

Sustainable development as a concept implies *forever*; this may be impractical to deal with and can even lead to a feeling of helplessness. There is some merit in seeking to develop programs that are sustainable in perpetuity, but such programs may require huge amounts of resources and considerable time for their implementation. It may be wiser and more effective to undertake a less demanding series of phased programs that initiate movement in desired directions rather than delaying action until longer-term programs can be put in place.

TABLE 17.2   Sustainable Development (SD) in Tourism: A Possible Allocation of Responsibility

Level/Organization	Responsibilities
Host community/region	Defining the tourism philosophy and vision for the community/region
	Establishing social, physical, and cultural carrying capacity for the host community/region
Destination management/community organization	Coordination of implementation of community SD plan for tourism
	Monitoring of levels and impact of tourism in the community/region
Individual tourism firms and operators	Fair contribution to implementation of SD plan for tourism
	Observance of regulations, guidelines, and practices for SD
Host community/region	Encouragement/acceptance of tourism within parameters of SD plan
Visitors/tourists	Acceptance of responsibility for minimal self-education with respect to values of host region
	Acceptance and observance of terms and conditions of host community SD plan for tourism

Although perhaps not the traditional image that most people might have of ecotourism, these kayakers in Lake Powell, Utah, are pursuing a low-impact activity that respects the well-being of the region they are visiting—the essence of the ecotourism concept. *Photo courtesy of Lake Powell Resorts and Marinas.*

Allocating Responsibility for Action

It should be apparent from the nature of the foregoing discussion that the allocation of responsibility for tourism-related sustainability issues and decisions will not be a neat and tidy exercise. The highly interdependent, multidisciplinary, multisector, and political nature of the decisions does not allow for simplistic answers. However, as long as this caveat is taken seriously, it may be possible to provide some guidelines as to how the process might be conducted and how the prime agents might be assigned to different areas of responsibility.

All this said, it then becomes necessary to propose an operational allocation of responsibility that remains true to the democratic model and the concept of resident-responsive tourism. See Table 17.2 for a proposed allocation of responsibilities.

MAJOR CHALLENGES FACING THE ACHIEVEMENT OF SUSTAINABLE TOURISM

While the previous sections have provided an understanding of the nature of sustainable tourism and the kinds of policies necessary to support its achievement, there nevertheless remain a number of major challenges that stand in the way of establishing and maintaining a sustainable tourism system. Five of these are identified here. Although they do not encompass all of the challenges facing tourism—and although they are not all of equal importance—they serve to illustrate the nature and range of issues facing tourism, as well as certain of the related opportunities that derive from sustainable tourism. These challenges include:

1. Managing the dynamic growth of tourism while maintaining sustainability
2. Poverty alleviation: meeting tourism's commitment to contribute to the UN's foremost millennium goal of halving world poverty by 2015[4]
3. Maintaining support for conservation
4. Ensuring the health, safety, and security of tourists
5. Addressing the effects of climate change

Each and every one of the five challenges will require great insight and effort to address them, but it is the final one on our list, namely **climate change**, that appears to currently be most pressing. As such, we shall now examine it in some detail and in depth.

The New Realities Facing Tourism in an Era of Global Climate Change[5]

Compelling evidence indicates that global climate has changed compared to the pre-industrial era—and that it is anticipated to continue to change over the 21st century and beyond. The Intergovernmental Panel on Climate Change (IPCC) declared that "[. . .] warming of the climate system is unequivocal." The global mean temperature increased approximately 0.76°F from 2001 to 2005 just as it did between 1850 and 1899—the same increase in temperature, but in a much shorter number of years, and the IPCC concluded that most of the observed increase in global average temperatures since the mid-twentieth century is very likely (>90% probability) the result of human activities that are increasing greenhouse gas concentrations in the atmosphere. Discernible human influences now also extend to other aspects of climate, including ocean warming, continental-average temperatures, temperature extremes, and wind patterns. Widespread decreases in glaciers and ice caps and warming ocean surface temperature have contributed to sea level rise of 1.8 mm (.071 inches) per year from 1961 to 2003, and approximately 3.1 mm (.122 inches) per year from 1993 to 2003. Thus, there has been a significant increase in sea level rise the last 10 years of the 42-year study period. The biological response of ecosystems and individual species has been recorded on every continent.

With its close connections to the environment and climate itself, tourism is considered to be a *highly climate-sensitive economic sector* similar to agriculture, insurance, energy, and transportation. The regional manifestations of climate change will be highly relevant for tourism destinations and tourists alike, requiring adaptation by all major tourism stakeholders. Indeed, climate change is not a remote future event for tourism, as the varied impacts of a changing climate are becoming evident at destinations around the world and climate change is already influencing decision making in the tourism sector—whether it would be ski resorts or beach destinations.

At the same time, the tourism sector is a nonnegligible *contributor to climate change* through greenhouse gas (GHG) emissions derived especially from the transport and accommodation of tourists. Tourism must seek to significantly reduce these emissions in accordance with the international community, which at the "Vienna Climate Change Talks 2007" recognized that global emissions of GHG need to peak in the next 10 to15 years and then be reduced to very low levels, well below half of levels in 2000 by mid-century.[6] The tourism sector cannot address the challenge of climate change in isolation, but must do so within the context of the broader international sustainable development agenda. The critical challenge before the global tourism sector is to develop a coherent policy strategy that decouples the projected massive growth in tourism in the decades ahead from increased energy use and GHG emissions, so as to allow tourism growth to simultaneously contribute to poverty alleviation and play a major role in achieving the United Nations Millennium Development Goals (MDG).

The Nature of Climate Change Impacts on the Tourism Industry and Destinations

There are four broad categories of climate change impacts that will affect tourism destinations, their competitiveness and sustainability.

1. **Direct climatic impacts:** Climate is a principal resource for tourism, as it codetermines the suitability of locations for a wide range of tourist activities, is a principal driver of global seasonality in tourism demand, and has an important influence on operating costs, such as heating-cooling, snow-making, irrigation, food and water supply, and insurance costs. Thus, changes in the length and quality of climate-dependent tourism seasons (i.e., sun-and-sea or winter sports holidays) could have considerable implications for competitive relationships between destinations and, therefore, the profitability of tourism enterprises.

2. **Indirect environmental change impacts:** Because environmental conditions are such a critical resource for tourism, a wide range of climate-induced environmental changes will have profound effects on tourism at the destination and regional level. Changes in water availability, biodiversity loss, reduced landscape aesthetic, altered agricultural production (e.g., wine tourism), increased natural hazards, coastal erosion and inundation, damage to infrastructure, and the increasing incidence of vector-borne diseases will all impact tourism to varying degrees. UNESCO has also identified several world heritage sites that are critical tourist destinations as being vulnerable to climate-induced environmental change (e.g., Venice, Italy—sea level rise; Great Barrier Reef, Australia—coral bleaching and mortality; Glacier-Waterton International Peace Park, USA and Canada—glacier retreat; and Chan Chan Archaeological Zone, Peru—El Niño-Southern Oscillation (ENSO) caused flooding and eroding).

3. **Impacts of mitigation policies on tourist mobility:** National or international mitigation policies—that is, policies that seek to reduce GHG emissions—are likely to have an impact on tourist flows. They will lead to an increase in transport costs and may foster environmental attitudes that lead tourists to change their travel patterns (e.g., shift transport mode or destination choices).

4. **Indirect societal change impacts:** Climate change is thought to pose a risk to future economic growth and to the political stability of some nations. The Stern report, *Economics of Climate Change,* concluded that although a global warming of only 1°C might benefit global GDP, greater climate change would eventually damage economic growth at the global scale, including the stark conclusion that unmitigated climate change could cause a reduction in consumption per capita of 20 percent later in the twenty-first century or in the early twenty-second century.[7] Any such reduction of global GDP due to climate change would reduce the discretionary wealth available to consumers for tourism and have negative implications for anticipated future growth in tourism; however, there has been no in-depth interpretation of the Stern report for the tourism sector.

Destination Level Adaptation

It is essential to emphasize that regardless of the nature and magnitude of climate change impacts, *all tourism businesses and destinations will need to adapt to climate change* in order to minimize associated risks and capitalize on new opportunities, in an economically, socially and environmentally sustainable manner.

Large tour operators who do not own the infrastructure are in a better position to adapt to changes at destinations because they can respond to clients and demands, and provide information to influence clients' travel choices. Destination communities and tourism operators with large investment in immobile capital assets (e.g., hotel, resort complex, marina or casino) have the least adaptive capacity.

Tourists Adaptation to Climate Change

Tourists have the greatest adaptive capacity (depending on three key resources: money, knowledge, and time) with relative freedom to avoid destinations impacted by climate change or shifting the timing of travel to avoid unfavorable climate conditions. Suppliers of tourism services and tourism operators at specific destinations have less adaptive capacity.

Industry Adaptation to Climate Change

The dynamic nature of the tourism industry and its ability to cope with a range of recent major shocks—including SARS, terrorism attacks in a number of nations, or tsunamis—suggest a relatively high adaptive capacity within the tourism industry overall. The capacity to adapt to climate change is thought to vary substantially between subsectors, destinations, and individual businesses within the tourism industry.

   The tourism sector has been adapting its operations to climate zones worldwide, using a diverse range of technological, managerial, educational, policy, and behavioral adaptations to deal with climate variability. However, adaptation has figured less prominently in climate change research on tourism than in some other economic sectors (e.g., agriculture).

Implications of Climate Change for Tourism Demand Patterns

Climate, the natural environment, and personal safety are three primary factors in destination choice, and global climate change is anticipated to have significant impacts on all three of these factors at the regional level. The response of tourists to the complexity of destination impacts will reshape demand patterns and play a pivotal role in the eventual impacts of climate change on the tourism industry. Understanding and anticipating the potential geographic and seasonal shifts in tourist demand will remain critical areas of research in the future.

The Way Forward to Adaptation and Mitigation in Tourism

Concern about climate change is increasing worldwide, and the IPCC has made it clear that global climate change is only just beginning. The impacts of climate change on the tourism sector will steadily intensify, particularly under higher emission scenarios. Climate change would redistribute climate resources for tourism geographically and seasonally and pose a risk to ecosystems worldwide. The nature and intensity of climate change impacts will differ for tourism destinations around the world. The most vulnerable regions are in developing countries, which generally also have less adaptive capacity, and this will be a particular challenge for their tourist destinations and their host communities. Climate change impacts on the tourism sector could influence other economic sectors, such as agriculture and local business networks supplying tourism. Conversely, the tourism sector must also be cognizant of the implications of climate change adaptation in other economic sectors, which could have significant impacts on tourism. As the financial sector incorporates a company's climate change strategy, or lack of one, into its investment criteria, it will influence credit rating and insurance rates.

Climate change mitigation requires the transformation of energy and transportation systems worldwide, with implications for the cost of travel and tourist mobility. Climate change also has the potential to have an adverse effect on the global economy and poses a security risk in some regions. Consequently, climate change is anticipated to have profound implications that could fundamentally transform aspects of the global tourism sector.

The unmistakable conclusion of studies in the field have shown that the significance of climate change to tourism is not in some distant and remote future. Climate change is already influencing decision making within the tourism sector, including that of tourists, forward-looking tourism businesses and investors, and international tourism organizations. The next generation of tourism professionals will need to contend with virtually all of the broad range of impacts of climate change.

This is the time for the tourism community to collectively formulate a strategy to address what must be considered the greatest challenge to the sustainability of tourism in the twenty-first century.

The Concept of Ecotourism and Its Role in Sustainable Tourism

Acknowledgment and acceptance of the importance of achieving sustainable tourism has given rise to the concept of ecotourism. Indeed, in the tourism world, the terms *sustainable tourism* and *ecotourism* tend to be used interchangeably. While they certainly are strongly related, each contains a particular nuance that many regard as significant. In our view, the concept of ecotourism conveys a greater concern for the fundamental obligation of all travelers to avoid harming, and indeed to protect, all sites that they visit. As such, ecotourism is highly value-laden in an intrinsic sense; that is, individual travelers must accept responsibility for their behavior and its impact. In contrast, the term *sustainable tourism* conveys a more functional societal obligation to ensure the conditions necessary to maintain the physical environment in a "preserved state" for future generations. These conditions are not simply economic and political factors; they include a recognition that desirable values and good intentions must be supported by hard cash and tough decisions.

View of Triplet Falls in Australia. It is this kind of pristine beauty that those responsible for tourism must constantly seek to preserve for the enjoyment of future generations. *Courtesy of Digital Vision.*

ECOTOURISM: COMMON TERMS USED

Ecotourism, geotourism, nature tourism, green tourism, low-impact tourism, adventure travel, alternative tourism, environmental preservation, symbiotic development, responsible tourism, soft tourism, appropriate tourism, quality tourism, new tourism, sustainable development, and sustainable tourism all are monikers for similar types of tourist activities and developments. Of all the terms, *ecotourism* and *sustainability* are most frequently used. The principle of both is to sustain or even enhance the quality and attractiveness of the natural environment.

Definitions of ecotourism abound. Conservation International states, "Ecotourism is responsible travel that promotes conservation of nature and sustains the well-being of local people."[8]

Dianne Brouse defines ecotourism as responsible travel in which the visitor is aware of and takes into account the effects of his or her actions on both the host culture and the environment.[9]

The International Ecotourism Society (TIES) (www.ecotourism.org) defines ecotourism as "responsible travel to natural areas that conserves the environment and improves the well-being of local people." This means that those who implement and participate in ecotourism activities should adhere to the following principles:

- Minimize impact.
- Build environmental and cultural awareness and respect.
- Provide positive experiences for both visitors and hosts.
- Provide direct financial benefits for conservation.
- Provide financial benefits and empowerment for local people.
- Raise sensitivity to host countries' political, environmental, and social climate.
- Support international human rights and labor agreements.

The Travel Industry Association of Canada (TIAC) (www.tiac-aitc.ca) adapted a nationally accepted definition of *ecotourism* to assist and protect the reputation of Canadian tourism. This led to its final definition:

> Ecotourism is a segment of sustainable tourism that offers experiences that enable visitors to discover natural areas while preserving their integrity, and to understand, through interpretation and education, the natural and cultural sense of place. It fosters respect toward the environment, reflects sustainable business practices, creates socioeconomic benefits for communities/regions, and recognizes and respects local and indigenous cultures, traditions, and values.

This is a powerful definition and the authors' favorite because it is succinct, yet covers the environmental, the economic, and the social—the three pillars required for sustainability. We encourage everyone to use it.

The definition of ecotourism adopted by Ecotourism Australia (www.ecotourism.org.au) is: "Ecotourism is ecologically sustainable tourism with a primary focus on experiencing natural areas that fosters environmental and cultural understanding, appreciation, and conservation."

Other definitions also reported in the Travel Industry Association of America's study, *Tourism and the Environment*, are as follows:

- Ecotourism is environmentally friendly travel that emphasizes seeing and saving natural habitat and archaeological treasures.
- Ecotourism is a tool for conservation.
- Broadly defined, ecotourism involves more than conservation. It is a form of travel that responds to a region's ecological, social, and economic needs. It also provides an alternative to mass tourism.

Adventure travel is a rapidly growing market, and one of the most popular activities is whitewater rafting. All tourists and especially these rafters on the Stanislaus River in California have a responsibility to leave only footprints and promote conservation. *Photo by Robert Holmes; courtesy of the California Division of Tourism.*

It encompasses all aspects of travel—from airlines to hotels to ground transportation to tour operators. That is, each component of the ecotourism product is environmentally sensitive.

■ As a form of travel, ecotourism nurtures understanding of the environment's culture and natural history, fosters the ecosystem's integrity, and produces economic opportunities and conservation gains.

Go to www.travelgreen.org to see the U.S. Travel Association's efforts on protecting the environment through sustainable travel.

National Geographic Traveler has created the term *geotourism,* which it defines as tourism that sustains or enhances the geographical character of the place being visited—its environment, culture, aesthetics, heritage, and the well-being of its residents. This definition tries to describe all aspects of sustainability in travel.

If these definitions sound like a case of the best of all possible worlds for the traveler, the destination, and the locals, to a degree it is. The problem is living up to the promises of the definitions and making ecotourism a reality. Otherwise, ecotourism becomes a paradox, bringing visitors to fragile environments and ruining them rather than preserving them. In fact, many people quarrel with the word *ecotourism.* If you consider the two parts of the word *ecotourism—ecology* and *tourism*—the inconsistencies are apparent. *Ecology* is defined as the science of the relationships between organisms and environment. When *tourism* is connected to it, a foreign entity is introduced and nature's relationships are changed. Ecotourism does not work when ecotours are so popular that they destroy the very environment they seek to protect.

Benefits and Importance of Ecotourism

Before we write off ecotourism as impossible, however, consider the benefits:

■ Provides jobs and income for local people

■ Makes possible funds for purchasing and improving protected or natural areas to attract more ecotourists in the future

- Provides environmental education for visitors
- Encourages **heritage preservation** and **environmental preservation** and enhancement (the creation of new or enlarged national and state parks, forest preserves, biosphere reserves, recreation areas, beaches, marine and underwater trails, and attractions)

Developing countries host many ecotourists. In Brazil, nature travel has become the country's largest new source of revenue. In south-central Africa, Rwanda's ecotourism is the third largest source of foreign exchange earnings. Much of this is generated by visitors to the Mountain Gorilla Project begun in the 1970s. The success of this project has convinced the national government to preserve and protect the critical habitat of the gorilla. It has also brought about support for other parks and reserves in that country.

In Costa Rica, 60 percent of visitors are interested in seeing the national park system, which is 11 percent of the country's land area. If biological and private reserves are added, the protected areas total 23 percent of the nation.

Dangers and Limitations of Ecotourism

A low-density rural population is typically found at ecotourism destinations. Most of these people depend on the use of the natural environment for their livelihood. Introduce tourism and it has an **effect on local populations**: There is the danger that tourism consumes resources and has the ability to overconsume. If an ecotour operator does not hire local people to perform services needed by the tour group and use local supplies, the financial benefits of ecotourism are not shared with the local population. This results in the local population and the tourists competing for scarce natural resources, which is unhealthy for the environment. To be successful as tour operators, it is imperative that the local people be involved. If not, their pressing need for survival will doubtless prevail, and this is very likely to damage the very natural attractions that first lured the visitors there.

Paos Volcano National Park in Costa Rica is a popular natural attraction. In addition to the giant volcano crater, the park also possesses abundant wildlife and unusual vegetation. *Photo by Richard Mills; courtesy of International Expeditions, Inc.*

Another problem is that scientific knowledge of visitor impacts on remote areas, nature areas, wilderness areas, and other relatively undisturbed natural areas in most countries is rather poor or nonexistent. Thus, tourism and land management decisions are made in the absence of good science. Once tourism starts, there is great pressure to allow more visitors. Consequently, the destinations face the danger of becoming overvisited. Carrying capacities need to be determined and enforced.

Finally, tourism is a multifaceted industry and, thus, is almost impossible to control. What starts out as well-planned ecotourism can turn into too popular an adventure and overwhelm the destination. To prevent this from happening, the basics of sustainable tourism must be practiced.

TRAVEL ORGANIZATIONS' EFFORTS

Although the UNEP and UNWTO have taken a lead role in encouraging sustainable tourism, there are other organizations that are working with them or independently to achieve sustainable tourism. The discussion of sustainable tourism deserves mention of some of these organizations and the resources they provide to accomplish the task.

Global Sustainable Tourism Council

The Global Sustainable Tourism Council (GSTC) is a global initiative dedicated to promoting sustainable tourism practices around the world. They work to expand understanding of and access to sustainable tourism practices, educate about practices, and advocate for a set of universal principles that define sustainable tourism. Visit its Web site at www.gstcouncil.org.

GSTC is currently active in all UNWTO regions—Africa, the Americas, East Asia and the Pacific, South Asia, Europe, and the Middle East. The membership represents a diverse global membership that includes UN agencies, major travel companies, hotels, country tourism boards, and tour operators.

The GSTC fosters sustainable tourism through the adoption of universal sustainable tourism principles. At the core of its efforts are the Global Sustainable Tourism Criteria, a set of voluntary principles that provides a framework for the sustainability of tourism businesses across the globe. To review the criteria, visit www.sustainabletourismcriteria.org.

Tour Operators Initiative for Sustainable Tourism Development

The Tour Operators Initiative for Sustainable Tourism Development has the mission to advance the sustainable development and management of tourism, and to encourage tour operators to make a corporate commitment to sustainable development. In carrying out this mission, the initiative addresses ways to minimize adverse impacts on, and to generate benefits for environment, culture, and communities in tourism destinations through the design and operation of tours and of the conduct of tour operators' business activities.

The initiative has been developed by tour operators for tour operators with the support of the United Nations Environment Programme (UNEP); the United Nations Educational, Scientific and Cultural Organization (UNESCO); and the United Nations World Tourism Organization (UNWTO), which are also full members of the initiative. Visit their Web site at www.toinitiative.org and review their publications, best practices, and, case studies.

Environmentally responsible tourism can be achieved through the combined efforts of private operators, travel organizations, and individuals. *Photo courtesy of The Inn By The Sea, Cape Elizabeth, Maine.*

U.S. Travel Association

The U.S. Travel Association tries to protect the environment through sustainable travel by maintaining the Web site www.TravelGreen.org that is a go-to source for information on sustainable travel. It is a site to learn how environmental sustainability is good for business and how travel companies and destinations are pursuing eco-friendly travel opportunities for their customers. The site lists sustainable tourism organizations, case studies, best practices, certification programs, social responsibility programs, and news items for all sectors of the travel industry. The site was developed by U.S. Travel in cooperation with American Express. Visit www.TravelGreen.org and discover a wealth of information.

BEST Education Network

BEST Education Network is an international consortium of educators committed to furthering the development and dissemination of knowledge on sustainable tourism. The organization is dedicated to developing innovative sustainable travel and tourism practices. The BEST Education Network emerged from a initiative known as Business Enterprises for Sustainable Travel, which was founded in 1998. The primary objective of BEST was to develop and disseminate knowledge in the field of sustainable tourism. In 2003, BEST went through organizational changes and the group overseeing the educational and curriculum aspects of the organization became independent and named itself the BEST Education Network.

The Network holds an annual three- to four-day Think Tank at various universities around the world. Its 2011 Think Tank XI titled "Learning for Sustainable Tourism" was held at Temple University. In addition to its annual Think Tank, BEST has developed sustainable tourism class modules as follows: Sustainable Tourism Marketing Module; Sustainable Tourism Planning Module; Sustainable Operations Management Module; Sustainable Festivals, Meetings, and Event Management Module; and The Bottom Line Reporting for Sustainable Development Module. These modules are available at Goodfellow Publishers, www.goodfellowpublishers.com. The Network is chaired by Dr. Dagmar Lund-Durlacher from MODUL University Vienna in Austria. MODUL University Vienna also houses the BEST Education Network Secretariat. Visit its Web site: www.besteducationnetwork.org.

SUMMARY

Responsible citizens of the world have cause to realize that all of humankind's activities must be increasingly examined in a very critical manner with respect to their impact or their sustainability of this planet. Tourism is only one of these activities, but it is an extremely important one. It follows that tourism must understand and accept those limitations that are essential to maintaining a high quality of life for all species. It is through the concept of sustainable tourism that the tourism sector seeks to play its role responsibly. This chapter has examined the fundamentals of sustainable tourism as well as the principles for its implementation and monitoring.

The main concept of ecotourism is responsible travel to natural areas that conserves the environment and sustains the well-being of local people. From the tourists' viewpoint, ecotourism is typically the gratification provided by a unique experience in an undisturbed natural environment, viewing flora, fauna, birds, animals, landforms, scenery, and natural beauty.

Benefits of ecotourism include providing jobs, helping preserve more areas, educating, and encouraging heritage and environmental enhancement. Benefits to the local people are maximized by hiring as many local people as possible and obtaining supplies and services locally.

Carrying capacity for visitors must be determined. It is defined as the maximum number of daily visitors that the area can receive without damaging its attractive features. Enforcement of this limit, along with good management and maintenance, is essential.

Sustainable tourism development is development that has been carefully planned and managed. It is the antithesis of tourism that has developed for short-term gains. Because of the expected continuing growth of tourism, sustainable development is the approach that will be needed. Because of the pressure on the world's resources, it is the only sensible approach.

No business sector has greater reason to promote and enforce environmental and business ethics codes than tourism. The environment is the resource base for tourism, and without protection, the natural attraction that brought the tourist in the first place will be lost.

❖ KEY CONCEPTS ❖

adaptive capacity
allocation of responsibility
benefits of ecotourism
carrying capacity
climate change
climate change adaptation
climate change mitigation
continuous monitoring

core indicators of sustainable tourism
dimensions of sustainable
  development
ecotourism
ecotourism development
effect on local populations
environmental preservation
heritage preservation

pillars of sustainable development
principles for implementing sustainable tourism
site protection
sociocultural authenticity
sustainable development
sustainable tourism

❖ INTERNET EXERCISES ❖

The Internet sites mentioned in this chapter plus some selected additional sites are listed for your convenience on the companion Web site for this book, www.wiley.com/college/goeldner.

ACTIVITY 1

Site Name: Ecotourism Australia

URL: www.ecotourism.org.au

Background Information: Ecotourism Australia was formed in 1991 as an incorporated nonprofit organization and is the major national body for the ecotourism industry.

Exercises

1. Describe the vision of Ecotourism Australia.
2. Describe its nature and ecotourism accreditation program.
3. Discuss its EcoGuide Certification Program.
4. What other activities does the association engage in?

ACTIVITY 2

Site Name: United Nations Environment Programme

URL: www.unep.org

Background Information: UNEP provides leadership and encourages partnerships in caring for the environment by inspiring, informing, and enabling nations and people to improve their quality of life without compromising that of future generations.

Exercises

1. What publications does UNEP have on ecotourism and sustainable tourism?

2. What kind of information can you find in its *Tourism Focus* newsletter?

3. How does UNEP define ecotourism?

4. What does UNEP say about the environmental impacts of tourism?

 QUESTIONS FOR REVIEW AND DISCUSSION

1. What is the definition of sustainable development?

2. What is the definition of sustainable tourism?

3. What is the agenda for sustainable tourism?

4. Why is climate change important to tourism?

5. What exactly is ecotourism?

6. Why are there so many different terms for this idea?

7. Why has this concept become so popular?

8. Give some examples of the resources necessary for an ecotourism destination.

9. Are resources other than natural ones involved? Are these meaningful? Explain.

10. Describe the role of local people in ecotourism and in sustainable development.

11. Why are preservation planning principles so important?

12. What should be the goals of ecotourism for a tour company? For the ecotourist? For the local population? For the local government? For a conservation organization?

13. Differentiate ecotourism policy in developing and developed countries.

14. Identify the principal limitations to ecotourism.

15. Referring to question 14, state some ways that these limitations might be ameliorated.

16. Why is capacity so important?

17. Why is it important to identify the values on which tourism development is based?

18. Of what use are "principles" in implementing recommendations to achieve sustainable tourism?

19. How much will consumers pay for environmental friendly tourism?

 CASE PROBLEMS

1. Bonnie S., CTC, is an agency travel counselor. She has decided that her agency's market area has a good potential to sell more ecotours. How should Bonnie proceed to identify prospective buyers of such tours?

2. As director of Ecuador's national park system, Ernesto B. has become increasingly concerned about the overuse of Galápagos National Park. He worries that the current popularity of the park—about 100,000 tourists each year—may actually be sowing the seeds of destruction. This situation may be inducing a disastrous future drop in visitor numbers. Outline some steps that he might take to:

   ▪ Ascertain the present quality of the visitor experience.

   ▪ Remedy some aspects of overuse of the park to ensure future success.

3. Nathan M. is the local managing director of a tour company specializing in ecotourism. His company operates big-game and bird photo safaris in Tanzania.

He has decided that his firm would be more socially responsible if his tours (by minibus) would obtain practically all needs from local sources. Give some examples of how he might do this and describe the benefits that would accrue locally. (When discussing this, include both economic and social benefits.)

4. Upon graduation, you have secured a job as tourism specialist with the World Wildlife Fund. Your first assignment is to be a team member charged with helping to formulate plans for some kind of wildlife protection area in Zambia. This country is located in south-central Africa. Its government is considering a new national park and has requested expert assistance from the fund. The president of the fund has made it very clear to the team that such plans must also aim to improve living standards for the local population. These standards, at present, are grievously low. Most local people are

subsistence farmers. They occasionally shoot big-game animals that damage their crops, and also for meat. After extensive field study, a particularly attractive area has been found in which the scenery is spectacular, the climate very pleasant, the natural history resources outstanding, and the local people friendly and hospitable. Thus, the proposed park seems to have an excellent potential for attracting substantial numbers of ecotourists. Propose some conceptual ideas as to how this challenge can be met successfully.

5. A very vocal environmental group has recently voiced harsh criticism of the state's tourism business. They claim that the industry rapidly consumes valuable natural resources, provides mostly low-paying unskilled employment, and degrades the culture of the main tourist centers. As the state's tourism director, how would you answer these charges?

6. Referring to case 5, the same environmental group has succeeded in convincing the state's attorney general that all roadside billboards be eliminated. The various state hotel, motel, restaurant, attractions, and tourist promotion organizations vehemently oppose such legislation. Can you think of some kind of compromise plan that might satisfy both of these opposing groups?

ENDNOTES

1. Material in this chapter is extracted from *Making Tourism More Sustainable: A Guide for Policy Makers*, (Paris, France and Madrid, Spain: United Nations Environment Programme, Division of Technology, Industry and Economics and United Nations World Tourism Organization, 2006). The authors acknowledge the value of this document and wish to convey their appreciation for the willingness of UNEP and UNWTO to reproduce the document in whole or in part for educational purposes.

2. *Our Common Future: The World Commission on Environment and Development* (The Brundtland Report, 1987; Oxford, UK: Oxford University Press).

3. *Making Tourism More Sustainable: A Guide for Policy Makers*, (Madrid: United Nations World Tourism Organization, 2005), p. 11.

4. Ibid, 12–14.

5. Extracted from *Climate Change and Tourism: Responding to Global Challenges*, (Paris and Madrid: World Tourism Organization and the United Nations Environment Programme, 2008).

6. The "Vienna Climate Change Talks 2007," international negotiations on GHG emission reductions, held under the auspices of the United Nations Framework Convention on Climate Change. www.unis.unvienna.org/unis/pressrels/2007/unisinf230.html.

7. N. Stern, *The Economics of Climate Change: The Stern Review* (Cambridge: Cambridge University Press, 2006).

8. Conservation International: www.conservation.org.

9. Dianne Brouse, "Socially Responsible Travel," *Transitions Abroad* (January–February 1992), p. 23.

PART 5

Essentials of Tourism Research and Marketing

Chapter 18 Travel and Tourism Research
Chapter 19 Tourism Marketing

Chichen Itza in the Yucatán has been named one of the new seven wonders of the world. *Photo courtesy of Corbis Digital Stock.*

Travel and Tourism Research

LEARNING OBJECTIVES

- Recognize the role and scope of travel research.
- Recognize the usefulness of different types of tourism research.
- Learn the travel research process.

- Study secondary data and how they can be used.
- Understand the methods of collecting primary data.
- Know who does travel research.

The ruins of Machu Picchu are one of the most beautiful ancient sites in the world. Machu Picchu stands 9,060 feet above sea level in the middle of a tropical Andes mountain forest. It is an amazing creation of the Inca Empire. Machu Picchu has been named one of the new seven wonders of the world. *Photo courtesy of Corbis Digital Stock.*

INTRODUCTION

Information is the basis for decision making, and it is the task of travel research to gather and analyze data to help travel managers make decisions. Travel research is the systematic, impartial designing and conducting of investigations to solve travel problems.

Travel research is broad in scope and covers all aspects of the travel environment. It examines consumers, competitors, products and services, market structure, economic trends, technological forces, government regulations, demographic trends, ecology, global forces, and other factors that make up the travel environment. Travel research is the foundation for developing your tourism strategy and marketing plan.

There are two main sources of data—primary and secondary. Primary research is original and collected to solve a problem. Secondary research already exists, as data have been collected for other purposes. There are two major types of research—exploratory and scientific. Exploratory research is qualitative and provides insights into the situation. One should draw conclusions from it only with extreme care. Scientific research is quantitative and follows a careful scientific process that allows the results of the study to be generalized to the population. To be useful, however, it must be carefully planned and rigorously executed, and thoughtfully interpreted.

Travel research provides facts that help travel decision makers operate more effectively. Managers can plan, operate, and control more efficiently when they have the facts. Thus, research, which reduces the risk in decision making, can have a great impact on the success or failure of a tourism enterprise.

TYPES OF TOURISM RESEARCH

Tourism research is conducted in many forms. Some illustrative types are presented next.

The Economic Impact of Tourism

Virtually every kind of tourism destination and attraction wants to know the level of economic activity and the benefits it is deriving from tourism within its boundaries. Frechtling provides a comprehensive treatment on assessing the economic impacts of travel and tourism.[1]

Awareness and Image Research

Another type of research that is very common in tourism is aimed at determining the level of awareness of the destination in key market segments. It is critical to know awareness levels of a destination since visitors are highly unlikely to choose to visit a destination if they are unaware of its existence when making travel plans.

Once awareness levels have been established, destination managers then wish to know the nature of the image of their destination in key market segments. Positive images can be used as the basis of marketing campaigns to induce decisions to visit—while negative images need to be carefully examined to determine how they can be improved.

Visitor Satisfaction Research

Studies that determine the level of visitor satisfaction regarding their visit—and the aspects of their visitation experience that were viewed most favorably and least favorably—can be extremely useful in helping to identify where action is required to rectify shortcomings in the destination's ability to host visitors and even the kind of improvements that are required to address the shortcomings.

Competitor Research

Competitor research is detailed competitor analysis that identifies both direct and indirect competitors in local, regional, national, and international markets. It examines company site, product offering, pricing, service levels, and marketing staff.

SWOT Analysis

This research determines the strengths and weaknesses of your company or destination and the opportunities and threats that exist in the local, regional, national, and international environments.

Consumer/Tourist Behavior Research

This form of research involves asking potential and/or current visitors to describe the decision process they normally go through in choosing a destination to visit, to identify the information used in making the decision and, if possible, to identify the factors that have the greatest influence on individual decisions.

Futures Research

Futures research, which commonly uses the Delphi technique, seeks to identify the factors that are most likely to influence destination performance and ultimately destination success in the future. This form of research is very useful for policy formulation and destination design.

Destination Vision Research

Visioning research seeks to define a consensus-based description of the kind of destination that residents would like to see some 20 to 50 years into the future. Destination managers can then set in place policies and programs designed to translate the vision into reality.

Social Impact Research

Social impact research, which is the counterpart of economic impact research, is intended to identify and subsequently determine the seriousness of the impact that tourism has had on the social fabric of the destination—and on the well-being of individual residents of the destination.

Promotion Conversion Studies

This research seeks to determine the degree to which a promotion has been successful in convincing those who were exposed to different kinds of messages to those who actually chose to visit the destination. The primary measure of interest is the conversion rate—the estimate of the number of people who saw the destination advertising and were converted to an actual visit. Conversion research has become a major accountability tool for evaluating media advertising and other promotions such as coupons. Conversion research is also useful in designing future promotion programs.

Operations Research

Operations research is designed to determine how best to design the internal operations of different types of tourism firms. Examples include the allocation of staff and equipment so as to attain maximum efficiency in room cleaning in a large hotel; the design and operation of a ski lift in a winter resort complex; and, finally, in major Disneyland-type attractions, operations research can provide managers with a better understanding as to how facilities should be designed and operated in order to obtain optimal returns.

Household Surveys and En Route Surveys

Household surveys are commonly used to examine the characteristics of travelers, the nature and frequency of past travel, the most preferred form of travel, and future travel intentions. In contrast, en route surveys obtain data from visitors while they are in the process of traveling. Such research, because it focuses on current activities and short-term memory, provides better measures of travel expenditures, sites visited, and most likely travel intentions during the current trip.

Human Resources Research

The kind of research that can examine a range of issues related to employees in tourism. These might include salary surveys, employee satisfaction surveys, studies on the effectiveness of different working conditions, skills requirements for different kinds of tasks, and assessing the level of education and training required to affectively deliver different kinds of tourism experiences.

Brand Studies

Brand studies look at how consumers view a brand, what attributes they associate with a brand, and their levels of brand awareness. Such studies may also examine brand preferences and product usage.

Demand Estimation and Forecasting

This tool helps to determine the approximate level of demand for a product or service. Based on the level of demand, such factors as arrivals, expenditures, and sales are then forecast for various time periods. Both short-range and long-range forecasts are needed.

Product Research

Product research examines what products and packages of products and services can be developed and assesses consumer reaction to them. This encompasses (1) idea generation, product design, required technology, and (2) market research and analysis. An example of new product development would be space travel.

ROI (Return on Investment) Research

ROI measures the effectiveness and return on investment in programs designed to attract visitors. Examples of such research include ad effectiveness, brand message, Web site performance, social media, conversion studies, and public relations.

Custom Research

Custom research is company specific and addresses the questions, issues, and solutions that are unique to a client. It is proprietary, conducted for a single company alone, and is specific to your products and services. Custom research could involve unique questions regarding market size, market share, demand forecast, brand performance, industry trends, pricing, market segmentation, or any other special subject.

THE TRAVEL RESEARCH PROCESS

The key to good *travel research* is to define the problem and work through it in a systematic procedural manner to a final solution. The purpose of this section is to describe briefly the basic procedures that will produce a good research result.

1. **Identify the problem.** First, the problem must be defined or identified. Then you are in a position to proceed in a systematic manner.

2. **Conduct a situation analysis.** (environmental scan). In this step, you gather and digest all the information available and pertinent to the problem. The purpose is to become familiar with all the available information to make sure that you are not repeating someone else's work or that you have not overlooked information that will provide a ready solution to the problem. The situation analysis is an exhaustive search of all the data pertinent to the company, the product, the industry, the market, the competition, advertising, customers, suppliers, technology, the economy, the political climate, and similar matters. Knowledge of this background information will help you to sort out the likely causes of the problem and will lead to more efficient, productive research. The organization will get the most from the research result when it understands the organization's internal environment, as well as its goals, strategies, desires, resources, and constraints. In addition to a trip to the library, the Internet is an ideal tool to use in conducting the situation analysis.

3. **Conduct an informal investigation.** After getting background information from available sources, you will talk informally with consumers, distributors, and key people in the industry to get an even better feel for the problem. During both the situation analysis and informal investigation, you should be developing hypotheses that can be tested. The establishment of hypotheses is one of the foundations of high-quality research and is a valuable step in the problem-solving process. A hypothesis is a supposition, a tentative proposal, or a possible solution to a problem. In some ways it could be likened to a diagnosis. If your automobile quit running on the interstate, you might hypothesize that: (1) you were out of gas, (2) the fuel pump had failed, or (3) you had filter problems. An investigation would enable you to accept or reject these hypotheses.

4. **Develop a formal research design.** Once adequate background information has been developed and the problem has been defined against this background, it is time to develop the specific scientific procedure or design for carrying out the total investigation or research project. This step is the heart of the research process. Here you have to develop the hypotheses that will be tested and determine the types and sources of data that are to be obtained. Are secondary sources available, or will it be necessary to conduct primary research? If primary research has to be conducted, then it is necessary to develop the scientific sample, the questionnaires, or other data-collection instruments and any instruction sheets and coding methods and tabulation forms. Finally, it is necessary to conduct a pilot study to test all of the foregoing elements. The results are then written up in a detailed plan that serves as a guide that any knowledgeable researcher should be able to follow and conduct the research satisfactorily.

One of the first things to do in examining a tourism problem is to review and discuss the problem with a research firm representative. Here, Suzanne Cook, senior advisor, U.S. Travel Association, is visiting with Terry Berggren, destination research manager, Ruf Strategic Solutions. *Photo courtesy of the Travel and Tourism Research Association.*

5. **Collect the data.** If the data are available from secondary sources, then collecting the data becomes primarily desk research. However, if primary data are collected, this step involves actual fieldwork in conducting survey research, observational research, or experimental research. The success of data gathering depends on the quality of field supervision, the caliber of the interviewers or field investigators, and the training of investigators.

6. **Tabulate and analyze.** Once the data have been collected, they must be coded, tabulated, and analyzed. Both this step and the previous one must be done with great care; it is possible for a multitude of errors to creep into the research process if collection, tabulation, and analysis are not done properly. For example, if one is going to use the survey method, then interviewers must be properly selected, trained, and supervised. Obviously, if instead of following the carefully laid out sample, the interviewers simply fill out questionnaires themselves, the data will not be useful. In today's environment, tabulation will take place on a computer. A number of excellent packages are available for this purpose. One of the most extensively used packages is SPSS, the Statistical Package for the Social Sciences.

7. **Interpret.** Tabulation results in stacks of computer printout, with a series of statistical conclusions. These data must now be interpreted in terms of the best action or policy for the firm or organization to follow—a series of specific recommendations of action. This reduction of the interpretation to recommendations is one of the most difficult tasks in the research process.

8. **Write the report.** Presentation of the results of the research is extremely important. Unless the data are written up in a manner that will encourage management to read them and act upon them, all of the labor in the research process is wasted. Consequently, emphasis should be put on this step in the research process to produce a report that will be clearly understood, with recommendations that will be accepted.

9. **Follow up.** Follow up means precisely that. A study sitting on the shelf gathering dust accomplishes nothing. Although many people will consider the researcher's task to be done once the final report or presentation has been made, the work is not completed until the results of the survey are put into action. Research is an investment, and an ultimate test of the value of any research is the extent to which its recommendations are actually implemented and results

achieved. It is the task of the researcher to follow up to make the previous investment of time and money worthwhile.

SOURCES OF INFORMATION

Primary data, secondary data, or both may be used in a research investigation. **Primary data** are original data gathered for the specific purpose of solving the travel research problem that confronts you. In contrast, **secondary data** have already been collected for some other purpose and are available for use by simply visiting the library or other such repositories of secondary data. When researchers conduct a survey of cruise passengers to determine their attitudes and opinions, they are collecting primary data. When they access Census Bureau information on travel agents, they are using a secondary source.

The situation analysis step of the **travel research process** is emphasized because it focuses on the use of secondary sources; however, their use is not confined to this step. One of the biggest mistakes in travel research is to rush out and collect primary data without exhausting secondary source information. Only later do you discover that you have duplicated previous research when existing sources could have provided information to solve your problem for a fraction of the cost. Only after exhausting secondary sources and finding that you still lack sufficient data to solve your problem should you turn to primary sources.

Secondary Data

In the last ten years, there has been a virtual explosion of information related to tourism, travel, recreation, and leisure. A competent researcher must be well acquainted with these sources and know how to find them. The Internet is a source that contains a wealth of information.

If you are fortunate enough to find secondary sources of information, you can save yourself a great deal of time and money. Low cost is clearly the greatest advantage of secondary data. When secondary data sources are available, it is not necessary to construct and print questionnaires, hire interviewers, pay transportation costs, pay coders, pay data inputers, and pay programmers; thus, it is easy to see the cost advantage of utilizing secondary data. Secondary data can also be collected much more quickly than can primary data. With an original research project, it typically takes a minimum of 60 to 90 days or more to collect data; secondary data could be collected in a library or on the Internet within a few days.

Secondary data are not without disadvantages; for example, many times the information does not fit the problem for which you need information. Another problem is timeliness; many secondary sources become outdated. For example, the Census of Population and Housing is conducted every ten years; as we get to the end of that time period, the data are not very useful.

Evaluating Secondary Data

Although it is not expected that everyone will be a research expert, everyone should be able to evaluate or appraise secondary data. Any study, no matter how interesting, must be subjected to evaluation: "Is it a valid study? Can I use the results to make decisions?" On such occasions the researcher must evaluate the secondary data and determine whether they are usable.

The following criteria may be used to appraise the value of information obtained from secondary sources:

1. **The organizations supplying the data.** What amount of time went into the study? Who conducted the study? What experience did the personnel have? What was the financial capacity

of the company? What was the cost of the study? An experienced research firm will put the proper time and effort into a study to yield results, whereas a novice or inexperienced organization might not.

2. **The authority under which the data are gathered.** For example, data collected by the Internal Revenue Service (IRS) are likely to be much better than data collected by a business firm. Data that are required by law, such as census data, are much more dependable than is information from other sources.

3. **Freedom from bias.** One should always look at the nature of the organization furnishing the data. Would you expect a study sponsored by airlines to praise the bus industry for providing the lowest-cost transportation on a per mile basis in the United States?

4. **The extent to which the rules of sampling have been rigidly upheld.** What is the adequacy of the sample? Adequacy is frequently difficult to evaluate because deficiencies in the sampling process can be hidden. One indication of adequacy is the sponsor's willingness to talk about the sample. Will the sponsor release sampling details? Are the procedures well-known, acceptable methods?

5. **The nature of the unit in which the data are expressed.** Here, even simple concepts are difficult to define. In defining the term *house,* how do you handle such things as duplexes, triplexes, mobile homes, and apartment houses? Make sure that good operational definitions have been used throughout the research so there will be no problems in understanding it. Research results that are full of terms such as *occasionally* and *frequently* are not likely to be useful; these terms have different meanings to different people.

6. **The accuracy of the data.** Examine the data carefully for any inconsistencies and inquire into the way in which the data were acquired, edited, and tabulated. If at all possible, check the data against known data from other sources that are accurate. For example, check the demographics in a study against known census data.

7. **Relevance to the problem.** You must be concerned with fit. You may have a very good study, but if it does not pertain to the problem at hand, it is not worth anything to you. The relevance of secondary data to the problem must stand up; otherwise, the study cannot be used.

D. K. Shifflet and Associates, Ltd., is one of the many firms available to conduct travel and tourism research studies and consult with clients. The firm has been providing research and consulting services to clients for more than 20 years. Jim Caldwell serves as vice president marketing and sales. *Photo courtesy of the Travel and Tourism Research Association.*

8. **Careful work.** Throughout your evaluation, always look for evidence of careful work. Are tables constructed properly? Do all totals add up to the right figures or to 100 percent? Are conclusions supported by the data? Is there any evidence of conflicting data? Is the information presented in a well-organized, systematic manner?

Primary Data

When it is not possible to get the information you need from secondary sources, it is necessary to turn to primary sources—original, firsthand sources of information. If you need information on travelers' attitudes, you would then go to that population and sample it. As stated earlier, you should collect primary data only after exhausting all reasonable secondary sources of information.

Once you have determined that you are going to collect primary data, then you must choose what method of gathering primary data you are going to use. The most widely used means of collecting primary information is the survey method. Other methods are the observational method and the experimental method. It is not uncommon to find one or more of these methods used in gathering data. These basic methods are discussed in a later section.

EXPLORATORY RESEARCH

Exploratory research is conducted to explore a problem, get a feel for the situation, and possibly come up with some ideas for a solution. Qualitative research is typically used for exploratory purposes. Here, one has a small number of respondents and the results are not generalizable to the population. Exploratory research information is collected by focus group interviews; in-depth interviews; projective techniques; reviewing literature, books, and Internet data; and discussions with experts. Of these, focus groups interviews tend to be the most used.

Focus Groups

Focus-group interviewing is a popular form of market research in tourism. Its primary purpose is exploratory: either to establish the parameters for subsequent survey research or to delve into the motivations and behaviors of travelers.

A focus group is a form of qualitative research that brings together a small number of individuals (usually about 8 to 12) for an in-depth discussion regarding the topic of interest to the client. Typical topics include the most-desirable/least-desirable characteristics of a planned attraction or service, reaction to a planned advertising theme or program, or the probable public reaction to developments in an environmentally sensitive region.

Focus-group participants are chosen to represent a cross section of the population having a likely interest or stake in the area to be studied. However, because they are not selected scientifically (usually availability and willingness to participate play a major role in focus-group composition), great care must be taken in extrapolating the findings of focus-group sessions to the general population. In addition, because the session facilitator can significantly influence the nature of the discussion, it is essential that the facilitator be well trained and very familiar with the underlying goals of the focus group.

Despite these cautions and concerns, focus-group interviewing remains one of the most insightful and valuable ways of gaining a true understanding of the factors affecting complex managerial situations and decisions.

The Internet continues to invade all aspects of our lives. This is now true for focus groups as market research firms are now conducting focus groups online. Proponents argue that you can gather qualitative feedback from hard-to-reach and geographically dispersed participants. Sophisticated Web-based technology has been developed for online focus groups that provide qualified participants, experienced moderators, transcripts, and recommendations. Because it is online, focus group findings have never been faster.

BASIC QUANTITATIVE RESEARCH METHODS

To qualify as quantitative research, a project typically tests specific hypotheses, uses random sampling techniques, involves a large number of respondents, and draws conclusions. Examples include surveys and questionnaires. Techniques include modeling, scaling, factor analysis, statistics, covariance analysis, and so on.

Technology is constantly changing the **research methods** and techniques being used in quantitative research. The computer, Internet, smart phones, and so on are influencing the way research is done. A look back at history finds that in the 1950s and 1960s it was the age of face-to-face and door-to-door personal interviewing, in the 1970s mall facilities and mall intercept interviews were prominent, in the 1980s it was computer-assisted telephone interviews (CATI) that was a great advance, in the 1990s it was the fax and e-mail attracting attention, in the 2000s it was Web communities via computer, and in the 2010s, handheld devices are combining the power of the Internet with the portability of the cell phone.

Thus, while the traditional methods of tourism research are still being used, they have been transformed by technology so as to be conducted more quickly and more efficiently. Think about the way traditional interviewing methods, personal, telephone, and mail are being conducted today. The computer and smart phones allow the researcher to conduct face-to-face interviews from great distances, e-mail allows the researcher to reach distant audiences inexpensively, and e-mail panels are replacing traditional mail panels. So the basic methods continue but are being performed in a very different way than in the past. Technology will continue to result in more refinements and efficiencies.

The Survey Method

If we look at the methods of collecting travel research data, we will find that the survey method is the most frequently used. The survey method, also frequently referred to as the questionnaire technique, gathers information by asking questions. The survey method includes factual surveys, opinion surveys, or interpretative surveys, all of which can be conducted by personal interviews, mail, telephone techniques, or the Internet.

Factual Surveys

A quick look at the types of surveys will reveal that factual surveys are by far the most beneficial. "In what recreational activities did you participate last week?" is a question for which the respondent should be able to give accurate information. Although excellent results are usually achieved with factual surveys, all findings are still subject to certain errors, such as errors of memory and ability to generalize or the desire to make a good impression. Nonetheless, factual surveys tend to produce excellent results.

Opinion Surveys

In these surveys, the respondent is asked to express an opinion or make an evaluation or appraisal. For example, a respondent could be asked whether tour package A or B is the most attractive or which travel ad is the best. This kind of opinion information can be invaluable. In studies of a ski resort conducted by the University of Colorado, vacationer respondents were asked to rate the performance of the resort's employees as excellent, good, average, or needs improvement. The ratings allowed resort management to take action where necessary. Opinion surveys tend to produce excellent results if they are properly constructed.

Interpretive Surveys

On interpretive studies the respondent acts as an interpreter as well as a reporter. Subjects are asked why they chose a certain course of action—why they participated in a particular recreation activity the previous week (as well as what activity), why they flew on a particular airline, why they chose a particular vacation destination, why they chose a particular lodging establishment.

Although respondents can reply accurately to *what* questions, they often have difficulty replying to *why* questions. Therefore, while interpretive research may give you a feel for consumer behavior, the results tend to be limited. It is much better to utilize motivational and psychological research techniques, which are better suited for obtaining this information.

In summary, try to get factual or opinion data via the survey method and utilize in-depth interviewing or psychological research techniques to get "reason why" data.

It was mentioned earlier that surveys can be conducted by personal interviews, telephone, mail, or Internet. The purpose of a survey is to gather data by interviewing a limited number of people (sample) who represent a larger group. Reviewing the basic survey methods, one finds the following advantages and disadvantages.

Using the Internet

The Internet has become increasingly pervasive in all aspects of life today—and the field of research is no exception. In an ongoing effort to reduce the cost and increase the effectiveness of survey research, many researchers have turned to the Internet. In general, the results of this move to online survey research have been impressive, to the point where Web-based research may even be the mode of choice for a large percentage of studies.

Despite its appeal, Web-based survey research does have certain shortcomings that need to be kept in mind when contemplating its use. One of the industry's current top concerns relates to growing consumer distaste for any unsolicited marketing messages, whether they come from researchers or not. This reality makes it increasingly more difficult for research organizations to recruit participants for both surveys and focus groups.

Another problem is that because Internet-based research is so easy and inexpensive to conduct, a lot of inexperienced, poorly qualified individuals are carrying out their own surveys online. Because it is easy to create a survey online and e-mail it out, research has gone through a damaging period during which untrained people have conducted surveys using unprofessional sampling or consolidation of results, and as a consequence have derived unreliable results.

Despite these problems, there is little doubt that the use of online surveys, primarily because of their economic efficiency, will continue to grow and to improve in quality. Research companies have developed excellent sophisticated Internet surveys.

Personal Interviews

Personal interviews are much more flexible than either mail or telephone surveys because the interviewer can adapt to the situation and the respondent. The interviewer can alter questions to make sure that the respondent understands them or probe if the respondent does not respond with a satisfactory answer. Typically, one can obtain much more information by personal interview than by telephone or mail surveys, which by necessity must be relatively short. Personal interviewers can observe the situation as well as ask questions.

A major limitation of the personal interview method is its relatively high cost. The U.S. Census, which uses a combination of mail and follow-up door-to-door interviewing, demonstrates the high cost of personal interviews. It tends to be the most expensive of the three survey methods. It also takes a considerable amount of time to conduct, and there is always the possibility of personal interviewer bias. Technology holds the promise of making personal interviewing less expensive.

Telephone Surveys

Surveys in which respondents are interviewed over the telephone are usually conducted much more rapidly and at less cost than are personal interviews. The shortcomings of telephone surveys are that they are less flexible than personal interviews, and of necessity they are brief. Further limitations of phone surveys are that not everyone has a telephone, land lines are disappearing, and cell phones introduce a new dimension. However, those with telephones tend to have the market potential to travel or buy tourism products. Consequently, phone users make a good sample for travel research.

Sampling is a critical element of research. ASDE Inc. provides sampling and related services to research professionals making Survey Sampler, which draws sample numbers through a random digit dialing methodology, available to clients doing phone surveys. Randa Bell, marketing director, serves client needs. *Photo courtesy of the Travel and Tourism Research Association.*

Speed and low cost tend to be the primary advantages of telephone interviews. Computer-assisted telephone interviewing using random dialing is still a much-used technique.

The survey questionnaire is entered into computer memory. The interviewer reads the questions from the computer screen and records the respondent's answers into computer memory by using a keyboard or by simply touching a sensitive screen. Because the data are recorded immediately, these systems tend to be faster and less expensive than old reentry of data methods.

Mail Surveys

Mail surveys have the potential of being the lowest-cost method of research, especially if e-mail is used. As would be expected, mail surveys involve mailing the questionnaire to carefully selected sample respondents and requesting them to return the completed questionnaires (see Figure 18.1). This survey approach has a great advantage when large geographical areas must be covered and when it would be difficult to reach respondents. With the advent of e-mail, these advantages are even more apparent.

Other advantages of this approach are that personal interview bias is absent and the respondent can fill out the questionnaire at his or her convenience.

The greatest problem in conducting a mail survey is having a good list and getting an adequate response. If a large percentage of the target population fails to respond, you will have to question whether those who did not respond are different from those who have replied and whether this introduces bias. Length is another consideration in mail questionnaires. Although they can be longer than telephone surveys, they still must be a reasonable length. Another limitation of mail surveys is that questions must be worded carefully and simply so that respondents will not be confused. Questions that are very clear to the person who wrote them might be very unclear to the respondent.

Observational Method

The *observational method* relies on the direct observation of physical phenomena in the gathering of data. Observing some action of the respondent is obviously much more objective and accurate than is utilizing

---

CAREY AMERICAN LIMOUSINE | Colorado Springs Shuttle Service

Please take a moment to respond to the following questions. This information will be used to evaluate areas of service to afford you quality service for your next trip. Thank you.

1. Was the vehicle on time? Yes _____ No _____ (Delay time: _____ Reason given _____)
2. What was the condition of the equipment? Clean _____ Average _____ Unkempt _____
3. Was your driver courteous? Yes _____ No _____
4. How was your service? Excellent _____ Fair _____ Poor _____ (Why? _____)
5. Was it easy to make your reservation? Yes _____ No _____ (Why? _____)
6. Where did you find out about our company? Travel agent _____ Advertisement _____ (Referred by _____)
7. Was the scheduled time convenient for you? Very _____ Acceptable _____ Inconvenient _____
8. Were you traveling on Business _____ Pleasure _____
9. Will you recommend our service to others? Yes _____ (Name & Address _____) No _____
Comments

Name: _____ If you represent a company or travel agency, please include

Address: _____ that information:

City: _____ State: _____ Zip: _____

COLORADO TRANSPORTATION GROUP   Telephone (_____) _____

Figure 18.1 A sample mail questionnaire.

the survey method. Under the observational method, information can be gathered by either personal or mechanical observation. Mechanical recorders on highways count the number of cars that pass and the time that they pass. Automatic counters at attractions observe and count the number of visitors.

PROFILE

BILL SIEGEL
Chairman, Longwoods International, Toronto, Ontario, Canada.

Bill is chairman and CEO of Longwoods International, a market research consultancy that is highly respected within the tourism industry. Since founding Longwoods in 1978, he has built an international organization that has assisted clients in 6 countries, 36 U.S. states, and 8 Canadian provinces.

His first career was as an experimental psychologist specializing in human perception and memory. After completing his B.A. (Honors) at the University of Toronto, he received his Ph.D. in psychology from the University of Michigan, where he was University Scholar, University Fellow, Springer Traveling Fellow, and Rackham Research Fellow. He went on to teach psychology and research methods as assistant professor at the University of Western Ontario, and was invited to be Distinguished Visiting Lecturer at the University of Western Australia. He authored articles in a number of scientific journals, including *Psychological Review, Journal of Experimental Psychology, Perception & Psychophysics,* and *Journal of the Acoustical Society of America.*

Bill switched his research interests from academia to the business world in the mid-1970s, when he was hired by Bell Canada as manager of marketing research to design and implement a groundbreaking study of the bottom-line effectiveness of advertising for the CEOs of the telephone companies across Canada.

His entry into tourism came in 1985, when his company was hired by the Canadian government to research Canada's image in the United States and to develop a communications strategy for overcoming a 15-year decline in market share. With more than 9,000 interviews, it was considered at that time to be the largest study of tourism to be conducted in the United States.

Today, Bill's company invites 2 million Americans annually to participate in its Longwoods Travel USA® syndicated research program. It has provided strategic counsel for a number of major brands, such as New York: *I ♥ NY*; USA: *You've Seen the Films, Now Visit the Set*; Hawaii: *The Islands of Aloha*; Colorado: *Mountains and Much More*; and Washington, D.C.: *Power Trip*.

His work has been cited in broadcast and print media around the world, including *The New York Times, USA Today, Newsweek, the Christian Science Monitor,* and *The Times of London*. He has been invited to speak at many industry functions, such as state governor's conferences, The Brookings Institution, the Travel and Tourism Research Association, the U.S. Economic Development Administration, the American Marketing Association, the Advertising Research Foundation, the Public Relations Society of America, and the European Society for Opinion and Marketing Research.

Bill has served on boards for the Travel and Tourism Research Association, Georgia Tech, Ryerson University, and Waterloo University, and was appointed Honorary Citizen of New Jersey by Governor Florio.

WORDS ABOUT THE FUTURE

Research will continue to play a key role for tourism marketers, providing them with the radar they need to navigate through the rapidly evolving world of travelers' decision making. However, the tools we use to survey consumers will continue to evolve to reflect the public's preferred modes of communication. In the past few years, we have witnessed a dramatic shift from mail and telephone as survey methodologies to online interviews. In 2007, my company migrated its syndicated Longwoods Travel USA® study from mail panel to online, where we now invite 2 million panelists to participate annually. The key benefits include unprecedented sample size, rapid turnaround, flexibility, interactivity, and greater respondent engagement.

Gazing at my crystal ball, I see continuing movement to the Web for survey research, with a growing challenge in reaching consumers on mobile devices. We will also struggle as an industry to better understand and measure the influence of social media. However, unlike most product categories, our scanners work at check-in, not check-out, and so for destinations, survey data will remain essential for understanding who comes, why, how much money they spend, the activities they enjoy, and, most importantly, how much business was generated by their marketing programs.

Advantages of the observational method are that it tends to be accurate and it can record consumer behavior. It also reduces interviewer bias. Disadvantages are that it is much more costly than the survey method, and it is not possible to employ in many cases. Finally, the observational method shows what people are doing but does not tell why they are doing it. It cannot delve into motives, attitudes, or opinions. If the why is important, this would not be a good method to use.

Experimental Method

The *experimental method* of gathering primary data involves setting up a test, a model, or an experiment to simulate the real world. The essentials of the experimental method are the **measurement** of variations within one or more activities while all other conditions and variables are being controlled. The experimental method is very hard to use in tourism research because of the difficulty of holding variables constant. Tourism researchers have no physical laboratory in which to work. However, it is possible for resort areas to run advertising experiments or pricing experiments or to develop simulation models to aid in decision making. Such test marketing is being conducted successfully, and as time passes, we will see the experimental method being used more.

WHO DOES TRAVEL RESEARCH?

Many organizations use and conduct **travel research**. The types of firms and organizations that engage in travel research include government, educational institutions, consultants, trade associations, advertising agencies, media, hotels and motels, airlines and other carriers, attractions, and food service organizations.

Research shows that in today's marketplace, both business and leisure travelers want a fitness room where they can exercise. *Photo courtesy of Glenwood Hot Springs Athletic Club in Glenwood Springs, Colorado.*

Government

The federal government has been a major producer of travel research over the years. The Office of Travel and Tourism Industries, in the U.S. Department of Commerce, conducts studies on international visitors, focusing on both marketing information and economic impact. State and local governments also employ travel research to assist in making marketing and public policy decisions. Examples are studies of highway users, the value of fishing and hunting, the economic impact of tourism in various geographic areas, inventories of tourism facilities and services, tourism planning procedures, and visitor characteristics studies. In other countries, research inaugurated by the official tourism organization of a state or country often has very significant ramifications for tourism development and promotion. Research done in Australia, Canada, Mexico, England, Spain, France, Poland, and Croatia has been outstanding.

Educational Institutions

Universities conduct many travel research studies. The chief advantage is that the studies are usually conducted by trained professionals without bias. Many of the studies have contributed greatly to the improvement of travel research methods.

Many departments of universities are qualified to accomplish pure research or applied research in tourism. Bureaus of business and economic research are often active in this field. An example is the research accomplished by the Business Research Division of the University of Colorado Boulder. This organization has published many tourism research findings, bibliographies, and ski industry studies. Departments of universities that can be helpful include psychology, sociology, economics, engineering, landscape architecture and urban planning, management, hotel and restaurant administration, theater, home economics, human ecology, forestry, botany, zoology, history, geography, and anthropology.

Consultants

Numerous organizations specialize in conducting travel research on a fee basis for airlines, hotels, restaurants, ski areas, travel agents, resorts, and others. Consultants offer the service of giving advice in the planning, design, interpretation, and application of travel research. They also provide the service of conducting all or a part of a field investigation for their clients.

The primary advantage of consultants or consulting firms is that they are well-trained, experienced specialists who have gained their experience by making studies for many different clients. They also provide an objective outsider's point of view, and they have adequate facilities to undertake almost any job. The disadvantage of consultants is that of any outsider: the lack of intimate knowledge of the internal problems of the client's business; however, management can provide this ingredient. Many travel firms with their own research departments find it advantageous to use consultants or a combination of their own internal staff and consultants.

Many well-known firms specialize in travel research. A few of these are ACXION; DataPath Systems; Davidson-Peterson Associates; Economics Research Associates; Forrester Research; TNS; Ipsos; D. K. Shifflet and Associates; Longwoods International; Mandala Research; Menlo Consulting Group; IPK International; Dean Runyan Associates; Ruf Strategic Solutions; Smith Travel Research; Strategic Marketing and Research, Inc.; TTC International UK; Tourism Economics; Western Management Consultants; and YPartnership.

Trade Associations

Extensive travel research is conducted by trade associations. The trade association often has facilities for carrying on a continuous research service for its members, particularly in the area of industry statistics. Many associations have excellent Internet sites and make their data available to the public.

Hotels and Motels

Hotels and motels constantly use current research findings concerning their markets, trends in transportation, new construction materials, management methods, use of electronic data processing,

TNS is another leading tourism research firm with more than 25 years of industry experience doing transportation, travel, hospitality, and leisure research. Shown here are Stephan Mayer, senior project director, and Richard Cain, vice president and account executive. TNS is a strong supporter of the Travel and Tourism Research Association (TTRA), and Richard Cain served as TTRA chairman of the board in 2009–2010. *Photo courtesy of the Travel and Tourism Research Association.*

human relations techniques, employee management, advertising, food and beverage supplies and services, and myriad other related information.

Airlines and Other Carriers

Airlines and other carriers offer services designed for the business and vacation traveler. Because of their needs and the importance of research to their operations, airlines and other carriers will usually have their own market research departments to conduct ongoing studies of their customers and the market. They are also frequent employers of outside consultants.

Attractions

The most ambitious private attractions in the country are the major theme parks, and research has played a major role in the success of these enterprises. That research has run the gamut from **feasibility studies** to management research. Walt Disney's thinking still dominates the industry. The Disney formula of immaculate grounds, clean and attractive personnel, high-quality shops, tidy restrooms, and clean restaurants is still the consumers' preference today. Research shows that if attractions are not clean, they are not likely to be successful.

Food Service

Much of the pioneering work in the use of research by restaurants has been done by franchises and chains because what will work in one location will typically work in others, resulting in a large payoff from funds invested in research. All travel firms, whether they are restaurants, airlines, hotels, or other hospitality enterprises, need to be in touch with their markets and find new and better ways of marketing to sell seats, increase load factors, and achieve favorable occupancy ratios.

THE STATE OF THE ART

Early tourism research was criticized for being too descriptive and lacking rigor. Today, travel research runs from simple fact gathering to complex mathematical models. Tourism researchers utilize virtually every quantitative and qualitative technique available. An examination of tourism research studies reveals that multidimensional scaling (MDS), conjoint analysis, correspondence analysis, cohort analysis, structural equation modeling (SEM), linear structural relationships (LISREL), analysis of variance (ANOVA), analysis of covariance (ANCOVA), multivariate analysis of variance (MANOVA), discriminant analysis, factor analysis, canonical correlation, cluster analysis, least squares, time series, repertory grid scaling, chi-square, multiple regression, simulation models, diary panels, case studies, content analysis, focus groups, word association, and ethnographic research techniques are in use by tourism researchers today.

Journals

The *Journal of Travel Research* was the first scholarly journal published in the tourism research field in North America in 1972. It was soon followed by the *Annals of Tourism Research* in 1973. Prior to 1972, only five journals related to tourism existed:

1. *Tourism Review*, which was the first tourism journal and was first published in 1946 by the International Association of Scientific Experts in Tourism (AIEST) in St. Gallen, Switzerland
2. *Turizam* (now *Tourism*), first published in Croatia in 1956
3. *World Leisure Journal,* first published by World Leisure in 1958

4. *The Cornell Hotel and Restaurant Administration Quarterly*, first published by Cornell University in 1960

5. *Journal of Leisure Research*, first published by the National Recreation and Park Association in 1968

Since then, there has been a virtual explosion of tourism and tourism-related journals. In a paper presented by Dr. James Petrick, Texas A&M University, at the 2005 Travel and Tourism Research Association conference in New Orleans titled "Examining Tourism Knowledge Development from Journal Topics," the authors identified over 150 tourism-related journals in the English language.[2] Journals have become more specialized over the years and now draw contributions from almost every discipline. Academic journals are the research showcase of a field. Journals present new findings, describe new discoveries, and track the development of the field. Continued growth in the number of journals is predicted.

Electronic Communications

Electronic communications have facilitated tourism research, and this area will continue to expand in the future. Currently, the most prominent tourism research bulletin board is TRINET. All tourism researchers owe Professor Pauline Sheldon at the University of Hawaii a huge debt of gratitude for establishing this electronic bulletin board, where hundreds of tourism researchers, both academic and practitioners, have the opportunity to exchange views, explore issues, and request help in research. Because of electronic communications, colleagues across the world are collaborating on research today.

CIRET

The International Center for Research and Study on Tourism (CIRET), in France, maintains the largest database on tourism in the world. Its Research and Documentation Center collects, catalogs, annotates, and distributes published tourism, leisure, outdoor recreation, and hospitality literature from around the world. Currently, the Documentation Center contains 155,844 documents. These documents are classified by theme and by country. Visit CIRET's Web site at www.ciret-tourism.com to see its thesaurus and geographical index.

In addition, databases are maintained on research centers, researchers, publishers, and congress calendars. The site lists over 773 research centers located in 106 countries and 4,594 researchers in 118 countries. More than 290 publishers are listed.

Dr. Rene Baretje-Keller, president of CIRET, makes its services available free to researchers and students in order to encourage networking among the global research community.

TRAVEL AND TOURISM RESEARCH ASSOCIATION

The **Travel and Tourism Research Association** *(TTRA)* is an international organization of travel research and marketing professionals devoted to improving the quality, value, scope, and acceptability of travel research and marketing information. The association is the world's largest travel research organization, and its members represent all aspects of the travel industry, including airlines, hotels, attractions, transportation companies, media, advertising agencies, government, travel agencies, consulting firms, universities, students, and so on.

TTRA's mission is to be the global leader in advocating standards and promoting the application of high-quality travel and tourism research, planning, management, and marketing information, with the following specific objectives:

- Serve as an international forum for the exchange of ideas and information among travel and tourism researchers, marketers, planners, and managers.

■ Encourage the professional development of travel and tourism researchers, marketers, planners, and managers.

■ Facilitate global cooperation between producers and users of travel and tourism research.

■ Promote and disseminate high-quality, credible, and effective research to the travel and tourism industry.

■ Foster the development of travel and tourism research and related curricula in institutions of higher education.

■ Advocate the effective use of research in the decision-making process of professionals in the travel and tourism industry.

TTRA has chapters in Asia, Europe, Canada, and the United States in the central states, Florida, Texas, the western states, the Southeast, Hawaii, and a student chapter at California University of Pennsylvania. TTRA contributes to the publication of the *Journal of Travel Research*, the TTRA newsletter, annual conference proceedings, and other special publications. TTRA has an extensive awards program that recognizes excellence and encourages professional development of researchers, marketers, planners, and students involved in the travel and tourism industry. Those wishing further information on TTRA should visit the association's Web site at www.ttra.com.

SUMMARY

Travel research provides the information base for effective decision making by tourism managers. Availability of adequate facts allows managers to develop policy, plan, operate, and control more efficiently and decreases risk in the decision-making process.

Useful travel research depends on precise identification of the problem; a thorough situation analysis supplemented by an informal investigation of the problem; careful research design; and meticulous collection, tabulation, and analysis of the data. The researcher must also present a readable written report with appropriate recommendations for action and then follow up to ensure that the recommendations are actually implemented so that results can be achieved.

The research itself may use secondary (preexisting) data or require collection of primary data (original research). Primary data may be gathered by survey—Internet, personal interview, mail, or telephone surveys—or by the observational and experimental methods. Numerous organizations and agencies use and conduct travel research. The Travel and Tourism Research Association is the world's largest tourism research organization.

 KEY CONCEPTS

research methods	information surveys	sources of data
decision making	measurement	Travel and Tourism Research
experimental method	observational method	Association
feasibility studies	primary data	travel research
focus groups	secondary data	travel research process

 INTERNET EXERCISES

The Internet sites mentioned in this chapter plus some selected additional sites are listed for your convenience on the companion Web site for this book, www.wiley.com/college/goeldner.

ACTIVITY 1

Site Name: National Laboratory for Tourism and eCommerce

URL: www.tourism.temple.edu

Background Information: The primary mission of the National Laboratory for Tourism and eCommerce is to foster quality inter- and multidisciplinary research in the varied aspects of tourism.

Exercise

1. Discuss how the laboratory supports its research mission.

ACTIVITY 2

Site Name: Travel and Tourism Research Association (TTRA)

URL: www.ttra.com

Background Information: TTRA is an international association of travel research and marketing professionals devoted to improving the quality, value, scope, and acceptability of travel research and marketing information.

Exercises

1. What resource links does TTRA list?
2. What conferences does TTRA hold?

ACTIVITY 3

Site Name: International Center for Research and Study on Tourism

URL: www.ciret-tourism.com

Background Information: CIRET is the leading database for tourism research, individual tourism researchers, and tourism research centers.

Exercises

1. How many researchers are listed in the site's *Encyclopedia of Worldwide Tourism Research?*
2. How many research centers?
3. How many publishers?

❖ QUESTIONS FOR REVIEW AND DISCUSSION ❖

1. What does a situation analysis cover?
2. What are some types of travel research?
3. When should you use primary data? Secondary data?
4. What are the basic research methods?
5. What are the strengths and weaknesses of focus groups?
6. Why would you choose survey research over focus groups?
7. Why are research findings so important to intelligent decision making?
8. If you were director of a major city's convention and visitors bureau, how would you use travel research?
9. As a consultant, you are researching the feasibility of a new resort hotel project. What procedures would you use, step by step?
10. How would a resort developer use a consultant's report when the report is completed? Once the resort is built, does the manager need further research?
11. What methods could be used by a state tourist office to survey out-of-state visitors?
12. Should a state tourist office conduct its own research or hire an outside supplier? Why?

❖ CASE PROBLEM ❖

You are the research director of the Colorado Tourism Office and plan to conduct a study of tourists visiting the state to create a profile of the Colorado visitor to help guide advertising and promotion decisions. What questions will you ask in the study? What demographic data will you collect? How will you sample visitors to ensure you have a representative sample? How will you tabulate the results? How will you present your findings?

ENDNOTES

1. Douglas C. Frechtling, "Assessing the Economic Impacts of Travel and Tourism: Introduction to Travel Economic Impact Estimation." Chapter in Ritchie, J. R. B. and C. R. Goeldner (eds.), *Travel, Tourism & Hospitality Research: A Handbook for Managers and Researchers* (New York: John Wiley & Sons, 1994), pp. 367–392.
2. C. Cheng, K. Li, J. Petrick, and J. O'Leary (2005), "Examining Tourism Knowledge Development From Journal Topics." Unpublished paper presented at the 2005 TTRA Conference in New Orleans.

CHAPTER 19

Tourism Marketing

LEARNING OBJECTIVES

- Appreciate the Internet's impact on tourism marketing.

- Become familiar with the marketing mix and be able to formulate the best mix for a particular travel product.

- Appreciate the importance of the relationship between the marketing concept and product planning and development.

- Understand the vital relationship between pricing and marketing.

- Be able to do market segmentation to plan a marketing program for the business you are the most interested in.

- Demonstrate the linkage between tourism policy and tourism marketing.

The Statue of Liberty is an internationally recognized tourism icon that greatly enhances market awareness of New York City—and the entire United States—as a travel destination. *Photo courtesy of New York State Division of Tourism.*

INTRODUCTION

The explosive growth of the Internet and mobile media technology has impacted how tourists make travel decisions and provided new tools and media for tourism marketing. The Internet helps people be more socially connected than ever before. Online social networks, social media, user-generated media, and e-commerce dominate the tourism marketing scene today. Phones are computers, Web sites offer tourism products and services, and sites such as TripAdvisor allow consumers to report on their travel experiences providing reviews and photos. It has been estimated that 80 percent of consumers have used the Internet in trip planning and today over 50 percent of travel is booked online. The impact of the Internet is pervasive, affecting all components of the four Ps of marketing—product, place, promotion, and price.

In today's marketplace, it is all about customer engagement and at the top of the list is social media. The sites and tools that need to be in a marketing plan today include blogs, wikis, widgets, tweets, mashups, photos, videos, podcasts, RSS feeds, profile pages on such sites as Facebook and MySpace, live chat/instant messaging, user-generated visual content, user ratings and rankings, and user comments and reviews. The U.S. National Science Foundation estimated there were 1.67 billion Internet users in 2010 and that this will grow to 5 billion in 2020.[1] Thus, tomorrow's tourism industry will be even more embedded in the Internet, playing an active role online and in social media to enhance all the traditional marketing activities and bring them to a new level. We will see continuous evolution of technology creating new tools, ideas, and marketing methods.

WHAT IS MARKETING?

Marketing has been defined in a variety of ways. The American Marketing Association defines it as "an organizational function and a set of processes for creating, communicating, and delivering value to customers and for managing customer relationships in ways that benefit the organization and its stakeholders."[2] Others have stated that marketing is the delivery of the standard of living to society. You are no doubt acquainted with the old adage, "Nothing happens until somebody sells something."

Most people have little idea what marketing is all about and would probably say that it has something to do with selling or advertising. However, marketing is a very broad concept, of which advertising and selling are only two facets. Marketing is goal-oriented, strategic, and directed. It both precedes and follows selling and advertising activities. Marketing is the total picture in getting goods and services from the producer to the user.

Unfortunately, the term *marketing* often conjures up unfavorable images of used-car salespeople, TV furniture advertisers, high-pressure selling, and gimmicks, leading to the perception of marketing in terms of stereotypes. In fact, marketing plays a critical role in all organizations, whether they are nonprofit educational institutions, tourist resorts, or manufacturers. The role of marketing is to match the right product or service with the right market or audience.

Marketing is an inevitable aspect of tourism management. Marketing can be done effectively and well, with sophistication, or it can be done poorly in a loud, crass, intrusive manner. The goal of this chapter is to discuss the basic elements of marketing so that it can be done effectively, with style, and with a favorable economic impact.

MARKETING CONCEPT

The heart of good marketing management today is the marketing concept, or a consumer orientation. Tourism organizations that practice the marketing concept find out what the consumer wants and then produce a product that will satisfy those wants at a profit. The marketing concept requires that management thinking be directed toward profits rather than sales volume.

Assume that you are going to develop a new major resort area. This is a difficult exercise in planning that requires that the designs that are developed be based on how consumers view the product. One of the first steps is to employ the marketing concept and do research to understand the consumers' (the market's) needs, desires, and wants. Designers of products and consumers of products often perceive them differently. Architects, for example, might see a hotel in terms of such things as space utilization, engineering problems, and design lines or as a monument; consumers may see the hotel as a bundle of benefits—as being attractive, as offering full service and outstanding food, as having recreational facilities, and so on. Once consumer views are determined, the task is to formulate strategic marketing plans that match the resort and its market. In today's competitive environment where consumers have many choices, firms need to employ the marketing concept. As indicated in the Introduction of this chapter, the Internet makes it much easier to engage the consumer and practice the marketing concept.

THE MARKETING MIX

The marketing program combines a number of elements into a workable whole—a viable, strategic plan. The tourism marketing manager must constantly search for the right **marketing mix**—the right combination of elements that will produce a profit. The marketing mix is composed of every factor that influences the marketing effort:

1. **Timing.** Holidays, high season, low season, upward trend in the business cycle, and so on, must be considered.
2. **Brands.** The consumer needs help in remembering your product. Names, trademarks, labels, logos, and other identification marks all assist the consumer in identifying and recalling information about your product.
3. **Packaging.** Although tourism services do not require a physical package, packaging is still an important factor. For example, transportation, lodging, amenities, and recreation activities can be packaged and sold together or separately. Family plans or single plans are other forms of packaging.
4. **Pricing.** Pricing affects not only sales volume but also the image of the product. A multitude of pricing options exist, ranging from discount prices to premium prices.
5. **Channels of distribution.** The product must be accessible to the consumer. Direct selling, via the Internet, phone, or office; retail travel agents; online travel agents; wholesale tour operators; or a combination of these methods are all distribution channels that can be developed. Online is now the dominant channel.
6. **Product.** The physical attributes of the product help to determine its position against the competition and provide guidelines on how to best compete.
7. **Image.** The consumer's perception of the product depends to a great extent on the important factors of reputation and quality.
8. **Advertising.** Paid promotion is critical, and the questions of when, where, and how to promote must be carefully considered.
9. **Selling.** Internal and external selling are essential components for success, and various sales techniques must be incorporated in the marketing plan.
10. **Public relations.** Even the most carefully drawn marketing plan will fail without good relations with the visitors, the community, suppliers, and employees.
11. **Service quality.** Outstanding service is necessary to have satisfied customers and repeat business.
12. **Research.** Developing the right tourism marketing mix depends in large part on research. See Chapter 18 on tourism research.

The preceding list makes it obvious that the marketing manager's job is a complex one. Using knowledge of the consumer market and the competition, the marketing manager must come up with the proper marketing mix for the resort, attraction, or other organization. The marketing manager's job begins with planning to allow direction and control of the foregoing factors.

The many elements in the marketing mix have been defined most frequently as the **four Ps**, a term popularized by E. Jerome McCarthy, coauthor of *Basic Marketing* and *Essentials of Marketing*.[3] While the four Ps are an oversimplification, they do provide a neat, simple framework in which to look at marketing and put together a marketing program. The four Ps are **product**, **place**, **promotion**, and **price**. The product includes not only the actual physical attributes of the product but also product planning, product development, breadth of the line, branding, and packaging. Planning the product should consider all these aspects in order to come up with the "right" product.

Place is really concerned with distribution. What agencies, channels, and institutions can be linked together most effectively to give the consumer easy access to the purchase of your product? Where is the "right" place or places to market your product?

Promotion communicates the benefits of the product to the potential customers and includes not only advertising but also sales promotion, public relations, and personal selling. The "right" promotional mix will use each of these promotional techniques as needed for effective communication.

Price is a critical variable in the marketing mix. The "right" price must both satisfy customers and meet your profit objectives.

Mill and Morrison have added another "three Ps" that they believe are particularly relevant to tourism.[4] **Programming** involves special activities, events, or other types of programs to increase customer spending or to give added appeal to a package or other tourism service. As noted in Chapter 15, tourism policy views programs as a strategic consolidation of a range of different activities designed to ensure a clear focus for development and marketing efforts.

The second of the additional three Ps concerns **people**. This P is intended to stress that tourism is a *people business*—that we must not lose sight of the importance of providing travel experiences that are sensitive to the human side of the visitor as well as to the functional requirements.

The final P is defined as **partnership**. This highlights the high degree of interdependency among all destination stakeholders, and the need for alliances and working relationships that build a cooperation—sometimes with competitors as well as colleagues. Edgell's concept of coopetition, discussed in Chapter 15, captures the value of partnership in a unique way.

Product/Experience Branding

A fundamental concept in traditional marketing is that of the product *brand*: "A distinguishing name and/or a symbol (such as a logo, trademark, or package design) intended to identify the goods or services of one seller, or groups of sellers, and to differentiate those goods or services from competitors who would attempt to provide products that appear to be identical."[5]

Recently, tourism marketers have been attempting to "brand" their destinations. Although the approach has considerable potential, the transference of its application from traditional products and services to the tourism setting is not without its difficulties.

One particularly useful transference of **branding** from products to tourism destinations postulates that *place branding* performs four main functions.[6] First, destination brands serve as *communicators*, where brands represent a mark of ownership and a means of destination differentiation that is manifested in legally protected names, logos, and trademarks. Second, they provide an image for the destinations, which is characterized by a set of associations or attributes to which consumers attach personal value. Third, brands serve as *value enhancers* that create brand equity for the destination in the form of improved streams of future income. Finally, a destination brand can be viewed as possessing a personality that enables it to form a relationship with the visitor.

PROFILE

MICHELE MCKENZIE
President and CEO,
Canadian Tourism
Commission,
Vancouver, B.C.

Michele McKenzie is the president and CEO of Canada's national tourism marketing organization, the Canadian Tourism Commission (CTC). The CTC markets and promotes Canada's extraordinary travel experiences internationally to increase export revenues in Canada.

Michele joined CTC in 2004, leading the Crown Corporation to its new home on the west coast of Canada, Vancouver. Under her leadership, Canada's new tourism marketing brand was developed and launched internationally. Canada's country brand recognition and tourism appeal has since risen from twelfth in the world, to sixth, to second place.

In 2009, CTC was named "Marketer of the Year" in Canada, a first for a Crown Corporation, a first for a West Coast corporation, and a great tribute to Michele's vision.

Backed by the government of Canada, Michele is leading her team to execute and deliver on an ambitious five-year strategy to help ensure that Canada's visitor economy is the greatest beneficiary of the 2010 Winter Games.

Michele is Ontario born, grew up in Nova Scotia, and is a graduate of Dalhousie University. Michele served as deputy minister for Nova Scotia Tourism, Culture and Heritage and has been an active director on several boards over the course of her career.

WORDS FOR THE FUTURE

What will tourism marketing look like in the future?

It is easy enough to envision where tourism will go in the future: travel will continue to be the world's fastest-growing industry; all destinations will have the opportunity to share in this growth, but new, exotic destinations will steal share from established destinations; air access will be intricately linked to destination growth, thus destinations with the most competitive air (and other government policies favorable to tourism) will win. Destinations will continue to adapt to security measures (and security decisions will begin to reflect tourism impacts), and sustainable practices will be expected.

However, envisioning what tourism marketing will look like in the future is another story altogether. Winning destinations will be those that build strong, sustainable brands and those that recognize that our customers are now fully in control. We must respect this new relationship with the customer, engage in meaningful two-way dialogue, and leverage the information explosion. And perhaps most important, we need to be nimble. We need to be skeptical of those who say they know what tourism marketing will look like in the future—no one really knows.

Together, we will invent the future of tourism marketing.

Product Planning and Development

The objective of most firms is to develop a profitable and continuing business. To achieve this objective, companies must provide products and services that satisfy consumer needs, thereby assuring themselves of repeat business. **Product planning** is an essential component in developing a profitable, continuing business and has frequently been referred to as the *five rights*—planning to have the right product, at the right place, at the right time, at the right price, in the right quantities.

Tourism icons, such as the Golden Gate Bridge in San Francisco, can be used to promote travel to a given location. Not all icons are bridges or statues, however. For example, the Southern belle of Mississippi is an enduring symbol of southern hospitality. *Golden Gate Bridge photo by Robert Holmes; courtesy of the California Division of Tourism. Southern belle photo courtesy of the Mississippi Department of Community Development/Division of Tourism Development.*

A product is much more than a combination of raw materials. It is actually a bundle of satisfactions and benefits for the consumer. Product planning must, therefore, be approached from the consumer's point of view. Creating the right service or product is not easy: Consumer needs, wants, and desires are constantly changing, and competitive forces typically carry products through a **product life cycle**, so that a product that is successful at one point declines and "dies" at a later time.

"Virginia Is for Lovers" is a destination branding tagline that has proven to be very successful, demonstrating the value of sticking with a successful theme over the long term. *Photo courtesy of Washington, D.C., and the Capital Region, USA.*

Figure 19.1 shows the phases that a new product goes through from inception to decline: (1) introduction, (2) growth, (3) maturity, (4) saturation, and (5) decline. Because of the rapidly changing consumer lifestyles and technological changes, the life cycle for products and services has become shorter, but the product life cycle remains a useful concept for strategic planning. Each stage of the product life cycle has certain marketing requirements.

Introduction

The introductory phase of the product's life cycle requires high promotional expenditures and visibility (the most productive time to advertise a product or service is when it is new). Operations in this period are characterized by high cost, relatively low sales volume, and a promotion program

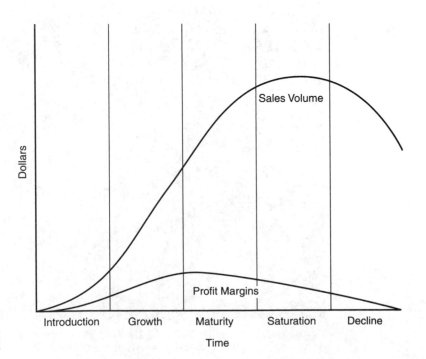

Figure 19.1 Product life cycle.

aimed at stimulating primary demand. In this stage of the life cycle, there will be a high percentage of failures.

Growth

In the growth period, the product or service is being accepted by consumers. Market acceptance means that both sales and profits rise at a rapid rate, frequently making the market attractive to competitors. Promotional expenditures remain high, but the promotional emphasis is on selective buying motives by trade name rather than on primary motives to try the product. During the growth stage, the number of outlets handling the product or service usually increases. More competitors enter the marketplace, but economies of scale are realized and prices may decline some.

Maturity

The mature product is well established in the marketplace. Sales may still be increasing, but at a much slower rate; they are leveling off. At this stage of the product's life cycle, many outlets are selling the product or service; they are very competitive, especially with respect to price, and firms are trying to determine ways to hold on to their share of the market. Ski resorts are an excellent example of a mature product. After years of spectacular growth, sales are now leveling off, and the resorts are looking for ways to hold market share and diversify.

Saturation

In the saturation stage, sales volume reaches its peak: The product or service has penetrated the marketplace to the greatest degree possible. Mass production and new technology have lowered the price to make it available to almost everyone.

Decline

Many products stay at the saturation stage for years. However, for most products, obsolescence sets in and new products are introduced to replace old ones. In the decline stage, demand obviously drops, promotional expenditures are lower, and there is usually a smaller number of competitors. Although it is possible for a product to do very well in this stage of the product life cycle, there is not a great deal of comfort in getting a larger share of a declining market. Hot springs resorts are a good example of a tourist product in the decline stage. These facilities, at their peak in the 1920s, are no longer the consumer's idea of an "in" place to go.

Service Quality

Service quality is the customers' perception of the service component of a product. Service quality is an important element of the marketing mix and in building and delivering a competitive advantage in tourism.

Outstanding service quality leads to customer satisfaction, which leads to repeat business. Customer satisfaction and loyalty are the keys to repeat business and long-term profitability. Keeping customers satisfied is everybody's job in an organization. Employees should strive to exceed customer expectations.

Since in tourism there are many service transactions over the course of a trip, or a vacation, it is increasingly useful to introduce the concept of the quality of the experience (QOE)—where tourism experience consists of a complex chain of service transactions and visitor participation in a broad range of activities and events. Using this framework, the goal of the tourism managers is to provide the visitor with a holistic combination of services, activities, and events from which he/she derives a high level of satisfaction.

Unfortunately, because the experience chain involves such a diverse mix of services, activities, and events, a great number of the links in the chain are outside of the control—or even the influence—of any single manager. Thus, it is important to develop management structures and processes that can assist in coordinating and enhancing the quality of the various services, activities, and events of the experience chain. It is here where the destination management organization (DMO) plays a critical role.

Pricing

One of the most important marketing decisions is the pricing decision. Price determines how consumers perceive the product and strongly affects other elements of the marketing mix.

Firms have a choice of three strategies in pricing their products. First, they may decide to sell their product at the market price, which is the same price that everyone else charges. They then compete on nonprice terms. Selling at a price equal to competitors' tends to prevent price cutting and protect margins, and customers are not driven away by price. However, because there is no price individuality, there can be no price demand stimulation.

Second, firms may decide to price below the current market price. Firms that adopt such a discount policy are trying to create the reputation of having the lowest prices and underselling all competitors. To be successful, such firms must make sure that demand is elastic; otherwise, they will gain only at the expense of their competitors and start a price war. This pricing strategy is more successful when it is based on the elimination of services. Motel 6, for example, took its name from its original $6-a-night charge and built its network on a no-frills philosophy. Today it is one of the top budget chains in the United States.

The third approach is to charge above-market prices. Premium pricing strategy must be coupled with the best service in the industry and other features and amenities to make this higher price attractive. Such an approach emphasizes quality, which many consumers think is a function of price; provides higher margins; generates more revenue for promotion; and makes better service

Southwest Airlines is well known for its low airfares, but it also has a reputation for going out of its way to deliver fun service to keep customers happy. *Photo courtesy of Southwest Airlines.*

possible. However, premium pricing reduces volume, raises overhead costs, and encourages substitution. Nevertheless, numerous tourism firms successfully use this approach, including the Ritz-Carlton (winner of the U.S. Malcolm Baldrige National Quality Award in 1992 and 1999), Fairmont, Hyatt, Marriott, and Westin hotels.

Some firms choose to employ two or three pricing strategies and develop a product to appeal to consumers in each market segment. The lodging industry began employing this strategy in the last decade. Intercontinental, Choice, Marriott, Hilton, Hyatt, and others have developed products to appeal to a broad range of market segments. The tourism marketing manager must consider 11 factors that influence price policies:

1. **The Internet.** A key impact of the Internet is that it has created transparency of pricing. The widespread availability of information and transparent pricing has increased

competition and made it a necessary for the marketing manager to deliver value. The Internet has made pricing strategy one of the most vulnerable parts of the marketing mix.

2. **Product quality.** The quality of the product really determines the price-value relationship. It is common sense that a product that offers greater utility and fills more consumer needs than a competitive product can command a higher price.

3. **Product distinctiveness.** A staple or standard product with no distinctive features offers little or no opportunity for price control. However, a novel and different product may be able to command higher prices. The Hyatt Corporation, for example, features lobby atriums; this attractive novelty combined with excellent service and facilities makes it possible for the Hyatt Hotels to command higher prices.

4. **Extent of the competition.** A product that is comparable to competitors' products must be priced with the competitors' prices in mind. The product's price to some extent determines its position in the market.

5. **Method of distribution.** The price of the product must include adequate margins for tour operators, travel agents, or the company's own sales force.

6. **Character of the market.** It is necessary to consider the type and number of possible consumers. If there is a small number of consumers, then the price must be high enough to compensate for a limited market. However, one must also consider the ability of consumers to buy and their buying habits.

7. **Cost of the product and service.** It should be obvious that price must exceed cost over the long run or else the business will not survive. Both cost and market conditions should serve as guides to pricing.

8. **Cost of distribution.** Distribution costs must also be included in the pricing equation. Unfortunately, in many cases they are much more difficult to estimate than other costs.

9. **Margin of profit desired.** The profit margin built into the price of the product must be more than returns realized on more conventional investments in order to compensate for the risk involved in the enterprise.

10. **Seasonality.** Most tourism products are affected by seasonality because of school-year patterns and vacation habits; consequently, the seasonal aspects must be considered in developing prices.

11. **Special promotional prices.** Many times it is good strategy to offer introductory prices and special one-time price offers to acquaint consumers with your product. However, these must be carefully planned so that they fill the proper intent and do not become a regular discount price. In today's tourism market we are seeing a number of *flash sales* that offer special prices that must be booked instantly or for short periods of time such as 2 hours, 6 hours, and 12 hours. The Internet and e-mail marketing are ideally suited to flash sales.

Price Skimming

When a new product or service is introduced, two pricing philosophies prevail: **price skimming** and **penetration pricing.** A price-skimming strategy sets the price as high as possible. No attempt is made to appeal to the entire market. The price is set to appeal only to the top of the market; consequently, this approach is frequently called skimming the cream. The strategy is to sell the product to as many consumers as possible at this price level, then, as either buyer resistance or direct competition develops, the seller will lower prices step by step. This approach typically results in higher profits and more rapid repayment of development and promotion costs. It also tends to invite competition. Skimming is appropriate when the product or service has the following characteristics: (1) price inelasticity, (2) no close substitutes, (3) high promotion elasticity, and (4) distinct market segments based on price. When space tourism is launched, it will use a price skimming approach.

Penetration Pricing

The opposite approach to price skimming is market penetration, in which the seller attempts to establish the price of the product as low as possible to penetrate the market as completely as possible. A low price makes the product available to as many income levels as possible, and the sellers are likely to establish a large market share quickly. When penetration pricing is used, this introductory price tends to become the permanent price of the product. It results in a slower recovery of fixed costs and requires a greater volume to break even. The factors that would recommend a penetration-pricing approach would be: (1) high price elasticity, (2) large savings from high-volume production (economies of scale), and (3) an easy fit of the product into consumer purchasing patterns. When Motel 6 was launched, the firm used a penetration approach, and it continues to use the low-price model.

Place (Distribution)

Another difficult decision for the marketing manager concerns what distribution channel or channels will be used. The distribution decisions affect the other elements of the marketing mix, and in the best marketing mix all aspects will be compatible with one another. Chapter 7 contains a description of the travel distribution system. The Internet is becoming the primary channel through which the travel industry engages the consumer. There is a move away from the traditional distribution channels to the Internet.

Channels of distribution are selected by: (1) analyzing the product; (2) determining the nature and extent of the market; (3) analyzing the channels by sales, costs, and profits; (4) determining the cooperation you can expect from the channel; (5) determining the assistance you will have to give to the channel; and (6) determining the outlets to be used. For example, if you want intensive distribution, exposing your product to maximum sale, you will use many travel agents. In contrast, with an exclusive distribution policy, you would sell your product yourself or through one or a few agents who would have the sole right to sell your product or service in a given area.

Promotion

The aim of promotion activities is to create demand for a product or service. **Promotion** is a broad term that includes advertising, personal selling, public relations, publicity, and sales promotion activities such as familiarization tours, giveaways, trade shows, point of purchase, and store displays.

To sell the product, it is necessary to: (1) attract attention, (2) create interest, (3) create a desire, and (4) get action. Either personal selling or advertising can carry out all of these steps in the selling process; however, the two used together tend to be more powerful. Advertising is ideally suited to attract attention and create interest in the products and services. Personal selling is best suited to creating desire and conviction on the part of the customer and to closing the sale. Advertising and personal selling are even more effective when supplemented by publicity and sales promotion activities. Familiarization tours (or *famtours*, as they are commonly called) are a form of promotion of particular importance in the travel industry. Travel agents, tour operators, and other persons who influence travel decisions are invited on a famtour in order to become more knowledgeable about the destination.

Advertising

Advertising has been defined as any nonpersonal presentation of goods, ideas, or services by an identified sponsor. In travel marketing, these paid public messages are designed to describe or present a destination area in such a way as to attract consumers. This can be done through the use

Not all promotion/advertising is on a billboard, in a newspaper, or on your large-screen television. Shown here is the state of New Mexico's automobile license plate: intense red numbers on a brilliant yellow background. This format provides thousands of in-state "impressions" every day for the "Land of Enchantment." *Photo courtesy of New Mexico Tourism Department.*

of the major advertising media such as the Internet, newspapers, magazines, direct mail, television, outdoor, or radio. Effective advertising gains the attention of the prospective visitor, holds the attention so the message can be communicated, and makes a lasting positive impression on the prospect's mind.

Each advertising medium has advantages and disadvantages. A key decision in developing promotional strategy is to select the right medium to maximize advertising expenditure. To assist in media selection, turn to Standard Rate and Data Service (SRDS), 1700 Higgins Road, Des Plaines, IL 60018. SRDS publications contain advertising rates and other media information required to make intelligent decisions (www.srds.com). The advantages and disadvantages of the major media are as follows.

Internet

E-mail marketing and Web sites have very rapidly established themselves as one of the most pervasive and most powerful means of directly communicating with individuals in the marketplace. They have the ability to be interactive, show rich multimedia, and be available 24/7. They are particularly valuable to small and medium-size tourism operators, who in the past had difficulty conveying information regarding their products and services to their many potential customers. Care must be taken, however, to ensure a well-designed Web site. Because of the ease of access to Web sites, many firms assume that a simple listing of products and services is adequate. This is far from true. The growing sophistication of Web site marketers means that both innovation and functionality must be carefully built into a Web site for it to be successful.

Spending on Internet advertising has grown rapidly in recent years, making it a major medium. The shift to the Internet as an advertising medium is illustrated by the Colorado Tourism Office, which has moved approximately 40 percent of its advertising budget to the Internet. It is estimated by *eMarketer* that global spending on Internet advertising will reach $61.8 billion in 2010 and $96.8 billion by 2014.[7] The Internet's gain is expected to come at the expense of print and television advertising.

Newspapers

Newspapers give comprehensive coverage of a local market area, are lower in cost than other media, are published frequently, are flexible (short lead time) and timely, have a wide audience, and get a quick response. Most newspapers have travel sections. The major disadvantages are low printing quality and short life. Newspapers also suffer from the image of being a dying industry.

Direct Mail

Although postage costs have increased rapidly, direct mail either by e-mail or the Post Office is one of the most important advertising methods for tourism enterprises. It is the most personal and selective of all the media; consequently, it is the most effective medium in minimizing waste circulation. Direct mail gets the message directly to the consumers that one wishes to contact. Direct-mail advertising is self-testing when it asks for a response.

The critical problem with direct mail is obtaining and maintaining the right mailing lists. Many types of lists are commercially available through firms specializing in this activity. (One source of such information is Standard Rate and Data Service.)

For the tourism industry, previous visitors are the most important mailing-list sources. However, names and addresses must be correct, and the lists must be kept in ready-to-use form on a computer. Other good sources of prospects are the inquiry lists.

Television

Television presents both an audio and a visual message and comes as close to approximating personal selling as a mass medium can. Television requires minimal exertion on the part of listeners and is very versatile. However, television is not a flexible medium, commercials have a short life, and advertising on television is expensive relative to the costs of using other media. Nevertheless, despite television's expense, many destinations are using television and finding it very cost effective. Cable television provides many opportunities for tourism advertising.

Magazines

The major advantage of magazines is their print and graphic quality. Other advantages are secondary readership, long life, prestige, and favorable cost per thousand circulation. Many special-interest magazines reach specialized market segments effectively, making it possible to target markets. Regional editions allow further selectivity, with a minimum of waste circulation. Some of the unfavorable characteristics of magazines are that they require long lead times and that changes cannot be made readily. Magazines also reach the market less frequently than do newspapers, radio, and television.

Frontier Airlines, a regional low-cost carrier headquartered in Indianapolis, Indiana, provides an excellent case study on creative advertising and branding. Frontier's planes are unique in that they have animals painted on their tails. With this part of branding in place, Frontier launched an advertising campaign focusing on Frontier being "a whole different animal." The multimedia campaign covers TV, radio, print, and the Web. The constant message of Frontier is: Affordable fares; newer, more comfortable planes; wider seats; expanded legroom; and DIRECTV service. Try the airline with the animals on its tails. *Photo courtesy of 2005 Frontier Airlines, Inc.*

Radio

Radio has the advantage of outstanding flexibility and relatively low cost. Although the warmth of the human voice adds a personal touch to the selling message, radio has the disadvantage that it presents only an audio message. Tourists driving in their automobiles are typically radio listeners, and many attractions find radio an excellent medium.

Outdoor Advertising

Outdoor advertising has been used with great success by many tourism organizations. It is a flexible, low-cost medium that reaches virtually the whole population. It has made the Wall Drug Store in Wall, South Dakota, world famous. Outdoor advertising has the disadvantage that the message must be short; however, it does reach travelers. An additional problem is highway signing laws, which are making it more difficult to advertise tourism attractions.

This outdoor sign at Ayers Rock Resort in Australia features the resort's logo, reinforcing a branded image in the consumer's mind. *Photo courtesy of the author.*

Using an Advertising Agency

Although promotion managers must know the fundamentals of marketing, advertising, personal selling, and public relations, the specialized skill and experience of an **advertising agency** can greatly increase business—and can do it profitably. An advertising agency will do the following:

- Work with ideas in copy and layout. *Copy* is the term used to describe written messages; *layout* refers to the arrangement of copy, art, and pictures.

- Advise on the choice of media to convey advertising messages, devising an organized and carefully worked-out plan using online, newspapers, magazines, radio, TV, guidebooks, posters, direct mail, postcards, folders, or other advertising media.

- Conduct market analysis and research so that advertising efforts can be directed to the best prospects.

- Assist in planning and carrying out a public relations program. The advertising program must be planned objectively by setting forth specific, achievable goals. The advertising agency can help to establish such goals. When seeking the services of an advertising agency, look at the agency's experience in promoting tourism, and check its past advertising campaigns and clients to determine the campaign's effectiveness.

The Advertising Budget

No magic formula exists for setting the advertising budget. How much to spend is always a perplexing question. Commonly used methods include a percentage of last year's sales, a percentage of potential sales, or the industry percentage. These methods are all flawed because advertising should create sales and cause things to happen, not react to what has happened in the past or in other companies. Consequently, the best method of setting advertising budgets is to determine the objectives to be performed and allocate the proper amount to reach these objectives.

Promoting a new tourist destination area will require more money than will promoting one with an established clientele. The specific amount to budget for advertising and promotion will depend on each situation. However, as a general rule, most resorts spend about 3 percent of sales on media advertising and about 3 percent on other promotion activities.

No matter what expenditures are, efforts should be made to coordinate the promotion program so it is consistent with the product offered and consumer expectations will be met. Word of mouth is the least expensive, most convincing form of personal advertising. A friendly and capable host encourages this type of communication. Visitors who are treated as very important persons will not only come back, they will recommend the area to their friends. All facilities, services, hospitality, and pricing policies must be directed to this one goal—a happy, satisfied visitor.

Personal Selling

Personal selling is the oldest method of creating demand. Because it is adaptable to the prospect, it is the most compelling and effective type of selling. In contrast to advertising, which is the impersonal component in the promotional mix, personal selling consists of individual, personal communication.

Personal selling is so widely used because it offers maximum flexibility. Sales representatives tailor their presentation to each individual customer. They can tell which approaches are working and which are not and adjust accordingly. Prospects can be identified so target market customers are approached and efforts are not wasted. Convention and Visitors Bureaus are especially successful in using personal selling.

Counterbalancing these advantages is the fact that personal selling is the most expensive means of making contact with prospects, and productivity gains are unlikely.

Public Relations

Public relations may be defined as an attitude—a *social conscience* that places first priority on the public interest when making any decisions. Public relations permeate an entire organization, covering relations with many publics: visitors, the community, employees, and suppliers.

Acceptance of any tourist destination by the public is of utmost importance. No business is more concerned with human relations than is tourism, and all public interests must be served. Serving one group at the expense of another is not sound public relations. Furthermore, each individual business manager and the group he or she represents must be respected and have the confidence of the community. There is no difference between a personal reputation and a business reputation.

Favorable public relations within the firm emphasize respect for people. Employees must have reasonable security in their jobs and be treated with consideration. Externally, tourism employees have a powerful influence on the public as they represent the owners in the public's eye. Employees should be trained to be courteous, respectful, and helpful to guests. Little things make a big difference, and the attitude of employees can make or break a public relations effort.

Not all promotion/advertising imitates New Mexico's license plates with intense red letters on a brilliant yellow background. In contrast, Howe Caverns, à la "HOLLYWOOD" (large white letters on a steep brown hillside) displays the HOWE CAVERNS name with large white letters—but on a gently sloping bright green lawn in New York State. While Howe's promotional strategy garners fewer impressions than does the New Mexico approach, it is definitely much harder to forget if you have ever seen it. *Photo courtesy of Howe Caverns, Inc.*

Considerations for the public relations effort include being aware of public attitudes toward present policies; ask some of the visitors for feedback. Communication is the lifeblood of good relations. In publicizing the firm, first do good things and then tell the public about them. Above all, give the public factual information about your area. False information is detrimental; you must describe conditions as they exist.

Internet Marketing

The Internet has changed travel and tourism forever. Tourism was one of the early industries to be transformed by the Internet as it first became a major information source and next as a major channel of distribution. The Internet has gone on to become pervasive in all areas of tourism marketing. Internet marketing is also called i-marketing, Web marketing, online marketing, and e-marketing. Internet marketing is being used by the tourism industry to perform multiple tasks and impact a number of areas of the marketing mix. Direct e-mail marketing, advertising, promotion, customer service, relationship marketing, providing information, distribution, selling, and research are all tasks being performed via the Internet. The Internet provides the same capabilities found in direct mail and telemarketing; it provides a new communication medium; it can provide interaction with the customer; and it has the ability to deliver a rich multimedia message 24 hours a day, 7 days a week, 365 days a year. A large segment of consumers are looking to the Internet for information, research, trip planning, and booking trips; therefore, the Internet will continue to grow as an important marketing tool.

To take advantage of people's desire to travel, companies and destinations need to present their brand and offerings online. The Internet gives every tourism operator and destination, regardless of size or resources, an opportunity to engage the traveler. It has become the new medium of the day—a medium where the rate of change is remarkably faster than traditional media. Things move quickly on the Internet with new technologies, new concepts, innovations, inspirations, and new approaches occurring frequently. Tourism marketers must stay on top of these changes and still balance the use with other media. One of the best ways to get visitors online is to use offline media—newspapers, magazine, brochures, and television—to drive visitors to your Web site. Also, your Web site should be search engine optimized (SEO). SEO is the process of improving the visibility of a Web site or Web page in several search engines. Once online, visitors need to find a site that is easy to navigate and gives them the same kind of answers they would get if they were sitting across the desk from a travel planner.

E-mail marketing messages, newsletters, Web sites, search engine marketing, banner advertising, mobile applications, e-partnerships, and Web 2.0 strategies are well-established Internet marketing activities. An area that is receiving increased attention is social media marketing. Recent surveys show that companies are planning new social media initiatives, are increasing budgets for social media, and are puzzled about how to measure the return on investment from this phenomenon. It is being argued that social media has become an important and necessary part of tourism marketing.

Social Media (Consumer-Generated Media)

Social media is online content created by Internet users themselves, anyone other than professional writers or journalists, and made available to other Internet users via interactive technology. It can take numerous different forms, including text, images, audio, and video. Social media has been described as instant word-of-mouth to mass markets.

Although traditional media is about providing content to an audience, social media is more like a two-way conversation, more interactive. Most types of social media thrive on their connectedness, making use of resources, people, and links to other sites. Participation in the form of comments, contributions, feedback and sharing information are encouraged. Social media includes social networks, blogs, wikis, podcasting, microblogging, forums, and content communities.

Social Networks

Using profiles, personal pages, photos, and messages users connect with friends and colleagues to share content and communicate. Prominent social networks are Facebook, YouTube, LinkedIn, MySpace, Reddit, and Delicious. Facebook now has more than 500 million users and if it were a country would be the third largest. Social networks have a global reach.

With expectation of a billion social network users by 2012, the travel industry will have to embrace networks, understand how they are being used by consumers, and grow their presence on these sites. The social network sites present the opportunity to promote the brand, solicit customer experiences, encourage testimonials, build loyalty, and create sales.

Blogs

A blog is a weblog, a Web site that is like a formal journal, diary, or newsletter. It is frequently updated and for public consumption. Most people can create a blog and then write on that blog. A blogger is a person who keeps a blog and writes about his/her opinions and thoughts. Blogging is the act of updating or reading the blogs and the blogosphere is where it all happens. From a marketing standpoint, blogging is a technology that lets a company have a one-on-one dialogue with customers and adversaries. Tourism firms can benefit from blogs by listening to what consumers are saying and gaining unfiltered insights into the customer experience. Blogs are used by travelers to post their experiences about places they visit, stay, enjoy, and eat. By monitoring sites that contain reviews and comments about an organization, one can immediately address any issues. Businesses can establish interactive relationship with the customer via company-sponsored initiatives. Examples are Starwood

❖ GLOBAL INSIGHT ❖

The Canadian Tourism Commission and Twitter

An outstanding example of social media marketing is the Canadian Tourism Commission's (CTC) use of Twitter and tweets in the U.S. cities of New York, Chicago, and Los Angeles. While a tweet is only 140 characters in length, one can share a lot in that little space. In the summer of 2010 the CTC teamed up with advertising agency DDB Vancouver to develop an interactive campaign involving digital storescapes (Twitter-based murals) transforming empty storefronts into social media platforms.

The storescapes included 8' by 10' monitors featuring a continuous stream of tweeted photos and conversations about Canada. These Twitter-based murals featured interactive touch screen interfaces that displayed tweets and photos from real travelers to Canada in real time. People passing by were encouraged to tweet back. The live billboards at the sites streamed information on Canada's endless to-do list of destinations, cultural experiences, events, and vacation packages inspiring Americans to book a Canadian vacation.

In addition, street teams equipped with iPads were on the sites to encourage passersby to enter a contest for a trip to a Canadian destination of choice, to interact with the touch screens, and post tweets on their favorite vacation destinations in Canada. The

digital storescapes built on the success of CTC's social media strategy and use of user-generated content in their traditional advertising. The storescapes campaign was part of a broader campaign targeting Americans to travel to Canada and was supported by television and broadcast spots, online advertising, social media, and print.

Although measurement is always difficult, Brunico Communications, LTD. reported consumer Web site visits were up 86 percent over the same period in 2009, Facebook fan signups increased by 3,500 percent, and the QR codes garnered 4,539 scans. Just two weeks into the digital storescape campaign, the CTC experienced an 86 percent increase in Twitter followers. The campaign also created extensive public relations coverage and YouTube activity. Given the success CTC plans to launch similar programs in other markets such as Mexico and Europe.

DISCUSSION QUESTIONS

1. If you could tweet something about Canada, what would it be?

2. How can you measure the effectiveness of social media marketing?

3. How does social media marketing fit with traditional media?

Hotels and Resorts, with its blog (the Lobby.com), and Sheraton's consumer experience and photo sharing. Marriott International has a program to reach bloggers that includes asking them to speak to its corporate communications team. Marketers can utilize the various types and formats of social media to promote their products and services. HotelChatter.com and TripAdvisor now accept display ads, and many discussion boards accept advertising. A problem here is that measuring ad spending effectiveness on social network sites is difficult and still being developed. *eMarketer* projects that global social network advertising will total $2.0 billion in 2010.

Wiki

A wiki is a type of Web site, like Wikipedia, that lets anyone create and edit its pages. The word is Internet slang. The word *wiki* is short for *Wikiwikiweb*. *Wikiwiki* is Hawaiian, meaning "fast" or "speed." In a wiki, people can write pages together. People can change or add something new to the pages. People can discuss as well and tell their views.

Podcasting

According to Wikipedia, the free encyclopedia Web site, a podcast is a media file that is distributed over the Internet using syndication feeds for playback on portable media players and personal computers. Podcasting is a combination of the words *ipod* and *broadcasting*, and it is a new way to share and information through MP3 audio files. The formats are downloaded, shared, and subscribed to using an MP3 player. The Apple iTunes store offers tens of thousands of podcasts that can be played on their iPod. Podcasts can be found for almost anything, including TV shows, movies, radio shows, blogs, books, and games to mention a few. A visit to podcast.com provides an indication of the variety available. Small businesses have discovered podcasting, with everyone from fitness experts to travel agents using podcasts to stimulate their business.

An Internet marketing strategy is composed of many tactics to grow the direct online distribution channel. Social media is a new tool to be added to this strategy. Consumer-generated media provides a unique value proposition to customers.

Microblogging

A microblog differs from a traditional blog in that its content is typically much smaller. A microblog entry could consist of just a short sentence, a sentence fragment, an image, or an embedded video. Twitter is the most prominent site. Some others are Qaiku, Google Buzz, Tumbir, and Plurk.

Forums

An Internet forum or message board is an online discussion site where people can hold conversations in the form of posted messages. From a technological standpoint, forums are Web applications managing user-generated content. Depending on the forum setup, a posted message may need to be approved by a moderator before it becomes visible. Discussion forums have been around for a long time and are a powerful and popular element of online communities. TRINET is a valuable forum for tourism scholars and researchers.

Content Communities

The purpose of content communities is the sharing of media content among users. Content communities exist for a wide range of media such as BookCrossing for books, Flickr for photos, YouTube for videos, and Slideshare for PowerPoint presentations. Users of content communities are typically not required to create a personal profile page.

Social media has become an important and necessary part of tourism marketing. For companies and destinations, social media can play a large role in online marketing success. While it is important to have a Facebook page and be on LinkedIn, it is equally important to join and participate in other travel forums. Used wisely and in the right place, social media can be integrated into a marketing plan and become a part of your marketing strategy for brand building, networking, customer service, promotion, and public relations.

Mobile Marketing

The next big thing in tourism marketing is mobile marketing. Instead of thinking Internet first, one will think of mobile first. It will be the combination of the two that will create a powerful force. One of the biggest keys to new marketing opportunities is the smart phone. A smart phone is a mobile phone that offers more advanced computing ability and connectivity than a typical mobile phone. They are best thought of as handheld computers integrated within a mobile phone that can run many applications. A ChangeWave Research survey press release dated July 14, 2010, reports smart phones are expected to be in the hands of half the U.S. mobile users by the end of 2011.[8]

Mobile technology today allows the user to access the Internet, to search, take photos, play videos, check in at the airport, and access GPS service, online mapping, location-based search, and geotagging. Mobile social networking sites join a mobile to the Internet via applications. Service providers such as Every Trail, Joobil, RightNow, Trazzler, and Next Step allow users to share experiences with others in the same network. For travelers and travel companies, Twitter has launched a geotagging service providing location-based search and socializing. Consumer expectations of mobile Internet use continue to rise.

Simplistic wireless application protocol (WAP) pages are increasingly being replaced by more sophisticated mobile Web sites. These mobile Web sites offer relevant and immediate content and services frequently replicating the functionality of online Web sites. Hotels such as Marriott, Hilton, and Fairmont offer booking via their mobile Web sites. It has been predicted that in time the number of Web-enabled phones in the United States will exceed the number of PCs.

With the new devices and formats, U.S. mobile advertising spending is expected to grow dramatically. *eMarketer* forecasts more than $1.1 billion spending in 2011, growing to $2.5 billion in 2014.[9] The new devices and ad inventory that Apple and Google have introduced have given mobile advertising new legitimacy.

The new applications and the growth of 24/7 access to the Internet via mobile phones has significant marketing implications. It is expected that the mobile will reach every segment of society and become the most common Internet access tool for the majority of the population by 2020. Currently it is estimated that over one-third of the U.S. population has smart phones and growth is rapid. Nokia forecasts that the total number of world mobile subscribers will rise from 4 billion in 2009 to 5 billion in 2015 and mobile data traffic will increase 300 fold by 2015.[10]

Today, a fraction of consumer travel transactions are via mobile with the majority being done on the PC. The future will see this reverse and the travel industry will adapt its offerings to serve the mobile user.

MARKET SEGMENTATION

The strategy of **market segmentation** recognizes that few vacation destination areas are universally acceptable and desired. Therefore, rather than dissipate promotion resources by trying to please all travelers, one should aim the promotional efforts specifically to the wants and needs of likely prospects. One of the early steps in marketing tourism, then, is to divide the present and potential market on the basis of meaningful characteristics and concentrate promotion, product, and pricing efforts on serving the most prominent portions of the market—the **target markets**.

An effective market strategy will determine exactly what the target markets will be and attempt to reach only those markets. The target market is that segment of a total potential market to which the tourism attraction would be most salable. Target markets are defined geographically, demographically

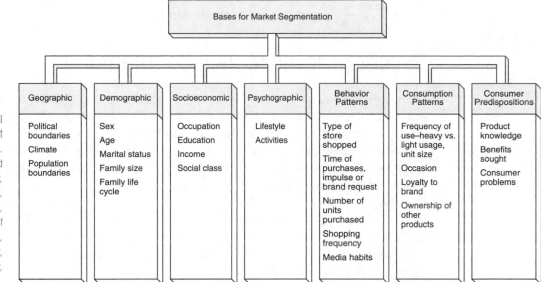

Figure 19.2 Typical bases for market segmentation. *Source:* W. Zikmund and M. D'Amico, *Marketing,* *3rd ed.,* copyright ©1984, New York: John Wiley & Sons, Inc.; adapted by permission of Prentice-Hall, Englewood Cliffs, N.J., from Philip Kotler, *Principles of Marketing,* copyright ©1980, p. 297.

(age, income, education, race, nationality, family size, family life cycle, gender, religion, occupation), or psychographically (values, motivations, interests, attitudes, desires) (see Figure 19.2).

Once target markets have been determined, appropriate media are chosen to reach these markets. For example, if tennis players are a target market, advertising in tennis magazines would give comprehensive coverage of this market. This "rifle approach" allows one to zero in exactly on the market of interest. In contrast, a "shotgun approach" would be to advertise in *Time* magazine, which would reach only a small number of the target market and result in large waste circulation.

Market segmentation must be employed in the marketing programs if a shotgun approach is to be avoided. Every tourism attraction can appeal to a multitude of market segments, and market segments can overlap a great deal. The marketing manager must look at market segments and determine which ones offer the most promising potential for his or her services. An excellent example of target marketing to a particular segment is provided by Courtyard by Marriott. The moderate price and attractive rooms were designed to appeal to the business traveler. Marriott has been very successful in attracting this market segment.

Tourist resorts typically segment in a variety of ways. One of the most common is geographic. Here, the segments tend to be destination visitors (those visitors traveling long distances to vacation at the resort), regional visitors (those who live within the region of the resort and can arrive within four hours' driving time), and local residents.

Proximity of the destination area to the market is an important factor. Generally, the nearer the tourist destination is to its major market, the more likely it is to attract large numbers of visitors. For example, Bob-Lo Island is just a few miles from Detroit and can be reached by excursion boat. As might be expected, this vacation destination receives many times the number of visitors from the greater Detroit area than does Bermuda or the Bahamas.

It follows, then, that the prime target area for promotion of any given tourist destination area will be that area of greatest population density nearest the vacation area. In the United States, the best concentration of markets for tourism promotion is in the metropolitan statistical areas (MSAs), formerly called standard metropolitan statistical areas (SMSAs). These are defined by the U.S. Bureau of the Census as a county or group of contiguous counties containing at least one city of 50,000 inhabitants or more. An authoritative source of market data concerning these areas is found in the **Survey of Buying Power** published by *Sales and Marketing Management Magazine,* 770 Broadway, New York, NY 10003.

Demographics also provide good segmentation variables. Demographics are the social statistics of our society. Age groups are an excellent example.

Psychographic Market Segmentation

Several models have been developed to classify people according to **psychographic** types. One such early model was developed by Stanley C. Plog, who classified the U.S. population along a psychographic continuum, ranging from the psychocentric at one extreme to the allocentric at the other.[11]

The term **psychocentric** is derived from *psyche-* or *self*-centered, meaning the centering of one's thoughts or concerns on the small problem areas of one's life. Such a person tends to be self-inhibited and nonadventurous. **Allocentric**, by contrast, derives from the root word *allo*, meaning "varied in form." An allocentric person is thus one whose interest patterns are focused on varied activities. Such a person is outgoing and self-confident and is characterized by a considerable degree of adventure and a willingness to reach out and experiment with life. Travel becomes a way for the allocentric to express inquisitiveness and satisfy curiosity. Table 19.1 shows personality and travel characteristics of psychocentrics and allocentrics.

Plog modified his model of destination preferences based on more recent research (1995).[12] According to Plog's findings, *Dependables* prefer a life that is more structured, stable, and predictable. These individuals would rather follow a set pattern or routine in order to be able to plan their lives. *Venturers* tend to go more places more often. Leisure travel occupies a central place in their lives, and they eagerly seek out new, exotic, and/or unknown places. Venturers are more likely to fly to their destinations, and they shun guided tours in favor of exploration. *Centrics* comprise the largest group, as one would expect. It is easier to move Centrics, because they possess characteristics of both Dependables and Venturers, and they tend to react favorably to destinations, activities, and events that appeal to travelers on either end of the lifestyle continuum. Both Plog's early work and current work are summarized in Table 19.1.

Camp Carnival kid's program features morning-till-night activities. These guests are obviously taking advantage and enjoying the many facilities available. Carnival is successfully appealing to the families-with-children market. *Photo courtesy of Carnival Cruise Lines.*

TABLE 19.1 Personality and Travel-Related Characteristics of Psychocentrics and Allocentrics

Psychocentrics/Dependables	Allocentrics/Venturers
Intellectually restricted	Intellectually curious
Low risk-taking	Moderate risk-taking
Withhold income	Use disposable income
Use well-known brands	Try new products
Territory bound	Exploring/searching
Sense of powerlessness	Feel in control
Free-floating anxiety/nervousness	Relatively anxiety-free
Nonactive lifestyle	Interested/involved
Nonadventurous	Adventurous
Lacking in confidence	Self-confident
Prefer the familiar in travel destination	Prefer nontouristy areas
Like commonplace activities at travel destinations	Enjoy sense of discovery and delight in new experiences, before others have visited the area
Prefer sun-and-fun spots, including considerable relaxation	Prefer novel and different destinations
Low activity level	High activity level
Prefer destinations they can drive to	Prefer flying to destinations
Prefer heavy tourist development (lots of hotels, family-type restaurants, tourist shops, etc.)	Tour accommodations should include adequate-to-good hotels and food, not necessarily modern or chain-type hotels, and few "tourist-type" attractions
Prefer familiar atmosphere (hamburger stands, familiar-type entertainment, absence of foreign atmosphere)	Enjoy meeting and dealing with people from a strange or foreign culture
Complete tour packaging appropriate, with heavy scheduling of activities	Tour arrangements should include basics (transportation and hotels) and allow considerable freedom and flexibility
Travel less	Travel more frequently
Spend more of income on material goods and impulse buys	Spend more of income on travel
Little interest in events or activities in other countries	Inquisitive, curious about the world and its peoples
Naive, nondemanding, passive traveler	Demanding, sophisticated, active traveler
Want structured, routinized travel	Want much spontaneity in trips
Expect foreigners to speak in English	Will learn language or foreign phrases before and during travels
Want standard accommodations and conventional (American) meals	Seek off-the-beaten-path, little-known local hotels, restaurants
Buy souvenirs, trinkets, common items	Buy native arts/crafts
Prefer returning to same and familiar places	Want different destinations for each trip
Enjoy crowds	Prefer small numbers of people

Source: Stanley C. Plog, *Leisure Travel: Making It a Growth Market . . . Again!*, (New York: John Wiley & Sons, 1991). Reprinted with permission of John Wiley & Sons, Inc.

Plog found that the U.S. population was normally distributed along a continuum between these two extreme types. This is illustrated in Figure 19.3. Other groups have been identified between the allocentrics and psychocentrics. Most people fall in the midcentric classification.

A new dimension was added with the establishment of an *energy versus lethargy* scale. It was determined that this dimension was not correlated, making it possible to place individuals into four quadrants based on how they scored on the two scales. The four quadrants were high-energy allocentrics, low-energy allocentrics, high-energy psychocentrics, and low-energy psychocentrics. High-energy allocentrics have an insatiable desire to be active on trips, exploring and learning what is new and exciting at a destination. Low-energy allocentrics would travel at a more leisurely pace, be

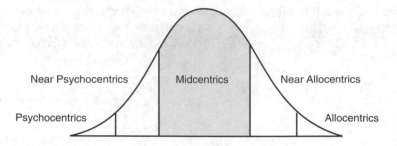

Figure 19.3 U.S. population distribution by psychographic type.
Source: Stanley C. Plog, ``Why Destinations Areas Rise and Fall in Popularity,'' *Cornell Hotel and Restaurant Administration Quarterly*, no. 3 (June 2001), pp. 13–24.

more intellectual, and delve into culture, history, and local customs. At the other end of the continuum, the low-energy psychocentrics were most likely to stay at home.

Through further research, Plog identified the travel preferences of psychocentrics and allocentrics. These are summarized in Figure 19.4. In studying the population on the basis of income level, Plog discovered another interesting relationship. At the lower end of the income spectrum, he discovered a heavy loading of psychocentrics.

People at the upper end of the income levels were found to be predominantly allocentric. However, for the broad spectrum in between—for most of America—interrelations are only slightly positive. This finding has several implications.

It is evident that at extremely low levels of family income, travel patterns may be determined largely by the income constraints. Regardless of the psychographic type, a person at the low end of the income spectrum might be compelled to take what Plog considers to be psychocentric-type vacations. College students are a good example of this. They may be allocentric by nature but cannot afford an allocentric-type vacation because such vacations are generally very expensive (a trip to Antarctica or a mountain-climbing expedition in Nepal). They travel, instead, to nearby destinations, spend less money, and participate in familiar activities. Therefore, it may be erroneous to conclude that a person with a low income is likely to be psychocentric. The severe income constraint may distort the person's classification in terms of psychographics.

Having defined types of destinations and types of tourists, one is tempted to link these two classifications directly, as Plog has done. Plog superimposed a list of destinations on the population distribution curve, suggesting that allocentrics would travel to such destinations as Africa or the Orient. Psychocentrics, by contrast, would vacation in nearby destinations (such as Cedar Point theme park for a psychocentric from Toledo, Ohio). The intervening psychocentric types are similarly identified with particular destinations (refer to Figure 19.4).

Such a direct linkage between the classification of tourists and of destinations does not consider the important fact that people travel with different motivations on different occasions. A wealthy

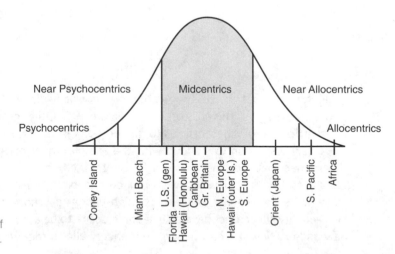

Figure 19.4 Psychographic positions of destinations.

allocentric might indeed travel to Africa on an annual vacation, but might also take weekend trips to a typically psychocentric destination during other times of the year. Similarly, though probably not as likely, psychocentrics could conceivably vacation in essentially allocentric destinations (with the exception of people with extremely low incomes). For instance, a psychocentric may travel to a remote area under the security provided by traveling with a group of similar tourists, which, being escorted at all times, may persuade a psychocentric to travel, say, to Asia.

What, then, is the link between the types of tourists and the types of destinations? To develop such a linkage, which will provide a method for predicting travel patterns, two things must be realized. First, as already pointed out, a tourist may travel for different reasons from one trip to the next. Second, a given destination can provide a variety of travel experiences, suitable to a wide range of tourists, depending on the manner in which the trip is planned. The only way in which a systematic linkage can be developed between the types of destinations and the types of tourists is to consider each trip in isolation and examine the motivations that have prompted the trip.

Plog first developed his model in 1972, about 40 years ago, and it has been widely cited in tourism literature since that time. It was one of the first attempts to provide a framework within which to analyze tourist behavior. The world has changed considerably since Plog introduced his model. For example, today there are fewer countries that are considered exotic. Also, there are now other ways to look at tourists, such as through lifestyle analysis or benefit segmentation. Plog's pioneering efforts, however, should not be overlooked. His model still provides a way to examine travel and think about developments using current market conditions. But most importantly, it served as a pioneering effort to motivate those who study tourist behavior to search for a theoretical basis for understanding why tourists behave as they do.

MARKETING PLANNING: THE TOURISM MARKETING PLAN

Couples on a honeymoon or celebrating an anniversary remain a popular target market for resorts and cruise lines, which have developed marketing campaigns promoting the romance of travel and the thrill of visiting exotic destinations.
Photo courtesy of Carnival Cruise Lines.

To this point, the chapter has examined a broad range of fundamental marketing concepts and attempted to give selected examples of their utilization in a tourism context.

In order to make these concepts truly valuable from a tourism standpoint, they must be applied in a comprehensive, integrated manner. The process of application is known as marketing planning. The end result of this process is the marketing plan.

The marketing plan for a destination or firm is one of the most important working documents that exists. It serves to translate the many ideals of tourism policy into an active process for attracting visitors and providing the range of experiences they seek from a destination.

The California Tourism Marketing Plan

Although tourism marketing plans can take different forms, an exemplary state tourism office plan is that of California. Its operational plan was first created in 1998 following the passage of the California Tourism Policy Act and has been updated annually because marketing plans are by nature *living* documents that change over time. The California plan conveys good comprehensive marketing planning.

One of the distinctive characteristics of the California Tourism Marketing Plan (CTMP) is the fact that it actually flows from a policy framework. The California Tourism Policy Act (CTPA) first provides a philosophical foundation for tourism development and marketing in one of the most significant tourism destinations in the world. It subsequently asserts the need for an effective marketing program (CTMP) to realize the ideals and goals of its philosophical foundation. Furthermore, it also sets out an organizational policy (in the form of the California Travel and Tourism Commission) to support implementation of its marketing goals. Finally, it takes the all-important step of providing for a funding policy (private assessments) to support the operations of the commission. To examine how California Travel and Tourism Commission operates, go to www.tourism.visitcalifornia.com/MPP, which will take you to the program page. Then, go to the "Essentials" section and examine the PDFs for its "Strategic Plan Final Draft" (2011–2016), its "Domestic Media Plan," "Canada Media Plan," and other plans.

JOINT MARKETING EFFORTS

In the majority of cases, a tourism organization will want to market its product and services individually; however, in other cases, joint cooperative efforts will be the most profitable. Typically, these efforts are launched through associations or government agencies. Colorado Ski Country USA and the Utah Ski and Snowboard Association are groups that jointly promote the services of their members, many of whom are in competition with each other. Publishing posters and directories, answering inquiries, and providing snow reports promote the industry in the most cost-effective way. In addition to these joint marketing efforts, the areas have their own individual marketing programs. They may also work with other private firms such as airlines, rental car companies, and credit card firms to stretch their marketing dollars.

Experience to date has shown that tourism promotion on a country or state basis is best accomplished by a cooperative effort of private industry and government. Joint promotion by private interests and official government tourist organizations is an effective and efficient procedure. One of the examples of the pooling of private and government funds is the Hawaii Visitors and Convention Bureau, an independent nonprofit organization that conducts tourism promotion under contract with the Hawaii Tourism Authority (HTA).

In some states, specific matching funds are provided by a government tourism agency for tourist promotion, such as the provision of a portion of advertising costs of a private regional tourist promotion association. Various combinations of matched funds are possible, depending on the amount of funds available and the provisions of the legislation that authorizes such expenditures of public funds. The Pennsylvania Tourism, Film, and Economic Development Marketing Office operates one of the largest matching-grants fund programs in the United States.

Private firms also find joint marketing efforts to be profitable. For example, in 2003, Universal Parks and Resorts entered into a ten-year marketing partnership with Coca-Cola. The partnership, first made in 1999, designates Atlanta-based Coke as Universal theme parks' official soft drink. The new agreement expands that to include Minute Maid as the parks' official juice. Coca-Cola and Universal plan a cross-brand promotional strategy targeted to teens and young adults, as well as themed beverage attractions in Universal's parks.

SUMMARY

Marketing can be defined as the performance of business activities that direct the flow of goods and services from the producer to the consumer or user. Such activities are vital to tourist businesses. The finest, most satisfying tourist facility would be unprofitable without marketing. People have to be informed about a travel destination and become interested in going there before a market can be created.

Basic to the marketing effort are the marketing concept, the marketing mix, product planning and development, pricing, branding, distribution channels, promotion, market research, personal selling, public relations, and market segmentation.

Joint marketing efforts among official tourism organizations, public carriers, and providers of accommodations or even with nearby competing destination areas are strategically sound and typically successful.

A destination and organization's marketing plan defines the approach by which prospective visitors are identified and selectively attracted through promotion and other marketing tools outlined in a destination or organization's marketing plan.

❖ **KEY CONCEPTS** ❖

advertising	marketing plan	product
advertising agency	marketing planning	product life cycle
allocentric	market research	product planning
branding	market segmentation	promotion
channels of distribution	partnership	psychocentric
consumer orientation	penetration pricing	psychographic
four Ps	place	public relations
Internet	people	service quality
joint marketing efforts	personal selling	social media
marketing	price skimming	Survey of Buying Power
marketing concept	pricing	target market
marketing mix		

❖ **INTERNET EXERCISES** ❖

The Internet sites mentioned in this chapter plus some selected additional sites are listed for your convenience on the companion Web site for this book, www.wiley.com/college/goeldner.

ACTIVITY 1

Site Name: MySwitzerland.com

URL: www.myswitzerland.com

Background Information: MySwitzerland.com provides information regarding tourism in Switzerland.

Site Name: Garda Lake

URL: www.gardalake.it

Background Information: This site provides tourism information on Lake Garda, Italy.

Site Name: New Zealand

URL: www.newzealand.com

Background Information: The Tourism New Zealand Web site is an introduction to tourism in New Zealand and how a visit can be a fantastic experience.

Site Name: Tour Egypt

URL: www.touregypt.net

Background Information: Tour Egypt provides information on Egypt's destinations and tourist attractions.

Site Name: Queen Victoria Market, Australia

URL: www.qvm.com.au

Background Information: The Queen Victoria Market is more than just Melbourne's shopping mecca; it is a historic landmark, a tourist attraction, and an institution for Melbournians.

Site Name: Travel Alaska

URL: www.travelalaska.com

Background Information: Travel Alaska provides vacation-planning information.

Site Name: Genuine Nebraska

URL: www.visitnebraska.gov

Background Information: This Web site offers extensive, database-driven information about places to go and things to see and do in Nebraska.

Site Name: Wyoming Forever West

URL: www.wyomingtourism.org

Background Information: This guide has been created with one goal: to help you find information about Wyoming quickly and efficiently.

Site Name: I Love NY

URL: www.iloveny.com

Background Information: This is the official site of New York State Tourism with information and deals on visiting New York.

Exercises:

Choose two state and two international tourism sites from the list above.

1. Which sites have the most powerful marketing concept in each category?

2. What characterizes the sites you have chosen?

3. What marketing concepts do these sites employ?

4. What is your opinion of using the Internet as a channel of distribution for advertising? Why?

5. How do the U.S. sites compare with the international sites?

ACTIVITY 2

Site Name: The Association of Travel Marketing Executives (ATME)

URL: www.atme.org

Background Information: ATME, established in 1980, is a nonprofit professional association of experienced and innovative travel industry marketers representing all segments of the industry.

Exercises

1. Why should a travel marketing executive join ATME?

2. What kind of information is contained in ATME's *Travel Marketing Decisions*?

QUESTIONS FOR REVIEW AND DISCUSSION ✦

1. What is the marketing concept?

2. Do you regard the concept of consumer-oriented marketing as a step forward? Why or why not?

3. What are the stages in a product life cycle? What are the marketing implications of each stage?

4. What are the key factors a tourism marketing manager must consider in setting price?

5. Discuss the conditions when penetration pricing should be used. Also price skimming.

6. Discuss how a tourism firm's pricing strategy may influence the promotional program.

7. How are channels of distribution selected?

8. How does the branding of a tourism destination differ from the branding of: (a) a tube of toothpaste, (b) an automobile, (c) a computer, (d) a fast-food restaurant, and (e) a hotel?

9. What does branding a tourism destination really mean?

10. What role do you see mobile Web sites, applications, and social technologies playing in the travel industry?

11. What are some examples of realistic objectives of a tourism marketing program? Use a resort hotel, a motorcoach company, and a tour company.

12. Explain the statement, "Tourism promotion efforts undirected by research are largely a waste of effort." Do you agree?

13. What are the advantages of marketing vacation packages?

14. Give an example of a vacation package that might be marketed in your area. How would you market it? To whom?

15. Why is marketing planning so important?

16. What value do you see in market segmentation? Give an example of "experience segmentation."

17. Describe examples in which mobile social networking has assisted growth in the tourism industry?

18. How can companies start listening to, using, and learning from the new social medium of blogging?

19. Is Google the world's most valuable online advertising agency disguised as a Web search engine?

20. As president of your local convention and visitors bureau, propose a joint marketing scheme that would have surefire results.

✦ **CASE PROBLEM** ✦

A Midwest lakeshore community is economically depressed. By 2010, industrial employment had fallen to 50 percent of its 1990 level. Tourism seems to be a logical industry to expand. The county has 25 miles of beautiful Lake Michigan sandy beaches and is adjacent to a 1.5-million-acre national forest. The forest has many fine rivers and inland lakes, offering bountiful year-round recreation. This area is only about a five-hour drive from Chicago or Detroit and has thrice-daily air service from Chicago.

The chamber of commerce has virtually no budget for tourism promotion. State law authorizes an added 2 percent local tourism promotion tax to the 4 percent state rooms tax. However, enacting the added tax must be approved by local lodging establishments. Vote is apportioned by number of rooms owned. Managers of the two larger resorts are in favor of the tax, but they suspect that the many smaller motel owners will not approve the tax. Added tourism is greatly needed to stimulate the local economy. How can this impasse be resolved? From where might the leadership for resolving the impasse originate?

ENDNOTES

1. Amadeus, *Hotels 2020: Beyond Segmentation* (Sophia Antipolis Cedex, France: Amadeus, November 2010).
2. American Marketing Association Web site/Resource Library/Dictionary. See: www .marketingpower.com/-layouts/Dictionary.aspx?dLetter=M.
3. William D. Perreault Jr. and E. Jerome McCarthy, *Basic Marketing,* 14th ed. (Boston: McGraw-Hill, 2002); and E. Jerome McCarthy and William D. Perreault Jr., *Essentials of Marketing,* 6th ed. (Burr Ridge, IL: Irwin, 1994).
4. Robert C. Mill and Alastair M. Morrison, *The Tourism System,* 4th ed. (Dubuque, IA: Kendall/Hunt, 2002).
5. D. A. Aaker, *Managing Brand Equity: Capitalizing on the Value of a Brand Name* (New York: Free Press, 1991).
6. Graham Hankinson, "Relational Network Brands: Towards a Conceptual Model of Place Brands." *Journal of Vacation Marketing*, vol. 10, no. 2 (2004), pp. 109–121.
7. eMarketer, *Worldwide Ad Spending* (New York: eMarketer, 2010) and www.emarketer.com.
8. ChangeWave Research, *New Smart Phone Survey Shows Explosive Industry Shake Up* (Rockville, MD: ChangeWave Research, 2010) and www.changewaveresearch.com.
9. eMarketer, *Mobile Advertising and Marketing: Past the Tipping Point* (New York: eMarketer, 2010) and www.emarketer.com.
10. Amadeus, *Hotels 2020: Beyond Segmentation* (Sophia Antipolis Cedex, France: Amadeus, November 2010).
11. Stanley C. Plog, "Why Destination Areas Rise and Fall in Popularity," *Cornell Hotel and Restaurant Administration Quarterly*, vol. 14, no. 4 (February 1974), pp. 55–58; Stanley C. Plog, *Leisure Travel: Making It a Growth Market . . . Again!* (New York: John Wiley & Sons, 1991); and Stanley C. Plog, "Why Destination Areas Rise and Fall in Popularity," *Cornell Hotel and Restaurant Administration Quarterly*, vol. 42, no. 3 (June 2001), pp. 13–24.
12. Stanley C. Plog, *Vacation Places Rated* (Redondo Beach, CA: Fielding Worldwide, Inc., 1995).

PART 6

Tourism Prospects

Chapter 20 Tourism's Future

Easter Island, in the South Pacific, is best known
for the giant stone monoliths that dot the coastline.
Photo courtesy of Corbis Digital Stock

CHAPTER 20 ✥

Tourism's Future

- Examine forecasts concerning the growth of international tourism.

- Identify the major global forces that are shaping tourism and the tourists of tomorrow.

- Understand the impacts, both positive and negative, that these forces are likely to have on tourism markets and on the ability of destinations to respond to the demands of these markets.

New technology keeps providing tourism with a bright, innovative future. The tourist of tomorrow can expect to have access to modes of travel that are unimaginable today. They will be provided by remarkable new concepts in transportation and accommodation such as the Aeroscraft, which provide a level of luxury and reliability never before seen. Although the Aeroscraft is nearly two football fields long, it will have an estimated top speed of 174 miles per hour and a range of several thousand miles. It is expected to be completed by 2018. *Photo courtesy of destination-design firm WATG.*

INTRODUCTION

We cannot make wise choices if we do not understand current world trends and their likely consequence for ourselves and the options we have for achieving our goals.

—Edward Cornish, Editor, *The Futurist* magazine[1]

Despite the current concerns caused by climate change, the future of tourism, at least for the next decade, continues to be full of promise. Projections concerning the levels of arrivals, receipts, and growth in employment for most destinations have all painted a fairly rosy picture. Although we will acknowledge the vulnerabilities of tourism, the contents of this chapter reflect the general optimism that continues to pervade the travel industry.

Over and above this optimism, what is especially important about this chapter is its attempt to define some of the more specific dimensions of future changes, and the challenges and opportunities they create. In addition, it seeks to indicate how the travel product may need to evolve in response to these challenges and opportunities.

Finally, we also wish to sound a cautious note. As shown by the recent economic crisis, even the most dynamic of economies can turn sour. On top of this, the events of September 11, 2001, continue to haunt the tourism industry. Severe acute respiratory syndrome (SARS) also drastically impacted Asian and Canadian travel in the last decade. Natural disasters such as the 2011 tsunami in Japan that affected its nuclear reactors can change a country in a day. While stability and growth almost always return to these regions and many forecasters are now optimistic that a full recovery from the "deepest recession since the great depression of the 1930s" is just around the corner, it is still clear that the lessons of history are that we must learn to manage effectively in bad times as well as good. So while readers should prepare for the optimistic future trends that this chapter presents, they should also ask themselves, "What if?" How might the travel industry take advantage of periods of climate change and lower economic growth? How might the travel industry be a catalyst for other sectors of the economy? And—as we said at the beginning of this text—bon voyage!

TOURISM IN THE THIRD MILLENNIUM

The purpose of this book has been to provide the student with a basic understanding of the principles, practices, and philosophies of tourism as they relate to the industry and society of today. To understand the present, it has, of course, been necessary to review the evolution and historical development of the field. Clearly, the tourism industry of today is the product of many forces that have shaped both its structure and the manner in which it functions. As has been pointed out on several occasions, the growth and development of tourism has been particularly rapid over the past half century:

- Since 1950, when international travel started to become accessible to the general public, tourist activity has risen from 25 million to 880 million arrivals in 2009.
- International tourism receipts have risen from US$2.1 billion to US$852 billion in 2009.[2]

The result is that tourism, as we entered the third millennium, was a very large and dynamic sector of the economy. On the one hand, because of the rapid growth and change of the past, one might be inclined to believe that tourism has now reached a mature phase of its development in which the rate of change and expansion will decrease. On the other hand, a realistic assessment of the probable future suggests that despite the challenges it faces (and has always faced), tourism is likely to continue to grow and develop more rapidly and more dynamically than many other sectors for many years to come.

WORLD TOURISM FORECASTS FOR 2020

As shown in Table 20.1, international tourist arrivals were forecast to top 1 billion in 2010 (they reached 880 million in 2009) and reach more than 1.6 billion in 2020. These volumes represent an overall average annual rate of growth between 1995 and 2020 of 4.3 percent, with no slackening of growth over the period (i.e., 1995–2000, 4.2 percent per annum [p.a.]; 2000–2010, 4.2 percent p.a.; 2010–20, 4.4 percent p.a.).[3] Europe will remain the largest receiving region, though its below-global average rate of increase will result in a decline in market share from 59 percent to 45 percent. East Asia and the Pacific, increasing at 7.0 percent p.a., will pass the Americas as historically the second largest receiving region, holding a 27 percent market share in 2020 against 18 percent by the Americas. The respective shares of Africa, the Middle East, and South Asia will all record some increase to 5 percent, 4 percent, and 1 percent by 2020.

■ Most significantly, World Travel and Tourism Council (WTTC) research shows that some 303.0 million people around the globe will be employed in jobs that exist because of demand generated by travel and tourism by 2020.

The bottom line is that travel and tourism is driving, directly and indirectly, more than 9 percent of employment today, globally, regionally, and nationally.

THE NATURE OF FUTURE GROWTH

As we have seen, tourism is expected to continue to grow. However, the nature of this growth and development may in many ways be quite different from that of the previous five decades. As has become abundantly clear over the past several years, we are a global community, living through widespread changes whose scope and significance are barely perceptible at this point in time. Yet somehow, we understand that what came to be known as the New World Order of the post–Cold War era evolved in some very fundamental ways as we passed the magical year 2000 and moved into the third millennium of Western history. And even though the Cold War now belongs to history, the reality of war is still with us. The wars in Afghanistan and in Iraq, are very visible indicators of the kind of social and economic disruption that tourism has constantly faced in the past—and perhaps serve as a segue into the new major disruptions that tourism managers face if the theory of climate change should morph into a confirmed reality. The ongoing war on terrorism that is being fought in our own lands, the civil wars throughout Africa and the Middle East, and the increasingly militant attitude toward the effects of travel on the environment have more than replaced the Cold War as a negative influence on people's desire and

TABLE 20.1 Forecasts of International Tourist Arrivals Worldwide and by Region: 2010–2020

Regions	Tourist Arrivals (millions)		
	2000	**2010**	**2020**
Europe	390	527	717
East Asia/Pacific	116	231	438
Americas	134	195	284
Africa	27	46	75
Middle East	19	37	69
South Asia	6	11	19
World	692	1,047	1,602

Source: United Nations World Tourism Organization.

In addition to the Aeroscraft, the tourists of tomorrow will be offered experiences that are "out of this world." These experiences will be realized in such facilities as the Space Resort. *Photo courtesy of destination design firm WATG.*

willingness to venture far from home. Until the threat of war is diminished, and until we adequately address the issue of climate change, tourism managers will have to develop a comprehensive destination policy, strategy, and management framework that adapts to and accommodates the reality of long-term terrorism and climate change.

Some of the dimensions of this adaptation and accommodation are already recognizable, and indeed, some are even predictable. Others are as yet but stirrings of anxiety or discontent. These stirrings are possibly the most disconcerting for the mature adults of the so-called developed nations—adults whose well-being and prosperity have improved constantly over their lifetime. For perhaps the first time, the fundamental changes occurring around them threaten to leap out of control and to undermine the foundations of their secure and attractive lifestyles. Others, in less fortunate circumstances, see these same changes as possibly the only glimmer of hope for what they view as a more equitable distribution of all the opportunities that life has to offer. Ironically, they may see these same changes as irrevocably condemning themselves to a life of endless poverty.

LEISURE, TOURISM, AND SOCIETY IN THE THIRD MILLENNIUM

A significant component of the high-quality lifestyle that characterized the last half of the twentieth century was access to, as well as the use of, increasing amounts of leisure time. Although the extent of this increase in leisure time has been questioned for decades,[4] there is little doubt that in aggregate terms the populations of the developed Western nations have had greater and more broadly based access to recreation and travel opportunities than has any previous society. As a result, tourism has grown to the point where it is now claimed that, with elderly populations being more frequent users of health-related goods and services, tourism and health care will be the world's largest industries by 2022.[5] While traditionally those in the tourism sector have lamented the lack of recognition received by the industry, from both governments and the public, this situation is changing dramatically—in many cases, to the chagrin of the tourism establishment. Suddenly, tourism is being blamed for the destruction of cultures, degradation of the environment, and homogenization of lifestyles. In brief, because of its growing economic and social importance, tourism has suddenly found itself thrust into the mainstream of societal concerns—this at a time when all aspects of society are being questioned as to their value, their continued relevance, and, perhaps above all, their sustainability over the long term.

It is against this background of global societal change that several leading organizations and individuals having a strong interest in the future of tourism have attempted to understand the important forces of change in the world and their likely implications for the future of tourism. A review and analysis of the conclusions of these efforts indicates that tomorrow's tourists will face a number of constraints and limitations that cannot be ignored. These new realities will force tourism policy makers and the tourism industry to alter dramatically the way it both develops and operates. They will also require that tourists themselves alter their demands and their behaviors. These changes that are now imposing themselves are, however, by no means entirely negative. Many can be viewed as corrections to the bad judgments and excesses of the past. Others represent opportunities for innovative and exciting new products and experiences. These new horizons in tourism may well prove more rewarding, and certainly more sustainable, than those of the past.

NEW REALITIES—NEW HORIZONS: GLOBAL FORCES IMPACTING THE FUTURE OF TOURISM

Tourism has had an illustrious past since the 1950s and currently has a dynamic present. It is not surprising that its future is equally optimistic. Despite this optimism, a large number of major

TABLE 20.2 Global Forces (Mega Drivers) that will Influence Tourism in the Third Millennium

Mega Drivers	Nature	Name
Mega driver 1	Social	A world of changing values
Mega driver 2	Social	Living with uncertainty and fear
Mega driver 3	Economic	The dichotomy between rich and poor
Mega driver 4	Political	The power of USA in the world
Mega driver 5	Economic	The power of the Asian block in the world
Mega driver 6	Economic	The power of EU in the world
Mega driver 7	Economic/Technological	A changing business world
Mega driver 8	Social	The global/local society
Mega driver 9	Political	The relationship between people and governments
Mega driver 10	Technological/Social	AIDS
Mega driver 11	Technological	Physical access: Transport of people and goods
Mega driver 12	Technological	Access to knowledge
Mega driver 13	Economic/Social	Changing labor and demographics
Mega driver 14	Economic/Political	Energy/oil
Mega driver 15	Environmental	The environment, natural resources, and climate
Mega driver 16	Basic Human Need	Food
Mega driver 17	Technological	New technologies

Source: Ian Yeoman with the Future Foundation, *Tomorrow's Tourists: Scenarios and Trends*, Amsterdam: Elsevier (2008).

influences (or what Yeoman has defined as mega drivers—see Table 20.2), will significantly alter the nature and shape of tourism in the coming years and decades.[6] These influences will present tourism managers with a number of new realities to overcome or adapt to. At the same time, they will also present new horizons that open up many new opportunities for growth and enhancement of the tourism experience. The specific forces that influence tourism are, of course, constantly changing. Some of the most influential for the present and into the foreseeable future are discussed next.

While all these mega drivers will influence the future of tourism, there are certain of them that will be particularly important for tourism—and in addition, there will be a number of changes that we should seek to understand in greater depth, as they involve changes that are fundamental to the well-being of the tourism sector.

Economic

Despite the current economic situation, tourism can optimistically anticipate continued moderate-to-good overall rates of global economic growth of the traditional economies, but with a special importance for certain emerging economies such as China, India, Brazil, Indonesia, and Russia. History may very well prove us wrong in the longer term, but in the foreseeable future, it is expected that competitive economic forces will continue to triumph over ideologies. Over the past several decades, we have seen throughout the world the emergence of what appear to be overpowering pressures to adopt the model of the market economy.

As part of another model, we have seen movements toward deregulation, privatization, regional economic integration, and toward a greater role for the global, or transnational, corporation. Whether these movements represent temporary change or a lasting restructuring of our economic system remains to be seen. However, for the moment, the direction of the tide is unquestionable.

Space tourism has already arrived. Dennis Tito has the distinction of being the first tourist to go into space. Others have been visiting land-based space attractions for years. Space shuttle launches were scheduled to end in 2011, but the Kennedy Space Center continues to draw thousands of visitors a year. *Photo courtesy of Kennedy Space Center Visitors Complex.*

As for tourism's immediate future, the *Economist* predicts that in 2011 the world travel industry will lift itself out of post-crisis decline as a 5 percent rise in international tourist arrivals brings activity back above its 2008 level (according to the World Travel and Tourism Council). France will see the largest absolute rise in international visitors, even with a growth rate a shade lower than China. The global airline industry, after good profit growth in 2010, will see earnings slow in 2011, despite higher traffic. Boeing will at last deliver its first 787 airliners—three years late. Facing claims for compensation due to delays, Boeing will hope to work quickly through its 850-odd order book for the next generation aircraft.[7]

Political

Historians will long debate exactly why the fall of the Berlin Wall in 1989 kicked off such a dramatic spread of the democratic movement. The record will show that few individuals (experts or ordinary people) foresaw the rapid transformations of the political systems that occurred in eastern and central Europe during the past few decades. Of course, all is not as simple as it seems. Many other forces were at work that allowed this rather focused **eruption of democracy** to occur. Indeed, it is highly likely that this very visible political shift was symptomatic of a much more fundamental and underlying desire by people all over the world to control more directly in the governing processes that affect their lives. From a tourism perspective, these forces have led to the very powerful concept of **resident-responsive tourism**. No longer can it be assumed that the residents of a tourism destination or region will automatically accept all (or any) forms of tourism development that the industry proposes or attempts to impose. Tourism development in the third millennium will actively have to seek the support of the communities it affects most directly. To do this, those responsible for tourism will have to involve a growing percentage of destination residents in the assessments of the costs and benefits associated with all forms of proposed (and even existing) facilities and activities. Unless a consensus is reached that the net benefits to the community are positive, it is questionable that tourism development in the coming years will have the support necessary to proceed.

The Continued Growth of ``Super-Europe''

To the surprise of many doubters, the European Union (EU) continues to grow, although admittedly, not without some serious problems areas. In 2004, the EU undertook a major step forward when it nearly doubled in geographic size with the long-awaited addition of ten new member countries: Cyprus, the Czech Republic, Estonia, Hungary, Latvia, Lithuania, Malta, Poland, Slovakia, and Slovenia. In 2007, Bulgaria and Romania further expanded this growing colossus. Currently, the EU has 27 member countries that have transferred some of their sovereignty—or law-making authority—to the EU: Austria, Belgium, Bulgaria, Cyprus, Czech Republic, Denmark, Estonia, Finland, France, Germany, Greece, Hungary, Ireland, Italy, Latvia, Lithuania, Luxembourg, Malta, Netherlands, Poland, Portugal, Romania, Slovakia, Slovenia, Spain, Sweden, and the United Kingdom (europa.eu/index_en.htm). Four more countries have applied to become members of the EU: Croatia, Macedonia, Iceland, and Turkey. Furthermore, five other countries (Albania, Bosnia/

Herzegovina, Kosovo, Montenegro, and Serbia) are considered to be potential candidates for future membership.

Although the EU has had to provide financial assistance to Greece and Ireland, it is currently the largest economic bloc and tourism region in the world.

A Decline in the Role of the Nation: The Rise of the City-State

As already noted, the increasing importance of regional trading blocs, such as the new borderless Europe, is now a reality. The North American Free Trade Agreement (NAFTA) has created another similar bloc. In response to these two initiatives, the Asian nations are moving toward an equivalent arrangement. Also, one can anticipate some similar form of free trade agreement in South America at some point in the future.

Although it is too early yet to reach firm conclusions regarding the changes that free movement of labor will bring to the social fabric of Europe, it does seem reasonable to anticipate that despite emotional attachment to the concept of national sovereignty, the importance of each existing individual nation-state will slowly decline. Indeed, one of the major goals of European integration is to arrive at common standards, a common currency, and a more common political system based on common values. At first glance, one might argue that the creation of the new Europe will result in a new meganation. In strictly pragmatic terms, this may be the case. However, it remains to be seen whether the emotional attachment to Europe as an entity comes anywhere close to the historical attachment that residents of the European nation-states had for their individual countries. Despite the famous depth of emotion underlying "Vive la France," this traditional "Crie de Coeur" (or cry from the heart) of every French citizen, now seems to be increasingly inappropriate. Certainly, the effective elimination of borders will greatly facilitate travel flows. At the same time, it will, over time, greatly reduce national distinctiveness and thus the appeal of a particular country as a unique travel destination.

Although speculative at this point, evidence exists that as a reaction to the decline of national identities, major metropolitan centers—or city-states—are rising in importance as competitive tourism destinations. These city-states, it is argued, may become the focal point both for economic development and for individual identity. Of direct relevance to tourism is the possibility that the new city-states may also become the primary basis for tourism destination development, branding, and promotion. Indeed, it can be argued that cities such as London, Rome, New York, Beijing, and a number of others have already achieved such a status.

Environmental Issues

As Chapter 17 examines in considerable depth, growing concern about carbon emissions and resulting climate change now occupies center stage in tourism. This tourism reality is, however, a reflection of a much broader societal realization that the world's population—all of it—must get serious about the health of our planet. The widespread ratification of the Kyoto agreement represented a move toward global acceptance and its ultimate implementation. Since the Kyoto agreement was never fully implemented, recent talks (late 2010) in Cancun, Mexico, were the latest attempt to make progress toward a new global deal on tackling climate change after the 2009 meeting in Copenhagen failed to secure a new legally binding treaty on cutting emissions, instead delivering only a voluntary accord. The Cancun Accord acknowledges the need to keep temperature increases to 2°C and brings nonbinding emissions cut pledges made under the voluntary Copenhagen Accord (hammered out in the dying hours of the 2009 conference in that city), into the UN process. It also includes an agreement to set up a green climate fund as part of efforts to deliver US$100 billion a year by 2020 to poor countries to help them cope with the impact of global warming and develop without polluting. The need for implementation of a successor to Kyoto makes it abundantly clear that spaceship Earth has a limited capacity to sustain life as we know it—and that definitive action needs to be taken to change the behavior of the world's population. Thus, policy makers in tourism must now acknowledge that development and behavior in the future will have to be compatible with the environment. At the same time, however, many believe that tourism is among the better alternatives for land use. Although such compatibility is laudable, it must also be stressed that other areas exist where compatibility between tourism and the environment is perhaps not so obvious. For example, the use of fossil fuels for transportation and their polluting effect cannot be denied. As a consequence, the sustainability of tourism in the long term may be questioned unless alternative nonpolluting energy sources become available.

In this regard, certain high-profile authors[8] have been particularly vehement in their criticism of travel as a major contributor to carbon emissions and global warming—to the point of even discouraging *love miles* (travel to visit family and friends). In recognition of the highly negative impact such authors are having on the image of air travel, the leaders of the world's airlines have decided to go on the offensive in the global warming debate, with a worldwide marketing campaign, new fuel efficiency targets, and a boldly stated goal to operate a zero-emissions "green" aircraft within 50 years.[9] One of the most promising steps in the achievement of this goal is Boeing's Subsonic Ultra Green Aircraft Research project—which has developed the SUGAR-Volt design for a passenger aircraft that uses a hybrid electric engine. The aircraft would take off using conventional—though much more efficient—jet engines. But in cruise flight, it would switch to electric engines, reducing the fuel burn by more than 70 percent and the total energy used in flight by more than half. It would have fewer emissions and be quieter as well.[10]

As per a report by the European Travel Commission,[11] the following impacts of climate change should be anticipated:

- To the extent that climate change does occur, it could lead to the loss of many destinations whose appeal depends on their natural environment.
- Many low-lying coastal regions are at risk from rising sea levels—as is already evident in the case of Venice.
- Climate change may also bring about increases in trips outside the summer season, and growing popularity of summer destinations during the traditional winter period can be anticipated.
- The cost of maintaining basic "natural" resources for tourism, such as beaches and national parks, will increase. Ski resorts will have an increased need for artificial snow, and marginal skiing areas may disappear.
- As governments seek to limit greenhouse gas emissions, there is a growing likelihood of climate/emission or carbon taxes being imposed. This will, in turn, increase the prices of transport and accommodation.
- The growing awareness of the finite nature of most natural products, and the need to conserve them, will place a premium on the remaining "unspoiled" destinations.
- The rising demand for ecotourism and nature-based holidays will increase the number and sophistication of products and destination experience on the market.
- Market activity will need to promote destination sustainability as an aspect of customer reassurance.

In addition to the airlines' efforts to fix their image as a global villain, a number of travel companies are embracing the concept of carbon offsets—just as a growing number of critics are questioning the real impact and viability of this creative accounting scheme.

Technology

As the United Nations World Tourism Organization (UNWTO) has noted, the world in the year 2020 will be characterized by the penetration of technology into all aspects of life. It will become

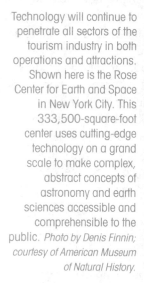

Technology will continue to penetrate all sectors of the tourism industry in both operations and attractions. Shown here is the Rose Center for Earth and Space in New York City. This 333,500-square-foot center uses cutting-edge technology on a grand scale to make complex, abstract concepts of astronomy and earth sciences accessible and comprehensible to the public. *Photo by Denis Finnin; courtesy of American Museum of Natural History.*

increasingly possible to live one's life without exposure to other people, with automated service being the norm and with full access to, and exchange of, information on everything being possible from one's own home. Even the emergence of the "tourism outlier," that is space tourism, will be, by definition, an activity that is undertaken largely in isolation. As a consequence, people will crave the human touch, and tourism will be a principal means through which they seek to achieve this.

In brief, while tourism has traditionally been characterized as a people industry, it is now coming face to face with the realities of the massive advances in technology that have occurred over the past several decades. During this period, industries that are less dependent on the human interactions (that characterize the tourism sector) have adopted labor-saving technology with a vengeance. As a consequence, these industries have been able to improve wage levels and enhance career opportunities for employees while keeping costs under control.

The travel industry has also been one of the most successful in utilizing the Internet to market its products. Both large and small firms have enhanced their ability to reach the consumer with their promotional messages; they have also surpassed other sectors in actually selling their product electronically.

Technology is having, and will continue to have, a pervasive impact on controlling the movement of travelers across certain international or interregional borders. Foreign visitors to the United States are currently required to have either a machine-readable passport or a visa. In addition, the new U.S. visas are required to contain biometric data in the form of fingerprints and a digital image of the traveler's face. Eventually it is envisaged that this kind of data will be required on all passports. Speaking of "digital images," the recent introduction and growing use of full-body airport scanner has introduced yet another hassle into the travel experience.

While the foregoing reflects a willingness on the part of governments to invest in technology to improve the efficiency of the travel system, many components of the travel industry have generally preferred to keep wages low, thus avoiding the need for technological innovation, particularly in the actual delivery of services. Although technology has been used extensively in a supporting role to keep wages low (e.g., computerized reservation systems, air control technology, kiosk check-in), there has been a great reluctance to replace human service providers with technologically driven alternatives (such as the banks did when replacing human tellers with automatic teller machines). Similarly, aside from fast-food restaurants, there has been relatively little focused effort to undertake a major rethinking or redesign of travel-related facilities and support systems so as to substantially reduce personnel requirements or to enhance the productivity of employees. While some tinkering has occurred in selected areas and sectors, we have not yet seen many of the benefits from technology that are possible. Until technology is adapted more widely, it will be difficult for the travel industry to make new travel experiences available to a mass audience and to do so at prices that are affordable to much of the population.

On the other side of the coin—and this is the dilemma—the introduction of technology is viewed as a job killer. Indeed, a common conclusion is that both skilled and not-so-skilled personnel in the labor force could be replaced by various forms of technology. While some argue that the increased use of capital and technology will require highly skilled labor; others argue that technology (particularly computer technology) may, in fact, increase the demand for a less-skilled labor force.

Service Robots Are Closer Than We Think

Despite the above reference about "job killer," most people really have no idea just how close we are to having highly functional robots available to carry out many of the large number of service tasks that tourism demands. On the one hand, robots have been in use in factories for decades—making an enormous impact on global productivity. On the other hand, the service sector has, to date, remained essentially untouched by robot hands. But now, a new generation of robots is minding children, caring for the elderly, and giving people baths or doses of medicine, as well as performing more basic tasks, like cleaning floors and mowing lawns—all tasks that are highly similar to many of those required in the tourism and hospitality sector—such as cleaning rooms, making beds, serving meals, and carrying luggage. Make no mistake about it, the shortage of reliable, low-cost labor, which has been the bane of the hospitality sector, is about to be addressed. Although it remains to be seen if robots can convey the therapeutic psychological support traditionally provided by one's favorite bartender, there are many other care-related tasks in which service robots will excel.

Hotels of the Future

Though there are lots of great hotels in most parts of the world, there are people who think we should go even further and build hotels in space for those who can afford paying thousands and thousands of dollars. We already know it would be an extraordinary experience, but would it be more fun and more comfortable than on Earth? Below are six hotels that humans are proposing to build in space:

1. Once a NASA collaborator in the building of space-based residences for the U.S. space program, *Bigelow Aerospace* is now on its own, and has already released prototypes of an inflatable hotel that should be ready (in space) in less than a decade. The company believes in its invention and claims that inflatable modules that will use several layers of vectran (twice as strong as kevlar) will be more solid than rigid ones, and will better sustain micrometeorite impacts. Rumors have it that Bigelow will commence operation in 2012. A four-week orbital stay will cost $15 million and $3 million more for another few weeks. The ultra-rich will be able to lease a full orbital facility for one year for $88 million.

2. *Galactic Suite* is a Barcelona-based private space tourism company that plans another orbital project. It should be up and running by 2012. Total cost is estimated at close to $5.27 billion, which explains why a three-night stay in its zero-gravity rooms will cost nothing less than $3.51 million, including special training. For this money, the suite spins around Earth every 80 minutes, so you get to enjoy the spectacular sunrise 18 times a day (Earth days). The Galactic Hotel is going to be small and will only include three bedrooms. The Spanish architects already have the plans figured out so that the hotel will include up to 22 pods (23 feet long by 13 feet high) clustered around a central nucleus.

3. *The Lunatic Hotel* is exactly what you think. It's a hotel on the Moon that explores the unique conditions and the building materials available there. The work of Hans-Jurgen Rombaut of the Rotterdam Academy of Architecture in the Netherlands, the hotel is going to feature two 160-meter-high slanting towers and teardrop-shaped "habitation capsules" looking like small airships (which, of course, are rooms). If it is entertainment you seek, the Lunatic Hotel is going to offer low-gravity games, abseiling, and flying using special suits with bat-like wings. It's one of the best solutions for a hotel on the moon so far, with user concerns being fully addressed. Expect something like that to be built by 2050.

4. Some 450 km above Tokyo, *Shimizu Construction* is interested in building a 64-room space hotel that should be opened to guests in 20 to 30 years. The 7,500-ton facility will rotate three times per minute to artificially produce a gravity of 0.7 g. Shimizu has been working on its Space Project since 1989. When ready, it should offer round-trip journeys in space for $83,000.

5. One of the most ambitious plans to offer regular people (rich regular people) the journey of their lives in space is the Martian Settlement. Japanese construction giant Obayashi Corporation has spent the last 10 years researching ways of building a *Martian colony*. It has gone so far as to develop estimations that that in 2057 there will be 500 people living on Mars. For a better picture of what is planned, Obayashi research data estimate that the Martian economy will make up 5 percent of the solar system's GDP by 2090, when there will be some 50,000 inhabitants.

6. If built, the *Aeroscraft*—a gigantic 400-ton blimp—may indeed be the flying luxury hotel of the future. A spacious luxury flying hotel, packed in a two-football-fields-big balloon that hangs in the air, thanks to 14 million cubic feet of helium, it's not really in "space." However, the fact that 250 passengers can enjoy a ride at 174 mph at 8,000 feet above ground while losing money in a casino, eating fine dishes in a restaurant, or just enjoying a great vacation, is quite remarkable.

The Transformation of the Airline Industry and the Modern Airliner

Underlying the transformation of the modern airliner is the ongoing competition between Boeing and Airbus, a result of the two companies' domination of the large jet airline market. In the decade between 2000 and 2009 Airbus received 6,452 orders, while Boeing received 5,927.[12] Airbus had higher deliveries between 2003 and 2009, but fell slightly short of Boeing's deliveries, delivering 3,810 aircraft compared to Boeing's 3,950. As the foregoing figures demonstrate, Airbus has recently edged out Boeing as the top commercial jet maker. The two companies are in a fierce battle for supremacy. As for the future, Airbus has chosen the path of building the world's largest airliner, the Airbus A380, a double-deck, wide-body, four-engine airline, the largest passenger airliner in the world. The A380 made its maiden flight on April 27, 2005, from Toulouse, France, and made its first commercial flight on October 25, 2007, from Singapore to Sydney with Singapore Airlines.

Boeing, in contrast, believes the future will see a need for smaller aircraft with a longer range. Its 787 Dreamliner, said to be the super-efficient plane of tomorrow, will have configurations flying between 3,500 and 8,500 nautical miles and with passenger capacities of 210 to 330. U.S. tour operator Thomson says that the range the 787 Dreamliner can achieve will "change the face of long-haul travel" in the future, enabling holidays to be offered in far-reaching destinations without the need to land and refuel. Thomson predicts that Borneo, Bali, Hawaii, and Mauritius are all future package holiday destinations from the United Kingdom with the 787.

The first 787 was unveiled in a roll-out ceremony on July 8, 2007, at Boeing's Everett assembly factory, by which time it had become the fastest-selling wide-body airliner in history, with 677 orders. By September 2010, 847 Boeing 787s had been ordered by 56 customers. As of 2010, launch customer All Nippon Airways has the largest number of 787s on order. The 787 is expected to enter commercial service in 2011.

In addition to the efforts of Airbus and Boeing, the United States National Aeronautics and Space Administration (NASA), which is basically a research organization, has created the Fundamental Aeronautics program to conduct cutting-edge research in the aviation field over the long term. Within the Fundamental Aeronautics program there are four subcategories of aircraft. The subsonic fixed-wing project conducts research on new designs for airplanes and their engines. Second, the subsonic rotary wing project aims to improve helicopters and other rotary wing aircraft, so that they can fly faster, further, quieter, and cheaper. Third, the supersonic project intends to create practical supersonic commercial airliners. Fourth, the hypersonic project seeks to design a vehicle that can fly from the surface of the earth directly into space, reaching many times the speed of sound. In addition, these hypersonic vehicles will eventually (in 30 to 50 years) achieve very-long-distance point-to-point travel in low-earth orbit, thus enabling about a three-hour trip from New York to Sydney, Australia. Such aircraft could also conceivably fly to Mars.[13]

Although all of the above are occurring in the realm of product development, the future of air travel is also likely to see a continuation of the growth of low-cost, reduced-service air carriers. Airlines such as Southwest Airlines (United States), Ryan Air (Ireland), EasyJet (United Kingdom), and WestJet (Canada) pose an ongoing threat to the traditional full-service airlines.

The Final Frontier? Space Tourism

Human curiosity about the stars predates travel and tourism as we know it today, so it is not surprising that travel into space should be gaining in popularity. In this regard, Brown identifies a number of studies demonstrating public interest in space tourism.[14] In addition, Wikipedia (2010, http://en.wikipedia.org/wiki/Space_tourism) provides a comprehensive list of references in an article dealing with the types of space tourists. Despite this interest, the prohibitively expensive cost of space travel makes it clear that not too many of us are likely to be getting a "moon-tan" in the near future. Nevertheless, seven individuals have flown as space tourists to date (see Table 20.3). Also, the continued interest in space tourism indicates that the concept is an emerging market. The $10 million "X Prize" (for two suborbital flights in space) has been won, and the establishment of many space tourism companies and the building or proposed building of spaceports in New Mexico, the United Arab Emirates, Sweden, California, Florida, and Singapore are clear signals that space tourism has a future. The most prominent companies seem to be Space Adventures, Virgin Galactic, Project Enterprise, and Dream Chaser.

Space Adventures (SA) is a privately owned space experiences company headquartered in Arlington, Virginia, with an office in Moscow, Russia. The company's mission is to open spaceflight and the space frontier to private citizens. Its goal is to benefit not only the private citizens who fly to space but also help open up the resources of space for all of mankind. SA continually aims to develop new spaceflight experiences that are exciting yet safe. In the process, they are constantly seeking new ways of arranging more reliable, affordable, and safer access to the resources of space.

In September, 2010, SA and the Boeing Company announced a memorandum of agreement regarding the marketing of anticipated transportation services to destinations in low Earth orbit (LEO) on Boeing commercial crew spacecraft. SA is a Virginia-based pioneer in space tourism that has already taken seven well-healed individuals to the International Space Station. Under this agreement, SA will market passenger seats on commercial flights aboard the Boeing Crew Space Transportation-100 (CST-100)

TABLE 20.3 List of Space Tourists Who Have Flown to Date

Space Tourist	Nationality	Year	Duration of Flight	Flight
Dennis Tito	American	2001	9 days (Apr 28 – May 6)	Launch: Soyuz TM-32
				Return: Soyuz TM-31
Mark Shuttleworth	South African	2002	11 days (Apr 25-May 5)	Launch: Soyuz TM-34
				Return: Soyuz TM-33
Gregory Olsen	American	2005	11 days (Oct 1 – Oct 11)	Launch: Soyuz TMA-7
				Return: Soyuz TMA-6
Anousheh Ansair	Iranian/American	2006	12 days (Sept 18 – Sept 29)	Launch: Soyuz TMA-9
				Return: Soyuz TMA-8
Charles Simonyi (two trips)	Hungarian/American	2007	15 days (Apr 7 – Apr 21)	Launch: Soyuz TMA-10
				Return: Soyuz TMA-9
		2009	14 days (Mar 26 – Apr 8)	Launch: Soyuz TMA-14
				Return: Soyuz TMA-13
Richard Garriott	American/British	2008	12 days (Oct 12 – Oct 23)	Launch: Soyuz TMA-13
				Return: Soyuz TMA-12
Guy Laliberté	Canadian	2009	12 days (Sept 30 – Oct 11)	Launch: Soyuz TMA-16
				Return: Soyuz TMA-14

Source: Wikipedia, "Space Tourism," en.wikipedia.org/wiki/Space_tourism.

Space Adventures, Ltd., which positions itself as the world's leading space experience company, seeks to be a unifying force for a generation of space explorers. Space Adventures, the only company to have launched seven private space explorers—to the International Space Station—launched a *Soyuz* rocket from Baikonur Cosmodrome in Kazakhstan. *Photo courtesy of Space Adventures.*

spacecraft to LEO. Potential customers for excess seating capacity include private individuals, companies, nongovernmental organizations, and U.S. federal agencies other than NASA. Boeing plans to use the CST-100 (or so-called "space taxi") to provide crew transportation to the International Space Station (ISS) and future commercial LEO platforms.

Boeing received US $18 million in NASA funding in 2010 to develop plans for a new capsule, the CST-100, which could transport crews to the International Space Station.

"By combining our talents, we can better offer safe, affordable transportation to commercial space flight customers," said Brewster Shaw, vice-president and general manager of Boeing's Space Exploration division.[15]

Preliminary plans would see four professional astronauts on each trip, leaving three seats available for space tourists, private companies or U.S. government agencies.

The SA-Boeing announcement is a boost to President Barack Obama's vision of a private space industry after he scrapped NASA's ambitious, but costly plans to build a new generation of rockets to return humans to the moon by 2020. President Obama laid out in June 2010 an overarching new U.S. policy on outer space, calling for more international and private-sector cooperation on exploration, climate change, and orbiting debris.

Once the shuttle program ends in 2011, the United States will rely on Russia's *Soyuz* spacecraft to carry astronauts to the space station until a commercial U.S. launcher can be developed.[16]

Boeing and Space Adventures have not yet set a price per seat, but said they would do so when full-scale development of the spacecraft is underway. Prices are expected to be in line with those paid by previous tourists who have spent up to $40 million for trips to the space station, so far aboard Russian *Soyuz* spacecraft.

In summary, SA's goal is to open the space frontier to everyone and promote private space exploration by building a series of successful, privately funded spaceflight missions. It has already sent seven space tourists to the International Space Station.

In addition, Virgin Galactic (VG), established by Virgin Group chairman Richard Branson, has undertaken the challenge of developing space tourism for everyone. VG represents the realization of a lifetime dream of "Sir Richard"—a dream that was born watching the U.S. moon landing in July 1969. In a manner similar to Space Adventure, Virgin Galactic's goal is to end the exclusivity attached to manned space travel, which means designing a vehicle that can fly almost anyone to space and back safely, without the need for special expertise or exhaustive, time-consuming training.

Terrorism and Crisis Management Becomes Integral to Travel and Tourism

The American Hotel & Lodging Association (AH&LA) and the Department of Homeland Security (DHS) have joined forces on an initiative to encourage and educate lodging employees to recognize, report, and react to suspicious and crisis situations that occur on property.[17]

In May 2010, DHS launched the "*If You See Something, Say Something*" campaign, which was originally implemented by New York City's Metropolitan Transportation Authority (MTA) and funded, in part, by $13 million from DHS's Transit Security Grant Program. It has since been customized and expanded for surface transportation (Amtrak), general aviation, several cities and states around the country, and now the lodging industry. With the assistance of AH&LA's Loss Prevention Committee, DHS has created public education materials for industry employees, including posters, table circulars and paystub inserts. It is a simple and effective program to raise public awareness of indicators of terrorism, crime, and other threats, and emphasize the importance of employees reporting suspicious activity to their supervisors and, in turn, to security or law enforcement authorities.

The need for Terrorism Awareness Training Courses developed by the Department of Homeland Security, directed toward hotels, is but one more clear indication that finding ways to counter **terrorism** has become an integral part of our daily lives. Nowhere is the significance of terrorism more important than in tourism. Because we, in the tourism industry, are encouraging the members of any population to travel on a discretionary basis, we have a special obligation to do all we can to take every step possible to provide travelers with security.

Why do terrorists attack tourism centers? According to *The Futurist,*[18] terrorists seek out tourist destinations for four primary reasons:

1. An attack on a tourism center is an attack on a nation's entire economy—a fact that further emphasizes the economic significance of tourism.

2. Tourism is highly media-oriented—terrorism seeks publicity, and tourist attractions like sporting events and festivals are likely to have media already at the site.

3. Tourist attractions such as museums, historic sites, and beautiful scenery represent the spirit and essence of a nation.

4. Tourist spots provide terrorists with relative anonymity. Police and security professionals rarely know the identities or motivations of visitors at sites and events.

As a consequence increasing security will be a must for airlines, hotels, restaurants, and other tourism services. Furthermore, security experts in the travel industry must address the possibility of a *suicide disease carrier* seeking to infect an entire population.

The tourism industry must, however, go beyond mere security management and put in place a **crisis management** system that is capable of dealing with a wide range of catastrophes.[19] Examples of recent tourism-related crises include:

- Britain: foot-and-mouth disease in cattle
- Cuba, Haiti, and Florida: the advent of earthquakes and successive major hurricanes
- China: SARS
- Bali: nightclub bombing
- Egypt: Luxor killings of tourists
- Thailand: avian (bird) flu and the threat of it spreading to humans
- Asia: tsunamis
- Europe: volcanic ash from Iceland

Terrorism affecting tourism has become so serious that costly efforts to develop missile warning systems and expendable decoys to protect commercial aircraft against shoulder-fired missile attacks are now taking place.

THE TOURIST OF THE FUTURE

The above sections dwelled on how technology may alter tourism facilities, products, and services—and indeed, the travel experience itself. In the meantime, the tourist who seeks to enjoy the experiences offered will also be changing. What changes can we expect?

Emergence of the Knowledge-Based Society and Workforce

One consequence of the rise of technology is that certain of the developed nations have already entered an era in which one of their greatest competitive advantages is the information or knowledge they possess, rather than their ownership of natural resources or their access to cheap labor. Assuming that such a trend continues and expands to other countries, it behooves the tourism industry to examine how the travel behavior of people in a knowledge-based society might differ from that of people from a manufacturing or more traditional service-based setting.

If the world's leading economies are any indication of trends in this regard, we can expect travelers from knowledge-based economies to be more experienced, more discerning, and more demanding—in brief, more sophisticated. In particular, we can expect that they will be seeking more individualized experiences, often characterized as special-interest travel. Such travelers are more interested in enriching their lives through experiences rather than hands-off entertainment. They seek authentic, interactive, highly involved, quality travel experiences, focusing on in-depth coverage of the special interest topic or destination at hand.

Pushing the limits even further, certain individuals and groups are now espousing the potential of virtual reality (VR) as a replacement for travel. This technology represents perhaps the outer limits of the knowledge-based industries in that it purports to provide simulated experiences that conceptually are equivalent to the real thing. It is asserted that by 2039, by merely strapping on the necessary technology, people will be able to "experience" a destination without actually visiting it. By this time, it is believed that personal computers will be sophisticated enough to bring *full immersion virtual reality* (FIVR) into the mainstream. At that point, tourism may be revolutionized since people no longer have to travel great distances or spend large amounts of money to explore the sights and sounds of another location—they can simply go online. For this reason, a number of travel firms will be going out of business around this time, or else drastically changing their business models to account for this new medium.

These online holidays are not necessarily as good as, or intrinsically better than, the real thing. Although on a different scale of technical wizardry compared to graphics of previous decades, they are still somewhat limited in their accuracy with respect to towns and cities. Currently, many of them lack sufficient detail, are often sparsely populated, and miss out on subtle characteristics of foreign culture—things that make real-life travel such an enriching, worthwhile experience. Decades of refinement will be needed before VR is entirely convincing.

Nevertheless, this new phenomenon is so profound in its depth of interactivity—as well as sheer convenience, accessibility, and ease of use—that it presents a serious threat to old-line travel agencies.[20]

Moving from a Service to an Experience Economy

Another fundamental change that has been occurring is what Pine and Gilmore refer to as the creation of the experience economy.[21] This change is seen as part of an ongoing evolution from the product and service economies of the past. In such an economy, consumers seek a quality experience from an investment of their time and money. In a related vein, there is also a changing relationship between hosts and guests. In brief, people are seeking genuine experiences rather than staged ones.

As visitors acquire an increasing number of travel experiences, they also become increasingly sophisticated, more discerning—and consequently, more demanding. Additionally, because of the foregoing enhancement in sophistication of tourists, travel itself may be losing some of its uniqueness, cachet, and status among well-educated, well-to-do individuals. To counter this possibility, policy makers and "experience designers" need constantly to seek equally sophisticated ways to challenge and stimulate the tourist of today. To do this, we simply need to keep in mind that the world and its peoples are endless sources of wonder. It is up to us to explore and find the deeper sources of wonder that have true meaning for the experienced, sophisticated traveler.

In many ways, tourism has been an important force underlying the creation of the experience economy. As Otto and Ritchie demonstrated some time ago, travelers seek a quality "experience chain" that links together the many service components of a complex travel experience.[22] The challenge facing the tourism industry is to ensure not only high-quality links in the experience chain but also an enjoyable, hassle-free passage from one link to another. Since each of the links is often managed by a different owner/operator, it is difficult to maintain a continuously high experience across the links. Because of this, destination management organizations (DMOs)—a role often assumed by convention and visitors bureaus (CVBs)—have become increasingly critical to the success of the destination visitation experience, as they seek to coordinate the many service/experience providers at a destination.

As Oxford Economics (www.oxfordeconomics.com) states somewhat differently, the tourists of tomorrow will be thrill seekers who want experiences not just visa stamps. The travel market is fragmenting. Activity-based travel (sailing, surfing, safaris, and entertainment events) are sectors that have shown strong growth—and will continue to do so in the future.

More generally, there is a trend from destination-based travel to experience-based travel. It is no longer enough to simply go to, say, France or Kenya—consumers want to immerse themselves more fully in local cultures and experiences to have a truly satisfying travel experience. This reemphasizes the fact that airlines and agents will need to shift to thinking of air travel as more of a total experience rather than as a functional A to B process. This is the route to substantial revenue opportunities by tapping into such shifting desires.

Demographic Shifts

Although very little in the social sciences is truly predictable, there is one notable exception: the demographics of the world's current population. In this regard, the forces of change that will drive and shape the face of the next generation are already evident. The populations of the developed Western world are aging and will decline in relative size. At the same time, the populations of the developing world continue to explode. While in the short term such changes may present opportunities for the tourism industry, they also raise some fundamental long-term questions. These questions concern not only the distribution of income and wealth on which travel depends, but also with respect to the geographic distribution of the world's population. One of the most profound shifts that is coming is that by 2020, Asia will represent one-third of global travel spending—up from 20 percent today.[23]

The above-noted aging of the populations of tourist-originating countries will bring about a number of significant changes in the choice of destinations and in the travel behavior of individuals. Just a few selected examples of such changes are:

- Leisurely, rather than highly programmed, vacations will increase.
- More grandparents will be traveling with children.
- Convenience will be paramount; airport delays due to increased security and overcrowded facilities will result in a trend away from short flights.[24]
- Many individuals will tend to turn inward toward family and friends (cocooning) as they seek protection in a hostile world.
- Concern for health and medical travel facilities will be driven by both physiological and psychological needs of older travelers.
- Travelers will seek "home hotels" where they can easily find most things they need, including shoes, clothing, and other necessities—so as to minimize the luggage they require.
- Educational hotels will meet the growing desire of tourists both to learn and to acquire new skills.[25]
- Since nearly half of all households in America are now headed by persons who are not married, this will increasingly change the need for travel facilities, events, and activities that were designed and developed to meet the needs of the traditional family vacation.

■ The evolving ethnic composition of the North American population is changing the choice and travel behavior of tourists. In the United States, one in three Americans belonged to an ethnic minority in 2010. At present, non-Hispanic whites comprise 67 percent of America's population, but this is a shrinking share. In 2030 and 2050, blacks will comprise a steady 13 percent of the U. S. population. Asians will grow to 6.3 percent in 2030 and to 7.8 percent in 2050. Hispanics (now 16 percent) will grow to 23 percent of the total population by 2030 and to 30.2 percent by 2050. Thus, by 2050 the ethnic population will total over 51 percent and the non-Hispanic white population will become a minority (48 percent) by 2050.[26]

The Long-Predicted "Chinese Elephant" Is Becoming a Tourism Reality

Chinese government travel restrictions on its population are continuing to be relaxed to the point where China is on its way to becoming one of the world's most powerful outbound tourism nations. According to the UNWTO, China is the fastest-growing outbound market in the world, and by 2020 it is expected that 100 million Chinese will make outbound leisure trips annually. This growth has resulted in tour groups from China quickly becoming a normal sight at the world's tourism destinations. Chinese visitors are important economically as they spend more than tourists from other Asia-Pacific countries.

China has an approved destination status (ADS) system where destinations are "sanctioned" by the Chinese government. Approved destination status is a bilateral agreement on tourism that greatly facilitates Chinese to travel to a destination. China currently has ADS agreements with 112 countries and additional agreements continue to be made. On December 11, 2007, the U.S. Commerce Secretary and the China National Tourism Administration signed a Memorandum of Understanding giving the United States ADS, while Canada did not receive approval until December 3, 2009.

Although there is growing evidence that China may soon become the world's leading economic power, several factors might affect its ranking. First, India shows signs of overtaking its powerful neighbor economically, largely because of its democratic free enterprise philosophy. Internally, China's one-child policy introduced in 1979, one of the most important social policies ever implemented, has led to a gender imbalance in the population, given a strong preference for male over female offspring.[27] This policy has led to positive results in the immediate term; however, it is also predicted to have negative implications over the longer term.

Diversity within a Homogeneous World

Despite the fact that the popularity of Coca-Cola and McDonald's contributes to the trend to "sameness" around the world, there are strong counterpressures to maintain individual and cultural distinctiveness. A visit to any major city in the world demonstrates how information, economic pressures, and the tendency to imitate has left the world "less different" than it was a century, or even decades, ago. It seems, however, that the human entity, while recognizing the pragmatic value of sameness, is determined at the same time to make every effort to preserve and enhance unique identity. Whether or not the culture that spawned the Bolshoi Ballet is threatened by the arrival of McDonald's restaurants remains to be seen. However, if the determination of those who are facing this issue is any indication, the existence of cultural diversity within a global society is a reality whose time has come.

The Quest for Stability and Security

After literally decades of economic growth and relative stability, many highly successful and valued persons are suddenly facing the impacts of the current economic recession and the prospect of decreasing economic well-being—and in many cases, even unemployment. This was not how it was supposed to turn out. We have seen, in response to this threat, a strong reluctance to spend, even by those who have the resources. Although the resulting increase in saving rates may provide the investments necessary for modernization and long-term economic growth, the more immediate impacts on leisure and tourism spending are already being felt.

In the area of physical (as opposed to economic) security, we have known for some time that risk of physical danger is certain to diminish the prospects of a given tourism destination or travel-related firm. War in the Middle East has affected tourism both locally and worldwide. Terrorism aimed at U.S. air carriers has diverted traffic to competitors. Concern for health is of increasing importance, particularly for older travelers. In a different but related vein, the threat of AIDS and other diseases has added yet another dimension of concern, only this time for younger segments of the population. We note without exaggeration that the wise tourist visiting certain regions of the world now seeks a traveling companion having a compatible blood type in case a blood transfusion is required. Such concern and attention to detail with respect to health care while traveling should not be dismissed as an aberration of the few.

The events of September 11, 2001, have vividly reinforced the critical significance of safety and security to people's desire to travel and, thus, to the well-being of the tourism industry. It follows that a primary goal of all sectors of the industry, as well as its government partners, must be to restore a pervading sense of confidence to travelers regarding all aspects of the travel experience.

Tourism-Driven Migration

"Migration and the formation of émigré communities can be a big driver of subsequent travel."

–John Kester, UNWTO[28]

While those in the developed world try to preserve their level of well-being, many millions in developing nations seek to better their lives. As fading borders increasingly facilitate population movements within trading blocs, there will be those who will first request, and then demand, the right for such freedom of movement to be extended. Recent events in Egypt, Tunisia, and Libya provide current evidence of the strength of this market. The day is not far off when freedom of movement of all peoples of the world may be termed a "basic human right." Although this certainly does not mean that this right will be granted, it will undoubtedly be asserted. Clearly, the implications of this still weak but emerging pressure go far beyond the concerns of those in the leisure and tourism field. This said, however, it is very clear that should such pressures succeed in even a modest way, the entire landscape of leisure and tourism could change dramatically.

The Digital Nomad[29]

Making use of the opportunities offered by mobile and online usage will be key in airline and customer interactions in the future.

—Marcus Casey, Lufthansa[30]

The travel experience will become increasingly digitized. **Digital nomads** have grown up with the Internet and are now traveling; their appetite for connecting with people and content at all times will be a major driver of changing tastes. They will base travel decisions on whether lodging has WiFi capability and whether they can get a cell signal from their car or canoe.

We are rapidly reaching a point in time whereby seamless travel is not only an opportunity but will indeed become an expectation. Such digitalization again raises the question of how F2F (face-to-face) travel agents can evolve.

All of these trends may themselves be affected by confounding factors such as new taxes and/or environmental concerns, though to date there is no substantial evidence that these will have major impacts on the growth of global travel.

When All Tourists Speak the Local Language

There are some 6,000 languages in the world. This confusing state of affairs has been documented throughout history, going back to Sumerian civilization more than 5,000 years before the birth of Christ. And since civilization began, translating one language into another has been a tedious and difficult task.

Of course, many people learn more than one language and can translate fluently, but learning languages takes years for most people, and there are always other languages that even the multilingual among us won't understand. The result of this complexity is that many tourists feel uncomfortable when traveling in a foreign language destination. However, it is anticipated that, within our lifetime, progress in machine-based translation will make **real-time voice-to-voice translation** a commonplace reality. The real game-changer for spoken language translation won't come until a system can translate in real time, as two speakers speak at a natural pace. This will likely come when the required computer power becomes cost-effective. That may happen in the next 10 years, but could take as long as 20 years.[31]

The Dichotomy of Comfort versus Authenticity

Many people are starting to "mix and match" their travel choices—choosing to use low-cost carriers but to stay in five-star hotels upon arrival.

Although Westerners, in particular, are likely to want new experiences, it is also likely that there will be something of a trade-off with infrastructure provision. Countries with better levels of infrastructure may be more attractive to travelers who are increasingly tired of the complexities of travel. However, countries with poorer infrastructure might offer a less crowded, more authentic experience. Ideally, airlines and agents who offer the optimal service package to their customers could

Although technology often takes the spotlight when talking about the future, it is equally important to take action to protect our environment, our heritage, and our animals for future generations. *Photo courtesy of Digital Vision.*

Shown here is a prime example of the "tourist of tomorrow," one who will be the prime beneficiary of the many exciting facilities and opportunities that are now on the drawing board. He has reason to smile. *Photo courtesy of Panama City Beach Convention and Visitors Bureau.*

benefit from this apparent trade-off (e.g., offering special assistance packages to travelers where infrastructure is poorer).

The Emergence of Extreme/ Adventure/Disaster or Dark Tourism

Yet another extreme form of tourism that has been recognized more recently is where individuals undertake to visit locations of mass destruction, where local uprisings, or even wars, create a unique type of destination experience that some travelers find exciting. In the same vein, major disasters such as floods, earthquakes, tornadoes, and hurricanes—despite or perhaps because of the danger they create—draw visitors to the disaster site. By their very nature, **dark tourism** events are inherently difficult to plan for, but it is not uncommon to see entrepreneurs selling T-shirts that make it possible for visitors to make everyone aware that they visited the site of the event/disaster or even mass killings (such as Auschwitz). The Global Insight in Chapter 11 has more detail on this topic.

MANAGING THE FUTURE EFFECTIVELY

Although it is impossible to truly "manage" the future, tourism policy makers and destination managers must make every effort to anticipate, adapt to, and take advantage of the future, as we understand it to be evolving. Based on the foregoing "best" understanding as to how the future is unfolding, the following are some of the most significant "action areas" for the tourism policy maker/ manager of today—and tomorrow:

- Tourism continues to grow. Seek to take advantage of the extent of this growth and its special areas of growth opportunities.
- How, and to what extent, is climate change likely to affect your destination and the experiences it is capable of offering?
- How is the aging of the tourism population in general—and the aging of tourists who have an interest in the experience you offer—likely to affect you and your destination?
- How does the increasing sophistication of the travel market apply to you and the experience offered by your destination? How do you feel you should/can respond?

SUMMARY

Despite the recent economic recession, social and economic megatrends in developed countries seem to favor long-term growth in both domestic and international travel demand. More long-term leisure, increased disposable income, higher levels of education, and more awareness of other countries and peoples are significant factors influencing a growing market for travel. The movement toward an experience economy is another fundamental change from which tourism can benefit if it plans and adapts appropriately.

Technological trends are also favorable. Transportation equipment is now more efficient and more comfortable; the airliner of the future will be much more fuel efficient, quieter, and capable of flying longer distances without having to make intermediate stops; hotel and motel accommodations have become more complete, attractive, convenient, and comfortable; and real-time voice translation may soon make tourists fully multilingual. In addition, the inevitable arrival of increasingly sophisticated robots will provide the hospitality sector with a reliable workforce capable of fulfilling many service functions in a very capable manner.

Political changes in the world are helping to open up travel to many new tourists. The expansion of Europe has itself broken down many barriers to travel. In parallel, the euro has become a second world currency, thus reducing yet another inconvenience of international travel—although removing some of the mystique as well.

Major international cities (true city-states) are increasingly becoming some of the world's most important travel destinations. They are easier to manage and have become very competitive through the development of strong destination brands.

Despite considerable progress, tourism is still facing the threat of climate change. Environmental regulations and the possibility of a carbon tax are making it both socially and practically more difficult to justify many types of travel. In addition, climate change is threatening to affect the appeal of low-lying beach destinations and high-altitude winter resorts.

Terrorism is yet another growing threat to the well-being of tourism. Incidents remain isolated and of relatively minimal impact, but terrorism activity continues to be in the background as a growing concern.

Finally, the tourist of the present is undergoing transformations that will make the tourist of tomorrow very different. Demography is currently the most powerful force at work. Most specifically, the populations of the developed world are aging rapidly—meaning that the facilities and experiences demanded are subject to many pressures for change in order to accommodate the preferences and needs of an older traveler. A second component of global demographics is the size of a rapidly emerging China—a China whose huge population increasingly has the desire and the means to travel. At the same time, China seeks to become a major travel destination itself, offering a whole new range of visitor experiences to compete with other new experiences—such as those provided by extreme, adventure, or disaster, known as dark tourism.

 KEY CONCEPTS

approved destination status	experience economy	service robots
city-state	knowledge-based society	space tourism
crisis management	migration and tourism	eruption of democracy
cultural diversity	need for stability	terrorism
dark tourism	real-time voice-to-voice translation	virtual reality
digital nomads	resident-responsive tourism	

 INTERNET EXERCISES

The Internet sites mentioned in this chapter plus some selected additional sites are listed for your convenience on the companion Web site for this book, www.wiley.com/college/goeldner.

ACTIVITY 1

Site Name: World Travel and Tourism Council

URL: www.wttc.org

Background Information: The World Travel and Tourism Council (WTTC) is the global business leaders' forum for travel and tourism. Its members are chief executives from all sectors of the travel and tourism industry.

Exercises

1. Visit the annual forecast (TSA Research) on the WTTC site and examine the worldwide employment forecast for the current year and the ten-year projection.

2. Do the same for the United States.

3. Do the same for the European Union.

ACTIVITY 2

Site Name: Space Adventures

URL: www.spaceadventures.com

Background Information: Space Adventures is a privately owned space experiences company headquartered in Arlington, Virginia, with an office in Moscow. Its goal is to open the space frontier to everyone and promote private space exploration by building a series of successful, privately funded spaceflight missions.

Exercises

1. Visit the site and determine its role in assisting the world's first two space tourists, Dennis Tito and Mark Shuttleworth.

2. Examine the space tourism opportunities that are available today.

ACTIVITY 3

Site Name: Virgin Galactic

URL: www.virgingalactic.com

Background Information: Virgin Galactic is a company established by the Richard Branson Group to undertake the challenge of developing space tourism for everyone.

Exercises

1. What do you see as the future of space tourism?

2. What do you see as the different roles of Space Adventures and Virgin Galactic?

❖ **QUESTIONS FOR REVIEW AND DISCUSSION** ❖

1. What might be an obstacle to the optimistic projections of increased international tourism forecast in this chapter?

2. Intelligent, creative, sensitive tourism developments can actually improve the environment and heighten the appeal of an area. Give examples of how this might happen.

3. Can tourism enhance and improve a destination area's cultural and hospitality resources? Provide actual or hypothetical examples.

4. What is the expected trend in health-oriented accommodations and programs? Food services?

5. What are the realistic prospects for a four-day work week?

6. Does early retirement appeal to most workers?

7. How can tourism interests obtain a growing share of leisure market expenditures?

8. What do you think the future of space tourism will be?

9. Would you or anyone you know pay $100,000 to travel in space? What would you pay?

❖ **CASE PROBLEM** ❖

As the newly appointed vice president of strategic planning of a large international hotel chain, you have been asked to prepare a report examining the future role that robots are likely to play in helping relieve the difficulties your company is currently facing in finding adequate numbers of interested, capable individuals to carry out the extensive housekeeping chores necessary to provide guests with the number of clean, well-kept rooms they expect.

Given the growing importance of sophisticated robots in many areas, the president of your chain has become a true believer in the contributions that robots are likely to make to improve the performance and productivity of your housekeeping staff. At the same time, the vice president of

human resources (VPHR) of your firm is very skeptical that robots will be able to clean rooms and make beds in a way that will please visitors.

In preparing your report, you have been asked to reconcile the enthusiasm of your president concerning the future role of robots and the skepticism of your VPHR regarding their likely performance.

■ How would you go about preparing this report?

■ What are your personal views on this issue before you start to study the issue?

■ What sources of information would you gather?

ENDNOTES

1. Cornish, Edward, *Futuring: The Exploration of the Future*. (Bethesda, MD: World Future Society, 2004), p. xi.
2. *UNWTO World Tourism Barometer*. Madrid: United Nations World Tourism Organization, vol. 8, no. 2 (2010), p. 3.
3. *Tourism 2020 Vision* (2000). Madrid: United Nations World Tourism Organization—see Web site: http://www.unwto.org/facts/eng.
4. Juliet B. Schor, *The Overworked American: The Unexpected Decline of Leisure* (New York: Basic Books, 1991).
5. Ian Yeoman with the Future Foundation, *Tomorrow's Tourist Scenarios and Trends* (Amsterdam: Elsevier, 2008).
6. Ibid.
7. "The World in Figures: Industries." *The Economist: The World in 2011.* London, UK: The Economist Intelligence Unit, p. 128.
8. George Monbiot, *Heat: How to Stop the Planet from Burning* (Toronto, ON: Doubleday Canada, 2006), and *Travel Weekly* (June 11, 2007).
9. International Air Transport Association, "IATA Calls for a Zero Emissions Future" (June 4, 2007), available at www.iata.org.
10. "The Transformation of the Modern Airliner," *Trends eMagazine* (October 2010), pp. 12–13.
11. European Travel Commission, "Tourism Trends for Europe" (September 2006), available at www.europe.com.
12. Competition between Airbus and Boeing, en.wikipedia.org/wiki/Competition_between_Airbus_and_Boeing.
13. "The Transformation of the Modern Airliner," *Trends eMagazine* (October 2010), pp. 12–13.
14. Frances Brown, "The Final Frontier? Tourism in Space," *Tourism Recreation Research*, vol. 29, no. 1 (2004), pp. 37–43.
15. Denise Chow, "Boeing Partners with Space Adventures to Market CST-100 Flights," *Space News*, September 20, 2010—see Web site: http://www.spacenews.com/venture_space/100920-boeing-partners-space-adventures.html.
16. Agence France-Press, Washington, from *Calgary Herald*, Friday, September 17, 2010, p. A27.
17. "AH&LA, DHS Launch Security, Terrorism Awareness Initiative," *Hotel News Resource*, November 16, 2010—see Web site: http://www.hotelnewsresource.com/article50228.html.
18. Edward Cornish (ed.), *The Futurist* (Bethesda, MD: World Future Society, 2002); online: www.wfs.org/futurist.htm.
19. Glaesser, Dirk, *Crisis Management in the Tourism Industry.* London, UK: Butterworth-Heinemann, 2003.
20. Will Fox, "21st century—2030–2039 timeline contents," FutureTimeline.net, 2011–see Web site: www.futuretimeline.net/21stcentury/2030-2039.htm.
21. B. Joseph Pine II and James H. Gilmore, *The Experience Economy: Work Is Theatre and Every Business a Stage* (Boston, MA: Harvard Business School Press, 1999).
22. Julie E. Otto and J. R. Brent Ritchie, "The Service Experience in Tourism," *Tourism Management*, vol. 17, no. 3 (May 1996), pp. 165–174.
23. Oxford Economics, "Changes in Tastes," in *The Travel Gold Rush 2020*, p. 5.
24. Peter E. Tarlow, "Tourism in the Twenty-First Century," *Futurist*, vol. 36, no. 5 (September–October 2002–2003), pp. 48–51.
25. Ivanka Avelini Holjevac, "A Vision of Tourism and the Hotel Industry in the 21st Century," *International Journal of Hospitality Management*, vol. 22, no. 2 (2003), pp. 129–134.
26. Population Division, U.S. Bureau of Census, Table 4. Projections of the Population by Sex, Race and Hispanic Origin for the United States: 2010 to 2050.
27. *British Medical Journal* (BMJ) (2006), vol. 333, no. 7564, pp. 361.
28. *The Travel Gold Rush 2020*, p. 31—www.amadeus.com/amadeus/goldrush2020.html.
29. *The Travel Gold Rush 2020*, Oxford Economics: Amadeus (2010), p. 29.
30. *The Travel Gold Rush 2020*, p. 29—www.amadeus.com/amadeus/goldrush2020.html.
31. "Trend #3: Undoing Babel," *Trends eMagazine* (May 2010), pp. 19–24.

Selected References

Chapter 1

Brown, F. *Tourism Reassessed: Blight or Blessing?* Oxford, UK: Butterworth-Heinemann, 1998.

Cook, Roy, Laura Yale, and Joseph Marqua. *Tourism: The Business of Travel*. Upper Saddle River, NJ: Prentice Hall, 2010.

Cooper, C., J. Fletcher, D. Gilbert, R. Shepherd, and S. Wanhill (eds.). *Tourism: Principles and Practice*. Essex, UK: FT Prentice Hall, 2008.

Degg, Richard (ed.). *Leisure, Recreation, and Tourism Abstracts*, quarterly. Wallingford, Oxfordshire, UK: CAB International.

Khan, Mahmood, Michael Olsen, and Turgut Var (eds.). *VNR's Encyclopedia of Hospitality and Tourism*. New York: Van Nostrand Reinhold, 1993.

Krippendorf, Jost. *The Holiday Makers*. London: Butterworth-Heinemann, 1989.

Leiper, Neil. "The Framework of Tourism: Towards a Definition of Tourism, Tourist, and the Tourism Industry." *Annals of Tourism Research*, vol. 6, no. 4 (October-December 1979), pp. 390–407.

Mill, Robert Christie, and Alastair M. Morrison. *The Tourism System*, 6th ed. Dubuque, IA: Kendall/Hunt, 2009.

Moutinho, L. *Strategic Management in Tourism*. Oxfordshire, UK: CABI Publishing, 2011.

Page, Stephen J., and Joanne Connell. *Tourism: A Modern Synthesis*, 2d ed. London: Thompson Learning, 2006.

Pearce, Philip, Sebastian Filep, and Glenn Ross. *Tourist, Tourism and the Good Life*. Oxon, UK: Routledge, 2010.

Richardson, John I., and Martin Fluker. *Understanding and Managing Tourism*. Frenchs Forest, NSW: Pearson Education Australia, 2004.

Smith, Stephen L. J. "Defining Tourism: A Supply-Side View." *Annals of Tourism Research*, vol. 15, no. 2 (1998), pp. 179–190.

Tribe, John. *Strategy for Tourism*. Oxon, UK: Goodfellow Publishers, 2010.

Tribe, John. *Philosophical Issues in Tourism*. Bristol, UK: Channel View Publications, 2009.

Turner, Louis, and John Ash. *The Golden Hordes*. London: Constable, 1975.

United Nations World Tourism Organization. *Compendium of Tourism Statistics*. Madrid: UNWTO, 2009.

United Nations World Tourism Organization. *Yearbook of Tourism Statistics*. Madrid: UNWTO, 2009.

United Nations World Tourism Organization. *Tourism in a Globalized Society*. Madrid: UNWTO, 2003.

United Nations World Tourism Organization. *Thesaurus on Tourism and Leisure Activities*. Madrid: UNWTO, 2001.

United Nations World Tourism Organization. *Concepts, Definitions, and Classifications for Tourism Statistics*. Madrid: UNWTO, 1995.

United Nations World Tourism Organization. *Implications of the UNWTO/UN Tourism Definitions*. Madrid: UNWTO, 1995.

United States Travel Association. *Tourism Works for America*. Washington, DC: USTA, annual.

Wall, Geoffrey, and Alister Mathieson. *Tourism: Changes, Impacts, and Opportunities*. Upper Saddle River, NJ: Prentice Hall, 2006.

Woodside, Arch G., and Drew Martin. *Tourism Management*. Oxfordshire, UK: CABI Publishing, 2007.

Young, George. *Tourism: Blessing or Blight?* Baltimore: Penguin Books, 1973.

Chapter 2

Aramberri, Julio. *Modern Mass Tourism*. Bingley, UK: Emerald Group Publishing, 2010.

Belasco, Warren James. *Americans on the Road: From Autocamp to Motel, 1910–1945*. Cambridge, MA: MIT Press, 1979.

Burkart, A. J., and S. Medlik. *Historical Development of Tourism*. Aix-en-Provence, France: Centre des Hautes Studes Touristiques, 1990.

Butler, Richard, and R. Russel. *Giants of Tourism*. Oxfordshire, UK: CABI Publishing, 2010.

Casson, Lionel. *Travel in the Ancient World*. London: Allen and Unwin, 1974.

Cooper, Chris. *Classic Reviews in Tourism*. Clevedon, UK: Channel View Publications, 2003.

Evans, Michael R. "Newport, Rhode Island—America's First Resort: Lessons in Sustainable Tourism." *Journal of Travel Research*, vol. 36, no. 2 (Fall 1997), pp. 63–67.

Fagan, Brian M. *The Great Journey: The Peopling of Ancient America*. New York: Thames and Hudson, 1987.

Friedhiem, Eric. *Travel Agents: From Caravans and Clippers to the Concorde*. New York: Travel Agent Magazine Books, 1992.

Gee, Chuck Y., and Matt Lurie (eds.). *The Story of the Pacific Asia Travel Association*. San Francisco: Pacific Asia Travel Association, 1993.

Jakle, John A. *The Tourist: Travel in Twentieth-Century North America*. Lincoln: University of Nebraska Press, 1985.

O'Gorman, Kevin. *The Origins of Hospitality and Tourism*. Oxon, UK: Goodfellow Publishers, 2010.

Rae, W. Fraser. *The Business of Travel: A Fifty Years' Record of Progress*. London: Thomas Cook and Son, 1891.

Robinson, H. *A Geography of Tourism*. London: Macdonald and Evans, 1976.

Rugoff, Milton. *The Great Travelers*. New York: Simon and Schuster, 1960.

Shaw, Steve. *The Delicious History of the Holiday*. London: Routledge, 2000.

Smith, Stephen L. J. *The Discovery of Tourism*. Bingley, UK: Emerald Group Publishing, 2010.

Sofield, Trevor, and Sarah Li. "Tourism Development and Cultural Policies in China." *Annals of Tourism Research*, vol. 25, no. 2 (1998), pp. 362–392.

Sofield, Trevor, and Sarah Li. "Historical Methodology and Sustainability: An 800-Year-Old Festival from China." *Journal of Sustainable Tourism*, vol. 6, no. 4 (1998), pp. 267–292.

Towner, John. "Approaches to Tourism History." *Annals of Tourism Research*, vol. 15, no. 1 (1988), pp. 47–62.

Towner, John. "The Grand Tour: A Key Phase in the History of Tourism." *Annals of Tourism Research*, vol. 12, no. 3 (1985), pp. 297–333.

Towner, John. "The Grand Tour: Sources and a Methodology for an Historical Study of Tourism." *Tourism Management*, vol. 5, no. 3 (September 1984), pp. 215–222.

Towner, John. "What Is Tourism's History?" *Tourism Management*, vol. 16, no. 5 (August 1995), pp. 339–344.

Walton, John K. *Histories of Tourism: Representation, Identity and Conflict*. Bristol, UK: Channel View Publications, 2005.

Chapter 3

Baum, Tom. *Human Resource Management for Tourism, Hospitality, and Leisure: An International Perspective*. Clifton Park, NY: Delmar Thomson Learning, 2006.

Business Travel News. Travel Manager Salary and Attitude Survey. New York: BTN—North America, annual.

Cook, Suzanne, and William Evans. *A Portrait of the Travel Industry Employment in the U.S. Economy*. Washington, DC: TIA Foundation, 1999.

Lee-Ross, Darren, and Josephine Pryce. *Human Resources and Tourism: Skills, Culture and Industry*. Bristol, UK: Channel View Publications, 2010.

Ninemeier, Jack, and Joe Perdue. *Hospitality Operations: Careers in the World's Greatest Industry*. Upper Saddle River, NJ: Prentice Hall, 2005.

Rubin, Karen. *Inside Secrets to Finding a Career in Travel*. Indianapolis, IN: JIST Works, 2001.

Skalpe, Ole. "The CEO Gender Pay Gap in the Tourism Industry—Evidence from Norway." *Tourism Management*, vol. 28, no. 3 (June 2007), pp. 845–853.

United Nations World Tourism Organization. *Human Resource Development in Asia and the Pacific*. Madrid: UNWTO, 2001.

U.S. Department of Labor. *Occupational Outlook Handbook*. Washington, DC: U.S. Government Printing Office, 2010.

Chapter 4

Lennon, John, Hugh Smith, Nancy Cockerell, and Jill Trew. *Benchmarking National Tourism Organizations and Agencies*. Oxford, UK: Butterworth-Heinemann, 2006.

OECD. *OECD Tourism Trends and Policies 2010*. Paris: OECD Publishing, 2010.

Pearce, Douglas G. *Tourist Organizations*. Essex: Longman Scientific and Technical, 1992.

Pike, Steven. *Destination Marketing Organizations*. Oxford, UK: Elsevier, 2004.

Soteriou, Evi C., and Chris Roberts. "The Strategic Planning Process in National Tourism Organizations." *Journal of Travel Research*, vol. 37, no. 1 (August 1998), pp. 21–29.

United Nations World Tourism Organization. *Yearbook of Tourism Statistics*. Madrid: UNWTO, 2009.

United Nations World Tourism Organization. *Compendium of Tourism Statistics*. Madrid: UNWTO, 2009.

United Nations World Tourism Organization. *Tourism and Poverty Alleviation*. Madrid: UNWTO, 2002.

United Nations World Tourism Organization. *Public-Private Sector Cooperation*. Madrid: UNWTO, 2001.

United Nations World Tourism Organization. *Budgets of National Tourism Administration*. Madrid: UNWTO, 1996.

U.S. Travel Association. *Survey of U.S. State and Territory Tourism Office Website Practices 2008*. Washington, DC: USTA, 2009.

World Travel and Tourism Council. *Progress and Priorities, 2009/10*. London: WTTC, 2009.

Chapter 5

Air Transport Association of America. *ATA Economic Report for the U.S. Airline Industry*. Washington, DC: ATA, annual.

Dickinson, Bob, and Andy Vladimir. *Selling the Sea*, 2d ed. Hoboken, NJ: John Wiley & Sons, 2007.

Dowling, R. K. *Cruise Ship Tourism*. Oxfordshire, UK: CABI Publishing, 2006.

Duval, David Timothy. *Tourism and Transport: Modes, Networks and Flows*. Bristol, UK: Channel View Publications, 2010.

Graham, Anne. *Managing Airports: An International Perspective*. Oxford, UK: Butterworth-Heinemann, 2003.

Lumsdon, Les, and Stephen J. Page. *Tourism and Transport: Issues and Agenda for the New Millennium*. Oxford, UK: Elsevier, 2003.

Tourism Industries. *In-Flight Survey of International Air Travelers*. Washington, DC: International Trade Administration, 2010.

United Nations World Tourism Organization. *Cruise Tourism: Current Situation and Trends*. Madrid: UNWTO, 2008.

Chapter 6

Amadeus. *Hotels 2020: Beyond Segmentation*. Sophia Antipolis Cedex, France: Amadeus, 2010.

Angelo, Rocco M., and Andrew N. Vladimir. *Hospitality Today: An Introduction*, 7th ed. Orlando, FL: Educational Institute of the American Hotel and Lodging Association, 2010.

Carlsen, Jack, and S. Charters. *Global Wine Tourism*, Oxfordshire, UK: CABI Publishing, 2007.

Croce, E., and G. Perri. *Food and Wine Tourism*. Oxfordshire, UK: CABI, 2011.

Deloitte and Touche. *Financial Performance 2010: A Survey of Timeshare and Vacation Ownership Companies*. Washington, DC: ARDA International Foundation, 2010.

Ernst and Young. *Economic Impact of the Timeshare Industry on the U.S. Economy*. Washington, DC: ARDA International Foundation, 2010.

Ernst and Young. *State of the Vacation Timeshare Industry: United States Study*. Washington, DC: ARDA International Foundation, 2007.

Kasavana, Michael L. *Managing Technology in the Hospitality Industry*, 6th ed. Lansing, MI: Educational Institute of the American Hotel and Lodging Association, 2011.

Lattin, Gerald W. *The Lodging and Food Service Industry*, 7th ed. Lansing, MI: Educational Institute of the American Hotel and Lodging Association, 2009.

Olsen, Michael, Eliza Ching-Yick Tse, and Joseph West. *Strategic Management in the Hospitality Industry*, 3d ed. Upper Saddle River, New Jersey: Prentice Hall, 2008.

Ragatz Associates. *Resort Timeshare Consumers: Who They Are, Why They Buy*. Washington, DC: ARDA International Foundation, 2006.

Ragatz Associates. *The Shared-Ownership Resort Real Estate Industry in North America: 2010*. Washington, DC: ARDA International Foundation, 2010.

Ragatz Associates. *Resort Timesharing in the United States*. Carmel, IN: RCI, 2003.

Ragatz Associates. *Resort Timesharing Worldwide*. Carmel, IN: RCI, 2003.

Research Intelligence Group. *Shared Vacation Ownership Owners Report: 2010 Edition*. Washington, DC: ARDA International Foundation, 2010.

Richard K. Miller & Associates. *The 2010 Restaurant, Food & Beverage Market Research Handbook*. Loganville, GA: RKMA, 2010.

U.S. Travel Association. *The Profile of the Culinary Traveler*. Washington, DC: USTA, 2007.

Chapter 7

Appelman, Jaco H. *Governance of Global International Tourism Networks: Changing Forms of Co-ordination Between the Travel Agency and Aviation Sector*. Rotterdam: Erasmus University, 2004.

Clarkson, Diane. *Extending Online Customer Service to the Mobile Channel*. Cambridge, MA: Forrester, 2010.

Evans, Nigel G., and Mike J. Stabler. "A Future for the Package Tour Operator in the 25th Century?" *Tourism Economics*, vol. 1, no. 3 (September 1995), pp. 245–264.

Friedheim, Eric. *Travel Agents: From Caravans and Clippers to the Concorde*. New York: Travel Agent Magazine Books, 1992.

Laws, Eric. *Managing Packaged Tourism*. Boston: International Thomson Business Press, 1997.

O'Connor, Peter, and A. J. Frew. "An Evaluation Methodology for Hotel Electronic Channels of Distribution." *International Journal of Hospitality Management*, vol. 23, no. 2 (June 2004), pp. 179–199.

Sheldon, P. J. *Tourism Information Technology*. Oxford, UK: CAB International, 1997.

Sheldon, Pauline, Karl Wöber, and Daniel Fesenmaier, (eds.). *Information and Communication Technologies in Tourism 2001*. Vienna: Springer-Verlag, 2001.

U.S. Travel Association. *Travelers Use of the Internet, 2010*. Washington, DC: USTA, 2010.

Chapter 8

Allen, Johnny, William O'Toole, Ian McDonnell, and Rob Harris. *Festival and Special Event Management*. Hoboken, NJ: John Wiley & Sons, 2002.

The American Gaming Association. *2009 State of the States: The AGA Survey of Casino Entertainment*. Washington, DC: AGA, 2009.

Clave, S. A. *The Global Park Industry*. Oxfordshire, UK: CABI Publishing, 2007.

Dallen, J. Timothy. *Shopping Tourism, Retailing and Leisure*. Bristol UK: Channel View Publications. 2005.

Douglas, N., W. Douglas, and R. Derrett (eds.). *Special Interest Tourism: Context and Cases*. Brisbane: John Wiley & Sons, 2001.

Erfurt-Cooper, Patricia, and Malcolm Cooper. *Health and Wellness Tourism: Spas and Hot Springs*. Bristol, UK: Channel View Publications, 2009.

Frost, Warwick. *Zoos and Tourism*. Bristol, UK: Channel View Publications, 2010.

Fyall, Alan, Brian Garrod, Anna Leask, and Stephen Wanhill. *Managing Visitor Attractions*, 2d ed. Oxford, UK: Butterworth-Heinemann, 2008.

Getz, Donald. *Event Studies: A Multidisciplinary Approach*. Oxford, UK: Butterworth-Heinemann, 2007.

Goldblatt, Joe. *Special Events*, 5th ed. Hoboken, NJ: John Wiley & Sons, 2008.

Goldblatt, Joe. *The Dictionary of Event Management*. New York: Van Nostrand Reinhold, 1996.

Hoyle, Leonard H. *Event Marketing*. Hoboken, NJ: John Wiley & Sons, 2002.

Hsu, Cathy H.C. *Casino Industry in Asia Pacific*. Binghamton, NY: The Haworth Press, 2006.

International Association of Scientific Experts in Tourism. *Sports and Tourism*. St. Gallen, Switzerland: AIEST, 2003.

Long, Patrick, Jo Clark, and Derek Liston. *Win, Lose, or Draw? Gambling with America's Small Towns*. Washington, DC: The Aspen Institute, 1994.

Moss, S. *The Entertainment Industry*. Oxfordshire, UK: CABI Publishing, 2009.

National Indian Gaming Association. *The Economic Impact of Indian Gaming in 2009*. Washington, DC: NIGA, 2010.

Picard, David, and Mike Robinson. *Festivals, Tourism and Social Change*. Clevedon, UK: Channel View Publications, 2006.

Robinson, P., D. Wale, and G. Dickson. *Events Management*. Oxfordshire, UK: CABI Publishing, 2010.

Swarbrooke, John. *The Development and Management of Visitor Attractions*, 2d ed. Boston: Butterworth-Heinemann, 2002.

Tarlow, Peter E. *Event Risk Management and Safety*. Hoboken, NJ: John Wiley & Sons, 2002.

Toohey, K. and A.J. Veal. *The Olympic Games*. Oxfordshire, UK: CABI Publishing, 2006.

U.S. Bureau of the Census. *Statistical Abstract of the United States: 2010*. Washington, DC: U.S. Government Printing Office, 2010.

Chapter 9

Anthony, I. *Verulamium*. Hanley, UK: Wood Mitchell, 1973.

Awaritefe, Onome D. "Tourists Values, Activities and Motivation for Travel to Third World Destinations: Case Study of Nigeria." *Tourist Review*, vol. 59, no. 1 (2004), pp. 34–43.

Bowen, D., and J. Clarke. *Contemporary Tourist Behaviour*. Oxfordshire, UK: CABI Publishing, 2009.

Casson, L. *Travel in the Ancient World*. London: Allen and Unwin, 1974.

Crouch, G. I., R. R. Perdue, H. Timmermans, and M. Uysal. *Consumer Psychology of Tourism, Hospitality and Leisure*, vol. 3. Oxfordshire, UK: CABI Publishing, 2004.

Earl, P. E., and S. Kemp (eds.). *The Elgar Companion to Consumer Research and Economic Psychology*. Northampton, MA: Edward Elgar, 1999.

Filep, Sabastian, and Luke Greenacre. "Evaluating and Extending the Travel Career Pattern Model." *Tourism*, vol. 55, no. 1 (2007), pp. 23–38.

Hibbert, C. *The Grand Tour*. London: Weidenfeld and Nicolson, 1969.

Iso-Ahola, S. "Toward a Social Psychological Theory of Tourism Motivation: A Rejoinder." *Annals of Tourism Research*, vol 9, no. 2 (1982), pp. 256–262.

Kim, Kakyom. "Understanding Differences in Tourist Motivation Between Domestic and International Travel: The University Student Market." *Tourism Analysis*, vol. 12, no. 1/2 (2007), pp. 65–75.

Loker, L. E., and R. Perdue. "A Benefit-Based Segmentation of a Nonresident Summer Travel Market." *Journal of Travel Research*, vol. 31, no. 1 (1992), pp. 30–35.

March, Roger, and Arch G. Woodside. *Tourism Behaviour*. Oxfordshire, UK: CABI Publishing, 2006.

Maslow, A. H. *Motivation and Personality*, 2d ed. New York: Harper & Row, 1970.

Mazanec, Joseph A., Geoffrey I. Crouch, J. R. Brent Ritchie, and Arch G. Woodside (eds.). *Consumer Psychology of Tourism, Hospitality, and Leisure*, vol. 2. Oxfordshire, UK: CABI Publishing, 2001.

Moscardo, G., P. Pearce, A. Morrison, D. Green, and J. T. O'Leary. "Developing a Typology for Understanding Visiting Friends and Relatives Markets." *Journal of Travel Research*, vol. 38, no. 3 (February 2000), pp. 251–259.

Pearce, Philip, Sebastian Filep, and Glenn Ross. *Tourist, Tourism and the Good Life*. Oxon, UK: Routledge, 2010.

Pearce, Philip. *Tourist Behaviour*. Bristol, UK: Channel View Publications, 2005.

Pearce, P.L."Fundamentals of Tourist Motivation." In D. G. Pearce and R. W. Butler (eds.) *Fundamentals of Tourist Motivation*, pp. 113–134. London: Routledge, 1992.

Pearce, P. L. *The Ulysses Factor: Evaluating Visitors in Tourist Settings*. New York: Springer-Verlag, 1988.

Pimlott, J. A. R. *The Englishman's Holiday*. London: Faber & Faber, 1947.

Plog, S. "*Understanding Psychographics in Tourism Research.*" In J. R. B. Ritchie and C. Goeldner (eds.). *Travel, Tourism, and Hospitality Research*, pp. 203–14. New York: John Wiley & Sons, 1987.

Plog, S. "Why Destination Areas Rise and Fall in Popularity." *Cornell Hotel and Restaurant Quarterly* (1974), pp. 55–58.

Rowling, M. *Everyday Life of Medieval Travellers*. London: B. T. Batsford, 1971.

Ryan, C. "The Travel Career Ladder: An Appraisal." *Annals of Tourism Research*, vol. 25, no. 4 (October 1998), pp. 936–957.

Swinglehurst, E. *The Romantic Journey*. London: Pica Editions, 1974.

Wolfe, R. I. "Recreational Travel: The New Migration." *Geographical Bulletin*, vol. 2 (1967), pp. 159–167.

Woodside, Arch G., Geoffrey I. Crouch, Joseph A. Mazanec, Martin Oppermann, and Marcia Y. Sakai (eds.). *Consumer Psychology of Tourism, Hospitality, and Leisure*, vol. 1. Oxfordshire, UK: CABI Publishing, 1999.

Chapter 10

Azmier, Jason J. *Culture and Economic Competitiveness: Emerging Role for Arts in Canada*. Calgary, Alberta: Canada West Foundation, 2002.

Chambers, Erve (ed.). *Tourism and Culture: An Applied Perspective*. Albany: State University of New York Press, 1997.

Clift, Stephen, and Simon Carter (eds.). *Tourism and Sex: Culture, Commerce, and Coercion*. London: Pinter, 1999.

Connell, J. *Health and Medical Tourism*. Oxfordshire, UK: CABI, 2010.

Cronin, Michael, and Barbara O'Connor. *Irish Tourism: Image, Culture and Identity*. Clevedon, UK: Channel View Publications, 2003.

Crotts, John, and Abrahm Pizam. "The Effect of National Culture on Consumers' Evaluation of Travel Services." *Tourism, Culture and Communication*, vol. 4, no. 1 (2003), pp. 17–28.

Graburn, Nelson H. H. "The Anthropology of Tourism." *Annals of Tourism Research*, vol. 10, no. 1 (1983), pp. 9–33. Special Issue on the Anthropology of Tourism.

Hanley, Keith, and John K. Walton. *Constructing Cultural Tourism*. Bristol, UK: Channel View Publications, 2010.

Harrison, D., and M. Hitchcock. *The Politics of World Heritage*. Clevedon, UK: Channel View Publications, 2005.

International Association of Scientific Experts in Tourism. *Tourism and Culture*. St. Gallen, Switzerland: AIEST, 2000.

Kerstetter, Deborah, John Confer, and Kelly Bricker. "Industrial Heritage Attractions: Types and Tourists." *Journal of Travel and Tourism Marketing*, vol. 7, no. 2 (1998), pp. 91–104.

Litvin, Stephen W. "Tourism: The World's Peace Industry?" *Journal of Travel Research*, vol. 37, no. 1 (August 1998), pp. 63–66.

Macleod, Donald, and James G. Carrier. *Tourism, Power and Culture: Anthropological Insights*. Bristol, UK: Channel View Publications, 2009.

Mandala, Laura. *Cultural and Heritage Tourism Study*. Alexandria, VA: Mandala Research, 2009.

Master, Hoda, and Bruce Prideaux. "Culture and Vacation Satisfaction: A Study of Taiwanese Tourists in South East Queensland," *Tourism Management*, vol. 21, no. 5 (October 2000), pp. 445–449.

McCool, S. F., and R. N. Moisey (eds.). *Tourism, Recreation, and Sustainability: Linking Culture and the Environment*. New York: CABI Publishing, 2001.

Morgan, Michael, Peter Lugosi, and J. R. Brent Ritchie. (eds.). *The Tourism and Leisure Experience*. Bristol, UK: Channel View Publications, 2010.

Moufakkir, O., and I. Kelly. *Tourism, Progress and Peace*. Oxfordshire, UK: CABI, 2010.

Nash, Dennison. *Anthropology of Tourism*. Kidlington, Oxford, UK: Pergamon Press, 1996.

Reisinger, Yvette, and Lindsay Turner. *Cross-Cultural Behaviour in Tourism: Concepts and Analysis*. Oxford, UK: Butterworth-Heinemann, 2003.

Richards, Greg. *Cultural Tourism*. Binghamton, NY: The Haworth Press, 2007.

Richards, Greg. *Cultural Attractions and European Tourism*. Oxfordshire, UK: CABI Publishing, 2001.

Shackley, Myra. *Managing Sacred Sites*. London: The Continuum International Publishing Group, 2001.

Smith, Valene L. *Hosts and Guests: The Anthropology of Tourism*, 2d ed. Philadelphia: University of Pennsylvania Press, 1989.

Smith, Valene, and Maryann Brent. *Hosts and Guest Revisited: Tourism Issues of the 21st Century*. Elmsford, NY: Cognizant Communication Corporation, 2001.

Walle, Alf H. *Cultural Tourism: A Strategic Focus*. Boulder, CO: Westview Press, 1998.

United Nations World Tourism Organization. *Handbook on Tourism Congestion Management at Natural and Cultural Sites*. Madrid: UNWTO, 2003.

Xie, Phillip E. *Authenticating Ethnic Tourism*. Bristol, UK: Channel View Publications, 2010.

Chapter 11

Aspostolopoulos, Yorghos, Stella Leivadi, and Andrew Yiannakis. *The Sociology of Tourism: Theoretical and Empirical Investigations*. Oxford, UK: Routledge, 2001.

Borocz, J. *Leisure Migration: A Sociological Study on Tourism*. Oxford, UK: Pergamon Press, 1996.

Botterill, David, and Trevor Jones. *Tourism and Crime*. Oxon, UK: Goodfellow Publishers, 2010.

Buhalis, Dimitros, and Simon Darcy. *Accessible Tourism: Concepts and Issues*. Bristol, UK: Channel View Publications, 2010.

Cohen, Erik. "Authenticity, Equity and Sustainability in Tourism." *Journal of Sustainable Tourism*, vol. 10, no. 4 (2002), pp. 267–276.

Cohen, Erik. *Contemporary Tourism: Diversity and Change*. Oxford, UK: Butterworth-Heinemann, 2004.

Cohen, Erik. "Traditions in Qualitative Sociology of Tourism." *Journal of Travel Research*, vol. 15, no. 1 (1988), pp. 29–46.

Dann, Graham M. S. *The Language of Tourism: A Sociolinguistic Perspective*. Wallingford, UK: CAB International, 1996.

Dann, Graham, and Erik Cohen. "Sociology and Tourism." *Annals of Tourism Research*, vol. 18, no. 1 (1991), pp. 155–169.

Darcy, Simon. *Setting a Research Agenda for Accessible Tourism*. Gold Coast, Australia: CRC for Sustainable Tourism, 2006.

deKadt, Emanuel. "Social Planning for Tourism in the Developing Countries." *Annals of Tourism Research*, vol. 6, no. 1 (January-March 1979), pp. 36–48. Special issue on Sociology of Tourism.

Guaracino, Jeff. *Gay and Lesbian Tourism: The Essential Guide to Marketing*. Oxford, UK: Butterworth-Heinemann, 2007.

Hall, C. M. *Tourism: Rethinking the Social Science of Mobility*. Upper Saddle River, NJ: Pearson Education, 2005.

Hiller, Harry H. "Toward an Urban Sociology of Mega-Events." *Research in Urban Sociology*, vol. 15 (2000), pp. 181–205.

Hughes, Howard L. *Pink Tourism: Holidays of Gay Men and Lesbians*. Oxfordshire, UK: CABI Publishing, 2006.

MacCannell, Dean. *The Tourist: A New Theory of the Leisure Class*. New York: Schocken Books, 1976.

Meethan, K., A. Anderson, and S. Miles. *Tourism, Consumption and Representation*. Oxfordshire, UK: CABI Publishing, 2006.

Pizam, Abraham, and Peter Tarlow. "Special Issue on War, Terrorism, Tourism." *Journal of Travel Research*, vol. 38, no. 1 (August 1999), pp. 4–65.

Pizam, Abraham, Peter E. Tarlow, and Jonathon Bloom. "Making Tourists Feel Safe: Whose Responsibility Is It?" *Journal of Travel Research*, vol. 36, no. 1 (Summer 1997), pp. 23–28.

Sharpley, Richard, BT and Philip R. Stone (eds.). *The Darker Side of Travel: The Theory and Practice of Dark Tourism*. Bristol, UK: Channel View Publications, 2009.

Smith, Valene L., and Maryann Brent. *Hosts and Guests Revisited: Tourism Issues of the 21st Century*. Elmsford, NY: Cognizant Communications, 2001.

Teuscher, Hans. "Social Tourism for All: The Swiss Travel Saving Fund." *Tourism Management*, vol. 4, no. 3 (September 1983), pp. 216–219.

Turner, Louis, and John Ash. *The Golden Hordes*. London: Constable, 1975.

Ury, John. *The Tourist Gaze*. London: Sage Publications, 2002.

Waitt, Gordon, and Kevin Markwell. *Gay Tourism Culture and Context*. Binghamton, NY: The Haworth Hospitality Press, 2006.

Wilks, Jeff, and Stephen Page. *Managing Tourist Health and Safety in the New Millennium*. Oxford, UK: Butterworth-Heinemann, 2003.

Wyllie, Robert W. *Tourism and Society: A Guide to Problems and Issues*. State College, PA: Venture Publishing, 2001.

Yeoman, Ian, and Cathy Hsu. *Tourism and Demography*. Oxon, UK: Goodfellow Publishers, 2010.

Chapter 12

Carter, R. W., G. S. Baxter, and M. Hockings. "Resource Management in Tourism Research: A New Direction?" *Journal of Sustainable Tourism*, vol. 9, no. 4, (2001), pp. 265–280.

Clawson, Marion, and Jack L. Knetsch. *Economics of Outdoor Recreation*. Baltimore: Johns Hopkins Press, 1966.

Keating, B. W. *Managing Ethics in the Tourism Supply*. Wollongong, Australia: Faculty of Informatics-Papers, 2008.

Pearce, Douglas G. "Islands and Coastal Tourism: Demand and Supply. Perspectives from Samoa, Sarawak and New Zealand." *Tourism*, vol. 49, no. 3 (2001), pp. 255–266.

Smith, Stephen L. J., and Honggen Xiaco. "Culinary Tourism Supply Chains: A Preliminary Examination." *Journal of Travel Research*, vol. 48, no. 3 (2008), pp. 289–299.

Travel Weekly. *Hotel and Travel Index, Worldwide*. Secaucus, NJ: Northstar Travel Media, 2010.

Tapper, Richard and Xavier Font. *Tourism Supply Chains*. Leeds, UK: Leeds Metropolitan University, 2004.

Waddell, Joseph M. "Hotel Capacity: How Many Rooms to Build?" *Cornell Hotel and Restaurant Administration Quarterly*, vol. 18, no. 2 (August 1977), pp. 35–47.

Chapter 13

Crouch, Geoffrey I. "A Meta-Analysis of Tourism Demand." *Annals of Tourism Research*, vol. 22, no. 1 (Summer 1995), pp. 103–118.

Crouch, Geoffrey I. "The Study of International Tourism Demand." *Journal of Travel Research*, vol. 32, no. 4 (Spring 1994), pp. 41–53.

Crouch, Geoffrey I. "The Study of International Tourism Demand: A Review of Findings." *Journal of Travel Research*, vol. 33, no. 1 (Summer 1994), pp. 12–23.

Frechtling, Douglas C. *Forecasting Tourism Demand: Methods and Strategies*. Oxford, UK: Butterworth-Heinemann, 2001.

Smeral, Egon. "World Tourism Forecasting: Keep It Quick, Simple and Dirty." *Tourism Economics*, vol. 13, no. 2 (June 2007), pp. 309–318.

Song, Haiyan, and Gang Li. "Tourism Demand Modeling and Forecasting—A Review of Recent Research." *Tourism Management*, vol. 29, no. 2, (April 2008), pp. 203–220.

Song, Haiyan, Stephen F. Witt, and Gang Li. *The Advanced Economics of Tourism Demand*. Essex, UK: Routledge, 2008.

Song, Haiyan, and Stephen F. Witt. "Tourism Forecasting: The General-to-Scientific Approach." *Journal of Travel Research*, vol. 42, no. 1 (August 2003), pp. 65–74.

Song, Haiyan, and Stephen F. Witt. *Tourism Demand Modelling and Forecasting: Modern Econometric Approaches*. Amsterdam: Pergamon, 2000.

Turner, Lindsay W., and Stephen F. Witt. *Asia Pacific Tourism Forecasts 2010–2011*. Bangkok: PATA, 2010.

Turner, Lindsay W., and Stephen F. Witt. "Forecasting Tourism Using Univariate and Multivariate Structural Time Series Models." *Tourism Economics*, vol. 7, no. 2 (2001), pp. 135–147.

United Nations World Tourism Organization. *Handbook on Tourism Forecasting Methodologies*. Madrid: UNWTO, 2008.

United Nations World Tourism Organization. *Tourism: 2020 Vision*. Madrid: UNWTO, 2001.

United Nations World Tourism Organization. *Measuring Total Tourism Demand*. Madrid: UNWTO, 2000.

U.S. Travel Association. *2011 Outlook for Travel and Tourism*. Washington, DC: USTA, 2010.

U.S. Travel Association. *Economic Review of Travel in America*. Washington, DC: USTA, 2010.

Witt, Stephen F., and Christine A. Witt. *Modeling and Forecasting Demand in Tourism*. London: Academic Press, 1992.

Chapter 14

Cannon, Thomas. "Relationship of Demographics and Trip Characteristics to Visitor Spending: An Analysis of Sports Travel Visitors Across Time." *Tourism Economics—Special Issue: Measuring the Economic Impact of Tourism*, vol. 8, no. 3 (2002), pp. 263–271.

Crompton, John L. "Economic Impact Studies: Instruments for Political Shenanigans?" *Journal of Travel Research*, vol. 45, no. 1 (2006), pp. 67–82.

Dwyer, Larry, Peter Forsyth, and Wayne Dwyer. *Tourism Economics and Policy*. Bristol, UK: Channel View Publications, 2010.

Dwyer, Larry, Peter Forsyth, and Ray Spurr. "Assessing the Economic Impacts of Events: A Computable General Equilibrium Approach." *Journal of Travel Research*, vol. 45, no. 1 (2006), pp. 59–66.

Dwyer, Larry, Peter Forsyth, and Ray Spurr. "Evaluating Tourism's Economic Effects: New and Old Approaches." *Tourism Management*, vol. 25, no. 1 (June 2004), pp. 307–318.

Dwyer, Larry, Peter Forsyth, John Madden, and Ray Spurr. "Economic Impacts of Inbound Tourism under Different Assumptions Regarding the Macroeconomy." *Current Issues in Tourism*, vol. 3, no. 4 (2000), pp. 325–363.

Dwyer, Larry, Robert Mellor, Nina Mistilis, and Trevor Mules. "Forecasting the Economic Impacts of Events and Conventions." *Event Management*, vol. 6, no. 3 (2000), pp. 191–204.

Faulkner, Bill, Laurence Chalip, Graham Brown, Leo Jago, Roger March, and Arch Woodside. "Monitoring the Tourism Impacts of the Sydney 2000 Olympics." *Event Management*, vol. 6, no. 4 (2001), pp. 231–246.

Frechtling, Douglas C. "An Assessment of Visitor Expenditure Methods and Models." *Journal of Travel Research*, vol. 45, no. 1 (2006), pp. 26–35.

Mak, James. *Tourism and the Economy: Understanding the Economics of Tourism*. Honolulu: University of Hawaii Press, 2004.

OECD. *OECD Tourism Trends and Policies 2010*. Paris: OECD Publishing, 2010.

Smeral, Egon. "Tourism Satellite Accounts: A Critical Assessment." *Journal of Travel Research*, vol. 45, no. 1 (2006), pp. 92–98.

Tyrrell, Timothy J., and Robert J. Johnson. "The Economics of Tourism: A Special Issue." *Journal of Travel Research*, vol. 45, no. 1 (2006), pp. 3–7.

United Nations World Tourism Organization. *Compendium of Tourism Statistics*. Madrid: UNWTO, 2010.

United Nations World Tourism Organization. *Travel and Tourism Barometer*. Madrid: UNWTO, 2010.

United Nations World Tourism Organization. *Enzo Paci Papers on Measuring the Economic Significance of Tourism*, vol. 1. Madrid: UNWTO, 2001.

United Nations World Tourism Organization. *Tourism Satellite Account: Recommended Methodological Framework*. Madrid: UNWTO, 2001.

United Nations World Tourism Organization. *The Tourism Satellite Account as an Ongoing Process: Past, Present, and Future Developments*. Madrid: UNWTO, 2001.

U.S. Travel Association. *Economic Review of Travel in America: 2008 Edition*. Washington, DC: TIA, 2009.

U.S. Travel Association. *Impact of Travel on State Economies 2010*. Washington, DC: TIA, 2010.

U.S. Travel Association. *Tourism Works for America 2010*. Washington, DC: TIA, annual.

Vanhove, Norbert. *The Economics of Tourism Destinations*. Oxford, UK: Butterworth-Heinemann, 2005.

Chapter 15

Agiomirgianakis, George (ed.). *International Journal of Tourism Policy*. Geneva: Inderscience Publishers, quarterly.

Andriotis, Konstantinos. "Tourism Planning and Development in Crete: Recent Tourism Policies and Their Efficacy." *Journal of Sustainable Tourism*, vol. 9, no. 4 (2001), pp. 298–316.

Becherel, Lionel. "The WTO Policy and Strategy Course." *TedQual*, vol. 4, no. 2 (2001), pp. 16–20.

Beirman, David. *Restoring Tourism Destinations in Crisis*. Oxfordshire, UK: CABI Publishing, 2003.

Blake, Adam, and M. Thea Sinclair. "Tourism Crisis Management: U.S. Response to September 11." *Annals of Tourism Research*, vol. 30, no. 4 (2003), pp. 813–832.

Bramwell, Bill, and Bernard Lane (eds.). *Tourism, Collaboration, and Partnership: Politics, Practice, and Sustainability*. Clevedon, UK: Channel View Publications, 2000.

Briassoulis, Helen, and Jan van der Straaten (eds.). *Tourism and the Environment: Regional, Economic, Cultural, and Policy Issues*, rev. 2d ed. Boston: Kluwer Academic Publishers, 2000.

Buckley, Ralf. "Pay to Play in Park: An Australian Policy Perspective on Visitor Fees in Public Protected Areas." *Journal of Sustainable Tourism*, vol. 11, no. 1 (2003), pp. 56–73.

Datzira-Masip, Jordi. "Tourism Policy in Spain: An Overview." *Tourist Review*, vol. 53, no. 1 (1998), pp. 41–50.

Department of Resources, Energy and Tourism. *National Long-Term Tourism Strategy*. Canberra: Australian Government, 2009.

Dredge, Dianne, and John Jenkins. *Tourism Planning and Policy*. Hoboken, NJ: John Wiley & Sons, 2007.

Edgell, David L., Maria DelMastro, Ginger Smith, and Jason Swanson. *Tourism Policy and Planning: Yesterday, Today and Tomorrow*. Oxford, UK: Butterworth-Heinemann, 2008.

Faulkner, Bill. "A Model for the Evaluation of National Tourism Destination Marketing Programs." *Journal of Travel Research*, vol. 35, no. 3 (Winter 1997), pp. 23–32.

Fennell, David, and David Malloy. *Codes of Ethics in Tourism*. Clevedon, UK: Channel View Publications, 2007.

Glaesser, Dirk. *Crisis Management in the Tourism Industry*. Oxford, UK: Butterworth-Heinemann, 2003.

Hall, D. *Tourism and Transition: Governance, Transformation and Development*. Oxfordshire, UK: CABI Publishing, 2004.

International Association of Scientific Experts in Tourism (eds.). Future-Oriented Tourism Policy: A Contribution to the Strategic Development of Places. *Proceedings of 49th Annual Congress of the International Association of Scientific Experts in Tourism, Portoroz, Slovenia*. St. Gallen Switzerland: AIEST, University of St. Gallen, 1999.

Kerr, William R. *Tourism Public Policy and the Strategic Management of Failure*. Oxford, UK: Elsevier, 2003.

Laws, Eric, Bruce Prideaux, and Kaye Chon. *Crisis Management in Tourism*. Oxfordshire, UK: CABI Publishing, 2007.

Laws, Eric, and Bruce Prideaux. *Tourism Crises*. Binghamton, NY: Haworth Hospitality Press, 2006.

OECD. *OECD Tourism Trends and Policies 2010*. Paris: OECD Publishing, 2010.

Parker, Steven. "Collaboration on Tourism Policy Making: Environmental and Commercial Sustainability on Bonaire, NA." *Journal of Sustainable Tourism*, vol. 7, no. 3–4 (1999), pp. 240–259.

Parker, Steven. "Ecotourism, Environmental Policy, and Development." In Dennis Soden and Brent R. Steel (eds.), *Handbook of Global Environmental Policy and Administration*, pp. 315–345. New York: Marcel Dekker, 1999.

Ritchie, Brent W. *Crisis and Disaster Management for Tourism*. Bristol, UK: Channel View Publications, 2009.

Ritchie, J. R. Brent, and Geoffrey I. Crouch. *The Competitive Destination: A Sustainable Tourism Perspective*. Oxfordshire, UK: CABI Publishing, 2003.

Ritchie, J. R. Brent. *"Interest Based Formulation of Tourism Policy for Environmentally Sensitive Destinations."* In Bill Bramwell and Bernard Lane (eds.), *Tourism, Collaboration, and Partnership: Politics, Practice, and Sustainability* pp. 44–77. Clevedon, UK: Channel View Publications, 2000.

Ritchie, J. R. Brent. "Policy Formulation at the Tourism/Environment Interface: Insights and Recommendations from the Banff-Bow Valley Study." *Journal of Travel Research*, vol. 38, no. 2 (1999), pp. 100–110.

Suder, Gabriele G. S. *Terrorism and the International Business Environment*. Cheltenham, UK: Edward Elgar Publishing, 2004.

Thomas, Rhodri (ed.). *Journal of Policy Research in Tourism, Leisure and Events*. Essex, UK: Routledge.

United Nations World Tourism Organization. *Making Tourism More Sustainable: A Guide for Policy Makers*. Madrid: UNWTO, 2005.

United Nations World Tourism Organization. *Co-operation and Partnership in Tourism: A Global Perspective*. Madrid: UNWTO, 2003.

United Nations World Tourism Organization. "India Introduces New Tourism Policy." *UNWTO News*, vol. 2, no. 10 (2002).

Vanhove, Norbert. "Tourism Policy between Competitiveness and Sustainability: The Case of Bruges." *Tourist Review*, vol. 57, no. 3 (2002), pp. 34–40.

Veal, A. J. *Leisure and Tourism Policy and Planning*. Oxfordshire, UK: CABI Publishing, 2002.

Chapter 16

Ashworth, G. J., and J. E. Tunbridge. *The Tourist-Historic City: Retrospect and Prospect of Managing the Heritage City*. Amsterdam: Pergamon, 2000.

Beeton, Sue. *Community Development Through Tourism*. Oxfordshire, UK: CABI Publishing, 2006.

Brown, Frances, and Derek Hall (eds.). *Tourism in Peripheral Areas: Case Studies*. Buffalo, NY: Channel View Publications, 2000.

Burns, Peter, and M. Novelli. *Tourism Development*. Oxfordshire, UK: CABI Publishing, 2008.

Chon, Kaye S. (ed.). *Tourism in Southeast Asia: A New Direction*. New York: Haworth Hospitality Press, 2000.

deKadt, Emanuel (ed.). *Tourism—Passport to Development?* New York: Published for the World Bank and UNESCO by Oxford University Press, 1979.

Dieke, Peter U. C. *The Political Economy of Tourism Development in Africa*. New York: Cognizant Communication Corporation, 2000.

Dredge, Dianne, and John Jenkins. *Tourism Planning and Policy*. Hoboken, NJ: John Wiley & Sons, 2007.

Egmond, T. Van. *Understanding Western Tourists in Developing Countries*. Oxfordshire, UK: CABI Publishing, 2007.

Gartner, William C. *Tourism Development: Principles, Processes, and Policies*. New York: Van Nostrand Reinhold, 1996.

George, E. Wanda, Heather Mair, and Donald G. Reid. *Rural Tourism Development: Localism and Cultural Change*. Bristol, UK: Channel View Publications, 2009.

Godde, P. M., M. F. Price, and F. M. Zimmermann. *Tourism and Development in Mountain Regions*. New York: CABI Publishing, 2000.

Godfrey, Kerry, and Jackie Clarke. *The Tourism Development Handbook: A Practical Approach to Planning and Marketing*. London: Continuum International Publishing Group, 2000.

Gunn, Clare A., and Turgut Var. *Tourism Planning*, 4th ed. London: Taylor and Francis, 2002.

Mill, Robert Christie. *Resorts: Management and Operation*, 2d ed. Hoboken, NJ: John Wiley & Sons, 2008.

Moscardo, Gianna. *Building Community Capacity for Tourism Development*. Oxfordshire, UK: CABI Publishing, 2008.

Murphy, Peter, and Ann Murphy. *Strategic Management for Tourism Communities*. Clevedon, UK: Channel View, 2004.

Nuckolls, Jonelle, and Patrick Long. *Organizing Resources for Tourism Development in Rural Areas*. Boulder: University of Colorado, 1993.

Tourism Center. *Community Tourism Development*. St. Paul: University of Minnesota Extension Service, 2001.

United Nations World Tourism Organization. *Tourism and Community Development: Asian Practices*. Madrid: UNWTO, 2008.

Chapter 17

Aronsson, Lars. *The Development of Sustainable Tourism*. London: Continuum International Publishing Group, 2000.

Bader, Elana. *Sustainable Hotel Business Practices: A Surface Examination*. London: HVS International, 2006.

Becken, Susanne, and John E. Hay. *Tourism and Climate Change: Risks and Opportunities*. Bristol, UK: Channel View Publications, 2007.

Buckley, Ralf. *Conservation Tourism*. Oxfordshire, UK: CABI, 2011.

Buckely, Ralf. *Environmental Impacts of Ecotourism*. Oxfordshire, UK: CABI Publishing, 2008.

Buckley, Ralf. *Case Studies in Ecotourism*. Oxfordshire, UK: CABI Publishing, 2003.

Bushell, R., and P. Eagles. *Tourism and Protected Areas*. Oxfordshire, UK: CABI Publishing, 2007.

Carlsen, Jack, Janene Giburd, Deborah Edwards, and Paddy Forde. *Innovation for Sustainable Tourism: International Case Studies*. Niels Bohrs, Denmark: BEST Education Network, 2008.

Dickinson, Janet, and Les Lumsdon. *Slow Travel and Tourism*. Oxfordshire, UK: CABI Publishing, 2010.

Dowling, Ross, and David Newsome. *Global Geotourism Perspectives*. Oxon, UK: Goodfellow Publishers, 2010.

Edgell, David L. *Managing Sustainable Tourism*. Binghamton, NY: The Haworth Hospitality Press, 2006.

Gossling, S., and J. Hultman. *Ecotourism in Scandinavia*. Oxfordshire, UK: CABI Publishing, 2006.

Harrill, Rich. *Guide to Best Practices in Tourism and Destination Management*. Lansing, MI: Educational Institute of the American Hotel and Lodging Association, 2005.

Harris, Rob, Tony Griffin, and Peter Williams. *Sustainable Tourism*. Oxford, UK: Butterworth-Heinemann, 2002.

Herremans, Irene M. *Cases in Sustainable Tourism*. Binghamton, NY: Haworth Hospitality Press, 2006.

Jones, Andrew L., and Mike Phillips. *Disappearing Destinations: Climate Change and the Future Challenges for Coastal Tourism*. Oxfordshire, UK: CABI Publishing, 2010.

Kütting, Gabriela. *The Global Political Environment and Tourism*. New York: Palgrave MacMillan, 2010.

McCool, S. F., and R. N. Moisey (eds.). *Tourism, Recreation, and Sustainability: Linking Culture and the Environment*. Oxfordshire, UK: CABI Publishing, 2008.

Miller, Graham, and Louise Twinning-Ward. *Monitoring For Sustainable Tourism Transition*. Oxfordshire, UK: CABI Publishing, 2006.

Mowforth, Martin, and Ian Munt. *Tourism and Sustainability: New Tourism in the Third World*, 3d ed. Essex, UK: Routledge, 2008.

Newsome, David, and Ross Dowling. *Geotourism: The Tourism of Geology and Landscape*. Oxon, UK: Goodfellow Publishers, 2010.

OECD. *OECD Tourism Trends and Policies 2010*. Paris: OECD Publishing, 2010.

Ritchie, J. R. Brent, and Geoffrey I. Crouch. *The Competitive Destination: A Sustainable Tourism Perspective*. Oxfordshire, UK: CABI Publishing, 2003.

Saaarinen, Jarko J., Fritz O. Becker, Haretsebe Manwa, and Deon Wilson. *Sustainable Tourism in Southern Africa: Local Communities and Natural Resources in Transition*. Bristol, UK: Channel View Publications, 2009.

Sharpley, Richard. *Tourism Development and The Environment: Beyond Sustainability?* Oxfordshire, UK: CABI Publishing, 2009.

Singh, Sagar. *Shades of Green: Ecotourism for Sustainability*. New Delhi: The Energy and Resources Institute, 2004.

Spenceley, Anna. *Responsible Tourism*. Oxfordshire, UK: CABI Publishing, 2010.

Stern, N. *The Economics of Climate Change: The Stern Review*, Cambridge University Press, Cambridge, 2006.

Stonehouse, Bernard and John Snyder. *Polar Tourism: An Environmental Perspective*. Bristol, UK: Channel View Publications, 2010.

U.S. Travel Association. *Geotourism: The New Trend in Travel*. Washington, DC: USTA, 2003.

United Nations World Tourism Organization. *Climate Change and Tourism*. Madrid, Spain: UNWTO, 2008.

United Nations World Tourism Organization. *Making Tourism More Sustainable: A Guide for Policy Makers*. Madrid, Spain: UNWTO, 2005.

United Nations World Tourism Organization. *Sustainable Development of Ecotourism: A Compilation of Good Practices in SMEs*. Madrid, Spain: UNWTO, 2003.

United Nations World Tourism Organization. *Sustainable Tourism in Protected Areas: Guidelines for Planning and Management*. Madrid: UNWTO, 2003.

United Nations World Tourism Organization. *The Canadian Ecotourism Market*. Madrid: UNWTO, 2002.

United Nations World Tourism Organization. *The French Ecotourism Market*. Madrid: UNWTO, 2002.

United Nations World Tourism Organization. *The German Ecotourism Market*. Madrid: UNWTO, 2002.

United Nations World Tourism Organization. *The Italian Ecotourism Market*. Madrid: UNWTO, 2002.

United Nations World Tourism Organization. *The Spanish Ecotourism Market*. Madrid: UNWTO, 2002.

United Nations World Tourism Organization. *The U. S. Ecotourism Market*. Madrid: UNWTO, 2002.

United Nations World Tourism Organization. *The British Ecotourism Market*. Madrid: UNWTO, 2001.

United Nations World Tourism Organization. *Guide for Local Authorities on Developing Sustainable Tourism*. Madrid: UNWTO, 1998.

Weaver, David B. (ed.). *The Encyclopedia of Ecotourism*. Oxfordshire, UK, CABI Publishing, 2001.

Zeppel, Heather. *Indigenous Ecotourism*. Oxfordshire, UK: CABI Publishing, 2006.

Chapter 18

Bruner, Gordon C., II, and Paul J. Hensel. *Marketing Scales Handbook: A Compilation of Multi-Item Measures*. Chicago: American Marketing Association, 2001.

Crompton, John L., and Shu Tian-Cole. "An Analysis of 13 Tourism Surveys: Are Three Waves of Data Collection Necessary?" *Journal of Travel Research*, vol. 39, no. 4 (May 2001), pp. 356–368.

Dann, Graham, Dennison Nash, and Philip Pearce. "Methodology in Tourism Research." *Annals of Tourism Research*, vol. 15, no. 1 (1988), pp. 1–28.

Jackson, Julie, Meg Houghton, Roslyn Russell, and Petra Triandos. "Innovations in Measuring Economic Impacts of Regional Festivals: A Do-It-Yourself Kit." *Journal of Travel Research*, vol. 43, no. 4 (2005), pp. 360–367.

Richard K. Miller & Associates. *The 2010 Restaurant, Food & Beverage Market Research Handbook*. Loganville, GA: RKMA, 2010.

Richard K. Miller & Associates. *The 2010 Travel & Tourism Market Research Handbook*, 9th ed. Loganville, GA: RKMA, 2010.

Richards, G., and W. Munsters. *Cultural Tourism Research Methods*. Oxfordshire, UK: CABI Publishing, 2010.

Ritchie, Brent W., Peter Burns, and Catherine Palmer. *Tourism Research Methods*. Oxfordshire, UK: CABI Publishing, 2005.

Ritchie, J. R. Brent, and Charles R. Goeldner (eds.). *Travel, Tourism, and Hospitality Research: A Handbook for Managers and Researchers*, 2d ed. New York: John Wiley & Sons, 1994.

Robinson, P. *Research Themes for Tourism*. Oxfordshire, UK: CABI Publishing, 2011.

Smith, Stephen L. J. *Practical Tourism Research*. Oxfordshire, UK: CABI Publishing, 2010.

Sturman, Michael (ed.). "*Special-Focus Issue on Research.*" *Cornell Hotel and Restaurant Administration Quarterly* vol. 44, no. 2 (April 2003), pp. 9–152.

Techneos. *Moving On: Leaving Paper for Mobile Survey Technology*. Vancouver: Techneos, 2010.

United Nations World Tourism Organization. *Compendium of Tourism Statistics*. Madrid: UNWTO, 2010.

United Nations World Tourism Organization. *Yearbook of Tourism Statistics*. Madrid: UNWTO, 2009.

United Nations World Tourism Organization. *Collection and Compilation of Tourism Statistics: Technical Manual no. 4*. Madrid: UNWTO, 1995.

United Nations World Tourism Organization. *Collection of Domestic Tourism Statistics: Technical Manual no. 3*. Madrid: UNWTO, 1995.

United Nations World Tourism Organization. *Collection of Tourism Expenditure Statistics: Technical Manual no. 2*. Madrid: UNWTO, 1995.

United Nations World Tourism Organization. *Concepts, Definitions, and Classifications for Tourism Statistics: Technical Manual no.1*. Madrid: UNWTO, 1995.

Chapter 19

Aaker, D. A. *Managing Brand Equity: Capitalizing on the Value of a Brand Name*. New York: Free Press, 1991.

Abbey, James R. *Hospitality Sales and Advertising*, 5th ed. Lansing, MI: Educational Institute of the American Hotel and Lodging Association, 2008.

Amadeus. *Hotels 2020: Beyond Segmentation*. Sophia Antipolis Cedex, France: Amadeus, 2010.

Beeton, Sue. *Film-Induced Tourism*. Bristol, UK: Channel View Publications, 2005.

Beckendorff, P. J., B. Moscardo, and D. Pendergast. *Tourism and Generation Y*. Oxfordshire, UK: CABI Publishing, 2010.

Clarkson, Diane. *Extending Online Customer Service to the Mobile Channel*. Cambridge, MA: Forrester, 2010.

Dickinson, Bob, and Andy Vladmir. *Selling the Sea: An Inside Look at the Cruise Industry*, 2d ed. Hoboken, NJ: John Wiley & Sons, 2007.

Fyall, Alan, and Brian Garrod. *Tourism Marketing: A Collaborative Approach*. Bristol, UK: Channel View Publications, 2004.

Guaracino, Jeff. *Gay and Lesbian Tourism: The Essential Guide to Marketing*. Oxford, UK: Butterworth-Heinemann, 2007.

Hallett, Richard W., and Judith Kaplan-Weinger. *Official Tourism Websites: A Discourse Analysis Perspective*. Bristol, UK: Channel View Publications, 2010.

Harrill, Rich. *Fundamentals of Destination Management and Marketing*. Lansing, MI: Educational Institute of the American Hotel and Lodging Association, 2005.

Hudson, Simon. *Tourism and Hospitality Marketing*. London: Sage Publications, 2008.

Kozak, Metin. *Managing and Marketing Tourist Destinations*. Essex, UK: Routledge, 2009.

Kozak, Metin, and Alain Decrop. *Handbook of Tourist Behaviour: Theory and Research*. Essex, UK: Routledge, 2008.

Kotler, Philip, John Bowen, and James Makens. *Marketing for Hospitality and Tourism*, 5th ed. Upper Saddle River, NJ: Prentice Hall, 2010.

Market Guide 2010. New York: VNU Business Publications, 2010.

Meethan, Kevin, Alison Anderson, and Steve Miles. *Tourism, Consumption and Representation*. Oxfordshire: UK: CABI Publishing, 2006.

Middleton, Victor T. C., Alan Fyall, and Michael Morgan. *Marketing in Travel and Tourism*, 4th ed. Oxford, UK: Butterworth-Heinemann, 2009.

Mill, R. C., and A. M. Morrison. *The Tourism System: An Introductory Text*, 6th ed. Dubuque, IA: Kendall/Hunt, 2009.

Morgan, Nigel, Annette Pritchard, and Roger Pride. *Destination Branding: Creating the Unique Destination Proposition*. Oxford, UK: Butterworth-Heinemann, 2004.

Nykiel, Ronald A. *Marketing in the Hospitality Industry*, 4th ed. Lansing, MI: Educational Institute of the American Hotel and Lodging Association, 2003.

Pike, Steven. *Destination Marketing Organizations*. Oxford, UK: Elsevier, 2004.

Plog, Stanley C. *Leisure Travel: A Marketing Handbook*. Upper Saddle River, NJ: Prentice Hall, 2004.

Reid, Robert, and David Bojanic. *Hospitality Marketing Management*, 5th ed. Hoboken, NJ: John Wiley & Sons, 2010.

Roesch, Stefan. *The Experiences of Film Location Tourists*. Bristol, UK: Channel View Publications, 2009.

Shoemaker, Stowe, Robert C. Lewis, and Peter Yesawich. *Marketing Leadership in Hospitality and Tourism: Strategies and Tactics for Competitive Advantage*, 4th ed. Upper Saddle River, NJ: Prentice Hall, 2007.

United Nations World Tourism Organization. *Handbook on Tourism Destination Branding*. Madrid: UNWTO, 2009.

United Nations World Tourism Organization. *Handbook on E-marketing for Tourism Destinations*. Madrid: UNWTO, 2008.

United Nations World Tourism Organization. *Handbook on Tourism Market Segmentation*. Madrid: UNWTO, 2007.

U.S. Travel Association, *Use of Mobile Travel Services by Destination Marketing Organizations, 2010 Edition*. Washington, DC: USTA, 2010.

U.S. Travel Association, *Travelers Use of the Internet, 2010*. Washington, DC: USTA, 2010.

U.S. Travel Association, *Emerging International Travel Markets: China 2008, Part II*. Washington, DC: USTA, 2009.

U.S. Travel Association, *Survey of U.S. State and Territory Tourism Office Website Practices, 2008*. Washington, DC: USTA, 2009.

U.S. Travel Association, *Domestic Travel Report*. Washington, DC: USTA, 2007.

U.S. Travel Association. *Gay and Lesbian Leisure Travelers in America*. Washington, DC: USTA, 2007.

U.S. Travel Association. *The Profile of Culinary Travelers*. Washington, DC: USTA, 2007.

U.S. Travel Association. *Travel Through the Generations*. Washington, DC: USTA, 2006.

Vladimir, Andy, and Bob Dickinson. *The Complete 21st Century Travel Marketing Handbook*. Upper Saddle River, NJ: Prentice Hall, 2005.

Wang, Youcheng. *Destination Marketing and Management*. Oxfordshire, UK: CABI Publishing, 2010.

Chapter 20

Canton, James. *The Extreme Future*. New York: Dutton, 2006.

Cornish, Edward. *Futuring: The Exploration of the Future*. Bethesda, MD: World Future Society, 2005.

Creton, Marvin, Fredrick DeMicco, and Owen Davies. *Hospitality 2010: The Future of Hospitality and Travel*. Upper Saddle River, NJ: Prentice Hall, 2006.

Crouch, Geoffrey I. "The Market for Space Tourism: Early Indications." *Journal of Travel Research*, vol. 40, no. 2 (2001), pp. 213–219.

Foot, David K., and Daniel Stoffman. *Boom Bust and Echo: Profiting from the Demographic Shift in the 21st Century*, rev. ed. Toronto, Canada: Stoddart Publishing, 2001.

Steffen, Alex. *Worldchanging: A User's Guide for the 21st Century*. New York: Abrams, 2006.

Weiermair, Klaus, and Christine Mathies. *The Tourism and Leisure Industry: Shaping the Future*. Binghamton, NY: Haworth Hospitality Press, 2004.

United Nations World Tourism Organization Business Council. *Public-Private Sector Cooperation: Enhancing Tourism Competitiveness*. Madrid: UNWTOBC, 2001.

United Nations World Tourism Organization. *Tourism 2020 Vision: A New Forecast from the World Tourism Organization*. Madrid: UNWTO, 2001.

Worldwatch Institute. *Vital Signs 2006–2007: The Trends That Are Shaping Our Future*. New York: W.W. Norton & Company, 2006.

Yeoman, Ian. *Tomorrow's Tourist: Scenarios and Trends*. Oxford: Elsevier, 2008.

Yeoman, Ian, and Cathy Hsu. *Tourism and Demography*. Oxon, UK, Goodfellow Publishers, 2010.

Glossary ✛

A

Accommodation   Facilities for the lodging of visitors at a destination. The most common forms are hotels, motels, campgrounds, bed and breakfasts (B&Bs), dormitories, hostels, and the homes of friends and relatives.

Adventure travel   A form of travel in which the perception (and often the reality) of heightened risk creates a special appeal to certain segments of the travel market. Examples include whitewater rafting and mountaineering.

Affinity group   A group bound together by a common interest or affinity. Where charters are concerned, this common bond makes them eligible for charter flights. Persons must have been members of the group for six months or longer. Where a group configuration on a flight is concerned, the minimum number of persons to which the term would apply may be any number determined by a carrier rulemaking body. They must travel together, on the departure and return flight, but they can travel independently where ground arrangements are concerned.

Agreement, bilateral   An agreement regulating commercial air services between two countries.

Agreement, multilateral   An agreement regulating commercial air services between three or more countries.

Airline Reporting Corporation (ARC)   A corporation set up by the domestic airlines that is concerned with travel agent appointments and operations.

Air Transport Association of America (ATA or ATAA)   The authoritative trade association maintained by domestic airlines.

Alliances   Associations to further the common interests of the parties involved.

Allocentric tourist   Outgoing and self-confident tourist who wants to see the world and do new things. The wish is to experience culture, lifestyle, and landscape that is totally different from their home place. Also called venturers.

American plan   A room rate that includes breakfast, lunch, and dinner.

Attractions   Facilities developed especially to provide residents and visitors with entertainment, activity, learning, socializing, and other forms of stimulation that make a region or destination a desirable and enjoyable place.

B

Balance of payments or trade   Practical definition of an economic concept. Each nation is assumed to be one tremendous business doing business with other big businesses. When a business (country) sells (exports) more than it buys (imports), there is a positive balance of payments. When a country buys (imports) more than it sells (exports), there is a negative balance of trade. Tourism is a part of balance of trade classified under services.

Built environment   The components or activities within a tourism destination that have been created by humans. These include the infrastructure and superstructure of the destination, as well as the culture of its people, the information and technology they use, the culture they have developed, and the system of governance that regulates their behaviors.

C

Cabotage   The ability of an air carrier to carry passengers exclusively between two points in a foreign country.

Carbon footprint   The effect that one's actions and lifestyle have on the environment in terms of carbon dioxide emissions.

Carrier   A public transportation company, such as air or steamship line, railroad, truck, bus, monorail, and so on.

Carrier-participating   A carrier over whose routes one or more sections of carriage under the air waybill or ticket is undertaken or performed.

Carrying capacity   The number of flights multiplied by the number of aircraft seats flown. Also the amount of tourism a destination can handle.

Charter   The bulk purchase of any carrier's equipment (or part thereof) for passengers or freight. Legally, charter transportation is arranged for time, voyage, or mileage.

Charter flight   A flight booked exclusively for the use of a specific group of people who generally belong to the same organization or who are being "treated" to the flight by a single host. Charter flights are generally much cheaper than regularly scheduled line services. They may be carried out by scheduled or supplemental carriers.

Clients   Those persons who patronize travel agencies, travel suppliers, and destinations.

Climate   The meteorological conditions, including temperature, precipitation, and wind, that prevail at, or within, a tourism region.

Code sharing   An agreement between two airlines that allows the first carrier to use the airline designation code on a flight operated by the second carrier.

Concierge   This is a wonderful European invention. Depending on the hotel, the concierge is a superintendent of service, source of information, and/or link between the guest and city or area.

Conservation   Management of human use of the environment to yield the greatest sustainable benefit to current generations while maintaining its potential to meet the needs and aspirations of future generations.

Consolidator   A travel firm that makes available airplane tickets, cruise tickets, and sometimes other travel products at discount prices. These are usually sold to retail travel agencies but are also sometimes sold directly to the public.

Consortium   A privately owned firm (not owned by its members as is a cooperative) that maintains a list of preferred suppliers. This list is made available to members, resulting in superior commissions earned.

Continental breakfast A beverage, roll, and jam. Sometimes fruit juice is added. In Spain, Holland, and Norway, cheese, meat, or fish is sometimes included.

Continental plan A hotel rate that includes a continental breakfast.

Cooperative A membership group of retail travel agencies that offers advantages to each agency member, such as lower prices on wholesale tour offerings, educational opportunities, problem solving, and other aids.

Coupon flight The portion of the passenger ticket and baggage check or excess baggage ticket that indicates particular places between which the coupon is good for carriage.

Culture The totality of socially transmitted behavior patterns, arts, beliefs, institutions, and all other products of human work and thought that are characteristic of the destination population.

D

Destination The ultimate stopping place according to the contract of carriage. Can also be defined as a place offering at least 1,500 rooms to tourists.

Destination management organization (DMO) Organization responsible for coordination, leadership, and promotion of a destination and its stakeholders, thus enabling it to provide tourists with an enjoyable and memorable visitation experience.

Development Modification of the environment to whatever degree and the application of human, financial, living, and nonliving resources to satisfy human needs and improve the quality of human life.

Domestic independent travel (DIT) A tour constructed to meet the specific desire of a client within a single country.

E

E-commerce The transaction of commercial dealings (advertising and promotion, sales, billing, payment, and customer servicing) by electronic means rather than through traditional "paper" channels.

Entertainment Performances, shows, or activities that attract and hold the attention of visitors. A successful destination will seek to integrate the travel, hospitality, and entertainment dimensions of tourism.

Environment All aspects of the surroundings of human beings, including cultural, natural, and manmade, whether affecting human beings as individuals or in social groupings.

Eurailpass A special pass sold overseas for unlimited first-class rail travel in 15 European countries for varying numbers of days. Youth and children's passes are also available.

European plan A hotel rate that includes only lodging, no food.

Events Includes a broad range of "occurrences," "happenings," and "activities" that are designed around various themes with a view to creating or enhancing interest in the destination. Local festivals and megaevents (such as the Olympic Games and world expositions) have proven to be most effective.

Excursionist A traveler who spends less than 24 hours at a destination.

F

Familiarization tour A tour with free or reduced-rate arrangements for travel agents or public carrier employees that is intended to stimulate them to sell travel or tours as experienced on the *famtour*.

Federal Aviation Administration (U.S.) A governmental regulatory agency concerned with airport operation, air safety, licensing of flight personnel, and other aviation matters.

Flag carrier An international airline often owned and/or operated by the government of its home country.

Flight, connecting A flight that requires a change of aircraft and flight number en route to a destination.

Flight, direct A flight that may make intermediary stops en route to a destination.

Flight, nonstop A flight that travels to a destination without any intermediary stops.

Food services Facilities that provide food and meals to visitors to a destination. The most common forms are restaurants, fast-food outlets, snack bars, cafeterias, food fairs, and the homes of friends and relatives.

Foreign independent travel (FIT) An individually designed tour by an individual or family rather than a predesigned package tour.

Frequent-flyer plan Program where bonuses are offered by the airlines to passengers who accumulate travel mileage.

G

Geotagging The process of adding geographical identification metadata to various media such as photographs, videos, Web sites, RSS feeds, and is a form of geospatial metadata.

Global Distribution System Worldwide computerized reservation network used as a single point of access for making airline, hotel, rental car, and other travel-related reservations by travel agents, online reservation sites, and large corporations.

Global warming The increase in the average temperature of the Earth's near-surface air and oceans in recent decades and its projected continuation.

Governance The system that defines the organizations, the processes, and the complex of political institutions, laws, and customs through which power and authority within a destination are exercised.

Ground arrangements All those services provided by a tour operator after reaching the first destination. Also referred to as land arrangements.

Group inclusive tour (GIT) A tour that includes group air and ground arrangements for a minimum of 15 persons. They may or may not stay together as a group for both the land and air portions of the trip.

H

High-speed rail (HRS) High-speed rail is a type of passenger rail transport that operates significantly faster than the normal speed of rail travel. The U.S. Federal Railroad Administration defines high-speed rail as having speed above 110 miles per hour (180 km/h).

Hub and spoke A system that feeds connecting passengers into major gateway airports from short-haul or point-to-point downline routes.

I

Incentive tour A tour arranged especially for employees or agents of a company as a reward for achievement, usually sales. Spouses are typically included on the trip.

Inclusive tour A travel plan for which prearranged transportation, wholly by air or partly by air and partly by surface, together with ground facilities (such as meals, hotels, and so on) are sold for a total price.

Information Knowledge obtained from investigation, study, or instruction.

Infrastructure The facilities, equipment, and installations needed for the basic functioning and daily lives of the residents of a region. These include communication systems, water and sewage facilities, public protection, health, transportation, and education systems.

International Air Transport Association (IATA) The authoritative trade association maintained by international and overseas airlines.

Internet service providers Companies that provide domain space for others on computer servers they own, companies that provide travel information that they develop, and companies that provide a combination of the two.

M

Mass tourism The act of visiting a destination with large numbers of people at one time.

Modified American plan A room rate that includes a full American breakfast and lunch or dinner, usually dinner.

O

Open jaw A pairing of two or more nearby destinations that allows a passenger to arrive at one airport and depart from a second.

Open skies An agreement between two or more nations that allows its air carriers to fly unrestricted within each other's borders; the United States and the Netherlands recently signed an open skies pact.

P

Package A prepaid tour that includes transportation, lodging, and other elements, usually meals, transfers, sightseeing, or car rentals. May be varied, but typically includes at least three items sold at a fixed price.

Passport A document issued by national governments to their own citizens as verification of their citizenship. It is also a permit to leave one's own country and return.

Pension A French word widely used throughout Europe meaning guesthouse or boardinghouse.

People Those humans who reside in, or visit, a tourism destination.

Physiography The physical geography of a tourism destination.

Planner Person whose job it is to oversee and arrange every aspect of an event. Person can be an employee or hired ad hoc by large companies, professional associations, or trade associations to plan, organize, implement, and control meetings, conventions, and other events.

Psychocentric tourist Nonadventurous tourists who tend to travel to developed areas and returns to the same vacation location often. They prefer the familiar. Also called dependables.

R

Reception agency A tour operator or travel agency specializing in foreign visitors. American Adventure Tours is such a company.

Resource audit A comprehensive cataloguing of the quantity and distribution of tourism facilities, events, programs, and services with the tourism system—and a subsequent assessment of their quality and appeal to the market segments of interest to a destination.

Retail travel agency A business that sells travel-related products such as package tours, cruises, accommodations, attractions, airline tickets, and rail transportation.

RSS A family of Web feed formats used to publish frequently updated works such as blog entries, news headlines, audio, and video in a standardized format. Commonly called *Really Simple Syndication*.

Run-of-the-house A hotel term to guarantee a firm price that applies to any room in the house. Often, a hotel will provide a superior room, if available, in an effort to please the guest and the tour operator.

S

Social media The online technologies and practices that people use to share content, opinions insights, experiences, perspectives, and photos. Examples are TripAdvisor, Facebook, Flickr, and YouTube.

Spa A hotel or resort providing hot springs or baths and other health-enhancing facilities and services.

Superstructure The equipment and facilities needed to meet the particular needs of the visitors to a region. These include accommodation and food services, visitor information and services, tourism attractions, special events, supplementary transportation, and special education and training programs for front-line staff and industry managers.

Supplier An industry term meaning any form of transportation, accommodations, and other travel services used by a travel agency or tour operator to fulfill the needs of travelers.

T

Tariffs The published fares, rates, charges, and/or related conditions of carriage of a carrier.

Technology The entire body of methods and materials used to achieve commercial, industrial, or societal objectives.

Timeshare Concept of dividing the ownership and use of a lodging property among investors.

Tour A trip taken by a group of people who travel together and follow a preplanned itinerary.

Tour-basing fare A reduced, round-trip fare available on specified dates, and between specified times, only to passengers who purchase preplanned, prepaid tour arrangements prior to their departure to specified areas.

Tourism (1) The entire world industry of travel, hotels, transportation, and all other components, including promotion, that serves the needs and wants of travelers. Tourism today has been given new meaning and is primarily a term of economics referring to an industry. (2) Within a nation (political subdivision or transportation-centered economic area of contiguous nations), the sum total of tourist expenditures within their borders is referred to as the nation's tourism or tourist industry and is thus ranked with other national industries. More important than just the total monetary product value of tourism is its role in the balance of trade. Here tourism earnings from foreigners truly represent an export industry. Tourism is an ''invisible'' export.

Tourist A person who travels from place to place for nonwork reasons. By the United Nations' definition, a tourist is someone who stays for more than one night and less than a year. Business and convention travel is included. This thinking is dominated by balance-of-trade concepts. Military personnel, diplomats, immigrants, and resident students are not tourists.

Tour operator A company that specializes in the planning and operation of prepaid, preplanned vacations and makes these available to the public, usually through travel agents. See Tour Wholesaler.

Tour organizer An individual, usually not professionally connected with the travel industry, who organizes tours for special groups of people, such as teachers, church leaders, farmers, and the like.

Tour package A travel plan that includes several elements of a vacation, such as transportation, accommodations, and sightseeing.

Tour wholesaler A company that plans, markets, and (usually) operates tours. Marketing is always through intermediaries such as retail travel agents, an association, a club, or a tour organizer—never directly to the public, as is sometimes done by tour operators. The wholesaler would not operate the tour if, for example, it was functioning as a wholesaler in the United States for tours operated by a foreign firm. In industry jargon, *tour operator* and *tour wholesaler* are synonymous.

Transportation The act or process of carrying or moving people or goods, or both, from one location to another.

Travel (see Tourism) Often interchangeable with *tourism*. Actually, this term should represent all direct elements of travel. Included in the term *travel* are transportation, vacations, resorts, and any other direct passenger elements, including but not limited to national parks, attractions, and auto use for any of the above purposes. To make a journey from one place to another.

Travel aggregators Aggregator Web sites are a way to simultaneously search several sources for the best travel deals that the Web has to offer. Some of the major players are Kayak.com, SideStep.com, CheapFlights.com, Mobissimo.com, and Farechase.com.

Travel industry services Includes those organizations, firms, and individuals that provide a diverse range of services that enable and facilitate travel as well as make it more convenient and less risky. Examples include computer support services, financial services, insurance, information, and interpretation.

Travel trade Includes those organizations, firms, and individuals that provide various elements of the total travel experience.

V

Vacation ownership A term often used to describe resort timesharing.

Visa Document issued by a foreign government permitting nationals of another country to visit or travel. The visa is usually stamped on pages provided in one's passport but may also be a document fastened to the passport or provided electronically.

Vouchers Documents issued by tour operators to be exchanged for accommodations, sightseeing, and other services.

W

Web 2.0 A perceived second generation of Web-based communities and hosted services such as social networking sites.

Y

Yield management The use of pricing and inventory controls, based on historical data, to maximize profits by offering varying fares over time for the same product.

SELECTED TOURISM ABBREVIATIONS

AAA American Automobile Association
ABA American Bus Association
ABC Advanced booking charter
ACME Association for Convention Marketing Executives
AHLA American Hotel and Lodging Association
AIEST International Association of Scientific Experts in Tourism
AIT Académie Internationale du Tourisme
Amtrak National Railroad Passenger Corporation
AP American plan
APEC Asia-Pacific Economic Cooperation
APEX Advance purchase excursion fare
ARC Airlines Reporting Corporation
ARDA American Resort and Development Association
ARTA Association of Retail Travel Agents
ASTA American Society of Travel Agents
ATA Air Transport Association of America
ATME Association of Travel Marketing Executives
BIT Bulk inclusive tour
BTA British Tourist Authority
CIC Convention Industry Council
CITC Canadian Institute of Travel Counselors
CLIA Cruise Lines International Association
COTAL Confederation of Tourist Organizations of Latin America

CRS Computerized reservations system
CTC Canadian Tourism Commission
CTC Certified Travel Counselor
CTO Caribbean Tourism Organization
DIT Domestic independent tours
DMAI Destination Marketing Association International
DMO Destination management organization
DOT (U.S.) Department of Transportation
ECOSOC Economic and Social Council of the United Nations
EP European plan
ETC European Travel Commission
FAA (U.S.) Federal Aviation Administration
FHA Federal Highway Administration
FIT Foreign independent tour
GDS Global Distribution System
GIT Group inclusive tour
HSMAI Hospitality Sales and Marketing Association International
IAAPA International Association of Amusement Parks and Attractions
IAF International Automobile Federation
IAST International Academy for the Study of Tourism
IATA International Air Transport Association
IATAN International Airlines Travel Agent Network

ICAO International Civil Aviation Organization
ICC Interstate Commerce Commission
ICCA International Congress and Convention Association
ICHRIE International Council on Hotel, Restaurant, and Institutional Education
ICSC International Council of Shopping Centers
IFWTO International Federation of Women's Travel Organizations
IH&RA International Hotel and Restaurant Association
IIPT International Institute for Peace through Tourism
IIT Inclusive Independent Tour
ILO International Labor Organization
ISMP International Society of Meeting Planners
ISTTE International Society of Travel and Tourism Educators
IT Inclusive tour
ITC Inclusive tour charter
IYHF International Youth Hostel Federation
MAP Modified American plan
MCO Miscellaneous charges order
MPI Meeting Professionals International
NACOA National Association of Cruise Oriented Agencies
NAPVO National Association of Passenger Vessel Owners
NARVPC National Association of RV Parks and Campgrounds
NCA National Council of Attractions
NRA National Restaurant Association
NRPA National Recreation and Park Association
NTA National Tour Association

OAG Official Airline Guide
OAS Organization of American States
OECD Organization for Economic Cooperation and Development
OTTI Office of Travel and Tourism Industries (U.S.)
PAII Professional Association of Innkeepers International
PATA Pacific Asia Travel Association
RAA Regional Airline Association
RPM Revenue passenger miles
RTF Rural Tourism Foundation
RVIA Recreation Vehicle Industry Association
SATW Society of American Travel Writers
SEO Search Engines Optimization
SITE Society of Incentive and Travel Executives
TIAC Tourism Industry Association of Canada
TTRA Travel and Tourism Research Association
UFTAA Universal Federation of Travel Agents' Association
UNDP United Nations Development Programme
UNESCO United Nations Educational, Scientific, and Cultural Organization
UNWTO United Nations World Tourism Organization
USTA United States Travel Organization
USTOA United States Tour Operators Association
WATA World Association of Travel Agencies
WHO World Health Organization
WTAO World Touring and Automobile Organization
WTTC World Travel and Tourism Council
WWW World Wide Web

Index ✛